2ND EDITION

ETHICS IN MEDIA COMMUNICATIONS: CASES AND CONTROVERSIES

Louis A. Day
Louisiana State University

 WADSWORTH PUBLISHING COMPANY

I(T)P® An International Thomson Publishing Company

Belmont, CA • Albany, NY • Bonn • Boston • Cincinnati • Detroit • London • Madrid • Melbourne •
.Mexico City • New York • Paris • San Francisco • Singapore • Tokyo • Toronto • Washington

Communication & Media Studies Editor: Todd Armstrong
Editorial Assistant: Michael Gillespie
Project Editor: Gary Mcdonald
Production: Robin Lockwood & Associates
Print Buyer: Karen Hunt
Permissions Editor: Robert Kauser
Copy Editor: Laura Larson
Designer: Wendy LaChance/By Design
Cover Designer: Harry Voigt
Compositor: TBH Typecast, Inc.
Printer: Quebecor/Fairfield
Cover Printer: Phoenix Color

For more information, contact Wadsworth Publishing Company:

Wadsworth Publishing Company
10 Davis Drive
Belmont, California 94002, USA

International Thomson Publishing Europe
Berkshire House 168-173
High Holborn
London, WC1V 7AA, England

Thomas Nelson Australia
102 Dodds Street
South Melbourne 3205
Victoria, Australia

Nelson Canada
1120 Birchmount Road
Scarborough, Ontario
Canada M1K 5G4

International Thomson Editores
Campos Eliseos 385, Piso 7
Col. Polanco
11560 México D.F. México

International Thomson Publishing GmbH
Königswinterer Strasse 418
53227 Bonn, Germany

International Thomson Publishing Asia
221 Henderson Road
#05-10 Henderson Building
Singapore 0315

International Thomson Publishing Japan
Hirakawacho Kyowa Building, 3F
2-2-1 Hirakawacho
Chiyoda-ku, Tokyo 102, Japan

Library of Congress Cataloging-in-Publication Data

Day, Louis A.
    Ethics in media communications : cases and controversies / Louis
A. Day. — 2nd ed.
        p. cm.
    Includes bibliographical references and index.
    ISBN 0-534-50716-6
    1. Mass media—Moral and ethical aspects.   I. Title
P94.D39   1997
174—dc20   96-8087

CONTENTS

PART TWO: CASES IN MEDIA COMMUNICATIONS 71

This book grew out of both a sense of frustration and a sense of optimism. After more than twenty years of college teaching, I am convinced that most students leave school without a meaningful understanding of the ethics of their profession or ethics in general, for that matter. There is even a general cynicism, as described in Chapter 1, concerning the value of ethics instruction within the public academy. In some cases, this cynicism has blossomed into outright hostility. *But skepticism about moral education produces skepticism about moral responsibility, which in turn produces leaders who lack a moral vision.*

Although many programs in journalism and mass communications offer instruction in ethics or social responsibility, students never really develop a framework for making ethical judgments. The need for a renewed emphasis on ethics in mass communications has never been greater. Evidence of a general decline in ethical standards is all around us: Wall Street brokers accused of insider trading, TV evangelists defrocked for sexual indiscretions, midshipmen expelled from the Naval Academy for cheating, sports figures accused of cheating, and news organizations blamed for "sleaze journalism" in pursuit of ratings and profits. My optimism, however, stems from the recent recognition of this ethical malaise by educators,

opinion leaders and even the general public. Within the academy, professional schools—law, business, and journalism, for example—have reinvigorated their curricula with a renewed commitment to the teaching of ethics. And ethics, which was once the concern primarily of scholars, philosophers, and theologians, has even taken on a populist quality as the ethical dimensions of virtually any issue of substance are publicly debated.

Ethics in Media Communications is one small contribution to this pursuit of ethical knowledge. It offers a systematic approach to moral reasoning by combining ethical theory with the practice of ethics by media professionals. A moral reasoning method is taught in the first three chapters, and in the rest of the book students are presented with hypothetical situations and asked to reach an ethical decision based on the principles they have learned. These cases represent a wide variety of moral dilemmas confronted by media practitioners. For example, a newspaper editor agonizes over whether to use digital technology to alter a photo that might contain information offensive to some readers. A television news director has to decide whether the undisclosed sexual orientation of a mayoral candidate is a matter of public interest. A public relations firm must decide whether to accept an account from a prospective client engaged in an activity that is offensive to some of the firm's employees. The staff of a college newspaper has to determine whether to continue to run ads promoting off-campus drinking establishments catering to college students. And a radio station manager must decide whether to cancel the controversial and hate-filled program of a popular conservative talk show host.

Some cynics may question the value of using classroom simulations to teach real-world ethics, especially given the fact that media practitioners operate under time deadlines in pressure situations. However, even football teams must endure hours of skull sessions before they do combat on the gridiron, and experience in moral reasoning—even hypothetical experience—will help students prepare for the day when they must make ethical judgments on the job.

A final note: I do have some evidence, though anecdotal, that this approach to teaching ethics is effective. After having used the moral-reasoning model in my classes, my students have told me that it made them more ethically aware of the consequences of their behavior. If this book accomplishes nothing more than that, it will not have been in vain.

ACKNOWLEDGMENTS

I wish to thank the following people for their helpful and constructive comments in preparing the Second Edition: Thomas Bivins, University of Oregon; Richard Goedkoop, La Salle University; John Hochheimer, Ithaca College; and Ruth Bayard Smith, Montclair State University.

In addition, I would like to thank the wfollowing reviewers of the First Edition: John De Mott, University of Memphis; Fred F. Endres, Kent State University; Richard Goedkoop, La Salle University; Milton Hollstein, University of Utah; Maclyn H. McClary, Humboldt State University; and David Protess, Northwestern University.

◀ INTRODUCTION ▶

The study of ethics may be new and unfamiliar to you. Although most of us are obedient disciples of the values we learned in childhood, we spend few of our waking hours pondering the importance of these moral rules and how they might lead to a more virtuous life. Prohibitions against lying, stealing, and cheating, for example, are platitudes to which we pay homage, but we don't always comply with them. Our ethical conduct is often "situational" because we have no comprehensive moral framework to guide us in making judgments. In short, we lack experience in moral reasoning.

This book is, first and foremost, designed to expose you to the process of moral reasoning. Of course, reading this book will not make you a morally mature individual. But it will provide a blueprint for improving your ethical awareness. Nowhere is the need for moral reasoning more acute than in journalism and other areas of mass communications. The polls continue to show an erosion of credibility and confidence in the mass media, some of which is no doubt due to the public's perception that the media ship is sailing without a moral compass.

Because the frenzied environment of the newsroom or the advertising agency is no place to start philosophizing about moral reasoning, the classroom must serve as our point of depar-

ture. The exercises in this book represent the moral dilemmas that you will face on the job. But more importantly, the practice in problem solving and critical thinking afforded by these hypothetical cases will make you a more confident decision maker. Before confronting the dilemmas posed by these case studies, however, you must be familiar with the terrain of moral philosophy. Thus, *Ethics in Media Communications: Cases and Controversies* is divided into two parts.

Part One, "Foundations and Principles," is devoted primarily to a consideration of moral development and the formulation of moral rules and principles within a social context. The third chapter of Part One also draws on a fusion of important concepts from moral philosophy, media practice, and critical thinking to construct a moral-reasoning "model" that will be used as the blueprint for analyzing the hypothetical cases in Part Two.

The chapters in Part Two, "Cases in Media Communications," present some of the major issues confronting media practitioners. The theme underlying this approach is that these issues affect all areas of mass communications. For example, moral principles involving truth-telling and deception apply to journalists, advertisers, and public relations executives alike (as well as to society at large). Likewise, conflicts of interest are certainly not the exclusive preserve of journalists.

The hypothetical cases involve ethical dilemmas confronted by both lower-echelon employees and management personnel. In many cases you will be asked to assume the role of a management-level decision maker. Some may question the value of this kind of exercise because, as a *future* media practitioner, you are likely to identify more closely with rank-and-file employees. However, role playing can be an effective means of stepping into another person's shoes. By so doing, you should at least come to appreciate the management perspective on ethical issues, even if you do not agree with it. This ability might prove valuable once you enter the job market. Also, keep in mind that the real purpose of this text is to expose you to the process of moral reasoning and not just to discuss ethical issues. To this end, it makes little difference what your role as ethical decision maker is as long as your judgment is based on sound moral principles.

In the book's Epilogue I provide a final comment on the current state of the practice of media ethics. There is also some crystal-ball gazing and a look at the future of the teaching of media ethics. Ethical studies have a long and honorable tradition in programs of journalism and mass communications. *Ethics in Media Communications* is designed to help you become part of that tradition.

PART 1

FOUNDATIONS AND PRINCIPLES

The first part of *Ethics in Media Communications* lays a foundation for the study of moral philosophy (ethics) and moral reasoning. To accomplish this ambitious objective, I have divided Part One into three chapters.

Chapter 1 begins with an overview of ethics as a subject worthy of exploration. It then documents the value of ethics instruction from the standpoint of both intellectual enrichment and professional practice, and also discusses how ethical values and attitudes are formed and how moral values sometimes collide. The theory underlying Chapter 1 is that an understanding of one's own ethical development—a development that should continue throughout one's lifetime—is a prerequisite for approaching the process of moral reasoning with confidence.

Chapter 2 focuses on the relationship between ethics and society. The need for a system of ethics is first established, followed by an examination of the requirements for a cohesive system of societal ethical standards. Because our ethical behavior is based, in part, on the rules and norms of society at large, the concept of moral duty and its relationship to virtuous behavior are examined. Chapter 2 also delves into the sometimes confusing relationship between law and ethics. The chapter concludes with a discussion of social responsibility and how individual standards of moral conduct are reflected in media institutions' corporate attitudes toward the public interest. Chapter 2 also considers the role of new technologies and the information superhighway on media ethics.

Chapter 3 provides the connection between ethics and moral reasoning. It examines the philosophical foundations of moral theory and the approaches to ethical decision making that have had the most profound impact on moral philosophy in Western civilization. These theories are then combined with the principles of critical thinking to develop a "model" for moral reasoning (the SAD Formula) that will be employed for analyzing the ethical dilemmas posed by the hypothetical cases at the end of Chapters 4 through 14.

CHAPTER

1

Ethics and
Moral Development

THE STUDY OF ETHICS:
AN OVERVIEW

Do I have a moral obligation to report cheating by a classmate? Do I have a duty to report a crime I witness? Is it ethically permissible for a TV reporter to use a hidden camera to document unlawful activity or scandalous behavior? Is it immoral for Hollywood to produce films containing graphic violence and sex aimed at a youthful audience? These examples are just a few of the many questions in today's society calling for an ethical response. Most of us could probably answer such questions based on our feelings about an issue. But could we defend our answer to anyone who is willing to listen? On what basis should these decisions be made?

The study of ethics can provide the tools for making difficult moral choices, in both our personal and professional lives. Through the teaching of ethical principles and moral reasoning, educational institutions can fulfill one of their historically important responsibilities, the "cultivation of morality."[1]

What exactly is *ethics*, and how does it differ from *morals*? *Moral* is derived from the Latin *mos, moris*, meaning (among other things) "way of life" or "conduct." It is often associated with religious beliefs and personal behavior.

Ethics, on the other hand, is derived from the Greek *ethos*, meaning "custom," "usage," or "character." It is often thought of as a rational process applying established principles when two moral obligations collide. The most difficult ethical dilemmas arise when there are conflicts between two "right" moral obligations. Thus, ethics often involves the balancing of competing rights when there is no "correct" answer. A case in point is a student who promises to remain silent when a classmate confides to her that he has cheated. If a teacher attempts to solicit testimony from that student regarding her friend's nefarious behavior, the student must then weigh the value of loyalty to the friend (a moral virtue) against commitment to the truth (another moral virtue).

Despite this historical distinction between morals and ethics, in recent years many commentators have merged the two concepts to such an extent that they have become virtually indistinguishable. *Ethics*, in fact, is the branch of philosophy that deals with the moral component of human life and is usually referred to as *moral philosophy*. This semantic alliance between *ethics* and *morals* is not altogether an unwelcome development and reflects the approach used in this text. Thus, the terms *ethics* and *morals* will often be used interchangeably.

This strategy is particularly useful in the study of media ethics (or any other profession, for that matter) because it reflects the growing realization that professional ethical behavior cannot be divorced entirely from the moral standards of society at large. A PR practitioner, for example, who deliberately distorts the truth is violating a fundamental principle that has its genesis both in the moral systems of various religions as well as ancient ethical canons.

Ethics reflects a society's notions about the rightness or wrongness of an act and the distinctions between virtue and vice. To accuse someone of laziness or incompetence is not to accuse that person of immoral conduct. On the other hand, such actions as lying, stealing, and cheating do imply the violation of ethical norms. Thus, ethics is often thought of as a set of principles or a code of moral conduct.[2]

Ethics involves the evaluation and application of those moral values that a society or culture has accepted as its norms. To suggest that individuals should set their own standards of conduct is to advocate ethical anarchy. One may derive a certain amount of satisfaction from adhering to a personal code of conduct, but the violation of this code does not necessarily raise serious ethical questions.

The study of ethics in the Western world began nearly 2,500 years ago when Socrates, according to his faithful student Plato, roamed Greece probing and challenging his brethren's ideas about such abstract concepts as justice and goodness. This Socratic method of inquiry, consisting of relentless questions and answers about the nature of moral conduct, has proved to be a durable commodity, continuing to touch off heated discussions about morality in barrooms and classrooms alike. Thus, the primary ingredient of ethical debate is conflict, because even within a given society or culture, opinions can differ on standards of proper moral conduct.[3] This moral diversity can be intellectually stimulating and personally enriching, as depicted colorfully in this editorial

comment from the *Quill*, the official publication of the Society of Professional Journalists:

> Ethical judgments are like that. No matter who makes them, they are seldom easy, and they are almost certain to strike some of us as perfectly proper while others regard them as wrongheaded, stupid, unfair, and—possibly—as evidence of intellectual and/or moral decay.
>
> All of which is a wonderful thing. Differing definitions of ethical behavior help keep our minds awake and our spirits inflamed. If everyone agreed on all ethical principles, life might be more orderly, but it surely would be more boring.[4]

Discussions of the ethical behavior of media practitioners are usually anything but boring. The study of ethics in mass communications is a noble heir to the Socratic tradition, because the activities of journalists, advertisers, and public relations executives are being subjected to critical inquiry as never before, even among their peers. We are in a constant state of agitation about the moral dimension of our lives. Our consciences tell us, often with brutal candor, that there is a real and important difference between actions that are right and those that are wrong. The knowledge of ethical principles and how they are derived can make a difference in our behavior.[5] However, the goal is not to make ethical decisions with which everyone agrees or, for that matter, to make decisions that are necessarily in keeping with societal expectations. The most challenging ethical dilemmas involve the balancing of competing interests when there is no "right" answer. Nevertheless, such moral reflection should result in at least morally defensible decisions even if those decisions prove to be unpopular. Ethics instruction refines our ability to make critical judgments and to defend those decisions on some rational basis.

For example, journalists, when delving into others' private lives, often justify their decision to publish embarrassing revelations on the ground of "the people's right to know." The problem with this kind of rejoinder is that it does not answer the questions of what the people have a right to know and why the public has a right to this kind of information in the first place.

The Three Branches of Ethics

Ethics, as a formal field of inquiry, attempts to put such questions into perspective and, in so doing, includes three different but conceptually related enterprises: metaethics, normative ethics, and applied ethics.[6] *Metaethics* is concerned with the study of the characteristics, or nature, of ethics. It also examines the meaning of such abstract terms as *good, right, justice,* and *fairness* and attempts to identify those values that are the best *moral* values. Metaethics is not concerned with making moral judgments but instead attempts to distinguish ethical values from those that involve merely matters of taste or attitude. For example, a commitment to truth has been identified by ethicists as a moral good, and this value underlies many of our societal norms. It is also the foundation of many media codes and standards of behavior, but it remains for media practitioners to adapt this rather abstract concept to specific moral dilemmas. Metaethics provides the broad foundation for ethical decision making, but it does not provide guideposts for how to get from point A to point B. When viewers or readers describe a news report as unfair, are they referring to an ethical concern or merely a matter of taste? Likewise, a media critic's description of a television series as "good drama" does not necessarily denote any observations concerning the program's moral stature. The function of metaethics is to define such vague concepts in ethical terms, providing precision of meaning so that all members of society can start with a level playing field in reaching moral judgments.

Normative ethics, on the other hand, is concerned with developing general theories, rules, and principles of moral conduct. The recent preoccupation with society's ethical malaise and demise of traditional values centers on some of the fundamental societal principles of moral behavior, that is, normative ethics. These theoretical rules and principles are the ethical markers of any civilized society, guideposts designed to bring moral order out of chaos. They provide the foundation for ethical decision making in the real world. Some of society's prohibitions against lying, cheating, and stealing flow from our concern with normative ethics. For example, a media institution's proscription against reporters' employing deception to get a news story derives from the general societal norm concerning lying. Nevertheless, under deadline and competitive pressures, journalists are sometimes tempted to abandon such broad principles because they want an exclusive article or perhaps because they truly believe that the public interest will be served by ferreting out the story, even at the expense of violating a fundamental rule of ethical behavior. When moral norms undergo their baptism of fire in the real world, the media practitioner enters the practical realm of applied ethics.

Applied ethics is really the problem-solving branch of moral philosophy. The task here is to use the insights derived from metaethics and the general principles and rules of normative ethics in addressing specific ethical issues and concrete cases. Suppose that a reporter is asked by an attorney representing a man accused of murder to reveal the names of the sources of information for an article that the reporter has written about the case. The reporter has promised the sources to keep their identities secret. However, the attorney believes that such information could lead to the acquittal of his client. One rule, or societal norm, in this case suggests that we should always keep our promises, because to do otherwise would violate the trust on which individual relationships are established. On the other hand, justice requires that we ensure a defendant a fair trial. In this case, these two rather abstract principles would be on a collision course, but *applied ethics* is designed to guide us through such a moral thicket by confronting issues within a real-world environment. There are not always right or wrong answers, but there should always be "well-reasoned" ones.

One reason, perhaps, why so many people are troubled and preoccupied with their moral existence is that they are unable to apply their beliefs to life's relentless barrage of ethical dilemmas.[7] Applied ethics is the vital link between theory and practice, the real litmus test of ethical decision making. Professional and occupational ethics reside here, and it is with this branch of ethics that the cases in Part Two are concerned.

Ethical Communication

The study of ethics would be futile if it did not promote understanding, and understanding can best be achieved by examining any ethical situation from the perspective of the following communications process:[8]

> A *moral agent* (communicator) with a particular *motive* commits an *act* (either verbal or nonverbal) within a specific *context* directed at a particular *individual or audience* usually with some *consequence*.

Moral agents are the ones who make ethical judgments, regardless of whether they are acting on their own volition or as institutional representatives. All communicators become moral agents when they confront the ethical dilemmas of their professions. However, agents must bear full responsibility for their actions, even if they are ordered to behave immorally, a painful lesson learned by those in positions of authority in Richard Nixon's administration during the Watergate era. An understanding of the moral agent role is essential because ethical standards often vary according to social roles. For example, most reporters and editors, because of their roles as agents for the public, could not in good conscience become politically active because to do so would compromise

their independence. Those who fail to observe this journalistic axiom may quickly fall from grace in the eyes of their employers. Such was the fate of TV anchorman Mike Snyder, who was suspended for two weeks from his position at the NBC affiliate in Fort Worth, Texas, for serving as master of ceremonies at a campaign rally for Republican gubernatorial candidate George W. Bush in 1994.[9] However, depending on their specific professional duties and the organizations for which they work, journalists have different obligations in this respect. A case in point is the editor of a politically conservative opinion magazine who is active in Republican party politics. The contract between such organs and their readers is different from the one between a general circulation newspaper and its audience.[10]

Ethical decisions are always made within a specific *context*, which includes the political, social, and cultural climate. Although the context does not necessarily determine the outcome of an ethical judgment, it exerts an influence that cannot be ignored. In fact, contextual factors often create the internal conflict that brings our conscience's admonition of what we ought to do into moral combat with what is the popular thing to do.

We must also examine the *motives* of the moral agent, because good motives can sometimes be used to justify what appears to be an unethical act. For example, a reporter may use deception to uncover governmental corruption, a journalistic technique most of us would be willing to tolerate (or perhaps even applaud) in the name of the public good. However, motives must not be examined based on their popularity or public acceptability; they should be viewed in conjunction with the consequences of the action. National leaders would not be justified in carrying out a policy of genocide, even if it were ratified by their constituents.

The *act* is the behavioral component of the communications process. It is what draws our attention to the actions of others and may lead us to describe their actions as either ethical or unethical. These acts may be verbal, as when a reporter lies to a news source. Or they may be nonverbal, as when an advertiser omits product information vital to informed consumer choice.

An ethical situation should also be evaluated in terms of the moral agent's relationship to the *individual(s)* or *audience* most directly affected by the ethical judgment. For example, a person's status as a public figure might justify reporting certain aspects of his or her personal life that would not be relevant if the subject were a private person. Or a magazine that appeals to a sophisticated audience might feel comfortable with including a quote containing offensive language, whereas a local community newspaper might sanitize such a quote. Likewise, the movie ratings system and the TV networks' "parental discretion" advisories, whatever their shortcomings may be, are a tacit recognition that these industries have a duty to alert the audience to morally offensive content.

Finally, ethical judgments produce *consequences*—either positive or negative—for both the moral agent and for others who may be touched by the agent's actions. These consequences may range from a stimulation of conscience to public approbation or disapproval of the moral agent's behavior. Sometimes these consequences are instantaneous and unambiguous, as when a newspaper's readers complain about a graphic photo of charred bodies on the paper's front page. But consequences may also be more subtle and long-term and usually form the foundations of individual and institutional reputations. A president's press secretary, for example, who consistently dispenses disinformation will eventually erode both his credibility and the integrity of the administration he represents.

THE VALUE OF ETHICS EDUCATION

Can ethics be taught? This is a difficult and controversial question but must be confronted directly. There are two schools of thought on this matter. Cynics contend that ethics is not a proper subject for study at all, because it raises questions without providing clear answers. Besides, the skeptics argue, knowledge of ethical principles and norms does not necessarily produce a more moral person. On the contrary, in this view, when confronted with real ethical dilemmas, people will ignore whatever wisdom was dispensed in an ethics course and act in their own self-interest. And there is some credible evidence, spanning the last fifty years, that character education classes and conventional religious instruction programs apparently have no significant influence on moral conduct.[11] Skeptics also argue that children's moral development is completed before they reach school and thus that such character education classes can have little effect. This view assumes, of course, that moral maturity, unlike psychological and physical maturity, ends at a very early age, a dubious proposition at best.

The cynical view is represented by the anecdote about the college student at a major university who was found guilty of plagiarism. Because this was his first offense, the student was sentenced to enroll in an ethics course taught by the philosophy department. He was finally expelled three months later, however, when he was caught cheating on an ethics exam.

Media practitioners, who are often skeptical of anything that smacks of ivory tower elitism, have another complaint about ethics courses. Classroom discussions and simulations, they argue, cannot duplicate the frenzied pace and pressures of the real world. They have a point. But even military units must drill before they engage in actual combat, and the fact that battlefield conditions are not identical to maneuvers does not diminish the value of those simulations. Some media institutions have altered their thinking in this matter and are sending employees to seminars to increase their ethical awareness. Considering that the media often make pronouncements on the ethics of others, such as politicians and business executives, it follows that their own moral conduct must be sound.

Obviously, ethics cannot be injected with a hypodermic needle, and there are no guarantees that formal instruction in moral philosophy will turn sinners into saints. But neither are there any guarantees that the lessons learned in history and political science courses will produce better citizens or serve the cause of democracy.

The other school of thought, represented by the optimistic proponents of formal ethics training, holds that ethics is a subject like math, physics, or history, with its own set of problems and distinctive methods of solving them.[12] Thus, the study of ethics is the key to understanding moral conduct and to improving the human spiritual condition. Surely, the optimists contend, this objective is worthy of attention in academic curricula. Socrates reflects this view when he remarks rather bluntly in Plato's *Apology* that "the unexamined life is not worth living." However, even Socrates apparently doubted at one time that morality was teachable.[13]

The urgent public criticism of the ethical standards of the professions in general, and the media in particular, compels us to accept the optimistic view of ethics instruction. We have little choice but to ponder, in a systematic and rational way, the ethical judgments being made in the newsrooms, advertising agencies, and public relations firms across this country. The media, it is safe to say, are operating in a hostile environment, although the polls differ on exactly how deeply public confidence has eroded.

Media practitioners are better educated and better trained than ever before. But many emerge from their college experience ill prepared to cope with the ethical exigencies of the real world. It is advantageous to the college student to confront the tough ethical calls first in the classroom, where they can be rationally discussed, rather than under deadline pressure later. Good professional ethics is a cherished commodity and builds respect among one's colleagues. Thus, the value of at least some formal ethics instruction would appear to be clear.

Contents of a Course in Media Ethics

What should one expect from a course in media ethics? An instructor probably cannot teach moral conduct in the sense that learning (or memorizing) ethical principles will produce a more virtuous person. But ethics instruction can *promote* moral conduct by providing the means to make ethical judgments, defend them, and then criticize the results of one's choices.[14] This process is known as *moral reasoning*, which is the primary focus of Chapter 3.

Our expectations should remain fairly modest, but there do appear to be several realistic and practical goals for a course in media ethics. The following five educational objectives are drawn from a study completed in 1980 by the Hastings Center, a pioneer in the ethics of medicine, biology, and the behavioral sciences.[15]

Stimulating the Moral Imagination A course in media ethics should promote the notion that moral choices constitute an important part of human existence and that the consequences of ethical decisions can lead to either suffering or happiness. Stimulating the moral imagination develops an emotional empathy with others that is not elicited by discussing ethical issues in abstract terms. Sometimes our moral imagination needs gentle prodding; at other times it needs shock therapy.

Recognizing Ethical Issues Although most of us would like to believe that we know right from wrong, we do not always recognize the moral dimensions of a situation. Anticipation of possible dilemmas is an important objective of ethics education and the moral reasoning process. For example, Terry Savage, a financial newspaper columnist and a commentator on Chicago's WBBM-TV, apparently failed to anticipate the salient ethical issues several years ago when she joined the corporate board of McDonald's. For the honor, she received a $24,000 stipend plus $2,000 for each meeting she attended. An editor for the *Chicago Sun-Times*, which published Savage's column, said he found the connection "troubling," but the reporter quickly denied any conflict of interest "as long as it's brought out into the open." She also pledged not to report on McDonald's or any of its competitors.[16] This response answers the question of honesty (i.e., disclosure), but it does not really address the ethical concern for journalistic independence (or at least the public's perception of independence).

Of course, some ethical strictures are subject to change. The standards of professional behavior, like the sands of time, are constantly shifting as media practitioners realign their moral compasses to account for changing circumstances. For example, at one time reporters, underpaid and overworked, routinely accepted gifts and gratuities from news sources. Today, this practice is generally frowned on, although there is still some disagreement over where to draw the line.[17]

Media professionals, like alcoholics, must first learn to acknowledge the problem before they can do something about it. Training in moral reasoning can assist all of us in recognizing the ethical implications of the decisions we are about to make. As Professor Louis Hodges of Washington and Lee University observes, in noting the long-term benefits of formal ethics training:

> A careful and systematic classroom experience with ethics can, I am convinced, be helpful. It does so by calling the mind's attention to important ethical issues, to the virtues, and, through cases, specifically to the needs of the audience. And that can help redeem the moral force of the profession.[18]

Developing Analytical Skills The ability to think critically about ethical issues is at the heart of the decision-making process. This goal involves examining fundamental abstract concepts such as *justice*, *moral duty*, and *respect for others* to see how they can be applied consistently and coherently to real-life situations. Critical examination of the arguments and justifications used to support one's moral deci-

sions is also an important consideration.[19] The ability to reason is essential to problem solving in mathematics and the behavioral sciences; the same can be said of moral philosophy. Case studies and classroom simulations, in which students role-play moral agents in a hypothetical or real ethical situation, can be effective tools in developing analytical skills.

Eliciting a Sense of Moral Obligation and Personal Responsibility President Harry Truman had a sign on his desk that said, "The buck stops here." The language was simple, the meaning profound. With these four words Truman was telling anyone who cared to listen that he accepted, without reservation, responsibility for all actions of the executive branch. He was also recognizing a simple moral truth: responsibility cannot be delegated. As moral agents we are all accountable for our actions, and should not blame others for our ethical lapses. Media practitioners often emphasize freedom at the expense of responsibility. A course in ethics can redress that imbalance.

Tolerating Disagreement Before moral agents can make informed ethical judgments, they must take into account and respect other points of view. A rational decision is based on a defensible moral foundation, ample deliberation, and consideration of the available options. As James Jaska and Michael Pritchard observe in an illuminating discussion on ethics in communications, "Tolerating differences in choice and refraining from automatically labeling opposite choices as immoral are essential. At the same time, seeking exact points of difference can help solve disagreements by eliminating false distinctions and evasions."[20] We live in an open and diverse society, and wisdom and reason suggest that we consult the moral views of others before rendering our personal judgments.[21]

Developing Ethical Fitness

Assume that you have read this entire text, comprehended all of the ethical principles, and agonized over the dilemmas posed by the various case studies. Assume further that you have excelled on all of the class assignments and examinations, and, for your diligence and hard work, you have received an A in your course on media ethics. You might be forgiven a certain amount of pomposity for your superior academic achievement, but does this achievement certify you as a more virtuous person than when you enrolled in the course?

Absolutely not! This text and any formal instruction in ethics are merely a point of departure. Through the formal experience of agonizing over the ethical dilemmas posed in hypothetical cases you can begin to cultivate your ethical awareness and to understand the moral reasoning process, as described more fully in Chapter 3. But just as watching videotapes will not make you physically fit or reading a book on the fundamentals of football will not make you a gridiron great, reading a text on media ethics will not make you a more virtuous individual. Athletes excel because of years of continuous practice. And so it is with character training and the learning of moral virtues. The only way to *be* a more ethical person is to *do* (i.e., practice) ethics. Rushworth Kidder, a journalist and the founder of the Institute for Global Ethics, refers to this as "ethical fitness."[22]

Virtuosity does not emerge from the endless philosophical debates about ethical issues or from analyzing a dilemma to death. Ethical fitness derives from confronting the tough moral issues of everyday existence and becoming an active participant in their resolution. To be ethically fit, according to Kidder's sage advice, you have "got to be mentally engaged" and "committed through the feelings as well as through the intellect."[23]

Kidder's point is worth pausing over for a moment. While the intellect is essential to rendering sound moral judgments (and the focus of this text *is* on moral reasoning), it is insufficient for the truly ethically fit individual. Moral decision making also requires compassion—or, in Kidder's words, "feelings." Without compas-

sion, ethical decisions might be reduced to sterile exercises in logic. But ethical fitness requires a holistic approach to character building in which both our intellectual and emotional aspects are fully engaged. Of course, our reason and emotions often disagree. An editor, for example, considering whether to publish a photo of a dead child, is torn between the journalistic value of newsworthiness and compassion for the child and his or her family, as well as the sensibilities of the readers.

Training for ethical fitness does not begin when you walk into a newsroom, advertising agency, or public relations firm. While it is true that professions impose certain unique duties on their members, what is often overlooked is that professional responsibilities cannot be completely divorced from society's fundamental values. The ethical decision-making process does not differ according to context or environment. In other words, there is not one ethical system for media practitioners and another for everyone else. The cultivation of moral virtue (i.e., the ability to distinguish good from evil and to make ethically defensible decisions) must be a lifelong commitment that at once engages our intellectual, intuitive, and emotional faculties. Ethics cannot be turned on and off according to the situation. The principles described in this text and the case studies that are designed to encourage your critical thinking are only catalysts. However, they will acquire real meaning only through *practicing* and *thinking about* what you have learned in the tranquility of the academic setting. That is how you become ethically fit!

THE ETHICS IMPERATIVE: RESPECTING THE INTERESTS OF OTHERS

If charity begins at home, so does the learning of social responsibility. A sense of moral obligation is the centerpiece of the child's early training. One of the first lessons of childhood involves sharing personal possessions and peaceful coexistence (if not absolute harmony) with one's playmates. Moral maturation begins early in life and continues in several stages until we are able, as fully autonomous individuals, to exercise our conscience and freedom of choice.[24] These early lessons can be described as the *ethics imperative*, because they are essential to becoming an ethical person. Morality involves taking into account the interests of others; an entirely selfish person cannot, by definition, make ethical judgments.[25] This is not to suggest that we should never be guided by self-interest. A request for a pay raise is obviously motivated by self-concern. Even striving to become a more virtuous individual involves a degree of self-interest. But one can achieve this goal only by factoring a concern for others into the decision-making equation.

Of course, not everyone agrees with this view. Some feel that self-interest should always be the *primary* determinant in choosing a course of action. Supporters of this belief are known as egoists. Egoists do not suggest that we totally ignore the impact of our behavior on others. After all, we often benefit when positive things happen to others. For example, when a business profits economically because of its record of public service to the community, the employees are likely to benefit through fatter paychecks. But egoists are always motivated by long-term self-interests, even if they have to resort occasionally to altruism to reach their goal.

Media practitioners are often viewed by the public as egoists, and this view has precipitated a crisis of confidence.[26] Attitudes concerning the media are increasingly negative, prompted no doubt by the perception that journalists will leave no stone unturned, even if it is an unethical stone, to uncover a story. Terms such as *ratings war*, *sleaze TV*, and *tabloid journalism* are now a familiar part of the audience's lexicon. In the competition of the market sensational, shocking and scandalous revelations have increasingly replaced serious and significant intelligence on the media's journalistic agenda.

This trend is reflected in such media circuses as the coverage of the O. J. Simpson trial, accusations of child molestation leveled against rock superstar Michael Jackson, and ice skater Tonya Harding's role in planning the attack against Olympic rival Nancy Kerrigan. Critics often accuse the media of pandering to the lowest common denominator in their relentless quest for greater profits. Whether or not these generalizations and criticisms are deserved is beside the point. In a country preoccupied with vicarious experiences through the mass media, perception becomes reality. It is a paradox of our libertarian civilization that the sense of cooperation and obligation instilled in us from early childhood is constantly being challenged by a society that values individualism and competition. Thus, media practitioners, many of whom graduate from colleges and universities where the grade point average is the measure of individual self-worth, come to their jobs with an ingrained competitive spirit. Of course, nothing is wrong with competition, but the ethical person draws the line where competition is motivated purely by self-interest that is likely to cause harm to others.

Perhaps the best way to reconcile these competing views of human nature is to acknowledge that there will always be a part of us that strives for recognition and fame in our own self-interest. But we should also acknowledge the necessity of taking into account the interests of others. An ethical person keeps these competing forces in balance, never allowing pure self-interest to dominate over the concern for others. In short, this *other-directed* interest should be a part of any decision with ethical overtones.

THE FORMATION OF ETHICAL VALUES AND ATTITUDES

In the preceding section, we noted the importance of developing a sense of altruism, that is, taking into account the interests of others. But how does one acquire moral conduct? The answer to this question lies in an understanding of how ethical values and attitudes are formed.

Defining Values and Attitudes

We must begin by defining what we mean by values and attitudes. Although there are many kinds of values and attitudes, this book will be concerned primarily with those that relate to ethical judgments. Thus, a *moral value* is something that is "esteemed, prized, or regarded highly, or as a good."[27] Autonomy, justice, and the dignity of human life are examples of values that are important to large segments of society. Objectivity and fairness are often cited as values underlying the practice of journalism.

Values are the building blocks of attitudes, that is, the "learned emotional, intellectual, and behavioral responses to persons, things, and events."[28] For example, the attitudes of abortion opponents may be predicated on such fundamental moral values as the sanctity of life. The attitudes of advocates of the right to choose, on the other hand, are based on such underlying values as individual autonomy and privacy. Thus, it is easy to see why ethical disagreements and debates generate such emotional rhetoric.

The ancient Greeks recognized the importance of *attitudes*, and since that time, many writers have described three components: the affective, the cognitive, and the behavioral.[29] The *affective* component of an attitude is the emotional side of our beliefs about a situation. It consists of our positive or negative feelings toward people or events, pleasure or displeasure, or perhaps even uncertainty. For example, some TV personalities may elicit positive emotional responses because of their charisma, charm, or interesting commentary. Others may evoke negative emotions because of their insensitivity and ill-concealed ego. Of course, one of the wonders of human nature is that the same individual is often capable of producing a variety of responses in different members of the audience. This emotional incongruity is reflected in the phenomenon of controversial talk show host Rush Limbaugh, who is either loved or reviled by radio and TV audiences. The affective component is important to the moral agent in making ethical judgments because it provides an emotional dimension to those decisions. It would be a callous reporter, indeed, who did not sympathize with the plight of the family of an airline-disaster victim and thus did not approach that family for an interview with great sensitivity.

The *cognitive* component is the intellectual side of an attitude. It consists of what the moral agent believes, knows, or reasons about a person, thing, or event. For example, one person may believe that TV evangelists pose a threat to mainstream Protestantism, whereas another may see television as an instrument for spreading Christianity around the world.

The *behavioral* component of an attitude relates to the individual's predisposition to respond. When we speak of ethical conduct, or behavior, we are referring to moral action reflecting the affective (emotional) and cognitive (rational) components of a moral agent's attitudes about a situation. Either of these may dominate at a given moment, but true moral reasoning takes into account both feelings and beliefs.

As a case in point, a newspaper editor's decision to publish a rape victim's name is never an easy one. Many papers have policies against doing so; others will publish the names under some circumstances. The emotional side of the attitude about this dilemma would probably evoke feelings of compassion and sympathy for the victim. The rational, or cognitive, component might lead to the conclusion that the victim's name was not essential to the story and that nothing would be gained by publishing it. In addition, a policy against releasing the names of victims of sex crimes might encourage other victims to report their experiences to the authorities.

On the other hand, some editors, despite feelings of compassion for the victim and even some misgivings about publishing her name, might reason that the crime victims have always been news and that their names should be published unless there is some unusual reason for not doing so. The media, they feel, should not be in the business of suppressing news; otherwise, their credibility will suffer. What is lost in this debate is the notion that the audience might support withholding the name of a rape victim without automatically assuming that news suppression was standard practice for the media. And, as we have previously seen, the audience is an important consideration in making ethical judgments. In any event, both the rational and the emotional sides of our being are instrumental in moral reasoning.

Attitudes about morality, then, can be viewed as packages of values that combine feelings, thoughts, and actions.[30] But where do our attitudes and values come from? What forces shape our moral development? The answers to these questions are important, because individual moral behavior forms the foundation of institutional and professional standards of conduct. *Institutions do not behave unethically; people do.*[31]

Sources of Values and Attitudes

Four influential sources directly affect our formation of values and attitudes: the family, peer groups, role models, and societal institutions. The extent to which each of these is responsible for our moral behavior depends on the unique circumstances of each individual.

Not surprisingly, *parents* provide the first and perhaps most important behavioral models for children. Parents are the primary influence in instilling a conscience, a sense of right and wrong. Some values and attitudes are learned by a child through instruction and discipline; others are acquired through imitating, or modeling, parental behavior. One popular explanation of the involvement and fascination of middle-class youths with drugs is that they are imitating a generation of parents who have relied heavily on prescription drugs, such as Valium, to deal with their stressful lifestyles. Likewise, a mother who writes an excuse to a teacher saying that "Johnny was sick yesterday," when in fact he was not, sends a cue to Johnny that lying is permissible. Ironically, such a parent would never instill deception in her child as a positive value, but her behavior sends a message that deception is socially acceptable in certain situations.

One measure of conscience is the ability to resist temptation.[32] This goal is achieved in the early stages of the child's moral development through a series of rewards and punishments,[33] but children increasingly internalize these lessons. At this stage children generally accept certain ideas advanced by their parents but are incapable of true moral reasoning. But in subsequent stages the beginnings of logical reasoning appear, and children's ever-developing moral blueprints become both reference points by which future ethical dilemmas can be resolved and defense mechanisms by which children can resist the challenges to their value systems.[34]

Peer groups are another important influence in moral development, especially among adolescents. The most significant peer groups are those encountered in the neighborhood, schools, churches, social clubs, and working environment. Peers can exert enormous, sometimes irresistible, pressure to conform. It is here that the individual's moral values may undergo their most rigorous challenge and that ethical compromises may occur because of the social role required of group members. Of course, some peer group memberships, such as participation in a religious organization, can reinforce an individual's value system.

Role models are those individuals whom we admire, respect, and wish to emulate. They can teach us the ways of righteousness or wickedness (e.g., drug dealers whose lavish lifestyles are sometimes attractive to impressionable youths), but they have a profound impact on the imitative behavior of others. Children and adolescents become psychologically involved with their role models and assume their ideas, attitudes, and conduct.

Sometimes, role models are ordinary people, such as teachers or ministers, who exert a subtle influence on those with whom they come in contact. Frequently, they are public figures who can set examples, either good or bad, for millions of followers. Shaquille O'Neal, Michael Jackson, and Oprah Winfrey appear to have very little in common except that they are all role models. Impressionable youths often take their ethical cues from such highly visible personalities. Beer commercials featuring well-known athletes, for example, convey a message that drinking is somehow a social virtue, a true test of masculinity. Likewise, the increased use of snuff by Little League and high school players can be attributed to the examples set by their major league heroes.

Role models and peers can exert as much influence, especially in later life, as families. The importance of selecting as models those individuals who exemplify positive ethical values was noted by the ethicist Michael Josephson in a conversation with the TV commentator Bill Moyers:

> We certainly get an inculcation from our parents, and that's a very important thing. But all that does is give us an orientation toward ethics. Now some people rebel against that orientation, and some people adopt it and follow it. We're also influenced by our peer groups. Ethics is taught from all sides, by a coach, for example, or a teacher, or a particular person who inspires someone to his highest self. . . . It is very important for leaders and role models, whether they be sports figures or politicians, to make positive statements of ethics, if they're not hypocritical.[35]

Do role models have any moral obligation toward their followers? Those who set bad examples are generally motivated by self-interest and thus are not worthy of emulation. But true moral leaders, those who are in a position to move the ethical development of others in a positive direction, have an obligation to set high standards of conduct for those who might be inclined to model their behavior.

Suppose that a college newspaper adviser, who is highly respected by the student staff and is thus somewhat of a role model, encourages his young reporters to do anything to get a story. Such advice can sometimes have the effect of instilling in journalistic neophytes the notion that reporters operate on an ethical plane separate from the rest of society. Likewise, a public relations instructor who counsels company loyalty over public responsibility is providing her students with a distorted view of the ethical conduct expected of PR practitioners.

Families, peer groups, and role models all exert powerful and demonstrable influences on our sense of ethics. But *societal institutions* should not be overlooked as another important influence in the moral life of the individual. Do such institutions alter our ethical standards, or do they merely reflect them? This is a complex question, but suffice it to say that society's institutions reflect the prevailing norms and at the same time are instrumental in bringing about changes in attitudes concerning standards of conduct. For example, the "sexual revolution" was well under way by the time television jumped on the bandwagon, but it is likely that TV programming had a role in expediting public acceptance of greater sexual freedom, even if we cannot prove it scientifically.

We said earlier that institutions do not behave unethically—people do. However, the decision making within the institutional structure is sometimes so diffuse that individual responsibility is difficult to ascribe. A case in point is the television drama, which necessitates a cadre of creative talent, each member with a stake in the moral tone of the content. The path of responsibility begins in Hollywood and flows to the network corporate offices. This division of creative labor within institutions often leads us to refer to the "ethical standards" of CBS, the

National Enquirer, or the *Washington Post.* Nevertheless, individuals make the moral judgments that emerge in the form of corporate policy or practice.

Institutions have a profound impact on their own members and set the ethical tone for their conduct. Within each organization there is a moral culture, reflected both in written policies and the examples set by top management, that inspires its members' ethical behavior. The socialization of journalists and the development of professional values do not end at the school door. The moral education of media practitioners begins early in life but is a never-ending process.

Institutions also have a profound influence on the ethical values and attitudes of societal members because of the pivotal role they play in the dynamics of any culture. Thus, we often speak of those institutions that respect the needs and sensibilities of the publics they serve (which sometimes include media organizations) as acting with a sense of social responsibility.

The media establishment has often been criticized for its lack of institutional values that might enhance the ethical stature of the industry. The traditional professions, such as law and medicine, have uniform codes of ethics, but journalists have shunned enforceable codes. They complain that such standards are antithetical to the independence demanded of reporters and are the first step down the path toward government licensing. However, media critics have used the absence of a uniform and enforceable code of ethics as evidence that journalism is not truly a profession.

The process by which all of these influences—families, peer groups, role models, and institutions—introduce the individual to the conventions and norms of a given society or subgroup is known as *socialization.*[36] For example, when an academic institution punishes students for cheating, it is reinforcing the value of honesty that is a first principle of our culture's moral code. Likewise, journalism students, through their enrollment in university-level journalism education programs, are quickly "socialized" into the conventions of their profession. Socialization is a lifelong activity and serves as an agent of social control by providing for a certain homogenization of moral values.

All of these influences contribute to the moral development of the individual in a combination that social psychologists do not yet fully comprehend. We do know, however, that our attitudes about a situation do not always determine our moral judgments, thus suggesting that peer pressure and institutional influences sometimes take precedence over the values we consider important.

A legislator who is an outspoken advocate of gun control may, for example, vote against a ban on handguns in order to gain some concessions from his legislative colleagues on another matter pending before them. A magazine editor who has campaigned aggressively for more federal resources to fight the "war on drugs" may, nevertheless, look the other way when the ad manager accepts ads for alcoholic beverages, the nation's number one drug. There are many reasons for this inconsistency between belief and behavior,[37] but at the very least it reflects a conflict of ethical values.

THE ETHICAL DILEMMA: A CONFLICT OF VALUES

A man named Heintz has a wife who is terminally ill with cancer. He has tried, without success, to raise money to buy a drug that might save her life. A druggist is charging $2,000 for such a potion. Heintz has been able to raise only $1,000, and the druggist refuses to extend him credit. Should Heintz steal the drug to save his wife's life?[38]

This famous hypothetical ethical dilemma was used by the social psychologist Lawrence Kohlberg and his associates to illustrate the conflicting values inherent in the notion of justice. On the one hand, Heintz loves his wife, and, in the interest of the sanctity of life, he may feel justified in stealing the drug. On the other hand, to do so would violate one of the fundamental moral tenets of the Western world, the proscription against stealing another's property.

Heintz dilemmas are all around us. They constitute the very essence of emotional debates about such diverse social issues as abortion, gun control, the death penalty, sex education, and pornography. Of course, not all moral judgments reflect the kind of life-or-death situation confronted by Heintz, but difficult ethical choices do involve conflicts in values. These conflicts can arise on several levels. Sometimes, there is an inner conflict involving the application of general societal values. For example, a public relations executive may have to decide between the value of revealing the *truth* to the public about her company's environmental blunder and the value of *loyalty* to the company.

Sometimes, a conflict arises between general societal values (e.g., minimizing harm to others) and professional values. Consider, for example, the public uproar in Columbia, South Carolina, when a local TV station honored a police request to withhold information as a matter of safety and the newspaper did not. In Columbia, a policeman was wounded in a stolen car chase. The case was not connected with his regular assignment as an undercover narcotics investigator, and the police chief asked the news media not to reveal the officer's name lest they endanger him or his son or pregnant wife. As result of the newspaper's decision not to comply, many subscribers were angry and some canceled their subscriptions.[39] In letters to defecting subscribers, editor Gil Thelen defended his decision: "We weighed the public's legitimate interest in the information with concerns about the officer's and his family's safety. No person in authority was able to provide specific information about any security threats to either."[40]

Another instance of conflicting values concerned Nike, which ran a billboard campaign in Chicago's South Side ghetto featuring famous African-American athletes wearing Nike ath-

letic shoes. Nike was careful to select athletes with squeaky clean images as role models for the African-American youths who were the target audience of this campaign. But when several black inner-city youths were assaulted or murdered allegedly because their peers wished to dress more like the celebrity role models, Nike was criticized in the media for selecting black athletes as spokespersons. Such advertisements created a desire for material goods that were beyond the economic means of the average juvenile in Chicago's South Side. A Nike representative defended the practice as good marketing to use such credible personalities in appealing to black youths. Thus, what appeared to be a sound advertising and marketing strategy, based on noble principles, unintentionally ran afoul of social values and the stark realities of life in the inner city.[41]

When neither conflicting value appears to be satisfactory, we may examine third options. Suppose the dean asks a journalism professor to reconsider a failing grade he awarded to a graduating senior in his media ethics course. *Loyalty* to the dean may propel him to honor his request. On the other hand, *honesty* suggests that the professor should not do so, especially if he is convinced of the correctness of the grade. However, he may appeal to a third value, *fairness*: would it be unfair to the other students to reconsider the grade of one student and not the entire class?

Ethical judgments involving the clash of competing principles generally arise in rather untidy situations.[42] Such was the case when a TV station and a newspaper agonized over whether to report a rather unusual adoption. The situation arose when a mother in Eugene, Oregon, Elizabeth Diane Downs, was convicted of shooting her three children. Although Downs told the police that she and the children—two of whom survived—had been shot by a "shaggy-haired stranger" who had flagged her down on a desolate road, an investigation led the police to conclude that she herself was responsible for the shootings. She was convicted of murder and attempted murder.[43] The two surviving children, both physically disabled after the ordeal, were entrusted to foster care. But more than three years after the shootings, rumors began circulating that the prosecutor in the case, Fred Hugi, was about to adopt the two youngsters. A reporter for KVAL-TV finally confirmed the rumor, and a crew was dispatched to the prison where Downs was serving her sentence to get her response to the prosecutor's plan. But the interview was never aired. Although the station recognized the public's interest in this development, it decided that the children's privacy was more important. The assistant news director at KVAL-TV, Gayle Mitchell, defended the decision on the ground that publicizing the prosecutor's involvement with the children would "thrust them back into the spotlight, just when things were starting to settle down for them." Besides, there was no reason to believe that Hugi would not make a good parent, and the children's disabilities would make finding another adoptive home difficult.[44]

The *Register-Guard* in Eugene, however, made a contrary decision, a decision that its managing editor, Doug Bates, vigorously defended on the paper's editorial page. Bates told his readers that publication of this story was in the public interest. Hugi's prospective role as the children's father, Bates asserted, raised questions of public policy and ethical conduct on the part of a participant in the judicial process that had sent the children's mother to prison. He also noted that the paper's readers expected to be informed and that any suppression of news, no matter how noble the reason, would result in a loss of journalistic credibility.[45] Shortly after this brouhaha died down, prosecutor Fred Hugi became the adoptive father of the two children. Thus, the newspaper's account apparently had little effect on the outcome of the case.

This scenario exemplifies a conflict of competing values. It also illustrates how two responsible news organizations made different ethical decisions, both of which could be defended on rational grounds.

The "free press/fair trial" issue provides another timely example of the conflict of ethical principles. Some court cases, particularly those involving heinous crimes or public figures, attract a lot of media coverage. Thus, the publication of certain damaging facts before the trial may make the selection of an impartial jury difficult, depriving the defendant of a fair trial. The First Amendment and an impressive array of legal precedents limit a judge's discretion in controlling media coverage of high-profile trials.[46] But the media cannot escape the ethical dilemmas that inevitably arise when they are caught between their professional obligations to provide responsible coverage of such events and a public that seems to have an insatiable appetite for the sordid aspects of such captivating dramas. A case in point was the O. J. Simpson trial in which both the tabloid and mainstream media transformed a tragic news event into a mass entertainment spectacle. This case is examined in greater detail in Chapters 7 and 11.

In ethical issues, no less than in legal ones, the key to dealing with Heintz dilemmas is to demystify the process by gathering as much evidence and formulating as many rational arguments as possible in defense of our ultimate decision. This is not to understate the difficulty of resolving conflicts between moral alternatives. Even after a decision is rendered, there will be some lingering uncertainty whether the choice was proper or wise. The goal of moral reasoning is not to reach agreement on the ethical issues of our time. Instead, moral reasoning is a tool designed to assist us, as moral agents, in working our way out of the ethical morasses encountered in our personal and professional lives.

SUMMARY

Ethics is the branch of philosophy that deals with questions of moral behavior. The study of ethics can provide the tools for making difficult moral choices, both personal and professional.

The goal is not to make ethical decisions with which everyone agrees but to increase our ability to defend our critical judgments on some rational basis.

Ethics, as a formal field of inquiry, includes three related subcategories. *Metaethics* attempts to assign meanings to the abstract language of moral philosophy. *Normative ethics* provides the foundation for decision making through the development of general rules and principles of moral conduct. *Applied ethics* is concerned with using these theoretical norms to solve ethical problems in the real world.

Ethical situations are usually complex affairs, in which a *moral agent* (the one making the ethical decision) commits an *act* (either verbal or nonverbal) within a specific *context* with a particular *motive* directed at an *individual* or *audience* usually with some *consequence*, either positive or negative. Each of these factors must be taken into account before passing judgment on the outcome of any moral scenario.

There are two schools of thought on whether ethics is a proper subject for academic consideration. Cynics disparage the study of ethics, because it is a discipline that raises many questions without providing concrete answers. They also argue that such character education classes will do little to influence those whose moral education is virtually complete before they enter the academy. Media practitioners sometimes see little value in such courses, because classes cannot duplicate the frenzied pace and pressure of the real world.

Proponents of ethics instruction believe that although moral conduct itself probably cannot be taught, such courses can promote virtuous behavior through the teaching of moral reasoning. However, the ability to make sound ethical decisions comes only through practice and a lifetime commitment to the principles of virtuosity. This condition is known as *ethical fitness*.

Although media ethics courses cannot simulate the realities of the competitive marketplace, they can offer an intellectual moral foundation for future generations of practitioners. A media ethics course has at least five realistic and practical educational objectives: (1) stimulating the moral imagination, (2) recognizing ethical issues, (3) developing analytical skills, (4) eliciting a sense of moral obligation and personal responsibility, and (5) tolerating disagreement. Thus, the teaching of moral literacy is just as vital to the curriculum as the skills courses that will train students for their first jobs.

However, the development of a sense of moral obligation does not begin in the classroom. Moral maturation starts early in life, when we begin taking into account the interests of others. This lesson is known as the *ethics imperative*, because purely selfish individuals cannot, by definition, make ethical judgments.

The study of ethics must include an understanding of how moral direction is acquired. Our ethical values form the foundation on which we make ethical decisions. These values underlie our attitudes about moral issues, and our attitudes are believed to consist of an emotional component, an intellectual, or rational, component, and a behavioral component. Thus, true moral reasoning takes into account both feelings and beliefs about an issue.

The acquisition of values and the formation of attitudes are a complex process that does not easily lend itself to scientific verification. However, for most of us the important forces that shape our moral development are the family, peer groups, role models, and societal institutions. Parents are our first encounter with discipline, but as we evolve into autonomous individuals, peer groups, role models, and institutional forces play an increasingly significant role in shaping our moral destiny.

With so many diverse forces bombarding us with ethical cues, it is inevitable that conflicts between competing values will emerge. The study of ethics and moral reasoning cannot necessarily resolve such conflicts for us, but it can provide the tools to make it easier to live with our difficult ethical choices.

Notes

1. Lindley J. Stiles and Bruce D. Johnson (eds.), *Morality Examined: Guidelines for Teachers* (Princeton, NJ: Princeton Book Company, 1977), p. xi.
2. Conrad C. Fink, *Media Ethics: In the Newsroom and Beyond* (New York: McGraw-Hill, 1988), p. 5.
3. *Ibid.*
4. Mike Moore, "Sports, Ethics and Ideas," *Quill*, January 1987, p. 2.
5. Baruch Brody, *Ethics and Its Applications* (New York: Harcourt Brace Jovanovich, 1983), p. 4.
6. See Joan C. Callahan (ed.), *Ethical Issues in Professional Life* (New York: Oxford University Press, 1988), pp. 7–9; John C. Merrill and S. Jack Odell, *Philosophy and Journalism* (White Plains, NY: Longman, 1983), p. 79.
7. For a good discussion of applied ethics see Brody, *Ethics and Its Applications.*
8. This model is based on one described by Richard L. Johannesen in *Ethics in Human Communication,* 3d ed. (Prospect Heights, IL: Waveland, 1990), p. 16.
9. "Conflict of Interest," *Quill,* November/December 1994, p. 13.
10. For an elaboration of this point, see Jeffrey Olen, *Ethics in Journalism* (Upper Saddle River, NJ: Prentice Hall, 1988), p. 25.
11. Stiles and Johnson, *Morality Examined,* pp. 11–12.
12. James Rachels, "Can Ethics Provide Answers?" in David M. Rosenthal and Fadlou She-haili (eds.), *Applied Ethics and Ethical Theory* (Salt Lake City: University of Utah Press, 1988), pp. 3–4.
13. This view was expressed, according to Plato, in the *Meno,* where Socrates stated that virtue is "an instinct given by God to the virtuous." See Stiles and Johnson, *Morality Examined,* p. 10; quoting Benjamin Jowett, Jr., *The Dialogues of Plato* (New York: Random House, 1920), Vol. 1, p. 380.
14. Reginald D. Archambault, "Criteria for Success in Moral Instruction," in Barry L. Chazan and Jonas F. Soltis (eds.), *Moral Education* (New York: Teachers College Press, 1973), p. 165.
15. Hastings Center, *The Teaching of Ethics in Higher Education* (Hastings-on-Hudson, NY: Hastings Center, 1980), pp. 48–52. These goals are also discussed in James A. Jaksa and Michael S. Pritchard, *Communication Ethics: Methods of Analysis,* 2d ed. (Belmont, CA: Wadsworth, 1994), pp. 12–18.
16. "From the Newsroom to the Boardroom," *Newsweek,* December 31, 1990, p. 65.
17. For a discussion of this issue, see H. Eugene Goodwin and Ron F. Smith, *Groping for Ethics in Journalism,* 3d ed. (Ames: Iowa State University Press, 1994), pp. 113–127.
18. Louis W. Hodges, "The Journalist and Professionalism," *Journal of Mass Media Ethics,* 1(2), Spring–Summer 1986, p. 35.
19. See Jaksa and Pritchard, *Communication Ethics,* pp. 15–16.
20. *Ibid.,* p. 9.
21. Hastings Center, *Teaching of Ethics,* p. 52.
22. See Rushworth M. Kidder, *How Good People Make Tough Choices* (New York: Morrow, 1995), pp. 57–76.
23. *Ibid.,* p. 59.
24. Edwin P. Hollander, *Principles and Methods of Social Psychology,* 4th ed. (New York: Oxford University Press, 1981), pp. 259–266.
25. For a discussion of this point, see Norman E. Bowie, *Making Ethical Decisions* (New York: McGraw-Hill, 1985), pp. 11–16.
26. Ted J. Smith III, "Journalism and the Socrates Syndrome," *Quill,* April 1988, p. 15.
27. Peter A. Angeles, *Dictionary of Philosophy* (New York: Barnes & Noble, 1981), p. 310.
28. Albert A. Harrison, *Individuals and Groups: Understanding Social Behavior* (Pacific Grove, CA: Brooks/Cole, 1976), p. 192.
29. *Ibid.,* pp. 192–195.
30. *Ibid.,* p. 193.
31. This notion is challenged by Thomas Nagel in "Ruthlessness in Public Life," in Callahan, *Ethical Issues,* pp. 76–83.
32. Hollander, *Principles and Methods of Social Psychology,* p. 258.
33. See A. Bandura, *A Social Learning Theory* (Englewood Cliffs, NJ: Prentice Hall, 1977); J. P. Flanders, "A Review of Research on Imitative Behavior," *Psychology Bulletin,* 69 (1968), pp. 316–337.
34. The psychologist Lawrence Kohlberg, in challenging theories advanced earlier by Sigmund Freud, maintains that a child's moral development occurs in six stages.
35. Bill Moyers, *A World of Ideas* (New York: Doubleday, 1989), p. 16.
36. See Hollander, *Principles and Methods of Social Psychology,* p. 174.
37. For a discussion of the various theories in social psychology relating to this topic, see Harrison, *Individuals and Groups,* pp. 195–218.
38. Reported in Jaksa and Pritchard, *Communication Ethics,* p. 99.
39. Richard P. Cunningham, "Public Cries Foul on Both Coasts When Papers Lift Secrecy," *Quill,* April 1995, p. 12.
40. Quoted in *ibid.*
41. For a more thorough discussion of this case, see Gail Baker Woods, "The Gym Shoe Phenomenon: Social Values vs. Marketability," in Philip Patterson and Lee Wilkins, *Media Ethics: Issues and Cases,* 2d ed. (Dubuque, IA: Brown & Benchmark, 1994), pp. 75–77.

42. For a more thorough discussion on this point, see Tom L. Beauchamp, *Philosophical Ethics: An Introduction to Moral Philosophy* (New York: McGraw-Hill, 1982), pp. 43–45.

43. For a discussion of this case, see Gayle Mitchell, "The Toughest Call," *Quill,* April 1987, pp. 27–28.

44. *Ibid.*, p. 27.

45. This editorial is reprinted in the *Quill,* April 1987, p. 29.

46. E.g., see *Nebraska Press Association v. Stuart*, 427 U.S. 539 (1976).

CHAPTER

2

Ethics and Society

THE NEED FOR A SYSTEM OF ETHICS

In August 1988, the *Seattle Post-Intelligencer* notified a Superior Court judge, Gary Little, that it was about to break a story detailing allegations that he had had sexual relations with boys. Other local news organizations were preparing similar stories. The day before the story was to be published, Little committed suicide. Some accused the press of "hounding the man to his death," especially in light of the fact that he had expressed his intention of leaving public life.[1] One reader blamed this outpouring of criticism of the press on a moral relativism in which judgments are "not as clear cut as they once were."[2] Richard Cunningham, a journalism professor who reviewed this case in the *Quill*, agreed: "It seems to this writer, at least, that it can be frightening for journalists and others to sail on a boundless sea without traditional anchors."[3]

Society and Moral Anchors

As this case illustrates, society is not always a gentle taskmaster when it comes to passing judgment on its moral agents. The standards against which society scrutinizes individual and institutional behavior are embedded in its code of moral conduct, its system of ethics. But if Cunningham is correct—if we are morally adrift without traditional anchors—that is sufficient justification to explore the following question: Why does society really need a system of ethics? At least four reasons merit attention.

The Need for Social Stability First, a system of ethics is necessary for social intercourse. Ethics is the foundation of our advanced civilization, a cornerstone that provides some stability to society's moral expectations. If we are to enter into agreements with others, a necessity in a complex, interdependent society, we must be able to trust one another to keep those agreements, even if it is not in our self-interest to do so.[4] Professional athletes who demand to renegotiate their contracts before they have expired may breed contempt and mistrust in the front office and the belief among the fans that they are placing self-interest over the interests of the team. The reading and viewing publics likewise expect journalists to report the truth, even when there is no formal agreement to do so. When reporters fail in this expectation, public confidence is eroded. And particularly where such ethical indiscretions are committed by respectable news organizations, the credibility of all media suffers.

Such was the case in 1981, for example, when the prestigious *Washington Post* returned a Pulitzer Prize for feature writing after the paper's editors discovered that one of their young reporters, Janet Cooke, had fabricated a dramatic account of an eight-year-old heroin addict, identified as "Jimmy." To the credit of the *Post,* the newspaper's ombudsman moved swiftly to make a full disclosure to the readers.[5] In still another highly publicized ethical debacle, driven as much by competitive pressures as an erosion of standards,[6] the producers of NBC's *Dateline,* in an episode broadcast in November 1992, rigged the results of a test crash involving a General Motors truck by equipping its outboard fuel tanks with explosive devices. Even after NBC News President Michael Gartner became aware of the deception, his first instinct was to defend the broadcast. Only after GM threatened to sue NBC did Gartner issue an apology.[7] He later resigned as a result of this ethical fiasco. But such betrayal of the public trust has consequences that extend far beyond this particular broadcast, as reflected in this observation by Rob Sunde, past chairman of the Radio-Television News Directors Association:

> Public confidence in NBC News was shattered. The affair seems to have given black eyes to the other major broadcast news organizations. Print journalists seemed to take special delight in the scandal, overlooking the fact all media had been smeared with NBC's tar brush, that people's trust in the news media in general had suffered.[8]

Fortunately, such instances are rare, but just one well-publicized ethical indiscretion can undermine respect from an already skeptical public.

The Need for a Moral Hierarchy Second, a system of ethics serves as a *moral gatekeeper* in apprising society of the relative importance of certain customs. It does this by alerting the public to (1) those norms that are important enough to be described as moral and (2) the "hierarchy of ethical norms" and their relative standing in the moral pecking order.

All cultures have many customs, but most do not concern ethical mores.[9] For example, eating with utensils is customary in Western countries, but the failure to do so is not immoral. Standing for the national anthem before a sporting event is a common practice, but those who remain seated are not behaving unethically. There is a tendency to describe actions of which we disapprove as immoral, although most of our social indiscretions are merely transgressions of etiquette. A system of ethics identifies those customs and practices where social disapproval is significant enough to render them immoral.

However, even those values and principles that have the distinction of qualifying as moral norms are not all on an equal footing. From time to time in this book I will refer to certain ideas, such as the commitment to truth and proscriptions against stealing, as *fundamental* societal values. This distinction suggests that some are more important than others. Trespassing, for example, although not socially approved, is generally viewed less seriously than lying. This may explain why the journalistic practice of invading private property to get a story, though not applauded in all quarters, does not usually meet with the same degree of condemnation as the use of outright deception.

The Need to Resolve Conflicts Third, a system of ethics is an important social institution for resolving cases involving conflicting claims based on individual self-interest.[10] For example, it might be in a student's own interest to copy from a classmate's term paper. It is in the classmate's best interest to keep her from doing so. Societal rules against plagiarism are brought to bear in evaluating the moral conduct inherent in this situation.

The Need to Clarify Values Finally, a system of ethics also functions to clarify for society the competing values and principles inherent in emerging and novel moral dilemmas. Some of the issues confronting civilization today would challenge the imagination of even the most ardent philosopher. A case in point is the battle over animal rights, a movement that has confronted researchers with this discomforting question: do the human benefits of animal research outweigh the suffering of the creatures themselves?[11] This issue also poses a thorny public relations problem, particularly for those companies using animals to test commercial products.

An ethical system encourages debate and the airing of differences over competing moral principles. In so doing, it crystallizes society's attitudes about ethical dilemmas and often leads to adjudication (if not a satisfactory resolution) of disputes. This point is illustrated by readers' complaints surrounding a California newspaper's coverage of a controversial ballot issue in 1994. The proposition, designed to cut off government services to illegal aliens, was supported by a group known as Save Our State (SOS), whose supporters were subjected to charges of racism and threats by militant opponents. Because of those threats, SOS sought to keep its address secret. But the Orange County *Register* learned the address and used it as the lead sentence in a story about the organization.[12]

Furious readers, fearing that bombers might be tempted to blow up the building, called the paper irresponsible. They believed the potential for harm, including possible loss of lives, outweighed any news value in revealing the organization's address. The *Register*'s topic editor defended the lead because of SOS's penchant for secrecy: "The decision to use the address as the lead was done to quickly focus on what has become a center of controversy about this group—its secrecy." But the paper's ombudsman was not impressed. "Leading the story with the address while knowing the group wanted secrecy for safety reasons," he wrote, "was a sorry example of in-your-face, gotcha journalism, precisely the type that has pushed

journalism to a low rung on the public opinion ladder."[13] Although there may have been no meeting of the minds between the *Register*'s editors and their disgruntled readers, the ombudsman served as a forum through which to clarify the competing values and to foster a rational deliberation of the ethical concerns.[14]

In another case, the *Times-Union* in Jacksonville, Florida, published a page-one article containing racist remarks by Chief Circuit Justice John E. Santora, Jr. Many readers were outraged, not at the remarks but at what they considered to be the newspaper's ill-considered judgment in printing them. Most callers said the *Times-Union* should not have published what the judge called "off-hand remarks," and some accused the paper of fanning the flames of racial intolerance. The paper responded that the judge was interviewed twice and knew that he was being taped when he made the intemperate comments.[15]

While the newspaper did apparently gain some public acceptance of the notion that it had done its job, the coverage precipitated a healthy debate about journalistic values and the media's role as community activist. For example, the paper's ombudsman, Mike Clark, criticized the *Times-Union* for not doing more to combat racial injustice in Jacksonville. "We had an obligation to show our involvement in the community, not just to report the news," he said. Clark believed that more space should have been devoted to solutions.[16] But John Seigenthaler, publisher emeritus of the Nashville *Tennessean*, in an interview for the *Quill* appeared to take issue with Clark when he said that exposing racism in the community is the duty of the paper, "and I'm not sure you have to go beyond that."[17]

The Functions of Media within the Ethical System

If a system of ethics provides moral cohesion for society's individual members and institutions, media practitioners are in particular need of one. Why? The mass media are among the most influential enterprises in a democratic society, standing at the crossroads between the citizens and their political, economic, and social institutions. In addition, they are instrumental in the transmission of cultural values. They set the agenda for which values are important and offer symbolic cues for standards of conduct, including ethical behavior. This process is conveyed through the three key functions that media practitioners play in American society: dissemination and interpretation of *information*, transmission of *persuasive* messages, and production and marketing of mass *entertainment*. Each of these functions brings with it an array of ethical expectations that are not necessarily the same. For example, should the standards for truth and accuracy be the same for advertising as for news? What values— entertainment or news—should govern the production of a docudrama? Under what conditions may PR practitioners withhold information from the media and the public and still maintain their own credibility and the credibility of their clients or companies?

First, the media are the primary source of *information* in a democracy. Accurate and reliable information is the lifeblood of the democratic process. Perhaps the most obvious players in this information flow are journalists, who gain access to the day's intelligence and attempt to provide accurate information for citizens to make informed and intelligent political decisions. But in a capitalist society, news media must also respect the demands of the marketplace, thereby satisfying the public's craving for the more sensational and tantalizing aspects of the human condition. This is exhibited in tabloid journalism's insatiable appetite for violent and sexually explicit content and its unremitting fascination with the private lives of social luminaries. The so-called mainstream media, however, are also the captive of marketplace forces and spend an increasing amount of time producing news content that has little to do with the democratic process.

Journalists are not the only media practitioners who perform the essential function of providing information in a capitalistic society. The economic messages of advertisers and the corporate image building of PR practitioners also provide relevant and beneficial information to consumers and other constituencies. The role of economic information in a democratic society was captured in a Supreme Court opinion recognizing the Constitutional status of advertising. "As to the particular consumer's interest in the free flow of commercial information," Justice Harry Blackmun wrote, "that interest may be as keen, if not keener by far, than his interest in the day's most urgent political debate."[18] He continued with his defense of advertising as a worthy contributor to the capitalistic system:

> Advertising, however tasteless and excessive it sometimes may seem, is nonetheless dissemination of information as to who is producing and selling what product, for what reason, and at what price. So long as we preserve a predominantly free enterprise economy, the allocation of our resources in large measure will be made through numerous private economic decisions. It is a matter of public interest that those decisions . . . be intelligent and well informed. To this end, the free flow of commercial information is indispensable.[19]

Regardless of the source of information, society has a right to expect a certain level of ethical behavior from its media institutions, and when this conduct is not forthcoming, a crisis of confidence occurs between these institutions and the public. At a minimum, media audiences demand information unencumbered by deliberate falsehoods, regardless of whether the source is a journalist or an advertising agency. But beyond that threshold, ethical expectations can vary, depending on the media practitioner's role. We expect reporters, for example, to include all relevant facts in their stories, unless there is a compelling reason for omitting some salient piece of information. We also expect their accounts of newsworthy events to be balanced—that is, not to favor one set of values over another. But society does not expect advertisers or PR practitioners to approach their tasks with a commitment to symmetry. They are mass marketers of products, ideas, and images, and their clients and audiences are fully aware that communications from these sources are motivated as much by self-interest as the public interest.

The second major function of media practitioners is the transmission of *persuasive* communications. Actually, persuasion enjoys a noble legacy, tracing its lineage to the ancient Greeks. Like the use of rhetorical persuasion in ancient Greece, contemporary persuasion techniques are considered an art form, particularly when they are adroitly used to alter public perceptions, attitudes, and even buying habits. However, unlike our Greek forbears, today's practitioners often use more subtle and sometimes indiscernible techniques to manipulate audiences and public opinion. Perhaps the most visible example are TV commercials, which often include visual cues that shrewdly and skillfully promote the values (some would say "superficial" values) of sex appeal, perpetual youth, and social conformity as essential to our psychological tranquility and self-esteem.

Editorials and news commentaries, advertising and public relations are the most prevalent sources for such content, although entertainment fare sometimes wraps persuasive messages in a sugar-coated genre. American society has embraced both advertising and PR as legitimate functions—after all, advertising is the economic mainstay of mass media in a capitalistic system—but they have increasingly become ethically controversial. Defenders of advertising and public relations derive their support from classical liberal marketplace theory that emphasizes the competition of competing voices and the supremacy of the autonomous and rational consumer. The most extreme form of this philosophy is "let the buyer beware," which in effect absolves purvey-ors of persuasive messages of any moral responsibility for the consequences of their actions. Critics respond that advertisers and PR practitioners are the true potentates in the communications process and take advantage of the inability or unwillingness of passive consumers to identify and discriminate among this relentless barrage of manipulative communications.[20] Thus, the public must be represented and protected by outside agencies, ranging all the way from government agencies like the Federal Trade Commission to various consumer watchdog groups. Because practitioners and their critics hold such dissimilar perspectives, ethical conflict is inevitable. In a free society, a reconciliation of these positions is unlikely. Perhaps the most that can be expected is to establish minimum standards of acceptable behavior (e.g., prohibitions against the intentional transmission of false or deceptive information) and to apportion moral responsibility among the various players in the chain of communication, from the disseminators of persuasive messages to the ultimate gatekeepers in the process, the recipients.

The third function of media practitioners —the production and dissemination of mass *entertainment*—poses an ethical challenge perhaps because there is little agreement on what its role in society should be. Unlike journalism, which is designed to scrutinize the political system and contribute to the democratic process, entertainment has no clear-cut rationale. Thus, the ethical question is whether the media have an obligation to elevate tastes and promote virtuous behavior or whether "giving the audience what it wants," even at the risk of reinforcing dysfunctional attitudes and behavior, is sufficient.

In a democracy, media practitioners produce material that they believe meets a perceived need of the heterogeneous audience. And the finicky public expresses its approval or disapproval in the marketplace.[21] In a pluralistic society with a diversity of artistic tastes, only an incurable optimist would argue that economic concerns and commercial motives do not matter. After all, one advantage of the mass production of entertainment is that a wide variety of content can be made available at little cost, thus providing an enjoyment for consumers of all socioeconomic classes. On the other hand, critics complain that the inevitable consequence of such mass production is an appeal to the lowest common denominator of artistic tastes. They argue commercialism should not be the only driving force in the production of popular entertainment and information and that producers of such material have a responsibility to contribute to an enrichment of cultural values. Thus, underlying any attempts at reconciling these two notions are two questions that must be confronted: Must all material produced for a mass audience have at least some modicum of social worth? Is it possible—or even morally desirable—to devise strategies that will meet the demands of a mass audience without resorting exclusively to content that does nothing more than trivialize the human condition and then provide an escape from it?

Perhaps the most troublesome trend in recent years has been the gradual blending of news, entertainment, and commercial values. For example, the integration of what used to be distinctive genres of news or public affairs and entertainment has elevated the uninhibited public examination of human transgressions and pathos to an art form and has trivialized and sensationalized the discussion of serious issues. The tabloid TV programs and talk shows are classic examples of this disturbing development. Likewise, "advertorials," which are ads that bear a striking resemblance to editorial content, and TV "infomercials" that resemble programming have also become ethically controversial. This trend toward blurring the line between the various media functions raises ethical concerns ranging from audience manipulation to outright deception.

Media practitioners, regardless of their societal function, are influential in that they touch the lives of all of us. Audience members, particularly those who are young and impressionable, often take their ethical cues from media personalities. Thus, they should serve as role models and should reinforce society's ethical expectations. When they fail in this responsibility, each ethical indiscretion further erodes society's confidence in the media.

REQUIREMENTS OF A SYSTEM OF ETHICS

If society's norms are to serve as moral guideposts, what criteria should be used in constructing a workable system of ethics? There may be some disagreement on this issue, but the following five criteria should form the foundation for any ethical system. These requirements pertain both to general societal principles and to codes of conduct reflecting the standards of professional organizations.[22]

Shared Values

An ethical system must be constructed, first and foremost, on shared values. Although individuals and groups within society may apply these standards differently to specific situations, they should at least agree on common ethical norms. For example, the fact that some members of society choose to lie under some circumstances does not diminish society's fundamental commitment to the value of truth. In other words, deviations from the norm may be excused for substantial reasons, but exceptions to the rule do not automatically alter its value.

This commitment to shared, or common, values is often reflected in the codification of those norms. The Ten Commandments, for example, are part of the code of moral conduct underlying the Judeo-Christian heritage. Many media institutions have codified their ethical principles, and such codes can at least provide the journalistic novice with some idea of the dividing line between acceptable and unacceptable behavior.

Wisdom

Ethical standards should be based on reason and experience. They should seek to strike a balance between the rights and interests of autonomous individuals and their obligations to society. In short, ethical norms should be reasonable. It would be unreasonable, for example, to expect reporters to remove themselves entirely from involvement in community affairs because of potential conflicts of interest. In fact, wisdom suggests that community involvement can enrich journalists' understanding of the stories they cover.

Wisdom also demands breathing room for advertisers who use "puffery" in their commercial messages, as long as the ads are not deceptive. Hyperbole is the handmaiden of salesmanship, and the marketplace suffers little from the introduction of exaggerated commercial claims of enhanced sex appeal and social acceptance. A code based on wisdom promotes ethical behavior while avoiding excessive and unreasonable moral propriety. Application of this criterion to a system of ethics results in flexibility, which shuns the extremes of an intransigent code at the one end and moral anarchy at the other. In journalism, for example, the proper balance is considered to be somewhere between the sensational and the bland.

Of course, wisdom based on experience suggests that the solutions derived from a moral code should be appropriate to the problem. Ethical quandaries sometimes call for drastic remedies. An affirmative action program, which in some cases might appear to be extreme, is sometimes justified to correct past discrimination. A university that suddenly discovers pervasive cheating on its campus might, in a moment of moral indignation, impose harsh new penalties for academic violations of the student code of conduct.

The idea of moderation could also be applied to the dilemma confronting the newspaper that carries ads for X-rated movies, especially if they contain offensive promotional material. Conservatives in the community would prefer that the ads be forever banned and have often been vocal on this point. Libertarians would argue, on the other hand, that any legal product or service should be allowed to promote its wares in the mass media. A publisher might take the temperate position—that is, between the extremes of banning the ads and accepting ads with graphic, tasteless displays—and accept ads with only movie title announcements.

Justice

Justice has to do with people's relations with one another and is often important to the resolution of ethical disputes. Central to the idea of justice is the notion of fairness, in which all individuals are treated alike in terms of what they deserve. In other words, there should be *no double standards*, unless there are compelling and rational reasons for discrimination.

This principle has important implications for the media. Media practitioners may employ it to decide what guidelines should be applied to using deception, establishing and maintaining confidential relationships, and intruding on others' privacy. For example, justice requires that journalists report the embarrassing behavior of others, both public and private figures, based on what they really deserve rather than for the purpose of titillating the morbid curiosity of the audience. Hollywood could also benefit from this idea of justice by using it to eliminate its dramatic renditions of racial and sexual stereotypes. And, in all fairness, substantial progress has been made in this area.

Freedom

A system of ethics must be based on some freedom of choice. A society that does not allow such freedom is morally impoverished. Moral agents must have several alternatives available and must be able to exercise their powers of reason without coercion. The first moral choice was made by Adam and Eve when they ate the forbidden fruit and were expelled from paradise. Of course, most ethical judgments do not result in such dire consequences. But without freedom there can be no moral reasoning, because moral reasoning, as we will see in Chapter 3, involves choosing from among several alternatives and defending one's decision based on some rational principle. In short, freedom provides the opportunity to raise one's ethical awareness, a goal that any system of ethics should encourage.

Accountability

As autonomous individuals, we are all responsible for our moral deeds and misdeeds, and the legitimacy of any ethical system depends on its facility in holding its participants to some standard of accountability. Accountability may range all the way from informal sanctions, as when an offending moral agent is tried in the court of public opinion, to more formal punitive measures, such as disbarment proceedings against attorneys who violate their codes of ethics or reprimands or dismissals of reporters who violate their companies' policies. An ethics system that does not include accountability encourages freedom without responsibility and thus lacks the moral authority to encourage virtuous behavior.

THE SOCIAL COMPACT AND MORAL DUTIES

When individuals emerge from their primitive stages of moral development and enter society, they assume certain obligations. There is a cost, in other words, of membership in a civilized society that values moral virtue. The ethics system is not a smorgasbord from which one can pick moral delicacies. Society imposes certain responsibilities on its constituents as a condition of membership. These responsibilities are known as *moral duties*. The idea of duty to others is important to moral reasoning because it is a way of paying homage to the triumph of virtue over self-interests.

The Two Levels of Moral Duty

Although there are many kinds of moral duties, for the sake of simplicity they can be divided into two categories: general and particularistic. *General ethical obligations* are those that apply to all members of society. Some are primary (or fundamental), in that they take precedence over other principles and should be violated only when there is an overriding reason for doing so.[23] Prohibitions against stealing, cheating, lying, and breaking promises are examples of fundamental duties. Others bind all of us, even though they do not occupy such a prominent position on the hierarchy of values as our primary general obligations. These secondary obligations, such as prohibitions against gambling and trespassing, have a weaker claim to moral permanence than our fundamental duties and are more likely to be violated or perhaps subordinated to competing interests. Charity bingo games and legalized state lotteries are two classic examples.

Of course, substantial disagreement persists among philosophers over the extent of our general obligations. Some believe, for example, that there is a moral duty to assist others in distress, to be a good samaritan. Others continue to ask, "Am I my brother's keeper?" and question whether such good deeds are really a general moral obligation. However, one could probably get agreement among philosophers and nonphilosophers alike that two general obligations underlie all others: to treat others with the respect and moral dignity to which they are entitled and to avoid intentionally causing harm to others.[24] You will notice that the latter duty is based on *intentional* harm, not *foreseeable* harm. For example, reporters know that scandalous revelations will harm others, but their *intent* is not to harm but to inform the public about matters of public interest. Even if their revelations are unwarranted, few journalists would embark on a story with the underlying motive of causing personal injury.

Particularistic obligations are determined by membership within a specific group, profession, or occupation. Practicing Roman Catholics, for example, have a moral duty to refrain from using artificial birth control. Doctors have a duty to maintain a confidential relationship with their patients, and attorneys have a responsibility to mount a vigorous defense for their clients, even if they believe them to be guilty. These are moral obligations that do not bind the rest of us.

A duty is often imposed on media practitioners to avoid certain conflicts of interest because of their unusual role within society. This obligation was apparently ignored several years ago when more than 5,000 media representatives and guests accepted invitations to visit Disney World for three days.[25] Although some insisted on paying their own way, others accepted Disney's offer to underwrite all expenses. The reporters and media executives who attended planned extensive coverage for Disney World's fifteenth anniversary, an event that might otherwise have gone unnoticed.[26] For Disney and central Florida, this arrangement was a publicity bonanza. For critics, including those inside the media, it was an ethical debacle. Michael Gartner, president of the American Society of Newspaper Editors, summed it up: "If Disney World wants to do this, it's fine, but I am disappointed that so many reporters and editors aren't troubled by the acceptance."[27] The editor of the *New York Times*, A. M. Rosenthal, lamented, "I thought we had cleaned ourselves up and we haven't. It is astonishing."[28]

Particularistic obligations for media practitioners, like those in other professions, are sometimes based on the more general societal obligations. Journalism's commitment to truth and fairness is a case in point. But occasionally the general and particularistic obligations collide, causing heated debate about which should prevail. Suppose, for example, that a reporter is covering a war in which American troops are fighting alongside those of an ally. The journalist is invited by the enemy forces to inspect evidence of allied atrocities. But instead of producing the evidence, the enemy sets up an ambush of American troops. Should the reporter cover the ambush?

This was the hypothetical scenario presented in early 1989 to Peter Jennings of ABC News and Mike Wallace of *60 Minutes*, who were participants on a ten-part Corporation for Public Broadcasting series, "Ethics in America." Jennings originally said he would not cover the ambush as part of his job and that he would warn the American troops. Wallace strongly disagreed and contended that reporters should cover this story just as they would any other. As the discussion progressed, Jennings moved closer to Wallace's position, but after wrestling with this moral dilemma, Wallace acknowledged his uncertainty. This hypothetical case produced an outpouring of interest and commentary within the journalistic community because of its graphic illustration of the conflict between reporters' journalistic (particularistic) obligations and their general duty as American citizens.[29]

Washington Post reporter Cindy Loose was confronted with such competing loyalties when she decided to break a cardinal rule of journalism in the interest of saving a life. Loose was covering the activities of an organization known as Helping Individual Prostitutes Survive (HIPS), when a prostitute named Sunshine decided to quit the streets. Fearing that the prostitute's pimp would show up and harm or perhaps even kill her, HIPS attempted to find an adequate hiding place for her. But as desperate as the situation was, they were unable to do so, and Loose decided to abandon her role as detached observer and to intervene in what she believed to be a life-threatening situation. She used her frequent flyer miles to move Sunshine to another city out of harm's way and in the process became a part of the story.[30]

Conventional journalistic wisdom would suggest that Loose should not have written the story. But the reporter did write the story, and the *Post* published it. Executive Editor Leonard Downie, Jr., described the decision as a "rare exception" to the no-involvement rule. And *Post* ombudsman Joann Byrd, who holds a graduate degree in philosophy, reviewed the ethical dilemma in a column and made this observation: "The choice is obvious when a journalist encounters a life-threatening emergency: Anyone should save a life when she has the wherewithal and is either the only one who can or the one best able." While the outcome here was uncertain, Loose was convinced that Sunshine's life was in danger and thus felt justified in subordinating her particularistic obligation of journalistic detachment to the universal moral duty to help save the life of another a decision applauded by those readers who called or wrote to comment on her decision.[31]

Deciding among Moral Duties

The duties just explored orchestrate our relations with one another and with society. Our moral calculations affect other humans, regardless of whether these individuals are known personally to us or are members of that amorphous mass known as the public. Thus, our ethical judgments must take into account all parties, including ourselves, to which we owe allegiance.

Ralph Potter, of the Harvard Divinity School, has referred to these duties as "loyalties" in constructing his own model for moral reasoning.[32] Lawyers, for example, have obligations to their clients, their professional colleagues, the judicial system, and society at large, as well as to their own sense of ethical conduct. Teachers have loyalties to the students, parents, academic colleagues, school officials, and the community at large. Sometimes these loyalties conflict, increasing the tension in the moral reasoning process. Clifford Christians and his coauthors in *Media Ethics: Cases and Moral Reasoning*, make this observation:

> Many times, in the consideration of ethics, direct conflicts arise between the rights of one person or group and those of others. Policies and actions inevitably must favor some to the exclusion of others. Often our most agonizing dilemmas revolve around our primary obligation to a person or social group. Or, we ask ourselves, is

my first loyalty to my company or to a particular client?[33]

The moral agent's responsibility consists of giving each set of loyalties its share of attention before rendering an ethical determination. Thus, as media practitioners we must identify those parties that will be most affected by our actions. For the purposes of the cases in this book, six categories of individuals and groups to which we are obligated must be examined:[34]

1. Individual conscience
2. Objects of moral judgment
3. Financial supporters
4. The institution
5. Professional colleagues
6. Society

First, we should follow the adage "Let your conscience be your guide." Our *conscience* often tells us, if we are willing to listen, the difference between right and wrong. In other words, we should feel personally comfortable with our decision or at least be able to defend it with some moral principle. Being able to look ourselves in the mirror without wincing from moral embarrassment is a sign of our virtue.

The *objects of moral judgment* are those individuals or groups most likely to be harmed or affected directly by our ethical decisions. For example, racial and ethnic minorities are the objects of moral judgment when films depicting them are based on stereotypes. Certain specialized audiences should also be taken into account, as when a sexually explicit program is aired during the time of the day when children are most likely to be watching or listening. A public official whose womanizing catches the fancy of the media would also be in harm's way, much to the delight of his political opponents. It may seem strange to suggest that a loyalty is owed to such unsavory topics of news coverage. But there is a duty to take into account the interests of others, even if we believe that the target of our action deserves punishment or public scorn.

Media practitioners also must be loyal to their *financial supporters*, who pay the bills and make it possible to compete in the marketplace. These include advertisers as well as individual subscribers. There will always be tension between the lure of profits and the ethical mandate to operate in the public interest, but the industry must sometimes strive to find an accommodation between them. This is not to suggest, of course, that the media must compromise their contract with society to present objective news coverage because of objections and pressure from advertisers or stockholders. It is an article of faith in many news organizations that advertisers should exercise no influence over editorial or news content. Thus, these loyalties to financial supporters must be carefully weighed, and in some cases the moral duty to society must override other considerations.

Allegiance to one's own *institution* is a noble gesture under most circumstances, because company loyalty is usually valued in corporate circles. Reporters often take pride in the news organizations for which they work and are concerned as much about their institutions' credibility as about their own. However, blind loyalty can work to the company's detriment. For example, a PR executive who recommends to management that the company "stonewall" the press concerning the effects of an environmental disaster disserves the company as well as the public. It should be noted that loyalty to one's organization may also take into account the stockholders (if any), because they are interested in preserving the company's financial well-being as well as in protecting their investments. Of course, media executives tend to be more concerned about the duties owed to investors than those owed to lower-level employees.

A practitioner's allegiance to *professional colleagues* is often powerful and unfaltering. When rendering a moral judgment, two questions are relevant: How will my actions reflect on my professional peers? Are my actions in keeping with the expectations of my colleagues? Suppose that a television news producer de-

cides to air graphic death scenes from a satanic ritual. Public protests would suggest that this ill-advised decision might reflect poorly on all broadcast journalists. On the other hand, reporters often look to the expectations and practices of their colleagues for moral support to legitimize their actions. Protection of news sources is a case in point, and some reporters have gone to jail rather than breach these confidential relationships and risk the ostracism of their peers.

For media practitioners, obligation or loyalty to *society* translates into a sense of social responsibility. It goes without saying that ethical decisions cannot be made without factoring the public interest into the equation. Because our own sense of moral propriety, that is, our conscience, is based on societal norms, our obligations to ourselves and society are often in concert. This is not always the case, however, as when reporters publish the contents of a stolen classified government document revealing American duplicity in foreign relations. In this case, their consciences might override the concern for social prohibitions against stealing. However, if their motivations for releasing this information are related to self-interest (personal recognition, increased ratings, and the like), they have acted unethically.

Considerations of societal duties are more complex than they appear. In the real world, society is not some monolithic entity but consists of many different groups, among which choices sometimes have to be made: news sources, public figures, minorities, senior citizens, children, people with disabilities. It is the balancing of these interests that presents a real challenge to media practitioners in the rough-and-tumble world of a diverse civilization.

THE NEXUS OF LAW AND ETHICS

Attorneys and judges tell us that laws are the cornerstone of our democratic civilization. They are wrong. It is the *moral respect* for the law that provides the foundation for our culture. Motorists do not refuse to run a red light just because there does not happen to be a law officer close at hand. They do so out of respect for legal authority (or perhaps fear of detection and punishment) and deference to the notion that limitations on individual liberty are sometimes necessary to bring order out of chaos in a complex society. Thus, there is what we might call a *nexus*, or connection, between the fields of law and ethics. But what is the scope of this relationship, and why should a media practitioner be concerned about this distinction?

We can begin by stating the obvious: not all moral issues can be, or should be, legally codified. The law permits many immoralities that transgress against friends and enemies alike, such as the breaking of promises, uttering of unkind words, and certain forms of deception. We often offend others' feelings, an act for which the law provides no restitution to the offended party. A high school student, for example, might break his date for the senior prom at the last minute, but the lady kept in waiting cannot resort to the courts for redress of her tearful ordeal. Even in a litigious society it would be undesirable to open the floodgates to such deep interference into individual relationships.

Nevertheless, legal obligations are based on moral ones. The criminal and civil statutes codify some of our most important moral obligations, for example, proscriptions against killing, stealing, raping, or maliciously defaming another's reputation. Most of these statutes involve punishing direct harm to others, but some laws are based on moral principles that are not concerned with the well-being of others. Laws regulating sexual behavior between consenting adults and prostitution fall into this category. The moral justification for such laws is not as widely shared within society, and thus compliance is less certain.[35] Nevertheless, a fundamental distinction between our legal code and moral obligations is that legal violations involve prescribed penalties and ethical indiscretions do not.

But if the laws themselves are based on moral respect, are there circumstances when we

are warranted in breaking a law? Does our ethical system provide for such waivers of our moral obligations?

Civil disobedience, in which citizens intentionally ignore laws that they feel are unjust, has received some moral respectability in recent years, particularly since the nonviolent civil rights demonstrations led by the Reverend Dr. Martin Luther King, Jr., in the 1960s. Most ethicists agree, however, that the legitimacy of civil disobedience depends on (1) the moral agent's true belief that the law is unjust, (2) nonviolence, and (3) the protesters' willingness to face the consequences of their actions.[36] In addition, some people justify civil disobedience only if the legal avenues of redress have been explored. For example, an antinuclear group, having exhausted all legal avenues to prevent the opening of a nuclear power plant that it considers to be unsafe, might resort to acts of civil disobedience to bring its concerns to the public's attention. In such cases, even when the legal questions have been settled, the moral issues persist.

What if the legal remedies have not been exhausted? Are moral agents then justified in violating the law? Perhaps, but it would appear that their actions are on shakier ground. A just law might be violated in emergency situations or when a higher moral principle is involved. For example, we would not think a husband immoral for running red lights to get his pregnant wife to the hospital in time for the delivery of their baby. On a more serious level, media practitioners may occasionally feel obligated to violate a just law if they believe that they must do so because of a more significant moral obligation. Journalists, for example, might be justified in ignoring a State Department ban on travel to a particular country if they felt compelled to document human rights abuses. Of course, the reporters would have to face the legal consequences of their transgressions, but their actions would still have some moral force behind them.

The point is this: journalists serve a unique function as representatives of the public and may feel that their obligations to the audience outweigh their legal duties. And this argument holds some merit. However, if a law has any moral force behind it—if it is a "just" law—it can be overridden only by a more compelling moral obligation.

This dilemma is exemplified by a case involving the Cable News Network and the prosecution of former Panamanian dictator Manuel Noriega in 1991. General Noriega, of course, had been taken into custody after a massive deployment of U.S. troops in Panama and was awaiting trial in Miami. During his incarceration, someone obtained tape recordings of jail cell conversations between Noriega and his attorney and provided them to CNN. After CNN announced that it had the tapes, U.S. District Judge William Hoeveler granted the defense's request for an injunction against the broadcast of the tapes,[37] an order that was upheld by the Eleventh Circuit Court of Appeals.[38] Despite the order, CNN did broadcast an excerpt from one tape. Judge Hoeveler, believing that the broadcast of the tapes was a violation of the attorney-client privilege and might be detrimental to Noriega's defense, eventually held CNN in contempt. In his opinion, which contained an exhaustive analysis of the competing claims of a free press and the general duty to respect judicial decrees, Judge Hoeveler appeared to be invoking the necessity for moral respect for the law when he made the following observation:

> I am ever mindful of the importance of an essentially unfettered press and the mandates of the First Amendment. But I must also be mindful of the vital importance of compliance with orders of the court. As is demonstrated regularly, not all District Court orders are correct. Those which are not can and should be corrected by appeal, not by the willfulness of those who disagree with a court's opinion. Without an unyielding adherence to this principle, the system could not survive.
>
> The thin but bright line between anarchy and order . . . is the respect which litigants and the public have for the law and the orders issued by

the courts. Defiance of court orders and, even more so, public display of such defiance cannot be justified or permitted.[39]

Journalists who complain bitterly that they have the right to ignore laws and court orders they believe to be unconstitutional miss the point. Statutes and court orders are legal until overturned by a higher authority. And in the CNN case, even the appellate court upheld the order because of the violation of a confidential relationship recognized by law and the possible threat to Noriega's right to a fair trial as a result of the broadcast of the jail conversations. Thus, most legal issues confronting reporters also have an ethical dimension, a fact that is sometimes overlooked by media practitioners.

For example, the refusal of reporters to reveal their confidential sources, even when ordered to do so by a court, often raises ethical questions that transcend the legal issues. Journalists usually appeal to their role as representatives of the public in reporting on matters of public interest, a role that could be jeopardized if the cloak of confidentiality were unavailable to sensitive news sources. But if reporters have information that could lead to the solution of a crime, they are then caught between the duty to cooperate with law enforcement officials and the moral obligation to keep their promises to their sources. Even when a court recognizes a legal privilege for reporters to maintain the confidentiality of their sources, the ethical question remains whether journalists have a moral obligation to assist in the fair administration of justice.

This inescapable alliance between law and ethics was evident when the editors for the Minneapolis *Star Tribune* and the St. Paul *Pioneer Press Dispatch* overrode a reporter's promise to a source and disclosed the source's name. During the campaign for lieutenant governor in Minnesota, an employee of an ad agency working for the Republican candidate had given reporters embarrassing information about the opposing candidate in the closing days of the race. The information, which had been provided on the condition that the source not be identified, revealed that the candidate had been arrested nearly twenty years earlier on a shoplifting charge.

Believing that the story lacked credibility without the source's name and that the source's motivation was more important than the arguably irrelevant shoplifting information, editors at both papers decided independently to disclose the source's name. He was fired from his position at the ad agency and sued the papers. He eventually won a U.S. Supreme Court decision that promises of confidentiality may be legally enforceable under state law.[40] The Court resolved the legal questions, but the ethical issues remain. Nevertheless, the editors of the *Star Tribune* and the *Pioneer Press Dispatch* learned how quickly ethical judgments can become troublesome (and costly) legal disputes (This case is also examined in Chapter 3 in explaining the moral reasoning process.)

Thus, most legal issues clearly have moral dimensions as well, and we cannot necessarily settle ethical questions merely by resolving the legal ones. Recent Supreme Court decisions overturning state laws penalizing the press for publishing lawfully obtained information are a case in point. In 1975, in *Cox Broadcasting Corp. v. Cohn*, the Court overturned a Georgia state court ruling holding an Atlanta TV station liable for broadcasting the name of a murder-rape victim obtained from the public record.[41] In 1989 the Court overturned a judgment against a Florida newspaper that had been sued under state law for publishing the name of a rape victim. Although the name was obtained from a press report available in the police department pressroom, a state law made it illegal to publish the names of rape victims. However, the Court held that the media cannot be punished for publishing information lawfully obtained, especially when the government itself releases the information.[42] But these cases did not settle the ethical question of whether the names of rape victims *should*

be published, even if they are a matter of public record. There are those who feel that the harm to the victims far outweighs the limited public good derived from release of this kind of information.

Four years after the *Cox* decision, the Supreme Court overturned a West Virginia statute making it unlawful for a newspaper to publish, without the written approval of the juvenile court, the name of a youth charged as a juvenile offender.[43] This ruling appears to have resolved the legal question of whether the media can publish or broadcast the names of juvenile lawbreakers, but the state's interest in rehabilitating youths who have gone astray appears significant enough to confront ethicists with some challenging issues.

These cases are, of course, indicative of the Supreme Court's sensitivity to the media's First Amendment rights. With some unusual exceptions, there is little that cannot be published. On its face, the First Amendment guarantees press freedom but has nothing to say about responsibility. It is left to the consciences of practicing journalists to decide whether to publish the names of rape victims or juvenile offenders. But constitutional freedoms are not just the point of departure for making ethical judgments. If irresponsible media come to be regarded as social parasites, these legal rights could be slowly eroded. The policy of the Federal Communications Commission regulating indecent content in the broadcasting industry and perennial Congressional threats to regulate televised violence are two examples. Even when the courts overturn these governmental initiatives on constitutional grounds, they usually reflect a belief that the media have gone too far in exercising their constitutional freedoms. Media practitioners should not assume, therefore, that the legal right to produce and distribute certain kinds of sensitive information is necessarily a moral imperative to do so. In fact, constitutional liberties place a greater responsibility on media practitioners to consider the ethical ramifications of their actions than if they were prohibited from exercising that freedom in the first place.

I conclude this section on the relationship between law and ethics as I began it, with the idea that it is the moral force of the law that provides the legitimacy for our legal codes. All parties have the same moral obligations to comply with the law. Thus, media practitioners are warranted in violating the law only if they can stand on some more important moral principle and are willing to endure the consequences of their disobedience.

INSTITUTIONAL AUTONOMY AND SOCIAL RESPONSIBILITY

"Institutions don't behave unethically; people do."[44] This statement from Chapter 1 would seem to suggest that any discussion of corporate morality is out of place here. However, despite the fact that ethical judgments are rendered by individuals within the corporate hierarchy, the public often associates images of moral or immoral conduct with the institutions themselves. Some media celebrities attract attention because of their conduct, but the institutional decision makers (the moral agents) are usually invisible to society. Nevertheless, the public has come to expect corporate sensitivity to their moral obligations.

In 1982 Johnson & Johnson, a manufacturer of over-the-counter medications, became embroiled in a public relations nightmare when several people died from taking cyanide-laced Tylenol. The company took quick and decisive action by recalling and later repackaging the product.[45] Seven years later a massive oil spill from an Exxon oil tanker off the coast of Alaska became a public relations debacle when the company was accused of reacting too slowly to this environmental crisis. Despite Exxon's offer to pay for the cost of the cleanup, the company's image suffered.

What do these two cases have in common? They both involve questions of social responsi-

bility, that is, a commitment to the public good that outweighs short-term individual self-interests. Lurking in this rather abstract concept of social responsibility is the principle of reciprocity, the notion that individuals and institutions have a moral obligation to the public's welfare, in return for which society bestows its respect and trust.

The Libertarian View

However, this last statement is still a controversial one. Although the "let the buyer beware" philosophy that dominated until the early part of this century has been diminished by the efforts of consumer activists like Ralph Nader, some still hold the libertarian view that "business is the business of business."[46] According to this view, a company is socially responsible if it provides employment and a stable financial base for the community. This notion is reflected in contemporary society by the economist Milton Friedman, who has adopted the view that both individuals and corporations pursuing their own self-interests in a competitive marketplace will, in fact, contribute to the public welfare.[47] Friedman believes that the only moral relationship is between management and stockholders and that society should interfere in this arrangement only to prevent deception or fraud.[48] In other words, the concept of the public interest is merely a byproduct of corporate autonomy.

This libertarian philosophy is based on the notion of self-reliance and individual autonomy, free from governmental or societal restraints. Libertarianism is characterized by the notion of freedom without enforced responsibility, and it was within this kind of environment that the American press matured in the nineteenth century. Thus, the system nurtured a press that was free but that also resisted the development of strong ethical codes.

Nevertheless, the libertarian press did subscribe to some fundamental values, many of which are still featured prominently in contemporary industry codes. As newspapers slowly acquired a reverence for facts and a preference for "hard news" over opinion, such notions as objectivity, fairness, and balance became a part of the journalist's ethical lexicon. Perhaps of primary importance was objectivity, a term that journalists began using in the twentieth century to "express their commitment not only to impartiality but to reflecting the world as it is, without bias or distortion of any sort."[49]

For most journalists, objectivity is an article of faith, but there is also a recognition that absolute objectivity is an illusion. Thus, they have settled for a philosophically less demanding definition that allows them to practice their profession without feeling as though they have sinned. According to this more realistic view of objectivity, reporters strive to keep their personal preferences and opinions out of news stories, to achieve balance in coverage, and to rely on credible and responsible news sources. According to this traditional view, the ethics of newswriting is concerned with facts and impartiality in the presentation of those facts.[50]

Nevertheless, libertarians are opposed to enforced responsibility, even when there is a danger that some unscrupulous journalists might infect the public arena with falsehoods and opinions disguised as facts. It is better to leave the remedy for such moral indiscretions, according to the libertarian view, to the marketplace and the consciences of individual media practitioners.

Social Responsibility

The idea of social responsibility has developed as a counterpoint to libertarianism. Although this theory continues to emphasize freedom, it holds that responsibility is necessarily a partner to freedom in institutional behavior. Codes of ethics are encouraged as a self-regulatory device to promote social responsibility. Some have taken issue with the traditional views of Friedman and believe that conducting business is not a right but a privilege granted by society.[51] Because the pursuit of profits has not automatically contributed to the public good, society has placed increasing demands on corporations to contribute to the correction of social ills. Affirmative action programs and the increased availability of affordable legal services for the poor are two examples.

There is little doubt that corporate responsibility in contemporary society includes emphasizing ethical behavior for both management and employees. Some companies have instituted ethics programs, both for legal and public relations reasons. Some have even devised codes of ethics for their personnel. But the formality of written codes does not ensure ethical conduct. For example, the Sundstrand Corporation, a multimillion-dollar military contractor, adopted an impressive code of ethics, which set high standards for contract pricing and performance, accounting, and numerous other issues. Nevertheless, the company was charged with having overbilled the federal government for military work, and it agreed to plead guilty.[52] It is safe to say that the corporate climate, the general attitudes of top management toward ethical behavior, is more important than codes of conduct in setting moral expectations within the institutional environment. This is as true for media organizations as it is for military contractors.

Social Responsibility in the Media It is unclear when the notion of social responsibility first entered the consciousness of media practitioners, but five historical trends contributed to its emergence. First, the Industrial Revolution forever altered the American social landscape, fostering the concentrations of capital and business ownership in fewer hands. Newspapers did not escape this reorganization of the free enterprise system, a trend that continues unabated.[53] Thus, with media control in fewer hands, some critics questioned whether the libertarian intellectual ideal of a true competition of ideas would continue to be a realistic expectation.

Second, despite this trend toward newspaper monopolies, an increasing number of media alternatives began to flood the marketplace in the form of magazines and radio. They placed pressure on newspapers to broaden their audience appeal. Thus, an economic imperative began to coexist with the media's journalistic mandate, and the idea of social responsibility became intertwined with commercial success.

Third, by the middle of the nineteenth century journalism had begun to attract people with strong educational backgrounds who established ethical standards for their industry and tried to live up to them.[54] In addition, a few publishers began to recognize that the freedom to publish carried with it a corresponding responsibility. Some, like the legendary Joseph Pulitzer, even viewed a sense of social responsibility as the salvation of their profession from the ravages of the economic marketplace: "Nothing less than the highest ideals, the most scrupulous anxiety to do right, the most accurate knowledge of the problems it has to meet, and a sincere sense of moral responsibility will save journalism from a subservience to business interests, seeking selfish ends, antagonistic to public welfare."[55]

This early recognition of media responsibility has been manifested more recently in the establishment of various institutes, sometimes funded by the media themselves, committed to enhancing the professionalism of practitioners. The Poynter Institute in St. Petersburg, Florida, which sponsors workshops on topics ranging from newswriting to ethics, is a prime example of this kind of continuing education for journalists and journalism educators.

Fourth, schools of journalism began to appear in the early part of this century, an idea also supported by Pulitzer, and they contributed to the sense of professionalism within the industry. The teaching of practical skills was supplemented with instruction in social responsibility, and a cadre of practitioners educated specifically in the discipline of journalism entered the marketplace. This rising sense of professionalism led to the development of a social conscience among media practitioners, a belief that responsibility should be a welcome companion to press freedom. This belief was formalized in 1923, when the American Society of Newspaper Editors (ASNE) at its first meeting adopted the "Canons of Journalism" as its journalistic standards. Although some state press associations had already adopted codes, this was the first national code of ethics advanced by any organization of journalists.[56] It also flunked its first test as an enforceable code.

One year after the formation of the ASNE code, F. G. Bonfils, publisher of the *Denver Post*, was accused of having accepted $1 million in bribes for suppressing information from his reporters about wrongdoing in the Teapot Dome scandal. This scandal involved allegations that government oil reserves in the Teapot Dome field in Wyoming were being sold to private oil companies. Several members of the ASNE accused Bonfils of having violated the codified principles of the organization, including truthfulness, fair play, accuracy, and impartiality, and demanded that he be punished for these violations. The debate over code enforcement lasted for five years, but in 1929, under the threat of a lawsuit from Bonfils, the newspaper editors voted for voluntary obedience rather than disciplinary action.[57]

The ASNE code was soon followed in 1928 by the first written principles for the electronic media, when the fledgling National Association of Broadcasters (NAB) adopted the industry's first radio code dealing with programming, advertising, and news. Since these early efforts at codification of professional ideas, such diverse groups as the Radio-Television News Directors Association, the American Advertising Association, the Public Relations Society of America, and the Society of Professional Journalists have adopted similar statements of ethical standards.

Social responsibility was also an outgrowth of the laissez-faire attitude of government, according to which the excesses of big business were allowed to run rampant. After the turn of the century, however, and particularly during the 1930s, wide government intervention in the marketplace brought applause from a public weary of economic and social turmoil and a business environment hostile to the interests of consumers. Advertising, the primary financial support for the media, was brought under governmental scrutiny in 1938 when Congress provided the Federal Trade Commission with new powers to oversee deceptive and unfair advertising practices. Some feared that the government might next turn its regulatory arsenal on the media themselves and force social accountability on institutions that were perceived as having abused their constitutionally granted freedom under the First Amendment. The fact that the newly emerging radio medium had been brought under government regulation in 1927 did little to dispel this fear.

Finally, the idea of media social responsibility was given credence after World War II through the work of the so-called Hutchins Commission on Freedom of the Press. In 1942 Robert W. Hutchins, chancellor of the University of Chicago, was commissioned to study the future prospects of press freedom. Funding was initially provided by Henry R. Luce, of Time, Inc., and later by Encyclopaedia Britannica. Hutchins appointed a panel of thirteen, including several distinguished educators, to carry out this ambitious assignment, and in 1947 the panel issued a report, "A Free and Responsible Press," which contained a well-reasoned and comprehensive analysis of the need for a socially responsible press.

Although the expression "social responsibility" was never mentioned in its report, the commission identified five obligations of the media in contemporary society.[58] Although some of them are applicable primarily to journalism, others are just as relevant to advertising and entertainment.

The first requirement, according to the commission, is to provide a "truthful, compre-hensive, and intelligent account of the day's events in a context that gives them meaning." The press must not only be accurate; it must also clearly distinguish between fact and opinion. But facts by themselves are insufficient. The media must also report the "truth about the facts" by putting stories into perspective and evaluating for the reader the credibility of conflicting sources. Interpretative reporting must extend beyond the pure facts and provide the relevant background surrounding the facts.

This was the issue when a reporter for a local newspaper covered a press conference in which the mayor accused a city councilman of distorting facts about the effects of certain pesticides on birds indigenous to the area and of being on the payroll of a local pesticide manufacturer. When contacted about the accusations, the councilman refused to comment except to say the mayor's accusations were "utter nonsense" and "politically motivated." The reporter's story included both the charges and the councilman's denial.[59] The paper's editor thought the story was fair and balanced, but the councilman was outraged. In a letter to the editor, he denied lying about the effects of pesticides or being on the payroll of any pesticide company. "The story may have been fair, balanced, and accurate," he wrote, "but it was not truthful."[60] The reporter should have held the story, in the councilman's view, until she had independently investigated the charges.

The commission's second recommendation is that the press serve as "a forum for the exchange of comment and criticism." This is an essential function in a system increasingly dominated by media giants. The press is urged to provide a platform for views that are contrary to its own while not abdicating its traditional right of advocacy.

A third requirement is that the press project "a representative picture of the constituent groups in society." In other words, racial, social, and cultural groups should be depicted accurately, without resorting to stereotypes. Social responsibility demands an affirmative role for the media in building positive images, both in their informational and entertainment content. Although some progress has been made in this area, stereotyping is still a common charge against the media.

The media should also, according to the commission, be responsible for "the presentation and clarification of the goals and values of society." They should transmit the cultural heritage, thereby reinforcing traditional values and virtues.

A journalism professor, Ted Smith, has rendered a strong indictment accusing the press of failing to live up to this obligation. Smith begins his critique by observing that the media, having ravaged most of the nation's established institutions, began a period of self-examination in the early 1980s. Several news organizations, he recalls, produced stories acknowledging the public's lack of confidence in the media. But after an initial flurry of stories on the subject of media credibility and ethics, he laments, the sense of urgency passed, and the self-scrutiny appeared to have no discernible impact on reporting practices. Although he attributes this renewal of self-assurance by the media to their perceptions that there is no "real crisis of credibility," he challenges this assertion and attempts to document the steady erosion of media believability since the early 1970s. This development represents a popular reaction against the mass media, which have come to view all traditional cultural values with some skepticism and have presented the public with a constant barrage of negative news coverage.

In comparing the media's skepticism with the critical dialogues of Socrates, Smith issues the following warning: "Some journalists may be flattered by the thought that they are perpetuating the illustrious tradition of Socrates. They would do better to remember his fate: He was tried, convicted and executed for subverting religion and for corrupting the youth of his city."[61] He accuses elite journalists of orchestrating "a relentless critique of all cultural affirmations as embodied in American policies, leaders and institutions."[62] Like Socrates, journalists have often reported from a vantage point outside the culture rather than as a part of it. This stance has led, he says, to a collapse of confidence in the media by the society of which they are supposedly a part. Although we must await historical confirmation of Smith's dire prediction that the press may suffer the same fate as Socrates, recent polls showing a continuing decline of media credibility suggest that there may be a cause for concern.

The final requirement of the Hutchins Commission is that the press should provide "full access to the day's intelligence." This notion is reflected in the media's championing of the public's right to know, although this so-called right has yet to find expression in the Supreme Court's interpretation of the constitution. From a philosophical standpoint, the right to know is predicated on the notion that the media are the representatives of the public, a fourth branch of government (along with the executive, legislative, and judicial) with responsibility for informing the citizenry about governmental activities. The increase in the number and scope of laws regarding public records and open meetings, at both the state and federal levels, is the manifestation of this right of access to government information. In recent years, however, the media have used the right to know to justify journalistic forays that extend beyond governmental activities into the private lives of individuals. This intrusion is sometimes viewed by an already skeptical public as social responsibility run amok, a sacrifice of personal autonomy for the sake of public curiosity.

Media Criticism and Social Responsibility
Almost from their inception, the mass media have attracted their share of criticism. Society's elites castigated the mass culture that resulted from the Industrial Revolution as being intellectually impoverished and destined to subvert

rather than elevate cultural tastes. They also decried the crass commercialism that seemed to be the animating principle of material mass produced to meet society's voracious appetite for such popular fare.

Today, media critics, particularly those representing the intellectual and cultural elite, still complain about the low quality of media content. But they have been joined by an assortment of public interest organizations with various agendas ranging across the political spectrum. For example, conservative critics of the media, concerned about the media's morally corruptive influence on society, have found a home in the Reverend Jerry Falwell's Liberty Foundation, the successor to his Moral Majority political lobby. Likewise, the coalition for Better Television, chaired by the Reverend Donald Wildmon, has been monitoring TV programs and serving as a moral watchdog over the television industry since 1977. Accuracy in Media (AIM), another influential conservative watchdog group, has also been frequently critical of broadcast standards and practices, particularly as they relate to news coverage of public affairs. AIM's counterparts on the political left are organizations like Fairness and Accuracy in Reporting (FAIR) and the Institute for Media Analysis (IMA), which have often been critical of the influence of commercial values in determining media content and the extent to which the media rely on government propaganda and handouts from the public relations industry.

Still other groups have attempted to persuade Congress to regulate televised violence, as well as allegedly obscene lyrics and satanic messages in recorded music. One of the most visible public interest groups, Action for Children's Television (ACT), has focused on the interests of the most impressionable segment of the television audience. Since its inception, ACT has been an influential voice in representing their youthful constituency before both the TV industry and government regulators.

In addition to these organized efforts by public interest groups at promoting their own views of social responsibility, individual voices within the media also serve as society's "in-house" critics. For example, PBS film critic Michael Medved; Howard Kurtz, the respected media reporter for the *Washington Post*;[63] and the *Chicago Tribune*'s Larry Wolters are among the most visible and perhaps influential media reviewers. As Professor Orlik has noted in commenting on the role of electronic media critics, such authorities "usually are in a much better position to propose change than are members of the public. That is because consumers seldom have the contacts and never have the time to acquire in-depth comprehension of radio/television workings for themselves. Consequently, it is the critic who must provide this knowledge for listeners and viewers."[64]

While the real impact of critics, both individuals and public interest groups, is sometimes difficult to assess, they do serve as one more pressure point to remind media managers of their moral responsibility to the society that has given them sustenance. In addition, various segments of the public, which may be individually impotent in influencing media decision makers and gatekeepers, can at least feel they have an advocate in the information and entertainment marketplace. And while readers and viewers may not always agree with the critics, they at least share a mutual interest in not allowing the performance of media institutions to go unchallenged.

A Threat and an Obligation It is clear, from the preceding discussion, that the idea of social responsibility has become a part of the U.S. corporate landscape. But can media institutions maintain their autonomous status, which is essential in a democratic society, while at the same time fulfilling their mandate of social responsibility? Some traditionalists argue that such concepts as *duty*, *accountability*, and *obligation* are incompatible with the independence and freedom necessary for dynamic and vibrant media institutions. They believe that social responsibility is a euphemism for "lowest common denominator," which will result in bland, noncontroversial content. According to this view, the media are captives of public opinion and have thus abdicated their role as social and political gadflies.

This argument is rather dubious. As noted earlier in this section, the media have been criticized precisely because they are such gadflies, constantly casting aspersions on society's cultural values. They have continued to function as autonomous institutions, despite some loss of public confidence. Nevertheless, fundamental changes within the American economic system have forced consideration of a more expansive vision of social responsibility for all institutions to the top of the public's agenda. As corporations grow larger, more visible, and more powerful, consumers are increasingly aware of these companies' impact on their daily lives. Society is interested as much in whether General Motors makes safe and fuel-efficient automobiles as in the financial contributions it makes to the economic system.

As we approach the twenty-first century, moreover, the media have witnessed some profound changes in their economic structures. The bottom line has become the ultimate barometer of success, and such terms as *merger*, *acquisition*, and *leveraged buyout* have become a part of the corporate lexicon. As *Newsweek* observed several years ago, "For the American news media, accustomed to thinking of themselves as a Fourth Estate, it has been something of a shock to be treated as Wall Street darlings instead."[65]

The media are among our most visible institutions, entering daily into the homes of millions of people. And because the bigness virus has also infected the media, it is only natural that consumers would place increasing demands on an institution that plays such a pivotal role in the formation of public opinion. In other words, there is an expectation—a moral

obligation, if you will—that the media will operate in the public interest. Thus, the concept of social responsibility has ethical implications when viewed in terms of moral duty.

THE CHALLENGES OF THE INFORMATION AGE

Although a thorough discussion of new technology and the information superhighway is beyond the scope of this text, a consideration of some of the ethical issues surrounding the application of this technology will be included in subsequent chapters. At this point, suffice it to say that the convergence of communications media and sophisticated technology has revolutionized the world in which we live. Society's lexicon is now fraught with such fashionable terms as *Internet*, *cyberspace*, *digitalization*, *E-mail*, and *information superhighway*. The implications of this astonishing cultural reformation are both magnificent and terrifying, posing challenges to policy makers, sociologists and philosophers alike.

The transition from traditional modes of communication, such as print and broadcast, to machine-to-machine distribution of information has spawned a growth industry in gathering and dissemination of information. This development has precipitated an explosion in the number of information consumers, as evidenced in the proliferation of on-line services, some of which are supplied by the news media themselves, where consumers can select useful information from an endless array of menus and data banks. This in turn has increased the number of links (i.e., potential moral agents) in the communication chain of data creation and distribution.

The ethical concerns evolving out of this technological revolution confronting twenty-first century media practitioners are staggering, and some of these are explored in subsequent chapters. In fact, we are already witnessing the tip of the iceberg, as media professionals and data collectors and distributors confront the moral intricacies of the information age. For example, the matter of privacy has always raised troublesome ethical issues for media practitioners, but privacy issues assume a renewed sense of urgency in the age of interactive media. Two-way media, electronic mail, computer database access, and home shopping networks are all mechanisms that facilitate the information-gathering process about individuals. Since information is considered an asset with economic value, it is often processed and sold to mass marketers. In addition, computer-generated information might provide valuable information or tips for news stories, particularly as they relate to public figures or other high-profile newsworthy persons. For example, during the 1993 winter Olympics, several reporters were accused of unethical conduct for reading American figure skater Tonya Harding's E-mail. Harding attracted intense media scrutiny while she was under investigation for allegedly participating in a plot to disable her U.S. rival, Nancy Kerrigan. Reporters obtained her E-mail password using a camera and then gained access to her electronic communications. The journalists claimed they did not read her messages; they just wanted to see if it was possible to get into her E-mail.[66] If that is true, then one wonders what public interest was served by this unwelcome intrusion into Harding's private messages.

Individual access to computer bulletin boards and the Internet has also created a concern, both legally and ethically, about the use of cyberspace for the unregulated spread of pornography, electronic shouting matches (known as "flaming"), and the uncontrollable theft of intellectual property. Unlike traditional modes of communication, the global Internet is a loosely organized information system (or "web") of thousands of voluntarily interconnected computer networks, reaching more than 100 countries and serving over 25 million individual users. Cyberspace differs from conventional media distribution systems in that there

is no central control or "ownership." Consumers now have access directly to the channels of distribution and thus have become major players in not only the mass consumption of information but also the creation and distribution of information. However, this could be a mixed blessing. On the one hand, the communication system is now one of pure democracy. We can all become direct participants in the energizing force for the democratic process—the cultivation and dissemination of knowledge. On the other hand, ethicists must now ponder whether such an "infomocracy" is antithetical to the creation of a virtuous society. For example, news organizations have traditionally been the primary gatekeepers in the information flow process in our democracy. Under such a system, the public can usually be confident of a fairly high level of reliability and "quality" of information because of the elaborate system of rigorous scrutiny by professional journalists and editors. But with unrestricted access to the Internet and other computer-generated data sources, both for individual communicators and recipients, there is a danger that the overall quality of the information generated will diminish.

Some of the most troublesome ethical dilemmas have resulted from the integration of computers and digital technology. *Digitalization* is a process by which pictures, sound, and text are converted electronically and stored as digits, which can later be decoded and reconstructed as the original product or an altered form of the original product. And because a "reconstructed" production is a perfect copy of the original, any transformation of the original content is impossible to detect. Simple alterations, such as the *St. Louis Post-Dispatch*'s decision in 1989 to remove a Diet Coke can from a Pulitzer Prize winner, can be accomplished with only a few keystrokes using technology widely available in today's newsrooms. The cliché "the camera never lies" has always been somewhat of a fallacy, but digital technology can be a seductive device in the hands of either overzealous or unethical media practitioners. Some of the ethical dimensions of digitalization and content alteration will be explored in Chapter 4.

Ethicists are only now beginning to examine, in a systematic way, the ethical dimensions of our newly created technological universe. The danger is that the technology itself will become the scapegoat for an increase in unsavory behavior of both media practitioners and others in the communications chain, when in fact it can only facilitate unethical conduct or perhaps offer a tempting excuse for such deportment. We might be impressed by the potential of the new media but should not be awed by their technological charisma. Such blind loyalty could lead to technological slavery. If indeed the high-tech revolution does lead to an increase in moral mayhem, it will be the result of unvirtuous moral agents and not the ethically passive tools of their trade. Thus, it is important to remember that traditional ethical values and principles (e.g., respect for persons, fairness, justice, honesty, etc.) transcend the innovations of the information age, and any strategies to harness the new technologies from an ethical perspective must place the individual at the center of the moral universe.

Unfortunately, with the accelerating tempo of technology and information transfer, quiet reflection is a luxury we cannot afford. Under such pressures it may be tempting to abdicate all responsibility to lawyers and policy makers. Of course, some legal regulation is inevitable and undoubtedly necessary. But a free, democratic society functions best when it leaves the resolution of its ethical quandaries to the reasoned judgment of its citizens rather than the regulatory authority of the government.

THE MEDIA AS SOCIALLY RESPONSIBLE INSTITUTIONS

Institutions, like individuals, must learn to be socially responsible. But there is no reason to

believe that, in so doing, they must sacrifice their corporate autonomy. Institutional autonomy, like individual autonomy, consists of freedom of choice, but there is a price to be paid for making decisions that do not at least take into account the interests of others. Of course, this realization sometimes necessitates changing corporate attitudes.

For the media, attitudes of social responsibility can be acquired through a two-step process. The first step is to promote a positive corporate image and to improve the chances of gaining public respect. This can be done through an aggressive campaign of external communications and a consideration of the impact on society of any ethical decisions made by media managers and employees. Although this step is based in part on self-interest—the idea that social responsibility is good for business—it creates a set of corporate values on which a more altruistic notion of responsibility can be built.

The second step is community involvement. This is accomplished by encouraging employees to participate in civic affairs and providing corporate financial support for community projects. It can also involve a high-level commitment to the resolution of social problems, even though it may not be economically advantageous to do so. Major newspapers, for example, might consider greater coverage of low-income and minority neighborhoods. Cable systems might increase their penetration in poor neighborhoods, thus enriching the program diversity for the lower rungs of society. Of course, these actions would necessitate restructuring the management philosophy of the communications industry. They are egalitarian ideas that may be hard for some corporate executives to swallow, especially when they have to confront the critical inquiries of stockholders, advertisers, or clients.

In addition to the involvement of some institutions in the communities of which they are a part, there are other visible signs that the media have at least recognized that freedom and responsibility can easily coexist on the same moral ground. The media have acknowledged that some self-regulation is essential because a failure to regulate will result in the further erosion of confidence and perhaps even public demands for governmental intervention. This recognition of social responsibility as a moral duty has been reflected in three self-regulatory mechanisms: codes of conduct, media ombudsmen (sometimes referred to as "readers' representatives"), and news councils.

Codes of Conduct

Although most media practitioners agree that ethical norms are important in their fields, formal codes of conduct are still controversial. Proponents of such codes argue that a written statement of principles is the only way to avoid leaving moral judgments to individual interpretations and that if ethical values are important enough to espouse publicly, they should be codified. Besides, codes provide employees with a written notice of what is expected of them.[67]

Opponents of such codes view them as a form of self-censorship, a retreat from the independence and autonomy necessary for a free and robust mass communication enterprise. In addition, the critics argue, such codes must, of necessity, be general and vague and thus are incapable of confronting the fine nuances of the ethical skirmishes that occur under specific circumstances.[68] Such luminaries in the field of journalism philosophy as John Merrill have dismissed codes as meaningful tools for ensuring accountability:

> The problem with such codes and creeds, however, is that they are not even sufficient in what they do—develop a consensus in thought and action; reason: the rhetorical devices of the codes of ethics and the creeds are so nebulous, fuzzy, ambiguous, contradictory, or heavy-handed that the few journalists who do read them are perplexed, confused, bewildered, angered, and scared off. Journalists, of all people,

should use the language skillfully, directly, and effectively, and in many instances they do. But when it comes to codes and creeds they seem to retreat into a kind of bureaucratese, or sociological jargon that benumbs the mind and frustrates any attempt to extract substantial meaning from the writing.[69]

There is also a fear, sometimes justified, that formal codes of conduct will be used against the media in legal battles as evidence that employees have behaved negligently in violating their own standards of ethical deportment. Finally, opponents contend that codes are nothing more than statements of ideals and are conveniently ignored in the competitive environment of the marketplace.

Nevertheless, codes are viewed as a serious attempt at least to recognize the fundamental values and principles for which media organizations stand. These codes are of two kinds: professional and institutional.

Professional Codes All of the major professional media organizations, representing a broad constituency, have developed formal codes. For example, the Society of Professional Journalists (SPJ) has adopted standards for such things as truth, accuracy, objectivity, conflicts of interests, and fairness. It is interesting to note that this code lists several areas of press responsibility and then devotes one subsection to ethics. This redundancy is a classic example of Merrill's concern with the "rhetorical ambiguity" of such codes.

A recurring debate has concerned whether the SPJ code should be enforced within the journalistic community, thereby ensuring adherence to the code's ideals. However, even the SPJ has resisted this idea, in part because it was afraid that attempts at making journalism a profession might encourage legislatures to license it, thus setting up a First Amendment confrontation. In 1985 its directors voted against enforcing the code on individual members because of a concern that such a stance would interfere with First Amendment freedoms. There was also a fear of litigation resulting from punitive action taken against some recalcitrant SPJ member for having violated the code.[70]

The American Society of Newspaper Editors, the Associated Press Managing Editors, and the Radio-Television News Directors Association have also adopted codes. The Advertising Code of American Business (developed by the American Advertising Federation and the Association of Better Business Bureaus International) sets forth the advertising industry's views on such things as truth in advertising, good taste and public decency, disparagement of competitors' products, price claims, and the use of testimonials. Likewise, the Public Relations Society of America (PRSA) has adopted a Code of Professional Standards to guide its members through the moral thicket of corporate responsibility. Hollywood has also mobilized its collective conscience in the form of the Motion Picture Association of America's rating system.

Codes of conduct, of course, are a prominent feature of the moral landscape for other professions. Lawyers, doctors, nurses, and psychologists all belong to professions with enforceable codes of ethics. The lack of enforceability, however, distinguishes media codes from those adhered to by other professional practitioners. While the PRSA *can* expel a member for violation of its code, it has no legal authority to prohibit an expelled member from continuing to practice public relations. In fact, the lack of an enforceable ethical code is cited by some as evidence of the media's lack of professional standing.[71]

Institutional Codes   In addition to these professional codes, many media institutions have their own policies regarding employees' conduct. These codes are often comprehensive and deal with such diverse matters as the acceptance of gifts and other gratuities from outside sources, conflicts of interests, the use of offensive or indecent material, the publication of rape victims' names, the staging of news events, the use of deceptive news-gathering techniques, and the identification of news sources. There are usually similar policies regarding advertising content, particularly in matters of decency and taste. Many of the issues covered by these codes will be dealt with in the hypothetical cases in Part Two.

Although these codes often reflect an organization's commitment to certain standards of conduct, they are sometimes criticized for failing to provide guidance for the myriad of ethical dilemmas that confront media practitioners under the pressure of time deadlines. Nevertheless, such codes are helpful in socializing new employees to the ethical values of the organization and can also be used as a neutral standard to which both sides can appeal in an ethical dispute.[72] In addition, unlike professional codes, which are just voluntary statements of principles, industry codes are usually enforceable, sometimes resulting in either warnings or dismissal of ethically recalcitrant employees.[73]

Unfortunately, in the heat of battle and under deadline pressures, some organizations ignore their own standards. Such was apparently the case in August 1993 when Jane Pauley, coanchor of *Dateline*, opened a segment on the murder of James Jordan, father of basketball superstar Michael Jordan. In the segment, she referred to criminal records of the two suspects charged in the murder and then introduced correspondent Brian Ross, who also dealt with the records and did so in the framework of "young criminals" moving through the justice system. This violated the NBC standards book, which cautions against using criminal records on the air.[74]

Of course, institutional policies are not self-effectuating and depend on the diligence and good faith of management personnel to oversee their adherence. Each violation, particularly if ignored by media executives, erodes the integrity of the published ethical guidelines. Should organizations drop their ethical standards if they no longer intend to observe them? Emerson Stone, a former CBS news executive, offers this advice:

> What should be done with standards that go unheeded? Should a news organization rewrite (or even completely drop) standards that it professes, that are valid, and that it no longer intend [sic] to observe? I think so.
>
> Oddly enough, a news operation must summon up ethical will in order to announce to the world that from then on it plans to be less critical. Standards are, or ought to be, ever-evolving, but the evolution should make them better, not water them down to make them easier to live with.[75]

The Ombudsman System

Perhaps the most visible example of a commitment to self-criticism is the presence, in some media organizations, of an ombudsman, hired to investigate questionable journalistic conduct and to recommend action. The idea originated in Sweden, where a government official with that title represents the public in its dealings with the bureaucracy.[76] There is also a press ombudsman, whose role it is to enforce journalistic ethics in Sweden's newspapers and periodicals. A board established by the country's main press associations actually considers allegations of media misconduct. If the board issues an adverse opinion, the editor of a reprimanded newspaper or periodical is ordered to publish the statement in its entirety in a clearly visible format. In the absence of legal procedures to enforce this decision, however, a publication's compliance is simply moral.[77]

Since these Scandinavian origins, ombudsmen have become a feature of the self-regulatory apparatus in other countries. Sometimes, they respond to complaints from irate citizens or the subjects of news coverage; at other times, they act on their own initiative. A case in point was the controversial decision by the *Edmonton Journal* to request letters from readers telling the dethroned Canadian Olympic sprinter Ben

Johnson what they thought of him. Johnson had been stripped of his gold medal because steroids had been detected in his urine during the 1988 summer Olympics in Korea. The best of the letters were to be published, and the rest were to be sent to Johnson. Several readers complained to the paper's ombudsman, John Brown, who shared their concerns and noted that those unpublished letters that did not meet the paper's publications standards should also have been considered unfit to pass on to Brown. Fortunately, the ombudsman's fears were apparently unfounded, because the paper reported that only one of the 1,000 letters received had been considered "offensive."[78]

The first newspapers to use an ombudsman in this country were the *Louisville Times* and *Courier-Journal* in 1967. By 1993 only about 30 of the more than 1,600 daily newspapers had ombudsmen.[79] Ombudsmen do not base their advice on fixed codes but are more interested in improving the social conscience of the institution than in adhering to a general and sometimes vague formal policy. Effective ombudsmen must be viewed both by management and the public as representatives of the community and should have access to space in the newspaper or airtime on the station to disagree with decisions by institutional personnel. Ombudsmen should also have seniority or some stature within the industry.[80]

Although ombudsmen are considered representatives of the public, they should also be even-handed in their handling of complaints. They must be fair to both readers and their newspapers and editors. One problem has been the public's perception of ombudsmen, who are sometimes viewed as a cosmetic response to reader criticism. Thus, an Organization of News Ombudsmen has been established to promote the positive role of these readers' representatives. Ombudsmen—or "readers' representatives," as they are called at some papers —can provide an avenue for constructive criticism and a platform for a reasonable dialogue with the faceless institutional gatekeepers. The presence of ombudsmen can be an effective tool of corporate management to demonstrate to a skeptical public that they are serious about the idea of social responsibility. Unfortunately, the future of ombudsmen, as a self-regulatory device, is somewhat in doubt. Several papers, apparently believing that too much self-criticism is destructive of corporate self-esteem, have recently fired or reassigned their ombudsmen for their brutal candor in assessing the ethical indiscretions of their employers.[81]

News Councils

News councils, arguably the most democratic of regulatory devices, are another breed of watchdog designed to foster a dialogue between the media and their various publics. These councils, which are usually composed of a cross-section of the community and the media, are designed to investigate complaints against the media, investigate the charges, and then publish their findings. However, although such bodies are common in Europe, news councils have become virtually an ethical anachronism in this country.

In the 1950s and 1960s, local councils sprang up in the United States, in large and small communities alike. The largest of these— the Minnesota Press Council—was statewide and remains the only visible force of its kind in investigating cases of alleged ethical wrongdoing. This grassroots movement provided the impetus for a national review panel, and in 1973 the National News Council came into existence. The council was initially funded by the prestigious Twentieth Century Fund and the Markle Foundation. Logically, the financial supporters should have been news organizations themselves, but the council was met with a predictable outpouring of disdain and even anger from print and broadcast journalists alike. Some felt that press freedom itself was being jeopardized, which in hindsight was a rather dramatic overreaction.

In 1984 the council died from neglect, a victim of media antagonism and dereliction. Richard S. Salant, a former head of CBS News and the council's president when it folded, noted that opposition to it reflected the deepseated hostility of the American media to any outside body looking over its shoulder and the belief that each news organization was capable of solving its own problems. An editorial comment from the *New York Daily News* was typical: "We don't care how much the Fund prates its virtuous intentions. This is a sneak attempt at press regulation, a bid for a role as unofficial news censor."[82] The publisher of the *New York Times*, Arthur Ochs Sulzberger, called the idea "simply regulation in another form."[83] However, not all members of the media were as pessimistic. For example, the *Washington Post*'s publisher, Katherine Graham, observed, "If properly handled, it won't do any harm and might do some good."[84]

The council's detractors may have felt that a little social responsibility is good for the soul but that an overdose of anything can be terminal. Considering the hostile environment in which they are now operating, the media may have lost a valuable ally in their fight to be perceived as institutions of social responsibility.

SUMMARY

A system of ethics is a cornerstone of any civilization. It is essential for (1) building trust and cooperation among individuals in society, (2) serving as a *moral gatekeeper* in apprising society of the relative importance of certain moral values, (3) acting as a moral arbitrator in resolving conflicting claims based on individual self-interests, and (4) clarifying for society the competing values and principles inherent in emerging and novel moral dilemmas.

Five criteria are the basis of any system of ethics. First, an ethical system must have shared values. Before ethical judgments can be made, society must reach agreement on its standards of moral conduct. Second, these standards should be based on reason and experience. They should seek to harmonize people's rights and interests with their obligations to their fellow citizens. Third, a system of ethics should seek justice. No double standard of treatment should be employed, unless there is an overriding and morally defensible reason to discriminate. Fourth, an ethical system should be based on freedom of choice. Moral agents must be free to render ethical judgments without coercion. Only in this way will the individual's ethical level of consciousness be raised. Finally, there must be some means of accountability, either formal or informal. An ethics system that does not include accountability encourages freedom without responsibility and thus lacks the moral authority to encourage virtuous behavior.

Society imposes moral duties on individuals as a condition of membership in that society. These duties are of two kinds. *General* obligations are those that apply to all members of society. *Particularistic* obligations are determined by membership within a specific group, profession, or occupation. A real moral dilemma can occur when there is a conflict between our general and particularistic duties, as when a reporter refuses to divulge the name of a confidential source to a court of law.

In fulfilling these moral duties, we must take into account all parties, including ourselves, who may be touched by our ethical decisions. For media practitioners, these include the individual's conscience, the objects of moral judgment, financial supporters, the institution, professional colleagues, and society at large.

Obviously a connection exists between law and ethics, inasmuch as many of our felony statutes, for example, those involving murder and theft, are based on the moral precepts of civilization. However, not all moral issues are legally codified. But since compliance with the law in a democratic society depends on moral respect for its legal institutions, violation of the law can be justified only by some higher moral principle. And even then lawbreakers must be willing to accept the consequences of their actions.

Individuals are the primary moral agents within society. They are the ones who make ethical judgments within the institutional hierarchy. Nevertheless, the public often associates ethical or unethical behavior with the institutions themselves, especially when corporate executives are invisible to a skeptical populace. Thus, we often speak of social responsibility when referring to a company's image.

Some traditionalists, such as the economist Milton Friedman, believe that the concept of the public interest is merely a by-product of corporate autonomy. According to this view, social responsibility consists primarily of serving the stockholders or other investors. Others have taken issue with this view and believe that conducting business is not a right but a privilege granted by society.

Because the media are now a big business feasting at the trough of Wall Street, the public has demanded accountability, just as it has from the rest of corporate America. This pressure for social responsibility, which has manifested itself through both mechanisms of self-regulation and external criticism, began around the turn of the century and has continued unabated.

The arrival of the information age has precipitated a new round of ethical soul searching and may challenge traditional concepts of social responsibility. Such unethical conduct as invasion of privacy, theft of intellectual property, and deception using digitalization are among the concerns of ethicists as the convergence of communications media and sophisticated technology continues unabated.

There is no reason to believe that institutional autonomy and social responsibility cannot coexist in the media, but this goal necessitates the restructuring of corporate attitudes.

This attitude realignment should begin, first, by convincing corporate executives that social responsibility is good for business and that little autonomy has to be surrendered in the process. Second, media institutions should be—and many already are—actively involved in the communities of which they are a part. Other promising signs indicate that the media have recognized that freedom and responsibility are not mutually exclusive. This recognition of social responsibility is reflected in two self-regulatory mechanisms: codes of conduct, both professional and institutional, and ombudsmen. News councils, perhaps the most democratic of self-regulatory devices, have all but disappeared from this country's ethical arsenal.

Predictably, all of these measures have met with some resistance from those who view social responsibility as a euphemism for censorship. But each, in its own way, has served to awaken the media to their obligations to the society from which they draw economic sustenance.

Notes

1. Richard P. Cunningham, "The Press as Moral Arbiter," *Quill*, November 1988, p. 16. Six years earlier, in 1982, the Washington Commission on Judicial Conduct had admonished Judge Little for having had out-of-court contact with juvenile offenders, but its decision was kept private.
2. *Ibid.*
3. *Ibid.*
4. Jeffrey Olen, *Ethics in Journalism* (Upper Saddle River, NJ: Prentice Hall, 1988), p. 3.
5. For a discussion of this case, see William L. Rivers and Cleve Mathews, *Ethics for the Media* (Upper Saddle River, NJ: Prentice Hall, 1988), pp. 232–233.
6. W. Dale Nelson, "Competition Casualty," *Quill*, May 1993, p. 38.
7. Rob Sunde, "Fake News: A Passing Scandal, or Here to Stay?" *Quill*, April 1993, pp. 10–11.
8. *Ibid.*, p. 10. On the decline of NBC's credibility, see "Gartner Resigns, NBC News Credibility Drops in Wake of 'Dateline'-GM Truck Scandal," *Broadcasting & Cable*, March 8, 1993, pp. 10, 12.
9. See John Hartland-Swann, "The Moral and the Non-Moral," in Tom L. Beauchamp, *Philosophical Ethics: An Introduction to Moral Philosophy* (New York: McGraw-Hill, 1982), pp. 7–10.
10. Olen, *Ethics in Journalism*, p. 3.
11. See "Of Pain and Progress," *Newsweek*, December 26, 1988, pp. 50–59.
12. Richard P. Cunningham, "Public Cries Foul on Both Coasts When Papers Lift Secrecy," *Quill*, April 1995, p. 12.
13. *Ibid.*
14. *Ibid.*
15. Richard P. Cunningham, "Judge's Racist Comments Rip Scab Off City, Readers," *Quill*, June 1992, p. 10.
16. *Ibid.*
17. Quoted in *ibid.*, p. 11.
18. *Virginia Pharmacy Board v. Virginia Consumer Council*, 1 Med.L.Rptr. 1930, 1935 (1976).
19. *Ibid.*, 1936.
20. For a more thorough examination of this controversy, see Clifford G. Christians, Mark Fackler, and Kim B. Rotzoll, *Media Ethics: Cases & Moral Reasoning*, 4th ed. (White Plains, NY: Longman, 1995), pp. 135–139.
21. For a discussion of the relationship between "popular" culture and "high" culture see Lee Thayer (ed.), *Ethics, Morality and the Media* (New York: Hastings House, 1980), pp. 19–22.
22. These criteria are based, in part, on the writings of ancient Greek and contemporary philosophers, as well as some recommended by the ethics scholar John Merrill.
23. See Olen, *Ethics in Journalism*, pp. 2–3. One author refers to these as *prima facie duties* in Beauchamp, *Philosophical Ethics*, pp. 188–190.
24. See Norman E. Bowie, *Making Ethical Decisions* (New York: McGraw-Hill, 1985), p. 100.
25. James C. Clark, "Many Reporters Couldn't Say No," *1986–87 Journalism Ethics Report*, Society of Professional Journalists (Chicago: National Freedom of Information Committee, Society of Professional Journalists, 1987), p. 4.
26. *Ibid.*
27. *Ibid.*
28. *Ibid.*
29. See "More on Jennings, Wallace, and the 'North Kosanese,'" *Quill*, April 1989, pp. 5–7.
30. Richard Cunningham, "Saving Life Becomes Ethical Dilemma for Veteran Reporter," *Quill*, May 1995, p. 14.
31. *Ibid.*
32. See Ralph Potter, "The Logic of Moral Argument," in Paul Deats (ed.), *Toward a Discipline of Social Ethics* (Boston: Boston University Press, 1972), pp. 93–114.
33. Christians, Rotzoll, and Mark, *Media Ethics*, p. 19.
34. Some of these categories are derived from those developed by Christians, Rotzoll, and Fackler in *Media Ethics*, pp. 20–21.
35. See Olen, *Ethics in Journalism*, p. 33.
36. *Ibid.*, p. 34.

37. 18 Med.L.Rptr. 1348 (S.D.Fla., 1990).

38. 18 Med.L.Rptr. 1352 (11th Cir., 1990).

39. *U.S. v. Cable News Network*, 23 Med.L.Rptr. 1033, 1045–46 (S.D.Fla., 1994).

40. *Cohen v. Cowles Media Co.*, 18 Med.L.Rptr. 2273 (1991).

41. *Cox Broadcasting Corp. v. Cohn*, 420 U.S. 469 (1975).

42. *The Florida Star v. B.J.F.*, 109 S.Ct. 2603 (1989).

43. *Smith v. Daily Mail*, 443 U.S. 97 (1979).

44. Not all ethicists agree with this view. Some believe that corporate morality exists apart from the ethical behavior of individual members. See Peter A. French, "Corporate Moral Agency," in Joan C. Callahan (ed.), *Ethical Issues in Professional Life* (New York: Oxford University Press, 1988), pp. 265–269.

45. This case is discussed in James A. Jaska and Michael S. Pritchard, *Communication Ethics: Methods of Analysis*, 2d ed. (Belmont, CA: Wadsworth, 1994), p. 48.

46. For a discussion of corporate social responsibility, see Conrad C. Fink, *Media Ethics: In the Newsroom and Beyond* (New York: McGraw-Hill, 1988), pp. 81–101.

47. See Milton Friedman, "Social Responsibility and Compensatory Justice," in Callahan, *Ethical Issues*, pp. 349–350.

48. *Ibid.*, p. 345.

49. Mitchell Stephens, *A History of News: From the Drum to the Satellite* (New York: Viking Penguin, 1988), p. 264.

50. *Ibid.*, pp. 263–268.

51. See Melvin Anshen, "Changing the Social Contract: A Role for Business," in Callahan, *Ethical Issues*, pp. 351–354.

52. See Jane Easter Bahls, "Beyond the Bottom Line," *Student Lawyer*, October 1988, p. 33.

53. See "Big Media, Big Money," *Newsweek*, April 1, 1985, pp. 52–59.

54. Fred S. Siebert, Theodore Peterson, and Wilbur Schramm, *Four Theories of the Press* (Urbana: University of Illinois Press, 1956), p. 83.

55. *Ibid.*, quoting Joseph Pulitzer, "The College of Journalism," *North American Review*, 178, May 1904, p. 658.

56. H. Eugene Goodwin and Ron F. Smith, *Groping for Ethics in Journalism*, 3d ed. (Ames: Iowa State University Press, 1994), p. 38.

57. Clifford Christians, "Enforcing Media Codes," *Journal of Mass Media Ethics*, 1, No. 1, Fall/Winter 1985–86, p. 14.

58. *Ibid.*, pp. 87–92.

59. Theodore L. Glasser, "When Is Objective Reporting Irresponsible Reporting?" in Philip Patterson and Lee Wilkins (eds.), *Media Ethics: Issues and Cases* 2d ed. (Dubuque, IA: WCB Brown & Benchmark, 1994), p. 34.

60. Quoted in *ibid.*

61. Ted J. Smith III, "Journalism and the Socrates Syndrome," *Quill*, April 1988, p. 20.

62. *Ibid.*

63. For an excellent book by Howard Kurtz that provides a penetrating and critical look at the newspaper industry, see *Media Circus: The Trouble with America's Newspapers* (New York: Times Books, 1993).

64. Peter B. Orlik, *Electronic Media Criticism* (Boston: Focal Press, 1994), p. 19.

65. "Big Media, Big Money," p. 52.

66. Catherine Mejia, "E-mail Access v. Privacy," *Quill*, April 1994, p. 4.

67. See Christians, "Enforcing Media Codes."

68. For a consideration of arguments against formal codes of ethics, see Jay Black and Ralph D. Barney, "The Case against Mass Media Codes of Ethics," *Journal of Mass Media Ethics*, 1, No. 1, Fall–Winter 1985–86, pp. 27–36.

69. John C. Merrill and S. Jack Odell, *Philosophy and Journalism* (White Plains, NY: Longman, 1983), p. 137.

70. Goodwin and Smith, *Groping for Ethics*, p. 35.

71. For a discussion of whether journalism is a "profession," see Goodwin and Smith, *Groping for Ethics*, pp. 34–41.

72. For a more thorough discussion of the pros and cons regarding media codes, see Richard L. Johannesen, "What Should We Teach about Formal Codes of Communication Ethics?" *Journal of Mass Media Ethics*, Vol. 3, 1988, pp. 59–64.

73. See Jay Black, "Taking the Pulse of the Nation's News Media," *Quill*, November 1992, p. 32.

74. See Emerson Stone, "Going, Going, Gone . . . ?" *Communicator*, December 1993, p. 16.

75. *Ibid.*

76. Goodwin, *Groping for Ethics*, p. 297.

77. For a discussion of press self-regulation in Sweden, see Hakan Stromberg, "Press Law in Sweden," in Pnina Lahav (ed.), *Press Law in Modern Democracies* (White Plains, NY: Longman, 1985), pp. 248–249.

78. Richard P. Cunningham, "Fall from Grace," *Quill*, December 1988, p. 7.

79. Emerson Stone, "Protecting Our Credibility," *Communicator*, May 1993, p. 17.

80. See Rivers and Mathews, *Ethics for the Media*, p. 231.

81. E.g., see Terry Dalton, "Another One Bites the Dust," *Quill*, November/December 1994, pp. 39–40; Richard P. Cunningham, "Third Canadian Paper Eliminates Ombudsman Post," *Quill*, September 1993, pp. 16–17; Richard P. Cunningham, "L.A. Riot Coverage Criticism Costs Ombudsman His Job," *Quill*, July/August 1992, pp. 12–13.

82. Rivers and Mathews, *Ethics for the Media*, p. 219.

83. "Judges for Journalism," *Newsweek*, December 11, 1972, p. 82.

84. *Ibid.*

3

Ethics and
Moral Reasoning

MORAL REASONING AND
ETHICAL DECISION MAKING

Discussions about religion and politics are sure to liven up any party. Ethics deserves a place on that list. Everyone has opinions about unethical and immoral conduct, and arguments about morality usually produce more heat than light. When ethical issues are confronted in the classroom or professional media seminars, the discussion often degenerates into passionate appeals for press rights or sympathy for the victims. Judgments are not well reasoned. In other words, they lack moral foundation.

Moral reasoning is a *systematic* approach to making ethical decisions. Like other forms of intellectual activity, it takes the form of logical argument and persuasion. Because ethical judgments, as we have seen in Chapters 1 and 2, involve the rights and interests of others, these decisions must be made with care and must be defensible through a reasoned analysis of the situation. An individual unschooled in the process of moral reasoning might assume that questions of ethical conduct, like those of personal taste, are nothing more than matters of opinion. Imagine trying to convince someone through rational argument that he should prefer colorful sports coats to more traditional blue business suits. Such an

undertaking would be an exercise in futility, because we cannot argue reasonably about matters of pure taste or opinion. We can, however, deliberate reasonably and persuasively about moral judgments.[1]

But moral reasoning consists of more than just offering reasons for our beliefs, opinions, and actions. After all, not all reasons are valid ones. Moral reasoning is a structured process, an intellectual means of defending our ethical judgments against the criticisms of others. This does not mean that reasonable people cannot disagree about the correct solution to an ethical dilemma. Two different moral agents may, through proper reasoning, arrive at opposing but equally compelling conclusions about the most virtuous course. The beauty of moral reasoning lies in the journey, not the destination.

Schoolchildren must master the three R's as the foundation for their later educational experiences. Likewise, truly ethical people must understand the process of moral reasoning. Otherwise, even if they exhibit virtuous behavior most of the time, they may be unable to defend their decisions in specific situations against countervailing influences. Knowledge of ethical principles is important, but the application and defense of these rules of conduct in the drama of human interaction is at the core of moral reasoning. In other words, an attempt at moral justification is successful if it can be vindicated on rational grounds.

But if moral reasoning is such a deliberate process—after all, thinking and analyzing are time-consuming—how can media practitioners (or harried managers and employees in other lines of work, for that matter) who perform under deadline pressures expect to apply it? That, of course, is the purpose of teaching moral reasoning techniques to aspiring practitioners within the relative tranquility of the classroom. The consciousness raising and training that occur there should help the student confront moral dilemmas in the real world with more confidence. In addition, knowledge of moral reasoning principles provides a framework within which moral agents, once they have made ethical judgments, can review them with an eye to improving their performance in the future. Some consistency in decision making will result, thus replacing the case-by-case approach that so often characterizes classroom discussions of ethical issues.

However, one word of caution is in order: no approach to moral reasoning, no matter how structured or thorough, is a guarantee of success in ethical decision making under all circumstances. Stephen Klaidman and Tom Beauchamp, in writing about moral virtue in *The Virtuous Journalist*, have this advice:

> No system of ethics can provide full, ready-made solutions to all the perplexing moral problems that confront us, in life or in journalism. A reasoned and systematic approach to these issues is all that can be asked, while appreciating that practical wisdom and sound judgment are indispensable components of the moral life. The absence of neat solutions may seem to prop up the views of those who are skeptical or cynical about the possibility of journalistic ethics, but such views are based on the false premise that the world is a tidy place of truth and falsity, right and wrong, without the ragged edges of uncertainty and risk. The converse is the case: Making moral judgments and handling moral dilemmas

require the balancing of often ill-defined competing claims, usually in untidy circumstances.[2]

Despite the rather untidy circumstances of some ethical dilemmas, the process of moral reasoning can be carried out if moral actors have knowledge and skills in three areas: (1) the moral context, (2) the philosophical foundations of moral theory, and (3) critical thinking. Each of these areas is important in its own way and plays an indispensable role in the moral reasoning model outlined later in this chapter.

THE CONTEXT OF MORAL REASONING

The making of ethical decisions does not take place in a vacuum. Moral agents must understand the *context* within which the dilemma has arisen. Before their powers of reason can operate at optimum efficiency, they must understand the issue itself, the facts of the situation, and the values, principles, and moral duties inherent in the case. In other words, the context consists of all of the factors that might influence an individual's resolution of a moral dilemma.

For example, White House press secretaries who knowingly disseminate "disinformation" to reporters in the interest of national security must not only be thoroughly familiar with the facts that might justify such deception; they should also keep in mind the societal proscriptions against lying and be prepared to justify their actions on some higher moral ground. But the general societal norms aside, they should also be aware of the standards of ethical conduct expected of government officials in these circumstances and the particularistic moral duties that govern their behavior. After all, these expectations do change over time, as evidenced by the recent heightened sense of moral indignation in Washington over conflicts of interest.

The context of an ethical dilemma might involve making decisions about either our personal behavior or our professional conduct. Lying to a friend, for example, involves different considerations than using deception in gathering a news story. Even an ethical purist might be forced to admit that lying is permissible in extreme circumstances, such as to prevent harm to another. But the justifications for this deviation from societal norms would be different for a media practitioner than for others operating within a dissimilar environment.

Contextual factors are often culturally determined, whether through association with a close circle of friends or through the "culture" of the newsroom. Company value systems and behavioral codes cannot be ignored in rendering moral judgments. Before promising confidentiality to a news source, for example, a reporter must be guided by company policy on the matter as well as the views and advice of professional colleagues. Likewise, decision makers must consider certain competitive and economic pressures that are common to media institutions. All of the considerations that are unique to a particular dilemma constitute the context of the ethical case.

Thus, before moral agents can argue rationally about media ethics, they must know something about the environment—that is, the social and cultural context—within which the media operate. They must bring to the decision-making process at least a minimum body of knowledge about the media. Otherwise, it will be difficult to evaluate the strength and legitimacy of the arguments put forth in defense of moral judgments made by media practitioners.

THE PHILOSOPHICAL FOUNDATIONS OF MORAL THEORY

Classical philosophy is directly relevant to ethical decision making in contemporary life. In identifying ethical theories that might be useful in constructing a moral-reasoning model, we might consult many philosophers, both ancient and contemporary. However, we will confine our discussion to a few who have had the most profound impact on moral philosophy in Western civilization.

The Greek Connection

Most would agree that the study of ethics had its genesis in the glory of ancient Greece. Socrates (ca. 470–399 B.C.) believed that virtue could be identified and practiced. He was dissatisfied with his contemporaries' opinions about moral conduct and wanted to discover those rules that could be reasonably supported. He believed that anyone, through careful reflection, could arrive at some insights into these rules.[3] Although he did not have a philosophical system of his own to pass on, his "Socratic dialogues" were a significant contribution to what we now refer to as moral reasoning. Of course, he would have been unnerved by the contemporary media environment, in which diatribes are as common as dialogues and reason often falls prey to intemperance.

Socrates' disciple, Plato (ca. 428–348 B.C.), argued in *The Republic* that justice is achieved through the harmony of wisdom, temperance, and courage. Translating into practice this philosophical observation from the ancient sage, we might say that moral conduct should be based on *experience and knowledge of the world, moderate behavior* as the means of achieving sound ethical judgments, and the *courage* to live up to those judgments. Plato believed that "good" was a value independent of the standards of behavior prevalent at any moment in society. An individual would be justified in defying conventional wisdom in the name of some higher moral good, even if that meant social ostracism. Thus, we might note these ancient seeds of the justifications that media practitioners (or any other moral agents) sometimes use for behavior that runs counter to societal norms.

Aristotle (384–322 B.C.) was for many years a student of Plato's, but he was more pragmatic in dealing with the world as he found it. He believed that moral virtue was obtainable but that tough choices had to be made in the process. The exercise of virtue, according to him, is concerned with means. Thus, the ends do not necessarily justify the means.

Aristotle's moral philosophy is sometimes referred to as *virtue ethics* and is based on the theory of the golden mean. He believed that virtue lay between the extremes of excess and deficiency, or overdoing and "underdoing." For example, courage is the middle ground between cowardice and foolhardiness. Pride is the mean between vanity and humility.[4] In contemporary journalism, such concepts as balance and fairness represent the golden mean. The banning of tobacco ads from radio and TV and the placement of warning labels on cigarette packages is a mean between the extreme of outlawing tobacco altogether and the other extreme of doing nothing to counteract the harmful effects of the product. The zoning of local communities to deal with the problem of "adult" movie theaters is another example of a temperate approach to a difficult and controversial problem.

But Aristotle admitted that not every action could be viewed in terms of the golden mean: "The very names of some things imply evil— for example, the emotions of spite, shamelessness, and envy and such actions as adultery, theft, and murder."[5] In other words, some actions are always wrong, and there is no mean to be sought. Thus, Aristotle's theory of the golden mean is helpful in resolving many of life's difficult ethical dilemmas but not the ones in which certain actions are clearly wrong.

Aristotle's virtue ethics emphasizes character. The development of a virtuous individual is the goal, not moral conduct in a particular situation or according to a specific rule. Aristotle believed that virtue was achieved through habit, perhaps an ancient expression of "practice makes perfect." Through repetitive moral behavior the notion of "good" is inculcated into the individual's value system. Thus, moral virtue becomes a way of thinking as well as a way of acting. Without perhaps being aware of it, Aristotle made a major contribution to moral reasoning, because the practice of moral reasoning, if it becomes habit forming, can realign one's way of thinking about ethics. This, at least, is one of the goals of this book.

The Judeo-Christian Ethic

The fundamental creed of the Judeo-Christian tradition is the admonition to "love thy neighbor as thy self." The Judeo-Christian ethic is characterized by a love for God and all humankind. According to this notion, all moral decisions should be based on a respect for the dignity of persons as an end in itself rather than merely as a means to an end. All individuals— rich and poor, black and white, famous and ordinary—should be accorded respect as human beings regardless of their status.

Although the Judeo-Christian ethic sounds rather utopian, it offers some practical advice for moral behavior: regardless of the approach we use to render ethical judgments, we should treat those affected by our decisions with dignity. In other words, the philosophy of respect for persons should underlie all ethical decision making. This advice certainly has relevance for journalists who scrutinize others' affairs and subject them to the glare of public examination.

Kant and Moral Duty

The eighteenth-century German philosopher Immanuel Kant ushered in the modern era of ethical thought. Kant's theories were based on the notion of duty and what he referred to as the *categorical imperative*. In *Foundations of the Metaphysics of Morals*, he wrote, "I should never act in such a way that I could not also will that my maxim should be a universal one."[6] In other words, moral agents should check the principles underlying their actions and decide whether they want them applied universally. If so, these principles become a system of public morality to which all members of society are bound.

Kant believed that moral behavior was measured by living up to standards of conduct because they are good, not because of the consequences that might result. He argued that although individuals should be free to act (a fundamental requirement for a system of ethics, as noted in Chapter 2), they have a responsibility to live up to moral principles. Because Kant's theories emphasize duty, his ideas are sometimes referred to as duty-based moral philosophy. In other words, one has a duty to tell the truth, even if it might result in harm to others.

Kant argued that we should respect the autonomy of others and should never treat them as means to our ends. But how can one respect the dignity of another while at the same time obeying the rule to tell the truth if it might injure the other party? Kant knew quite well that obeying universal rules of conduct could result in harm to others. However, a reasonable interpretation of his writings is that he believed that we should never treat such persons exclusively as means and should accord them the respect and moral dignity to which everyone is entitled at all times.[7]

Kant believed that one's motives for acting must be based on acceptance of the duty to act rather than just on *performing* the correct act. The intent of the act is as important as the act itself. A reporter who "hypes" an article in the hope of winning an award or prize money would not, in Kant's view, be acting from sound motives. Likewise, an advertiser that avoids deceptive commercial messages just to escape detection by the Federal Trade Commission cannot be said to be acting from any sense of moral duty.

Some wonder how Kant's absolutist view of the ethical landscape can be applied in today's complex society. A more liberal interpretation of Kant, one that still pays homage to his sense of moral duty, is that universal ethical principles—for example, truth telling, fairness, and honesty—should be obeyed unless a compelling reason arises for deviating from the norm. In addition, some contemporary duty-based philosophers have come to accept consequences as an important consideration in ethical decision making, as long as such consequences are not the primary determinant of one's moral behavior.[8]

The Appeal of Utilitarianism

Another approach to morality, one that is popular in contemporary American society, is the idea of utilitarianism. Two nineteenth-century British philosophers, Jeremy Bentham and John Stuart Mill, are credited with introducing utilitarianism into the mainstream of modern Western ethical thought. Mill's version of this philosophy is often referred to as creating the greatest happiness for the greatest number of people. Later utilitarians have argued that happiness is not the only desirable value and that others should be considered as well.[9]

However, all versions of utilitarianism have one thing in common: they are concerned with the *consequences* of an ethical judgment. Rather than looking at the intention behind the act, as Kant suggested, one must explore the best outcome for the greatest number of people.

A case in point is a rather unusual situation that arose in Juneau, Alaska, in 1985. Two reporters searching a courthouse trash can discovered copies of a court clerk's notes on grand jury proceedings that were still under way. Of the four newspapers to which they offered the information, three refused to publish it, because they did not want to violate the integrity of the grand jury's secret proceedings. The editor of the fourth paper, however, had no such qualms and published the story. His job was to learn what was happening, according to the editor, and tell his readers,[10] thus suggesting that he had breached grand jury secrecy because of the utility of the information to the public.

Likewise, reporters who use deception to uncover social ills often appeal to the principle of utility on the ground that, in the long run, they are accomplishing some moral good for the public they serve. In other words, the positive consequences for society justify the devious means in gathering the information.

The Ethics of Egalitarianism

Egalitarianism is based on the notion that all individuals should be treated equally in terms of rights and opportunities. In this respect, egalitarianism resembles the Judeo-Christian ethic.

One contemporary version of the egalitarian idea is outlined by the philosopher John Rawls in his book *A Theory of Justice*. Rawls recommends that self-interested individuals enter into a social contract that minimizes harm to the weakest parties. They should step into what he calls an "original position" behind a hypothetical "veil of ignorance." They are temporarily deprived of knowledge about themselves that is likely to influence judgments in their favor, such as sex, age, race, and social standing.[11] Minority views are to be accorded the same standing as those of the majority. Behind this veil, individuals who have some stake in the outcome of an ethical dilemma propose their own principles of justice for evaluating the basic social and political institutions of their society. When the veil is lifted, they are asked to visualize what it would be like to be in each of these sociopolitical positions.[12] The goal is to protect the weaker party in the relationship and minimize harm. This process forces self-interested moral agents to think impartially and consider the views of others without regard to their own cultural biases. Thus, ethical decisions can be made independently of social, political, economic, and other distinctions. An example is the TV executive (the powerful party) who decides to air commercial-free programming for children (the weaker party) out of respect for the psychologically vulnerable youthful segment of the audience. In such cases, the moral agent accomplishes a noble objective while justifying his decision economically by having the commercial lucrative fare

subsidize the sustaining programs directed at children.

This veil of ignorance, though perhaps a romanticized parable, encourages the development of a system of ethics based on equality according to what individuals deserve rather than special privilege. This is an egalitarian idea, an admonition that king and knave alike must submit to the throne of moral judgment and that justice should not be meted out arbitrarily. In other words, no double standard of ethical treatment should exist *unless there is an important and morally defensible reason to discriminate*. This principle is particularly relevant to journalists, who must make decisions about news coverage of individuals of diverse backgrounds, from the famous to the ordinary.

The Rise of Relativism

Partially in response to Kant's absolutist ideas, a school of philosophers has arisen espousing the virtues of relative values. These thinkers have rejected the approach of basing moral choice on immutable values.

Bertrand Russell (1872–1970) and John Dewey (1859–1952) are the most notable proponents of this philosophy, sometimes referred to as *progressivism*. Dewey, in particular, is credited with (or blamed for, depending on the point of view) convincing U.S. public schools that they should not be preoccupied with inculcating moral values in their students. Of course, some people believe that this progressivist movement has worked to the detriment of the moral stability of youth. This movement may also explain why, until recently, the teaching of ethics in public schools was looked on with suspicion.

Relativists believe that what is right or good for one is not necessarily right or good for another, even under similar circumstances. In other words, moral agents determine what is right or wrong from their own point of view but will not judge the adequacy of others' ethical judgments.[13] Relativists have the attitude that "I'll determine what's right for me, and you can decide what's right for you."

Carried to its outer limits, relativism can lead to moral anarchy in which individuals lay claim to no ethical standards at all. A less extreme view, however, is held by those who believe in certain moral principles, such as telling the truth, but are willing to deviate from them if certain circumstances warrant. Thus, the term *situation ethics* has entered our moral lexicon.[14] Situationists decide on a case-by-case basis whether it is expedient to deviate from the rule. This is ad hoc decision making at its worst and can hardly be used as a model of ethical decorum. Professor Bert Bradley offers this negative assessment of situation ethics: "It appears . . . that situation ethics has an unsettling ability to justify a number of diverse situations. It is not difficult to see how situation ethics can be used to rationalize, either consciously or unconsciously, decisions and actions that stem from selfish and evasive origins."[15]

John Merrill, one of the nation's leading scholars on the philosophy of journalism, agrees with Bradley. Writing in *The Imperative of Freedom*, he refers to this approach as "nonethics" and makes this observation:

> When the matter of ethics is watered down to subjectivism, to situations or contexts, it loses all meaning as ethics. If every case is different, if every situation demands a different standard, if there are no absolutes in ethics, then we should scrap the whole subject of moral philosophy and simply be satisfied that each person run his life by his whims or "considerations" which may change from situation to situation.[16]

In an earlier book, Merrill observes that the "temper of the times has thrust the subjectivist into a dominant moral position, or at least to the point of being in the majority. And for many persons today, if the majority believes something is ethical, then it is ethical."[17] This is not an encouraging observation for those who believe that obedience to the causes of relativism and situation ethics is part of the prob-

lem, rather than part of the solution, for society's moral malaise.

ETHICAL THEORIES IN MORAL REASONING

From the foregoing discussion, one could construct many different approaches to evaluating ethical behavior. But the perspective to which I am committed in this text is derived from three kinds of ethical theories, based primarily on the teachings of Aristotle, Mill, and Kant. Thus, the guidelines that will be used in the moral reasoning model presented later in this chapter fall into three categories: *deontological* (duty-based) theories, *teleological* (consequence-based) theories,[18] and *virtue theories*, represented by Aristotle's golden mean.

Deontological (Duty-Based) Theories

Deontologists (derived from the Greek word *deon*, or "duty") are sometimes referred to as *nonconsequentialists* because of their emphasis on acting on principle or according to certain universal moral duties without regard to the good or bad consequences of their actions. The most famous deontologist is Kant. As noted earlier, his fundamental moral principle is his categorical imperative, which is based on moral rules that should be universally applied and that respect people's dignity.

According to this duty-based theory, prohibitions against certain kinds of behavior apply, even if beneficial consequences would result. Rather than focusing on the consequences (after all, foul deeds might produce good results), deontologists emphasize the commitment to principles that the moral agent would like to see applied universally, as well as the motive of the agent. Thus, in this view Robin Hood would have been a villain and not a hero for his rather permissive approach to the redistribution of the wealth. Duty-based theories do not approve of using foul means to achieve positive ends. In other words, the ends do *not* justify the means.

Because of their emphasis on rules and commitment to duty, deontological theories are sometimes referred to as "absolutist," admitting of no exceptions. Under a duty-based approach to ethical decision making, for example, reporters would not be justified in using deception in ferreting out a story, and Hollywood producers could not defend their use of gratuitous sex or violence just to achieve higher ratings or audience appeal. It is little wonder that many media practitioners dismiss this absolutist approach as unrealistic and even as a threat to their First Amendment rights.

Nevertheless, duty-based theories do have some advantages. First, concrete rules that provide for few exceptions take some of the pressure off moral agents to predict the consequences of their actions. There is a duty to act according to the rules, regardless of the outcome. Second, the deontological theories are more predictable, and one who follows these ideas consistently is likely to be regarded as a truthful person.

In addition, rules can be devised for special circumstances to take some of the ambiguity out of ethical decision making.[19] For example, in cases where reporters refuse to divulge the names of their sources to a court, even when these sources may have information relating to the innocence of a criminal defendant, a special rule might be devised to compel disclosure on the ground of justice to the defendant. Such rules would then have to be applied in all such circumstances, without regard to consequences in particular situations. The problem is that such rules often collide with other fundamental principles, such as the obligation to keep one's promises.

This situation illustrates one of the shortcomings of duty-based theories. In cases where there is a conflict between two equally plausible rules, deontologists have a difficult time resolving the moral standoff. The "Heintz dilemma" described in Chapter 1, in which

Heintz was trying to decide whether to steal an expensive lifesaving drug for his terminally ill wife, illustrates such a rule conflict. Deontologists do not provide very satisfactory solutions to this problem.

In addition, even when there is no rule conflict, it is sometimes difficult to apply general principles to specific unusual circumstances. For example, should a TV reporter knowingly broadcast false information at the request of the police to save the life of a hostage being held at gunpoint! Most of us would probably vote in favor of doing anything to save the life of the hostage, but strictly interpreted duty-based theories might suggest otherwise.

It can also be argued that moral duties cannot be separated from the consequences of fulfilling those obligations. For example, the reason that the duty to tell the truth is such a fundamental principle is that truth telling produces good consequences for society. And even Kant, despite his condemnations of consequential reasoning, sometimes acknowledges the link between universal moral duties and the positive consequences of carrying out those ethical responsibilities.[20]

Nevertheless, from this description it would appear that the Kantian approach to ethical decision making is too uncompromising for the complex world in which we live and would thus not provide a sound theoretical foundation for moral reasoning. However, the contemporary interpretation of deontological morality reflects a more liberal attitude and suggests that there is a duty to obey specified rules unless there is a *compelling* reason not to do so. In any event, the burden of proof is on the moral agent to prove that an exception is justified in extreme or rare circumstances, such as telling a lie to prevent a murder.

Teleological (Consequence-Based) Theories

Teleological, or consequentialist, theories are popular in modern society. They are predicated on the notion that the ethically correct decision is the one that produces the best consequences. Consequentialists, unlike deontologists, do not ask whether a particular practice or policy is right or wrong but whether it will lead to positive results.

Of course, variations on the teleological theme are possible. At one extreme are the *egoists*, who argue that moral agents should seek to maximize good consequences for themselves. They should, in other words, *look out for number one*.[21] But as suggested in Chapter 1, egoism should be rejected as a viable avenue for moral behavior because it is based essentially on self-interest.

At the other extreme are the utilitarians, represented primarily by the writings of philosophers such as Mill. As noted previously, utilitarians believe that we should attempt to promote the greatest good (the most favorable consequences) for the greatest number of people. Utilitarianism is appealing because it provides a definite blueprint for making moral choices. When confronting an ethical dilemma, moral agents should analyze the benefits and harms to everyone (including themselves) affected by the decision and then choose the course of action that results in the most favorable outcome for the greatest number.

Appeals to the public interest to justify certain unpopular decisions by media practitioners is a contemporary manifestation of utilitarianism at work. Thus, a socially beneficial consequence is sometimes used to justify an immoral means. Reporters who accept and publish stolen classified government information on the ground of the "public's right to know" are attempting to justify what they believe to be good consequences, even though the means of accomplishing the ends are rather questionable.

Another aspect of teleological theories, particularly utilitarianism (and one that is often overlooked), is the focus on minimizing harm. Consequentialists recognize that difficult moral choices sometimes cause injury to others.

When news stories are published that reveal embarrassing facts about private individuals, the potential for harm is great. On balance, the consequences for the public might be greater than the harm to the subject of the story, but the reporter has a moral obligation to inflict only the harm required to put the story into perspective. To do more would only appeal to the public's morbid curiosity. For example, a story concerning a malpractice suit should not include allegations concerning the doctor's personal life unless these facts relate directly to questions of the physician's negligence or professional competence.

A classic example of the "minimization of harm" principle at work is a station manager's allowing a news anchor to resign rather than be fired. The termination (a kind way of avoiding the word *firing*) of an on-air personality might be in the best interest of the station and the public, but clearly some harm would result to the anchor because of the loss of employment. However, resignations (rather than firings) restore some dignity to the process and, in many cases, facilitate the job-hunting process for the unfortunate TV star.[22]

The consequentialist approach to resolving ethical questions does have a certain appeal. It is more flexible than the duty-based theories and allows greater latitude in prescribing solutions in difficult situations. Teleological theories also provide a clear-cut procedure for confronting moral choices through listing the alternatives, evaluating their possible consequences, and then analyzing each option in light of its impact on others.

However, some people object to these theories on the ground that they rely too much on unknown results and the predictive powers of moral agents. How can we know, for example, that the government's withholding of vital information relating to national security will be in the best interest of the American people? Another objection to consequentialism is that it does not always take into account the special obligations to individuals or small groups that may conflict with our moral duties to society at large. Media practitioners who are intent on producing the greatest good for the greatest number of people often overlook the needs of special audiences. This neglect results in a form of artistic majoritarianism, in which minority needs are slighted in the media marketplace.

Despite these objections, consequentialist ethics is a valuable tool in moral reasoning, because it does force us to weigh the impact of our behavior on others. It provides a rational means for extricating ourselves from the confusion of rule conflict and thus helps demystify the process of ethical decision making.

Virtue Theories: Aristotle's Golden Mean

Although duty-based theories and consequence-based theories differ in many respects, they have one thing in common: they are concerned with standards and principles for evaluating moral behavior. They focus on what we should do, not on the kind of person we ought to be. The ancient Greeks, on the other hand, were more concerned with character building than with what we think of as moral behavior. Plato and Aristotle viewed the acquisition of virtuous traits as central to morality. They believed that acts performed out of a sense of duty did not necessarily reflect a virtuous character. Theories that emphasize character are often referred to as *virtue theories.*

However, if virtue theories are directed at the building of moral character (a long-term proposition, at best), what relevance can they have for moral reasoning, which is a systematic means of arriving at ethical judgments in specific situations? How can virtue ethics assist us in confronting the moral dilemmas posed by the cases in this book?

It is true that many writers in philosophy have rejected the idea that virtue ethics has an independent and primary status—that it can be useful in the process of moral reasoning.[23] However, one helpful theory can be extracted

from virtue ethics: Aristotle's theory of the "golden mean." As noted earlier, he believed that virtuous conduct involved learning to avoid the extreme in any given situation. Thus, the golden mean provides a moderate solution in those cases where there are identifiable extreme positions, neither of which is likely to produce satisfactory results.

Aristotle's golden mean, however, is not analogous to the kind of weak compromise or middle-of-the-road "waffling" that one finds in political circles. The mean is not necessarily midway between the two extremes, because there are times when a moral agent must lean toward one extreme or the other to correct an injustice. Thus, an employer might be justified in giving larger pay increases to some workers than others in order to remedy the effects of past salary inequities. As Clifford Christians and his colleagues have observed in their casebook, *Media Ethics,* "The mean is not only the right quantity, but it occurs at the right time, toward the right people, for the right reason, and in the right manner. The distance depends on the nature of the agent as determined by the weight of the moral case before them."[24]

Aristotle's approach to achieving a virtuous resolution of a dilemma is exemplified by the Federal Communications Commission's approach to regulating broadcast indecency. Although federal law prohibits the transmission of indecent material over radio and television,[25] the Commission has decided to prohibit such content only during times of the day when children are likely to be in the audience—an approach that was endorsed by the Supreme Court in 1978.[26] This time period, which has actually shifted over the years, is referred to as the "safe harbor."

At one extreme is the "vice" of doing nothing and allowing the airwaves, which carry programs into the privacy of the home, to become a twenty-four-hour repository of scatological language indiscriminately broadcast to children and adults alike. At the other extreme is a total ban on such program fare, which could result in censorship of some speech with literary and artistic value, as well as speech lacking in any discernible social worth. Thus, the safe harbor is an attempt, in a libertarian society, to achieve a balance between the extremes of moral anarchy on the airwaves and moral prudery that manifests itself through overzealous government regulation. Although the remedies are legal ones, clearly the golden mean has widespread application in the unpredictable drama of human affairs. Aristotle, it seems, continues to speak to us through more than 2,000 years of history, thus affecting our destiny and our views on moral virtue.

CRITICAL THINKING IN MORAL REASONING

Understanding the context of an ethical situation and the philosophical foundations of moral theory are necessary but insufficient for sound moral reasoning. There must also be critical thinking about the dilemma. Critical thinking is the engine that drives the moral reasoning machinery and thus leads us away from the knee-jerk reactions and toward a more rational approach to decision making. Nothing is more frustrating than classroom discussions in which students express their opinions about ethical issues without having thought critically about them. This is not to suggest that such discussions should end with a consensus on the correct course of action. It does mean, however, that most of the time should be devoted to analyzing and evaluating the reasons for the ethical judgments rendered.

Critical thinking is not a mysterious phenomenon, available only to philosophers and others of superior intellect. We do not all possess the talent to become athletes, musicians, or great literary figures, but each of us does have critical thinking abilities.[27] And because critical thinking is a skill, it can be learned. The moral reasoning model outlined in the next section is designed to encourage the learning of this skill.

Critical thinking, like the moral theories described earlier, has a long and honorable tradition in Western history, tracing its origins to the ideas of Socrates, Plato, and Aristotle. Like his teacher Plato, Aristotle believed that moral principles separating right from wrong could be derived through the power of reason. To these ancient Greeks, skepticism was a healthy occurrence, because it led to relentless questions about the meaning of moral virtue. Thus, critical thinking involves, to some extent, learning to know when to question something and what sorts of questions to ask. Some of the recent Wall Street insider-trading scandals might have been avoided if the deviant investment brokers had critically questioned the propriety of their conduct.

Critical thinking begins, first of all, with something to think critically about. In other words, there must be knowledge of the subject to be evaluated. For media practitioners engaged in moral reasoning, this knowledge would include an understanding of the facts and context surrounding a particular case, some comprehension of the principles and practices of their own profession as well as the moral theories that might be brought to bear on ethical decision making. For example, students of critical thinking about media ethics (and this includes you, as you attempt to resolve the hypothetical cases in this book) cannot critically examine the use of deception in news gathering unless they understand the role of the media within society and the ethical norms that the industry itself has established for sanctioning or condemning such behavior. It would be expedient to offer an opinion that reporters should be held to the same standards as the rest of us, but this statement neither answers the question of "why" nor allows for any reasonable defense of an exception to the general rule.

Second, critical thinkers must be able to identify problems (or in the case of this text, to recognize ethical issues) and gather, analyze, and synthesize all relevant information relating to that problem. They must also be able to identify all stated or unstated assumptions concerning the problem.

Finally, critical thinking also requires that alternatives be evaluated and that decisions be made. In so doing, the critical thinker must examine the consequences and implications of the alternatives, each of which may have at least some validity. In some respects, this is the most intimidating aspect of critical thinking, because it requires that we make choices, choices that may be subjected to severe criticism from others. However, successful salespeople learned long ago that the best techniques in the world fail without the ability to close the sale. The same is true of critical thinking. One can analyze (or study) an issue to death, but at some point a decision must be made. The hope is that it will be a well-reasoned decision, based on the most rational analysis of the situation.

Students must not only be aware of the concepts of critical thinking but also practice them. Students do not become good writers because they learn (or memorize) the rules of good writing; they do so through practicing them. As Chet Meyers has written succinctly in an illuminating work, *Teaching Students to Think Critically*:

> Just as students will not become proficient writers merely by taking a year of composition but must be required to practice good writing in all their classes, so students will develop good critical thinking skills only by being challenged to practice critical and analytical thinking in the context of all the different subjects they study.[28]

In summary, the critical thinking component of moral reasoning involves a three-step process: (1) acquisition of knowledge and an understanding of the context of the ethical dilemma, (2) critical analysis of that knowledge and a consideration of ethical alternatives, and (3) a decision based on the available alternatives.

The moral reasoning model outlined in the next section reflects the notions about critical thinking described earlier and should be utilized in exploring the hypothetical cases in Part Two. Thus, the integration of this model for ethical decision making with the case study method is a functional vehicle for retreating from an ivory tower approach to teaching media ethics and developing critical thinking abilities that should awaken the powers of reason within even the most reluctant individual.

A MODEL OF MORAL REASONING

As noted earlier, moral reasoning is a systematic process. It involves numerous considerations, all of which can be grouped into three categories: (1) the situation definition; (2) the analysis of the situation, including the application of moral theories; and (3) the decision, or ethical judgment. For the sake of simplicity, I will refer to this as the *SAD Formula*.[29] Of course, other models are available, but the SAD Formula seems particularly adaptable to the needs of the moral reasoning neophyte.

However, this model can also be a valuable tool in creating a discourse among media professionals. Some news organizations, for example, regularly conduct sessions or hold discussions on ethical problems. The SAD Formula could be used to respond to either hypothetical or real ethical issues, with individual reporters and editors working through these problems. A dialogue with professional colleagues and a critique from management personnel or an ombudsman could follow.

The following explanation of this model is designed with written case studies in mind, although it can be used for oral discussions as well. But written analyses, at least until one becomes comfortable with the moral reasoning process, help attune the mind to logical thinking and sharpen the intellectual faculties. Following the discussion of the SAD Formula, a sample case study is presented (in abbreviated form) to illustrate this approach to moral reasoning.

The Situation Definition

The situation definition is designed to identify the ethical issue and list or describe those facts, principles, and values that will be important to the decision-making process. The first step is to describe the facts and identify the relevant conflicting values and principles implicated in this ethical dilemma. Sometimes the conflicting values and principles will be obvious; at other times their discovery may require some thought. They will obviously vary from case to case, but such things as truth telling, the right to privacy, conflict of interest, the right of the public to receive information, fairness, justice, loyalty, media credibility, harm to others, and confidentiality are representative of the values and principles lurking in the hypothetical cases in this book.

Students of media ethics should also have an appreciation for the role that competition and economic factors play in decision making in a deadline-oriented environment. These "values" are at the heart of the media enterprise and will be a consideration in most ethical judgments. In the real world, such factors often dominate. But experience in moral reasoning, even within the more sanitized classroom situation, can create an appreciation for other values that should be considered in rendering moral judgments.

In any event, the facts and competing values and principles should be described in the *situation definition* section so that they can be easily applied to the analysis portion of your written case study.

Second, there should be a clear statement of the ethical question or issue involved. This step can be done only after some understanding of the facts, and it provides a logical lead-in to the analysis section. The question should be specific, not general. For example, an issue statement regarding whether a reporter should go undercover in a Veterans' Administration hospital to investigate rumors of unsanitary conditions might be written as follows: "Is it ethical for reporters to conceal (or lie about) their identity to gain employment at a VA hospital for the purpose of investigating rumors of unsanitary conditions at the facility?" When dealing with individual cases, this form is preferable to a more general question (e.g., "Is it ever permissible for reporters to use deceptive news-gathering techniques?) because it relates to the specific circumstances and thus provides a more solid foundation for debate. Of course, more general questions are acceptable when debating broader issues of ethical significance, such as "Is society justified in passing laws that limit the distribution of sexually explicit material?"

A statement of the ethical issue would appear to be a simple task. But if you do not fully understand the dilemma, clarity of moral vision will be replaced by confusion and uncertainty, and the reasoning process will become defective. It is imperative that you spend a great deal of time fleshing out all of the relevant considerations for inclusion in the situation definition. The time spent in brainstorming here will diminish the likelihood of faulty reasoning during the analysis phase.

Analysis of the Situation

Analysis is the real heart of the decision-making process within the SAD Formula. In this step, you will use all of the available information, as well as your imagination, to examine the situation and evaluate the ethical alternatives.

There is surely no limit to the things that might be included here, but any analysis of a media ethical dilemma should include at least four considerations. First, there should be a *discussion*, pro and con, of the relative weights to be accorded to the various conflicting values and principles. This is a fertile field for imagination, and you should not be afraid to engage in a certain amount of intellectual experimentation, as long as your arguments are reasonable and defensible.

Second, there should be an examination of *factors external to the case situation itself* that might influence the direction of moral judgment. An external factor is one that was there prior to the particular case at hand and is likely to be there after the specifics of this case are resolved. Illustrative of such factors are company policy, legal constraints, and the demographic composition of the local community, which may determine how the citizens will react to decisions made by media practitioners. For example, reporters who electronically eavesdrop on unsuspecting public officials in violation of company policy (and possibly the law) may undermine their claim of moral virtue unless they have an equally persuasive countervailing reason for doing so. Demographic considerations might, for example, lead a TV station manager in a predominantly conservative Catholic community to preempt a controversial network movie reflecting the pro-choice view on the issue of abortion for fear of protests.

One external factor that is sometimes valuable in rendering moral judgments is an appeal to precedent: "What do we normally do under similar circumstances?" For example, if a newspaper usually reports all misdemeanor violations, even those of public figures, on an inside page, it must justify deviating from that practice in a particular circumstance. Otherwise, it will be suspected of ulterior motives or perhaps even malicious intent.

Third, you should examine the various individuals and groups likely to be affected by your ethical judgments. In Chapter 2 we explored the moral duties and the loyalties owed to several parties: individual conscience, objects of moral judgment, financial supporters, the institution, professional colleagues, and the various segments of society. These parties should be weighed, or evaluated, in terms of their relative importance and impact on the ethical issue under consideration. Of course, some may not figure in the moral equation at all in some situations. Financial supporters (advertisers, stockholders, subscribers), for example, are usually concerned with issues that affect their own well-being, the financial viability of

the institution, or, in some cases, issues in which they have a vested interest.

In Chapter 1 we noted the role that emotions play in attitudes about ethical behavior. With all of this talk about reason in moral decision making, does that mean that our emotional side has no role to play? Not at all. In fact, emotions often do, and should, influence the evaluation of our duties or loyalties to others. A reporter's sympathy (or perhaps empathy) for a victim of tragedy, even when the reporter feels obliged to intrude into the victim's privacy, is an emotional response but also certainly a rational one. It should be factored into the decision-making equation, because actions taken with the interests of others in mind (rather than self-interests) are a product of both our intellectual and emotional components.

Finally, the ethical theories discussed earlier should be applied to the moral dilemma. Examine the issue from the perspective of consequences (teleology), duty-based ethics (deontology), and Aristotle's golden mean. In those cases where a particular approach might not be applicable (e.g., where there does not appear to be a middle ground), this point should also be noted in the analysis. Each of these theories should be evaluated with the idea of rendering what, in your opinion, is the most satisfactory ethical judgment.

Decision

In the final section, you must make your decision and *defend* your recommendation. Your discussion should include an appeal to one or more of the moral theories outlined earlier. Keep in mind that a deontologist and teleologist might arrive at the same decision, but they do so for different reasons. For example, if you apply deontological ethics to a case involving the use of undercover reporting, you would categorically oppose deception as an acceptable news-gathering device. Applying teleological ethics, you would weigh the harms and benefits and might still conclude that the use of deception in

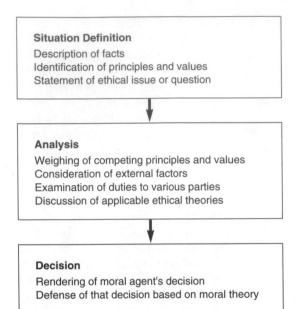

Situation Definition
Description of facts
Identification of principles and values
Statement of ethical issue or question

Analysis
Weighing of competing principles and values
Consideration of external factors
Examination of duties to various parties
Discussion of applicable ethical theories

Decision
Rendering of moral agent's decision
Defense of that decision based on moral theory

Figure 3.1   The SAD Formula:
a moral reasoning process

the case under consideration is more harmful than beneficial. But in this instance, you are focusing on the consequences rather than the universal rule that says lying (i.e., deception) is always wrong. In your decision-making section of some cases, you might also wish to point out that a particular course of action could never be justified under any of the ethical theories described in this text.

Although your defense may be somewhat redundant of some of the points outlined above, that will serve to reinforce your arguments and allow you to justify them with greater moral certainty. In summary, the SAD Formula for moral reasoning can be diagrammed as shown in Figure 3.1.

A SAMPLE CASE STUDY

The following sample case, which was described briefly in Chapter 2, is based on actual circumstances.[30] It concerns a decision by edi-

tors at two newspapers to break promises of confidentiality made to a news source by their reporters. This discussion is not intended to exhaust all possibilities for resolving the issue; you are encouraged to add your own perspectives. For example, one issue that could be considered in this case is whether the reporters should have made the promises in the first place. However, since the discussion below focuses on the conduct of the editors as the moral agents, any consideration of whether the promises should have been made is omitted. Of course, in this case we are playing the role of neutral observer (and critic), whereas in the hypothetical cases in Part Two you are asked to assume the role of the moral agent.

Situation Definition

Six days before the Minnesota gubernatorial election, Dan Cohen, an employee of an advertising agency working for Republican candidate Wheelock Whitney, approached reporters from four news organizations, including the *Minneapolis Star Tribune* and the *St. Paul Pioneer*, and offered to provide documents relating to an opposition candidate for lieutenant governor in the upcoming election. Cohen had been encouraged by a group of Republican supporters to release this information. In exchange for a promise that he not be identified as the source of the documents, Cohen revealed to the reporters that Marlene Johnson, the Democratic-Farmer-Labor candidate for lieutenant governor, had been convicted of shoplifting twelve years earlier, a conviction that was later vacated.

After discussion and debate, the editorial staffs of the two papers independently decided to publish Cohen's name as part of their stories concerning Johnson. The Minneapolis paper made this decision after their reporter had contacted Cohen to ask whether he would release the paper from its promise of confidentiality. Cohen refused. In their stories, both papers identified Cohen as the source of the court records, reported his connection to the Whitney campaign, and included denials by Whitney campaign officials of any role in the matter. The same day the stories were published, Cohen was fired by his employer. The editors justified their decision on the grounds that (1) Cohen's actions amounted to nothing more than a political dirty trick, thus his motives were suspect; (2) Cohen's name was essential to the credibility of the story; and (3) reporters should not make promises of confidentiality without authorization from their superiors.

Cohen sued the papers for breach of contract and won a jury award of damages. The U.S. Supreme Court eventually ruled 5–4 that such promises of confidentiality are legally enforceable. Although Cohen won his lawsuit, the ethical issues surrounding the newspapers' decision to break the promise of confidentiality and publish his name remain.

The moral agents in this case are the editors of the two papers, since they are the ones who breached the promise of confidentiality. In this case the conflicting values and principles are not too difficult to identify. On the one hand, there is the right of a source to expect a news organization to honor a promise of confidentiality. And closely connected to this expectation is the value of reporter autonomy (i.e., a news organization's obligation to honor promises made by their reporters). The value of loyalty is also implicated, since a newspaper's refusal to honor commitments made by its reporters could create morale problems and discord within the newsroom. Since arguably the public has a "need to know" anything about political candidates that might affect their fitness for office, the use of anonymous sources can sometimes be justified to obtain such information. On the other hand, using anonymous sources can erode the credibility of a news organization. Thus, the "need to know" principle might also be used to justify publication of Cohen's name so that readers can consider the source's motivation in releasing this information. And since the editors felt that Cohen's

motivation was newsworthy, they believed that it provided journalistic *balance* (or symmetry) to the potentially damaging information concerning the Democratic candidate.

The harm principle is also implicated in this case. At a minimum, the parties who might be harmed through a breach of confidentiality are Cohen, Cohen's employers, and the credibility of the reporters themselves and perhaps their paper. On the other hand, if the promise is kept, Johnson could be injured in her electoral bid, although what effect such a specious charge might have on her campaign is not clear.

Thus, the ethical issues are as follows: (1) Were the editors ethically justified in breaching the promises of confidentiality made by their reporters? (2) Are such promises made by reporters, without authorization from management, morally binding on their news organizations?

Analysis

Evaluation of Values and Principles One could argue that the reporters should never have made the promise in the first place, but the fact is that they have done so and now the editors (the moral agents) must decide whether to honor that promise. Since the breaking of promises should never be taken lightly, any breach of a promise must be based on some other overriding principle. Can the editors absolve themselves of responsibility simply by refusing to honor the promises made by other staff members? Probably not, since the average news source is unlikely to distinguish reporters from the organizations for whom they work. If they enter into an agreement with a reporter from the *New York Times*, for example, they assume that the newspaper will honor that agreement. Even if a paper's policy requires an editor's approval before any such agreement is made—and the reporter violates that policy— that is a management problem for the paper and should not have to be a concern for the source.

Thus, if the editors in this case are justified in breaching confidentiality, their decision must be based on some more compelling principle. Was the information provided by the source of such overriding public interest that a promise of confidentiality was warranted? In this case, the public's "need to know" that Johnson was convicted of shoplifting twelve years ago, a charge that was later vacated, is questionable. In fact, the editors could have refused to publish the story, thus avoiding the ethically controversial decision to breach the promise of confidentiality. But in so doing they might also be accused of suppressing information.

Nevertheless, the editors apparently felt the story was newsworthy because of Cohen's motivation in damaging the Democratic ticket just prior to the election. Cohen is obviously a key figure in this campaign, and his involvement in "dirty tricks" (in the editors' view) is newsworthy, which in turn justifies publishing the information concerning Johnson's past. And because of Cohen's tactics and out of fairness to Johnson, the editors have concluded that the source's name must be included. They are appealing, in other words, to the fundamental journalistic principle of balanced coverage of newsworthy events. While the paper might risk some loss of credibility in not standing behind their reporters and perhaps even an erosion of loyalty among their staff, the editors might argue that the story itself lacks credibility without the source's name. In addition, the editors might include some explanation to the readers concerning the promise of confidentiality and the reasons that they decided not to honor this pledge.

Regardless of the editors' decision, harm will accrue to some of the parties involved. If Cohen's name is included in the story, he will probably be fired. In addition, the credibility of the reporters and the paper might suffer. Johnson could be harmed, perhaps needlessly, by the release of this information, although it is not clear whether the electorate will hold her past against her, especially since her record for shoplifting was expunged. But the editors might argue that including Cohen's name and letting the readers evaluate his motivation for themselves might work to Johnson's advantage, thus negating any potential harm to her from the story.

External Factors One important factor external to the facts of this particular case might be the absence of any clear-cut policy on source confidentiality. (This point is considered an external factor because it is a situation that apparently existed prior to this case and will remain so after this issue is resolved, unless the newspaper moves to implement a written policy on the matter.) The reporters apparently did not feel that they needed to seek management approval, and this factor could be cited in favor of reporter autonomy. One might also point to society's attitude toward political dirty tricks as an external factor in favor of including Cohen's name in the story.

Moral Duties (Loyalties) Owed The editors in this case owed a duty, first of all, to their *consciences* to do what is morally right. Unfortunately, professional obligations and pressures sometimes lead us away from what we would consider to be the ethically virtuous course of action under other circumstances. In this case, the editors' consciences should have spoken to them clearly on the matter of breaking promises. However, they might also have rationalized their decision on the grounds that Cohen was acting from impure motives. But, again, if this were a concern, they could have chosen to suppress the story. At this point, however, competitive pressures could become a factor. If the story is suppressed, other news organizations might run the story, thus causing some journalistic embarrassment to the Minneapolis and St. Paul papers.

The moral agents in this case (the editors) also owe a duty to those who are most likely to be directly affected by this decision. These parties are identified in the SAD Formula as the *objects* of the ethical judgment. In this case Cohen, Johnson, and the reporters are the major objects. The reporters promised Cohen anonymity, and he acted on that promise in good faith. Regardless of Cohen's motives—which were known at the time the promises were made—the editors owed a duty to the source to keep this promise and minimize harm. On the other hand, a duty is also owed to Democratic candidate Johnson, the target of the information provided by Cohen. While this information had the potential for harming Johnson, the editors apparently believed that out of fairness Cohen's name should be included. In this way readers could decide for themselves, based on the source's questionable motives, what relevance to accord this information in terms of the campaign. In this way the harm to Johnson might be minimized. The reporters are also *objects* in this case since their editors' failure to support them could cause harm to their professional credibility. It has certainly eroded their relationship with the management staffs of their respective newspapers. One could argue that, in the absence of any policy requiring management approval of promises of confidentiality, the editors were duty bound to support their reporters.

Media practitioners must also be loyal to their *financial supporters* (i.e., those who pay the bills). In the case of a newspaper, the supporters are primarily advertisers, although some revenues are also derived from subscribers. Advertisers rely on the media to help sell their products. Newspapers have only their credibility to sell, and a loss of credibility could result in an erosion of circulation and reader support. It is unlikely that, regardless of the decision rendered by the editors in this case, merchants would withdraw their advertising, unless perhaps if they were staunch supporters of one candidate or the other. But over time an erosion of credibility could hurt the newspaper's bottom line.

The editors also owed a duty to their *institution.* Whatever their decision, they must take into account how it will reflect on their respective newspapers. Since promises of confidentiality have become a mainstay of investigative reporting, any breach of such a promise will reflect unfavorably on the institution, unless this decision is based on some overriding and more important principle.

In most ethical dilemmas involving professionals, there is always the nagging question of whether moral agents have complied with the standards of their profession. Thus, they must be loyal to their *colleagues.* In this case the editors clearly violated acceptable practice, although the breaking of promises to sources is not unheard of. Each such ethical lapse tends to erode the profession's credibility. Of course, editors must have the flexibility to render judgments contrary to acceptable practice for compelling reasons. How would most editors have responded in this situation? The question is whether the reasons given for breaking the promise were compelling enough to satisfy most journalists who have always considered anonymous news sources to be an essential ingredient in the news-gathering process.

Finally, a duty is owed to *society.* Some journalists apparently believe that their unique roles in society entitle them to special moral exemptions. But all media practitioners are bound by the same fundamental principles as the rest of us, and any deviation must be justified (as in the case of any other societal member) by some overriding principle. In this case, the reporters made a promise, and any breach of that promise, without some compelling reason, is a violation of cultural norms. On the other hand, the editors could argue that the reporters had no right to make such a promise and that their obligation lies in the direction of journalistic fairness and balance, which necessitated the inclusion of Cohen's name.

Moral Theories When one is rendering a moral judgment, there is no benefit of hindsight. A Kantian (deontologist) evaluating this case would follow a rule that can be universally applied. The very fabric of society is predicated, in part, on faith in others' promises. Thus, "Never break a promise" becomes a maxim that should be applied universally and that includes promises of confidentiality made by reporters to news sources. And, in this case, the editors could not absolve themselves of responsibility simply by refusing to honor promises made by their reporters. The fact is that Cohen believed that he was dealing in good faith with reporters who came to the bargaining table with the full authority of their employers. A deontologist would argue strenuously that the editors had a moral obligation to honor the promise and that perhaps they should use this case as a catalyst for devising a company policy requiring reporters to obtain management approval before entering into a moral contract (and perhaps a legal one as well) with a news source.

This case can also be viewed from the perspective of anticipated consequences (teleology), that is, the relative benefits and harms for the individuals or groups affected by this decision. If the source's name is included in the story, the greatest harm, of course, will accrue to Dan Cohen. He will probably lose his job. On the other hand, his motives are suspect. His willingness to release such questionably relevant information so close to the election is nothing more than a campaign dirty trick. Therefore, perhaps he deserves the consequences of his ethically dubious behavior.

The Democratic candidate, Marlene Johnson, could be hurt by the revelations, although the electorate may attach little importance to a twelve-year-old conviction on a minor charge that was overturned anyway. And whether Cohen's name is included in the story probably will not alter this equation substantially.

Morale in the newsroom—and hence employee loyalty to the paper—could suffer as a result of the failure of the editors to support their reporters. Perhaps the reporters used poor judgment in making the promises in the first place. But considering the questionable newsworthiness of the information, perhaps the story should have been killed. One could argue that the breaking of a promise (which is a serious matter) could not, in this case, be justified just for the sake of journalistic balance when the story itself is of questionable validity in the overall scheme of the campaign.

Is there any real benefit to be derived from this breach of confidentiality that would outweigh the harms? One might argue that the inclusion of Cohen's name might serve to inform the public about the character of those who are running the Republican campaign. And it still is not clear as to whether this character flaw is confined to Cohen or whether it reflects on the ethical stature of his employer. Therefore, the various harms that will occur from this breach of confidentiality appear to outweigh any modest benefit that might result.

Decision

The foregoing analysis strongly opposes the editors' breach of confidentiality. The breaking of a promise is a serious matter. Credibility is a mainstay of the journalistic enterprise, and the failure of the editors to support their reporters, even if the promises were ill advised, erodes the credibility of both the reporters and the newspapers. Promise keeping is a fundamental societal value. And in this case a great deal of harm can occur without any comparable benefit. In addition, an evaluation of the duties owed to the various parties in this ethical dilemma point, on balance, in the direction of keeping the promise. The sanctity of promises and credibility seem to permeate the discussion of the loyalties to the six parties discussed. And these were more important, in this case, than the editors' concern for journalistic balance. Thus, the editors' decision to break their reporters' promises cannot be supported under either a deontological or teleological perspective.

SUMMARY

Moral reasoning is a systematic approach to making ethical decisions, relying primarily on logical argument and persuasion. Moral judgments should be based on sound ethical theories and should be defensible through a reasoned analysis of the situation. The process of moral reasoning requires knowledge and skills in three areas: (1) the moral context, (2) the philosophical foundations of moral theory, and (3) critical thinking.

First, the moral agent must understand the context within which the dilemma has arisen. This understanding includes some comprehension of the issue, the facts of the situation, the values and principles inherent in the case, and the social and cultural environment within which the media operate.

Second, moral theory must be brought to bear on the problem. The writings of the ancient Greeks—Socrates, Plato, Aristotle—and John Stuart Mill and Immanuel Kant provide the philosophical foundations for the moral theories described in this chapter. These theories are of three types: *teleological*, based on the consequences of the moral agent's actions; *deontological*, in which moral duties and the actors' motives are more important than the consequences of their actions; and *virtue*, focusing on character rather than moral behavior in specific situations. For the purpose of the moral reasoning model outlined in this book, Aristotle's golden mean, which seeks a solution between the extremes in a given situation, has been selected as a practical representation of a virtue theory.

Third, critical thinking is essential to moral reasoning. Success in critical thinking requires some knowledge of the subject, practice in analyzing and reasoning, and the willingness to make decisions.

Although there are many approaches to moral reasoning, the model employed in this book is the *SAD Formula*, consisting of the situation definition, the analysis, and the decision. The situation definition entails a description of the facts, identification of the principles and values inherent in the case, and a clear statement of the ethical issue under review. The analysis section is really the heart of the moral reasoning process. In this tier of the SAD model, the moral agent weighs the competing principles and values, considers the impact of factors external to the case facts themselves, examines the moral duties owed to various parties, and discusses the application of various ethical theories. The final step consists of rendering the moral decision. Here the moral agent makes a judgment and defends it.

Notes

1. For a discussion on the differences between morality and other forms of human activity, see Joan C. Callahan (ed.), *Ethical Issues in Professional Life* (New York: Oxford University Press, 1988), pp. 10–14.
2. Stephen Klaidman and Tom L. Beauchamp, *The Virtuous Journalist* (New York: Oxford University Press, 1987), p. 20.
3. Anders Wedberg, *A History of Philosophy, Vol. 1: Antiquity and the Middle Ages* (Oxford: Clarendon, 1982), p. 139.
4. For other examples of virtuous behavior, see W. T. Jones, *The Classical Mind* (New York: Harcourt, Brace & World, 1969), p. 268.
5. "Moral Virtue," in Tom L. Beauchamp, *Philosophical Ethics: An Introduction to Moral Philosophy* (New York: McGraw-Hill, 1982), p. 161. This writing is an excerpt from Aristotle's *Nichomachean Ethics*, Book 2, Chaps. 1, 2, 4, 6, 7, 9.
6. Immanuel Kant, "The Good Will and the Categorical Imperative," in Beauchamp, *Philosophical Ethics*, p. 120. This is an excerpt from Kant's *Foundations of the Metaphysics of Morals*, trans. Lewis White Beck (Indianapolis: Bobbs-Merrill, 1959), pp. 9–10, 16–19, 24–25, 28.
7. Beauchamp, *Philosophical Ethics*, pp. 123–124.
8. Callahan, *Ethical Issues*, p. 20.
9. Clifford G. Christians, Kim B. Rotzoll, and Mark Fackler, *Media Ethics: Cases and Moral Reasoning*, 4th ed. (White Plains, NY: Longman, 1995), p. 15.
10. Conrad C. Fink, *Media Ethics: In the Newsroom and Beyond* (New York: McGraw-Hill, 1988), pp. 53–54.
11. See John Rawls, *A Theory of Justice* (Cambridge, MA: Harvard University Press, 1971), pp. 11–13, 30–31, 118–192.
12. For a discussion of Rawls's theory, see James A. Jaska and Michael S. Pritchard, *Communication Ethics: Methods of Analysis*, 2d ed. (Belmont, CA: Wadsworth, 1994), pp. 111–112; Norman E. Bowie, *Making Ethical Decisions* (New York: McGraw-Hill, 1985), pp. 268–269.
13. Deni Elliott, "All Is Not Relative: Essential Shared Values and the Press," *Journal of Mass Media Ethics*, 3, no. 1, 1988, p. 28. See also William Frankena, *Ethics* (Upper Saddle River, NJ: Prentice Hall, 1973), p. 109.

14. See Joseph Fletcher, *Situation Ethics: The New Morality* (Philadelphia: Westminster, 1966). For a discussion of various views of situation ethics, see Richard L. Johannesen, *Ethics in Human Communication*, 3d ed. (Prospect Heights, IL: Waveland, 1990), pp. 79–88.

15. Quoted in Johannesen, *Ethics in Human Communication*, p. 79. See Bert E. Bradley, *Fundamentals of Speech Communication: The Credibility of Ideas*, 3d ed. (Dubuque, IA: Brown, 1981), pp. 27–29.

16. John C. Merrill, *The Imperative of Freedom: A Philosophy of Journalistic Autonomy*, 2d ed. (New York: Freedom House, 1990), p. 169.

17. John C. Merrill, *The Dialectic in Journalism: Toward a Responsible Use of Press Freedom* (Baton Rouge: Louisiana State University Press, 1989), p. 175. Merrill also proposes a synthesis of deontological and teleological ethics to form what he refers to as "deontelic ethics." See pp. 195–214.

18. *Ibid.*, pp. 167–170; Baruch Brody, *Ethics and Its Applications* (New York: Harcourt Brace Jovanovich, 1983), pp. 9–35.

19. See Brody, *Ethics and Its Applications*, p. 31.

20. Although Kant often condemned consequential reasoning, most scholars seem to agree that even he did not believe that an action could be universalized without universalizing its consequences. Thus, the consequences of an action sometimes cannot be separated from the action itself. For example, the reason that the duty to tell the truth is a fundamental societal value is that truth telling has general positive consequences for society. See Beauchamp, *Philosophical Ethics*, p. 139.

21. James A. Jaksa and Michael S. Pritchard, *Communication Ethics: Methods of Analysis*, 2d ed. (Belmont, CA: Wadsworth, 1994), p. 115.

22. There are two variations of the utilitarian philosophy. *Act utilitarians* are interested in the most favorable consequence in a specific case, whereas *rule utilitarians* appeal to the rules or principles that will achieve the most desirable outcome. However, for the sake of simplicity, the discussion and cases in this text will not attempt to distinguish between these two variations of the utilitarian philosophy.

23. For a discussion of this idea, see Beauchamp, *Philosophical Ethics*, pp. 163–166.

24. Christians, Rotzoll, and Fackler, *Media Ethics*, p. 13.

25. 18 U.S.C.A. sec. 1464.

26. *FCC v. Pacifica Foundation*, 438 U.S. 726 (1978).

27. For more discussion of critical thinking, see Robert E. Young (ed.), *New Directions for Teaching and Learning: Fostering Critical Thinking* (San Francisco: Jossey-Bass, 1980).

28. Chet Meyers, *Teaching Students to Think Critically* (San Francisco: Jossey-Bass, 1986), p. 5.

29. This model is based, in part, on ideas advanced by Ralph B. Potter in "The Logic of Moral Argument," in Paul Deats (ed.), *Toward a Discipline of Social Ethics* (Boston: Boston University Press, 1972), pp. 93–114.

30. E.g., see *Cohen v. Cowles Media*, 18 Med.L.Rptr. 2273, 2274 (1991). For different ethical perspectives on this case, see "Confidentiality and Promise Keeping," *Journal of Mass Media Ethics*, 6, No. 4, 1991, pp. 245–256; Theodore L. Glasser, "When Is a Promise Not a Promise?," in Philip Patterson and Lee Wilkins (eds.), *Media Ethics: Issues and Cases*, 2d ed. (Dubuque, IA: WCB Brown & Benchmark, 1994), pp. 104–106; Jay Black, Bob Steele, and Ralph Barney, *Doing Ethics in Journalism: A Handbook with Case Studies* (Needham Heights, MA: Allyn & Bacon 1995), pp. 205–206.

PART 2

CASES IN MEDIA COMMUNICATIONS

The chapters in this part examine some of the most important ethical issues confronting media practitioners. Each chapter begins with some background and an overview of the issue. Where appropriate, examples are provided to illustrate a point, but there is no attempt to discuss fully every possible ethical dilemma that might arise in connection with the issue. The goal of this book is to help you become a critical thinker, regardless of the specific moral dilemma that might confront you.

Each chapter also includes several hypothetical cases designed to challenge your moral imagination and let you apply the moral reasoning model outlined in Chapter 3. The cases are followed by some suggestions on how to deal with the issues, but you are expected to make a serious effort to reason out the solutions and to defend your decisions based on the ethical approaches suggested in Chapter 3.

4

Truth and Honesty
in Media Communications

TRUTH AS A
FUNDAMENTAL VALUE

Are lying and deception ever justified? If you put this question to your friends, you would probably receive several different responses. Some would answer with an unqualified "Never!" Others would say that it depends on the circumstances. Still others would try to evade the question directly by cautiously noting that the answer depends on the definition of the word *lie*. These responses, as simplistic as they are, represent the wide range of answers provided by moral philosophers in their tireless efforts to answer this question.

At the outset, it should be acknowledged that lying and deception are related but not necessarily the same thing. For the purposes of this chapter, *deception* means "the communication of messages intended to mislead others, to make them believe what we ourselves do not believe."[1] Deception may result not only from words but also from behavior, gestures, or even silence. Thus, under some circumstances the withholding of information from the public might be considered a deceptive act.

Lying is really a subcategory of deception and involves the communication of false information that the communicator knows or believes to be false. Although media practitioners have been known to transmit false information deliberately, many of the contemporary ethical problems involving the ethics of truth telling fall under the broad category of deception.

The commitment to truth is perhaps the most ancient and revered ethical principle of human civilization. Despite our constant temptation to lie and use deception in our self-interest, the idea of truth as a positive value is well entrenched in moral and legal philosophy. Some of the earliest condemnations of lying were contained in judicial laws against false witnesses and perjury, such as the ancient Code of Hammurabi, which stated unequivocally: "If a citizen appears as a false witness in court . . . , he shall be put to death."[2] We find the Judeo-Christian expression of this ideal in the Ninth Commandment's dictum, "Thou shalt not bear false witness against thy neighbor."

On a more secular level, both ancient and modern philosophers have been preoccupied with the role of truth in human affairs. Of course, Socrates was eventually sentenced to death for his critical inquiry, thus becoming possibly the first martyr to free speech.[3] Kant, as noted in Chapter 3, felt that the truth was a universal value that should be brought to bear in all circumstances, regardless of the consequences.

John Milton, in his *Areopagitica*, published in 1644, made a compelling argument for freedom of thought when he depicted truth and falsehood as combatants in the marketplace of ideas. The truth, Milton felt, would always win in a fair fight. More than two hundred years later, John Stuart Mill was still promoting this idea in arguing for people's right to express opinions free from government censorship: "If the opinion is right, they are deprived of the opportunity of exchanging error for truth; if wrong, they lose, what is almost as great a benefit, the clearer perception and livelier impression of truth, produced by its collision with error."[4] Of course, Milton and Mill were perhaps more interested in the *intellectual* meaning of truth than its application to moral philosophy.

The U.S. legal system, which owes much to the work of these early philosophers, revolves around a never-ending search for the truth, and even the Deity is invited to stand guard over this sacred trust when the officer of the court looks sternly at the witness and asks, "Do you swear to tell the truth, the whole truth, and nothing but the truth, *so help you God?*" Our libel laws have come to recognize truth as an absolute defense in most states, a tacit admission that the news media should not be punished for reporting the truth, regardless of what their motivations are for doing so. Although the U.S. Constitution's guarantees of freedom of speech and press do not mention truth, the Supreme Court has interpreted this majestic document to mean that publishing or speaking the truth should receive more protection than the public dissemination of falsehoods.[5] Truthful advertising (commercial speech), for example, is accorded greater legal protection than false or deceptive advertising, though not to the same extent as political speech. Thus, in a sense the truth has become an important part of the "supreme law of the land."

The idea of truth has also found a comfortable resting place among our literature and folklore. We are all familiar with the mythical account of George Washington's frank admission of chopping down the cherry tree, a youthful lesson in the rewards of choosing honesty over falsehood. Mark Twain put the value of truth telling in a humorous context: "When in doubt, tell the truth. It will confound your enemies and astound your friends."[6] Shakespeare advises us that lying is self-contradictory. In *Hamlet* he puts it this way: "This above all: to your own self be true. And it must follow, as the night the day, You cannot then be false to any man."

Our first real lesson in truth telling usually comes from our parents, who admonish us to "always tell the truth." The churches and schools reinforce these childhood values, although there has been a lot of debate about whether educational institutions should teach moral values. The punishments for dishonesty are obvious and demonstrable, as when a student is expelled from school for cheating on an exam or when a witness is sentenced to jail for perjury. Unfortunately, the rewards for telling the truth are sometimes more elusive. Nevertheless, there is little doubt that the commitment to truth continues to be an important societal norm.

But if the truth is so sacred, why is honesty so often the first thing to be compromised when it is in our self-interest to do so? The answer may lie, in part, in the fact that the tendency toward dishonesty is as much a part of human nature and our societal norms as telling the truth. In fact, the art of deception enjoys a history at least as ancient (if not as honorable) as the commitment to truth. Deception was linked irrevocably with the idea of original sin when the serpent deceived Eve, who in turn persuaded Adam to eat the forbidden fruit of the Tree of Knowledge. This propensity for lying was passed on to Adam and Eve's offspring, as evidenced by Cain's response when the Lord questioned him regarding his slain brother's whereabouts: "I know not. . . . Am I my brother's keeper?" And still later in the Old

Testament, Jacob's children, in a fit of jealousy directed against their brother Joseph, deceived their father by telling him that Joseph had been ravaged by a wild beast, when in fact they had sold him into bondage.[7]

As we saw earlier, the ancient philosophers may have been committed to the ideals of truth, but even Plato questioned whether the truth was always beneficial. When confronted with the proposition whether one should lie to save someone from a murderer, Plato said yes. And in those situations where the truth is unknown, we can even make falsehood appear to be truth and thus turn it to our advantage.[8] This advice, of course, blurs the distinction between fact and fiction and raises contemporary ethical questions concerning such issues as the use of composite characters in news stories and the use of the docudrama—the dramatic blending of fact and fiction—as a credible TV format for communicating historical events.

Our mythology, folklore, and literature are replete with dramatic examples of deception and lying as legitimate means of fulfilling one's self-interest. As consumers of fictional drama we are generally impressed with the cunning and cleverness of acts of deceit of some of our favorite characters. In fact, it is safe to say that deceit, rather than truth, is featured more prominently in literature as a reflection of the human condition.

Thus, those who are prone to deception have an impressive array of witnesses in their corner. Moreover, many contemporary philosophers, unlike their ancient predecessors, have virtually ignored the importance of truth in human intercourse. We are living, it seems, in an age of relativism, when accusations of moral misconduct are met with the rather cavalier retort, "Everything's relative." The problem is not that the relativists are entirely wrong; there are times when deception may be justified. But if we are to remain moral beings, both in our personal and professional lives, we should be prepared to defend our deviations from the path of truth based on some firm moral foundation.

Telling the truth never needs any moral justification; lying and deception do.[9]

THE IMPORTANCE OF TRUTH

Some ethicists are uncompromising in their defense of truth as a fundamental value and adhere to the Kantian view that lying is inherently wrong. Others are more forgiving but still insist on a heavy burden of proof to justify any lie. Ethicist Sissela Bok, for example, adheres to what she refers to as the *principle of veracity*, which does not condemn every lie but requires that moral agents prove their lies are necessary as a last resort. And even then, alternatives to lying must be explored and chosen if available.[10] Nevertheless, because so many of the contemporary writings on moral philosophy have failed to establish the continuing importance of truth as an essential ingredient in our value systems, it would be instructive to do so here. There are several reasons that civilized society should embrace the commitment to truth as a fundamental principle.

First, a lack of integrity in human communications *undermines the autonomy of the individual.* As rational beings, we depend on truthful and accurate information to make informed judgments about a whole host of activities, including the election of public officials, what products to buy, what TV programs to watch, and even the selection of friends and professional colleagues. Because many of our waking hours are spent consuming the visual and auditory stimuli provided by the mass media, we have a right, as autonomous individuals, to expect media practitioners to behave with the same degree of integrity as the rest of society.

The notion of individual autonomy is based, in part, on freedom of choice. Deception may undermine the confidence we have in our choices, which may make us reluctant to exercise our autonomy in the future.[11] For example, a lack of veracity among advertising and public relations practitioners would understandably create a climate of public distrust of the business community. Thus, the term *social responsibility* has entered the lexicon of media practitioners alongside the word *freedom*, a concept that is also reflected in the codes of the various media professions.

The second reason for a commitment to truth is that it demonstrates a *respect* for persons as ends rather than as tools to be manipulated. Deception usually places self-interest over the interests of others. There are exceptions, of course, such as when a doctor refuses to tell a patient the truth about a terminal illness. But by and large a lack of veracity in the communication process places the recipient of the deceptive information at a competitive disadvantage. Where media practitioners are involved, the problems are magnified, because consumers are either more unlikely to discover the deception than they would be in person or have no way to register their disapproval immediately with any real hope of having an impact.

Of course, the fallacy in this "respect for persons" rationale for truth telling is that it can also be used to *justify* deception, as when someone avoids unbridled candor to salvage the feelings of others. At a higher level, journalists sometimes defend their deceptive practices in the name of the public interest. Some investigative reporters use misrepresentations to uncover official corruption or other unsavory activities inimical to society's well-being. From an ethical standpoint, this practice is defended on the ground that it will benefit the public at large while harming (deceiving) a small number of unsuspecting persons. Those who question the practice believe that reporters are too inclined to become undercover sleuths before exhausting other means of getting the story. From a duty-based perspective, two wrongs do not make a right (even in the name of the public interest), and deception as standard fare for investigative reporting should be rejected.

This practice is still a point of contention within the journalistic community, but many news organizations have their own policies against misrepresentation of the reporter's identity except in rare circumstances. And even then, approval must usually be sought from some higher authority.

The belief in the truthfulness of communications *also* builds *trust* between individuals and between individuals and society's institutions. Deception constitutes a breach of faith and makes it less likely that relationships based on trust and credibility will succeed in the future.[12] One writer has even described the practice of lying as "parasitic on the social process."[13] For example, a public relations practitioner for a chemical company who is not completely honest with the press concerning a toxic spill may have something to gain in the short term but will soon discover that the company's (as well as her own) credibility has suffered a serious blow. Likewise, misleading or deceptive advertising practices constitute a breach of faith with the consumer, because it is usually more difficult for the consumer to discover the truth about commercial speech than about political speech, which receives such intense scrutiny from the press. Because trust is built on truthful communication, lying and deception undermine the very foundations of society.

Finally, truth is *essential to the democratic process*. Democracy depends on an informed citizenry, one that approaches the political and economic marketplace armed with the knowledge that inspires studious deliberation. In a complex democratic society, the media are the primary conduits of information flow, and to the extent that they do not provide truthful, accurate, and meaningful information, they deprive their audiences of the intellectual nourishment necessary for rational decision making. The recent trends toward "sound bite" journalism and the displacement of thoughtful reporting and analysis with the sensationalism and triviality of the tabloid media are troubling manifestations of how truth is often vulnerable to the lure of commercial values. Certainly nothing is ethically amiss in the media's appealing to the popular tastes of their audiences. And to the extent that the public abandons serious content for banality, they must share the moral responsibility for the depreciation of democratic values. But when the media are not faithful to the democratic mandate to service the political and economic system that has provided them sustenance in the first place, they become culturally dysfunctional and deprive the system of its vitality.

MEDIA PRACTITIONERS AND THE TRUTH-FALSEHOOD DICHOTOMY

In theory, it would appear that absolute truth is an ideal for which all media practitioners should strive. In practice, however, the application of this principle often depends on the circumstances and the role of the moral agent. Although outright falsehoods can seldom be justified, exactly how much truth is good for the public soul depends on our expectations. For example, we expect journalists to be unbiased and report the truth (i.e., as many of the known facts as possible that are important to a story). On the other hand, consumers realize that public relations practitioners and advertisers are advocates and do not expect them to do anything that would be contrary to their self-interest or their clients' interests. This is not surprising considering the fact that advertisers and PR professionals come from a different tradition than journalists. Thus, the question becomes one of how much of the truth should be revealed and under what circumstances PR professionals and advertisers may withhold information that might be important to consumers.

In assessing the role of truth as it pertains to the various forms of media practice, Professor Frank Deaver of the University of Alabama suggests that we construct a continuum, a form of ethical "gray scale," from one extreme to the other.[14] Absolute truth will reside at one end

and deception and blatant lies at the other. Those whose purpose it is to provide facts and information (e.g., ethical journalists) will lie near the "truth" end of the scale. Those who intend to deceive, even if for justifiable purposes, will occupy the other end of the continuum. Unethical journalists and advertisers and public relations practitioners who knowingly dispense falsehoods are the most prominent inhabitants of this position on the scale. Somewhere between these two extremes, according to Deaver, are two other points: those who intend to persuade by using selective information (i.e., not the whole truth), such as advertisers and PR professionals, and those who engage in nontruths without intent to deceive. Fiction (e.g., media entertainment that does not purport to be a truthful account of events), parables, allegories, and honest error fall into this latter category. *New journalism*, which achieved popularity in the 1960s, resides here because it often uses parables, allegories, and fictional characters to achieve a "greater truth." It is often justified on the grounds that a fictional approach to real events and ideas appeals to a larger and more diverse audience than the more conventional structured approach to journalism.[15]

Truth in Journalism

The Standard of Journalistic Truth Expert opinion abounds on what constitutes a truthful news account. At the minimum there appear to be three concepts that underlie the notion of truth in reporting.[16]

First, and most obviously, the reporting of a story must be *accurate*. The facts should be verified; that is, they should be based on solid evidence. If there is some doubt or dispute about the facts, it should be revealed to the audience. This is a threshold requirement, because inaccurate information can undermine the credibility of any journalistic enterprise. Quotes should also be checked for accuracy. From the standpoint of ethical practice, altering direct quotes to avoid embarrassment to the speaker is questionable. If there is a problem in this respect, indirect quotes or paraphrases should be used. Nevertheless, some reporters believe that "cleaning up" an interviewee's faulty grammar is justified out of fairness to the person.

What is *not* acceptable within the industry and is indeed considered to be a mortal journalistic sin is the fabrication or alteration of the substance of quotes, even when they reflect the essential truth of what was said. Several years ago, writer Janet Malcolm created a controversy within the journalistic community (as well as a lawsuit that wound up at the Supreme Court) when she was accused of fabricating quotes. She had interviewed Jeffrey Masson, a psychoanalyst, concerning his views on Freud and had included his remarks in an article for the *New Yorker* and a book for Knopf. Masson accused Malcolm of peppering her writings with phantom quotes that damaged his reputation. Malcolm denied that she had made anything but minor changes in the quotes. In any event, she was abandoned by most of the mainstream press in her quest for journalistic redemption.[17]

What if the quotes are accurate but contain assertions that the reporter believes may be untrue? Is there an obligation to investigate the truthfulness of every statement (often an impossibility during the frenzy of a political campaign), or does the reporter's obligation end with quoting the speaker accurately? Surely the failure to investigate may deny the audience some access to the truth, but there is some question whether this duty amounts to a moral imperative. Nevertheless, when reporters do not personally witness an occurrence or when the information is not general knowledge, they should be sure to attribute the source of their information. This is a fundamental requirement of accurate reporting.

Second, in addition to being accurate, a truthful story should *promote understanding.* Time and space limitations preclude providing a comprehensive understanding of any situation. The goal should be to provide an account that is *essentially* complete. A story should contain as much relevant information as is available and essential to afford the average reader or viewer at least an understanding of the facts and the context of the facts. This places the working journalist somewhere between the extremes of full disclosure and no disclosure.[18]

The fact is that the whole truth can probably never be known about any situation, but ethical issues arise when moral agents *intentionally* withhold all or some facts relevant to the public interest. This practice is antithetical to the journalistic imperative of reporting all of the known relevant facts, but there are times when threats to individuals' lives or the public's welfare lead to the withholding or delaying of certain kinds of information. Fast-breaking stories relating to kidnappings and hostage takings are two prime examples.

Other occasions may arise when the journalistic imperative to report the truth is held hostage by more powerful forces that are just as determined, for their own ends, to control the flow of information to the public. Media coverage of military conflicts is a troublesome and recurring example. Chastened by what they believed to be unrestrained negative coverage of the Vietnam War, the Pentagon, many of whose senior brass were veterans of that unpopular conflict, was determined not to repeat its earlier mistakes in Operation Desert Storm, which successfully thwarted Iraq's aggressive intentions in Kuwait. In this relatively short six-week campaign, the military severely limited media access to the combat zone. And reporters, many of whom were covering their first war, seemed so hypnotized by the Pentagon's relentless flow of sanitized information that *Newsweek* described them as "callow children of the video arcades, stupefied by the high-tech at press briefings." "At times," *Newsweek* observed, "news organizations seemed so busy courting generals they forgot to ask questions. Competing correspondents, papers and networks played right into the Pentagon's hands."[19] The more restrained commentators chided them for being uncritical. Their less charitable critics accused them of being government collaborators.[20]

The third criterion for a truthful article is that it be *fair and balanced*. These twin concepts involve more than just avoiding reporter bias, although that is certainly desirable. Journalists should attempt to accord recognition to those views that enhance the understanding of the issue. Every effort should be made to represent them fairly and not to use quotes out of context.

Deception in Journalism Any ethical debate about the use of deception in news gathering and reporting must take into account its various nuances and forms. Some moral purists argue that, since truth is an animating principle of the journalistic profession, any form of deception is taboo. According to this Kantian view, such behavior erodes the bond of trust between reporters and their audiences. Others are not so austere in their ethical approach and acknowledge that there are times when deception must be used to uncover stories of overriding public importance.

As the media continue to be plagued by a public crisis of confidence, certain journalistic devices have increasingly been put under an ethical microscope. One such practice is the use of surreptitious investigative techniques, such as undercover reporting and the use of hidden cameras and microphones. Journalists defend such tactics on the grounds that as fiduciaries of the public, they must sometimes use deception in order to uncover a greater truth. In other words, the end justifies the means. Such was the case when freelance reporter Jonathan Franklin posed as a mortician and entered Dover Air Force Base, where casualties of the Persian Gulf War were processed. In so doing, he confirmed that the military had underestimated the number of casualties. Franklin's article was eventually published in the *Bay Guardian*, a weekly paper in San Francisco. The managing editor, acknowledging that he usu-

ally turned down stories based on undercover work, justified this exception on the grounds that the deception was directed against government misconduct, not an individual.[21]

Despite the continued use of undercover reporting, many news managers are uncomfortable with the practice. The watershed event occurred in the mid-1970s when the *Chicago Sun-Times* decided to go into the tavern business to document a pattern of government corruption in the Windy City. Two reporters posed as an out-of-town couple and purchased a tavern named the Mirage. With help from a private government watchdog group, they rigged the tavern with plumbing and electrical problems and then surreptitiously photographed dozens of electrical and building inspectors as they solicited bribes to ignore the deficiencies. The *Sun-Times*' dramatic exposé resulted in the indictment of scores of electrical and building inspectors. While the newspaper's editor hailed the series as a magnificent piece of investigative reporting,[22] the Pulitzer board refused to give the *Sun-Times* an award because of the reporters' methods in gathering the information.

Since the highly publicized Mirage story and the Pulitzer board's refusal to endorse the tactics employed by the *Sun-Times*, many news organizations have questioned the use of undercover reporting except in extraordinary circumstances. For example, former *Philadelphia Inquirer* reporter Rick Tulsky, in referring to the newspaper's policy manual that specifically mentions the Mirage Bar incident, has offered the following advice: "I would say that, if by announcing you're a reporter you cannot do what any other member of the general public can do, it's OK to pretend to be a member of the general public and not a reporter. It's *not* OK to represent yourself as anything other than a general citizen."[23] David Lawrence, publisher of the *Miami Herald*, agrees that the use of deception should be a journalistic rarity: "We don't believe in using deceit. But if we were to ever find a circumstance where it was necessary, and I emphasize that it would be extraordinarily rare, we . . . would tell our readers what we did to get the story."[24]

Although the use of deception is probably as old as journalism itself, the tabloid TV shows, less inhibited by ethical squeamishness over deceptive investigative practices, have turned undercover reporting into an art form. And their insatiable appetite for visual shockers has made the hidden camera an essential ingredient in the tabloids' daily diet of sensationalism.

But the tabloid genre is not alone on this ethically slippery slope. They enjoy some fairly respectable company in the form of the numerous (and mostly profitable) prime-time network magazine shows. They too have embraced concealed cameras as a prominent newsgathering device in their search for visual intensity and ratings. So much so, that in 1993 the prestigious *Columbia Journalism Review* singled out ABC's *PrimeTime* for scrutiny of its persistent use of hidden cameras in many of its investigative pieces.[25] Clandestine recording can indeed provide dramatic and powerful documentation of nefarious conduct of various kinds, as evidenced in a 1992 *PrimeTime* episode on racism. The show sent out two investigators, one black and one white, and surreptitiously recorded their disparate treatment by both prospective employers and merchants. When Diane Sawyer confronted the bigots, they were speechless.[26] The episode was a stark reminder of the vestiges of racism. In another episode on the Food Lion supermarket chain, millions of Americans eavesdropped via a camouflaged camera as store employees relabeled old meat and chicken and sold it as fresh. The program, a contemporary reflection of the muckraking tradition, appalled an enormous audience and shocked the conscience of the industry.[27]

One could hardly fault a news organization if it chose to ban the use of deceptive undercover reporting practices altogether. After all, adherence to the truth hardly needs any justification. But those who find such moral conservatism too restrictive in a highly competitive

media environment must still defend their use of deception based on some overriding principle and some fairly demanding criteria. Investigative techniques, such as undercover reporting and the use of hidden cameras, should be employed only after a full and deliberate discussion and moral reasoning process in which the decision maker(s) (1) are convinced that the information sought is of compelling public importance, (2) have considered all alternatives to the use of deception, (3) are convinced that the benefit to be derived from the deceptive practice outweighs the possible harm to the various parties involved, and (4) are willing to disclose to their audience the nature of the deception and their reasons for using such tactics.[28]

News staging is another deceptive practice that is not that uncommon in both print and electronic journalism. Of course, people watch TV news because they want to be vicarious eyewitnesses to events and are usually confident that reporters are on the scene as their representatives to provide firsthand insights and gather relevant information. Unfortunately, the demand for pictures, time deadlines, and even budgetary constraints push news organizations beyond the bounds of ethical propriety.

For example, a fairly common technique is for reporters, who are not at the scene of a news event, to narrate an account of the event (known as a *voice-over*) as if they were present with video supplied by someone else—either other news organizations or perhaps even amateur photographers. The practice has become so common at the network level, particularly in their foreign coverage, that CBS correspondent Martha Teichner complained that she spends less time reporting from the scene and more time writing voice-overs at the London bureau.[29] Needless to say, the source of such video should be identified for the viewer. However, when journalists abdicate their newsgathering responsibilities and do no more than narrate a story, they become performers or news "readers" rather than investigative reporters. Moreover, there is a danger in using video supplied by outside sources. The frustration level among network correspondents concerning such practices is reflected in this comment from CBS News's Betsy Aaron published in the *Columbia Journalism Review*:

> I do know that when I look at the tape and I don't see what's beyond that tape, I am not seeing the story. I'm relying on someone else to gather that story for me. I have no idea what the person's agenda was—and there always is an agenda. And we're putting that on the air with the CBS label or the NBC label or the ABC label and we're doing it in a cavalier fashion that we never would have done twenty years ago or ten years ago or even five years ago.[30]

Although such slovenly journalistic practices raise important ethical concerns, they pale in comparison with those surrounding the outright staging of news events. Such practices are virtually indefensible under any ethical construct. Nevertheless, the media have been plagued lately by a rash of such ethical lapses. In Chapter 2, I referred to the case in which NBC, in a story on *Dateline* relating to a design flaw in GM pickup trucks, filmed a demonstration in which one of the trucks was rigged to burst into flames upon impact. Following the brouhaha over this staged event, coanchors Jane Pauley and Stone Phillips, who apparently were not privy to the deception, promised that the program would never again use such "unscientific demonstrations." At about the same time, however, NBC was again caught with ethical egg on its face when anchor Tom Brokaw was forced to apologize for a story about the environmental damage resulting from clearcutting in the Clearwater National Forest by the timber industry. The accompanying video showed fish floating belly up in a river that, according to NBC, had died as a result of clearcutting. A few days later the network acknowledged that the fish were not in Clearwater National Forest. In addition, they were not dead but had been stunned by forestry officials as part of a fish count in another stream.[31]

Print journalists like to chide the electronic media for their obsession with ratings and visual impact, which often encourage such questionable practices as staging. But staging is not the exclusive province of electronic journalists. Print reporters and photographers are sometimes tempted to present the news in a dramatic fashion. Such was the case when the Associated Press ran a story concerning three young girls who were killed in a house fire in Hampton, Virginia. The anguish of the event was illustrated with a picture of a doll on the floor beside a rumpled bed. However, the photographers of the *Newport News*, who were also present at the scene, did not recall seeing such a doll. After an inquiry from the paper's editors, a photographer for the *Virginian Pilot*, who had actually taken the photograph, acknowledged that a fire inspector had tossed the doll onto the bed, and when it fell on the floor, he had snapped a picture of it.[32]

The allegation that the electronic media are more prone to staging than their print colleagues is based on the notion that they are often too willing to sacrifice journalistic values for entertainment values, as reflected in their preoccupation with surviving the competitive brutality of the ratings war. Electronic journalists, quite naturally, are defensive about such claims. Consider, for example, the case of Wendy Bergen, an award-winning reporter for KCNC-TV in Denver, who was prosecuted for staging a pit-bull dogfight and then lying about it. The station wanted to expose the illegal sport of dogfighting and ran a story featuring video that allegedly had been mailed to them by an anonymous source. But after a police investigation, the reporter, who denied any wrongdoing, was convicted of arranging the dogfight, which was filmed by two station cameramen. Print critics diagnosed the ethical disease as "ratings mania."

But KCNC News Director Marv Rockford was quick to respond: "It's a really facile conclusion . . . that this had something to do with ratings. Did Wendy Bergen care whether we were No. 1? Absolutely. Is that what motivated her?

No."[33] And former KCNC Assignment Editor Anne Gordon, a newspaper editor before moving to television, chastised her print colleagues for what she perceived to be a self-righteous ethical posture: "I still believe very strongly that the basic tenet of what we do is trusting our reporters. The print people who have made fun of that are just lying to themselves."[34]

As noted in Chapter 2, the introduction of computer-assisted digital technology poses still another challenge to the moral imagination of media practitioners. Digital imaging technology itself is ethically neutral, but its deceptive capabilities are worrisome. Alteration of still pictures, of course, predates the arrival of digitalization, but the new technology makes such manipulation of both still and moving pictures easier and virtually undetectable. Because of these factors, will news professionals now be more tempted than ever to alter visuals?

The jury is still out on that question, but some disturbing trends are already apparent. For example, on the January 26, 1994, ABC newscast correspondent Cokie Roberts was introduced as reporting from Capitol Hill and was shown standing in front of the famous landmark bundled in winter clothing. But in fact she was standing before a projected photographic image of Capitol Hill inside the network's Washington studio.[35] Three weeks later, during the 1994 winter Olympics, *New York Newsday* got a drop on its competitors by publishing a dramatic front-page photograph of figure skating rivals Tonya Harding and Nancy Kerrigan together on the ice. Although the magazine identified it as a "composite" photo, the event had yet to take place. *New York Newsday*'s editor, David Forst, defended the use of the fantasy photo because it was clearly labeled.[36]

Likewise, in a more high-profile case, *Time* magazine's June 27, 1994, cover featured a computer-retouched police mug shot of O. J. Simpson, the former football star and accused murderer. The altered photo was darker and more sinister looking than the original, leading some critics to describe it rather uncharitably as misleading, racist, and perhaps legally prejudicial.[37] The magazine identified the cover shot on the contents page as a "photo-illustration" and later described how the illustrator had altered the "cold specificity" of the mug shot and had subtly smoothed and shaped it into "an icon of tragedy."[38] *Time*'s managing editor, James R. Gaines, said he felt the retouched photo "lifted a common police mug shot to the level of art, with no sacrifice of truth."[39]

Certainly the alteration of the "content" of visuals in such a way as to distort the reality of the event raises serious ethical questions and erodes the confidence that readers and viewers have in the editorial process. But what if the alterations are made primarily for considerations of design or taste, as when the editors of *American Photo* digitally removed for matters of "taste" the nipples of model Kate Moss who appeared on the magazine's cover in a tight-fitting gauzy?[40] Under such circumstances, the ethical slope becomes more slippery as media practitioners balance competing concerns.

Many news organizations have policies against altering the content of photographs, and the need for new ethical constructs to deal with the deceptive capabilities of digital imaging is not yet manifest. After all, if certain forms of manipulation are unacceptable under current policies, the arrival of a new technology should not alter the unethical nature of that practice. The ultimate test is still, purely and simply, one of *honesty*.

Infotainment: Where Truth and Fiction Collide

In recent years there has been a noticeable and controversial blending of fact and fiction in the media, which has created a predictable outpouring of criticism. Ethical purists would prefer a rigid "church-state" separation between news and entertainment, but thus far they appear to be losing the battle. One version of this kind of media format is the so-called "new journalism," the technique of writing factual accounts as if they were short stories or novels. The dramatic impact and entertainment value of the articles are enriched through the use of fiction-writing devices. Although some writers have successfully maintained the essential truth of their stories, others have employed a liberal dose of poetic license to make their works more marketable. The audience, unable to separate fact from fiction, may be the ultimate loser.[41]

The docudrama is another popular version of fact-based entertainment. Docudramas have appeal because they are based on current events, and the audience can usually identify with the featured characters. However, the producers of these films are not journalists. Their goal is to create an interesting story. The question then arises whether the writers and producers of docudramas should have the same degree of ethical commitment to the truth as practicing journalists. The docudrama genre is not new, but it has become increasingly controversial. Some producers have been careful to note the fictionalized nature of their creations. But when a producer markets a revisionist version of history and cleverly disguises theories and rumors as fact, then serious ethical concerns must be addressed. Such was the case with Oliver Stone's film *JFK*, which was savaged by critics as entertainment masquerading as history and as little more than propaganda for a huge conspiracy theory of the Kennedy assassination.[42] Stone himself acknowledged that his version of events was not a "true story" but said his film spoke to "an inner truth." And *JFK* star Kevin Costner admitted that the film's whole case might be dismantled and discredited but that the "movie as a whole has an emotional truth."[43] Such linguistic spins led columnist John Leo, writing in *U.S. News & World Report*, to offer the following rebuttal:

> But inner truths and emotional truths are the stuff of fiction, or used to be. What I think Stone and his actor are saying here is that it doesn't much matter whether this is literally true or not, so long as it steers the culture where we want to go. This has become an increasingly modish opinion as the line between fact and fiction grows ever more blurry in the culture.[44]

Leo also took issue with Robert Redford's version of the truth in *Quiz Show*, Hollywood's dramatic re-creation of the quiz show scandals of the 1950s in which the TV networks stood accused of coaching contestants and providing answers to the difficult questions in advance. He faulted Redford for taking liberties with the facts, altering sequences, collapsing time frames, and in general oversimplifying a complex story.[45] Redford himself acknowledged the docudrama problem, noting rather casually in an interview with Ken Auletta of the *New Yorker* that "[t]he danger with all of this is that the truth gets futzed around so much that people will accept fiction as fact."[46] But Leo was unforgiving in his assessment of the use of so much artistic license in the dramatic rendition of real events:

> Imposing the dramatic structure here is a form of dishonesty that blunts the attack on dishonesty in television that inspired the movie in the first place. If Redford absolutely needed so many fictional fixes, there was an obvious thing to do: Change all the names and call it fiction. The problem comes from wanting to have it both ways, offering the allure of real-life drama, with some theatrical alterations to boost the story's power. It's the basic source of dishonesty in docudrama.[47]

While docudramatists may not be held to the same standards of truth as journalists—after all, some artistic license is inevitable in transforming historical events into a dramatic structure—they nevertheless owe a duty to their audiences to present a faithful re-creation of at least the substantive aspects of those phenomena. They should not offer as fact what is clearly fiction or mere theories or unsubstantiated rumors.

Of course, time is an ally of producers who wish to tap the rich annals of history for arresting topics that lend themselves to dramatic re-creation. Reflection and perspective are essential to the search for truth. Unfortunately, the recent plethora of TV docudramas, ripped from today's headlines, is lacking in both.[48] No event or personality, it seems, is beyond the pale, and the docudrama feeding frenzy has included everything from re-creations of the sensational Jennifer Levin/Robert Chambers "preppie murder" case in New York and the rescue of an eighteen-month-old girl from a well in Texas, to the emotionally charged and fatal confrontation between federal agents and the Branch Davidians in Waco, Texas—the first docudrama about a real-life tragedy that was filmed *while the tragedy was still unfolding.*

Critics complain that such docudramas pulled from today's headlines are driven more by ratings than any allegiance to balance and proportion and that these made-for-TV movies simply repackage real-life tragedies as home entertainment.[49] In the process, as *Newsweek* observed in its rather terse assessment of what it referred to as "headline TV," truth often falls prey to fantasy.[50] Such was the case in ABC's rendition of the highly publicized "Baby M" custody battle when writers depicted surrogate mother Mary Beth Whitehead to be "a near-lunatic monster." Whitehead later complained that the only true thing in the docudrama was her dog.[51]

Defenders of docudramas based on current events respond that such programs often address important social issues. The executive producer of an ABC movie about the *Challenger* space shuttle disaster, in which the entire crew perished, has even described such subjects as "the true operas of our culture."[52] Indeed, contemporary docudramas can illuminate social issues and even provide psychological insights into the dimensions of human tragedy. In a highly competitive marketplace, using today's headlines as the artistic cue for a TV movie is not inherently unethical, as long as producers adhere to a "truth in labeling" standard. They should not promote as reality a product that is nothing more than a fictionalized account of events. But ethical concerns do arise when fantasy subtly and skillfully replaces truth and the audience remains an unenlightened hostage to the producer's deception.

If the rap against docudramas is that they sometimes pass off fantasy as fact, "reality" programming suffers from no such malady. This genre, which rivals the docudrama in popularity, provides the audience with an unfiltered flow of real-life misery, voyeurism, raw emotion, and human drama. Representative of this new wave of reality programming is *Rescue 911*, *Unsolved Mysteries*, *America's Most Wanted*, and *Emergency*. One of the more popular entries in the crowded field of reality programming is *Cops*, a contemporary video rendition of the police reporter's beat. *Cops*, which is recorded by cameras that ride with the police in their squad cars and follow them as they respond to calls and make arrests, offers no narration. No journalist provides a detached perspective.[53] In this respect, such shows are vulnerable to the charge that they are little more than public relations for the police since they depend on the police's voluntary cooperation. But supporters might respond that this is a bogus accusation since *Cops* is produced primarily for entertainment and thus not subject to the same ethical mandates as news broadcasts.

One criticism leveled against such graphic depictions of reality is that they exploit human misery and foibles. But the fact remains that they probably could not exist without the cooperation of those who are featured in the programs. Producers attempt to obtain releases from their subjects, either before or after cameras roll. And, as *Newsweek* observed rather cynically in its critique of the reality TV craze, "The fact that so many comply, no matter how indecently they're being exposed, offers one more depressing proof that getting on TV has become our strongest biological urge."[54]

But as noted in Chapter 2, ethical behavior should not be determined by simply what is legal. Securing of releases might provide media attorneys with a certain degree of emotional tranquility, but producers of such programs, as well as their network, station, and cable clients, must still confront the ethical dimensions of their behavior. For example, in the first episode of ABC's *American Detective*, the three-year-old son of a cocaine dealer bursts into tears when police break into his home to arrest his father. The father subsequently agreed to the televising of his arrest, which included an exploitation of his son's anguish before a nationwide audience.[55]

Beyond the ethical concerns involving exploitation, of course, are the effects of packaging such unfiltered events and emotions within an entertainment structure. In the long chain of moral responsibility surrounding the communications process, perhaps it is not asking too much for the TV audience to use its critical faculties to distinguish entertainment from truly useful information, to separate fact from fiction. But as media practitioners, who owe a duty to our audience and society in general, we might also consider the following assessment:

> As the boundary between information and entertainment breaks down, as television pumps out an undemarcated flow of fact-based fictions and fictionalized facts, viewers . . . "are having a harder time determining what's real life and what's somebody's imagination. The result is that they're being desensitized to reality."[56]

Truth in Advertising and Public Relations

Clearly, the standards outlined for journalists cannot be entirely applicable to the other forms of media practice with which we are concerned in this book. Advertisers and public relations practitioners, for example, are in the business of persuading. They come to the marketplace with a bias, and there is nothing wrong with that. PR practitioners have a right to defend their client's interest in the court of public opinion, and in such circumstances the audience expects that the dissemination of information will be more selective.

Although the ethical expectations of mass persuaders may vary from journalists, we still expect advertisers and PR personnel to adhere to the threshold requirement of truth—that is, that they not knowingly disseminate inaccurate information. The various professional codes of the public relations and advertising industries commit their practitioners to standards of truth and accuracy. Unfortunately, such standards are ignored when company executives allow their allegiance to the bottom line and loyalty to stockholders to eclipse their responsibility to the society that has given them their corporate privilege. Such was the case when officials of Dow Corning denied for several weeks that its breast implants were harmful to recipients and then later announced that the company had known for some time the potential hazards of the implants. Such public falsehoods are counterproductive because they eventually damage the corporate reputation that the false statements were designed to protect in the first place.

Although mass persuaders are just as morally culpable as journalists for deliberately telling a lie, they are under no ethical obligation to provide balance in their public proclamations. A cereal company, for example, while extolling the health benefits of its oat bran flakes in a TV campaign, is unlikely to acknowledge the presence of sugar in its product.[57] Nor would a spokesperson for a "low-fat" product, which appeals to the health-conscious consumer, voluntarily admit to its high caloric content resulting from sugar. Likewise, a PR spokesperson for a corporation will attempt to put the best foot forward and not dwell on the company's shortcomings.

In other words, mass persuaders—PR practitioners and advertisers—employ selective truth to construct their messages, and there is nothing inherently unethical about this. As noted in Chapter 2, persuasion is one of the legitimate functions of mass communication, and society does not expect the same level of truth here as they do from practitioners of the information function (i.e., journalists). We expect accurate information, but we do not expect balance or objectivity. PR professionals, for example, in order to retain credibility, should provide accurate information but, as Professor

Deaver cautions us, "we should know that it is not necessarily objective and unbiased; that it is certainly not the whole story."[58]

Advertising is a little more problematic because of two related and controversial techniques: linguistic ambiguity, in which no specific product claims are made (e.g., "Bayer works wonders" or Ford's "Quality is job one"), and puffery, or the use of superlatives and exaggerations, and subjective opinions that do not implicate specific facts (e.g., "the best deal in town" and "number one in sex appeal"). Most people would probably agree that intentional ambiguity is unethical in situations "where accurate instruction or efficient transmission of precise information is the acknowledged purpose."[59] But in a competitive media environment often driven by entertainment values, advertising's purpose transcends the provision of accurate information. Its purpose is to create a favorable image about the product or company and thus to increase sales or hold on to market share. In most advertising messages, therefore, ambiguity is usually recognized as such and accepted by consumers.[60]

Puffery is also a ubiquitous technique in contemporary advertising, but it is not without its critics. Ivan Preston, for example, in his book *The Great American Blow-up*, argues that all puffery is false by implication and should be illegal. Philip Patterson and Lee Wilkins, in their illuminating discussion of the ethics of persuasion, assert that "[t]he absence of a verifiable claim, for example ads employing ridicule or commercials promoting 'image,' should alert the consumer to a potentially unethical approach to persuasion."[61] Opponents might counter, however, that this is ethical prudishness and that such a narrow posture is neither realistic nor desirable. And indeed, it is not at all clear as to why an advertising message designed to create an image or a "feel good" mood among consumers is unethical, even if it is devoid of information (unless, of course, the advertiser promises accurate information and fails to deliver). If consumers expect informa-

tion from ads, they will demand it. In a marketplace economy, the audience should assume some degree of responsibility and must be discriminating and ponder commercial messages with a healthy degree of skepticism.

However, when advertisers omit important information that could mislead consumers and actually affects a consumer's purchasing decision, such ads are deceptive and raise more serious ethical concerns. For example, in 1989 the Federal Trade Commission accused the Campbell Soup Company of deceptive advertising when the company contended that its soups, which were low in fat and cholesterol, could reduce the risk of heart disease. What it did not disclose was that the soups were also high in sodium, a key culprit in the development of high blood pressure.[62]

PR and Journalism: A Love-Hate Relationship

Public relations practitioners and journalists often view each other with suspicion. Some journalists consider the practice of public relations as parasitic, populated by "flacks" who derive their livelihood by using the media to their own advantage. PR practitioners, on the other hand, often look at newsrooms as repositories of cynicism, where journalists eagerly survey the landscape for governmental or corporate malfeasance or irresponsibility. "Good news," according to this view, is an oxymoron.

The fact is, however, that neither profession can claim moral superiority over the other because they derive their principles from different intellectual moorings. The mission of journalists is to uncover facts, report on society's institutions, and present a fair and balanced account (some would describe this as "objectivity") of the day's intelligence. Ethical journalists, according to the traditional view, should have no causes to promote, no axes to grind. PR practitioners, on the other hand, are by definition advocates and are committed to achieving organizations' goals. They too provide information for public consumption, but they usually do so in a manner to achieve the most favorable results for their company or client.

The journalist's stock in trade is revelation, the public dissemination of as much relevant and significant information as possible. On the other hand, confidentiality of information and relationships plays an important role in the life of the PR practitioner. Proprietary information that might work to the advantage of a competitor is one example. As advocates, PR practitioners usually view a certain degree of confidentiality as essential to advancing a positive image for their companies and clients. Thus, they are more likely to be selective in the information they provide the public and the media. However, when the public interest requires full disclosure (as noted earlier), even when to do so might be initially detrimental to the public image and corporate profits, the long-term PR benefits can be tremendous. Sincerity and self-criticism can be ethically invigorating in the arena of public opinion.

Despite this apparent mistrust between reporters and PR practitioners, the relationship is really more symbiotic than adversarial. News organizations depend on public relations information (in some cases quite heavily) for both economic and journalistic reasons. The cost of gathering information from every possible organization within a community would be prohibitively expensive without the assistance of representatives from those organizations.[63] In addition, company officials and their PR representatives are good sources of information that might not be available elsewhere, providing a constant flow of free information to the news media. In this respect, PR practitioners serve as extensions of the news staff: "They play a specific, functional, cooperative role in society's information-gathering network, even though they owe no loyalty to specific news outlets, are not paid by them, and may never set foot in the building in which the news is produced."[64]

In return, the media serve as a willing and sometimes uncritical forum for the dissemination of governmental and corporate messages and information. PR releases provide an opportunity for companies to tell their side of the story, especially in an environment where PR practitioners distrust the media's objectivity in their own accounts of events. The most visible and controversial evidence of this symbiotic relationship is the widespread dissemination and use of video news releases (VNRs). VNRs resemble typical TV news stories in their packaging but are produced on behalf of a client in an attempt to get free airtime to promote a cause, product, or service.[65] They are distributed free to stations and often come with scripts for local anchors or reporters to read as "voice-overs." In other cases, they are downlinked from satellites. For example, in 1991 on the occasion of Cheerios' fiftieth anniversary, the company transmitted by satellite to stations across the country a colorful report on the event. General Mills reached an audience of almost 17 million, and no local station had to send a news crew to General Mills' Minneapolis headquarters.[66] VNRs are an efficient, effective way for PR firms to represent their clients to a mass audience. Furthermore, especially in economically hard times, VNRs are a cost-effective means for a station to produce more material for local broadcast without adding more employees.[67]

The production and use of VNRs imposes ethical obligations on both PR practitioners and the stations to whom they disseminate this material. Some practitioners believe, for example, that as long as the information contained in a VNR is accurate and true and the production standards are high, they have conducted themselves in an ethical manner. The rest is up to the journalists.[68] News organizations then have an ethical obligation to identify the source of the VNR, regardless of whether it is substantially edited or aired in its entirety. Yet, in a Nielsen survey of news directors several years ago, only 60 percent of the respondents said VNR sponsors should be identified when a VNR is aired.[69] And, unfortunately, unattributed VNRs are not that rare among news departments.

Of course, local stations are not the only ones that are delinquent in their ethical obligation to attribute material provided by outside sources. For example, on June 13, 1991, the *CBS Evening News* broadcast featured a segment on the hazards of automotive safety belts. The shoulder straps, according to correspondent Mark Phillips, are a "labor-saving device that may be costing lives instead of saving them." He offered as proof a videotape of a car being tipped on its side, the door opening, and the strap allowing a dummy to fall out and be crushed beneath the car. But the tape was not a CBS news product, although viewers were never told otherwise, and the CBS eye was featured prominently throughout the piece. It was a video news release supplied by the Institute for Injury Reduction, a lobby group largely supported by lawyers whose clients often sue automobile manufacturers for crash-related injuries.[70]

INTELLECTUAL DISHONESTY

The unauthorized or unacknowledged use of someone else's literary or artistic creation is dishonest. Society does not abide the theft of the fruits of one's physical labors. There is no reason that it should be any more tolerant of the piracy of intellectual property. For the sake of simplicity, intellectual dishonesty generally falls into two categories: plagiarism and misappropriation. While misappropriation also has a specific legal meaning, within the ethical context we shall take it to mean the *unauthorized use* of someone else's literary or artistic expression. Plagiarism, on the other hand, refers to the taking of another's ideas or expression and passing it off as your own. Plagiarism often revolves around the question of attribution, whereas misappropriation occurs when a use of intellectual property is not authorized by the owner. It reflects the creator's moral right to control the use and dissemination of his or her intellectual property. However, misappropriation often involves both lack of authorization and lack of attribution. Such misappropriation not only raises ethical concerns but can also run afoul of copyright law.

A case in point is the controversial technique known as *digital sampling*, which is increasingly used in the production of rap music. Using the sophisticated computer technology discussed in Chapter 2, music and words can be "lifted" from previous recordings to use in new recordings. Thus, although a new number has been created, it is substantially a composite of other more original works.[71] A federal court in New York has recently ruled that digital sampling could result in copyright liability for the sampler. Needless to say, a commitment to ethical propriety (doing the right thing) can also protect against legal problems.

Plagiarism has been described as "the unoriginal sin."[72] Take, for example, the following unfortunate events: A reporter for the Associated Press resigned after it was discovered that, without attribution, she had used several anecdotes and passages taken verbatim from *New West* magazine. In her story about high-speed chases on California highways, she had led readers into thinking she had witnessed the race described in *New West*.[73] During the 1991 David Duke campaign for the Louisiana governorship, the Fort Worth *Star-Telegram* published a story under the byline of political writer James Walker, a thirteen-year veteran at the paper. Quotes in the story were attributed to various speakers but not to the Louisiana television report and the New Orleans *Times-Picayune* from which they were lifted. Walker resigned, attributing his indiscretion to an "error in judgment."[74] A reporter for the *St. Petersburg Times* resigned after she claimed as her own about a third of an article on credit cards from *Changing Times* magazine. On the day of her resignation, she apologized to her colleagues, describing her indiscretion as a "stupid mistake."[75]

Each fell from journalistic grace for allegedly committing the unspoken mortal sin in media communications: *plagiarism*. Each was accused of using someone else's intellectual property without attribution. College students are all too familiar with the "crime" of plagiarism. Nothing is more intellectually odious to the academic community than the pirating of someone else's literary work, and most colleges and universities deal with such transgressions swiftly.

But such concerns with intellectual dishonesty are not confined to the ivory tower. Plagiarism should be just as morally offensive to media practitioners. Since their stock in trade is artistic originality and creativity, the unattributed use of someone else's work violates the virtue of honesty. When it is necessary to borrow from another source, that source should be attributed. As the authors of a leading media ethics text have observed, "Ethically, then, the only defensible position is to identify the work as coming from someone else other than the author. There should be no question of whether the source is so obscure it will not be recognized."[76]

Although attribution is the cornerstone of media credibility, the practice of nonattribution is quite common. Some reporters, for example, often incorporate information from stories in their newspapers' morgues for historical background and perspective without sufficient verification or attribution. Wire stories sometimes appear under the bylines of local reporters. Broadcast and print reporters often steal from each other to preserve the myth of exclusivity.[77] But ethicist Deni Elliott, commenting on plagiarism in the news business, says there is a greater need for attribution today and in the future, "not because of declining morality, but because our notion of news is changing."[78] In the days when news was "out there" waiting to be discovered, observes Elliott, everyone was chasing the same story, and not much counted for plagiarism. Competitive reports often resembled each other. But in today's journalistic culture, reporters' accounts are more likely to be individualized, the result of painstakingly synthesizing, analyzing, and interpreting.[79]

A lively debate within journalistic circles concerns what actually constitutes plagiarism. The excuses range all the way from "a lack of clear industry standards" to "the line between ethical behavior and plagiarism depends on context." However, such relativistic arguments are nothing more than an attempt to rationalize both the predatory practices of charlatans, as well as those who surrender to deadline pressure or moments of weakness. It is ironic that journalists, who have always embraced attribution as one of the "first principles" of ethical reporting, should equivocate on the issue of plagiarism. According to Elliott, such ethical indiscretions violate the moral duty owed to at least three parties:

> A reporter who passes off some other reporter's reporting as her own cheats her boss by violating a rule of research that she knows she is expected to follow. She cheats the original author by not recognizing her claim of ownership. Most importantly, she cheats her reader because she doesn't have the background that she implicitly promises with her byline or on-air appearance.[80]

Like most ethical thickets concerning media practitioners, there is undoubtedly some room for ambiguity in what constitutes plagiarism. But in searching for guidelines, you might ask yourself two questions: (1) Have I clearly attributed all information derived from other sources? (2) Will the average reader, viewer, or listener be able clearly to distinguish my work from others in terms of style, structure, and expression? These two questions should not exhaust your inquiry into what constitutes plagiarism, but they can serve as a barometer in measuring the intellectual honesty of your own work.

TRUTH TELLING AND APPROACHES TO MORAL REASONING

In working your way through this ethical thicket involving truth telling, you should return to the various approaches to moral reasoning discussed in Chapter 3. You may recall that deontologists, represented by the views of such philosophers as Kant, hold that something other than consequences should determine the rightness or wrongness of an act. The important thing is the "rule" against lying, despite the fact that telling the truth might result in bad consequences, as when a journalist reports the facts about a public figure that might injure his reputation. Kant maintains that the test of a moral principle is whether it should be universalized to apply to every situation. Therefore, the principle of truth telling is an absolute that should be relevant in all circumstances, regardless of the consequences. This approach would clearly rule out all deception by media practitioners, even by reporters who argue that deception is sometimes necessary to root out corruption in government.

However, this duty-based approach to ethical decision making encounters rough waters when passive, rather than active, deception is involved. Active deception involves overt misrepresentation. But passive deception occurs whenever moral agents do not reveal their true identity or purpose. Newspaper restaurant critics, for example, do not alert the manager to their presence for fear of influencing the quality of food and service accorded them. This practice may be justified, because the critic is there to view the culinary landscape from the perspective of the average consumer. But what if reporters, in order to research a story on hospital emergency-room care, were to don white jackets and stand around in an emergency room for an evening, allowing others to believe that they were on the medical staff. Would this form of passive deception be ethically justified?

From a duty-based perspective, the moral agent's motive is always significant. The restaurant critic's motive clearly is not to deceive but simply to avoid altering the outcome of the dining experience. On the other hand, the reporters' entry into the emergency room, even if not accomplished through active deception, would be more suspect, because their intent is to allow others to believe something that is in fact not true. Of course, this kind of ethical hairsplitting usually provides for an animated

discussion about the limits of deception in moral reasoning.

Because of its absolute prohibition against lying and deception, the Kantian (nonconsequentialist) model has been rejected by some as unrealistic and even undesirable. However, some contemporary authors have suggested that we should not construe Kant's categorical imperative so narrowly.[81] All lies or acts of deception are not, after all, on the same moral footing. Under this more moderate Kantian view, the touchstone test would be whether there was a compelling reason to deviate from the truth, and even then the burden of proof would be on the one who was engaging in the deception. This *compelling-reason* test would require that (1) the reason(s) for the deception be important, (2) the deception be done for humanitarian purposes devoid of self-interest, and (3) the arguments in favor of deception far outweigh the arguments against the compromising of the principles of truth telling.

A different perspective on the question of truth and deception is provided by the teleologist. As noted in Chapter 3, teleologists (represented by the utilitarians) are sometimes referred to as consequentialists, because they gauge the consequences of an act before making an ethical judgment. Because utilitarians believe in promoting the greatest good for the greatest number, a media practitioner following this approach would weigh the relative harm or good done to various individuals or groups as a result of his deceptive behavior. However, utilitarians do not assume that lies and deception are harmless. In fact, "lies are presumed guilty until proven innocent, rather than innocent until proven guilty."[82] In other words, the burden of proof is still on the moral agent to prove that a lie or deceptive act will promote the greatest good for the greatest number of people and that the benefits outweigh the harmful consequences.

One question that often arises is whether journalists stand apart from the general population in ethical situations like the use of deception. If we assume that reporters act on behalf of the public, the answer must be no. Only if the average citizen, faithful to the ethical norms of society, would be willing to use deception to get a story could a journalist justify doing likewise. And regardless of what justifications are used for occasional deceptions, the line should always be drawn at violations of law, because illegal conduct by reporters undermines the respect for law.[83]

Aristotle's golden mean, the example of *virtue ethics* described in Chapter 3, is also a valuable approach in providing a sense of balance and proportion in cases involving how much truth to reveal about a situation or the kind and scope of coverage to provide for a news story. In news stories in which there is a tendency toward excessive and sometimes sensational coverage (e.g., in the case of a terrorist hijacking), the golden mean can be a helpful guideline in exercising more restraint in reporting. Sometimes this approach can be applied by advertisers and PR executives in an attempt to maintain that delicate balance between social responsibility and corporate self-interest. A case in point are beer commercials that contain a subtle admonition to the audience not to drink and drive.

TRUTH AND DECEPTION: HYPOTHETICAL CASE STUDIES

The cases here give you an opportunity to examine a variety of issues dealing with the principle of truth. The scenarios cover a wide range of deceptive practices, from communicating outright falsehoods to withholding information and using the literal truth to deceive an audience. Several kinds of moral agents are represented in these cases: reporters, advertisers, PR practitioners, and those who make decisions regarding television entertainment.

Each case begins with a set of facts and an outline of the ethical dilemma. Next, I briefly discuss the case study and the role that you are asked to play. You are asked, in some situations, to assume the role of a moral agent. In every case you should apply the material and the moral reasoning model outlined in the first three chapters of this book.

CASE STUDIES

▶ **CASE 4-1**
Hidden Cameras and the Journalist as Social Conscience

Proposition 120, a rather innocent-sounding label for a very controversial ballot initiative, had been the brainchild of State Senator Hugh Wilson. Wilson, a conservative lawmaker and perennial opponent of big government, was determined to stem the flow of illegal immigrants into his state from Mexico. And the most effective means of accomplishing this goal, in Wilson's view, was to deny them access to the state's bountiful social services.

His supporters championed Wilson as a fiscal knight in shining armor. His detractors disparaged his proposal as an assault of draconian proportions on innocent human beings.

Nevertheless, Wilson's proposal struck a responsive chord among a large segment of the electorate and was soon featured prominently as Proposition 120 on the November ballot, along with the plethora of state and local elections and the hotly contested races for the U.S. House of Representatives. Specifically, Proposition 120 would cut off most social services to illegal immigrants, including educational opportunities for their children. Although the rather formal language of the proposition obscured the emotional and human dimensions of the debate, the message to the nation's lawmakers in Washington was unmistakable: *stop the flood of illegal immigrants into our state, or we'll do it for you!*

Manny Fernandez watched with concern on election night as the returns were tabulated by his newsroom computers. Within a couple of hours after the last polls closed, it was clear that Proposition 120 would pass overwhelmingly. As news director of Channel 5 in San Jacinto, one of three network affiliates located in a metropolitan center of 650,000 near the Mexican border, Fernandez knew that Proposition 120 would just exacerbate the city's growing ethnic strife. With its proximity to the Mexican border, San Jacinto was the entry point for many of the immigrants. On election night the Hispanic population stood at 40 percent; the city had become a true melting pot. And the pot was beginning to boil.

San Jacinto voters had defied the trend statewide and had narrowly defeated the proposal. But an influential and very vocal minority had campaigned aggressively for Proposition 120. The best-case scenario, in Fernandez's view, would be a court injunction that would halt the implementation of the measure until its constitutionality could be decided. This step would allow time for the cooling of passions. But what Fernandez feared most was a violent uprising by the Hispanic community and perhaps even a defiance of the measure by local school officials, who considered the denial of educational opportunities to the immigrants' children as tantamount to child abuse.

Channel 5's news staff had reported on the "immigrant problem," as it was referred to in the newsroom, almost from its inception. The alarming drain on the state's dwindling financial resources precipitated by the staggering costs of social services to the immigrants had been the centerpiece of the station's coverage. And although the hiring of these immigrants was illegal, the station had documented repeatedly the rather casual violation of the law by local merchants. Of course, neither employers nor employees were willing participants in these stories, and Channel 5 had often relied on confidential sources and concealed identities to

document this illegal behavior. One of the station's reporters had even spent a few days in jail rather than reveal a source to a grand jury investigating the situation.

Fernandez viewed these reports with mixed emotions. As a journalist, he felt an undeniable commitment to the first principles of journalism, fairness and balance. This was a complex and contentious issue, and he was determined that all credible voices should be heard. On the other hand, as the son of Mexican immigrants himself, he felt an emotional bond with those who had crossed the border, either legally or illegally, in search of a better life. Fernandez had harbored expectations that the newly ratified trade agreement between the United States and Mexico would improve economic conditions south of the border, but the continuing pilgrimage of immigrants into his state had dampened his cautious optimism.

As expected, within a week after the passage of Proposition 120, a federal court blocked implementation of the measure until its constitutionality could be tested. And with the endless hearings likely to ensue, Fernandez felt relieved that other stories could at last compete for top billing in his station's newscasts. Ron Mackey had other ideas.

Mackey was the producer of Channel 5's top-rated early evening newscast. Mackey had joined the staff three years ago, quickly molding a rather lethargic news operation into an aggressive, creative journalistic enterprise. But Mackey was not one to be complacent, and his antennae were constantly scanning the horizon for visually appealing, dramatic, and controversial story ideas. His enthusiasm sometimes tested the limits of ethical propriety, but his arguments in favor of the public's right to know were usually convincing to his superiors, particularly in Jan Jacinto's competitive marketplace.

Two weeks after the election, Fernandez turned first to Mackey during his morning staff meeting. "I'll discuss tonight's lineup in a minute," he said. "But we have something new on the immigrant problem. Ortego has confirmed the rumors." Fernandez recognized Ortego as a confidential source the station often relied on in covering the hiring of illegal immigrants. And the *rumors* referred to unsubstantiated accounts of manufacturers that had set up sweat shops in San Jacinto.

"We have confirmation from a second source," Mackey continued. "There may be more than one shop in the area, but the one that's been identified is Alton Enterprises on Third Avenue." Alton was a locally owned company that produced a line of cheap ready-to-wear garments with its own label. But it also did contract work for several major retailers and discount stores, and it was in this manufacturing arena that illegal immigrants were forced to work fifteen to eighteen hours a day for less than the minimum wage. Some workers, according to the information provided by the sources, were under eighteen years old. And there was also evidence that some plant supervisors physically abused the workers when they fell behind the company-imposed production quota.

Fernandez realized that, if the charges were true, the issue of employment of illegal immigrants would reach a new plateau. It was one thing for small merchants, who often worked on small profit margins and experienced a large employee turnover, to ignore the sometimes complex requirements in documenting the legal status of immigrants. But it was quite another for a large company to exploit their workers under such inhumane conditions.

"So how should we handle this?" Fernandez directed the question to Mackey, but he welcomed suggestions from Assistant News Director Andrea Cobb and Assignment Editor Marci Gonzalez.

"We can't just rely on sources in this case. We have to name the company, and we need authentic visual evidence. This is different from the other stories, where some small merchants are too busy eking out a living to document the legal status of their employees. In this case, Alton is running a sweatshop; they're exploiting and abusing their workers. We have to go in undercover with concealed cameras. Jose can be our mole."

Jose was a young photographer who had been with the station for two years. With his youthful appearance and fluent Spanish, he should have little trouble, in Mackey's judgment, in passing himself off as an undocumented immigrant and gaining employment at Alton. His concealed camera could record the plant's daily activities, including the alleged abusive behavior of the plant's supervisors. Eventually Jose could also gain the confidence of his coworkers in order to capture, on tape, their own personal testimonials of economic woes.

"Don't we have other options?" Fernandez responded. "Jose will obviously have to lie on his job application to get hired. And besides, I've always been uncomfortable with the use of hidden cameras. Let's face it. Most of our network's magazine shows have used concealed cameras and microphones, and now they're being accused of practicing tabloid journalism. This isn't good for our credibility." In staking out the moral high ground, perhaps Fernandez was remembering a tongue lashing he had suffered on this issue at the hands of a student during a visit to a journalism ethics class at a local college.

"I agree," Cobb said. "Surely there must be other ways to approach this story. Perhaps our sources can arrange for us to talk to some of the employees; we could even interview them on tape and mask their identities. And keep in mind, some of these people may not be illegals. We have to be careful to document each worker who appears on tape. If we go into this plant and surreptitiously record these employees on tape, even if we don't identify them, we may never again get cooperation from the Hispanic community. Even if there is some exploitation, at least the company does provide employment.

"Many of our Hispanic citizens may not appreciate this kind of public exposé and breach of trust with these immigrant workers," he continued. "In their view, after all, these sweatshops may be no worse than the conditions they left in Mexico. I would feel more comfortable if there were other companies involved—if the practice were widespread. Alton is a large company, but it *is* only one manufacturer among many in this region."

"Interviewing them really isn't an option," Gonzalez responded, in apparent agreement with Mackey. "They aren't likely to talk; they need the job, and they're afraid of retribution. Besides, television is a visual medium. We need to use the tools of our trade. The hidden camera is our way of documenting this story. We can mask the faces of the workers. So who will get hurt? The public needs to know that this kind of exploitation is occurring here in San Jacinto, even if only one company is involved. Isn't it our job to call attention to a problem before it spreads? And I don't really have a problem with Jose's using deception to get this job or using a hidden camera, for that matter. There are times when reporters must take extraordinary measures to help cure society's ills. *And this is one of those times."*

Fernandez was not so sure. But he promised to keep an open mind on the subject. After all, his station had acquitted itself well, in his judgment, in its coverage of the immigrant problem over the past several years. The Hispanic community had given Channel 5 high marks, overall, for its balanced treatment of the issues. Would this story be greeted with similar acclaim? Fernandez ended the staff meeting and pondered the ethical concerns raised by Mackey's proposal.

THE CASE STUDY

Are journalists ever justified in using deception to collect information in the name of the public interest? Investigative reporting demands documentation, and, as a visual medium, television is at its best when it provides photographic evidence of its discoveries. And as technological advances have produced small cameras that can shoot in poor lighting conditions, the temptation to use concealed cameras has, in many cases, been irresistible. But despite the widespread use of hidden cameras and other forms of deception in news gathering, these techniques remain controversial.[84] Misrepresentation and deception, of course, are a violation of society's norms. Thus, such practices must be justified based on some overriding moral principle.

Two salient values in this case appear to be the "public's need to know" and the "minimization of harm." Some would argue that the information in this story is of profound public importance. It certainly represents a new chapter in the ongoing saga of the illegal immigrants. But at this point the evidence points to only one company that is engaged in worker exploitation. There are many oth-

ers that hire legal immigrants and appear to be law-abiding. Is the station justified in going undercover to expose one company? Mackey might argue that such aggressive journalism would prevent others from setting up sweatshops in San Jacinto to take advantage of the abundant labor supply.

Anticipating the consequences in ethical dilemmas of this kind is fraught with uncertainty, and the question of harm is certainly problematic in this case. Channel 5's news staff may truly believe that they are coming to the aid of these workers by exposing their life of misery and abuse. Under most circumstances, the station would be applauded for such journalistic enterprise. But if the illegal workers are identified by immigration officials and returned to Mexico, some Hispanic viewers may be less than enthusiastic about the station's role in unmasking the sweat shop. After all, are the conditions here much worse than the poverty in their homeland? But should Fernandez be concerned about such consequences? After all, Alton's actions are morally and legally indefensible. If the station does not confront publicly such affronts to human decency, then it might be accused of abandoning its mandate as the guardian of the public's interest.

Fernandez should be convinced that the harm prevented by the misrepresentation and use of hidden cameras outweighs the harm that may occur from the act of deception. As news director, Fernandez is concerned with the station's credibility. On the one hand, the failure to investigate this story for fear of alienating the viewers with the use of deception could damage the station's reputation as an aggressive journalistic enterprise and a defender of the public's interest. On the other hand, the use of hidden cameras and undercover reporters could result in a loss of credibility for the station, especially if the station's viewers consider such tactics as unnecessary or unreasonable.

Using the SAD Formula for moral reasoning described in Chapter 3, assume the role of Channel 5's news director, Manny Fernandez, and ponder whether you will approve the use of misrepresentation and hidden cameras to document the existence of sweatshops and the exploitation of illegal immigrants in San Jacinto.

▶ **CASE 4-2**
National Security and the Public's Right to Know

For the first time in his life Fred McGee was not sleeping well. In fact, he had been sleeping very little in the three months since he discovered the truth about the project he was working on. McGee had worked as a chemical engineer for ten years for Landmark Industries, a company that specialized in the production of commercial fertilizers and pesticides. Landmark was located in Concordia, a New England town of 25,000 just fifteen miles from the state capital. The company was Concordia's largest employer and, in view of the state's depressed economy, might have been considered the salvation of the town.

But even Landmark was not recession-proof, and the company felt obliged to look for additional sources of revenue. A management consultant advised Landmark to consider bidding on some of the government contracts that were so readily available. The company took the consultant's advice and soon entered into a lucrative contract with the Defense Department to develop and test a sophisticated chemical agent that could be used against enemy soldiers in times of war. Both the State Department and the Pentagon considered the Middle East and the former Soviet empire to be unstable and were committed to diversifying the nation's weapons inventory. Of course, most of Landmark's employees were not told the specific purpose of the project.

McGee was one of 150 employees selected to work on the project. All were given top-secret clearances. They were told that the chemical (referred to as Agent X) was being developed as a defensive weapon to be used as a last resort in case of an attack on the United States. At first, McGee enjoyed the challenge of his new assignment, but he soon began to worry. What if there were an accident and the gas escaped into the local community? He also had moral reservations about what he was doing. McGee was a patriot, but in his more reflective moments, he wondered whether the government should be involved in this kind of project, especially considering that it

might be putting the unsuspecting citizens of Concordia at risk. After many sleepless nights McGee decided to take action. He surreptitiously copied several of the key documents related to the project and called Ralph Collins.

Collins was an investigative reporter for a TV network affiliate located in the state capital. As one of the "stars" and anchors of a local magazine news show, Collins was used to receiving calls from cranks who claimed to have inside information. But the caller on this particular day sounded agitated—and credible. Collins agreed to meet with McGee in a bar around the corner from the station.

During the meeting, McGee told Collins about the research at Landmark and offered some documents as proof. He said he was concerned about the safety of the residents of Concordia, including his own family. He also evoked a promise from Collins that he would not divulge where he had gotten the information or the documents.

On returning to the station, Collins briefed his news director, Brent Myers, on what he had been told, without revealing his informant's name. He also called some sources in Washington, who confirmed that Landmark was working on a top-secret project. They also told Collins that any research related to chemical weapons was an apparent violation of a treaty signed fifteen years before with the former Soviet Union and still in force with the Russian Republic. The release of this information, Collins was told, would cause "acute international embarrassment" for the United States and "irreparable harm" to its national interests. The reporter then called the president of Landmark, who refused to discuss the matter.

Collins met again with Myers. More research needed to be done, he said, but the story should be released. In fact, this was a story of international importance, not to mention the local impact on Concordia residents. Myers hesitated. He admitted that Collins had a point. But a story of this kind might injure national security. And closer to home, there could be severe economic repercussions. Once the Defense Department realized there was a security leak at Landmark, it might cancel the contract, which, in turn, could result in the company's financial failure. With the heavy layoffs that would result, Concordia's very existence could be in jeopardy. This was not a remote prospect, considering the recent fate of several New England towns as the result of the demise of their primary industries. Still, did the citizens of Concordia not have a right to know of the possible dangers posed by the chemical weapon project? If the people were asked to choose between jobs and public safety, how would they vote? This was a true dilemma, and there was no easy answer.

One other concern nagged at the news director. As a representative of management, Myers was aware of the potential dangers to the station itself. The station, like all broadcast stations, is federally licensed, and the release of classified information could conceivably jeopardize its license. But should this prospect, as ominous as it was, stand in the way of what Myers knew to be an important news story? He told Collins that he would talk with the general manager and then let him know whether the story should be reported.

THE CASE STUDY

This case involves the question of whether journalists should report what they know to be true even if significant harm might result. In this situation, the potential harm is obviously greater than in the typical run-of-the-mill news story. If this were a story involving the drinking habits of a public official, for example, a reporter might resolve the dilemma by evaluating the impact of the drinking on the politician's official duties. Because the reporter's duty is to inform the society, the public interest must be given precedence. If the public interest is marginal and the potential for harm great, the story should be withheld.

But in this case, the scales appear to be evenly balanced. Both the potential for harm and the public benefits are apparent, regardless of whether the story is released. The local community would suffer economically by the loss of its primary industry. But the American public needs to know that its government is violating an international agreement and, in the process, is posing a health risk to human life. However, one might conceivably argue that such violations are a fact of life in international relations and that the release of this story would serve no identifiable public benefit.

From the standpoint of the station's economic interests, the news director also understands the competitive pressures inherent in this situation. If his station refuses to report the story, McGee will probably contact some other news organization. The opportunity for an exclusive will be lost.

Put yourself in the place of the general manager. Because the release of this story involves grave consequences, the decision is yours to make. Assume that Myers has set forth the arguments pro and con outlined in the case. You should also consider others that may have escaped the attention of the news director. For example, does the fact that part of the story will be based on stolen documents undermine the station's moral credibility? If the residents later discover that the station knew of the project and its potential danger and failed to report it, will you be able to defend your decision from an ethical standpoint?

Subject this dilemma to the moral reasoning model and the ethical approaches discussed in Chapter 3. Be sure to defend your decision.

▶ **CASE 4-3**
Digital Photography and the Manipulation of Reality

It was a classic confrontation in the abortion wars. The Reverend Joshua Saint Clare, the national leader of the Lifeline Coalition, had rallied his anti-abortion legions for another skirmish in front of the Maplewood Women's Pavilion, one of only two abortion clinics in Lewiston. Carla Alvarez was just as determined to defend the women of Lewiston against the moral onslaught of the Reverend Saint Clare. As a prominent attorney committed to rekindling the feminist liberation movement of the 1970s, Alvarez was uncompromising in her view that the right for a woman to control her own body was precedent to all other rights.

The drama that was unfolding at the Maplewood Women's Pavilion was a reenactment of similar confrontations between Saint Clare and Alvarez in five other cities, three of which had sparked sporadic violence but no serious injuries. And each time, local and national media descended on the scene with an unquenchable thirst for conflict, emotional impact, and undeniable visual appeal. The fanaticism displayed on both sides had resulted in a cult of personalities that virtually silenced the more moderate voices on the abortion issue. The high-decibel verbal sparring between the charismatic Saint Clare and the combative Alvarez was irresistible in the competitive journalistic marketplace. The characters had overshadowed the plot on the nation's front pages and the evening newscasts.

As usual, correspondents from the TV networks, several large newspapers and the news magazines were on hand in Lewiston to chronicle the next chapter in this morality play. The *Lewiston Gazette* was on hand too. This story was made to order for Chief Photographer Brian Fogle.

Fogle had joined the staff of the *Gazette* ten years ago after serving a three-year apprenticeship on a small-town weekly just seventy-five miles from Lewiston. He had thrived at a paper that was increasingly becoming more visual in its coverage and where color was often featured conspicuously on both the front page and the metro page. The *Gazette*'s impressive list of awards for photojournalism since Fogle's arrival at the paper bore testament to the photographer's talent as both journalist and artisan. Fogle prided himself on his journalistic instincts in ferreting out the "real" story and then packaging it in the most vivid, dramatic way possible.

The abortion story was no exception. Fogle, along with reporter Mickey Chambers, had arrived early at the Pavilion, and with the police standing by in case of violence, the two groups of demonstrators soon began to exchange insults. And once again, the Reverend Saint Clare and Carla Alvarez squared off in their all too familiar public exhibition of mutual disdain. Fogle moved quickly through the mob, capturing the growing hostility in color and preserving this dramatic confrontation for posterity. Most of his pictures, Fogle knew, would simply wind up in the newspaper's morgue. But not the profile shot of Saint Clare and Alvarez standing toe-to-toe engaged in their verbal dual in front of the abortion clinic, while their supporters, armed with placards bearing a variety of messages, cheered them on. Fogle was confident that this photo had captured the very essence of the story that was un-

folding at the Maplewood Women's Pavilion and that it would be featured prominently in color on the *Gazette*'s front page.

Editor Samuel Gates was not so confident. In reviewing the front-page layout for the next day's edition, Gates was immediately impressed by the hostility that radiated from the photo. This shot was certain to convey the electric atmosphere surrounding the confrontation to the reader. But it was not the profile shot of the two combatants that concerned Gates. While it was clear from the photo that Saint Clare and Alvarez were surrounded by demonstrators, one was featured more prominently than others. In the center of the photo, in the background but clearly visible, was a placard with an aborted fetus in a jar.

With the deadline approaching, Gates quickly summoned Fogle and photo editor Bill McBride to his office and expressed his concern. "This is a fantastic shot, Brian," Gates declared sincerely, "but there is a problem. Quite frankly, I feel uneasy with running this photo on the front page with the aborted fetus. This could offend some of our readers, especially if we run it in color. Do you have another shot without any signs?"

"Not really," Fogle responded somewhat defensively. "I had to move in a hurry, and the crowd was making it difficult to get near enough for any kind of closeups. I was lucky to get this. Besides, Saint Clare and Alvarez were surrounded by demonstrators carrying signs. This is part of the story."

"If there's a problem with the sign, we can take it out or smear the message on the sign," McBride volunteered. Gates knew that McBride was referring to the SCITEX machine, part of a multimillion-dollar investment in computer technology the paper had made just five years ago. The SCITEX, using digital technology, allowed technicians to reconstruct or alter photographs without the faintest hint of hand retouching.

"But that's deceptive to the readers," Fogle responded indignantly. "The photo should run as it is, or it shouldn't be used at all. But I'm opposed to just killing it because it's essential to give our readers a feel for the hostility that I felt at the clinic." At this point Gates was not sure whether his chief photographer was taking the ethical high road or just reacting from a sense of artistic pride.

"We have other pictures," Gates said. "Of

course, they are mostly crowd scenes, and they aren't as personal or dramatic. But there are some where the messages on the signs are not as visible."

But Fogle persisted. "This story is no longer just about abortion. It's about the personal animosity between Saint Clare and Alvarez. And this photo captures this hostility. This picture *is* the story."

"Then if that's the case," Gates responded, "why not remove or smear the sign? It detracts from the focus of the story. This sign might be offensive to our readers without adding anything to the photo. Why take a chance?"

The photo editor had to concede the validity of this argument. "If you're concerned about offending the readers," McBride said, "then what's the difference between altering this photo and deleting foul language from quotes in news copy? This is common practice at this paper."

As the deadline approached, Gates began to feel the tug of competing ethical loyalties. As a journalist and editor, he was usually opposed to deleting substantive content that contributed to an understanding of the story. The sign may not have been essential to the photo, but it did provide context. And he did not believe that this background sign necessarily detracted from the dramatic face-to-face encounter of the two antagonists. And even if it did, the paper might still be accused of altering reality just for the sake of dramatic effect. Would removing or smearing the sign through digital manipulation be deceptive to the readers? Would they really care?

But editors often edit stories for length, tastes, and even superfluous content. Was this offensive visual message really important to the story? If the story was no longer abortion itself but the repeated and increasingly vociferous confrontations between Saint Clare and Alvarez, then perhaps the background sign in the photo *was* superfluous. Besides, the *Gazette* was a family newspaper and owed a duty to its readers to treat them with civility, while providing them with an accurate account of the day's events. This could be accomplished in the narrative part of the coverage without such a morally challenging photograph. On a couple of occasions, the paper had "cleaned up" the background and composition of feature photos. Was this any different?

As Gates pondered his decision, he realized that the temptation to take advantage of his technology's capabilities was almost irresistible. But he had to remember that his computers and software were only tools and that machines were incapable of making ethical judgments. Digital technology, he knew, should be the servant, not the master, of practicing journalists.

THE CASE STUDY

This case does not involve digital manipulation just to delete extraneous material or adjust a photo for space considerations. The editor is concerned about readers' potential reaction to this offensive sign between the profile shots of the two abortion combatants. On the one hand, the alteration of any photo might be considered deceptive unless the readers are informed as to how and why the photo was altered. On the other hand, if one accepts McBride's argument, then deleting material from photos is really no different from editing news stories for content for overriding ethical reasons (e.g., deleting offensive language or cleaning up the grammar in a quote).

Under time pressures, such ethical dilemmas are often subjected to ad hoc decision making, without concern for long-range consequences. But as editor, Gates must protect the integrity of his enterprise. If the *Gazette* acquires a reputation, for example, of doctoring photos, even if the readers are informed of such manipulation, then the paper has sacrificed its only stock in trade: the truth. Nevertheless, there are those rare exceptions when journalists must deviate from standard ethical practice for other overriding considerations. Is this such a situation? If so, what are the overriding considerations?

Under the scenario outlined here, Gates has four choices. First, he could publish the photo in color on the front page. He would then run the risk of offending some readers.

Gates's second option is to alter the photo, either removing or smearing the sign. In this case, the paper will avoid offending its readers. But on the other hand, if the *Gazette*'s readers learn of this manipulation, the paper's credibility could suffer.

Third, Gates could decide to omit the photo from the paper's coverage entirely. This would avoid his ethical quandary. But would this decision be journalistically sound, especially since the photo is important to the overall story? In addition, the omission of this dramatic photo would certainly undermine the *Gazette*'s goal of improving its visual coverage in order to enhance the paper's marketing potential.

Finally, the paper could publish the photo in black and white or perhaps move it to an inside page in order to lessen its impact. Would this lessen the chance that it might offend some readers?

As the deadline approaches, assume the position of Editor Samuel Gates, and, using the SAD Formula for moral reasoning outlined in Chapter 3, decide how you would handle this ethical dilemma.

▶ **CASE 4-4**
A Local Hero Comes Home

Elizabeth Singletary was the pride of Bakersfield, a small midwestern town that could have been the setting for a Norman Rockwell painting. Singletary, the daughter of an Air Force sergeant stationed at Townsend Air Force Base near Bakersfield, had graduated as the valedictorian of her high school class. Her academic achievements had not gone unnoticed by her Congressman, and he offered her an appointment to the Air Force Academy in Colorado Springs. Singletary's ambition was to be a fighter pilot, a career path that had made her a novelty among her more conservative high school classmates. She finished fifth in her class at the Academy and then promptly qualified for flight school, where she also gained high marks from her instructors. When Lieutenant Singletary went on active duty, she joined only a handful of women who had earned the right to command a cockpit.

Singletary's first assignment was at an Air Force base on the East Coast, but within six months her squadron was dispatched to the Middle East to confront the aggressive activities of the Iraqi military. Iraq was once again threatening its neighbors and had marshalled its elite Republican Guard units along its borders with Kuwait in an apparent preparation for another invasion. The President's warnings had been ignored, and once the Pentagon's plans were complete, he had ordered a joint naval-air assault against the Iraqi forces.

The operation lasted for five days. The Iraqi air force had mounted a rather meager challenge to the air superiority of the American air assault, but two Navy and three Air Force jets were shot down in the fiercest surface-to-air missile response since the Persian Gulf War. The deadly accuracy of the missiles confirmed intelligence reports that Iraq's military rehabilitation had been at least partially successful.

Singletary's squadron had been at the vanguard of the mission on the third day when, according to the Pentagon, her aircraft was struck by a missile and crashed. The Pentagon initially listed her as "missing in action," but her body was soon retrieved by an Army rescue team specifically trained for that purpose. Her remains were sent to Dover Air Force Base for processing and then returned to Bakersfield for burial in a local cemetery.

The residents of Bakersfield had been divided on whether American forces should attack the Iraqi military within its own borders, but they were not divided on Lieutenant Singletary's role in this assault. She had returned to her hometown as a hero, the first woman pilot to give her life for her country in combat.

Marvin Anderson had worked for the *Sentinel* for two years and was assigned to cover this unfortunate episode. Anderson liked the relative tranquility of working for the *Sentinel*, Bakerfield's biweekly account of local politics, ribbon cuttings, and the social registry. But he also welcomed the opportunity to cover a story with national dimensions and high drama, even if the drama was of tragic proportions.

Since Lieutenant Singletary was the nation's first woman air combat casualty, the *Sentinel*'s interest in the story was shared by the national media. Jim Singletary, Elizabeth's brother, was appointed as family spokesperson to confront the relentless questions from the assembled journalists. As the only local reporter covering the story, Anderson pressed Singletary for a personal interview, and he agreed. The insights gained during the interview would make a perfect sidebar, in Anderson's judgment, to the account of the funeral. Singletary had provided insights into his sister's character that would be ignored by the national correspondents who had focused, as they usually do, on the family's grief and the continuing controversy over whether women should be assigned combat roles in the military. Jim Singletary had even shared the contents of his sister's only two letters sent to her family from the Middle East. They revealed a very optimistic young woman, with a profound commitment to her Christian faith and a great deal of pride in her work and serving her country. Lieutenant Singletary's sacrifice would soon disappear from the national consciousness as other stories competed for inclusion on the media's agenda, but the *Sentinel*'s coverage would be significant, Anderson knew, in establishing the young pilot's heroic legacy to the Bakersfield community.

Anderson departed from the interview with a feeling of confidence concerning Lieutenant Singletary's niche in local history. What he discovered at Townsend Air Force Base made him feel less confident. The day before the paper's next publication date and three days before the funeral, Anderson contacted the public affairs officer at the air base, Major Michael Shelton, to confirm some of the details of the mission and the events that led to the death of the young female pilot. Shelton restated the Pentagon's version of the story but then told the reporter that the situation was under review. "There apparently is some doubt," he said, "whether her aircraft was actually downed by an Iraqi missile. There is a strong possibility that she was hit with a missile from an American F-16 that mistook her aircraft for an Iraqi fighter. This might be a friendly fire incident."

Friendly fire incident Anderson recognized as the Pentagon's euphemism for the tragic consequences of a military mistake. The reporter was determined to investigate this rather disturbing news through other channels. The readers of his paper had a right to know the truth. A call to the Pentagon provided little new information except to confirm that the incident was under investigation.

Anderson's next call was to Jim Singletary, who admitted that his father had learned through a colleague at Townsend that the military was investigating the possibility that Lieutenant Singletary had been killed with friendly fire. "I don't know how this will turn out," he told the reporter, "but please don't publish this in the *Sentinel*. My sister is a hero to her friends and the residents of Bakersfield. She died in the line of duty. What good will it do to reveal now that she was killed by her own comrades? She's still a hero to our family."

Anderson told the pleading Singletary that he would think it over but made no promises. As a reporter for a small-town biweekly, Anderson was a neophyte in ethical decision making. The rather mundane journalistic existence of chronicling the activities of small-town America did not provide the moral challenges of his colleagues on metropolitan dailies. However, the paper had not retreated entirely from its journalistic responsibilities. Managing Editor Ed Garf made sure of that. In fact, he appeared to delight in exposing the foibles of local politicians and community leaders but only if they truly deserved public sanction. And in those cases the readers generally applauded the paper for holding them accountable. But these occasional forays notwithstanding, Garth was fully aware that his readers' continued support depended on the *Sentinel*'s role as community booster. And for the most part, Garth was comfortable in that role. He would leave the excitement of enterprise journalism and investigative reporting to his daily newspaper counterparts.

As the publication deadline neared, Anderson briefed Garth and Assistant Editor Sylvia Hightower on his fact-finding mission at the Air Force base and the follow-up interview with Jim Singletary. "He wants us to hold the story," Anderson told the two editors, in describing the plea from the family spokesperson.

"But if the story is true—if the Pentagon is investigating Lieutenant Singletary's death as a friendly fire incident—then we have to report it," Hightower said. "This is news. And our readers have a right to know. They think she was shot down by an enemy missile."

"But she's also a local hero," Garth said. "The last resident of Bakersfield to be killed in action died in Vietnam—and he certainly didn't return as a hero. The community has really embraced this cause and rallied around her family. What difference does it make how she died? We should be more sensitive to the family."

"If we sit on this story, then the paper might lose credibility," Anderson responded rather forcefully. "I realize there's a danger that the public might view the reporting of this friendly fire investigation as causing unnecessary grief for the family. But the national media will report the story as soon as they find out. We're closer to the story; we should report it first, in tomorrow's edition. We should include the information from our source, the acknowledgment from Jim Singletary, and the Pentagon's brief statement. We should be out front on this. Tomorrow we go to press."

Garth had to acknowledge the validity of his young reporter's argument, but he was concerned about dropping such an emotional bombshell before the funeral. "Perhaps there's a middle ground here," he proposed. "We aren't a daily newspaper. Why not just hold the story for a week until the family has had a chance to recover from the funeral? What's the difference whether the story is published now or next week?" However, even Garth was not entirely comfortable with his proposal because the family did not want the story published at all. A week's delay in publication would not address their concerns. Besides, by this time the national media would probably have the story.

Hightower then retreated to the newsroom, and Anderson returned to his computer to file his story if Garth should give the green light on publication. Despite his long tenure at a paper that often served as a community booster, Garth's journalistic instincts remained as keen as ever. He was aware that most reporters considered the withholding of information to be a violation of the public trust, except in exceptional circumstances. Was this such a circumstance? After all, the Pentagon investigation was essential to an understanding of the circumstances surrounding Lieutenant Singletary's death.

On the other hand, Garth pondered the harm that might be done to the family and even the legacy that Lieutenant Singletary's death had left to Bakersfield as a local hero. As the deadline approached, Garth attempted to balance his journalistic responsibilities with those of community supporter and humanitarian.

THE CASE STUDY

This case raises some troubling questions concerning truth telling, maintaining journalistic independence, and minimizing harm to innocent parties. Many requests for withholding information originate with law enforcement or other government officials who wish to solicit the media's cooperation in some investigation or other enterprise. Most reporters are reluctant to cooperate with such officials for fear of compromising their independence and role as government watchdogs.

But the request in this case appears to reflect Jim Singletary's sincere concern for his family's welfare rather than some self-serving attempt to protect his sister's public persona as military hero. Nevertheless, the publication of the friendly fire story could have the inevitable effect of tarnishing her image as local hero. Does the community's need to know the truth outweigh the harm that might occur from publication of this story? Should the answer to this question depend on whether the paper is a metropolitan daily, which is generally considered to be more independent of community involvement, or a biweekly, such as the *Sentinel*, which is viewed as a community booster?

The managing editor has three choices. He can kill the story, he can delay publication for a week, or, for the sake of timeliness, he can run the story before the funeral in the next edition. For the purpose of resolving this ethical quandary, assume the role of Managing Editor Ed Garth. And then, using the moral reasoning model described in Chapter 3, decide whether you should publish the information on the friendly fire incident or honor Jim Singletary's request and withhold the story.

 CASE 4-5

Selling a Pain Remedy: Literal Truth as Deception

By industry standards, the Erlbaum and Smathers Advertising Agency was a late entry into the commercial marketplace. Its birthplace was Chicago, the brainchild of disaffected advertising executives from two agency giants who had left their former employers because of what they perceived as creative complacency and undisguised arrogance at their dominant position within the industry. E&S entered the arena in the early 1980s, prospering during the economic boom years of the Reagan Administration. The agency's initial client list was fairly modest, but its enterprising, energetic spirit had quickly caught the attention of the larger and more lucrative advertisers. Their ambitious young cadre of writers and artists, many of whom had been lured away from larger, more prominent agencies, were among the best and brightest in the industry. As the winner of several Clio awards, E&S's credentials were well established a little more than a decade after its inception. The agency's products now covered the commercial landscape, from toothpaste to automobiles.

The latest addition to its client list was Lycol, an over-the-counter pain reliever that competed aggressively with other similar pain remedies for the consumer's attention. Lycol's advertising budget was impressive, and E&S's creative staff went to work to develop an effective campaign to persuade a health-conscious public of the relative effectiveness of their client's product. Alicia Foster was the final gatekeeper in the chain of quality control to which all E&S campaigns were subjected.

With five years in the promotion department of a Chicago TV station and three years of agency experience under her belt, Foster had been with E&S since its inception. Her work ethic, imaginative ideas, and relentless pursuit of excellence had propelled her through the ranks and into her present position of vice president of creative services. In an industry whose credibility usually fares poorly in public opinion polls when compared to other occupations, Foster disputed those who believed that deception is inevitable in the competitive arena of the marketplace. She believed that integrity should figure prominently in the moral vision of her own agency. Nevertheless, the young executive had made an ethical accommodation with puffery and so-called *weasel words* (e.g., *virtually*, *as good as*) as acceptable industry practices. She had confidence in the consumer to ignore such rhetorical hyperbole in ferreting out the cleverly presented key selling points.

As the Lycol TV campaign was set for its preproduction review, Foster once again presided over the congregation of her talented staff. She looked forward to these meetings because they afforded an opportunity to offer constructive criticism, reinforce a sense of collegiality, and even reinvigorate her own creative tendencies.

After an initial round of pleasantries, Foster quickly focused on the storyboard displayed before them. The commercial's theme was the popularity of Lycol as the number one over-the-counter pain medication. There were no specific scientific claims in terms of the effectiveness of Lycol compared to its competitors. It began with a well-known TV talk show host interviewing several public figures on the benefits of Lycol. The host opened the commercial by looking into the camera and proclaiming, "America has discovered Lycol. More people are choosing Lycol for fast and effective pain relief than any other brand. Just listen to what these people had to say when I asked them why they use Lycol." This scene was quickly followed by a series of testimonials from the assembled guests. For example, in one a pro football quarterback stated, "As an NFL quarterback, I need quick pain relief after a rough game, and so I always keep a bottle of Lycol in my locker." In another an aging but popular movie star touted the benefits of Lycol in keeping her active. At the end of the commercial, the talk show host declares convincingly, "A recent survey found that three out of four hospitals use Lycol for their patients. If it's good enough for the nation's health care experts, it's good enough for me."

"Is our research solid on this campaign?" Foster directed the question to Les Mitchell, the researcher in the group.

"Yes. Lycol *is* number one in terms of over-the-counter sales. And these stars do actually use the product now. We also have the hospital survey results," Mitchell responded. "Lycol is used by most hospitals—it isn't the only over-the-counter remedy used, but it's the most common. Part of the reason is cost, and the Lycol sales reps have done a brilliant marketing job with the hospitals. In addition, Lycol is only one of a handful of general-purpose nonnarcotic pain relievers. Most of the others are for particular kinds of pain, such as backache or muscle aches."

"Is there any evidence that the hospitals use Lycol because it's that much more effective in fighting pain than competitive brands?" Foster asked with growing concern.

"No. The survey results appear to be the direct result of costs and aggressive marketing by the manufacturers of Lycol," Mitchell acknowledged.

"Then let me pose this question to the group," Foster said. Her staff recognized the prelude to her familiar role as devil's advocate. "The theme of this campaign—the key selling point of this ad—is the popularity of Lycol as an over-the-counter pain reliever. We never make any scientific claims as to whether Lycol is more effective than other brands. Nevertheless, if we then insert the statement about the hospital survey results, doesn't that imply that hospitals consider Lycol more effective than other brands? And isn't that misleading the consumer?"

"I don't think so," volunteered George Lico, the copywriter who had worked diligently on the campaign. "The hospital claim is accurate. We have the study to prove it. And it's just one of many appeals in the ad. In essence, we're promoting the popularity of Lycol as a pain remedy. If it were not effective, then hospitals would not use it, regardless of cost. And we never say, in the ad, that Lycol is the *only* one used by hospitals."

"I admit the claim is literally true," Foster responded. "It's the context that bothers me. I'm still afraid that this campaign leaves the impression that hospitals consider Lycol to be more effective than other nonprescription pain killers. And in our health-conscious society, this might be a persuasive argument."

But Lico was unmoved. "The key selling point is the product's apparent popularity with the consuming public. Let the viewers judge for themselves whether the drug is more effective than its competitors. And the hospital survey is only one more piece of evidence of the drug's popularity. We never state that hospitals purchase Lycol because they consider it medically more effective than other brands."

At this point Foster solicited comments from other staff members who were evenly divided between Lico's "literal truth" philosophy as the only threshold of moral obligation and Foster's paternalistic concern for consumer understanding. Foster was still troubled but thanked her staff for their

comments and promised to give them serious consideration before deciding whether to approve the Lycol campaign for release.

THE CASE STUDY

The advertising campaign in this case appears to be accurate, but is it true? The claim concerning hospital usage is supported by scientific evidence, although the reasons undoubtedly vary among hospitals and may have little to do with whether they believe that Lycol is medically more effective than other brands. Are advertisers expected to supply evidence that undermines their own claims?

As representatives of the public, journalists are expected to provide as much information as possible to help the consumer understand the context of the story. But advertising agencies owe their primary loyalties to their clients. Unlike the practice of journalism, fairness and balance are not a part of the advertising ethical lexicon. Ad agencies are expected to construct strategies and create effective advertising campaigns that will help distinguish their clients' products from similar products in the competition of the market.

Nevertheless, in a consumer-oriented society, advertisers and their agencies cannot simply ignore the moral obligation imposed on all institutions to act in a socially responsible manner. In a capitalistic society, persuasion and manipulation are essential ingredients of the advertising process. And society has given its reluctant acceptance if not enthusiastic endorsement in return for advertisers' support of the mass media system.

One approach is to limit the advertiser's moral responsibility to the avoidance of outright falsehoods. This view is represented by author Theodore Levitt, who contends that distortion is one of advertising's legitimate and socially desirable purposes, because the audience demands symbolic interpretation of everything it sees and hears.[85]

An opposing view is represented by Philip Patterson and Lee Wilkins in their insightful commentary on the importance of sincerity in advertising: "Sincerity in advertising means that claims are made within a context clearly understood by both the advertising copywriter and the consumer. If the ad's claims fall either outside the contextual capabilities of the audience, or if the context is incomplete or misleading, then the ad is suspect."[86]

In this scenario, the claims are literally true, but Alicia Foster has a concern that, when the hospital survey statement is juxtaposed next to the other claims, the audience will believe that hospitals use Lycol because of its medical rather than cost effectiveness. But is it incumbent on advertising agencies to clarify every ambiguity in an ad?

Using the SAD Formula for moral reasoning outlined in Chapter 3, assume the role of moral agent Alicia Foster and evaluate this ad campaign from an ethical perspective. The goal is to achieve a balance between allowing creative license and breathing space for commercial persuasion while protecting an unsuspecting public from unreasonable and predatory exploitation. Keep in mind that the realities of the advertising marketplace demand a role for all parties in the chain of moral responsibility: the advertiser, the advertising agency, and the consumer.

▶ **CASE 4-6**
The Computer Virus: A PR Challenge

When the president of the First National Bank, Myron Fitzsimmons, was told that the bank's mainframe computer had been infected with a "virus," he recognized the problem for what it was: a public relations nightmare. Shortly after the bank opened that day, a team of computer experts was called in when the employees were unable to retrieve the records stored in the bank's computer. The verdict: someone had apparently accessed the computer and then planted the virus, thus making the records unusable. It was too early to tell how much information had been stolen, but Fitzsimmons was prepared for the worst.

Fitzsimmons notified the other bank officers and then called in Fran Sizemore, the bank's director of public relations. Sizemore had been with First National for five years, after six years of experience in PR with a local hospital and a chemical company. During her tenure at First National, she had cultivated good relations with the local media and was well respected. She had always considered it

to be good PR to be up-front with reporters and contact them as soon as the facts were clear.

However, Sizemore had never lost sight of the fact that her first loyalties were to the institution for which she worked and the bank's customers. She had attempted to educate reporters to this reality and gain some empathy on their part. She could not, she constantly reminded them, divulge confidential bank information or release information that would be detrimental to her own company.

Fitzsimmons briefed Sizemore on the problem and asked her to develop a plan for dealing with the media. Despite her propensity for openness, Sizemore wondered whether it would be advisable to notify reporters right away. Under policy guidelines that she had prepared when she took the job, information was to be released to the media as soon as it had been verified for accuracy and completeness and cleared for release. From her experience at the bank, Sizemore knew that this last part of her policy might be a problem in this case. Bank officials were perfectly willing to cooperate in releasing information unless they felt that it would reflect poorly on the bank's corporate image.

In this case, little was known except that a virus had infected the computer system. It was too early to know who was responsible or, for that matter, how the intrusion had occurred. The release of the story before more facts were known might fuel speculation and create panic among some of the bank's customers. In fact, on further reflection Sizemore was not sure that there was any value in having the story appear at all. The apparent success of this electronic invasion might just plant the idea in the minds of others.

On the other hand, the media might find out anyway, especially if the situation warranted a criminal investigation. Bank customers would be outraged if the story broke without any apparent cooperation or comment from bank officials. First National might lose credibility with its customers, as well as the media. Sizemore's standing with the media would probably suffer, and considering the "bad press" that the banking industry in general (and First National in particular, which had suffered economic losses due to several outstanding bad loans) had received during the previous few years, she needed good relations with the reporters who covered the financial institutions in her community. Perhaps the best approach would be for Sizemore to recommend to bank management that the story be released, with a statement about what the bank was doing to get to the bottom of the problem. This course would perhaps reflect favorably on the bank's image as a socially responsible institution while reassuring customers.

In evaluating the situation Sizemore realized that she had three options to present to the bank president. She could recommend that the story be (1) released immediately, (2) withheld entirely, or (3) withheld until all the facts were known, even if they reflected unfavorably on bank security procedures. This last option would entail releasing as much of the information as possible without divulging confidential company procedures. Each of these options had risks, and Sizemore retreated to her office to consider the alternatives.

THE CASE STUDY

Like most public relations dilemmas, this case involves moral duties to three publics: the institution, the media, and society at large. However, unlike reporters, whose primary responsibility is to their audience, PR practitioners owe their first allegiance to their clients or the organizations for which they work. They are both an advocate and a source of information. The PR practitioner becomes the initial gatekeeper who decides how much of the truth should be released and under what circumstances.

From an ethical standpoint, nothing is inherently wrong with being an advocate.[87] Outright lying may be wrong, but no one expects an advocate to release information that would be detrimental to his or her own interest. PR practitioners are expected to foster a positive image for their clients or companies. The question is how to accomplish this goal while continuing to serve the public interest. And one means of serving the interests of society is through releasing information to the media.

For the purpose of analyzing the ethical dilemma outlined here, assume the role of Sizemore. Then, applying the moral reasoning model in Chapter 3, select one of the three options available to you and defend it on ethical grounds. As a practical matter, how much relative weight should be accorded to Sizemore's philosophy (openness with the media) and to the bank management's tendency to withhold embarrassing information if it might reflect unfavorably on the bank's image? In examining this case, keep the following underlying question in mind: Is there anything ethically objectionable in withholding a story (i.e., the truth) when it is in your company's best interest to do so?

▶ CASE 4-7
AIDS in the Operating Room

As the largest and most progressive health care facility in the state, the Greensboro Regional Medical Center was the jewel in the state's medical crown. Its state-of-the-art technology, impressively credentialed staff of physicians, nurses, and technicians, and reputation for a consumer-oriented approach to the practice of medicine had touched a responsive chord among the health-conscious citizens of Greensboro and its environs. The employees of Greensboro Regional were, of course, pleased with their hospital's standing in the community. But no one was more pleased than Arlen Corbett, the hospital's irrepressible administrator.

Corbett had come to Greensboro Regional ten years ago after stints at two smaller hospitals within the state. He had taken the reins of an organization that was in financial disarray and where patients often fell victim to the bureaucratic maze of processing their involuntary attendance. These conditions had taken their toll on staff morale, and patient care had suffered.

The hospital's board had given Corbett a "mandate for change," and he quickly took advantage of this window of opportunity. He streamlined the hospital's top-heavy bureaucracy by significantly reducing the staggering amount of paperwork, reduced the size of the administrative staff, and budgeted sufficient sums for investment in state-of-the-art equipment. Corbett's most impressive accomplishment, however, was in changing the culture of the workplace, and he had scoured the landscape for medical recruits who shared his commitment to consumer-oriented health care. He also hired Katrina Evans as director of public relations to help *sell* his facility in the competition of the medical marketplace.

Evans had joined the staff of Greensboro Regional with rather limited experience. Armed with a degree in public relations, she had spent just two years with a small PR firm in her hometown. But during the interview, Evans had impressed Corbett with her enthusiasm and creative ideas, and he had decided to take a chance on this public relations neophyte. Corbett was not reticent about taking credit for changing the hospital's working environment and introducing a patient-oriented health care philosophy. But he also recognized Evans's indispensable contributions in marketing these changes to a still skeptical public.

Evans's success derived not only from her unswerving loyalty to her employer and a true belief in the quality of health care it provided. She was also extremely opportunistic, seizing on every public relations advantage to cultivate further the hospital's public persona. For example, following a series of newspaper articles documenting several cases of health care workers in other cities who had tested positive for the HIV virus, Greensboro Regional had promptly instituted an HIV testing program for all of its employees. The hospital could have quietly implemented the program, but Evans had decided to publicize it vigorously as an another example of Greensboro Regional's commitment to providing quality health care in a risk-free environment. While some employees had initially resisted the mandatory HIV testing, most had resigned themselves to this periodic and inevitable intrusion into their privacy. From time to time local reporters had queried Evans about the testing program. Fortunately, for the four years since its inception, the results of the blood samples had been uniformly negative—that is, until Dr. George Mason's test results returned from the lab.

Mason was among Greensboro Regional's most skilled cardiac surgeons. He had arrived at the hospital seven years ago with impressive credentials, one of the consequences of Corbett's aggressive recruiting campaign. As a graduate of Johns Hopkins University, he had interned and served his residency at a prestigious hospital in Boston before beginning his career as a cardiovascular specialist in New York. Although Greensboro Regional could not compete financially with its big-city counterparts,

Corbett had lured Mason to Greensboro with the promise of a new cardiac care unit, which was then on the drawing board, and a lab that would support the physician's research interests.

Once the test results were confirmed, Dr. Robert Boutwell, the hospital's chief of staff, suspended Mason's operating room privileges. While there was not yet any evidence that the physician actually had AIDS, his medical colleagues reluctantly concurred in this decision as a precautionary measure. Mason was allowed to treat patients, but his practice was limited to procedures that did not run the risk of contact with bodily fluids. The doctor was not pleased with his exile from the operating room, but he had temporarily accepted the judgment of the medical staff. Boutwell had also ordered his staff to begin a "lookback" to identify Mason's most recent surgery patients. A decision would then be made on whether any of them should be notified and invited to come to the hospital for testing.

Corbett was sympathetic to Mason's plight, but he also recognized a potential public relations disaster when he saw one. He was uncomfortable with the situation, but he knew that an abrupt dismissal or resignation from one of the hospital's most celebrated surgeons would pique the public's curiosity. Corbett was content with the physician's limited role until some decision could be made on Mason's future. Apparently judgment day was at hand.

"I've just gotten off the phone with Matt Dunn," Katrina Evans declared during a hastily arranged meeting with Corbett and the chief of staff. Corbett and Boutwell both recognized Dunn as a reporter for the *Greensboro Gazette*. "He's on to the story about George Mason and wants confirmation. Dunn says two sources have told him that one of our surgeons has AIDS and is still practicing here at the hospital."

"Who are these sources?" demanded Corbett. Boutwell was also curious.

"I don't know," responded Evans. "But we have to assume that they are hospital employees. Remember that not everyone here was thrilled when we implemented the HIV testing program. And there is still a fear of working with someone who has tested positive for the HIV virus, even among some health care workers."

"But Dunn's information is inaccurate," said Boutwell. "Dr. Mason does not *have* AIDS. He just tested positive for the HIV virus. Also, Dunn is technically correct when he says Mason is still practicing here, but he makes it sound like Mason is continuing to perform surgery. That's certainly not true. In my judgment, we have taken all reasonable precautions to minimize medical risks, while being fair to Dr. Mason. At the appropriate time Dr. Mason will probably resign anyway."

"Dunn already has the story," Evans noted. "But since some of his information is inaccurate or misleading perhaps we need to seize the initiative just to set the record straight." Her *proactive* public relations instincts were now fully awakened. "We might release the story without identifying Dr. Mason. We could emphasize the fact to Dunn that one of our staff physicians tested positive for the virus but does not have AIDS—and that he has been suspended from any surgical responsibilities and that the situation is under review and all appropriate precautions will be taken. We could even mention our lookback investigation to determine if any recent patients should be invited in for testing. We could also put a positive spin on the story by pointing out that in four years this is the first case of a positive HIV virus test result, and that once it was discovered, the hospital was quick to respond."

"I don't understand what makes this so newsworthy," Corbett said. "Why does Dunn feel this information has to be published?"

"It's probably because of the way we initially promoted this program," Evans responded. "And since then I have truthfully denied to reporters that any of our staff members have ever tested positive for HIV. I've also made it clear that it's the policy of the hospital not to comment on individual personnel matters. Of course, Dunn may not name Mason for fear of a lawsuit."

Corbett's humanitarian tendencies leaned toward Mason's professional salvation. But his administrative responsibilities propelled him in the direction of protecting the reputation and credibility of the hospital. "If we stonewall and Dunn publishes an inaccurate story, regardless of whether he names Mason, then there may be panic among those who have recently undergone surgery here. On the other hand, if we confirm the story we might be able to reassure the public that all precautions have been taken. But that may not satisfy them if they discover that Mason is still on staff. We'll then be under a great deal of pressure to terminate Mason immediately, and that could destroy whatever professional future he has remaining."

Arlen Corbett knew that the moment of decision was rapidly approaching and instructed his director of public relations to have a recommendation on his desk the next morning. Katrina Evans then retreated to her office to ponder this ethical dilemma.

THE CASE STUDY

Like all moral agents, PR practitioners must have an allegiance to the truth. This commitment is codified in the professional code of the Public Relations Society of America: "A member shall not knowingly disseminate *false or misleading information* and shall act promptly to correct erroneous communications for which he or she is responsible." But what about correcting erroneous information for which the PR practitioner is *not* responsible in order to set the record straight? In this case, two sources, perhaps hospital employees, have provided the reporter with essentially truthful but misleading information, the publication of which could harm the hospital's standing in the community. If Katrina Evans confirms the story, with the proper clarifications, she will then violate her policy against commenting on individual cases, even if she does not identify Mason. This tactic could sow the seeds of mistrust among employees. But if she abides by the policy, then the public may feel the hospital has something to hide when Evans's "no comment" is included in the *Gazette*'s story.

Evans also doubts the public interest of this story since there appears to be no health risk to the public and the hospital has acted reasonably under the circumstances. However, she does acknowledge that the high profile of the HIV testing program as a result of her own PR initiative has perhaps added a public interest dimension that would not have been otherwise apparent.

Whichever course of action is selected, Dr. Mason will be harmed through the public revelation of his condition, even if he is not identified in the story. The hospital's hand will certainly be forced in deciding his fate sooner rather than later.

For the purpose of analyzing the ethical dilemma described in the scenario above, assume the role of Katrina Evans and prepare your response to hospital administrator Arlen Corbett. In so doing, you should apply the moral reasoning model contained in Chapter 3. Keep in mind that you should resolve this issue in such a way that will reflect most favorably on your employer and minimize the harm to the hospital's reputation.

▶ **CASE 4-8**
A PR Dilemma: The Terrorist Threat

Thirty-one-year-old Delbert Worthington was not known as a cautious entrepreneur. He made his fortune in the junk bond market and used part of the proceeds to finance his latest venture: a no-frills, low-cost, transcontinental airline. Worthington took advantage of the fallout from airline deregulation to purchase a bankrupt carrier that had operated in the Northeast corridor. Financial investors on Wall Street were not particularly surprised at the young entrepreneur's entry into the competitive airline marketplace, but a few eyebrows were raised when he decided to turn his latest acquisition into an international carrier.

However, U.S. International, as the airline was called, was not designed as a prestige operation. Its low-overhead operation allowed Worthington to change the bottom line from red to black in just three years. Much of the profit margin depended on the peak summer tourist season, when thousands of economy-minded American families and college students invaded Europe.

Worthington knew a lot about making deals and devising marketing strategies. Those were things over which he had some control. He cared little about international politics, except when it interfered with the way he did business. And so it was with some annoyance that he pondered the communiqué from the State Department alerting him to a terrorist threat against U.S. International. According to the communiqué, a woman claiming to be a member of a rather obscure radical organization with Iranian ties had phoned the American embassy in Paris and said that a bomb would be placed on board a U.S. International flight departing from one of the European capitals within the following two months.

The threat could not have come at a worse time. The start of the tourist season was just three weeks away, and any leak to the public concerning the threat could have disastrous economic consequences for the airline. Of course, that is what the terrorists had in mind. Either way they would win. The communiqué noted that it was the policy of the U.S. government not to release or publicly discuss communications from terrorists. Such threats were routine. Thus, it remained up to each airline to respond.

Robert McDonald, public relations director for U.S. International, had never seen a more somber-looking Delbert Worthington. Worthington had just convened an emergency meeting of his young staff. The company president opened the meeting by reading the communiqué and reassuring the staff that all of the European airports had been placed on a heightened state of alert and had also strengthened security. Worthington then turned to McDonald for advice on the crucial question: Should there be a press conference to inform the public of the threat and to reassure travelers that all precautions had been taken? The press had already received some inkling of the threat but had not yet identified the airline or the specifics. Should the airline, Worthington wanted to know, get out front on this one?

McDonald had had five years of PR experience before joining U.S. International, but crisis management was not his forte. He graduated with a public relations degree (actually his diploma said journalism, but he preferred to emphasize his PR major on job applications) from a prestigious university and had been offered a position with a large paper company. However, he retreated to the relative obscurity of a mobile phone manufacturer and distributor and signed on as director of marketing and public relations. A small operation, he believed, would allow him more autonomy in the formulation of company policy. After five years in this position, during which his most challenging inquiry from the media had to do with the next generation of car phones, McDonald decided to seek more interesting, if not greener, pastures. McDonald had been with U.S. International from the outset, and his marketing acumen, as well as his savvy in dealing with the media, had been instrumental in the phenomenal growth of the carrier. Worthington, McDonald knew, was mostly interested in profits. He would leave whatever trappings of social responsibility were required to his young PR associate.

But the dilemma confronting McDonald now involved more than just corporate image building. First, there were matters of foreign policy. The U.S. government had made it clear that it favored a policy of nondisclosure. A panic by the American flying public would play into the hands of the terrorists by depriving the airline and the European economies that depended on tourist dollars of much-needed revenue. Second, the threat in this case was general. No date was cited, and no particular flight was targeted. As the State Department pointed out, such threats are common, and most of them turn out to be hoaxes.

On the other hand, if the threat turned out not to be a hoax—if a plane were bombed, with the inevitable loss of life—this situation could be a public relations (not to mention a legal) debacle. After a Pan American jet was blown out of the sky over Scotland in late 1988, some segments of the public, including the families of those who had died in the tragedy, wondered why the airline had not revealed the numerous warnings that apparently had been issued before the incident. In addition, in the previous several months the Passengers' Rights Association, a consumer group, had stepped up the pressure on all international carriers to be more candid with the flying public about terrorist threats.

As the meeting drew to a close, Worthington noted that there were still three weeks before the start of the tourist season. He wanted a recommendation from McDonald within ten days. McDonald, feeling truly beleaguered for the first time in his young professional life, retreated to his office to ponder the situation.

THE CASE STUDY

The code of the Public Relations Society of America pledges that members will "conduct ourselves professionally, with truth, accuracy, fairness and responsibility to the public." But how much truth does the public need to know? Should passengers be apprised of threats against airlines so that they can make an informed decision on whether to use those carriers? Should airlines hold press conferences every time there is a general threat against an airline? Is this reasonable? Clearly such paranoia plays into the hands of terrorists and, in some respects, undermines U.S. foreign policy regarding terrorism.

On the other hand, if the threats are not a hoax and lives are lost, as in the case of the Pan American tragedy, the corporate conscience will be besieged by an outraged traveling public. It is perhaps ironic that "truth" and "responsibility to the public" appear in the same plank of the PRSA code. Under normal circumstances, these would be mutually reinforcing values. But what if the truth, especially when there is no proof of immediate danger, causes a panic and irreparable economic harm? Has the cause of responsibility to the public been served?

Assume the role of the PR director for U.S. International. Using the SAD Formula for moral reasoning outlined in Chapter 3, make a recommendation to Worthington about the prudent (and ethical) course of action. In so doing, remember your loyalties to the company, the European countries that have granted you landing rights (prompted by the incentive of American tourist dollars), and the American flying public.

▶ **CASE 4-9**

News Packaged as Entertainment: *The O. J. Simpson Story*

The newsroom staff watched with disbelief as the surrealistic pictures flickered across their monitors at network headquarters in New York. O. J. Simpson, the NFL superstar famous for running from defensive backs, was now running from the Los Angeles Police Department. Simpson had failed to surrender to police after having been charged with the murders of his ex-wife, Nicole Brown Simpson, and her friend, Ronald Goldman.[88] He was subsequently spotted riding in his white Bronco on a Los Angeles freeway, and TV cameras were soon on hand to transmit this bizarre spectacle as several police cruisers followed Simpson in hot pursuit toward an unknown destination.

In another wing of network headquarters, the sales staff watched the proceedings with no less curiosity but with some concern. The heavy demand for airtime from the news division that would inevitably flow from this high-profile case would result in heavy revenue losses as a result of program preemptions. But their economic indigestion was tempered somewhat by the knowledge that their competitors would suffer a similar fate and by the fact that the public's insatiable appetite for the sensational would manifest itself in a ratings bonanza.

After Simpson was taken into custody, the news executives were in perpetual motion during the ensuing weeks preparing for what they knew would be an unprecedented media blitz, and the sales department began evaluating the financial repercussions. But Darrell Hannah recognized the story for what it really was: a made-for-TV movie. Hannah, the network's vice president for programming, harbored little doubt as to the entertainment value of this unfolding tragedy. It had all of the ingredients: sex, race, beautiful women, and a football superstar turned Hollywood celebrity caught in a stormy marital relationship. It would begin appropriately as a legitimate news story only to be commandeered by the sensationalistic tabloid press and would then be reincarnated as a prime-time blockbuster.

Hannah's fears soon materialized as the various news organizations, driven by irresistible competitive pressures, began to include both fact and rumor in their daily regimen. This was accompanied by a thriving cottage industry in checkbook journalism among the tabloid media as they unashamedly offered financial inducements to potential witnesses to tell their stories to a national audience. Hannah was no journalist, but he sympathized with his more traditional journalistic counterparts who were chagrined at the increasing prominence of entertainment values in the news product of the electronic media. Within his own sphere of influence, Hannah also harbored some misgivings about the so-called docudrama, the skillful blending of fact and fiction in which dramatic license often obscures the search for truth and understanding. Nevertheless, Hannah had reluctantly accommodated himself to these fashionable perversions of reality as a sound economic investment. During ratings periods, docudramas were among the network's more popular offerings, marketed by the sales staff with undisguised zeal.

Calvin Taylor's proposal for a dramatic rendition of the O. J. Simpson story came as no surprise to Darrell Hannah. Taylor was an independent Hollywood producer who had a proven track record in network television. He had sold five made-for-TV movies to Hannah's network, including two highly successful docudramas. One of these, a brutally frank emotionally wrenching account of an infantry unit during the Vietnam War, had even won an Emmy for its stark portrayal of that unpopular conflict.

The network programming chief perused Taylor's latest proposal with more than casual interest. It would require expeditious evaluation and approval since production was scheduled to begin in mid-October, only four months after Simpson was charged with the double murders. According to the materials that were attached to the script outline, the plot development and dialogue would be based on actual transcripts and records, interviews with witnesses and friends of the football hero and his ex-wife, police officials, sources inside the defense team and the Los Angeles County prosecutor's office, and a recently published book on the subject.

The movie, tentatively titled *Fallen Hero: The O. J. Simpson Story*, would begin with a reenactment of the murder itself, with the actual assailant skillfully concealed, and then proceed to the initial police investigation, the car chase, Simpson's arrest and incarceration, the massive media publicity, the continuing police investigation and collection of evidence, and the strategic moves of the prosecutors and Simpson's defense team. Simpson's personal life—his legend as a football superstar, his status as a Hollywood sex symbol, his first marriage, and stormy and sometimes abusive relationship with Nicole Brown Simpson, and his intimate relationship with his children—were to be revealed through a series of skillfully contrived flashbacks as the legal drama was unfolding around the fallen hero.

Hannah was impressed with the producer's determination to be fair and avoid rendering any moral judgment on Simpson. Like most docudramas, there was a danger that the actors might overshadow the actual evidence and historical facts that surrounded the case. But human motivation, behavior, and emotions are also a part of history, Hannah reasoned, and it would be up to the actors to maintain the integrity of the interpretive process.

Taylor's proposal called for a fast track production schedule that would dramatically re-create and interpret events even as the real-life scenario continued to unfold. The movie would end with the trial and the verdict itself, which were still months away. However, Taylor had developed three possible conclusions, depending on the jury's decision. If the network approved the project, it would be scheduled for four hours of airtime spread over two nights within a month after the trial.

As usual, Hannah sought his staff's advice before rendering final judgment on Taylor's proposal. He savored their counsel but knew that he would be the ultimate gatekeeper in the disposition of the producer's ambitious venture.

"This is a good proposal. It skillfully weaves all of the key elements together," volunteered Manuel Sanchez. In Hannah's view Sanchez was among the best and brightest in the business, and his programming acumen was directly responsible for his network's dominance in the prime-time lineup during the past three years. "I particularly like the use of flashbacks to portray Simpson's private life. Much of the dialogue may be contrived, but with Taylor's attention to detail, I'm sure it reflects more or less accurately the characters' personalities and views. Besides, the audience understands that this is a somewhat fictionalized account of real events. They understand that some dramatic license is necessary."

"I'm not so sure," responded Sandra Greenberg. Hannah liked Greenberg because of her candor and willingness to challenge Sanchez or anyone else who offended her sense of propriety or morality. "As you know, most docudramas carry a disclaimer to alert the audience that they are a fictionalized account or dramatic re-creation of real events. And in many cases that may be sufficient. But not here. The coverage in this case has been so pervasive that I'm not sure anyone can separate fact from fantasy or news from entertainment. And many people are only too willing to believe what they perceive to be the 'real' story behind the O. J. Simpson saga."

But Sanchez was not deterred. "Docudramas are seldom historically accurate. They're based on real events, and many of them do come close to the truth. But the reality is that they take liberties with the facts and with dialogue. And the actors themselves affect the audience's perception of the real characters and events. But after all, these programs are primarily entertainment. We've run docudramas before, and they've usually been a ratings success. What's so different about the O. J. Simpson story?"

"The difference," Greenberg responded, "is that docudramas—at least those that purport to reflect reality—should have the advantage of historical perspective. Taylor's Emmy-winning film certainly fit that mold. It was produced fifteen years after the fall of South Vietnam. But the O. J. script is being written virtually as events unfold. That just increases the chance of distortion. Quite frankly, I'm not crazy about docudramas that show up on national TV just a couple of months after the actual events. They're usually superficial and even sensational."

"Granted, there is a danger of distortion. But overall, Taylor's proposal is balanced," said Sanchez. "It depicts Simpson as both hero and villain, which is probably accurate, but only time will tell on that score. The bottom line here is that this could be a ratings bonanza. And if we don't buy this proposal, one of our competitors will."

Hannah retreated to his spacious office overlooking midtown Manhattan to ponder this exchange between Sanchez and Greenberg. On the one hand, he was the captive of his own success. Made-for-TV movies, including docudramas, had fared well in his network's prime-time menu, and Calvin Taylor had contributed to that success. And Sanchez was right. *The O. J. Simpson Story* would probably be a ratings triumph. Hannah was also pleased that Taylor had avoided the temptation to depict Simpson in rather stark terms as either hero or villain; the proposal was balanced in this respect. He was troubled by the focus on the gridiron great's celebrity status and the lack of attention paid to the victims and their families. But he reasoned that, even under the best of circumstances, docudramas can only reflect one aspect of reality. Even many of the reporters covering the story had been guilty of celebrity journalism and had overlooked the repulsive nature of the crime and the impact on those who were closest to the victims. Of course, this was small comfort to Hannah as he pondered his own dilemma.

On the other hand, he shared Greenberg's distaste for the docudrama plucked from today's headlines. Of course, his network had aired movies based on current events, but usually a year or more after the actual incident—not a perfect historical vantage point but certainly time for *some* reflection and perspective. He was troubled by the "instant" docudrama that was rushed into production just to ride the crest of public obsession. Were such dramatic depictions of real events designed to promote understanding or merely garner commercial success? Hannah was part of his network's entertainment division. Was his responsibility limited to catering to the mass audience's insatiable appetite for entertainment, or did he have a moral obligation to ensure that docudramas aired over his network provided the audience with at least a reasonable reflection of historical truth?

THE CASE STUDY

The docudrama is a controversial vehicle because it resides on that slippery slope between historical interpretation and fiction. At its best the docudrama can both enlighten and entertain; at its worst it can carry revisionism to such an extreme that the story loses all historical truth. The docudrama has become an increasingly popular format for prime-time television, and as such it raises some ethical questions concerning the balance between truth and entertainment. Can the moral ambiguities of history, for example, be adapted to television, which must quickly attract an audience and tell an interesting story within such a short time period?

Nevertheless, the docudrama can be a powerful vehicle for reviving society's important stories for a mass audience.[89] Perhaps some truth, even

when seen through a refracted lens, is better than ignoring political and social problems altogether.

When docudramas revive historical events, they at least have the benefit of perspective and reflection. But *The O. J. Simpson Story* poses different questions: Is a TV docudrama "pulled from today's headlines" inherently unfair because of its lack of perspective? Are producers of such "instant history" more likely to distort the truth in their search for ratings?

For the purpose of rendering an ethical judgment on this matter, assume the role of network programming chief Darrell Hannah. And then, applying the SAD Formula for moral reasoning described in Chapter 3, decide whether you will accept the proposal from Calvin Taylor for *The O. J. Simpson Story*. Keep in mind that your job is not to evaluate the accuracy or fairness of the movie or to separate fact from fiction, since that is impossible to do based on the information provided. On the one hand, you are concerned that a docudrama that is in production as the events themselves are unfolding enhances the chances for distortion and sensationalism. Because of time pressures, more dramatic license might be taken than would otherwise be the case. On the other hand, as your network's chief programmer, you also recognize the marketability of hot news stories packaged in an entertainment format. Thus, the issue might be framed as follows: Since you are part of your network's entertainment division, should you simply apply entertainment values in deciding whether to air movies based on current events, or do you have a moral obligation to ensure that docudramas aired over your network at least have the advantage of historical "distance" from the actual events reflected in the presentation?

Notes

1. See Sissela Bok, *Lying: Moral Choice in Public and Private Life* (New York: Vintage Books, 1978), p. 14; Richard L. Johannesen, *Ethics in Human Communication*, 3d ed. (Prospect Heights, IL: Waveland, 1990), p. 110.
2. Quoted in Warren Shibles, *Lying: A Critical Analysis* (Whitewater, WI: Language, 1985), pp. 19–20.
3. For a good scholarly analysis of the trial of Socrates,

see I. F. Stone, *The Trial of Socrates* (Boston: Little, Brown, 1988).

4. John Stuart Mill, *On Liberty* (New York: Bobbs-Merrill, 1956), p. 21.

5. See *Gertz v. Welch*, 1 Med.L.Rptr. 1633, 1640 (1974); *New York Times Co. v. Sullivan*, 376 U.S. 254, 270 (1964); *Chaplinsky v. New Hampshire*, 315 U.S. 568, 572 (1942).

6. This quote and variations thereof have been attributed to Mark Twain. See "Pudd'nhead Wilson's New Calendar," quoted in Mark Twain's Works: *Following the Equator* (New York: Harper, 1925), p. 12; and Bok, *Lying*, p. 153.

7. *Genesis* 4, 37, cited in Arnold M. Ludwig, *The Importance of Lying* (Springfield, IL: Thomas, 1965), p. 7.

8. See William L. Rivers and Cleve Mathews, *Ethics for the Media* (Upper Saddle River, NJ: Prentice Hall), p. 15.

9. Clifford Christians, Kim B. Rotzoll, and Mark Fackler, *Media Ethics: Cases and Moral Reasoning*, 4th ed. (White Plains, NY: Longman, 1995), p. 80.

10. Bok, *Lying*, pp. 32–33.

11. Johannesen, *Ethics in Human Communication*, p. 110.

12. James A. Jaska and Michael S. Pritchard, *Communication Ethics: Methods of Analysis*, 2d ed. (Belmont, CA: Wadsworth, 1994), p. 132.

13. Shibles, *Lying*, p. 19.

14. See Frank Deaver, "On Defining Truth," *Journal of Mass Media Ethics*, Vol. 5, No. 3, 1990, pp. 168–177.

15. *Ibid.*, p. 174.

16. Some of these are discussed by Stephen Klaidman and Tom L. Beauchamp in *The Virtuous Journalist* (New York: Oxford University Press, 1987), pp. 34–55.

17. See "When Is a Quote Not a Quote?" *Newsweek*, January 21, 1991, p. 49; Paul McMasters, "Hold Your Nose and Defend Janet Malcolm, *Quill*, January/February 1991, pp. 8–9.

18. See *ibid.*, pp. 31–32.

19. "Not Their Finest Hour," *Newsweek*, June 8, 1992, p. 66.

20. For a critical analysis of the role of the media in Operation Desert Storm, see John R. MacArthur, *Second Front: Censorship and Propaganda in the Gulf War* (New York: Hill & Wang, 1992).

21. Jay Black, Bob Steele, and Ralph Barney, *Doing Ethics in Journalism: A Handbook with Case Studies*, 2d ed. (Boston: Allyn & Bacon, 1995), p. 121.

22. See Gene Goodwin and Ron F. Smith, *Groping for Ethics in Journalism*, 3d ed. (Ames: Iowa State University Press, 1994), p. 206.

23. "End Doesn't Justify Means," *FineLine*, October 1991, p. 7.

24. *Ibid.*

25. Russ W. Baker, "Truth, Lies, and Videotape," *Columbia Journalism Review*, August 1993, pp. 25–28.

26. *Ibid.*, p. 26.

27. *Ibid.*, p. 27.

28. These criteria are based, in part, on some of the ones devised by participants in an ethics seminar at the Poynter Institute for Media Studies. See Black, *Doing Ethics in Journalism*, p. 108.

29. "The New Unreality: When TV Reporters Don't Report," *Columbia Journalism Review*, May/June 1992, pp. 17–18.

30. *Ibid.*, p. 18.

31. Jonathan Adler, "On the Ropes at NBC News," *Newsweek*, March 8, 1993, p. 49.

32. Richard P. Cunningham, "The Ombudsmen," *Quill*, April 1989, p. 9.

33. *Ibid.*

34. *Ibid.*

35. "Darts and Laurels," *Columbia Journalism Review*, May/June 1994, p. 23.

36. *Ibid.*

37. "To Our Readers," *Time*, July 4, 1994, p. 4.

38. *Ibid.*

39. *Ibid.*

40. Several such examples of digitally altered photos based on design or taste considerations are contained in a paper delivered to the 1994 annual convention of the Association for Education in Journalism and Mass Communication in Atlanta, Georgia: Tom Wheeler and Tim Gleason, "Digital Photography and the Ethics of Photofiction: Four Tests for Assessing the Reader's Qualified Expectation of Reality," pp. 5–6.

41. For a discussion of the new journalism, see Goodwin and Smith, *Groping for Ethics*, pp. 226–227.

42. E.g., see "Twisted History," *Newsweek*, December 23, 1991, pp. 46–49.

43. *Ibid.*, citing comments made to the New Orleans *Times-Picayune* and *Vanity Fair*.

44. *Ibid.*

45. John Leo, "Faking It in 'Quiz Show,' *U.S. News & World Report*, October 17, 1994, p. 24.

46. Quoted in *ibid.*

47. *Ibid.*

48. See "Racing the News Crews," *Newsweek*, May 24, 1993, p. 58.

49. E.g., see "Ripping Off the Headlines," *Newsweek*, September 11, 1989, pp. 62–65.

50. *Ibid.*, p. 63.

51. *Ibid.*

52. *Ibid.*, p. 65.

53. See Jon Katz, "Covering the Cops," *Columbia Journalism Review*, January/February 1993, pp. 25–28.

54. "Whose Real Life Is This Anyway?" *Newsweek*, February 25, 1991, p. 46.

55. *Ibid.*

56. *Ibid.*, quoting Dan Gingold, University of Southern California journalism professor, p. 47.

57. For those who care to read them, however, the ingredients will be listed on the product package itself.

58. Deaver, "On Defining Truth," p. 172.

59. Johannesen, *Ethics in Human Communication*, p. 113.

60. *Ibid.*, p. 115.

61. Philip Patterson and Lee Wilkins, *Media Ethics: Issues and Cases* (Dubuque, IA: WCB Brown & Benchmark, 1994), p. 55.

62. Don R. Pember, *Mass Media Law*, 6th ed. (Dubuque, IA: WCB Brown & Benchmark, 1993), p. 523.

63. For a discussion of this notion of mutual dependence, see Baskin and Aronoff, pp. 207–208.

64. *Ibid.*, p. 207.

65. For a good discussion on the ethics concerns involved in the use of VNRs, see K. Tim Wulfemeyer and Lowell Frazier, "The Ethics of Video News Releases: A Qualitative Analysis," *Journal of Mass Media Ethics*, Vol. 7, No. 3, pp. 151–168.

66. David Lieberman, "Fake News," *TV Guide*, February 22, 1992, p. 11.

67. See Joan Drummond, "Ethics vs. the Economy," *Quill*, May 1993, pp. 35–38.

68. Wulfemeyer and Frazier, "The Ethics of Video News Releases," p. 156, citing "VNR's—A New Tool Needing the Same Care," *PR Week*, September 5, 1988, p. 4.

69. Doug Newsome, Alan Scott, and Judy VanSlyke Turk, *This Is PR* (Belmont, CA: Wadsworth, 1989), p. 353.

70. Lieberman, "Fake News," pp. 10–11.

71. For a discussion of some of the ethical questions raised by digital sampling, see Don E. Tomlinson, "Digital Sound Sampling: Sampling the Options," in Patterson and Wilkins, *Media Ethics: Issues and Cases*, pp. 248–250.

72. See Roy Peter Clark, "The Unoriginal Sin," *Washington Journalism Review*, Vol. 5, March 1983, pp. 43–48.

73. *Ibid.*, p. 43.

74. Black, *Doing Ethics in Journalism*, p. 172.

75. Clark, "The Unoriginal Sin," p. 47.

76. Black, *Doing Ethics in Journalism*, p. 176.

77. Clark, "The Unoriginal Sin," p. 45.

78. See Deni Elliott, "Plagiarism: It's Not a Black and White Issue," *Quill*, November/December 1991, p. 16.

79. *Ibid.*

80. *Ibid.*, p. 16.

81. Ray Eldon Hiebert, Donald F. Ungurait, and Thomas W. Bohn, *Mass Media IV: An Introduction to Modern Communication* (White Plains, NY: Longman, 1985), p. 549.

82. Jaska and Pritchard, *Communication Ethics*, p. 128.

83. See Paul Braun, "Deception in Journalism," *Journal of Mass Media Ethics*, 3, no. 1, 1988, pp. 82–83.

84. E.g., see Russ W. Baker, "Truth, Lies, and Videotape: *Prime Time Live* and the Hidden Camera," *Columbia Journalism Review*, July/August 1993, pp. 25–28; Jay Black, Bob Steele, and Ralph Barney, *Doing Ethics in Journalism: A Handbook with Case Studies*, 2d ed. (Needham Heights, MA: Allyn & Bacon, 1995), pp. 123–125.

85. Theodore Levitt, "The Morality (?) of Advertising," *Harvard Business Review*, July–August 1972, pp. 84–92.

86. Philip Patterson and Lee Wilkins, *Media Ethics: Issues and Cases*, 2d ed. (Dubuque, IA: WCB Brown & Benchmark, 1994), p. 54.

87. For a discussion on this point, see Raymond Simon, *Public Relations: Concepts and Practices*, 3d ed. (New York: Wiley, 1984), pp. 380–383.

88. For an interesting account of the news coverage of the O. J. Simpson case, see Jacqueline Sharkey, "Judgment Calls," *American Journalism Review*, September 1994, pp. 16–26.

89. E.g., see Clifford G. Christians, Kim B. Rotzoll, and Mark Fackler, *Media Ethics: Cases & Moral Reasoning*, 3d ed. (New York: Longman, 1991), p. 368.

The Media and Privacy:
A Delicate Balance

ETHICS AND PRIVACY:
THE SEARCH FOR MEANING

Privacy is an ambiguous concept that does not lend itself easily to definition.[1] One common view is that the right to privacy means the right to be left alone or to control unwanted publicity about one's personal affairs. Of course, the media are in the business of *not* leaving people alone. Their tendencies are in the direction of revelation, not concealment. Thus, the balancing of the individual's interest in privacy against the interest of the public in access to information about others is one of the most agonizing ethical quandaries of our time.

Invasions of privacy by the media encompass a broad spectrum, ranging from incursions on another's physical solitude, or "space," to the publication of embarrassing personal information. Some invasion of privacy is essential to the news-gathering process and a well-informed public. But the ethical dilemma arises in deciding where to draw the line between reasonable and unreasonable media conduct.

Reporters are not the only media practitioners who invade our private domain. Most disseminators of mass media content, including advertisers and those who produce entertainment, are inherently intrusive. They seek us out in an effort to dominate our aesthetic tastes and economic choices. In a highly competitive media environment, this process is probably inevitable, but its very pervasiveness adds an ethical dimension to the relationship between media professionals and their audiences.

Most of us value privacy, yet we are ambivalent about how much we should retain and how much we should relinquish. We object to government spying and intelligence gathering on private citizens but are willing to tolerate TV cameras and two-way mirrors to discourage shoplifting. Some workers object to polygraph exams as a condition of employment but accept drug testing as a necessary evil, although society is certainly divided on this issue. The media are frequently accused of unwarranted invasions of privacy, but the fact is that incursions into our private domain are rampant. We seem to relinquish more privacy with each passing year, turning over to governmental and private agencies volumes of data about our personal affairs.

Society's concern about invasions of privacy by the media lies just beneath the surface of public discourse and, like an active volcano, occasionally erupts into a raging debate whenever the standards of proper decorum appear to have been transgressed. Such was the case in May 1987 when the *Miami Herald*, after "staking out" the apartment of a Democratic presidential contender, Gary Hart, reported that Hart had put himself in a compromising position with a woman friend. Hart's wife was in Colorado at the time. This story served as a catalyst to bring to the forefront rumors that Hart was a "womanizer," thus legitimizing inquiries into the former U.S. senator's fitness for national office. Although Hart retaliated by accusing the *Herald* of untruthful and biased reporting, his popularity plummeted, and he soon withdrew from the Democratic race. The debate that followed concerning the *Herald*'s news-gathering techniques and whether Hart's personal life was legitimate news was almost as intense as the controversy about the candidate himself.

Five years later it was then presidential candidate Bill Clinton who provided tantalizing coverage as reporters relentlessly pursued allegations of his twelve-year affair with Gennifer Flowers. While the networks basked in the glow of sizable ratings, news executives had to defend themselves against charges that they had lost sight of other campaign issues.[2]

Such cases generate a lot of heat but are not always illuminating in our search for the delicate balance between public and private interests. Privacy is usually a prominent feature of media ethics texts and professional seminars in which hypothetical and real-life ethical issues are explored. Yet precise rules remain elusive, although some broad guidelines have emerged. The frustration of confronting ethical situations like the Hart affair, as well as those involving private individuals, is described by Conrad Fink in *Media Ethics: In the Newsroom and Beyond*:

> Infinite variations of ethical dilemmas arise in privacy issues. Here, perhaps more than in any other area of journalistic ethics, you will have no precise guidelines, and often will find little solace in what other journalists did in similar cases. Make your best judgment call, balancing your responsibility to your reading or viewing public against the individual's right to privacy, and expect to awaken in the night, even years later, with the gnawing feeling you made the wrong call.[3]

This is not a very promising assessment for media practitioners who must make difficult judgments under deadline pressures. In all likelihood the search for the meaning of privacy will proceed unabated, and the distinction between reasonable and unreasonable violations of privacy will continue to elude us. Nevertheless, sensitivity to the privacy interests of others is an essential ingredient of moral reasoning.

THE VALUE OF PRIVACY

Why do we value privacy? Why is it so important to us?[4] First, the ability to maintain the confidentiality of personal information is the hallmark of an autonomous individual. It can be taken as an article of faith that others are not entitled to know everything about us. To the extent that this principle is breached, we lose control, and our sense of autonomy is undermined. Several years ago the *Cocoa Today*, in Florida, ran a picture of a kidnapping victim virtually nude as she was being escorted by police officers from the home where her estranged husband had been holding her hostage. The kidnapping itself was a newsworthy event, but readers questioned the sensitivity of the paper in running the photo. The victim questioned it, too, and sued for invasion of privacy. Although the appellate court eventually ruled against her, the publication of this photo undoubtedly compounded her feeling that she had lost some control over her private life.

The principle of autonomy is also at the core of the prohibitions against false and deceptive advertising. When TV commercials, for example, enter the privacy of our home, we have the right to expect messages that will assist us in making informed product choices. Deceptive ads undermine our autonomy in making those decisions in the marketplace.

Second, privacy can protect us from scorn and ridicule by others. In a society in which there is still intolerance of some human tragedies, lifestyles, and unorthodox behaviors, no one wants to be shamed. Alcoholics, homosexuals, and AIDS patients, for example, know only too well the risk of exposing their private lives to public scrutiny.

Third, privacy produces a mechanism by which we can control our reputations. "Who cares what others think?" is a common refrain, but the fact is, we do care. The more others really know about us, the less powerful we become in controlling our destiny. John Tower found this out the hard way in 1989 as he was subjected to the most exacting senatorial scrutiny of any cabinet nominee in history and was ultimately rejected because of his previous bouts with alcohol and persistent rumors of womanizing. Several months later, Jim Wright became the first speaker of the House to resign under a cloud after one of his congressional colleagues accused him of unethical activities.

Fourth, privacy, in the sense of being left alone, is valuable in keeping others at a distance and regulating the degree of social interaction we have. Our laws against trespassing and intrusion reflect this concern. Electronic eavesdropping and telephoto lenses have rendered personal solitude more difficult, but our interest in maintaining some semblance of privacy remains undiminished.

Finally, privacy serves as a shield against the power of government. Knowledge is power! As the individual relinquishes his or her privacy interests to the government, the dangers of manipulation and subservience to the state increase, as in a totalitarian society. Thus, privacy is a value that lies at the heart of a liberal democracy and an essential ingredient in protecting the individual's political interests.[5]

There is, then, a moral right to privacy that has value for those who wish to maintain a sense of individuality. However, as a *fundamental value,* it is of recent vintage. As such it must compete aggressively with other values (such as truth and justice), particularly in our information society. We are curious about the activities of others, and revelations of facts by the media and other agencies have eroded our expectations of privacy. In other words, we are at once *private* beings and *social* beings, and these two roles collide, sometimes to our detriment.

The Emergence of Privacy as a Moral Value

The concept of privacy, unlike that of truth, does not find its root in ancient history. In discussing such fundamental cultural values as privacy, it is always tempting to search Genesis for confirmation, as when Adam and Eve covered themselves with fig leaves. However, Adam and Eve's sense of modesty was in no way comparable to the contemporary meaning of privacy. Anthropologists tell us that our modern ideas about privacy were absent from ancient and primitive societies.[6] The origins of the word *private* in classical antiquity suggest that it was not a term of endearment. Because citizens were expected to be involved in public affairs, to refer to someone as a "very private person" (as we sometimes hear today) was to disparage that individual's sense of citizenship.[7] The average American voter would have failed miserably this rigid test of public responsibility.

It took centuries for the idea of privacy to gain respectability, but we find some appreciation of the advantages of physical solitude in the seventeenth century, as landholders retreated to their estates and gardens to escape the concerns and pressures of public life.[8] The birth of the United States was founded, in part, on the lack of religious privacy in England, and demands for religious tolerance—the privacy of one's conscience—were later codified in the First Amendment's guarantee of religious freedom. The colonists were also concerned with protecting their homes from unreasonable searches by government agents and preventing forced quartering of troops in their private residences, both of which are also dealt with in the Constitution.

Nevertheless, protection against unwanted invasions of privacy by their fellow citizens was not an overwhelming concern to the colonists, because their agrarian society was characterized by considerable physical distance between villages and farms. On the other hand, within homes and public accommodations there was little real privacy, no sense of one's own space. Don Pember has noted this paradox in *Privacy and the Press*:

> While man had progressed a long way from caves and tentlike dwellings, homes with living, eating, and sleeping facilities in the same room were often the rule. In public inns, travelers shared many of the same facilities. If man could exalt his solitude, his isolation, his own little world in spacious colonial America, he might also regret on occasion his inability to find a place where he could withdraw within his own home.[9]

The press of the late eighteenth and early nineteenth centuries was also vastly different from the contemporary mass media. Newspapers contained more commentary and opinion than news, and the lives of average citizens attracted little attention. With education still the preserve of the elite,[10] the press was unavailable to the illiterate mass audience. The emergence of mass public education in the 1830s greatly expanded the potential newspaper audience and paved the way for the "penny press," thus democratizing the media's content for the masses. Following the Civil War, rapid urbanization revolutionized the economic, social, and cultural underpinnings of American society. The rugged individualism and frontier mentality of Jefferson's day retreated as city dwellers became dependent on their neighbors for survival. In addition, the overcrowded cities virtually precluded any sense of real privacy, and fascination with the intimate lives of one's neighbors became a spectator sport.

These population centers created a lucrative marketplace for the development of the urban mass media. Advertisers eagerly sought space in the thriving press to tap the buying power of the newly affluent consumers. For millions of readers, newspapers became a welcome daily diversion from the humdrum existence of the workplace, and editors and publishers adjusted their content accordingly. They retreated from the intellectually appealing articles of colonial America and replaced them with stories selected more for their excitement, entertainment, and human interest than their news value.[11] Of course, not all papers succumbed to these temptations, but there is no doubt that those that did profoundly influenced the course of American journalism.

This new brand of sensational reporting was characterized, in part, by frequent exposure of the affairs of both public and private figures, as the collective audience became increasingly fascinated with the foibles and misfortunes of both the famous and not-so-famous members of society. This form of journalistic enterprise was no laughing matter to the victims of such publications, especially the "blue bloods," who rapidly grew tired of the press's nosy inquisitions. Media critics were quick to accuse the press of engaging in sensationalism and boorish behavior to satisfy the morbid curiosity of some segments of society.

Thus, as the United States entered the twentieth century, the value of privacy as a moral right increased dramatically because there was less of it. The right to privacy became an ethical concern in a complex urban society that still prized individual autonomy. The Industrial Revolution had resulted in crowded cities with little space and privacy, and newspapers had subjected human foibles to the glare of publicity as never before. This situation posed a moral dilemma for a culture that valued both privacy and press freedom: whereas the press defended its intrusions on the ground of newsworthiness, its critics sought to impose public accountability on what they perceived to be unethical breaches of journalistic decorum. It was within this environment that the right to privacy became a legal concept as well as a moral one.

Privacy as a Legal Concept

Until the turn of this century, there was no legal right to privacy in the United States. By common agreement, the contemporary notion of privacy as a legal concept began in 1890 with the publication of an article in the *Harvard Law Review*. In this scholarly treatise, two young lawyers, Samuel D. Warren and Louis D. Brandeis, propose a legal recognition for the right to be left alone. Offended by newspaper gossip and what they see as violations of the standards of decency and propriety, the authors suggest monetary damages for citizens who suffer from the prying and insatiable curiosity of an unrestrained and unrepentant press.

The Warren and Brandeis proposal initially fell on deaf ears. Nevertheless, if its authors were alive today, they would surely be humbled by contemporary privacy law, which has greatly exceeded their modest proposal. In the hundred years since the publication of the *Harvard Law Review* article, the courts or the legislatures in most states have recognized some legal protection for the right to privacy. In American jurisprudence, however, the right to privacy has actually developed into four separate and distinct torts.

Intrusion is what many people think of when the subject of invasion of privacy arises. The media can be held liable for an unwarranted violation of one's physical solitude. A journalist who enters a private home uninvited, even at the invitation of law enforcement authorities, may be sued for intrusion. The use of telephoto lenses to capture the private moments of an unsuspecting subject and electronic eavesdropping can also pose legal problems.

The second area of privacy law is *publicity of embarrassing private facts*. This is the kind of privacy protection that Warren and Brandeis

had in mind when they published their treatise on the subject. The media can be held liable for publicizing embarrassing revelations about someone if the information (1) would be highly offensive to a reasonable person and (2) is not of legitimate concern to the public.[12] Legal victories for disgruntled plaintiffs are rare, however, because most courts are reluctant to impose liability against the media for the reporting of truthful information. But this attitude has angered some people, who believe that the media use this freedom to rummage, often irresponsibly and unnecessarily, through the private domains of both the famous and the obscure. Although most journalists may not do this, those who do create feelings of animosity and distrust.[13]

The media can also be held liable for publishing information that places someone in a *false light*. Legal problems can arise when a newspaper, magazine, or broadcast station reports falsehoods or distortions that leave an erroneous impression about someone. False light cases often arise within the context of the mismatching of stories and pictures. A newspaper should use extreme caution, for example, in using a file photo to illustrate a current story unless its purpose is clearly identified. TV stations are sometimes confronted with a legal problem when the audio and video are not properly matched and an erroneous impression is left concerning an individual who happens to be included in the news coverage.

Appropriation is the oldest of the four types of invasion of privacy. Appropriation consists of the use of a person's name, picture, or likeness without that person's permission, usually for commercial exploitation. This is the least ambiguous area of privacy law and is designed to protect the right of individuals, both public and private figures, to exploit their personal identities for commercial and trade purposes. However, news coverage is not considered a trade purpose, and those who are featured in news stories cannot collect damages for appropriation.

This framework of civil privacy law, designed to shield us from the excesses of the press and one another, has been supplemented by some constitutional protection from the excesses of government. In the past thirty years the Supreme Court has discovered, among other things, a constitutional guarantee of access to contraceptives without government interference and a right to enjoy pornography within the privacy of our homes.[14]

Privacy is also a concern of our criminal laws, and although these statutes serve as legal restraints on all of us, they are particularly relevant to the news-gathering process. Our laws against criminal trespass are of ancient vintage and should serve as a strong deterrent to any reporter considering a transgression against private property, especially over the objection of the property owner. Electronic eavesdropping and recording have become commonplace within the journalistic community. Although the law is fairly tolerant of the use of such techniques in public places, some states prohibit the recording of a conversation without the consent of both parties. The ethical problems associated with surreptitious recording will be dealt with in a subsequent section.

Such legal proscriptions are a reflection of society's public policy on the matter of privacy. Thus, media practitioners have a moral obligation to respect the solitude of others unless they have relinquished their privacy (either voluntarily or involuntarily) through participation in some newsworthy event or unless there is some overriding public interest in violating this right in a specific instance.

It is clear, therefore, that our preoccupation with privacy and the legal protection against violations of our right to privacy have increased dramatically as we seek solitude and attempt to maintain some modicum of autonomy over our personal affairs. It is equally clear, however, that privacy law has not achieved the balance between public and private interests envisioned by media critics at the turn of this century. Thus, there is a need for an "ethics" of privacy

that goes beyond the legal principles and provides a moral compass for media practitioners in fulfilling their obligations to society.

THE NEED FOR AN ETHICS OF PRIVACY

Legal principles are not a worthy foundation for making ethical judgments concerning the lives of others. They cannot be fitted neatly to individual cases, and, where the media are concerned, the courts have gone out of their way to ensure a minimum of interference with reporting and news gathering. It is a rare invasion of privacy case indeed that does not go the way of the media defendant. In view of the law's strong presumption in favor of the media, several convincing arguments are put forth for a system of ethics that transcends legal considerations.[15]

The law of privacy, first of all, has virtually stripped away protection from public officials and public figures. Little about the lives of public people is sacred in the eyes of the law. The fact that they have chosen to inject themselves into the public arena suggests a willingness to undergo rigorous scrutiny and to suffer the consequences of embarrassing revelations.

From a legal standpoint this argument has some merit; from an ethical perspective it is suspect. Undoubtedly, public figures must expect some fallout from the glare of publicity, and it is true that their "zone of privacy" is more narrow than that of the average citizen. But this is not to say that they must sacrifice all privacy and relinquish all autonomy over their personal affairs. Unfortunately, the media, believing they are satisfying their audiences' insatiable appetite for probing accounts of the sinful ways of public persons, have often justified their behavior by refusing to recognize any zone of privacy for such individuals. One recent study, however, suggests that those who argue that everything about a public official should become public do not have the weight of public opinion on their side. According to this study, the concept of private information still has a strong place in the minds of the public.[16]

From the standpoint of ethics, a key question should be to what extent the public information relates to the individual's public performance or image. Focusing on the relationship of private concerns to matters of public interest will not resolve all of the ethical dilemmas in this area, but it does provide a point of departure. For example, the private sex life of Senator Bob Packwood, under this standard, would not normally be a matter of public interest. But when several women accused Senator Packwood of sexual harassment—a charge that eventually led to an investigation by the Senate Ethics Committee—the accusations became a latter of legitimate public concern. The fact that readers and viewers are interested in such fare is not, within itself, sufficient justification for reporting private information about public persons.

Of course, the media's fascination with the lives of public figures is not new. Pember, in *Privacy and the Press*, describes a situation in which an insensitive press actually followed President Grover Cleveland and his bride on their honeymoon in 1886.[17]

The second reason that an ethics of privacy is needed revolves around one of the primary legal defenses for the publishing of embarrassing private information: newsworthiness. The courts have taken a very liberal approach in allowing the media to define what they consider to be news or matters of public interest. Taken to the extreme, anything that is disseminated by a news organization might be considered news. But from an ethical standpoint, more precise criteria are needed. More attention should be paid to what the public needs to know rather than merely to what it has a curiosity about.

One problematic situation arises when a private person is not inherently newsworthy but is included in a story by way of illustration. A case in point is a story published by a South Carolina newspaper on the problem of teenage pregnancies. A sidebar article identified a teenager as the father of an illegitimate child. In a rare invasion of privacy victory for a plaintiff, the juvenile's guardian sued and won damages because the jury was apparently not convinced that the teenager had voluntarily relinquished his right to privacy. The South Carolina Supreme Court, in upholding the verdict, noted that public interest does not mean mere curiosity.[18] This principle also has application for reporters and editors called on to make ethical decisions.

This case illustrates that there are offenses that even the law will not tolerate. But legal permissiveness aside, an ethics of privacy should be concerned with the real public interest value in information rather than how much appeal to mere curiosity can be tolerated under the law. As Christians and his colleagues have observed in their casebook on media ethics, "Clearly, additional determinants are needed to distinguish gossip and voyeurism from information necessary to the democratic decision-making process."[19]

Finally, the law of privacy has accorded substantial latitude for news gathering in public places. The general rule is that anything that takes place in public view can be reported. The idea is that activities that transpire in public are, by definition, not private. But even in public we sometimes covet some degree of solitude. Take, for example, lovers seated on a park bench. From a legal standpoint photographers might be within their rights to capture this moment on film and publish it as an item of human interest. A sense of ethics would suggest, however, that they obtain permission from the couple, for two reasons: (1) common decency requires permission before intruding into this private moment, and (2) minor inconvenience may turn to acute embarrassment if these two lovers are married, but not to each other.

Beyond the human interest realm, even "hot" news stories may require some restraint. The seminude photo of the kidnapping victim described earlier was snapped in public, but its publication remains questionable. Sometimes good taste and simple compassion for the victims of unfortunate circumstances require a heightened degree of moral sensitivity on the part of media practitioners. This is particularly true in situations involving accident victims or victims of other tragedies. The public, of course, has an interest in learning about accidents and tragedies. But such an interest does not, in every circumstance, demand a public airing of a tape of an accident victim or an interview with a grief-stricken parent who is probably still in a state of shock. From an ethical perspective, Jeffrey Olen, in Ethics in Journalism, makes the following salient observation regarding the ethical conduct of reporters covering accidents: "If we take seriously the claim that journalists are our representatives, then their moral rights at the scene are no greater than our own."[20]

An offshoot of this public-property defense is the use of material obtained from public records. Such information has generally been privileged, and the media have enjoyed some immunity from liability for the fair, accurate, and nonmalicious publication of this material. In 1975 the U.S. Supreme Court provided a constitutional dimension to this defense when it ruled that an Atlanta TV station could not be held liable for invasion of privacy in broadcasting the name of a rape-murder victim listed in a public record.[21]

The theory underlying this principle is simple: a state is not *required* to place such embarrassing information in the public record, but once it does so, the matter is no longer private. Any citizen could conceivably examine this record. Thus, the press is merely providing publicity for what individual citizens could see for themselves if they had a mind to.

This is a convincing argument from a legal standpoint. From an ethical perspective, it is less so. The reality is that most private facts committed to public records remain unknown to society unless publicized by the media. Lawyers may rest easier if their clients rely on public records for their stories, but moral agents should still balance the public benefits against the possible harm that will accrue under such circumstances.

PRIVACY AND THE JOURNALIST: SOME SPECIAL PROBLEM AREAS

Any story, even one that appears to be innocuous, has the potential for raising complaints from those who are featured in it. Some people might object to a funeral notice, for instance, for fear that a burglar might use that information to invade their home while they are at the service. Sensitive elderly citizens might even object to the publication of their age. Because some members of the public view such innocent intrusions as matters of privacy, the media should be sensitive to their concerns. But some areas of news coverage dealing with private and sensitive information and certain techniques of news gathering raise special problems for journalists. News stories about contagious diseases and disabilities, homosexuality, rapes and other sex crimes, juvenile offenders, and suicides are among the most problematic.

Contagious Diseases

When Dorothy Barber entered a Kansas City hospital in 1939, she did not anticipate that her medical condition would be of sufficient interest to attract the press's attention. Barber was being treated for a disease that caused her to eat constantly but still lose weight. A wire service reporter entered her hospital room and snapped her picture despite her protests. The local media carried articles for several days on her illness, and Time magazine purchased the picture from the wire service and published it along with a story and a picture cutline that read: "Insatiable-Eater Barber; She Eats for Ten." Because of the magazine's insensitivity, Barber won $3,000 in damages for invasion of privacy.[22]

Perhaps no area of privacy is more closely guarded than facts about the state of a person's medical health. Barber's medical condition might have held some morbid curiosity for some readers, but the media's behavior could not have been defended on the ground of newsworthiness. Where private individuals are concerned, journalists must be particularly careful in revealing embarrassing medical conditions or contagious diseases.

At one point in history, leprosy was considered one of the most loathsome diseases. And today, of course, AIDS presents a real challenge for the media.[23] Despite a widespread public education program about AIDS, a stigma is still attached to the disease that often results in loss of job, an alienation from friends and relatives, and even expulsion from school. There is usually no public interest rationale for publishing the names of AIDS patients unless their disease is directly related to some newsworthy event. A case in point is estranged lovers who sue their sex partners for the failure to have warned them that they had AIDS.

Where public figures are concerned, of course, society's interest in their private lives is more acute. One could not argue with any degree of confidence, for example, that the public should be kept ignorant of a medical condition that threatened the life or well-being of the nation's president. But even public figures are entitled to a certain zone of privacy, and the journalistic treatment of their medical conditions should be approached with caution.

In 1987 news accounts of the first congressman known to have died from AIDS touched off a debate about the media's treatment of this public servant. Representative Stewart McKinney was known as a crusader for the poor during a distinguished seventeen-year House career, but his supporters feared that his accomplishments would be overshadowed by a *Washington Post* report that he might have contracted AIDS through homosexual contacts rather than the blood transfusions cited by his doctor.[24] McKinney's congressional colleagues were quick to jump to his defense and to accuse the press of having played up the form of his death while ignoring his accomplishments. This angry comment by Senator Christopher Dodd was typical: "Here's another example of a person whose contribution will not be remembered. He'll be defined by what a couple of reporters decided to write about what they had to go out and discover from some undisclosed sources in town."[25]

Leonard Downie, Jr., managing editor of the *Post*, defended his paper's decision to publish the story. He pointed out that McKinney's doctor had raised the issue by announcing that he believed the AIDS had resulted from multiple blood transfusions that the congressman had received during heart bypass surgery in 1979, before the testing of blood for the AIDS virus. Downie said the *Post* had learned of McKinney's homosexual contacts through credible sources. "If the doctor's conjecture about the blood supply was let stand, we knew we would be publishing a story that was incomplete, inaccurate and misleading," Downie said. "On as important a subject as the safety of the blood supply and the causes of AIDS, we felt we should not do that."[26]

Former tennis great Arthur Ashe died of AIDS-related complications in February 1993 but not before bitterly denouncing *USA Today* for invading his privacy. As an African American, Ashe had overcome racial barriers to win the U.S. Open and Wimbledon tennis championships. He retired from tennis because of heart problems and later tested positive for the HIV virus as a result of a blood transfusion during one of his open-heart bypass operations. In April 1992 Ashe was contacted by a *USA Today* reporter about a rumor that he had AIDS. During the interview Ashe asked to speak with the managing editor/sports, Gene Policinski. In response to a question from Policinski concerning whether Ashe had AIDS, the former tennis star answered "could be" but said he would neither confirm nor deny the information. He then asked whether he could have some time to call friends and other journalists and to prepare a public statement. Believing that he had no choice but to confront the issue directly, he met again with a *USA Today* reporter and confirmed he had AIDS. The story was quickly provided to *USA Today*'s international edition and circulated to other news organizations.[27]

During his follow-up news conference, Ashe issued what could be considered an epiphany on reporting personal information about celebrities who are no longer in the public limelight:

> I have it on good authority that my status was common knowledge in the medical community, especially here in New York City, and I am truly grateful to all of you, medical and otherwise, who knew, but either didn't even ask me or never made it public.
>
> What I actually came to feel about a year ago was that there was a silent and a generous conspiracy to assist me in maintaining my privacy. . . .
>
> Then sometime last week, someone phoned *USA Today* and told the paper. After several days of checking it out, *USA Today* decided to confront me with the rumors. It put me in the unenviable position of having to lie if I wanted to protect our privacy. No one should have to make that choice. I am sorry that I have been forced to make this revelation now at this time. After all, I am not running for some office of public trust, nor do I have stockholders to account to. It is only that I fall in the dubious umbrella of, quote, public figure, end of quote.[28]

Like most difficult ethical decisions, the Arthur Ashe case divided the journalistic community. Jack Shafer, editor of the Washington, D.C., *City Paper*, was sympathetic to Ashe but nevertheless found no fault with the *USA Today*'s decision: "My heart goes out to Ashe for whatever anguish the news stories caused him, but news stories cause anguish all the time." But *Washington Post* writer Jonathan Yardley disagreed: "Arthur Ashe was absolutely right to insist on his privacy and *USA Today* was absolutely wrong to violate it. No public issues

were at stake. No journalistic 'rights' were threatened. The fight against AIDS will in no way be hastened or strengthened by the exposure to which Ashe has been subjected." Even *USA Today* columnist DeWayne Wickham was not supportive of his paper's controversial decision: "Journalism teeters on the edge of a very slippery slope when, by confronting Ashe with rumors of his infection, and thus forcing him to go public or lie, it attempts to pass off voyeurism for news judgment."[29]

Columnist Murray Kempton has decried what he regards as reporters' willingness to apply their own standards of newsworthiness, often to the detriment of simple respect for others. "Journalists sometimes forget they are reporting on human beings," he said.[30] This respect for persons notion is always at the heart of the privacy debate and can be pivotal in the search for the delicate balance between news values and the value of individual autonomy.

Homosexuality

In the fall of 1977, the editors of the *Washington Post* and the now defunct *Washington Star* were confronted with an ethical dilemma: how far should they go in identifying the victims of a fire at a homosexual club?[31] The dead and injured had been watching all-male, X-rated films on the second floor of the Cinema Follies and had been unable to escape the flames, which were blocking the only unlocked exit. Eight men died in the fire, and six others required hospitalization. Most of the men were married, but none was well known in the city.

The *Star* decided to fully identify the eight men who had died because of the tragic circumstances surrounding their deaths. The Post published some of the names but buried them in the middle of the story about the fire.[32] Both papers reported the nature of the club, but neither published the names of the injured. Both papers also later carried feature articles on the previously identified victims, delving into their backgrounds, their families, and what their friends had to say. The *Star* used the full names of the deceased, whereas its competitor published only the first names. The *Post*'s managing editor, Howard Simons, said that the paper's primary motivation in not using the names was compassion for the wives and children of the men. The *Star*'s editor, James Bellows, said he felt that the names were news and should be published.[33]

About a week after the tragedy, the *Post*'s ombudsman, Charles Seib, in an editorial, criticized the paper's decision to omit the names from the feature article. His comments are worth noting:

> The *Post* decision not to use all the names and not to repeat those names previously published is not entirely without precedent. Rape victims are rarely identified and the names of juvenile offenders are customarily withheld unless the charges are extremely serious.
>
> Nevertheless, I can recall no tragedy of the magnitude of the Cinema Follies fire in which a local newspaper did not publish the names of all the identified dead.
>
> The handling of this story goes beyond pure news judgment, of course. It involves public and personal attitudes toward homosexuality, which appear to be changing rapidly. It is here that there is a disquieting side to the *Post*'s decision.
>
> In effect, *Post* editors said that homosexuality is so shameful that extraordinary steps had to be taken to protect the families of the victims. We will report the tragedy fully, they said, and tell you what we know about the men who died. But we won't tell you who they were.
>
> Question: Does this have the effect of underscoring the stigma of homosexuality, of shoving it back into the closet at a time when efforts are being made to bring it out and address it as a social fact?[34]

Seib also contended that the victims' names should have been reported because they were news, according to the paper's conventional yardsticks for measuring newsworthiness.[35]

The *Star* did not escape Seib's ethical examination. He raised the question of whether the conventions of simple justice had been violated by the *Star*'s decision to publish the names of the dead while apparently not attempting to obtain the identities of the injured, which had not been released by the authorities. He wondered whether this action was fair to the families of those who had died in the fire. He also observed that the publication of the names could have resulted in a form of guilt by association, because it was conceivable that some of the victims were not homosexual but had just attended the film exhibit out of curiosity.[36]

The ethical concern surrounding sexual orientation and privacy has become even more contentious because of an attack on sexual privacy from an unexpected source: gays themselves. In a controversial new tactic known as "outing," gay activists are publicizing the names of alleged homosexuals who have chosen to conceal their sexual preferences. The activists claim that by forcing reluctant gays into the open (i.e., to force them out of the "closet"), their numbers will swell, thus helping to eradicate the stigma attached to being gay.

A defining moment in the outing movement came in 1990 when Michelangelo Signorile, writing in *OutBack*, a New York–based gay weekly, detailed the secret homosexual life of Malcolm Forbes, following the publishing tycoon's death. Some paper's picked up on the story, others refused to publish the information.[37] But this episode exemplifies the ethical double standard practiced at some mainstream newspapers. *The New York Times*, for example, declined to include Forbes's name in their accounts of the *OutBack* story, explaining that "any individual's sex life is his own business." But the *Times* and other publications displayed no such moral scruples in covering the sexual escapades of real estate magnate Donald Trump, which led *Newsweek* magazine to remark that the "implicit assumption is that adultery is more acceptable."[38]

Although public attitudes toward homosexuality may have softened somewhat since this case, labeling someone as a gay or lesbian can still be harmful. The key test for the moral agent is whether a person's sexual orientation is *relevant* to the story, such as when a police officer is fired for being homosexual. This test of *relevance,* a key ingredient of newsworthiness, was at the heart of the debate over whether to reveal the sexual orientation of Pentagon spokesperson Pete Williams. While the rumors had circulated for months, the first revelation came in a column from Jack Anderson and Dale Van Atta in which they reported that Williams was considering resigning in the face of efforts by a "radical homosexual group" to out him as a closet gay.[39] Many of the 800 papers that subscribed to the column published the story, while others "spiked" it. In Williams's home state, six dailies in 1991 subscribed to the column and all six ran it. The Wyoming editors unanimously agreed that Williams's sexual preference was irrelevant to his ability to perform as assistant secretary of defense. But they also saw some irony in the fact that gays were being ousted from the military while being allowed to serve as civilian employees of the Pentagon.[40] This apparent contradiction, in the minds of the editors, met the requirement of *relevance*—in other words, it was newsworthy.

Sex Crimes

The coverage of sex crimes is one of the most troublesome for journalists.[41] Crime, of course, is by virtually any definition of news a matter of public interest, and the identities of crime victims are usually included in the accounts of these events. But the tradition among journalists in the United States is to omit the names of rape victims unless the victims have been murdered or are well known.

In 1975 the U.S. Supreme Court held that the media cannot be held liable for invasion of privacy when they publish the name of a rape victim from the public record.[42] As noted previously, the fact that sensitive information is public does not automatically justify its publication from an ethical standpoint. But some

journalists have taken issue with the conventional standard of automatically protecting women who allege rape. Rape has lost some of its social stigma, they maintain, and the traditional rationale that women must be protected is no longer valid.[43] Others point out, perhaps with some justification, that once the charges are filed and as long as the issue is an open one before the courts, the media should be evenhanded in their coverage. This policy necessitates the publication of the names of both the victim and the accused, because the question of guilt or innocence has yet to be determined.[44] Reporters and editors who subscribe to this view are appealing to our sense of justice.

Despite the increasing attempts to destigmatize rape victims in the collective minds of the public, a 1991 *Newsweek* poll revealed that most Americans do not believe that news organizations should reveal the names of rape victims. An overwhelming 86 percent said that society still attaches a certain amount of shame to being raped and that reporting victims' names creates a "special hardship" for women.[45]

But what are the long-term consequences for society in releasing the names of victims of sex crimes? One could argue that such a policy helps protect the innocent and deter frivolous and malicious accusations. On the other hand, publication could further traumatize the victims and perhaps even make them uncertain witnesses against their alleged attackers once the case goes to trial. In addition, such publicity could deter others from reporting similar attacks. And the increasing presence of TV cameras has done little to reassure rape victims in their search for both privacy and justice. This is particularly true of high-profile cases, which are the only ones likely to merit the attention of electronic media coverage.

A classic example is the highly publicized 1991 rape trial in West Palm Beach of William Kennedy Smith. Under Florida law, identifying rape victims through the media was illegal,[46] and the televised coverage featured a blue dot to mask the features of Smith's accuser.[47] The fact that this sensational trial, featuring the nephew of Senator Edward Kennedy, was televised nationally provided the catalyst for still another debate on whether rape victims should be identified. Nevertheless, when a supermarket tabloid, the *Globe*, published the victim's name, NBC, the *New York Times*, and several other newspapers followed suit. But overshadowing the controversy about naming the alleged victim was the decision by the mainstream media to take its ethical cues from the tabloid press. Both NBC and the *Times* were accused of using the *Globe*'s revelation as an excuse for their own journalistic deportment. For example, in his on-air intro to the story, Tom Brokaw explained, "While Smith has become a household word, the identity of the woman has been withheld by the news media until now, and this has renewed a journalistic debate over naming names."[48] The next day the *New York Times* not only named the victim and members of her family but also profiled her sex life.[49] But even within the *Times* organization feelings ran high, and more than a hundred staffers signed a petition expressing "outrage" over the naming of the woman.[50]

To the extent that a news organization predicates its own judgments on the decisions of others, it is on rather shaky ethical terrain. Such behavior deprives the moral agent of the requisite degree of independence to formulate ethically reasonable, defensible judgments. And in this case, there was undoubtedly some of the copycat journalism mentality involved in the decision-making process. But in fairness to NBC and the *Times*, we should note that the decisions within both news organizations were arrived at after exhaustive discussions and a great deal of soul searching. For example, NBC News President Michael Gartner, in spite of some powerful arguments against doing so from his senior staff, decided after a thirty-six-hour debate that his network should report the name.[51] Gartner, who has always been a strong advocate of naming rape victims, defended his decision in a column in the *Communicator*, the publication of the Radio Television News Di-

rectors Association. Since these reasons constitute the most compelling arguments in favor of naming rape victims, they are worth noting.

First, according to Gartner, names and facts are news and they add credibility to the story. They round out the story and give the reader or viewer all the information he or she needs to understanding issues. Second, producers, editors, and news directors should make editorial decisions, including what information to include in a news account, not those involved in the news. In no other category of news do news managers and journalists give the newsmaker the option of being named. Third, by withholding the names of rape victims, journalists become a part of a conspiracy of silence, reinforcing the idea that being raped is shameful. "One role of the press is to inform, and one way of informing is to destroy incorrect impressions and stereotypes." Finally, since news organizations always name the suspects in a rape case, fairness demands that the accusers should also be identified.[52]

Juvenile Offenders

Youthful lawbreakers have also traditionally been protected from the glare of publicity. Since the nineteenth century, such offenders in the United States have been dealt with through a separate juvenile justice system committed to rehabilitation rather than punishment. To this end most states have historically closed juvenile proceedings to the press and the public, although this practice has begun to change. And until recently, the media have honored this code of silence by withholding the names of juvenile offenders. But with the increase in the commission of serious crimes by juveniles, a trend that has led some states to try youthful perpetrators of violent crimes as adults, journalists have begun to challenge these ethical norms and even state laws that threaten the press with punitive measures for publishing the names of juvenile offenders. On the legal front, the Supreme Court provided the media with an important victory in 1979 by ruling that a state cannot punish the press for identifying a juvenile accused of a crime when the information is lawfully obtained.[53]

Despite this reinforcement by the nation's highest court, some reporters and editors are still reluctant to publish the names of juvenile offenders. Traditionalists argue that the release of this information will impede rehabilitation by subjecting such youths to the embarrassing glare of publicity. In addition, children and adolescents, whose moral guideposts may not yet be firmly anchored, are entitled to a mistake without being stigmatized in their later social relationships and employment opportunities.

Nevertheless, the increase in juvenile crime has piqued the public's interest, and there seems to be a growing feeling that many juvenile offenders, particularly teenagers, know the difference between right and wrong and that there is no compelling ethical justification to shield them from the consequences of their deeds, including the media spotlight. This does not mean, of course, that the media should retreat entirely from their sensitivity in coping with juvenile offenders. Whether to include the identity of a youth accused of breaking the law will depend, among other things, on the nature of the crime, the age of the juvenile, and perhaps the circumstances surrounding the incident. Nevertheless, in view of recent court decisions stripping away the cloak of anonymity from youthful criminals and the trend in some states toward a presumption of public openness in their legal dealings with juveniles, media practitioners can no longer use the law as a crutch in their ethical decision making. They are now confronted directly with the dilemma of balancing the privacy interests of youthful offenders against the public's need to be apprised of one of the nation's most serious social ills.

Suicides

The right to die with dignity is almost an article of faith in our society. For this reason, most news stories concerning the deaths of people and obituaries reflect an acute sensitivity to the circumstances surrounding the death. Except in the case of a public figure, the cause of death is often unreported, and the media will generally defer to the wishes of the family in deciding what to include in the published account.

Suicides present a ticklish problem for reporters and editors. When the suicide is that of a public figure or when it occurs in public view, it should probably be reported. But even here journalists should approach such stories with a sense of compassion for the family and friends of the victim. And where suicides or suicide attempts are captured on videotape, a likely occurrence in today's electronic age, TV stations should use such footage with caution. Competitive pressures and the excitement of such dramatic footage can lead to a moral lapse on the part of some producers and news directors. Not only is the respect for persons an important value in the ethical decision-making process under such circumstances; matters of taste, especially where the suicide is graphic or gruesome, require that the moral agent be sensitive to the viewing audience as well.

In addition, journalists should report on suicides in a straightforward manner, without romanticizing or sensationalizing the act or presenting it as an attractive alternative to depression or pain.[54] Some commentators urge a more aggressive journalistic stance in combatting suicides by going beyond the threshold mandate of serious, fact-based reporting and balancing the tragic aspects with information for their audiences on where to go for help in resolving their problems. In 1992, for example, the Nashville *Tennessean* reported the contents of a suicide note left by Deputy Police Chief John Ross. Ross defended suicide as "a rational act (Japanese style) when one brings disgrace to those whom he loves."[55] Frank Ritter, the *Tennessean*'s reader advocate (ombudsman), justified the publication of the suicide note but criticized the paper for not doing more:

It was news, and the newspaper is obligated to report the news, no matter how painful that might be for us, or for the suicide victim's family. But I would have felt more comfortable if the story had been accompanied by information on where people can seek help for problems that bring them to the brink of self-destruction. . . . [W]e needed to give expression to a voice of sanity: Suicide is not "a rational act."[56]

Of course, as morally noble as this tactic is, it is likely to be controversial since it requires news organizations to abandon their traditional posture of neutrality and in a sense become activists within their news coverage.

When a suicide occurs within the privacy of one's home, the public's need to know such details may be less compelling than when the victim is a public figure or commits the act in public view. One might inquire, for example, why a cause of death by suicide is any more essential to a news story or obituary involving a private person than the revelation that the deceased died of cancer or a heart attack. Nevertheless, some newspapers do report routine suicides, at least in news accounts if not in the obituaries. It would appear that suicides are no longer sacred cows for the press, but this does not lessen the moral responsibility of media practitioners to weigh the news value of such sensitive facts against the possible loss of dignity for the victim and the intrusion into the privacy of family and friends.

Secret Cameras and Recorders

The ethics of privacy is just as concerned with *how* reporters acquire their information as with the distribution of the embarrassing facts themselves. Journalists are quite inventive, or even ingenious, in their detective work. The electronic age, plus a continuing interest in and demand for investigative reporting, has made video and audio recording devices an important part of journalists' arsenal for documenting their discoveries.

Reporters sometimes lie in wait in unmarked vans or other inconspicuous positions, waiting for their prey to engage in some illegal or other form of nefarious conduct. When a hidden camera merely records a transaction in a public place, such news-gathering techniques can usually be justified from an ethical standpoint, although reporters must be careful not to implicate innocent persons in their surveillance. Of course, the use of hidden cameras should be the exception and not the rule, lest reporters be accused of becoming electronic "snoops" rather than protecting the public's interest.

The surreptitious recording of a conversation between a reporter and a source also poses an ethical dilemma as well as a legal one. Under federal law and in some states, a conversation may be recorded with the consent of only one party to the exchange. In other states both parties must consent. But legal considerations aside, journalists disagree on the seriousness of the ethical dilemma involved in secret recordings or even whether an ethical problem exists at all. On the one hand are those who view secret recordings of conversations and interviews to be more of a practical aid in the news-gathering process than an attempt to subvert the privacy rights of the individual being interviewed. Tape recordings assist in documenting the accuracy of the facts and quotations to be included in the story and are used by both print and broadcast journalists. As long as the interviewees know that they are talking to a reporter, a recording device is no more intrusive than the reporter's questions. Of course, assuming the validity of this view the question then arises as to whether the reporter, having secretly recorded the conversation, should obtain the subject's permission before airing the recorded interview. Of course, one could counter this argument by raising the following question: if a secret recording device is just an aid in the news-gathering process, why not ask the interviewee for permission to record the conversation? Needless to say, this would be foolish when a reporter is attempting to procure evidence of wrongdoing, and under such circumstances surreptitious taping of a conversation might be justified.

A recent article in the *Journal of Mass Media Ethics* offers a reasonable approach to the ethical dilemma posed by surreptitious recordings. The author suggests that the proper focus for determining the morality of secret tapings should be based on the rules governing privacy, confidentiality, and source attribution:

> Rules about privacy require that both the reporter and the source are in their public roles as journalist and source, not in their private roles as human beings. Rules about confidentiality establish what information is intended for public consumption and what is not. And rules about attribution establish the extent to which the source will be publicly known.[57]

Thus, according to this view, journalists who engage in surreptitious recording "do not engage in deception and they do not violate a source's privacy."[58] The ethical issues are settled by the rules established for the interview. If the source strongly objects to a recorded interview, journalists who do so anyway are on shaky ethical terrain without some compelling justification. Such practices may also violate company policy. This was the case in 1994 when *60 Minutes* correspondent Mike Wallace and producer Bob Anderson were reprimanded by CBS News President Eric Ober for secretly taping a story source, who made it clear she did not want to do an on-camera interview. Ober said this was a clear-cut violation of CBS News rules. Wallace said the tape would not have been used without the source's permission.[59]

"Ambush" Interviews

Is it fair to descend on an unsuspecting news source with embarrassing questions? The "ambush" interview—catching sources on the street and peppering them with unexpected questions—has become a dramatic instrument for investigative reporters, especially when portrayed on television.

As with most techniques of news gathering, some disagreement exists within the journalistic community over the ethics of ambush interviews. Some would answer the question about fairness by inquiring into the nature of the

news source. A public official or someone suspected of involvement in illegal activity might be fair game for a journalistic ambush, according to this view.

But some journalists object to ambush interviews under any circumstances, perhaps with good reason. First, when the ambush is captured on tape for broadcast, the element of surprise often results in an appearance of guilt on the part of the source. Particularly when the interviewee is inexperienced in dealing with the media, the attempts to fend off the unexpected interrogations of the determined, aggressive reporter can project a visual image of uncertainty and guilt.

Second, ambush interviews can violate the basic journalistic standards of balance and fairness. Anyone who becomes the subject of a media inquiry, which includes even sources suspected of illegal activity, has the right either to reject an interview altogether or at least provide a reasoned response to the reporter's questions. Answers generated through ambush interviews are usually not well-reasoned ones and thus cannot achieve the balance required in the journalistic enterprise.

The issue of fairness was at the heart of a brouhaha that surrounded a Connie Chung interview with Kathleen Gingrich, mother of House Speaker Newt Gingrich. During the interview aired in January 1995 on *Eye to Eye with Connie Chung*, Chung asked Gingrich what her son thought of First Lady Hillary Clinton. At first she refused to answer, but Chung persisted, saying it would be "just between you and me," as the cameras continued to roll. The interviewee, in a whisper that was picked up on camera, revealed that her son, "Newty," had told her that the First Lady was a "bitch."[60]

Everette Dennis, executive director of the Freedom Forum Media Studies Center at Columbia University, accused Chung of "ambushing" Gingrich. "What we have here is a short-term rating gain for CBS and a long-term black mark for media credibility," he said. Not surprisingly, David Bartlett, president of the Radio-Television News Director's Association, disagreed. "Mrs. Gingrich," he said, "clearly made the revelation in a stage whisper, 'with full knowledge that the cameras were rolling.' There was no attempt to deceive or trick anyone into saying something on camera they didn't want to."[61] Meanwhile, as journalists, ethicists, and academics debated the ethical dimensions of this on-air exchange, the program managed only a modest increase over its recent dismal ratings performance.

Accidents and Personal Tragedies

Accidents and personal tragedies are often newsworthy, but victims may be unsophisticated in dealing with the media. Thus, reporters should be careful not to take advantage of the situation and to respect the privacy of those who find themselves in such unfortunate circumstances. Sometimes, of course, it is necessary to acquire certain information and to interview the victims of accidents or personal tragedies. But such requests should be handled with diligence and sensitivity. A TV reporter, for example, should not stick a microphone in the face of an unsuspecting grieving relative of an accident victim just to capture this dramatic and emotional moment on tape.

The media are particularly vulnerable to charges ranging from insensitivity to prurience when they publish "broken-heart" photos that capture an individual's private grief. Such was the case when the Minneapolis *Star Tribune* published a photo of Esteban Marques kneeling in grief over the slaying of his eight-year-old daughter. Readers complained that the picture shredded the man's right to privacy. Shortly thereafter, the paper published the picture of Curt Hanson weeping when he learned that his former girlfriend had been found dead in her wrecked car. Readers again objected to the publication of the photos.[62]

The protests, however, did not come from the people whose pictures were published. And Executive Editor Joel Kramer defended the use of the photos as essential elements of the sto-

ries. *Star Tribune* ombudsman Lou Gelfund, while advocating a moratorium on broken-heart photos, also noted that neither picture had been taken surreptitiously. Marques fell to his knees as he was talking with the photographer, and Hanson was aware of the presence of the photographer in the restaurant where he and his friends and other news people awaited word from the search for his former girlfriend.[63] Thus, while it might be emotionally tempting to discard such visual portrayals of life's most tragic moments, contextual factors such as those described here are always essential ingredients in the moral reasoning process. In this way prurient interest becomes more readily distinguishable from the public interest.

The coverage of large tragedies is particularly challenging to the media. Under such circumstances a herd instinct often takes over as reporters and photographers camp out in front of the homes of surviving family members. Such was the case when journalists set out to interview the relatives of some of the 241 American marines who were killed in the bombing in Beirut in 1983. The families of the American Embassy personnel who were taken hostage in Iran four years earlier were subjected to similar media scrutiny.

At times, some invasion of privacy may be justified, especially when a firsthand account is essential to the audience's understanding of the story. But competitive pressures can also lead to unwarranted invasions of privacy and harassment. Such journalistic vigils are sometimes seen as rather ghoulish by members of the public. And such glaring displays of moral insensitivity, even if they are unusual or relatively rare, can further erode media respectability.

Computers and Database Journalism

Several years ago, the *Seattle Times* used computer data on everything from parking tickets to detectives' expense vouchers to prove how a police investigation into the deaths of forty-six women was botched. At about the same time, reporters at Knight-Ridder's Washington bureau uncovered unusually high death rates at several hospitals around the country by analyzing computerized Medicare records of open-heart surgeries. And when three Rhode Island children were hit and killed in three separate school bus accidents, the *Providence Journal* cross-checked its list of bus driver licenses to a tape of traffic accidents. The paper discovered that some bus drivers had been ticketed as many as twenty times over a three-year period. That information, coupled with the tape of criminal convictions, showed that several drivers were convicted felons. As a result, licensing procedures were improved and buses were made safer.[64]

These are all examples of investigative journalism in the finest tradition of the craft. But these stories would have been difficult, if not impossible, without the use of computers. Computer networks have revolutionized investigative reporting with their virtually endless storage and retrieval capacity. But when government accumulates so much data on so many people—information that is easily assessible by third parties (e.g., reporters)—the potential for mischief is intensified. Under such circumstance, public knowledge must sometimes give ground to other competing values. And chief among these moral claimants is the individual's interest in privacy.

The now famous Warren and Brandeis article, described earlier, arguing for legal recognition of a right to privacy, was written in response to reporters crashing a party at Warren's house. In writing the article, the authors undoubtedly sensed that something significant and pernicious had forever altered the standards of etiquette. If they were alive today, they would undoubtedly have the same sense of moral foreboding in confronting the challenges of computer technology.

Government public records have traditionally provided a bountiful repository of information for investigative reporters, but the use of computers and government databases has expanded their horizons exponentially. The sheer drudgery of physically perusing "hard copies" of documents has been replaced by the facility of accessing data banks directly from the newsroom or even from the comfort of a reporter's home.

Like any technology, computers provide a seductive tool for improving the quantity and quality of communication. But no innovation has so crystallized the conflicting values inherent in the individual's right to privacy, media access to information, and the public's right to know. Journalists have long relied on the wealth of information available in public records, but members of the public are discovering, much to their consternation, that a lot of identifying information about themselves can be accessed from government files. And they are beginning to fight back. In response to pressure from their constituents, legislators across the country have begun to seal some databases, such as voter registration lists, vital statistics, and land transfer records. Perhaps the most visible example of this frenzied legislative activity was the Congressional passage, in 1994, of the Driver's Privacy Protection Act, a federal mandate requiring the states to limit access to driver's license and car registration records containing personal information.[65]

But these legislative initiatives, the result more of political pressure than intelligent deliberation of policy issues, have left the ethical questions unresolved. As noted earlier in this text, technology is ethically neutral. It enters society in neither a virtuous nor a corrupt state. Thus, computers are the obedient servants of the moral agents that use them. The most visible example of this is the Internet, which is a repository of useful consumer information while also serving as a platform for the dissemination of hate speech and pornography.

On the positive side, computer databases can assist journalists in fulfilling their role as government watchdogs. The media's exposure of government wrongdoing instills confidence in the media as fiduciaries of the average citizen and assures them of some degree of governmental accountability.[66] The use of computers can also bring reporters to "a new level of activism" in their reporting,[67] providing quick access to a wealth of information, reducing the time for data collection, and freeing them up to analyze the data, develop relationships and correlations among diverse information, and reflect on its significance.

On the other hand, indiscriminate access to government data banks does raise privacy concerns, particularly when the information is used for a purpose other than that for which it is retrieved. For example, as private economic enterprises media might be tempted to use news-gathering computer tapes for marketing purposes, such as developing a potential subscriber list from the wealth of demographic information yielded by the tapes.[68] In addition, the inaccuracy of some of the database information is well documented, as evidenced by the trials and tribulations of those who have attempted to get a false credit record expunged. Thus, the fact that information is retrieved, through an elaborate computer network, from government data banks does not relieve news organizations of the responsibility of corroborating the accuracy of that information. The use of computer data banks is no substitute for fact checking, as the *Boston Globe* discovered several years ago in preparing a series on money laundering across the United States. In analyzing the data, the paper discovered large and unexplainable swings in cash transactions reported in certain cities. Ultimately the discrepancies were traced to a clerk in Detroit, who occasionally added five zeroes to the actual figures—just to ease boredom.[69]

THE SEARCH FOR JOURNALISTIC GUIDELINES

The infinite variety of situations in which concerns about privacy can arise precludes the identification of specific criteria that will accommodate every contingency. But at least three moral values should provide the foundation for an ethics of privacy for media practitioners.

The first guideline is based on the notion of *respect for persons* as an end in itself. This idea is based, in part, on the Judeo-Christian creed described in Chapter 3. As autonomous individuals, we are all entitled to a certain amount of dignity, which should not be arbitrarily compromised for the sake of some slogan such as "the people's right to know." When invasions of privacy are inevitable, as when someone involuntarily becomes a subject of public interest, the goal should be to minimize the harm.

The second value is that of *social utility*. The moral agent must decide what information is essential or at least useful to the audience in understanding the message being communicated. This principle eliminates appeals to sensationalism, morbid curiosity, ridicule, and voyeurism as a justification for invasion of privacy.

The third principle is based on the notion of *justice*. You may recall that in Chapter 2, I defined justice in terms of what one deserves. Moral agents are obliged to render judgments based on how much privacy their subjects really deserve under the circumstances. Public officials who are accused of violating their oath of office would, under most circumstances, deserve less privacy than victims of human tragedy. Certainly, the degree of "voluntariness," or purposeful behavior, is a consideration in deciding what kind of treatment an actor really deserves.

Unfortunately, the industry codes offer little guidance or practical advice in the area of privacy. But many news organizations do have policies related to particular kinds of sensitive information, for example, the publication of the names of rape victims, the identification of juvenile offenders and victims of crime, and the coverage of tragedies and accidents. But the effectiveness of such guidelines, even where they exist, depends on the good-faith efforts of management and staff to abide by them day in and day out. A continuous in-house review of ethics policies and an ongoing dialogue of dilemmas that arise within the newsroom can increase the moral sensitivity of company personnel to privacy concerns.

ADVERTISING AND PRIVACY

Advertising is ubiquitous. It not only intrudes into the privacy of our homes. It competes for our attention on billboards at athletic events, in the skies overhead on the sides of blimps, at movie theaters, and in public transportation. Advertising relentlessly seeks us out, marketing everything from fast foods to feminine hygiene products.

Since we willingly relinquish a certain amount of privacy by venturing into public places, advertising prominently displayed in such arenas does not generally give rise to privacy concerns. But advertising that enters our home—even by tacit approval through the purchase of a radio or TV set or a computer—does implicate privacy interests. Under such circumstances, advertising might be viewed as a guest. It is welcome to stay (or at least tolerated) as long as certain minimum standards of decorum are maintained. Ads that are too loud or offensive in their delivery offend these standards. Likewise, exaggerated claims that exploit consumer ignorance or insult their intelligence are problematic.[70] But what about ads that are simply in poor taste? Some commentators believe that matters of tastes are not serious enough to raise ethical concerns.[71] In their view, concerns about taste belong to the more genteel domain of etiquette rather than the more probing realm of morality. And this argument certainly holds some appeal. But when advertisers seek us out in our private spheres and offend our sensibilities with tasteless messages, then the line between etiquette and ethics is at the least ambiguous. If advertisers have any responsibility for their content—and they certainly do—then part of that responsibility must be moral in character.

Advertising has also been accused of promoting superficial values, such as sex appeal, the connection between materialism and happiness, self-esteem and stereotypes. To the extent that this accusation is true, advertising competes with the primary societal unit (the family) for control of the socialization process. For advertising critics, this is particularly troublesome when children are exposed to such unfiltered commercial messages.

In the not too distant past, certain advertising "guests" were never welcome, particularly in the electronic media. At one time, for example, feminine hygiene and condom ads were considered taboo. Today, it seems, there are few legal products that have not found their advertising niche. Defenders of unfettered access argue that any lawful product should have the right (both legally and ethically) to advertise. Opponents contend that, at least where the electronic media are concerned, advertisements for some personal products (e.g., condoms) should be rejected because they are *inherently offensive*, even if the ads themselves are in good taste. In other words, because radio, TV, and computer-transmitted ads do seek us out in the privacy of our homes, privacy concerns should be greater than in other situations.

PRIVACY: HYPOTHETICAL CASE STUDIES

The cases that follow represent a wide range of privacy issues, although they are by no means exhaustive. In applying the moral reasoning model outlined in Chapter 3, you should keep in mind the three primary philosophical approaches. Because privacy is a fundamental value, duty-based moral agents (deontologists) believe that the consequences of one's actions are always subordinate to the ethical principle itself. Thus, invasions of privacy cannot always be justified on the ground that society will somehow benefit. The value of privacy can be overridden only in the face of some more compelling principle. For example, a reporter might feel obliged to report a case of apparent child abuse even if it meant intruding into the privacy of a family relationship. Thus, a journalist's commitment to truth, which also embraces a moral duty, can justify invasions of privacy when individuals become newsworthy and can then be said to have relinquished their privacy. As always, duty-based theorists confront difficult choices when two equally compelling principles compete for their allegiance.

A consequentialist (teleologist), as noted earlier, examines the potential consequences of the decision. The public good is always a consideration here. Teleologists, although certainly not oblivious to the harm to individuals, look at the impact of the moral choice. In some cases, such as the utilitarian variety of teleology, the moral agent will consider the consequence to the greatest number of people. At other times the consequence to individuals or small groups will be of primary concern. In applying the guidelines outlined for an ethics of privacy, however, even consequentialists must justify invasions of privacy based on some competing principle(s) and, in so doing, should not cause more harm than is justified by their decision.

A virtue ethicist, in applying Aristotle's golden mean, searches for some mean position between two extremes. Of course, in invasion of privacy cases, this course is not always possible, but some situations do provide an opportunity to limit the intrusion or to make its impact more palatable. Television advertising, for example, is by its nature intrusive and invades the privacy of our home. Of course, commercials are here to stay, but the advertisers have an obligation not to offend the sensibilities of the audience. In other words, making TV a welcome guest in the home is a reasonable accommodation between banning intrusive advertising altogether and not having any standards at all.

◄ C A S E   S T U D I E S ►

► CASE 5-1
Lesbianism as a Private Matter in Public Life

Newport Ridge is a thriving community of 250,000 on the eastern fringe of the Midwest farm belt. Like most communities, the Great Depression had left its legacy in Newport, and the city's political leaders had been quick to embrace the economic salvation of Franklin Roosevelt's New Deal. For fifty years Newport had been a Democratic Party stronghold, and Republican challengers were routinely denied access to the corridors of power at the local level. But the "Reagan revolution" of the 1980s had dramatically changed Newport's political landscape. Weary of double-digit inflation, the perceived permissiveness, and the increasingly higher tax burden to pay for the endless menu of social programs, Newport's voters had abandoned traditional party loyalties for the more conservative Republican agenda.

But as the November elections approached, two-term Republican incumbent Howard Sasser was in trouble in his bid for a third term as Newport's mayor. The mayor's failure to fulfill a campaign promise to reduce local property taxes and a high unemployment rate had led to voter disaffection, resulting in a popularity rating of less than 50 percent according to the latest polls. For the first time in fifteen years, the political pundits saw an opportunity for the Democrats to recapture the reins of city government.

And Democratic challenger Linda Blairstone was certainly an opportunist. Blairstone was the daughter of five-term senator Jason Blairstone, who had been swept out of power in 1994 when the Republicans seized control of both houses of Congress for the first time in forty years. The senator's close association with the policies of the Clinton Administration were certainly to blame for his political demise, but his sponsorship of a controversial bill to prohibit the military from discriminating against gays had also offended many members of his increasingly conservative constituency. His supporters defended the senator's actions as a manifestation of his nonjudgmental character. But the Washington rumor mill was less charitable: the senator had identified with the victims of homophobia because of his own daughter's sexual orientation. The rumors surfaced among journalists and some political insiders in Newport just as Linda Blairstone was beginning her bid for public office but went unreported in the local media.

Linda Blairstone was *not* her father's daughter, politically speaking. She had not used her father's influence to gain favor with local party leaders and had carefully avoided any association with the senator's liberal agenda. Blairstone was a thirty-two-year-old attorney whose political experience consisted primarily of a seat on the local school board, but she had never concealed her interest in a career in public life. The mayor's office, in her judgment, was an ideal point of departure for an education in grassroots politics en route to more substantial political rewards.

Blairstone felt confident as she approached the first of three televised political debates with Sasser just six weeks before the election. As an attorney, she was a skilled debater and prepared to exploit the incumbent's political vulnerabilities. Most of the hour of allotted airtime was spent responding to reporters' questions and in verbal sparring over such local concerns as property taxes, sewage and drainage repairs, unemployment, and more effective police and fire protection. But the last question came from the political correspondent for the *Newport Ridge Gazette*, who wanted to know the candidates' position on the state's antigay initiative that would also be on the November ballot. The measure would deny citizens a variety of civil rights

based strictly on sexual orientation. Without hesitation, Sasser said he supported the proposition because he did not believe anyone should be given special privileges just because of his or her lifestyle. And the public agreed, Sasser noted confidently, because polls conducted among registered voters in Newport revealed a two-to-one margin in favor of the proposition. But Blairstone was less resolute in her response: "I was under the impression the purpose of this debate was to solicit our views on local issues. I don't want to get into all of the state propositions on the ballot, although I am concerned that the antigay measure may run afoul of the state's constitution. In any event, the state's voters will have an opportunity to express themselves on this matter in November."

Mike Tross viewed this reply with more than passing curiosity, particularly in light of the rumors that had surfaced shortly after Blairstone's entry into the race six months ago. Tross was the chief political reporter for Channel 5 in Newport, one of three network affiliates that served the community. He had been among the panelists interrogating the two candidates during the debate and decided that Blairstone's rather evasive response to the last question justified a follow-up phone call. The reporter reasoned that either the candidate had no opinion on the antigay initiative, which was unlikely, or that there were ulterior motives for her lack of candor. Tross decided to confront Blairstone directly concerning the rumors about her personal life and called her two hours after the debate. "I won't respond to such questions," she declared. "My personal life is none of your business."

Early the next morning, Tross briefed Channel 5's news director, Nathan Howser, on his conversation with the young mayoral aspirant. Howser then convened a meeting with Tross, Assignment Editor Louis Sinclair, and News Producer Cindy Lake to discuss the matter.

"The rumors are still out there that she's a lesbian," volunteered Tross, in referring to Blairstone's rather oblique response at last night's debate. "And I have several sources who can confirm this. Most don't want to go on the record, although one of her former campaign workers is willing to talk. I also know that she once represented a client who sued his employer for firing him because he was gay. However, nothing has been reported in the media, and at this point there doesn't appear to be much public discussion of the matter. Most of the voters probably aren't even aware of the rumors."

"Then is there any reason to refer to her lifestyle in our reporting of the campaign? Is it newsworthy or a matter of public interest?" asked Howser.

"It may be," replied Tross. "Her last response during the debate raised the issue, even if somewhat indirectly. She clearly did not want to answer the question truthfully. As a lesbian, she *must* be opposed to this antigay initiative. But if Blairstone had been candid, she could lose the election— and her answer might even raise questions concerning her private life, particularly if the rumors become more widespread. For the sake of fairness, of course, we should include her 'no comment' in any report that we do about her alleged lesbianism."

"Speaking of fairness," said Howser, "I wonder if your brief telephone interview was fair. Blairstone really had to make a choice between lying or telling the truth, in which case she could kiss the mayor's race good-bye. She chose to say 'no comment,' but you know how our viewers will interpret that response."

"I agree with Nathan," declared Lake emphatically. "This is a private matter that has nothing to do with her fitness for public office. And so what if she were less than candid during the debate! I'll admit that Blairstone was probably concerned about the political fallout if she were to come out strongly in opposition to the measure. But it's just as likely that she was afraid of being 'outed' if there were follow-up questions concerning what clearly would have been an unpopular position."

"But Blairstone is a public person. She is seeking elected office. There are rumors out there concerning her sexual orientation, and I think we have a responsibility to deal with them. Public officials should not expect the same treatment as private persons. And there's another angle," continued Tross. "Keep in mind Senator Blairstone's sponsorship of the bill to prohibit discrimination against gays in the military. Perhaps his daughter's sexual orientation influenced his thinking on this issue. If

so, that would certainly make this a matter of public interest."

"But even if it's true that his daughter's lifestyle influenced his thinking on this issue, the senator's sponsorship of this legislation, does this justify our delving into her private life?" asked Sinclair. "I don't see the connection. Does the public need to know about her sexual orientation?"

Tross was unmoved. "Yes. I think it's newsworthy because the voters are about to approve this antigay measure by a two-to-one margin, if the polls are accurate. The voters certainly have a right to know that one of the candidates on the same ballot as the antigay initiative is a lesbian. This is certainly unusual—and that makes it news."

Howser was not so sure, but he had to admit that Tross had a point. There was a certain irony in the voters expressing their disapproval of the gay and lesbian lifestyle, while unwittingly electing a candidate who is a lesbian. Should the voters be told in advance? Or would this be an unwarranted intrusion into Linda Blairstone's private life? Everyone in Channel 5's newsroom had an opinion, but Nathan Howser was the moral agent who would have the responsibility of rendering an ethical judgment in this matter.

THE CASE STUDY

This case represents a classic ethical debate concerning the private lives of public persons. Some argue that those who seek public office relinquish all rights to privacy. And, certainly, the relentless snooping of both the mainstream and tabloid media into the private affairs of public officials—a preoccupation that often borders on journalistic voyeurism—lends credence to this argument. The zone of privacy for public officials and public figures has certainly shrunk and perhaps dissipated in recent years. But such an absolutist position is devoid of sound moral reasoning because it ignores the respect for persons that is due for any object of our ethical decision making, including those in public life.

On the other hand, those running for public office must expect more rigorous scrutiny than the ordinary citizen, particularly when private matters relate to their fitness for office or some other matter of public interest. But even reasonable people can disagree over the application of these standards, as evidenced in this scenario.

For example, the political reporter, Mike Tross, believes that the candidate's sexual orientation is newsworthy because it helps explain her evasive response to the question concerning her stance on the antigay measure. He also appears to believe the voters have a right to know about her lesbianism, even if it does not relate to her fitness for office, since they are about to approve this initiative.

However, assignment editor Louis Sinclair and news producer Cindy Lake have some strong reservations about revealing her sexual orientation. They see little public purpose to be served by revealing this aspect of her private life. While they admit that Blairstone was less than candid during the debate, they are more willing than Tross to accept this moral indiscretion out of fairness to the candidate.

Assume the role of news director Nathan Howser. Should your station include the candidate's sexual orientation in your coverage of this campaign? If so, can you justify this decision on the grounds of newsworthiness, or would it be an unjustified invasion of privacy? Using the moral reasoning model outlined in Chapter 3, render an ethical judgment in this matter, and defend your decision.

▶ CASE 5-2
The Unwilling Witness

Traci Cameron was one of the most highly recruited academic prospects to enroll at Briarwood College for the fall semester. As the valedictorian of her high school class and with a composite ACT score of 32, Cameron was among the best and the brightest in Briarwood's freshman class. She had arrived at the prestigious liberal arts school with an optimistic outlook and undisguised confidence. Within two weeks after her arrival on campus, Traci Cameron was dead, the victim of a rape and strangulation. Her brutal murder shocked the usually tranquil Greenville community. It also set off a spirited ethical debate within the newsroom at the *Greenville Enquirer*.

Martin Johnson had joined the staff of the *Enquirer* three years before as a general assignment reporter after receiving his BA in journalism from Briarwood. After only a few months, he had moved to the police beat, a task he found to be agonizingly mundane in light of the community's impressively low crime rate. The police blotter was usually nothing more than a monotonous chronicle, and Johnson's daily accounts of shoplifting, automobile thefts, and brawls at the County Line Bar did little to cultivate his reportorial talents. But Traci Cameron's murder had revitalized his journalistic enterprise.

Johnson had first been alerted to the crime through an unusual amount of frantic chatter on the police scanner. When he arrived on the scene at the Woodlawn Apartments, where the young freshman co-ed shared a two-bedroom flat with her roommate near the Briarwood campus, the police investigation was in full swing. A reporter from a local radio station was already peppering detective Lieutenant Mark Davidson with questions. Johnson respected Lieutenant Davidson because of his sincere desire to assist the media, within the bounds of law enforcement propriety of course.

Johnson quickly joined the impromptu interrogation, forcing the usually patient detective to repeat many of the details of the murder. Davidson told the young reporter that the victim's name was Traci Cameron, a freshman at Briarwood. Her roommate, Mona Lambert, had returned late from the library and saw a man standing over Cameron's nude body. Lambert then fled to a neighbor's apartment and called police. As Davidson concluded the interview and prepared to return to the crime scene, he asked Johnson not to include Lambert's name in his story. "The killer is still at large," he said, "and it might help our investigation if we can keep her name off the front pages for awhile."

Johnson made no promises and quickly retreated to the *Enquirer*'s newsroom to record his notes in his computer's memory. As he translated his handwritten notes into electronic images, he heard his broadcast competitor's account of the murder. The station reported that Cameron's body had been discovered by her roommate who, according to police, had seen the killer. However, the story did not include the roommate's name.

Later in the day Johnson went to the police station and examined the report on the murder and then made a stop at the coroner's office, where he was greeted by the usually affable staff assistant who normally handled media inquiries. "Our preliminary investigation reveals the victim was raped and then strangled," he was told.

"Traci Cameron's roommate—the one who found the body—has requested anonymity," Johnson said. Johnson was seated at a small conference table with City Editor Don Gordon and Managing Editor Darrell Poindexter. The reporter had relayed the young woman's request to Gordon, who had hastily arranged a meeting with the managing editor. Johnson knew from experience that Poindexter, who relished a spirited newsroom discussion on journalism ethics, would be the moral agent in this case. Johnson welcomed the opportunity, even under deadline pressure, to deliberate the ethical dimensions of his report. But he was surprised at the apparent disagreement between his two more experienced journalistic brethren, both of whom had impressive professional credentials.

"The roommate's name is Mona Lambert," continued Johnson. "Lambert says she's having a hard time dealing with this and doesn't want her name in the paper. She just wants to be left alone."

"Where did you get the name?" asked Gordon.

"Lieutenant Davidson gave me the name but asked that it not be included in the story," responded Johnson. "The police report just lists her as 'Jane Doe,' but it does describe her as the victim's roommate. When I called Lambert to get some additional information, that's when she said she didn't want her name in the paper."

"Lambert obviously wants to protect her privacy," responded Poindexter. "And she's had a traumatic experience. Publication of her name might just cause more grief. Is it really essential to the story? Why don't we just identify her as 'Jane Doe' without referring to her as Cameron's room-

mate?" At times like this Poindexter's journalistic instincts pushed him in the direction of full disclosure, but he enjoyed challenging the moral acumen of his staff. Besides, as a manager his decision making always focused on what was in the paper's best interest, which did not always harmonize with the predispositions of his reporters and editors.

"Because she's newsworthy, whether she wants to be or not," replied Gordon rather testily. "Lambert is a part of the puzzle. It's significant that she discovered the body. Besides, the police report, which is a public record, has already listed her as Cameron's roommate, and the radio station has included this in its report of the murder. It seems to me she has already lost whatever privacy she might desire."

"I agree," said Johnson. He felt uncomfortable in this ethical crossfire between Gordon and the managing editor, but he summoned the courage to defend his turf. "I'm sympathetic to Lambert's predicament. But since the radio station has reported that Cameron's body was discovered by her roommate, for all practical purposes she has been identified, even if her name doesn't appear in the record. And since the police report does list the relationship of the witness to the victim, then this makes Lambert newsworthy. She is part of the investigation."

But Poindexter was not prepared to concede the point. "I don't think we should take our ethical cues from our competitors—in this case a radio station—even if they have reported that Cameron's body was discovered by her roommate. And I'm not so sure that the privacy issue is moot, just because the witness has been identified as Cameron's roommate. Lambert is new on campus. How many people know who she is or where she lives? Only a few friends. If her name is published in connection with this murder, the whole world will know. I still think her privacy concerns are important. I realize she's part of the story. And in this sense Lambert is newsworthy. But sometimes we have to weigh these news judgments against the potential harm that a story might cause to an innocent third party."

"There may be some risk of harm to Lambert,"

admitted the city editor. "But she appears more concerned with her own privacy than anything else. If we acquiesce to every request for anonymity from those who, through no fault of their own, become newsworthy, then our coverage will become an exercise in self censorship. The *Enquirer* will cease to be an independent voice; we'll lose credibility with our readers."

"You may have a point; credibility is a concern," Poindexter admitted in acknowledging his role as institutional gatekeeper. "Yet, there are times when journalists need to exercise more compassion—innocent parties still have a right to their privacy. But is this really such a case?"

During the debate, Poindexter was not insensitive to the arguments of Johnson and his city editor, and he had played devil's advocate in order to sharpen their critical skills. But he also felt a moral responsibility to those who might be harmed by the news coverage provided by the *Enquirer*. As the deadline approached, the managing editor reflected on the competing interests and values implicated in this ethical dilemma.

THE CASE STUDY

This case involves one of the more troublesome ethical dilemmas for journalists: an innocent person who unwillingly becomes linked with a newsworthy event and then expresses a desire to protect her privacy. The conflict that results from journalists' ethical imperative to balance their professional responsibilities with the need for compassion is captured in this observation on privacy in *Doing Ethics in Journalism*:

> Harm from privacy invasion is almost certain, but it is more difficult for a journalist to fully identify benefits from an intrusion. Thus, it is important to recognize that the primary ethical obligation of journalism is to *inform the public by seeking truth and reporting it as fully as possible.* That obligation must then be balanced against the obligation to respect individuals and their privacy.[72]

In this scenario, Lambert is apparently having difficulty coping with her roommate's untimely death and would like to maintain some semblance of solitude, despite the personal tragedy that has interrupted her peaceful existence. Lambert's plea for anonymity is an appeal to compassion and respect for her as an innocent person. Lambert believes that there is still a zone of privacy that needs protecting, even though her relationship to the victim has been established in the public record and the broadcast report of the crime. This concern is also reflected in Poindexter's comment that if her name is published in the paper, then "the whole world will know" of her connection to this brutal homicide.

Johnson is not unsympathetic, but the reporter's professional training and experience impel him toward including all relevant information in his account of Traci Cameron's murder. There are occasions, of course, when privacy concerns should prevail where an individual's inclusion in a story is of little demonstrable public interest. But in this case the victim's roommate, who discovered the body and is also a material witness, is a central figure in this investigation. She is clearly newsworthy. Nevertheless, the murderer is still at large, and Lambert is still apparently traumatized by her ordeal. Will the paper's credibility really suffer if they honor her request? The paper might consider withholding Lambert's identity until the murderer is apprehended, but that may do little to assuage her privacy concerns.

You are Managing Editor Darrell Poindexter and have assumed the role of moral agent in this case. Analyze this ethical dilemma, applying the moral reasoning model outlined in Chapter 3. In making your decision, you should consider the following questions:

1. Is the name of the witness essential to the story? Is the story incomplete without the name?

2. If the name is important to the story, are the privacy concerns sufficiently compelling to overcome the "newsworthiness" arguments in favor of inclusion?

3. Although Lambert's name is not specifically included in the public record report of the crime, does the fact that she is identified as the victim's roommate undermine her privacy claims?

4. Does the fact that a broadcast competitor has already identified Lambert as the victim's roommate justify a similar decision by the newspaper?

▶ **CASE 5-3**
Rape and Race: A Double Standard

The attack on Senator Jerome Mencer's young aide might have remained a little-noticed local crime story on the inside pages of the *Washington Post* had it not been for the senator's verbal harangue about the lack of law and order in the nation's capital. The twenty-one-year-old assistant had been bicycling in Rock Creek Park when, according to police reports, she was accosted by five or six black youths and savagely beaten and raped. This attack prompted Mencer, whose committee was considering support for local law enforcement agencies, to unleash a colorful rhetorical broadside against the already beleaguered Washington police establishment.

"We have the highest crime rate in the nation," the senator lamented during an impromptu press conference. "This kind of attack on innocent citizens is an outrage. No one is safe here. It's clear that whatever the police are doing isn't working." The senator's remarks, along with the brutality of the attack in the nation's capital, propelled the story into the national consciousness. It soon became front-page copy and figured prominently in the network newscasts for several days.

The juvenile suspects were apprehended, and their names were reported in most of the media. Although many news organizations have policies relating to the publication of names of youthful offenders, it is not unusual for the identities of juveniles involved in serious crimes to be reported. But this story about violent crime and brutality against women was soon consumed by a new, potentially explosive twist. Undercurrents of racism crept into the public debates about the case. Many newspapers (including the *Washington Post*) were flooded with letters demanding swift and harsh punishment for the suspects. The airwaves were filled

with similar calls, and the various talk shows were peppered with tough law-and-order rhetoric, some of it filled with racial epithets.

Black leaders, in a city where racial tensions were already high, responded by accusing the "white-dominated news media" of fanning the flames of racism by publishing the juveniles' names and identifying them as black while not publishing the name of their accuser, the victim of the attack. One black minister even voiced the opinion that the whole thing was a hoax, alleging that the woman had really been the victim of "rough sex" during a date but needed some scapegoats to conceal the reality of her embarrassing predicament.

Jeremiah Jacobi, managing editor of the *Afro-American Beacon*, felt the harsh tug of competing loyalties as he pondered how this paper should cover the story. The Beacon is a black Washington weekly that was established as a voice of moderation within the black community. Its news and editorial policies are designed to walk the delicate tightrope between appealing to the sense of cultural identity within the black community and at the same time promoting a sense of mutual understanding between blacks and whites. For the most part, the paper has been successful and enjoys respect and credibility among both whites and blacks.

As a journalist, Jacobi feared that the aura of racial politics might obscure the real story about this heinous crime. It would just damage further the already strained relations between blacks and whites if this became a racial issue.

Although the *Beacon* published an account of the incident (including the fact that the attackers were believed to be black), it followed its long-standing policy of not publishing the names of the juvenile suspects or the victim. Jacobi believed that publishing the names of youthful offenders was an unwarranted invasion of privacy that could have a long-lasting effect on the recalcitrant juveniles and thus impede the process of rehabilitation. As for victims, the editor saw no value in publishing their names and magnifying what was already a traumatic experience.

However, Jacobi was being pressured by certain members of his constituency, including several influential advertisers (black-owned businesses) to publish the name of the victim. Some black journalists echoed this sentiment and accused the "establishment media" of a bias toward white rape victims by withholding their names while publicizing the identities of black youths accused of serious crimes.[73]

Although the *Beacon* had always followed a policy of not publishing the names of rape victims, in the past both the victims and the assailants had been black, and the stories had attracted little attention outside the community. But this was a crime story of national import, a controversy with racial overtones.

If Jacobi did not publish the name of the victim, he might be accused of acquiescing to the journalistic "standards" imposed by the mainstream white media. On the other hand, to do so would invite charges from the white community of an unwarranted intrusion into her privacy. This, Jacobi knew, would be viewed as an irresponsible act and might damage the paper's credibility within the white community. He would be accused of having subordinated professional judgment to racial loyalty. In addition, if he revealed the name of the victim, would he not, for the sake of even-handedness, be obliged to publish the names of the suspects?

Either way, his decision, like the story itself, would appear to be motivated by racial considerations. Was there, Jacobi wondered, an ethical way of dealing with this story without alienating either the black or white communities? Were the privacy interests here more important than the public's need to know the identities of all parties for the sake of balanced coverage?

THE CASE STUDY

This is not a typical privacy case involving the publication of the names of youthful offenders and rape victims. It raises the issue of questionable motivations on the part of the moral agent. Assume the role of Jacobi, and, using the SAD Formula for moral reasoning, decide how this story should be covered. You might begin with the broader question of why rape victims or juvenile suspects should or should not be publicly identified as part of any legitimate news story. If your response is a qualified one, note the exceptions, and then ask yourself whether this case falls within those exceptions.

The identities of the suspects have already been published in other media outlets. Does this diminish the ethical responsibility of the Beacon if it should follow suit?

Perhaps one way to refocus the public's attention on this incident as a crime story is to play down the race of the suspects and attempt to humanize this drama from the victim's perspective. But this tactic might necessitate revealing her identity and perhaps even attempting to interview her. Would this invasion of her privacy be justified under the circumstances?

Finally, as the managing editor of the *Afro-American Beacon*, your decision will come down to this: should you resolve this privacy issue based on the paper's role as a voice of the black community or as a responsible member of the journalistic community at large? Are the two roles necessarily incompatible?

▶ ## CASE 5-4
AIDS and the Right to Privacy

To the citizens of Scotlandville, football was more than a weekend diversion. It was a way of life, a passionate preoccupation to which both religion and politics gave way as topics of conversation during the autumn season. Attendance at the Friday night clashes between Scotlandville High and their usually outmatched opponents was a patriotic duty not unlike a Memorial Day barbecue or a Fourth of July fireworks display.

Scotlandville was a community of only 25,000, but its high school's reputation as a football factory was legendary, thus making it a favorite haunt for college recruiters. The Scotlandville Wildcats were undefeated in forty-four games, the longest winning streak of any high school team in its class. The last time the Wildcats had suffered two losing seasons in a row was fifteen years before, a debacle that had led to the early retirement of the team's long-suffering coach.

It did not take the present coach, Stan Morrell, long to renew the winning spirit of the Wildcats. In his first season the team lost three games, but in the thirteen subsequent years the Wildcats won three state championships. Morrell was a no-nonsense disciplinarian who used both verbal and physical abuse to motivate his young charges. He would brook no "sissies" on his team, but his coaching techniques were of little concern to the school board or the avid fans of Scotlandville as long as he produced champions.

Expectations were again high as Morrell stepped to the podium to conduct his first press conference before the season's opener. Scotlandville was not large enough to deserve a TV station of its own, but the coach's winning record, good humor, and dramatic flair attracted the attention of both radio and television stations from surrounding communities. In addition, Scotlandville's only licensed radio station and the local paper, the Scotlandville Courant, were always on hand.

But this was not to be a typical Morrell press conference. Usually the coach would begin these sessions with a wisecrack and then discuss the prospects for the upcoming season, understating the team's talent and experience so as to lower the expectations of the loyal Wildcat supporters. Of course, this approach was a common practice among coaches, and the fans had learned to ignore his warnings about impending doom. This time his remarks could not be ignored. After a few preliminary comments, Morrell announced that Billy Hargus, the star running back and all-state prospect, would not start the season because of treatment for a debilitating illness. He would not elaborate but said the decision had been made after consultation with the Harguses' family physician. Normally, this might not have been devastating news for a team with a depth chart of the caliber of the Wildcats, but the second- and third-stringers were inexperienced and lacked the confidence of a Billy Hargus. Wildcat supporters—which included virtually every Scotlandville citizen—speculated publicly about the effects of the young running back's absence on the team's prospects for another championship. They were also curious about what adjustments Morrell would make to compensate for the loss.

Raymond Anderson was curious, too. Anderson was sports editor of the Scotlandville Courant and looked forward to his exclusive weekly interviews with Morrell. Anderson had majored in journalism at the University of Missouri, but his enthusiasm for sports had quickly overshadowed the coverage of politics, civil rights, and poverty as a lifetime commitment. On graduation he had returned to his hometown and for the previous ten years had covered sports for the Courant.

At Morrell's first interview after the press conference, the coach spent the first few minutes briefing Anderson on what changes he would have to make to compensate for Hargus's loss. The sports editor then inquired about the nature of the young football star's illness. Anderson was not prepared for the coach's response: Hargus had AIDS and would not return to the team that season. Morrell told Anderson that Billy's condition had been diagnosed by the family physician three months before. His parents had confided in the school principal, a compassionate and sympathetic man, who had agreed to allow Hargus to continue to attend classes. He had also promised confidentiality in the matter but felt duty bound to inform Morrell, because he had the responsibility for the young athlete's well-being on the football field. It was Morrell who had recommended to Hargus's parents that he quit the team.

The coach had not made his comments off the record and had solicited no promise of confidentiality from Anderson. And now the sports editor was confronted with the most troubling ethical dilemma of his career: should he report the real cause of Hargus's absence from the team?

On the one hand, Anderson had already heard speculation about the star athlete's medical condition, speculation that was prompted by Morrell's public declaration of the illness, even if no details were provided. Besides, Anderson reasoned, even at age seventeen Hargus was a local celebrity, a youthful public figure whose football exploits were highlighted weekly by the sports-hungry press. His absence from the team was certainly a matter of public interest. It was probably only a matter of time before other reporters picked up the scent and began asking questions. Anderson could not even be sure that the coach had not fed this story to his competitors. Was Hargus entitled, then, to the same right to privacy as his lesser-known classmates?

On the other hand, despite his celebrity status, Hargus was still an adolescent, in need of nurturing and in search of maturity. How would he handle the revelation of his condition emotionally? Despite the publicity campaigns regarding AIDS, the public's ignorance concerning the disease was astounding. Hargus might even be shunned by his classmates, and, in the worst-case scenario, some parents might withdraw their children from school. This had certainly been the pattern in some communities where youthful AIDS victims had attempted, often under court order, to reclaim their rightful places in the public school system.

But did the parents of Scotlandville not have a right to know that an AIDS victim was attending their school, even if the scientific evidence suggested that the disease was not contagious through casual contact? What were the sports editor's obligations to the community? Perhaps, Anderson rationalized, it should be the school principal's responsibility to deal with this problem, not his.

Anderson knew that Scotlandville was a traditional, Bible Belt community, with conservative religious values. Having AIDS was tantamount to an admission of homosexuality, a mortal sin in the eyes of the pious citizens of Scotlandville. This might have explained the motivation of Morrell, hardly a paragon of tolerance, in cavalierly releasing this information to Anderson.

The day following the interview, Anderson sat in his small office at the *Courant* pondering the situation. He did not feel pressured to make a quick decision, but his mind soon became preoccupied with the ethical dimensions of his dilemma.

THE CASE STUDY

The coverage of AIDS presents one of the most difficult ethical problems confronting the news media. The disease itself is a matter of acute public interest, thereby making its victims the subject of social curiosity. When the case concerns celebrities or public officials, this curiosity is intensified. Of course, most people with AIDS are not newsworthy, but when they are involved in news stories or

matters of public interest, ethical considerations enter the picture. Under what conditions should the names of patients be identified in the media?

The scenario involving Hargus is, perhaps, a little unusual, but the questions posed by this case are not. At its most basic level, the case involves a clash between two competing principles: the right to privacy and the public's right to know that a person with AIDS is attending its high school.

Most ethical dilemmas can be approached by posing a series of relevant questions and answering them to your satisfaction. For example, the following questions would appear to be relevant to this inquiry:

1. Does the story concern a matter of public interest?

2. Should the fact that Morrell first publicly broached the issue of Hargus's condition (even though he provided no details) be viewed as an argument in favor of following up on the story and reporting details of the illness?

3. Should the fact that Hargus is a high school football player alter his "expectation of privacy"?

4. Does the public have a right to know that there is a youth with AIDS attending a public high school?

5. Is the fact that Hargus is a minor and a student, as well as an athlete, relevant to this issue?

6. Will the harm in disclosing the information be greater than withholding it?

Assume the role of the sports editor, Anderson, and render an ethical judgment in this matter. Your discussion should take into account the questions raised here, although you may wish to pose some of your own.

▶ ### CASE 5-5
The Teenage Runaway and Family Privacy

Overton's new law-and-order district attorney had promised to rid the community of pornography and "filth," and he was making good on his promise. After only one year of operation the Twin

Arts, Overton's only adult theater, had been raided by a team of plainclothes officers led by Sergeant Paul David, and its films had been confiscated.

Before the films were impounded, the DA decided to view the evidence in the privacy of his office. Also on hand were David and Louis Sanders, the police reporter for the *Overton Chronicle*. Sanders was covering the raid and its aftermath for the paper, and the DA saw nothing wrong with allowing the young reporter to look at the spoils of war. David watched the first film with some interest and then some boredom. But the second film, a poorly produced piece of sleaze entitled *Beast of Love*, caught his notice. The female star of the film was listed as Monique Maguire. He knew her as Sally Hawkins.

By all accounts Hawkins had had a happy childhood. As the daughter of a prominent family in Overton, she had been a model student at Knightwood Academy, a private grammar school. She had then opted to attend one of the public high schools in Overton, and it was there that her parents began to detect some disturbing changes in their daughter. She began running with the wrong crowd, experimenting with drugs, and skipping school. She became sullen, withdrawn, and uncommunicative. Her parents, in a desperate attempt to reach their daughter, even scheduled a couple of sessions with a therapist, but they seemed to magnify her apparent resentment. Finally, at sixteen, she dropped out of school entirely and ran away from home.

Donald and Martha Hawkins contacted the police and asked for help in finding their daughter, providing a recent school picture of her. David, who took the report, promised the couple that the police would do everything possible but said that the chances of retrieving her were not good.

Now, two years later, Hawkins had apparently returned to Overton, though not in the way her parents would have liked. Despite the makeup and some significant changes in the young porn star's appearance, David was convinced that Hawkins and Monique Maguire were the same. A comparison between the film and the two-year-old photo in the police files confirmed his belief. He mentioned his discovery to both the DA and Sanders.

David then contacted Donald and Martha Hawkins and told them he had a lead on their daughter. They were, of course, shocked at the details but relieved that there had finally been some word of Sally. At least she was alive!

Sanders also contacted Hawkins's parents and asked whether he could get some background information on their daughter. He told them he was preparing a story on the police raid for the next day's edition. Donald Hawkins asked the reporter not to reveal the real identity of the film star. Sanders made no promises but said he would consider the request.

The reporter recognized the conflict between privacy considerations and matters of public interest. Surely the story about the raid merited attention, but was it necessary to reveal the true identity of the porn star? On the other hand, news is based on the "unusual," and the fact that Monique Maguire was from a local family was certainly an interesting angle. Was the family more concerned about their privacy (and embarrassment) than that of their daughter? Would he be hesitating, Sanders wondered, if she had come from the "wrong side of the tracks" rather than the affluent area where she had been born? Also, possibly some of Hawkins's former acquaintances had seen the movie before it had been confiscated and even recognized her. Was total privacy really possible under the circumstances?

Sanders also wondered whether a story of this kind might serve as a warning to other parents of the perils of unrestrained adolescence. Much had been written and broadcast about runaways who had drifted into prostitution and the porno film industry, but here was a dramatic local example. Perhaps there was some social benefit to reporting the whole story.

Still, Sanders recognized the ethical pitfalls of this position, and he knew that a safe harbor would be simply to report the raid without unmasking the true identity of Monique Maguire.

THE CASE STUDY

Although this case would appear to be about Sally Hawkins, the privacy issue really revolves around her parents. One could argue that she "relinquished" her right to privacy (especially since she is no longer a juvenile) by appearing in a pornographic movie.

On the other hand, the Hawkinses are a prominent family, and they are fearful of having their privacy invaded by association with the film stardom of their estranged daughter. Of course, if she is identified, her parents' privacy will invariably be invaded. Are parents responsible for the sins of their children? In the public's collective mind, they sometimes are.

But Sanders does have a point. As the star of this film, Monique Maguire herself would probably have little news value, but the fact that a local runaway has been identified from the film is a matter of public interest. Should the family's privacy override this consideration?

For the purpose of resolving this ethical dilemma, assume the role of reporter and moral agent, and make a decision on this matter. In evaluating the pros and cons of this issue, utilize the SAD Formula.

▶ **CASE 5-6**
The Right to Die with Dignity

To his supporters, Dr. Michael Dvorak was an angel of mercy. To his detractors, he was possessed of a God complex that manifested itself in his arrogant defense of euthanasia as a morally acceptable solution for terminally ill patients. Dvorak, a rather controversial internist, had acquired a reputation as a medical gadfly and had lobbied relentlessly with the legislature for a "right to die" law that would institutionalize physician-assisted suicide for the terminally ill who freely chose to end their lives with dignity. He was viewed with some annoyance by the medical establishment, who still believed that euthanasia was an assault on the Hypocratic oath's prescription to *do no harm*. But opinion polls reflected increasing public support for Dvorak's legislative agenda and a law that would legalize physician-assisted suicide.

Nevertheless, the legislature, under pressure from the medical establishment, repeatedly rebuffed the right to die initiative while various special interest groups debated the ethics of euthanasia. But Dvorak grew impatient with the tediousness of the political process and decided to take matters into his own hands. When one of his patients, a woman, age fifty-four, who was in the terminal stages of multiple sclerosis, asked for his assistance in ending her life, he readily agreed. Dvorak's participation in the carbon monoxide death of his patient brought a quick response from Riverside County District Attorney Robert Nix. As a conservative Christian, Nix was a foe of euthanasia and relished the opportunity of bringing the unrepentant physician to justice. The DA obtained a murder indictment against Dvorak, but, following a six-day trial, with both national and local media in attendance, the jury acquitted him of the charge.

Emboldened by this legal triumph, Dvorak pledged to continue his assistance to any terminally ill patient who expressed a desire to die with dignity. District Attorney Nix was equally determined to resist what he considered to be the doctor's insane disregard for the sanctity of life and the laws of the state.

Three months after his acquittal, Dvorak was again front-page copy with reports that he had assisted a terminally ill cancer patient, sixty-two-year-old widow Helen Tate, to commit suicide, and again he was indicted for murder. The opening salvo was fired in this high-profile trial when the district attorney released statements by two of the woman's children disputing the doctor's claims that their mother wanted to die. "At times she did express a desire to end her life," according to one of the statements, "but in the couple of weeks prior to her death she told me she had had second thoughts because of what this might do to her family." Nix knew that the children's testimony would be crucial during the trial.

Dvorak's attorney, Melvin Sanderson, also a veteran litigator in the court of public opinion, retaliated by releasing to the media, a week before the commencement of Dvorak's trial, a videotape of his patient's "last wish" that was allegedly made about an hour before the time of death listed on the coroner's report. The tape showed an emaciated, pathetic woman, whose body and spirit had been ravaged by the months of chemotherapy treatments. On the tape Tate was heard, in a barely audible whisper, apologizing to her children for causing them so much grief and begging their forgiveness. But the sound track also contained an unmistakable desire to end her life and a request for Dvorak's assistance in doing so. "This tape should remove any doubt as to Ms. Tate's desires to end her suffering," the defense lawyer announced confidently in his public statement accompanying the video's much publicized release. "And my client is not guilty of murder," continued Sanderson. "He did not kill Helen Tate. He just provided a means for her to end her own suffering."

This statement was quickly followed by one from Tate's children denouncing Sanderson's disgraceful behavior and asking the news media to repudiate this "blatant and sensationalistic attempt to manipulate public opinion." "This tape was made as a personal farewell to her children," the statement said. "We believe that the expression of her wish to die was coerced by Dr. Dvorak when our mother was no longer in full control of her faculties. To broadcast this tape or to publish pictures of our mother in this condition would constitute a gross violation of her privacy, as well as that of her family."

To Sanderson, this videotape was defense exhibit A in the case of *The People v. Dr. Michael Dvorak*. To Sandra Feinstein, it represented a challenging ethical dilemma. Feinstein was the news director of Channel 8, a CBS affiliate in the competitive three-station market of Harrisburg, the Riverside County seat. Two hours before Channel 8's *News at 6*, Feinstein was huddled with producer Bruce Baxter and Stephanie Hunter, the reporter who was covering the criminal proceedings against Dvorak. The tape they were watching was a solemn testament to the ravages of disease and the pathos of human suffering.

"We have to decide whether to put this tape on the air." Feinstein broke the silence with her usual air of authority. "Both Channel 3 and Channel 12 have this tape; I don't know what their plans are, but we must assume that at least one of them will run this tape—especially Channel 12. They run a lot of graphic video and tabloid-type stories."

"This *is* news," responded Hunter. "This tape represents one of the key issues in this case. Was Ms. Tate's desire to die unequivocal, or did she, as

her children claim, have second thoughts about her decision?"

"But what about the privacy issue?" responded Baxter. "Her children have asked the media not to use the tape. Despite the fact that Dvorak's attorney released this tape, I certainly don't think Ms. Tate expected her dying moments to become a public spectacle. This tape was clearly intended as a personal farewell message to her children."

"Ms. Tate is dead," said Hunter. "I don't see this as a privacy issue in her case. As far as her children are concerned, they are key witnesses in this trial. Whether they like it or not, they have become matters of public interest. Besides, once this tape is entered into evidence at the trial, it will become a public record—and anyone can attend this trial and see the tape. Hasn't the privacy surrounding this case really been lost because of the criminal proceedings against Dr. Dvorak?"

"I'm not so sure," replied Baxter with increasing defiance. He enjoyed challenging Hunter, with whom he often disagreed, and probing for the weaknesses in her arguments. "It's true that this tape will become a matter of public record and that those in the courtroom can view the tape. But the fact is that most of our viewers will not be in the courtroom. They'll be watching this tape at home. Obviously, we should report the proceedings of the trial itself. But if Channel 8 airs this graphic videotape that was not originally intended for public dissemination, then we're the primary culprits here. Ms. Tate might be dead, but she has a right to die with dignity. And as far as her children are concerned, they didn't ask to become a part of this spectacle."

"I question Sanderson's motives in releasing this tape," said Feinstein. "But I'm also concerned about our viewers' reaction. They might see this as nothing more than journalistic exploitation and a ratings ploy. The tape is a good visual. But is it *essential* to the content of the story?"

But Hunter was persistent. "Perhaps Sanderson's motives are less than pure in releasing this tape at this time. But we just have to bite the bullet and run it anyway. This is a key piece of evidence in a murder trial; our viewers should understand this. The tape is essential to the story and provides context. We are a visual medium. Pictures can't be divorced from the other content of the story. In this case the news value of this tape outweighs any privacy interests of Ms. Tate or her children."

As Hunter made her final plea for what she viewed as the integrity of the station's news judgment, Feinstein began pondering this ethical dilemma. It was now only an hour until air time. The notion of delaying a decision on the matter and perhaps airing the tape on another night occurred to Feinstein, but she knew that at least one of her competitors, and perhaps both, was likely to include the tape in that night's newscast. She regretted that her reporter and producer had brought different perspectives to the table. A consensus would have made Feinstein feel more comfortable if not fully confident in her role as moral agent.

THE CASE STUDY

Helen Tate made this tape as a private farewell message to her children. She apparently never anticipated the public scrutiny to which this visual account of her last moments of suffering might be subjected. She is not alive to express her own wishes, but one might argue that the airing of the tape could serve to remove any doubt in the public's mind as to her desire to die with dignity. On the other hand, the graphic image of this frail, pathetic woman might raise some questions about whether she made this declaration with a clear mind. Would the airing of this tape undermine the respect that is due Tate, even in death?

Reporter Stephanie Hunter argues that the privacy question as it pertains to Tate is moot, since she is deceased. From a legal standpoint, Hunter is essentially correct. Is this also a compelling ethical argument?

The privacy of Tate's children is also at stake here. They argue that the tape contains a personal communication to them from their mother and that their own privacy should be respected. Have they relinquished this privacy through their public statements concerning the tape or their willingness to serve as prosecution witnesses against Dvorak?

Assume the role of News Director Sandra Feinstein, and, applying the SAD Formula for moral

reasoning discussed in Chapter 3, render an ethical judgment as to whether you will include this videotape in tonight's rendition of *News at 6*. From an ethical perspective, you must decide whether the news value of this tape and its importance to the trial coverage outweigh the family's request for privacy. As the moral agent, you must decide whether the tape is essential or useful to the audience in understanding the context of the story. It is a key piece of evidence in this case. The tape could be instrumental in the jury's deliberations, and Tate's children have challenged the defense's explanation of the tape. The tape clearly does have news value.

But since the case has not yet gone to trial, it is not entirely clear as to how this evidence will be used or explained to the jury. Sanderson's claim that this tape shows an autonomous woman expressing, with a clear mind, her desire to die will certainly be challenged by the prosecution. Thus, is it even possible to really place this tape into the overall context of the story? On the other hand, the station is faced with competitive pressures. Channel 8 could air the tape and let the audience render its own judgment concerning its meaning.

▶ ## CASE 5-7
The Televangelist with a Past

Jerry Gantry was an apostle of God, and television was his pulpit. The Reverend Gantry's ministry had debuted on the electronic stage at a time when several of his scandal-riddled brethren had fallen from grace. But despite some disillusionment among supporters of these televangelists, Gantry's faithful had never deserted him, and his fundamentalist message, delivered with a vigorous blend of theatrical timing and God-fearing grace, was on prominent display in ninety-seven TV markets and on several cable channels.

Gantry had graduated from Pineville Theological Seminary twenty years ago and had toiled for several years in the rural hinterlands and small towns of West Virginia before abandoning this poverty-stricken region for the more attractive and cosmopolitan environment of Charlotteville, located along the densely populated eastern seaboard. He had assumed the ministry of an established church, whose membership was faithful but static. Gantry's charismatic style and dramatic applications of the scriptures to the problems of everyday life had reenergized his congregation, who had responded enthusiastically.

But Gantry's considerable talents were not confined to the spiritual. He quickly seized on what he viewed as the marketing opportunities available in the Charlotteville community to extend his outreach and negotiated a contract with Channel 4 to televise his Sunday morning services. This exposure soon attracted new worshippers who had come to bear witness to the Reverend Gantry's fiery Biblical admonitions. His success in expanding his membership rolls was matched only by his lucrative fund-raising efforts, and the Reverend Gantry embarked on an ambitious building project that included a huge panoramic cathedral that would double as a TV studio. It was here that the most famous graduate of the Pineville Theological Seminary began his career as a nationally acclaimed televangelist.

The Reverend Gantry's syndicated messages about sin and salvation were quite diverse, biblically speaking, but his most recent favorite theme was what he termed "sins of the flesh": prostitution, pornography, and adultery. He had even taken the unusual step of publicly condemning a fellow televangelist for having to resign from his church when church elders discovered his marital infidelity. "Sins of the flesh" was a theme that also pervaded many of his columns that were carried by 350 daily newspapers across the country. And it was a theme that caught the attention of Andy Byars.

Byars was the news director for Channel 4 in Charlotteville, where the Reverend Gantry had made his television debut. The station was still among those that carried his popular program. As the Reverend Gantry's teleministry began its tenth year in syndication, Byars began to hear rumors that, before becoming an ordained minister, Gantry had led less than an exemplary life. An investigation by John Caldwell, the station's investigative reporter, had turned up the following facts: As a

nineteen-year-old college sophomore, Gantry had pleaded guilty to one count of propositioning an undercover police officer in a rather sleazy neighborhood just adjacent to the campus where he was attending college. According to court records, the judge had sentenced him to two years' probation. But less than a year after graduation, his life took a turn for the worse when he was arrested for ordering several videotapes and magazines featuring child pornography from state undercover agents. This time, Gantry served three years in prison and then sought psychological counseling, which had lasted for eighteen months. One of Caldwell's sources told him that Gantry's problems with pornography were more severe than his one conviction. He had voluntarily gone into therapy because of what he believed was an addiction to such material. It was during this time that Gantry had decided to seek redemption in the service of the Lord and to enroll at the Pineville Theological Seminary.

Byars was confident of the thoroughness of Caldwell's investigation. Channel 4 paid Caldwell well for his considerable talents as an investigative reporter, and the investment had paid off. The station had won some well-deserved recognition from its journalistic peers as well as public approbation for its relentless pursuit of governmental and corporate corruption scandal. Caldwell produced only one story, usually a multipart series, every eight weeks, but he more than offset his lack of on-camera appearances with the ratings bonanzas that usually accompanied his highly promoted reports.

As Byars reviewed the situation with Caldwell and news producer Myra Sanchez, he was not surprised at the reporter's interest in pursuing the results of the investigation. "This is a good story," Caldwell declared emphatically. "His offenses occurred when he was young, before he began his ministry. But his convictions are a matter of public record. His counseling records are confidential, but I have two sources who are willing to talk about them. One says he doubts whether Gantry was really 'cured' of his fascination with child pornography."

"But this happened twenty years ago in a community 700 miles from here," responded Byars. "If this were a private citizen, we wouldn't even be discussing this issue. Assuming the individual had kept his nose clean, we would consider it a matter of privacy. Should we treat Gantry any differently just because he is a public figure—and a minister at that?"

"But that's the point," said Caldwell. "He *is* a minister—one who has built his reputation condemning, among other things, prostitution, pornography, and sex outside of marriage. I don't believe Gantry is entitled to any zone of privacy in this case since his prior conduct—even though it occurred twenty years ago—undermines the credibility of his messages. And even assuming that he has stayed clean during his ministry, his past does help explain his preoccupation with the so-called sins of the flesh."

But Sanchez had some reservations. She had produced several of Caldwell's investigative triumphs, and she admired and respected his enthusiasm for his work. But this story was risky from both a journalistic and public relations standpoint. Gantry was a popular television personality, both nationally and locally. His supporters would undoubtedly be surprised by the revelations of his past, but most would probably forgive him for these indiscretions that occurred before his ordination. The station could be accused of sensationalism and tabloid journalism. On the other hand, the story could be another ratings bonanza. Coming on the heels of scandals involving other televangelists, this story could attract the attention of mainstream Protestants and Catholics, who had never really accommodated themselves to what they perceived as the electronic marketing of religion. The fact that the Reverend Gantry's criminal vices had occurred twenty years ago was a detail that many of the station's viewers would probably overlook.

"What's the real news value in these revelations?" Sanchez wanted to know. "Some of our viewers will find them fascinating and will use this as an opportunity to take their shots at Reverend Gantry. Gantry obviously views his arrests, imprisonment, and therapy as episodes from his past that should remain private. Otherwise, he would have introduced them in his sermons as examples of his own fallibility. But he has never mentioned them to my knowledge. Some of this may be public record in the community where his crimes oc-

curred, but they certainly aren't public knowledge here or among his followers."

"But his sermon topics themselves have been controversial," rebutted Caldwell. "His preoccupation with such things as prostitution and pornography in his sermons, often to the exclusion of other sins, has attracted the attention of even the mainstream religious community. And some civil libertarians and other detractors have accused him of trampling on the First Amendment because of his calls for greater law enforcement efforts to 'eradicate the evils of pornography and sexual violence.' And we have included some of this controversy in our news coverage. It seems to me that we now have a responsibility to put this story into context. The fact is that Gantry's guilt about his past could help explain his public outcry against such vices."

Sanchez had to concede the point. Channel 4 had carried a couple of stories documenting the disenchantment of some viewers with Reverend Gantry's relentless crusade against pornography, prostitution, and adultery. Since the televangelist had recently made these issues the centerpiece of his electronic church, perhaps he was fair game in the rough-and-tumble arena of investigative journalism. Did he really have a right to privacy on matters that pertained, even in some remote way, to his public ministry?

Byars respected the views of his award-winning investigative reporter. If the Reverend Gantry had been a private person, then his youthful involvement with various forms of vice would have been newsworthy only at the time of his arrests and convictions in the community where the transgressions occurred. But as a high-profile minister and public figure, did Gantry have the same right to expect his past to remain forever concealed from public scrutiny? Were his convictions for solicitation for prostitution and possession of child pornography at least twenty years ago and his subsequent treatment for what may have been an addiction to pornography relevant to some matter of public interest?

The news director was not unaware of the ratings potential of such a story. Channel 4 had slipped to number two in the last ratings book. This report, which would require more thorough investigation, could be a ratings bonanza, particularly if produced within the context of the current controversy over the Reverend Gantry's crusade against "sins of the flesh." On the other hand, Byars also recognized the harm that might result from this exposé. Despite the Reverend Gantry's flashy style and the enormous wealth he had accumulated from his electronic pulpit, his ministry had influenced the lives of millions of people. Was the news value in events that had transpired so long ago sufficient to justify the harm that would result from this intrusion into the Reverend Gantry's private past? As the moral agent in this case, Andy Byars agonized over the question of whether to give his investigative unit the green light to pursue this story.

THE CASE STUDY

This case requires the moral agent to weigh the news value in reporting the past misdeeds of a public figure against his privacy interest in preventing disclosure of these activities. The public interest in this proposed journalistic enterprise must also be balanced against the potential harm that accrue to both the station and the Reverend Gantry's ministry.

As a public figure, Reverend Gantry has a zone of privacy clearly less than that of a private citizen. If Gantry were not in the public limelight, then there would be no news value in his past criminal conduct for which he has paid his price to society, although it is a matter of public record in a community 700 miles from the minister's home base. And even as a public figure, Gantry might claim some privacy interests in transgressions that occurred before he was admitted to the seminary. But Gantry is now a high-profile minister. Does the *nature* of his transgressions justify the station's resurrection of his past, particularly if they might explain his preoccupation with such "sins of the flesh"? Or is reporter John Caldwell stretching the concept of *news relevance* in attempting to link the minister's past misdeeds with the current controversy over his crusades against prostitution and pornography?

Assume the role of News Director Andy Byars, and then, using the SAD Formula for moral reasoning outlined in Chapter 3, decide whether you will commission investigative reporter John Caldwell to disclose the skeletons in the closet of televangelist Jerry Gantry.

 ## CASE 5-8
Condom Ads and Viewer Privacy

Although condom advertising was now featured prominently in the American mass media, some of the TV networks and national magazines were still reluctant to carry the controversial ads. Howard Sellers was no exception. As the general sales manager of a medium-market TV station, Sellers was responsible for setting policy on advertising standards and practices. He was no prude, but he could read the pulse of the viewing public in his conservative community. In a city where the school board, under public pressure, had retreated from its intention of offering sex education, he wondered whether his audience was prepared for the intrusion of condom ads into their living rooms.

But some members of his sales staff were beginning to exert pressures on their boss for a change of heart. Many of them were young and college educated, products of the so-called sexual revolution, and failed to understand the reluctance of some media organizations to accept condom ads. The national sales manager, Harold Phelps, had recently been contacted by a large agency with $2.5 million to spend on a national spot campaign for Safety-First, the latest entry into the condom market. He, too, felt the urge to accept the advertising of the increasingly visible and lucrative condom industry. He had seen some of the commercials and found nothing offensive about them.

But outside opposition to the proliferation of condom ads in the mass media was strong and well organized. Citizens for Decency on Television, for example, got wind of the proposed Safety-First campaign and was pressuring local TV stations to reject the ads. Sellers also granted an audience to some local religious leaders, including a Catholic priest and a bishop, to discuss the station's policy on the advertising of birth control devices.

Even putting aside the Catholic clergy's opposition on moral grounds to artificial means of birth control, the arguments boiled down to this: The advertising of condoms promotes promiscuity. Furthermore, because children make up an important segment of the TV audience, unrestricted access of immature youths to contraceptive product advertising and information violates their parents' rights to provide appropriate sex education. It intrudes into the private relationship between parents and their children. In addition, contraceptive advertising invades the privacy of the home and offends the sensibilities of some segments of the adult audience.

Phelps had also attended the meeting between the clergy and Sellers and had tried to counter the ministers' arguments by appealing to the social responsibility of promoting condom usage in light of the AIDS epidemic. No less of an authority than the U.S. surgeon general, Phelps argued, had endorsed their use to protect against the AIDS virus. However, Phelps failed to win any converts.

Sellers was caught between the conflicting claims of his own staff and the advertising industry, on the one hand, and the citizens and religious groups, on the other. Was condom advertising an unwarranted intrusion into family privacy? In some respects all advertising fell into this category, but the issue of contraceptive ads had moral dimensions not found in the typical product campaign. On the other hand, condom ads were now a mainstay of cable television, and, despite continued resistance from the television networks, some local stations had relented. Sellers wondered whether his station, too, should change its policy, risking the ire of those segments of the viewing public that considered such advertising to be an offensive intrusion into their privacy. He had always believed that, as a general rule, local television stations were the conscience of the community and should give the public what it wanted (and not give it what it objected to). But there were also times when the audience should be given what it "needed," even if some segments objected. Because AIDS was truly an epidemic of national proportions, perhaps this was one of those times.

THE CASE STUDY

Although much of this chapter is devoted to the matter of journalistic ethics, I noted early in the chapter that advertising and other forms of content can also raise privacy issues. And because advertising seeks us out, it is by definition intrusive. We are constantly bombarded by a litany of commercial messages, both in public and in the privacy of our homes, and are unable to retreat completely from their persuasive appeals. Everything from blimps to billboards to T-shirts is used to capture our attention.

Because advertising is part of the machinery that drives the free-market economy, there is no way to avoid the intrusiveness of some advertising. Perhaps the goal should be to avoid unreasonable invasions of our privacy, which raises the question of responsibility and taste in advertising. Of course, the audience has some accountability in this process, and the audience can be fickle and unpredictable. Doug Newsome, Alan Scott, and Judy VanSlyke Turk, in a discussion of public relations ethics, have noted the discrepancy between what is allowed in commercials and what is permitted in programming with this critical observation:

> The list of no-no's includes not showing someone taking pills, drinking alcohol or kissing passionately; not picturing the toilet or using the name (the reason you see commercials showing someone in the grocery store squeezing the paper); not showing or suggesting the purpose of deodorants; not showing or saying what feminine hygiene products look like or identifying what they are for. It can be exasperating for those preparing commercials that can cost more than a million dollars.[74]

A double standard is at work here. The audience is indeed fickle, but perhaps it has a right to call the shots, because it is the target of media messages. As for the advertisers and other media practitioners, they must attempt to satisfy the interests and demands of some audience segments while minimizing the offense created to others.

Assume the role of Sellers, and, using the SAD Formula, decide whether you will accept condom advertising on your station. In so doing, construct arguments to explain your decision to those who are most likely to be unhappy with it.

Notes

1. For a fairly wide-ranging discussion on various ethical concerns of privacy, see *Journal of Mass Media Ethics*, 9, Nos. 3–4, 1994.
2. "Clinton Coverage: Media Get Mileage, Flak," *Broadcasting*, February 3, 1992, p. 13.
3. Conrad C. Fink, *Media Ethics: In the Newsroom and Beyond* (New York: McGraw-Hill, 1988), p. 30.
4. For a good discussion on the value of privacy, see W. A. Parent, "Privacy, Morality, and the Law," in Joan C. Callahan (ed.), *Ethical Issues in Professional Life* (New York: Oxford University Press, 1988), pp. 218–219.
5. Louis Hodges, "The Journalist and Privacy," *Journal of Mass Media Ethics*, Vol. 9 (No. 4), 1994, p. 201.
6. For a discussion of this point, see Alan Westin, "The Origins of Modern Claims to Privacy," in Ferdinand David Schoeman (ed.), *Philosophical Dimensions of Privacy: An Anthology* (Cambridge: Cambridge University Press, 1984), pp. 59–67.
7. Richard A. Posner, *The Economics of Justice* (Cambridge, MA: Harvard University Press, 1983), pp. 268–269.
8. *Ibid.*, p. 268.
9. Don R. Pember, *Privacy and the Press* (Seattle: University of Washington Press, 1972), p. 5.
10. *Ibid.*
11. *Ibid.*, pp. 12–13.
12. William L. Prosser, *Handbook of the Law of Torts*, 4th ed. (St. Paul, MN: West, 1971), pp. 810–811.
13. See Don R. Pember, *Mass Media Law*, 6th ed. (Dubuque, IA: Brown, 1993), p. 235.
14. See *Griswold v. Connecticut*, 381 U.S. 479 (1965); *Stanley v. Georgia*, 394 U.S. 557 (1969).
15. Clifford G. Christians, Kim B. Rotzoll, and Mark Fackler also discuss the need for a system of ethics in *Media Ethics: Cases and Moral Reasoning*, 4th ed. (White Plains, NY: Longman, 1995), pp. 116–117.
16. See James Glen Stovall and Patrick R. Cotter, "The Public Plays Reporter: Attitudes toward Reporting on Public Officials," *Journal of Mass Media Ethics*, Vol. 7, No. 2, 1992, pp. 97–106.
17. Pember, *Privacy and the Press*, p. 16.
18. *Hawkins v. Multimedia*, 12 Med.L.Rptr. 1878 (1986).
19. Christians, Rotzoll, and Fackler, *Media Ethics*, p. 116.
20. Jeffrey Olen, *Ethics in Journalism* (Upper Saddle River, NJ: Prentice Hall, 1988), p. 71.
21. *Cox Broadcasting Corp. v. Cohn*, 95 S.Ct. 1029 (1975).
22. *Barber v. Time, Inc.*, 159 S.W.2d 291 (Mo. 1942).
23. For a discussion of this issue, see Estelle Lander, "AIDS Coverage: Ethical and Legal Issues Facing the Media Today," *Journal of Media Ethics*, 3, No. 2, Fall 1988, pp. 66–72.
24. "Report on AIDS Death Sparks Debate," (Baton Rouge) *Morning Advocate*, May 11, 1987, p. 3A.
25. *Ibid.*
26. *Ibid.*
27. "Sports Editor: It's a News Story," *USA Today*, April 9, 1992, p. 2A.
28. "Ashe: Privacy at Stake," *USA Today*, April 9, 1992, p. 2A (excerpts from a partial transcript of Arthur Ashe's news conference).
29. "Arthur Ashe AIDS Story Scrutinized by Editors, Columnists," *Quill*, June 1992, p. 17.
30. "AIDS and the Right to Know," *Newsweek*, August 18, 1986, p. 46.
31. For a more in-depth treatment of this case, see Goodwin and Smith, *Groping for Ethics*, pp. 243–245.
32. Charles B. Seib, "How the Papers Covered the Cinema Follies Fire," *Washington Post*, October 30, 1977, p. C-7.
33. *Ibid.*
34. *Ibid.*
35. *Ibid.*
36. *Ibid.*
37. "'Outing': An Unexpected Assault on Sexual Privacy," *Newsweek*, April 30, 1990, p. 66.
38. *Ibid.*
39. Sue O'Brien, "Privacy," *Quill*, November/December 1991, p. 10.
40. *Ibid.*
41. For a thorough examination of news media treatment of sex crime victims, see Helen Benedict, *Virgin or Vamp: How the Press Covers Sex Crimes* (New York: Oxford University Press, 1992).
42. *Cox Broadcasting Corp. v. Cohn*, 420 U.S. 469 (1975).
43. H. Eugene Goodwin and Ron F. Smith, *Groping for Ethics in Journalism*. 3d ed., (Ames: Iowa State University Press, 1994), p. 247.
44. *Ibid.*, p. 251.
45. "Right to Privacy," *Newsweek*, April 29, 1991, p. 31.
46. The Florida courts have now declared certain aspects of this law unconstitutional.
47. See David A. Kaplan, "Remove That Blue Dot," *Newsweek*, December 16, 1991, p. 26.
48. Judy Flander, "Should the Name Have Been Released?" *Communicator*, June 1991, p. 10.
49. *Ibid.*
50. "Naming," *Newsweek*, April 29, 1991, p. 29.
51. "NBC Creates Stir with Rape Report," *Broadcasting*, April 22, 1991, p. 25.
52. Michael Gartner, "Why We Did It," *Communicator*, June 1991, pp. 11–12.
53. *Smith v. Daily Mail*, 443 U.S. 97 (1979).
54. Frank Ritter, "Reporting on Suicide Is Not Easy, and Needs Sensitivity," *Tennessean*, January 12, 1992, p. 5-D.
55. *Ibid.*
56. *Ibid.*
57. Louis W. Hodges, "Undercover, Masquerading, Surreptitious Taping," *Journal of Mass Media Ethics*, 3,

No. 2, Fall 1988, p. 34, citing T. L. Glasser, "On the Morality of Secretly Taped Interviews," *Nieman Reports*, 39, Spring 1982, pp. 17–20.

58. *Ibid.*

59. "In Brief," *Broadcasting & Cable*, November 21, 1994, pp. 80–81.

60. "Controversy over Chung-Gingrich Interview," *Broadcasting & Cable*, January 9, 1995, p. 16.

61. These remarks are quoted in *ibid.*

62. Richard P. Cunningham, "Seeking a Time-out on Prurience," *Quill*, March 1992, p. 6.

63. *Ibid.*

64. Gregory Stricharchuk, "Computer Records Become Powerful Tool For Investigative Reporters and Editors," *Wall Street Journal*, February 3, 1988, p. 25.

65. "When Privacy Trumps Access, Democracy Is in Trouble," *News Media & the Law*, Spring 1995, p. 2.

66. Karen Reinboth Speckman, "Using Data Bases to Serve Justice and Maintain the Public's Trust," *Journal of Mass Media Ethics*, 9, No. 4, 1994, p. 236.

67. *Ibid.*

68. *Ibid.*, p. 237. For an example, see Karen Reinboth Speckman, "Computers and the News: A Complicated Challenge," in Philip Patterson and Lee Wilkins (eds.), *Media Ethics: Issues and Cases*, 2d ed. (Dubuque, IA: WCB Brown & Benchmark, 1994), pp. 134–135.

69. Stricharchuk, "Computer Records Become Powerful Tool," p. 25.

70. For a discussion of ethical standards in advertising, see Richard L. Johannesen, *Ethics in Human Communication*, 3d ed. (Prospect Heights, IL: Waveland, 1990), p. 93.

71. E.g., see Richard T. DeGeorge, *Business Ethics*, 2d ed. (New York: Macmillan, 1986), p. 274.

72. Jay Black, Bob Steele, and Ralph Barney, *Doing Ethics in Journalism: A Handbook with Case Studies*, 2d ed. (Needham Heights, MA: Allyn & Bacon, 1995), p. 181.

73. Similar charges were made when a white female jogger was attacked in 1989 in New York's Central Park. See "Opinions, but No Solutions," *Newsweek*, May 15, 1989, p. 40.

74. Doug Newsome, Alan Scott, and Judy VanSlyke Turk, *This Is PR: The Realities of Public Relations*, 4th ed. (Belmont, CA: Wadsworth, 1989), p. 233.

CHAPTER

6

Confidentiality and the Public Interest

THE PRINCIPLE OF CONFIDENTIALITY

In 1992, Senator Brock Adams abandoned his reelection campaign after the *Seattle Times* reported allegations by eight female associates or employees that he had sexually abused and harassed them. The paper did not publish their names, and Adams said he quit the race because he could not fight back without confronting his unnamed accusers. His press secretary was even more caustic in his denunciation of the paper's tactics, accusing the *Seattle Times* of sinking to "a new low of journalistic terrorism." Michael R. Fancher, executive editor of the *Times*, defended the paper's decision to publish the anonymous women's allegations on the grounds that "all were credible, and offered credible people . . . to corroborate the circumstances of their stories."[1]

In December 1991, Libby Averyt, a reporter for the Corpus Christi *Caller-Times*, went to jail rather than answer questions about her interviews with murder defendant Jermarr Arnold. During the interviews, Arnold had admitted slaying a twenty-one-year-old jewelry store clerk in 1983 but expressed no remorse over the killing. A state district judge held the reporter in contempt when she declined to answer questions from Arnold's attorney during a pretrial hearing.[2]

In the same year, the *Wall Street Journal* reported that a Procter & Gamble official had resigned under pressure and that part of the company's food and beverage division might be sold. The reporter attributed the information to "current and former employees." At the request of P&G, a Cincinnati grand jury subpoenaed the telephone company's toll records of local customers who called the newspaper's Pittsburgh bureau and one of its reporters. The company complained that the paper's sources had violated an Ohio law prohibiting the disclosure of a company's confidential or proprietary information.[3]

What do these three situations have in common? All are based on the value of confidential relationships or information, an important principle in the practice of media communications. The principle of confidentiality imposes a duty to withhold the names of sources of information or the information itself from third parties under certain circumstances. Although this obligation is not absolute, neither is it a mere rule of thumb. The consensus among philosophers is that confidentiality is a prima facie duty that can be overridden only by other, weightier considerations.[4] Thus, the burden of proof is generally on those who wish to override it.[5] This is familiar terrain for media practitioners, who must decide, in an endless variety of situations, whether confidentiality or candor is the more desirable servant of the public interest. Of course, these ideas are not mutually exclusive, because a promise of confidentiality to a news source can lead to candor in the uncovering of corruption or other illegal activities.

The notion of confidentiality, however, goes beyond the protection of news sources. Sometimes news organizations must decide whether to publish secret or confidential information provided to them by a source. Classified government documents and grand jury investigations are two prime examples. Under such circumstances, the issue is not just one of *source* confidentiality but whether the media should release *information* to which they may not be entitled in the first place.

Because media practitioners are in the information business, there is often an irresistible urge to prefer disclosure over secrecy. But the notion that revelation and openness are always in the public interest is presumptuous at best. There are times when the court of public opinion is not entitled to information, the release of which could offend or perhaps even cause harm to other parties. Thus, the case for confidentiality as an important societal value worth salvaging is a compelling one.

The role of confidentiality in our social relationships is one that we learn early in life. Our parents instill in us the value of keeping secrets and admonish us never to break a promise. This is part of the socialization process by which we develop loyalty to our peers. In fact, secrets can provide a sense of power, because we are privy to information that is not widely shared by others. But promises of confidentiality also limit our freedom of action. An oath of secrecy places a burden on the moral agent to withhold information even in the face of conflicting (and sometimes more compelling) demands.

Suppose, for example, that you have promised a friend accused of a crime that you will not reveal to anyone what you know about his or her dastardly deed. If you were subpoe-

naed to testify in the case, would you refuse to do so? Could you justify on moral grounds your recalcitrance in thwarting the administration of justice? Likewise, if your pregnant teenage girlfriend told you in confidence that she was considering an abortion, would you tell her parents? Clearly, such promises of confidentiality should not be made lightly, because there is always the risk that they will run afoul of other moral obligations that may tempt us to violate our pledge. Such is the dilemma when a reporter elects to withhold from a court information that may bear on the guilt or innocence of a defendant.

Confidential relationships usually arise in three circumstances. First are *express promises*, as when a reporter promises anonymity to a news source. These are often verbal commitments, but they may also be written. The oaths of secrecy signed by CIA agents are a case in point.

A promise of confidentiality from a reporter, however, involves more than just a pledge not to reveal a source's identity. The conditions of this "contract" of secrecy should be clear to both reporter and source. To this end the journalistic establishment has developed its own lexicon to describe the different kinds of confidential relationships.

"Off the record," for example, is supposed to mean that the information provided to the reporter is not for public release. But sources sometimes interpret this to mean that they do not want to be identified with the information, which in the journalist's mind is usually defined as "without attribution." Thus, when some sources say "off the record," they really mean that they do not want to be quoted.

"On background" generally refers to an arrangement by which government officials or other sources call in reporters to brief them on some matter of public interest. The source is then usually identified in the story by such references as a "White House aide," "a senior Pentagon official," or "a State Department spokesman."[6] It is not unusual for journalists to negotiate with their sources over which of these forms of confidentiality will be employed. Nevertheless, such ground rules are subject to interpretation, and it is important that reporter and source have a meeting of the minds on the conditions of their contract before any agreement on confidentiality.[7]

Confidential relationships may also be formulated out of a sense of *loyalty*. In such cases there may not be an express promise of secrecy in every situation, but a sense of loyalty to an individual or company propels the moral agent in that direction. A personal secretary to a recently deceased celebrity who refuses to write a kiss-and-tell book and thereby eschews personal enrichment is acting out of a sense of loyalty. Public relations practitioners are expected to serve the best interests of their companies and not to release information detrimental to the corporate welfare. They are expected, in other words, to be loyal. But how should ethical PR practitioners respond when their company is engaged in behavior inimical to the public welfare? The PRSA Code of Ethics obligates a member not to "place himself or herself in a position where the member's personal interest is or may be in conflict with an obligation to an employer or client" and also requires that a member "shall, as soon as possible, sever relations with any organization or individual if such relationship requires conduct contrary to the articles of this Code." In other words, the PR practitioner should resign if the employer's conduct is such as to erode his or her loyalty to the company.

Resignation is a drastic remedy, however, for conflicting loyalties, and as a staff member a greater good can probably be derived from staying on the job and arguing one's case directly to corporate management. Some practitioners elect to stay but become frustrated in their failure to change the system from within and become *whistle-blowers*. In other words, they secretly inform the media about their employer's irresponsible deportment in order to bring public pressure on the organization.[8]

Whistle-blowing, however, is a controversial practice. Some argue that if practitioners cannot be loyal to their employers, they should resign as soon as they become disaffected with the company's questionable conduct. Practitioners themselves may also actually participate in the unethical or illegal activities before acting on their moral qualms, thus subjecting them to charges of "unclean hands" in leveling the charges against the company. In addition, although whistle-blowing might stop the unethical corporate practice, it will still usually cost the whistle-blower his or her job in the long run. Such was the case when a PR practitioner charged his company, a multinational fruit conglomerate, with the manipulation of media coverage, as well as with political and military action in a Latin American country where the company was operating.[9]

It should be pointed out that loyalty in the marketplace is not always based on genuine affection but is more often a reflection of a feeling of obligation. Thus, such loyalties are transitory and may lose their moral force when the circumstances under which they are formed are altered. What if PR representatives, for example, move from one agency to another. Are they acting unethically if they use the knowledge of their former employer to lure away clients? The PRSA Code admonishes members to "scrupulously safeguard the confidences and privacy rights of present, former, and prospective clients or employers." Nevertheless, loyalty, like patience, does have its limits, but the use of confidential information from a now-terminated relationship poses some intriguing moral dilemmas.

The third type of confidential relationship is one *recognized by law*. Society has determined that some relationships are so important that they deserve legal protection. The protection accorded to confidential communications between doctors and patients, lawyers and their clients, and priests and penitents are examples. It is unnecessary for an attorney to make an express promise of confidentiality to a client; this relationship is automatically protected by law. In addition, many states and courts now recognize a privilege for reporters to maintain the confidentiality of their sources, a tacit acknowledgment of the role of the media as representatives of the public.

Unlike other society privileges, however, a reporter's privilege is not predicated on the danger of personal embarrassment or a threat to the privacy rights of the parties per se. Instead, the rationale is that compulsory disclosure would lead to serious consequences for both the reporter and the source. For example, sources who pass on information about government or other corruption may fear for their jobs or even their physical well-being. On the other hand, reporters may be subject to contempt charges if they refuse to divulge the source's identity.[10]

In those confidential relationships recognized by law, journalists share moral obligations similar to those imposed on the society they serve. For example, reporters who testify before grand juries are subject to the same oaths of secrecy as other witnesses. Thus, they should not divulge in the media the contents of their testimony, unless they are released from their commitment to confidentiality through due process of law.

One reporter who chose to honor his commitment to confidentiality until it could be challenged through the legal system was Michael Smith, of the *Charlotte-Herald News* in Florida. In 1986, Smith was subpoenaed to testify before a special grand jury investigating activities in the Charlotte County state's attorney's office and the sheriff's department. The reporter was warned that disclosure of his testimony was prohibited by Florida law. On completion of the grand jury's investigation, Smith wanted to publish a news story and possibly a book about the investigation, including his observations of the grand jury process and the matters about which he had testified. To the reporter's credit, he did not simply ignore the statutory ban on publication but sued in federal court to have the law declared unconstitutional as a prior restraint on his First Amendment right of free speech. The U.S. Supreme Court eventually upheld Smith's constitutional claim.[11]

THE JUSTIFICATION FOR CONFIDENTIALITY

The principle of confidentiality has taken a beating in recent years. In our information-rich society, the public's demand for knowledge about all manner of things is insatiable. Thus, other duties are sometimes seen as more important than secrecy. This trend, which is disturbing to some, is described by the ethicist Sissela Bok in "The Limits of Confidentiality":

> So much confidential information is now being gathered and recorded and requested by so many about so many that confidentiality, though as strenuously invoked as in the past, is turning out to be a weaker reed than ever. . . .
>
> Faced with growing demands for both revelation and secrecy, those who have to make decisions about whether or not to uphold confidentiality face numerous difficult moral quandaries.[12]

Despite this assessment, there are several justifications for a reaffirmation of the principle of confidentiality.[13] First, there is a concern for human autonomy in safeguarding personal information and knowledge. The ability to keep secrets—and to feed information to others selectively—provides a sense of power over the individual's sphere of influence. In fact, most disputes over secrecy boil down to conflicts over power, the power that comes through controlling the flow of information.[14]

This power is of particular relevance to journalists, who value openness over secrecy in a democratic society. The press is the most important counterbalance against the natural tendencies of government and other institutions to control the flow of negative or sensitive information. The media, therefore, have a much clearer *public* mandate to challenge such policies of concealment than some other members of society, such as social scientists and private detectives.[15]

News sources are exerting their sense of autonomy (or power) when they channel confidential information to reporters. This is an important concept for journalists to remember, because anonymous sources act with a variety of motives. Some have an ax to grind, and others may breach confidentiality with the public's interest in mind, as in the case of a whistleblower. Of course, the idea of autonomy in maintaining confidentiality does have its limits. For example, an individual who knows that a crime is about to be committed (and this includes reporters) is obliged to relinquish this secret to the proper authorities.

The second justification for confidentiality is that it establishes a feeling of trust among individuals within society. The respect for others' secrets is essential to maintaining relationships. Trust, the keeping of promises, and loyalty are the foundations of confidentiality, and it is against these cherished values that third parties who seek to breach the cloak of confidentiality must compete. Reporters who insist on complete candor from their public relations contacts in sensitive situations are asking them to place truth over institutional loyalty. Likewise, law enforcement authorities who insist on knowing reporters' confidential sources are asking that promises be broken in the name of an overriding principle, the fair administration of justice.

Confidentiality is also sometimes necessary to prevent harm to others. Committee personnel decisions, even at public institutions, are usually closed to the press and the public because of the potential harm flowing from the rather candid and sometimes brutal comments during the deliberations. Reporters' offers of confidentiality to news sources are usually grounded in the perceived harm that might accrue to those individuals if their identities should become known.

Finally, confidentiality serves the ends of social utility. Without assurances of confidentiality, the trust surrounding certain professional relationships would be eroded. Clients would be less than candid with their attorneys, which could undermine the cause of justice. Patients might lose confidence in their doctors, which would diminish the quality of personal health care. And, of course, reporters argue that confidential sources are often essential to uncovering crime and bringing it to the public's attention. Thus, for a journalist secrecy can become a tool for ensuring the public's access to the day's intelligence.

SEEKING DISCLOSURE: THE MORAL POSITION OF THE ACTOR

Because of the value attached to the principle of confidentiality within our society, the moral positions of the party seeking disclosure and the one claiming confidentiality must be considered in deciding whose claim should be accorded greater significance. Motivation is helpful in evaluating whether there are overriding reasons for disclosure. For example, an individual whose neighbor pleads that she cannot afford to repay a loan might desire a peek at the neighbor's income tax returns, but his moral position is a weak one. Likewise, a reporter who seeks copies of a company president's personal financial statement is also in a weak position unless the executive is involved in a matter of public interest to which the statement might relate.

Public interest (as opposed to merely private curiosity or self-interest) is perhaps the most compelling justification for disclosure. Information is the lifeblood of democracy, and where certain knowledge is essential either to rational consumer choice or collective political decision making, the arguments favoring publicity over confidentiality assume critical dimensions.

A case in point is Hill & Knowlton's representation of "Citizens for Free Kuwait," a lobbying group that sought to foster Kuwait's interests in the United States at a time when this country was contemplating military action against Iraq to free Kuwait. According to the PR firm, it made prompt disclosure under the Foreign Agents Registration Act of its relationship with the lobby and the fact that the bulk of its fees were being paid by the Kuwaiti government.[16] Among President Bush's justifications for initiating military action against Iraq were Saddam Hussein's atrocities against the Kuwaiti people. Perhaps the most sensational claim was that Iraqi soldiers removed hundreds of Kuwaiti babies from incubators and left them to die on the hospital floors.[17]

In October 1990, the Congressional Human Rights Caucus held a public hearing on conditions in Kuwait under Iraqi occupation and heard testimony from witnesses who had escaped from Kuwait after the Iraqi invasion. The most dramatic incubator story—and the one that attracted the most media coverage—was that of Nayirah al-Sabah, the fifteen-year-old daughter of the Kuwaiti ambassador to the United States. Hill & Knowlton had offered her to the committee. At the request of her father, the girl's last name and her relationship to the Kuwaiti ambassador were omitted from public testimony for fear of reprisals against her family in Kuwait. The claims of incubator atrocities were apparently influential in convincing some senators to support the resolution authorizing war.[18] Several news organizations later challenged her testimony, suggesting that the girl had committed perjury and questioning whether she had even been in Kuwait and whether there had been any atrocities. Hill & Knowlton, citing evidence of atrocities after the liberation of Kuwait, stood by the maligned witnesses' testimony.[19]

Regardless of the truth of Nayirah al-Sabah's testimony, the more significant ethical question, from the PR's firm's perspective, was Hill & Knowlton's relationship with members of the Congressional caucus conducting the hearings. In an op-ed piece in the *New York Times,* John R. MacArthur wondered why the caucus did not investigate Nayirah's story. As it turned out, the committee's chairman, California Democrat Tom Lantos, and John Edward

Porter, an Illinois Republican, had a close relationship with Hill & Knowlton. The company's vice president had helped organize the Congressional Human Rights Caucus hearings in meetings between the two congressmen and the chairman of Citizens for a Free Kuwait. In addition, Hill & Knowlton provided office space in Washington at a reduced rate and phone message service for the Congressional Human Rights Foundation, a group founded in 1985 by Congressmen Lantos and Porter. Also, a year after al-Sabah's appearance before Lantos's committee, the foundation named Frank Mankiewicz, Hill & Knowlton's vice chairman, to its board. Although the PR firm came in for a great deal of public censure for representing a controversial client and a questionable cause, it was the use of the Kuwaiti ambassador's daughter in Congressional testimony without full disclosure that raises serious ethical concerns. As Susanne Roschwalb observes in her rather exhaustive examination of the PR firm's involvement in the Kuwaiti hearings:

> Hill & Knowlton becomes the focal point for the discussion of ethics because the basic concerns about public relations, media management and lobbying were magnified during a time when the country was debating war and Hill & Knowlton's client was a foreign country with a direct interest in the outcome of the debate.[20]

The moral position of mass media institutions is often at issue when they seek the release of confidential information. From the standpoint of motivation, the media are at least on respectable moral ground when they publish sensitive information because they believe it to have news value. Such decisions, of course, do involve subjective judgments, but they are at least news judgments born out of public interest considerations.

This is not to suggest that public interest concerns are the only noble ethical motivations. Obviously, the potential for harm to individuals, small groups within society, or even large institutions can provide a morally justifiable rationale for breaching confidentiality. But the moral position of actors is an important consideration in evaluating their claims of access to confidential information.

In staking out a claim to openness, as opposed to secrecy, journalists should beware of moral hypocrisy. Reporters serve a legitimate function as government watchdogs, and in this capacity they correctly view secrecy as antithetical to the democratic process. But, from an ethical perspective, this claim is undermined somewhat by the use of clandestine operations, surreptitious surveillance, and reliance on confidential sources whose veracity may never be subjected to public scrutiny. These practices may lead to credibility problems for the media, as noted by Bok in her book dealing with secrecy and confidentiality:

> The press and other news media rightly stand for openness in public discourse. But until they give equally firm support to openness in their own practices, their stance will be inconsistent and lend credence to charges of unfairness. It is now a stance that challenges every collective rationale for secrecy save the media's own. Yet the media serve commercial and partisan interests in addition to public ones; and media practices of secrecy, selective disclosure, and probing should not be exempt from scrutiny.[21]

CONFIDENTIALITY IN JOURNALISM: SOME SPECIAL CONCERNS

The issue of confidentiality confronts all media practitioners. But because reporters' privilege, the right to maintain the confidentiality of news sources, has become so controversial in recent years, we must spend some time examining the journalistic dimensions of this issue.

The Case for and against Confidentiality

In 1972, the U.S. Supreme Court denied constitutional protection for the reporter-source re-

lationship. In *Branzburg v. Hayes*, which was really a combination of cases involving three reporters, a 5-to-4 majority ruled that the reporters had no privilege under the First Amendment to refuse to testify before grand juries.[22] The *Branzburg* decision sent a shiver through the journalistic community. However, the impact of this decision has been offset in recent years by the recognition of a First Amendment privilege in the lower federal courts and many state courts. In addition, over half the states have extended protection to journalists through "shield laws," statutory privileges designed to protect reporters from having to reveal the identities of their confidential sources to judicial or investigatory bodies. In some jurisdictions, the privilege is absolute; in others, the shield laws provide only qualified protection.

Some reporters have welcomed the arrival of shield laws within their states (there is no federal shield law), because such legislation reflects public policy and recognizes the importance of the reporter-source relationship. Others oppose shield laws, preferring to base a reporter's privilege on the First Amendment, which is not subject to legislative whims. Even a liberal or absolute statute can be amended or repealed, depending on the political makeup of the law-making body.

In carving out a privilege for reporters, some states and courts have relied on the dissenting opinion by Justice Potter Stewart in the *Branzburg* case. Stewart noted that he would require the government to demonstrate three things before compelling grand jury testimony from a reporter regarding a confidential source: (1) that there is probable cause to believe that the reporter has information "clearly relevant to a specific probable violation of law," (2) that the information sought cannot be obtained by alternative means less destructive of First Amendment values, and (3) that there is a "compelling and overriding need" for the information.[23] This three-part test, because it has been embraced in one form or another by lower courts and some states through their shield laws, represents an important summary of the circumstances under which journalists might be required to divulge their sources.

Nevertheless, even where the law works to reporters' advantage, the ethical quandary regarding the protection of sources remains problematical. The threshold issue is whether to promise anonymity in the first place. This is a critical decision because it sets in motion a potential conflict with other competing interests, particularly when the information provided by the sources relates to criminal or civil investigations or litigation. Thus, a promise of confidentiality should be used with extreme caution in the news-gathering process.

News sources are the cornerstone of good investigative journalism. And sometimes reporters feel compelled to promise confidentiality in order to solicit candid testimony from those who bear witness to the unsavory conduct of others. Reporters point out, perhaps correctly, that without the assurance of anonymity, some sources would dry up. Thus, the audience would be deprived of valuable information about matters of public interest. In such cases, reporters are laying claim to a fiduciary relationship with their readers and viewers, in which they serve as representatives of the public in its quest for information.

There is also resentment in the journalistic community at being used as an arm of law enforcement, a pawn for lazy prosecutors and other officials who are unable or unwilling to develop their own sources. Sometimes, however, no alternative sources are available, and thus this argument loses some of its appeal as a defense for reporters' privilege. But, in general, confidentiality in a reporter-source relationship does serve a valid social purpose, and a promise to a source should be broken only when there are overriding reasons for doing so.

Nevertheless, some serious reservations have been advanced about the use of confidential sources. Because the credibility of sources is one of the barometers of truthful communica-

tions, confidentiality deprives the audience of the opportunity to decide for themselves how much faith to put in the information. In addition, news sources, as noted earlier, act from a variety of motives, some of which are not commendable. Some like to influence public opinion by leaking information to reporters in exchange for a promise of confidentiality. Such sources are described variously as "authoritative," "highly placed," "unimpeachable," or "well informed." Others act from self-interest or with such objectionable motives as hatred or revenge. Still other sources are more altruistic and appear to be acting out of a legitimate concern for the public interest.

Another concern is that sources sometimes use their cloak of confidentiality to attack third parties who cannot defend themselves against an unidentified opponent. They venture opinions and observations that might remain unexpressed if the source were quoted by name.

There is also concern that such a privilege could serve as a license for irresponsible behavior by the media. Instead of searching for facts, they could spin webs of fantasy, maligning both public officials and private citizens in the process. No means of redress would be available, because the reporter could not be called as a witness to corroborate the allegations.[24]

Critics of reporters' privilege, especially as it relates to criminal cases, also contend that journalists should not be exempt from the moral and legal duties imposed on the citizenry at large. According to this view, one has a general obligation to assist the cause of justice by offering any evidence at one's disposal, and there is no compelling reason to relieve reporters of this moral responsibility. And the critics may have a point: journalists, who are quick to point out that politicians are not above the law, are often reluctant to apply the same egalitarian ideals to their own professional conduct.

A promise of confidentiality might also exempt a reporter from the normal editorial review processes, at least insofar as the credibility of sources is concerned. In the strictest sense, the promise precludes disclosure even to the reporter's employer, but some debate prevails within the journalistic community over whether promises of anonymity are really the reporter's or the institution's. For example, if reporters reveal their sources to an editor, has the promise of confidentiality been breached? Regardless of the views of individual journalists and editors on this issue, journalists have a moral obligation to clarify this point with the source before extending an offer of unqualified confidentiality. In addition, at the risk of offending the sense of reportorial independence and autonomy, news organizations should develop a written policy on this matter to serve as a moral beacon for employers and employees alike.[25]

Indeed, most news organizations now routinely require reporters to reveal their sources to their editors, a practice that was once opposed by both editors and independent-minded reporters. Some news organizations have specific policies stating that promises of confidentiality can flow only from the institution itself, not from individual reporters. An editor at the *Washington Post*, for example, would probably demand to know a source's identity. This policy, which would not have existed a decade earlier, was probably precipitated by the Janet Cooke affair, described in Chapter 2, when the *Post* discovered that she had fabricated a story about an eight-year-old drug addict. Her work of fiction almost went undetected because she was not required to divulge her sources to the paper's editors.[26]

Many news organizations discourage the use of confidential sources altogether. Only when all other "on-the-record" avenues of investigation have failed, according to these policies, should confidentiality be considered. It is also common practice to confirm the information provided by a confidential source with at least one other source. And when a story is based on a confidential source, the reason for the source's anonymity should be explained to the audience.

A Delicate Balance: Confidentiality and Competing Interests

The ethical dimensions of the reporter-source relationship are anchored in two important principles. First, the moral duty to keep a promise of confidentiality to a source is derived from the general obligations imposed on each member of society. Keeping promises, as pointed out earlier, is a value considered worthy of protection. A breach of secrecy should be the exception, not the rule. Second, the confidentiality of the reporter-source relationship is based on the reporter's *particularistic* obligations (see Chapter 2) to the field of journalism. Such obligations are set out in the professional codes.

Given this impressive array of moral support, some reporters have apparently concluded that their duty to protect their sources overrides all other obligations. And it is true that the special nature of the reporter-source relationship serves important societal functions, a reality that does not apply to most citizens in terms of their confidential relationships. Thus, the burden of proof is on those parties seeking the breach of confidentiality and the revelation of the sources' identities.

It does not follow, however, that journalists are *exempt* from competing obligations. A system of ethics cannot excuse any group from the rules of moral reasoning predicated simply on the *role* of that group within society. Reporters must engage in the same process of moral reasoning as the rest of us, in which competing values are weighed against the principle of confidentiality.[27] If confidentiality is then deemed to override other duties, reporters will have some justification for defending these decisions against the critics of their ethical behavior.[28]

In summary, ethical concerns affecting the reporter-source relationship arise at three points: (1) when the reporter decides whether to promise anonymity to a source; (2) when the reporter decides whether to divulge the source's identity to an editor or other supervisor, especially when there is no clear-cut company policy on this matter; and (3) when the journalist contemplates the breaking of a promise of confidentiality because of some conflicting moral principle or perhaps under penalty of law. The existence of a reporter's privilege is, for some members of the journalistic community, an essential tool of investigative reporting. But this does not exempt reporters from the obligation to follow the normal procedures of moral reasoning and to acknowledge that there are competing moral claims to their promises of confidentiality.

CHANGES IN THE REPORTER-SOURCE RELATIONSHIP

Clearly journalists are under more pressure than ever before to reveal their sources of information. In the past, some reporters have gone to jail rather than reveal their confidential sources, but the reporter-source relationship has changed perceptibly. Floyd Abrams, a prominent First Amendment attorney, believes that breaking promises to sources is more common than one might suspect and that a lot of "fibbing" is done about this practice because news organizations do not want to acknowledge it to the rest of the journalistic community.[29]

Perhaps the greatest source of pressure comes from the legal community, especially in libel suits. In such cases, journalists and their employers are confronted with the prospects of huge damage assessments, particularly when a plaintiff argues that the truth or falsity of an allegation can be determined only if the source's identity is revealed. If reporters refuse to comply with a court order to divulge the source's name, the judge may well enter a default judgment in favor of the plaintiff, a judgment that could run into the millions of dollars.[30]

Another reason sometimes cited for revealing a source is the professional obligation to set the record straight. Such was the case during the Iran-*Contra* hearings, when Lieutenant Colonel Oliver North complained that leaks had led to a *Newsweek* cover story concerning the details of the interception of an Egyptian plane carrying the suspected hijackers of the cruise ship *Achille Lauro* in 1985. *Newsweek* later identified North himself as the leak in order to set the record straight on the publication of the article.[31]

A journalist moral agent might also plead "altered circumstances" in justifying a broken promise to a source. This was the dilemma faced by Howard Weaver, editor of the *Anchorage* (Alaska) *Daily News*, when he was confronted with whether to break a promise to an AIDS patient and his family. A hemophiliac was suing a blood supplier, alleging that he had contracted AIDS from tainted blood he bought. In response to a plea from the man and his family, Weaver agreed not to use his name in the paper's coverage of the story. The stigma of having AIDS, the family argued, was equal to that of being raped. But the paper later discovered the man was having unprotected sex after he found out he had AIDS. "We were faced with the question of violating our pledge of confidentiality," said Weaver, "stacked up against what could have been obvious life-and-death circumstances to his partners." The editor told his mother he had a moral responsibility to warn the man's partners, and if he did not the paper would take action. The man later notified his partners, and the paper was taken off the horns of an ethical dilemma.[32]

Some reporters are also more likely today to breach a promise of confidentiality if they believe that the public has a right to particular kinds of information. Milton Coleman, a national reporter covering politics for the *Washington Post* in 1984, chose to publish some embarrassing remarks made by a Democratic presidential candidate, the Reverend Jesse Jackson, in a private conversation and then felt compelled to defend his decision on the editorial page of the *Post*. The conversation involved the relationship of American Jews with the state of Israel. According to Coleman's version of the meeting, Jackson said, "Let's talk black talk," which Coleman interpreted as speaking "on background" or not for direct attribution. At one point Jackson referred to Jews as "Hymies" and New York as "Hymietown." Coleman did not use the material but passed it along to Rick Atkinson, another *Post* reporter, who was preparing a lengthy article on Jackson's running feud with the Jewish community on domestic and foreign policy issues.[33] The references were included near the end of Atkinson's article, references that Jackson at first denied but later acknowledged.

Coleman defended his decision to break his implied "not for attribution" agreement with Jackson because Atkinson's article dealt with long-standing problems between blacks and Jews as well as statements by the Democratic candidate that offended Jews. Coleman offered another reason to justify his breach of confidentiality:

> Moreover, Jackson was running for the president of the United States. Even in context, even in "private" among reporters, even "off the record," the remarks suggested an insensitivity to those he referred [*sic*] in the sense that he believed that in unguarded moments with other blacks or with disarmed reporters it was acceptable to make such references.[34]

Coleman's defense raises the question of whether the status of a source as a public figure, particularly a presidential contender, justifies less respect for the value of confidentiality. Are there times, as he suggests, when the public interest should take precedence over the reporter-source relationship? In reviewing the Jackson controversy, Klaidman and Beauchamp question the subordination of the value of trust that underlies this relationship for the sake of the public interest:

> We admire his courage and his legal right to choose the course of disclosure, and we acknowledge the immorality of Jackson's comment, but Coleman's decision still casts some

doubt on his trustworthiness in reporter-source relationships, and it is difficult to estimate the consequences of the skepticism that naturally arises as a result. In the short term, the public utility was undoubtedly served by Coleman's disclosure. But public service is not always an overriding moral value, and the long-term judgment is more difficult to make.[35]

Although confidential sources will probably continue to occupy an important niche in investigative reporting, the trend away from the traditional view that the reporter-source relationship is sacred is unmistakable. News organizations have tightened their policies and have reined in reporters who might, in their enthusiasm to get an exclusive, make unnecessary promises of confidentiality to their sources. Nevertheless, in those cases in which promises are made—wisely or unwisely—reporters who are asked to break their pledge of confidentiality must still wrestle with the moral dilemma of whether to do so.

THE PRINCIPLE OF CONFIDENTIALITY: HYPOTHETICAL CASE STUDIES

The cases in this chapter provide the opportunity to examine several issues involving the principle of confidentiality. Although the scenarios deal primarily with the relationships between reporters and their sources and the ethical responsibilities of PR practitioners, confidentiality is a value that affects all of us, regardless of our professional interest.

In analyzing these cases, keep in mind the three approaches to ethical decision making described in Chapter 3: deontological (duty-based) ethics, teleological (consequence-based) ethics, and Aristotle's golden mean. Of course, any ethical dilemma involving confidentiality must begin with the general rule as outlined at the outset of this chapter: the burden of proof for breaching confidentiality is on the party seeking disclosure.

A duty-based theorist would consider confidentiality a basic right grounded in the principle of autonomy. Thus, a breach of secrecy, especially when made pursuant to a promise, would be justified only when confidentiality must be overridden by some other basic right. An example would be the right to a fair trial, the outcome of which depends, in part, on a defendant's access to a reporter's sources of information. But even here there is a duty to keep promises, and the abrogation of a promise can seldom be justified, according to the deontological perspective.

Consequentialists, on the other hand, would examine the potential impact of disclosure before breaching confidentiality. This process involves, first, measuring the *short-term harm (or benefits)* of the decision. Second, the *long-term consequences* must be evaluated. For example, in deciding whether to break a promise of confidentiality, a reporter should weigh not only the relative harm to the source and other interested parties but also the long-term impact on the journalist's (and perhaps the institution's) credibility and future effectiveness as an investigative reporter.

Aristotle's golden mean requires a search for a "mean" between two extremes. In most cases, however, there may not be a middle ground for exploration, because any release of information effectively violates the principle of confidentiality.

CASE STUDIES

▶ CASE 6-1
AIDS Patients and Confidentiality

Sandy Beach is a resort community located along the Atlantic shore of the United States. Its year-round residents number 75,000, but these figures mushroom during the summer tourist season. Sandy Beach also sports a small but growing gay population that migrated from the surrounding urban centers to escape the feeling of isolation and the "gay bashing" that had been the sport of street gangs and other idle teenagers. Sandy Beach is frequented by the rich and famous as well as ordinary tourists, and no lifestyle is beyond the bounds of tolerance.

But as the number of gays residing in Sandy Beach grew, so did the reported incidences of AIDS. Within five years the problem rose to epidemic proportions, mirroring the experiences of the larger cities around the state. A few cases of AIDS among heterosexuals began to emerge, alarming the conservative majority in the state legislature. As long as the AIDS virus had been confined to the gay community, it had been viewed as a medical problem. Now that it was being detected among other members of society, the issue had taken on political overtones. Thus, the legislature, in an action that some described as one of desperation rather than enlightenment, passed a law making it a criminal offense to "intentionally or knowingly expose another to the AIDS virus through sexual contact, without the knowledge and consent of the partner." Proponents of the measure argued that the statute would bring about some measure of responsibility and reduce sexual promiscuity. Critics countered that the law would just drive people with AIDS underground and make them reluctant to seek treatment.

Nevertheless, the AIDS epidemic certainly caught the public's attention. It also caught the eye of Jack Summerfield, a reporter for the Arlington *Sun-Times*, the only daily paper in a city just twenty miles from Sandy Beach. Summerfield spent several weeks gathering facts and figures from various state agencies, including the health department, in preparation for a series of articles on the epidemic. But the reporter knew that statistics alone only serve to sterilize a story and rob it of its human dimension. Summerfield wanted to produce a series that enlightened the audience about the personal suffering and tragedy and the feeling of hopelessness that attended the disease. To do so, he needed to tell the story from the perspective of the victims themselves.

Summerfield had already cultivated some contacts in Sandy Beach from a previous article on the gay community. After some initial hesitation, these sources led him to three friends who were afflicted with the AIDS virus. However, all three insisted on anonymity in exchange for their frank exchanges with the reporter. Summerfield agreed not to divulge their identities to anyone. The three told their own stories of growing up with a sexual identity crisis, learning to cope with public ostracism, and battling with AIDS. During the interviews, one of the men admitted that he had had several sexual partners following his diagnosis for AIDS and that he had probably infected at least two of them.

A couple of weeks later, a five-part series on the AIDS epidemic began in the *Sun-Times* under Summerfield's byline. The editor was so impressed with the articles that he entered them in an AP contest. The district attorney of Sandy Beach liked them, too. He invited Summerfield in to chat about the articles, especially the admission by one of his unidentified sources that he had probably infected others after his diagnosis for AIDS. Frank Cordes, never one to engage in idle chatter, got right to the point: he needed the name of Summerfield's source in order to decide whether there was probable cause to believe that a crime had been committed. The DA pointed to the new law concerning the illegal spreading of the virus and pointed out that, according to the source's own admission, he had had several sexual partners after he had been informed of his affliction.

Summerfield sympathized with the DA's predicament but responded that he had promised his source confidentiality. He could not, in good conscience, divulge the identity of the gay interviewee who had made the candid confession. Besides, the reporter noted, any forced disclosure would violate his rights as a reporter. But Cordes

was in no mood for constitutional niceties and told Summerfield, in language filled with colorful expletives, that it was his job to prosecute lawbreakers and that, like any other private citizen, the reporter had a duty to tell what he knew about possible criminal conduct. The DA then threatened to get a court order compelling Summerfield to reveal his sources for the story but gave the reporter forty-eight hours to reconsider his refusal before taking such drastic action.

Summerfield departed Cordes's office feeling both drained and ambivalent about his confrontation with the DA. In his four-year tenure with the *Sun-Times*, he had never used sources who had insisted on anonymity, and the prospect of choosing between breaking his promise and a contempt-of-court citation was not an appealing one. The state's shield law, which had recognized a privilege for the reporter-source relationship, was highly qualified and merely heightened the legal uncertainties of the investigative reporting process. Summerfield could not feel confident of being sustained in his refusal to cooperate with the DA, but, the legal issues aside, the young reporter was also concerned about the ethical dilemma posed by his predicament.

On the one hand, he felt confident of his ethical posture. As a reporter investigating a matter of public interest, he had made a promise not to reveal the sources of his information. It was an act of faith in the journalistic community that reporters should not break promises to confidential sources. To do so would erode the trust that reporters must rely on to fulfill their social mandate as representatives of the public. The DA should develop his own sources, Summerfield believed, rather than relying on the good offices of journalists. Otherwise, reporters would be viewed as arms of the law. In addition, without the promise of confidentiality, the paper's readers would have been deprived of this firsthand and tragic account of the devastating impact of the AIDS virus within the gay community.

However, Summerfield also wondered whether his personal dislike for the AIDS statute had clouded his moral vision. He did believe that the law was ill advised and would simply deter AIDS carriers from seeking assistance, especially if they believed that they might be prosecuted for their alleged promiscuity. But the epidemic posed an immediate danger to all of society, and those who ignored the well-being of their sexual partners needed to be restrained. Perhaps the threat of criminal sanctions was the only effective deterrent. Summerfield had been aware of the law when he made his promises, and, with the clarity of hindsight, he wondered whether he had been hasty in doing so. He had to admit that the DA's concerns were legitimate. Perhaps journalists did have the same obligations as other citizens to assist in administering justice. The legislature, after all, made public policy, and perhaps this was one of those rare instances when public policy should take precedence over the reporter's privilege. Would justice be better served by his silence or a breach of confidence?

As a journalist Summerfield felt a moral obligation to those victims who had trusted him. But he also wondered whether the greater social good was being served by his stubborn refusal to cooperate with the district attorney.

THE CASE STUDY

The cost of protecting one's news sources can be high. Some reporters have gone to jail rather than divulge the identities of their sources. Although more than half the states now have shield laws recognizing a journalist's privilege, many of these laws are qualified in the protection they afford. There are, however, ethical issues that go beyond the legal ones.

The so-called reporter's privilege is really just a special application of a moral principle that applies to all of us: the obligation to keep promises. But it is also true that the motivation for reporters' promises sets them apart from the rest of us. When confidentiality is guaranteed to a source, it is normally done with the public interest in mind. If some sources cannot be assured of remaining anonymous, the public may be deprived of vital information.

But what if the moral agent had no right to make the promise in the first place? A case in point would be college professors who promise to waive graduation requirements for students when they have no authority to do so. Surely there are limits

to the circumstances under which reporters should feel free to promise their sources confidentiality. In this scenario, Summerfield was aware of the existence of the criminal statute concerning AIDS carriers and yet chose to conceal the identity of his sources anyway. If he had not done so, of course, he would have had no story, or at least not one with the same dramatic impact.

Assuming that a journalist feels justified in making a promise, the question arises whether the duty as a citizen should take precedence over reporters' privilege. Can a journalist ethically defend the breach of confidentiality? When the threat of legal sanctions hangs over the reporter, as in this case, does it add moral weight to the breaking of a promise to a source? Conversely, if reporters should refuse to obey a court order to divulge their sources, are they morally justified in doing so? Do their ethical obligations outweigh their legal ones?

There are essentially two ways of approaching a case involving reporters' privilege from an ethical perspective. One way is to decide that journalists, like everyone else, must weigh the relevant factors and decide which obligations are important in each case. The other approach is to decide that protection of sources is essential to the practice of journalism and that confidentiality must override all other obligations.

This is not an easy dilemma and poses some rather fundamental questions about the functions of journalists within our society. Assume the role of Summerfield, and, using the model for moral reasoning, decide whether you will comply with the district attorney's request to reveal your sources.

▶ CASE 6-2
Satellite Photography and Military Security

The Middle East had again become a dangerous place. Still chastened by its humiliating defeat in the Persian Gulf War, Iraq had devoted its energies and resources to rebuilding its once formidable military machine and was poised to resume its aggressive role as a major player in the region. The Iraqi people had suffered enormous economic and personal hardships in the wake of the United Nations sanctions imposed following the liberation of Kuwait, and the country's leadership was unrepentant in its determination to avenge its national honor. Despite the UN sanctions, the Iraqis had once again launched an assault against Kuwait. But this time, according to intelligence reports, the aggressors planned to strike at the heart of American national interests in the Gulf: the Saudi Arabian oil fields.

The Americans had maintained a military presence in Kuwait following the liberation of that country, and the Defense Department quickly implemented its contingency plan to counter the Iraqi invasion. The Pentagon, along with its allies, ordered substantial reinforcements to all ground, air, and naval forces as American troops prepared to thwart the aggressive designs of the Iraqi government and to protect the nation's vital national interests in the region. And with the smell of war in the air, media managers quickly began to reassess their budgets in anticipation of committing considerable resources to another "high-tech" American military engagement in the Middle East. In the meantime, journalists, many of whom were veterans of the Persian Gulf War, began to speculate among themselves as to whether they would be eyewitnesses or mere spectators in this country's latest military engagement.

The Gulf War had been accompanied by a highly controlled flow of information from the battle zone. Senior military officers, many of whom blamed the media for the American "defeat" in Vietnam, were determined not to repeat the indignity of losing public support while American lives were being sacrificed on foreign soil. The Gulf War lasted only six weeks, but the media's adversarial role had been effectively neutralized as reporters obediently filed government-supplied accounts of the impressive allied engagement and rapid defeat of the Iraqi military. But the Fourth Estate's postmortem on its uncritical coverage of the war concluded that this had not been journalism's finest hour.[36] This assessment had prompted a dialogue between the Pentagon and the media over war coverage, and in 1992 the Defense Department adopted new rules allowing journalists more ac-

cess to military operations than they had during the Persian Gulf War.[37] With the new threat in the Middle East, reporters were anxious to test the new rules under combat conditions.

As the American and allied military presence in the Persian Gulf region increased, the Pentagon's public relations machinery went into overdrive to accommodate inquiries from both the Washington press corps and those who sought credentials to report from the war zone. Both the State Department and the Pentagon conducted daily briefings, attempting to assure the nation that the aggressor would suffer the same fate as it had several years earlier. These briefings were dutifully attended by the cadre of journalists hungering for any journalistic morsels that might be gleaned from these daily rituals in spin control.

The Pentagon's briefings were usually conducted by General Donald McBride, a thirty-year veteran who seemed to relish his role as information gatekeeper in what could be the next American military engagement. McBride's responses to reporters' questions were usually terse as he skillfully avoided offering any significant insights into the Pentagon's battle plan for Operation Desert Hope, as it was designated by the Defense Department.

As hostilities resumed on Kuwaiti soil and the military buildup continued, rumors began to circulate that a new, sophisticated missile known as the SST-120 had been deployed to Saudi Arabia. The SST-120 exceeded anything currently in the American arsenal in terms of range and accuracy, but its destructive capabilities were controversial. The missile's warhead could be packed with a substance known as a "nerve-blocking agent," which would be released on impact and paralyze all living organisms within a three-mile radius for a limited period of time. The Pentagon had been proactive in its public assessment of its new weapon, describing it as "a humane way to neutralize enemy forces without great loss of life on either side, thus reducing the need for surgical nuclear strikes in a limited theater of operations." But environmentalists and human rights groups had challenged the Pentagon's optimistic appraisal, alleging that the blocking agent could cause permanent nerve damage and possibly death in some cases. The Defense Department had beaten an orderly public relations retreat, and the controversy soon disappeared from the nation's headlines. *Until now!*

"Are the rumors true," an AP correspondent asked during one of the daily briefings, "that the United States has dispatched SST-120 missiles to the region, and, if so, will the warheads be loaded with this new nerve blocking agent?"

"I don't want to comment on the details of our military operations," General McBride declared, "except to note that we expect our conventional weapons should be sufficient to accomplish our military objectives in the region." The general's remarks were dutifully reported by all of the news organizations represented at the briefing.

Sandra Macvey was among those who had witnessed General McBride's response to her colleague's question concerning the missile's role in the Pentagon's war preparations. As her network's Pentagon correspondent for eight years, Macvey had accommodated herself to the inevitability of attempts at what she considered media manipulation by the military establishment. But she prided herself on her independence and tenacity in ferreting out information from other sources to balance the Pentagon's relentless public relations assault in times of crisis. She was unapologetic for her adversarial role as government watchdog but had still managed to cultivate the respect of her Pentagon connections.

McBride's refusal to confirm the deployment of the SST-120 was understandable, particularly in light of its controversial military capabilities. But Macvey's journalistic intuition convinced her that the newest, most sophisticated offensive missile in the Army's arsenal would indeed figure prominently if the hostilities in the Middle East did not end in a swift victory for the allied forces or if American casualties began to mount. Her network's latest acquisition from Satellite Images, Inc. (SI), confirmed her suspicions.

Satellite Images was a commercial company that specialized in gathering data from the most technologically advanced remote sensing satellite that was capable of photographing and mapping intricate details on the earth's surface. All of the networks had used SI's photographs in covering

such newsworthy events as the nuclear disaster in Chernobyl, Russia, and the war in Bosnia-Herzegovina. But neither of those events had involved American military security, a distinction that was not lost on Sandra Macvey and her network colleagues.

"These images are unmistakable," declared Macvey as she reviewed the photographs with producer Lydell Thompson and Washington network bureau chief Robert Bradley. "The SST-120 has been deployed—here, along the Saudi border.

"The question is where do we go from here," said Bradley. "The Pentagon refuses to comment on this missile system and its possible use in the Middle East. But we know it's capable of carrying this nerve-blocking agent. Bill Mathews has examined these pictures and says the way the SST-120 is deployed, it probably is packed with the chemical. Otherwise, there would be no real advantage to using the missile in this type of engagement." Mathews, a former Defense Department intelligence analyst, was the network's military consultant, who had provided valuable insights during the Persian Gulf War.

"If we use these photographs in our coverage, there will be some very unhappy people in the Pentagon," remarked Thompson. "Sandra has a good relationship with the top brass. But that could change if we air this story."

"That's true," responded Macvey, recognizing the gravity of the situation. "And we could leave ourselves open to charges of posing a threat to the Pentagon's military strategy or endangering the lives of American troops. But, on the other hand, in a sense the press corps has been misled; McBride said he expects conventional weapons to do the job, but the fact that the SST-120 is already deployed raises some serious doubts. Perhaps we need to air these photographs to set the record straight. Our competitors probably have the same photos; we're going to look foolish if we sit on this story. And we could look like pawns if we can document this story and still don't run it."

"I agree this story is newsworthy, and it's not clear to me as to how such a report would impact on our military strategy," said Bradley. "Also, only time will tell whether the new rules will really work, whether reporters will have more access to the battle front than in the 1991 war. So far, most of our information has come from the Pentagon. We need something more.

"But we have to ask ourselves," Bradley continued, "whether there is a need to broadcast these photos now. If the missiles are brought into play in the conflict, that will be time enough to report on their use. Are we compromising our military position in the region by revealing to the world—and, of course, the Iraqis—that this new weapon is operational and available for use in the event that Saudi Arabia is seriously threatened. The Iraqis may find out anyway, but should we make their task any easier?"

"I don't really see this as a security issue," responded Macvey. "The whole world knows about the SST-120. It's controversial, and it's been in the news. The only question is whether the missile has become a player in this military conflict. And, besides, reporting this information might even act as a deterrent to an Iraqi invasion of Saudi Arabia. If they know this missile has been deployed, maybe they'll think twice before continuing with this suicide mission."

"Perhaps," said Bradley, "but is it really up to us to release these photos? The Pentagon has chosen, for its own reasons, to maintain confidentiality over any information regarding deployment of the SST-120. We really can't be sure of how this fits into their overall military strategy."

As the bureau chief, Bradley was afflicted with moral ambivalence. It was times like this that he resented the very satellite technology that had revolutionized his own network's role as a player on the international stage. He had always been a staunch defender of the public's right to know and had exalted his staff to use every means at their disposal to lay bare the inner workings of the government agencies they covered. But as his network's representative in the nation's capital, Bradley was concerned that his news operatives would be accused of violating military security and would thereby become part of the story rather than detached observers of the drama unfolding in Kuwait and Saudi Arabia. He was also aware that opinion polls revealed strong public support for America's role in the Middle East. The news media were not held in

such high esteem. Bradley pondered this ethical dilemma as he attempted to balance his network's responsibility to its viewers against the government's need to maintain confidentiality in matters of military security.

THE CASE STUDY

As the twenty-first century nears, both the opportunities and the problems awaiting humankind in the information age are becoming manifest. The new technologies have expanded our horizons and altered the very essence of civilization, but they have also confronted us with some staggering ethical dilemmas.

The conflict between the media and the military over war coverage and operational security assumes different dimensions with each new crisis. But satellite technology, particularly the privatization of outer space, has altered the equation in favor of the media, making it more difficult for the Pentagon to control the flow of information about its military activities. However, because of the potential harm to the national interest accruing from the rather casual and perhaps irresponsible dissemination of this information, the media are more obliged than ever to engage in sound moral reasoning before violating the cloak of confidentiality surrounding the development and deployment of military hardware.

In the scenario outlined here, the network's Pentagon correspondent, Sandra Macvey, believes the satellite images of the military's most sophisticated weapon should be included in her news coverage. She believes, first, that such a position is justified to "set the record straight" because of what she believes was a rather evasive response from the Pentagon's spokesperson during a briefing. Second, Macvey notes correctly that this missile is controversial (i.e., it is already newsworthy) because of the dispute over the destructive capabilities and the safety of the nerve-blocking agent that can be delivered in the warhead of the SST-120.

On the other hand, the network's bureau chief, Robert Bradley, has sounded a note of caution. He is obviously concerned about the breach of military security that could result from Macvey's report if the satellite images are included and whether his network's aggressive pursuit of the public's right to know might result instead in a public relations disaster. He appears to view this dilemma in rather stark terms, as a conflict between the public's interest and the need to maintain some confidentiality over military information. In this case, are these two values necessarily inconsistent?

For the purpose of resolving this "hi-tech" ethical quandary, assume the role of network bureau chief Robert Bradley. And then, using the SAD Formula for moral reasoning outlined in Chapter 3, decide whether you will approve Sandra Macvey's inclusion of the satellite photos in her news coverage of the latest episode in America's military presence in the Middle East.

▶ **CASE 6-3**
The Grand Jury and Secrecy

Fran Mason had waited eagerly and somewhat impatiently for the results of the grand jury's investigation, and the moment of truth was almost at hand. Mason covered city hall for the Arlington *Sun-Times* and had been intrigued by the allegations of a "sex for hire" scheme being operated right out of the police department's own vice squad. Rumors had circulated for several years concerning unsavory off-duty activities of vice squad detectives, but investigations had produced nothing concrete until one of those involved, apparently in a moment of moral repentance, decided to strike a deal with the district attorney. Armed with the evidence provided by his informant, the DA impaneled a grand jury to investigate the charges.

However, the case was a hard one to crack, and the grand jury convened off and on for several months to hear evidence. But now the grand jury was about to issue its report, and indictments would probably follow. Mason's wait was about over—or so she thought.

In a surprise move, a state district judge, Eldon McCray, dismissed the grand jury for apparent irregularities in the investigatory process and ordered the report sealed. He declined to elaborate on his action or to provide any hint of what was in

the report. Mason called the DA, but he was also evasive, citing an order by the judge not to discuss the case or the contents of the report. The judge had similarly admonished the members of the grand jury not to discuss the report until he lifted the "gag order."

Mason was frustrated. She believed that the public had a right to know what was in the report. Had the grand jury itself been compromised? The body had spent months listening to evidence and testimony, and now its findings had been sealed from public view. Mason was well aware of the state law that ensured the secrecy of grand jury proceedings. There were good reasons for this enforced confidentiality, and the reporter had no real quarrel with the intent of the law. It covered virtually everyone associated with the grand jury, including the jurors themselves. The law, however, did not extend to the media, because to do so would raise constitutional questions. Nevertheless, the secrecy imposed by state law was by and large effective.

Mason had obtained a list of the grand jury members from the courthouse and considered contacting them to see whether they could shed some light on this bizarre turn of events. Some would undoubtedly obey the judge's order, but others might be willing to offer some informative insights. But Mason was unsure what her course of action should be. On the one hand, she understood the need for secrecy during an investigation. Even though the grand jury had completed its work, the judge had still imposed a cloak of confidentiality over the investigation and the final report. Perhaps there were individual rights to be protected if another grand jury was impaneled.

However, Mason also believed that the public had a right to know at least why the investigation had been terminated and the report sealed. Should she ask the jurors to break the law in order to provide this information? The end was a noble one, but in the process she would have to rely on immoral means.

THE CASE STUDY

Reporters often rely on the principle of confidentiality in defending the use of anonymous sources.

A breach of that privileged relationship between reporter and source would (according to some journalists) erode the flow of valuable information to the public.

In this case, however, the reporter is considering asking others to breach secrecy in order to inform the public about the results of a criminal investigation. Can encouraging grand jurors to break the law because of some perceived higher moral good be defended on ethical grounds?

Assuming the role of Mason, use the formula for moral reasoning to decide whether you will seek the information you need from the grand jurors.

▶ CASE 6-4
The Search for a College President

Middleton College had been without a president for a year, but the search was beginning to bear fruit. Following the resignation of Susan Hoglin last summer, a search committee had been formed and a nationwide search conducted. Although Middleton was a small community college, its reputation was solid, and the committee was confident of attracting a good pool of talent.

They were not disappointed. After an extensive advertising campaign, 150 applicants had filed their résumés with the committee by the January 15 deadline. With the college's affirmative action officer looking on, the committee had then culled from the pile those who clearly were unqualified. Within six weeks, another cut was made, and the pool had been narrowed to twenty.

It was then that Maria Lightfoot, the education reporter for the *Middleton Sentinel*, began paying more attention to the candidates. Although she had followed the committee's activities since its inception, the paper had not seen fit to publish the names of the applicants until some narrowing of the list had been accomplished. Lightfoot was aware that the list of twenty would eventually be cut to five finalists, but she believed that the time had come to apprise her readers of the credentials of those who appeared, in the judgment of

the committee, to be the best qualified for the position.

With this in mind, Lightfoot asked the search committee chairman to provide her with a list of names and copies of the résumés of the twenty applicants who remained viable candidates for the position. He refused, saying that some of the applicants had specifically requested that their applications remain confidential, because their current employers were unaware of their interest in the position at Middleton.

Lightfoot persisted, noting that she was entitled to the information under the state's liberal public records law. On the advice of Middleton College's attorney, the chairman relented but asked the reporter to withhold publication of the names until the five finalists had been selected. He was afraid that if their applications became known through a breach of their request for confidentiality, some of the most qualified candidates would withdraw from consideration. This, said the chairman, would harm the college and bode ill for future faculty and administrative searches.

Lightfoot had always had good relations with Middleton College administration and staff and was hesitant to do anything that would impair that relationship. Thus, the reporter made no promises but said she would consider the chairman's request.

THE CASE STUDY

This case involves a disturbing ethical dilemma that has developed in recent years. As more and more information is made available to the media and the public through public records, the principle of confidentiality has been sorely tested. From a legal standpoint, of course, the media are free to disseminate information from public records without fear of liability. But should they use this legal right to justify publishing facts that may be inimical to public or private interests?

On the other hand, in this scenario Lightfoot could take the position that if the legislature had wanted to exempt college search procedures from the reach of the public records law, it would have done so. Otherwise, it must be presumed that the intent was to open those procedures and records to public scrutiny. But in any case the reporter must consider the committee chairman's concerns about harm to the presidential search and those candidates who requested confidentiality. These concerns, of course, must be balanced against the public's right to know about the results of the search (for which public funds have been expended).

Assume the role of Lightfoot, and, using the moral reasoning model, make a decision on whether you will honor the committee chairman's request or go ahead and publish the names of the twenty applicants remaining on the list.

▶ **CASE 6-5**
Attorney-Client Privilege and the Public's Right to Know

The FBI was still basking in the publicity of its latest law enforcement triumph. Mohammed Ahmed, who had been indicted in absentia for masterminding the bombing of the Empire State Building, had finally returned to confront his accusers. Ahmed, a Palestinian by birth, had been a rather shadowy figure and a minor player on the international stage of terrorism until he had publicly claimed credit for the brutal bombing of a commercial jetliner over Greece in February 1995, which had resulted in the deaths of 325 passengers and crew. Ahmed was subsequently linked to a rather obscure Iranian-sponsored fundamentalist group committed to the destruction of Israel and its Western supporters.

But Ahmed apparently had not been content to confine his terrorist activities to the Middle East and Europe. According to the FBI, he had slipped undetected through U.S. customs using a fake passport and had quickly organized a group of followers who had preceded him. Their goal was to carry out attacks on symbols of American power and prestige and humiliate their antagonists in their own backyard. The Empire State Building was the first of several landmarks targeted by Ahmed's

group, but the mission had not been entirely successful. Although the first two floors of the structure were gutted in the explosion that had killed three people, the edifice remained defiantly intact in response to this unprovoked assault.

An FBI informant fingered Ahmed as the mastermind behind this plot, and the agency moved quickly to take him into custody. However, even as his lieutenants were planting the bomb in a remote corner of the Empire State Building, the elusive Ahmed had crossed the border into Canada and had returned to his base of operations in the Middle East. Within a few weeks, the FBI had compiled enough evidence on Ahmed to link him to the crime, and a grand jury indicted the terrorist for his role in the bombing. The State Department was determined to bring Ahmed to justice and offered a $2 million reward for information that would lead to his arrest.

This rather lucrative financial incentive soon produced results, as an informant in Pakistan, motivated more by self-interest than principle, led police to a local hotel where Ahmed had registered under an assumed name. The Pakistanis were anxious to rid themselves of this controversial guest and quickly extradited the terrorist to the United States and into the custody of the FBI.

Ahmed was housed in a maximum-security cell just a few blocks from where the bombing that had led to his arrest occurred. He was arraigned before a federal magistrate in New York, who appointed an Arab-speaking attorney, Yassir Assad, to represent the unrepentant defendant. During the next several weeks, Assad met repeatedly with Ahmed to forge a meaningful attorney-client relationship and plan an aggressive defense against what Assad believed was a rather dubious chain of evidence against the accused.

As the trial date approached, the media prepared for the high drama that was sure to emerge as Mohammed Ahmed was given his constitutional right to due process. Network reporter Daniel Thorn was among those journalists who eagerly awaited the jury selection process, which would signal the official beginning of the trial. Thorn had paid his dues as a foreign correspondent for twelve years in the Middle East and was culturally attuned to, if not a master of, the rather mysterious workings of the Arab fundamentalist mind. He had never met Ahmed, but during his tenure in the Persian Gulf region, he had often visited the breeding grounds of such religious and political fanatics. Since his return to his homeland, his fascination with and revulsion of state-sponsored terrorism remained undiminished.

Thorn was looking forward to his journalistic role in this high-profile drama and had prepared thoroughly for his engagement. Three weeks before the commencement of the trial, the veteran correspondent was reviewing some notes in his New York office when he received a call from a government source, Jacob Marley, who had often supplied Thorn with inside information. Marley again asked for a meeting with Thorn.

"I have something you might be interested in," said Marley as he sipped a cup of black coffee in a diner just a few blocks from network headquarters. "You're covering the Ahmed case, aren't you?" Thorn responded affirmatively to what he considered a rhetorical question.

"The government has been monitoring the conversations between Ahmed and his attorney," continued Marley. "I'm sure they know nothing about this. I have dubs of two of the tapes here. I don't know if they contain anything interesting. Most of it's in Arabic. But you can have it translated."

As usual, Thorn did not inquire into how Marley had acquired the tapes. In the past Marley had been a valuable source of information, and he was confident that this would prove to be no exception. Thorn retreated to what he often described as the organized chaos of the network newsroom, where he found Joel Silverman, the executive producer of the evening news, huddled with several writers. He briefly described his journalistic coup to Silverman. The producer was impressed but immediately recognized the ethical and legal implications of the network's use of these surreptitious recordings. Silverman asked for a meeting with Malcolm Sikes, whose position as news division president compelled a divided loyalty between the journalistic imperative and corporate responsibility. Unfortunately, sometimes the two seemed incompatible.

Sikes, Silverman, and Thorn were joined in the meeting by a translator, who was also a network consultant on the Middle East. They listened intently as the recordings disclosed, often in barely audible tones, the confidential conversations in Arabic between Ahmed and his attorney in his maximum-security residence. The two tapes, which ran for a total of 10 hours, focused primarily on the credibility of two government witnesses, both of whom had been former lieutenants of the accused terrorist. Apparently Assad had succeeded in forging a bond of trust with his reluctant client as Ahmed chattered incessantly and candidly about his relationship with those he termed "traitors." There was no admission of guilt on the tapes, but on two occasions he expressed sympathy for the Holy War being waged against the "enemies of Palestine" and repeatedly accused his former associates of duplicity in attempting to undermine his leadership among his fundamentalist followers. To his attorney, Ahmed denied any involvement in the bombing of the Empire State Building.

Sikes finally broke the silence. "You're sure these tapes are authentic?" he asked Thorn.

"Yes. I got them from a source who has always proved to be reliable in the past. And I recognize the voices on the tape. In addition, since receiving these tapes I've heard through other contacts that the feds have been monitoring the conversations between Assad and Ahmed."

"The tapes are quite interesting," replied Sikes. "I don't know whether Ahmed is telling the truth, but these conversations really raise some interesting questions about the credibility of the government's two key witnesses. But if we air these tapes, we could be asking for trouble."

"But these recordings provide a rare glimpse into the defense strategy in this case," responded Thorn. "The FBI, at least publicly, has always maintained that a conviction is a virtual certainty. But the defense apparently plans to attack the credibility of the two key witnesses. If they succeed, this case could come apart. The FBI has other circumstantial evidence, but in my judgment these witnesses are crucial to their case. I think these tapes are newsworthy. They relate to a high-profile case. The public interest here is high."

"I'm not so sure," said Sikes, who held a law degree but had never joined the legal community. "This could be a violation of the attorney-client privilege. This network did not actually monitor these conversations—that was the government's misconduct—but if we air these tapes we'll certainly have to share part of the blame. And we could take a public beating on this, especially from the legal profession. And they won't have any trouble catching the attention of our competitors and our print colleagues."

"But like you said, we didn't make these recordings," replied Silverman. "If Assad has a complaint, he should direct it against the government. These tapes provide a rare insight into this case even before it goes to trial. Our job should not be to worry about the attorney-client privilege. The breach of confidentiality occurred when the recordings were made. But this case—every aspect of it—is a matter of public interest. We shouldn't be in the business of suppressing relevant and newsworthy information relating to such an important story."

"Exactly where is the public interest?" asked Sikes rather testily. He did not disagree with Silverman entirely, but he felt compelled to play devil's advocate out of allegiance to his managerial responsibilities. "Ahmed may be a despicable human being to the average American, but he is still entitled to a fair trial. And that's what the public interest really is. I don't see any compelling news value in violating attorney-client privilege and airing part of the defense strategy on national TV. There will be plenty of grist for the journalistic mill as the trial unfolds."

But Thorn was persistent. "But there's more to this story than just this confidential conversation. Doesn't the public have a right to know about possible government misconduct in prosecuting this case?"

Sikes conceded that there was merit in both points of view. The tapes did add a dimension to this story that would certainly be of interest to the network's viewers—an inside look at the defense strategy—as well as the government's role in monitoring the conversations between Ahmed and his attorney. On the other hand, if they aired the tapes, the news division would become a major player in this breach of confidentiality. The network could suffer a public relations debacle. In addition, Sikes wondered if Ahmed's emotional and often fanatical recorded comments contributed much to the underlying search for truth that is the cornerstone of the American justice system. While the accused terrorist and his attorney continued their preparations for trial unaware of this breach in their privileged relationship, the head of one of this country's premier news organizations wondered whether the public's need to know was sufficient to justify this violation of the attorney-client privilege.

THE CASE STUDY

The attorney-client privilege represents one of the most strongly defended confidential relationships in American society. It is considered fundamental to our system of justice. However, in this case the news organization is not responsible for the initial violation of the attorney-client privilege. The government, apparently without the knowledge of Ahmed and his attorney, secretly monitored their conversations, and these tapes wound up in the network's hands. Are the networks also guilty of exacerbating the problem by airing these tapes to a national TV audience? Malcolm Sikes, the news division president, questions whether the network should participate in this breach of confidentiality. After all, *both* the government's alleged misconduct and the broadcasting of these confidential conversations might adversely affect Ahmed's constitutional guarantee of a fair trial. He is also concerned about the public relations fallout from what some might perceive as journalistic arrogance in the handling of this matter.

But the network's correspondent, Daniel Thorn, is less concerned with the constitutional implications and the intricacies of the attorney-client privilege than with what he feels is the journalistic imperative to evaluate the newsworthiness of the recorded conversations themselves and accommodate the public's need to know about alleged government misconduct in the case.

As noted earlier in this chapter, "Confidentiality is a prima facie duty that can be overridden only by other, weightier considerations. Thus, the burden of proof is generally on those who wish to override it." Can the network justify its participation in this breach of the attorney-client privilege on some overriding moral principle?

Respond to this question by first assuming the role of news division president Malcolm Sikes. And then, applying the formula for moral reasoning outlined in Chapter 3, render a judgment on whether you feel the network is ethically justified in breaching the attorney-client privilege between Yassir Assad and his controversial client.

▶ **CASE 6-6**
Public Relations and Whistle-Blowing

Like many other hospitals, Avondale General had at one time suffered from an abundance of beds and a shortage of patients. Dramatic advances in health care, an increase in outpatient treatment, and a substantial reduction in the number of elective surgery cases had reduced the average daily hospital occupancy to 60 percent. The economic impact on the medical facility had been staggering, with cutbacks in services and a reduction of staff. The future of Avondale General, one of two hospitals in the city, had not looked promising—until the installation of the region's first cardiac critical care unit.

By general agreement of the hospital staff, the cardiac wing had been the hospital's "white knight." A team of heart specialists had proposed Avondale General as the site of the region's first cardiac facility because of its central location and its adaptability for expansion. The unit had opened its door six years before and had already compiled an impressive number of open-heart surgery cases. Avondale's public relations director, Barbara Hale, made sure that the cardiac unit was featured prominently and often in press releases and the hospital's quarterly magazine.

Even members of the veteran medical staff were impressed by the success of the cardiac unit. The hospital administrator, Maxwell Johnson, was also impressed. Income from expensive heart operations was essential in maintaining the solvency of the hospital, and the cardiac wing had once again put Avondale General on sound economic footing. "Thank goodness for blocked arteries!" Johnson sometimes mused in his more morbid moments.

But Martha Blackwell was not as impressed as the hospital administrator. A surgical nurse for ten years, Blackwell had been assigned to the cardiac unit since its inception. She was concerned that the number of operations far exceeded the national average for open-heart surgery, and her years of experience as a nurse told her that some of the procedures were unnecessary. Blackwell was aware of the risks of bringing this concern to the attention of the hospital administration. Nurses were respected for their abilities, but their opinions, especially those concerning staff physicians, were unwelcome. Nevertheless, she took her fears to Dr. James Mitchell, the chief of staff and the surgeon under whom she had worked before joining the cardiac unit. She also confided in Hale while having lunch with the PR director in the hospital's cafeteria.

Mitchell was not particularly surprised. One of the residents in the cardiac wing had (perhaps foolishly) complained about unnecessary surgery and had been reassigned to another department. Mitchell promised a review of the procedures and appointed a committee composed of doctors and nurses to look into the matter. Within a few weeks the committee had completed its assignment and issued a report. Its conclusion: no unnecessary surgery had been performed in Avondale General's cardiac unit.

Hale acquired a copy of the report, stamped confidential, and was perusing its contents when she received a call from John Thorndike, a reporter for the *Avondale Telegraph*. A source had told Thorndike that the hospital was conducting an investigation of the cardiac care unit, and Thorndike was seeking confirmation. Hale wondered if the source could be Blackwell. Nevertheless, the PR director told her caller that she would check into the story and get back to him.

Hale was puzzled by the committee's conclusions. Blackwell was an experienced surgical nurse and was unlikely to have made such serious allegations unless there was some substance to the charges. But the report was more interesting for what it did not contain than for what it did. There was no direct testimony from Blackwell or the resident who had lodged the complaint and had been reassigned. Was this a cover-up?

Hale was in an ethical quandary. She could stonewall Thorndike and deny the existence of the investigation. However, that would be a lie, and she might lose the high credibility that she had worked long and hard to establish with the media. She could leak the report to Thorndike, but that move would be disloyal to the hospital for whom she worked. The document was marked confidential, an unmistakable message that its contents were not intended for public consumption. Nevertheless, Hale could try to convince Johnson to release the report, because its findings were favorable and would perhaps convince a skeptical public that the hospital was policing itself. This would be good PR, Hale could tell the hospital administrator.

The third alternative was the most drastic. Hale could blow the whistle on the committee's credibility. She could leak the document to the reporter and tell him (under a promise of confidentiality) that the committee's findings were probably a whitewash. With the cover-up (if that is what it was) exposed in the press, the scandal could have an adverse impact on the operation of the financially successful cardiac unit. And Hale was painfully aware of the role played by the facility in subsidizing the rest of the hospital's operations.

Since she had undertaken Avondale General's public relations efforts five years ago, Hale had grown to like and respect the hospital staff and had developed a loyalty to the hospital. But what about her obligations to the media, the public, and the patients who had possibly undergone needless surgery? Leaking the committee's findings would be a breach of confidentiality and an act of disloyalty. Perhaps she should try first to deal with the problem internally and express her concerns to the hospital administrator and maybe the board. But considering the financial stakes involved in reducing the number of surgical procedures in the cardiac unit, her complaints would probably fall on deaf ears.

THE CASE STUDY

This case concerns whistle-blowing, a relatively new word in the ethical lexicon. Whistle-blowers sound an alarm from within the very organization for which they work, with a goal of calling attention to some act of neglect or perhaps even criminal activity that threatens the public interest.[38] Most whistle-blowers originally file their complaints within the management structure, but when this route fails to produce action, they may go public or seek some other forum for a hearing.

Whistle-blowing, like so many other acts of moral import, involves competing loyalties. This dilemma has been described by Bok in "Whistle-blowing and Professional Responsibilities":

> The whistleblower hopes to stop the game; but since he is neither referee nor coach, and since he blows the whistle on his own team, his act is seen as a violation of loyalty. In holding his position, he has assumed certain obligations to his colleagues and clients: stepping out of channels to level accusations is regarded as a violation of these obligations. Loyalty to colleagues and to clients comes to be pitted against loyalty to the public interest, to those who may be injured unless the revelation is made.[39]

Unlike many whistle-blowers, Hale might never be known as the source of the leak, because the reporter has promised her anonymity. Nevertheless, her sense of loyalty has been pitted against her obligation to prevent harm and injustice to others, that is, those patients who may have undergone unnecessary surgery and the insurance carriers that had to assume the costs. Hale cannot be entirely sure that the committee's report is a whitewash. But there are times when one must act on the basis of probability.

PR practitioners are in a particularly vulnerable position, because they are the organization's communications link to the media and the public. The code of the Public Relations Society of America requires members to conduct their "professional life in accord with the public interest." But determining what is in the public interest is sometimes a frustrating exercise. On the one hand, the public should be made aware of at least the possibility of excessive surgery at Avondale General, with the attendant underlying profit motive. On the other hand, how much of a problem really exists is not clear, and any forced cutbacks in cardiac surgery could undermine not only the unit itself but also the economic viability of the entire hospital. Would this be in the interest of the community, which depends heavily on this modern surgical facility?

Assume the role of Hale, and decide whether you will breach the confidentiality of the hospital report. You should weigh clearly your competing loyalties before rendering your judgment.

▶ **CASE 6-7**
The Student Newspaper and Faculty Evaluations

As a senior at Southwestern State University, Jonathan Southall was feeling more impoverished than he had as an entering freshman. For four years he had subsisted on a series of low-interest student loans and the meager income from his part-time job as a waiter. But each year Southall watched helplessly as the relentless tuition increases exceeded the cost of inflation, further eroding his confidence in the administration's financial management capabilities. Southall did not dispute the chancellor's defense that competitive salaries, funded in part by the tuition hikes, were essential to attracting and keeping quality faculty. He was not convinced, however, that the tuition increases had been accompanied by a comparable increase in the quality of education.

But now, as the newly elected president of the Student Government Association, Southall demanded accountability. He had been elected overwhelmingly on a platform committed, among other things, to "opening up" the faculty evaluation process and publicizing the results of the student surveys required in all courses at the end of each semester. Within the first two weeks of his nine-month tenure as SGA president, Southall moved expeditiously to fulfill his passionate campaign promise. However, his overtures to the university's administration were rebuffed, as they invoked various claims of confidentiality, privacy rights, and academic freedom. "The faculty evaluation results are for the eyes of administrators and faculty only," said the vice chancellor for academic affairs in summarily dismissing Southall's initiative. "They are used in the university's tenure and promotion process, and that ensures sufficient accountability to Southwest-

ern's teaching mission." The vice chancellor also cited a court decision four years ago that, in effect, exempted faculty evaluations from the coverage of the state's public records law.

Undeterred by what he perceived as the administration's cloak of secrecy designed to protect the substandard performance records of some of the university's faculty, Southall continued to pressure the chancellor's office through statements made to the SGA that were dutifully reported in the student newspaper. His flirtation with liberalism, albeit on a rather modest scale, had challenged one of the university's sacred cows. He acknowledged to his political allies in the SGA that his campaign might not produce instant intellectual gratification, but he would not be denied his day in the court of public opinion.

If the Southwestern State administration did not share Southall's unbridled enthusiasm for complete faculty accountability, Felicia Cobb did. Cobb was the *Watchdog*'s SGA correspondent and was an unapologetic advocate for openness in government (including student government) and public accountability. She believed strongly that her classmates had a right to know how their peers assessed the faculty's pedagogical handiwork.

Andrew Jenner thought so, too. Jenner was a graduate assistant assigned to work in the Office of Data Processing and Retrieval, which was responsible for feeding the results of the faculty evaluations into the university's mainframe computer. Cobb was intrigued when Jenner contacted her in her dorm and requested a rendezvous in a coffeehouse just off campus. "Shades of Watergate," she thought in recalling the historical accounts of the clandestine meetings and anonymous sources surrounding the downfall of the Nixon presidency.

Jenner was nervous but got right to the point. "I support Southall's campaign to release the results of the faculty evaluations," he began. "But that'll never happen, at least not in the near future. I feel strongly that we students have a right to know. This is all the data on the individual faculty evaluations," he told Cobb pointing to a package in his hand. "I have access to this information in my position as a graduate assistant. You can have this on the condition that you not reveal the source. If my department head finds out, I'll lose my assistantship and be kicked out of school." Cobb readily agreed to Jenner's insistence on anonymity as she savored her journalistic triumph.

"I've finally recovered from my bout with information overload," Cobb told Lyle MacArthur, the student editor of the *Watchdog*. "There are more than 1,200 faculty included in this survey from last semester, and most of them taught two or three courses. We can publish the results in a tab insert, and then include a story highlighting the results in a front-page story." The paper's faculty adviser, Richard Hammock, was not sure the evaluations should be published at all.

"We'll take a lot of heat from the administration *and* the faculty if we publish these faculty evaluations," stated Hammock matter-of-factly three days before the scheduled publication date in a hastily arranged meeting with MacArthur, Cobb, and student managing editor Amanda Tedrick. "The results of these evaluations are supposed to be confidential."

"I have no doubt that we'll be under a lot of pressure," acknowledged Cobb, who had acquired the controversial data in the first place. "But the students have a right to know about the quality of teaching at this university and how their classmates rate their teachers. This is one factor that students use in choosing their classes, particularly when they have a choice of more than one instructor."

"This may be true," said Tedrick. "But why is this news? Even if we assume that students have an interest in knowing how their teachers rate, I'm not sure that the results of the faculty evaluations are newsworthy. There's even some doubt as to their reliability. I'm a senior, and I've filled out these forms faithfully every semester. But, quite frankly, I'm convinced that the way students evaluate their teachers is related to the difficulty of instruction. That may not be true in all cases, but there's certainly a tendency in that direction. The point is that faculty evaluations are inexact. I doubt that the results necessarily identify the good or the bad teachers. There are too many other factors involved. Such surveys sometimes are nothing more than popularity contests that do not necessarily measure teaching effectiveness."

"That may be true," acknowledged MacArthur, who was impressed by his reporter's enterprise,

"but it's not our job to be concerned about whether these surveys measure teaching effectiveness. The only issue is what students think of their teachers. And this university has made the results of these surveys a part of the tenure and promotion process. And since the quality of faculty affects all students, that makes these surveys newsworthy."

"I am concerned about how we acquired this information," said Hammock. "The university has determined that these evaluations should be confidential. We haven't done anything illegal, but the publication of these survey results will violate university policy. And it could cause a rift between the faculty and the administration concerning a lack of security for what the faculty assumed was confidential information."

"That's not our problem," countered Cobb. "If we believe the students have a right to know this information, then we should publish it. The professional media often publish confidential information if there is a legitimate public interest in doing so. What makes us so different?"

"We are different," responded Hammock, "because of the relationship of the *Watchdog*'s staff. You are all students, and the faculty still hold the keys to your academic future here. This could blow over, and perhaps there won't be any retribution. But most of our paper's staff are enrolled in journalism courses. A professor whose evaluations are poor could find ways to retaliate. In that respect, our reporters do not stand in the same relationship as the professional media in terms of the newsworthy individuals they cover."

"That could be a problem," agreed Tedrick. "Of course, I don't believe our paper should avoid controversy just because it makes the administration unhappy. Otherwise, we lose credibility with our readers. On the other hand, if we break the rules, we're putting ourselves into an adversarial relationship with the administration *and* the faculty. They provide much of our information. The fact is that we breached the confidentiality of these evaluations. The faculty have always assumed that they would be seen only by the department chairs and deans."

"It's true that we gained access to confidential information, and in so doing perhaps we broke the rules," said Cobb, who was a true believer in *the people's right to know.* "But these evaluations are paid for by public funds. In addition, we pay tuition and have a right to demand accountability. In covering the SGA, I have discovered that there is a great deal of concern about recent tuition hikes, but there's a perception that the quality of education hasn't improved. We're the voice of student expression. It's our responsibility to look into these questions. And the only measure of teaching effectiveness currently employed to evaluate professors is this student survey."

"It's your call," Hammock said to MacArthur. "You're the editor. As the faculty adviser, I have no control over what you publish. I can only advise. All I ask is that you weigh the benefits—that is to say, the news value of these evaluations—against the potential harm of releasing this confidential information."

While the editor had sided with Felicia Cobb during this rather intriguing discussion, he now found his role as moral agent more challenging. Since the faculty evaluations were confidential under university policy and academic freedom and even perhaps professional reputations were at stake, MacArthur knew that the burden of proof was on the student newspaper to justify any breach of confidentiality on the grounds of newsworthiness or public interest. In addition, MacArthur harbored no illusions concerning the consequences of publishing these evaluations: the access that the *Watchdog* had enjoyed to sources in the upper administration would evaporate. Of course, that was the risk that any newspaper confronted in offending their news sources.

It was true that the surveys were conducted at taxpayer expense and that his classmates had a vested interest in the quality of their educational experience at Southwestern State University. But student grades were also the product of a heavy investment of public funds, and yet they were confidential. What was the difference, he wondered? As a student, would he be happy if his grades were available for public inspection?

In confronting the ethical dimensions of publishing this confidential information, MacArthur was troubled by his conflicting loyalties. As a student, he had faithfully filled out these student questionnaires each semester, and he believed that he had the right to see the results. But he was a participant in the process, not an entirely disinterested observer. His role as a journalist-in-training also propelled him in the direction of disclosure, but, unlike most professional journalists, MacArthur was a part of the institution whose policies favoring confidentiality were about to be breached. Nevertheless, the *Watchdog* was a student newspaper independent of administration control. It was supported by student fees and advertising, not state funds. The paper owed its primary allegiance to its student readers. And undoubtedly this information would be helpful to students in selecting their professors and courses. But he wondered whether even this justification were sufficient to overcome the officially imposed shroud of secrecy surrounding the faculty evaluation process at Southwestern State University.

THE CASE STUDY

Most colleges and universities do not release the results of student evaluations of individual faculty members, although student governments sometimes conduct their own surveys and publish the results. School administrators view confidentiality of such material as essentially a personnel matter predicated on privacy and academic freedom concerns. But such a system can also conceal substandard performance records by public employees. Thus, students might argue that they have a vested interest in the quality of their education and a right to know how their professors measure up in the classroom.

In this scenario, both university policy and the state's public records law (as interpreted by the courts) exempt faculty evaluations from disclosure. In addition, in most cases involving confidentiality the party seeking disclosure must carry the burden of proof. Thus, the *Watchdog*'s moral claim in support of its decision to publish—particularly since the information was obtained through an anonymous source—must be based on some overriding principle. While the promise of confidentiality and the circumstances under which the paper received the material also raise ethical concerns, these issues are not central to this case study since they are a *fait accompli*.

In contemplating his decision, the editor, Lyle MacArthur, might consider the following questions: (1) Are the results of the individual faculty evaluations a matter of public interest? (2) Are students entitled to this information because the surveys are publicly funded? (3) Are the students entitled to this information because they pay tuition and have a right to demand accountability? (4) Should the paper decline to publish the evaluation results because they are an inaccurate barometer of the quality of teaching, or is the fact that they are taken seriously by the administration in their tenure and promotion decisions sufficient justification for reporting students' collective opinions regarding the quality of their instruction?

Assume the role of student editor Lyle MacArthur, and then, using the moral reasoning model outlined in Chapter 3, render a judgment on whether you will publish the results of Southwestern State University's faculty evaluations.

▶ CASE 6-8
Scandal in the Ivory Tower: A PR Dilemma

Jackie Sundberg had graduated near the top of her journalism class at Washington College and had been recruited by the Greenville *Sun-Times*. After only a year as a general assignment reporter, she had been elevated to the prestigious governmental affairs position following the retirement of the paper's only Pulitzer Prize winner, Brewster Harps. She had approached her new assignment with the same dogged determination that she had demonstrated in her studies at Washington College and first year on the job, and she had rapidly gained the respect of her colleagues at the paper as well as her competitors.

But after six years of covering city hall, Sundberg grew weary of the long hours, rather modest pay, and tiresome redundancy of the partisan wrangling of the city and county commissions and the numerous other local governmental bodies. Her journalistic skills remained undiminished, but

her curiosity and fascination with the political process had slowly evaporated.

Sundberg decided it was time to pursue her interest in public relations. She had majored in print journalism at Washington but had taken two PR courses as electives. Sundberg believed that her writing skills, seven years of newspaper experience, and ability to deal with people would provide an entry into the world of public relations. She was right, and the timing could not have been better. The PR director's position at Washington College had just been vacated, and Sundberg immediately submitted an application, along with a resume and a "string book" of her best articles from the *Sun-Times*. Six weeks later she was hired and assumed her new duties with enthusiasm.

Her first seven months on the job were leisurely, a welcome refuge from the frenzied pace of the newsroom. Most of her time was occupied with writing press releases, publishing the college's alumni magazine, and answering an occasional inquiry from the media concerning some activity at the college. But this situation changed as what the faculty referred to as the Sanford Affair began to unfold.

Preston Sanford had been appointed president of Washington College six years before and had come to his new job with impressive academic and professional credentials. However, he had taken the reins of power with a vengeance that shocked even some of his most ardent supporters on the search committee. His managerial style did not accommodate itself to faculty governance, and soon rumblings of discontent were heard among the faculty rank and file. Most troubling of all was his apparent insensitivity to the moral integrity of the institution.

The faculty's disenchantment came to a head in the Faculty Senate with the appointment of an ad hoc committee to investigate "the competence and character of President Preston Sanford." Specifically, the committee was charged with looking into (1) the president's readmission, over the objections of the faculty, of an English student expelled for plagiarism; (2) a presidential cover-up of indiscretions by two administrators who had submitted phony credentials when applying for their positions; and (3) the misuse of university funds for personal travel. The committee was to conclude its investigation within four months with a written report, at which time the senate would decide whether to ask for a vote of no confidence from the faculty.

The ad hoc committee, after reviewing stacks of documents and interviewing dozens of witnesses, had completed its investigation on time. Sundberg had received a copy of the committee's draft report, but David Berry, as provost the second in the chain of command at Washington College, had instructed her not to release it until it could be reviewed and "sanitized," a euphemism for deleting some of the material that reflected poorly on the overall college administration.

Sundberg had dutifully arranged a press conference for the next day, during which the provost would present an oral summary of the findings and answer reporters' questions. She was skimming the draft report again, wondering how much of it would find its way into the press conference, when the phone rang. It was Paul Davis, a former colleague on the *Sun-Times*. Davis, according to Sundberg's recollection, had always been a determined reporter, and today was no exception. He was aware of the existence of the draft report and had called the provost's office in search of a copy. However, it had refused to release the document, Davis said, in violation of the state's public records law. And it was probably too late to get a court order before the press conference (a fact probably not lost on the provost). Would Sundberg get him a copy, Davis wanted to know?

Sundberg had been the beneficiary of the public records law many times as a reporter for the *Sun-Times*, but now the tables were turned. The law was generally acknowledged to be one of the more liberal state public records statutes and covered virtually all documents produced by governmental bodies, including colleges and universities. Draft reports were also open for public inspection. The provost, Sundberg realized, was maneuvering for damage control. He would have to confront the media on the results of the report, which would undoubtedly result in the eventual termination of Sanford, but he would like to preserve what modicum of integrity remained for the institution itself. In some respects Sundberg could not blame him.

The report did, in places, wander aimlessly among the intricacies of college decision making and reflected adversely on some higher-level administrators, some of whom were probably just following orders from the president. It also indicted the faculty and staff for not maintaining vigilance and allowing the wanton deeds of the president to continue unabated for so long. There was certainly plenty of blame to go around.

Sundberg had told David that she would "look for" a copy of the report and get back to him within the hour. But most of the hour was spent pondering her ethical dilemma. Her journalistic instincts, which had not deserted her during her short tenure as PR director, led her in the direction of openness. The press and the public had a right to know the unblemished truth about the committee's findings, she reasoned. Besides, state law required disclosure.

On the other hand, was this really her decision to make? She was not the "custodian" of the report, as defined by the law, and to release the document without authorization would violate university policy. Besides, she had read the draft report and had to admit that the provost's concerns were justified. The committee had traveled a rocky road in approaching the president's ethical indiscretions, and its report would undoubtedly cast aspersions—perhaps unfairly—on the faculty and institution.

This dilemma was new to Sundberg. As a reporter she had always been driven by the desire to inform the public. Her moral vision had always been clear on this point. But now she was torn between her obligations as a public servant and her responsibilities as PR director for the institution that demanded her loyalty.

THE CASE STUDY

Public policy in the form of the state's public records law clearly demands release of this report. But is it the PR director's responsibility to do so, especially if she has been directed not to do so by the college administration, apparently for justifiable reasons?

On the other hand, the report, which will probably result in the termination of Sanford, is of public interest and should be released. However, the document apparently exceeds the committee's mandate and is likely to cause harm to the integrity of the institution itself. Can PR practitioners withhold information for justifiable reasons if institutional harm is the likely result?

Assuming the role of Sundberg and using the SAD Formula, render your decision on this ethical dilemma. As always, be sure to defend your judgment.

▼

Notes

1. Lou Hodges, "Cases and Commentaries: Brock Adams and *The Seattle Times,*" *Journal of Mass Media Ethics,* 7, No. 4, 1992, pp. 246–247.
2. "Reporter Jailed for Refusal To Testify," *News Media & The Law,* Winter 1991, p. 30.
3. "P&G Calls in the Law to Trace Leaks," *News Media & The Law,* Fall 1991, p. 2.
4. Nancy J. Moore, "Limits to Attorney-Client Confidentiality: A Philosophically Informed and Comparative Approach to Legal and Medical Ethics," *Case Western Law Review,* 36, 1985–86, p. 191.
5. Sissela Bok, "The Limits of Confidentiality," in Joan C. Callahan (ed.), *Ethical Issues in Professional Life* (New York: Oxford University Press, 1988), p. 232.
6. For a more thorough discussion of these categories of confidentiality, see H. Eugene Goodwin and Ron R. Smith, *Groping for Ethics in Journalism,* 3d ed. (Ames: Iowa State University Press, 1994), pp. 148–150.
7. For an interesting discussion of the reporter-source relationship, see John L. Hulteng, *The Messenger's Motives: Ethical Problems of the News Media,* 2d ed. (Upper Saddle River, NJ: Prentice Hall, 1985), pp. 79–96.
8. Otis Baskin and Craig Aronoff, *Public Relations: The Profession and the Practice,* 3d ed. (Dubuque, IA: Brown, 1992), pp. 90–91.
9. *Ibid.,* p. 91.
10. Maurice Van Gerpen, *Privileged Communications and the Press* (Westport, CT: Greenwood, 1979), p. 171. In recent years some courts have held that agreements of confidentiality between reporter and source constitute an enforceable contract. See *Cohen v. Cowles Media Co.,* 16 Med.L.Rptr. 2209 (1989).
11. *Butterworth v. Smith,* 17 Med.L.Rptr. 1569 (1990).
12. Bok, "Limits of Confidentiality," p. 231.
13. *Ibid.,* pp. 232–234.
14. Sissela Bok, *Secrets: On the Ethics of Concealment and Revelation* (New York: Pantheon, 1982), p. 19.
15. *Ibid.,* p. 249.
16. Cornelius B. Pratt, "Hill & Knowlton's Two Ethical Dilemmas," *Public Relations Review,* Vol. 20, 1994, p. 286.
17. Susanne A. Roschwalb, "The Hill & Knowlton Cases: A Brief on the Controversy," *Public Relations Review,* Vol. 20, 1994, p. 271.
18. *Ibid.*
19. Pratt, "Hill & Knowlton's Two Ethical Dilemmas," p. 287.
20. Roschwalb, "The Hill & Knowlton Cases," pp. 271–272.
21. *Ibid.,* p. 264.
22. *Branzburg v. Hayes,* 408 U.S. 665 (1972).
23. *Ibid.,* 743 (Stewart dissenting).
24. Van Gerpen, *Privileged Communications,* p. 172.
25. For an examination of one newspaper's approach to this problem, see Richard P. Cunningham, "Should Reporters Reveal Sources to Editors?" *Quill,* October 1988, pp. 6–8.
26. Monica Langley and Lee Levine, "Broken Promises," *Columbia Journalism Review,* July/August 1988, p. 22.
27. See Jeffrey Olen, *Ethics in Journalism* (Upper Saddle River, NJ: Prentice Hall, 1988), pp. 40–41.
28. For a discussion of the reciprocal nature of the reporter-source relationship, see Stephen Klaidman and Tom L. Beauchamp, *The Virtuous Journalist* (New York: Oxford University Press, 1987), pp. 163–177.
29. Langley and Levine, "Broken Promises," p. 21.
30. *Ibid.,* p. 22.
31. "Two Leaks, but by Whom?" *Newsweek,* July 27, 1987, p. 16.
32. Howard Weaver, "Unnamed Problem," *FineLine,* November/December 1990, p. 7.
33. Rick Atkinson, "Peace with American Jews Eludes Jackson," *Washington Post,* February 13, 1984, pp. A1, A4–A5.
34. Milton Coleman, "18 Words, Seven Weeks Later," *Washington Post,* April 8, 1984, p. C8.
35. Klaidman and Beauchamp, *Virtuous Journalist,* p. 170.
36. E.g., see Christopher Dickey, "Not Their Finest Hour," *Newsweek,* June 8, 1992, p. 66.
37. For a list of these guidelines, see "New War Coverage Rules," *Quill,* October 1992, p. 22.
38. Sissela Bok, "Whistleblowing and Professional Responsibilities," in Callahan, *Ethical Issues in Professional Life,* p. 331.
39. *Ibid.,* p. 333. For a discussion of the moral dimensions of confidentiality as it relates to whistle-blowing, also see Bok, *Secrets,* pp. 210–229.

Conflicts of Interest

CONFLICTS OF INTEREST: REAL AND IMAGINED

Disturbed by the growing number of pro-choice church members, the usually conservative National Conference of Catholic Bishops in 1990 solicited the help of Hill & Knowlton, the nation's largest public relations firm, to help recruit antiabortion Catholics and non-Catholics. When it was discovered that Hill & Knowlton also represented organizations that support abortion rights, the firm's management was accused of violating Article 10 of the code of the Public Relations Society of America, which prohibits a member from representing "conflicting or competing interests without the express consent of those concerned after a full disclosure of the facts." Hill & Knowlton was also castigated by many of its female employees for accepting an assignment "whose ultimate goal is to limit our fundamental rights."[1]

When several female reporters for the *New York Times* and the *Washington Post* joined thousands of marchers in a Washington, D.C., abortion rights demonstration, they apparently believed they were exercising their constitutional right to free speech. Their goal was to protect a woman's "right to choose" as guaranteed in the Supreme Court's 1973 *Roe v. Wade* decision. This prompted the *Post*'s managing editor, Leonard Downie, Jr., and executive editor, Benjamin C. Bradlee, to issue a memo or-

dering anyone who had participated in the march to refrain from further coverage of the debate. But *Times* reporter Linda Greenhouse caused the most controversy because she had written about abortion for almost twenty years and also covered the Supreme Court for the country's most prestigious newspaper.[2]

These cases share common ground in their concern for the morally devisive abortion issue. They also share one of the most troublesome ethical terrains for media practitioners: conflicts of interest. Simply stated, a *conflict of interest* is a clash between professional loyalties and outside interests that undermines the moral agent's credibility. Conflicts generally arise from the roles we play within society and, for that reason, appear to involve *particularistic* duties (see Chapter 2) rather than our general societal obligations. Unlike the value of truth, there does not appear to be any all-encompassing moral rule urging our consciences to reject all conflicts of interest. A reporter, for example, should avoid endorsing political causes, but the rest of us are not so constrained.

It is tempting, therefore, to say that divided loyalties do not involve any fundamental moral values. Our parents tell us never to lie, cheat, or steal. They say nothing about conflicts of interest. The fact is, however, that a conflict of interest raises some basic questions concerning fairness and justice, two important and fundamental values. A judge who owns stock in a company accused of violating the antitrust laws, for example, could not be counted on to conduct a fair and impartial trial. Likewise, a reporter who is married to a city official might be tentative in uncovering local governmental corruption.

Many news organizations have specific policies relating to conflicts of interest, such as banning the acceptance of perquisites and "freebies" from news sources or the participation in political and community organizations by members of the editorial staff. The professional codes also admonish media practitioners to avoid conflicts of interest. The code of the Public Relations Society of America, for example, prohibits members from representing conflicting or competing interests without the express consent of those involved or placing themselves in a position where the member's interest might conflict with those of a client. The code of the Society of Professional Journalists reflects a concern with *potential* conflicts of interest, as well as actual conflicts, when it observes that journalists and their employers "should conduct their personal lives in a manner which protects them from conflict of interest, real or apparent." The SPJ code also discourages secondary employment, political involvement, holding public office, or service in community organizations "if it compromises the integrity of journalists and their employers."

Some are troubled by the sweeping nature of these restrictions and believe that they are not required by our ethical system. Jeffrey Olen, for one, writing in *Ethics in Journalism*, has this to say about the code's pronouncement: "If media organizations wish to adopt that policy in order to protect an enhanced image of trustworthiness to their audiences, that is one thing. But such a policy is not morally required. All that is morally required is that journalists, like anyone else, be trustworthy."[3] What Olen ignores is that even the appearance of impropriety can undermine the credibility of moral agents in the eyes of an ever-skeptical public. A music critic who accepts free tickets to an opera may be perfectly capable of writing a detached and objective account of a performance, but there will be lingering doubts in readers' minds.

But Olen is right about one thing. The appearance of conflict is often difficult to avoid. And there are reasonable or acceptable conflicts of interest that do not necessarily undermine the credibility of the moral agent. But at a minimum the public should be apprised of the situation. A case in point is the control that professional baseball teams often exercise over the selection of announcers to broadcast their games on local stations. This fact is made known to the audience through a "disclaimer" broadcast during the game. The audience has no aversion to this practice, because it usually expects local commentators to be supportive of the home team. In other words, these announcers, like advertisers and PR practitioners, operate with an acknowledged vested interest, and they are not expected to abandon the goals of their employers in the name of objectivity.

One problem with confronting the ethical behavior of individual media practitioners is that potential conflicts of interest begin at the top. The mass media are big business and depend on advertisers for their support. The editorial side of the ledger is beholden to the commercial side for its daily bread. And many of these advertisers, particularly large corporations, could someday be the subject of news stories. Whereas large newspapers and broadcast entities are better able to insulate their journalistic integrity from commercial pressures, smaller news operations might be forced to pull their punches to avoid coverage that would reflect unfavorably on an advertiser.

Some news organizations are also owned by parent companies whose allegiance is more to the bottom line than to journalistic independence. NBC, for example, is owned by General Electric. Could the network's news division be expected to aggressively cover a scandal involving GE? Perhaps, but the impact of this relationship remains to be seen. In a world of conglomerates, the possibilities for conflicts of interest are boundless, and it becomes even more incumbent on media managers at the corporate level to be sensitive to the ethical dilemmas posed by such conflicts.

RECOGNIZING CONFLICTS: THE MOST TROUBLESOME TERRAIN

If we are to avoid conflicts—or at least learn how to deal with them—we should acknowledge them for what they are. Some people become ensnared by competing loyalties without even recognizing the ethical dimensions of their actions. Life is full of such traps awaiting the uninformed and unwary. In other cases we are aware of the potential conflict but are helpless to do anything about it. All college journalists, for example, are at the mercy of the administration. Even if administrators have limited powers of censorship over the student press, there are more subtle ways of dealing with recalcitrant student reporters, both inside and outside the classroom. Thus, a potential conflict emerges between the roles of student and journalist.

Although conflicts of interest can arise in many situations, those confronting media practitioners tend to fall into three broad areas: conflicting relationships, conflicting public participation, and vested interests and hidden agendas.

Conflicting Relationships

It is always difficult to serve two masters. Our independence of action is severely limited when we are involved in conflicting relationships. The code of the PRSA, for example, admonishes its members not to place themselves "in a position where the member's interest is or may be in conflict with a duty to a client, or others, without a full disclosure of such interests to all involved." Advertising agencies' and PR practitioners' primary duties are to their clients, and, when conflicting loyalties intrude, their independence of action on behalf of those clients is compromised. It would clearly be a conflict of interest, for example, for a PR firm to represent both an oil company and an environmental group in their dispute over what to do about developing a wilderness preserve. The following subsections describe some of the more common conflicts confronting practicing journalists.

Gifts and "Perks" Journalists' primary responsibility is to their readers and viewers, and, when they accept favors, gifts, or other special considerations from vested interests or news sources, it raises serious questions about their objectivity. Although unspectacular freebies, such as meals provided by a news source, may not be problematic, over time, the reporter's professional detachment could be undermined. In the eyes of the public, the appearance of a conflict can be as damaging as the conflict itself. The mere acceptance of the thing of value raises questions about the moral agent's credibility and future independence of action, even if no favor is promised in return.

At one time reporters, who tended to be underpaid, less educated than they are now, and less attuned to the ethics of the profession, routinely accepted gifts from news sources. The rules, to the extent that they existed, were lax, to say the least. Many reporters are still underpaid, of course, but they have become more sensitized to ethical concerns. Many news organizations have specific prohibitions against accepting gifts or anything else of value. Although the specific language of these policies may vary, a basic text on news broadcasting has captured the practical flavor of their concerns: "Reporters shouldn't accept any gifts from the people they may have to write about—no bottles of Scotch, vacations, fountain pens or dinners. Reporters don't even want to be in a position of having to distinguish between a gift and a bribe. Return them all with a polite thank you."[4]

An ethical purist might reject the idea of accepting even a cup of coffee from a news source. Although most reporters might not go this far, many now refuse to accept meals from outside parties. One of the most troublesome kinds of freebies, from an ethical point of view, is the "junket," a free trip (and perhaps food and lodging) paid for by some vested interest or a news source. The expenses-paid trip is a valuable PR tool for some organizations, and in the past reporters have not been loath to take advantage of such offers. The movie industry and the television networks participate in the junket game to promote their new films and shows, although more and more news organizations are now paying their reporters' own way to these extravaganzas.

And the public relations profession, which is the source of many of the organized media visits, is not without its ethical scruples in the matter. For example, Article 6 of the PRSA code admonishes members not to "engage in any practice which has the purpose of corrupting the integrity of channels of communications or the processes of government." The PRSA code has also been interpreted to prohibit "any form of payment or compensation to a member of the media in order to obtain preferential or guaranteed news or editorial coverage in the medium."[5] However, the code does not prohibit media tours when media representatives "are given the opportunity for an on-the-spot viewing of a newsworthy product, process, or event in which the media . . . representatives have a legitimate interest." But what about an all-expenses-paid tour? Thus, PR initiatives that include an all-expenses-paid trip are acceptable as long as they have a legitimate news purpose.[6] Such trips for no purpose other than pleasure (i.e., junkets) would be unacceptable.

Reporters who travel with those they cover have also fallen prey to conflicts. Sports reporters, for example, sometimes travel with the teams they are covering, although this practice has been viewed with increasing skepticism. Some news organizations now either pay the way for their employees or require that they travel separately from the team. However, those reporters who still ride free with the team seldom reveal this fact to the public, exacerbating an already serious conflict of interest.

At one time political reporters eagerly took advantage of free rides with the candidates they were covering, but this practice has virtually disappeared.[7] The acceptance of any such gift from a candidate or any governmental agency is one of the most flagrant examples of a conflict of interest. Under such circumstances, the objectivity of the reporter immediately becomes suspect. Of course, there is an exception to any rule, and reporters operating in a war zone are usually at the mercy of the military for transportation. Such was the case in the Persian Gulf War, where journalists had to depend on the military to provide access to the combat zone, but even then under tightly controlled reporter "pools."

Like any other profession, journalism has its share of "perks." Some special interests try to curry favor with reporters by offering them discounts, special memberships, and the like. However, reporters, like public officials, should never use their positions for personal gain. A rather tragic case in point is R. Foster Winans, a reporter for the *Wall Street Journal*, who was fired when it was learned that Winans had violated the paper's policy against trading in stocks they were writing about or providing outsiders with advance knowledge of what they planned to publish. Winans had alerted friends and others in the investment community as to what he planned to write about in an upcoming column. As a result, they benefited from this "inside information." If Winans had been sensitive to the ethical principles described in this chapter, he might still be covering the investment community for the *Wall Street Journal*.

Government officials, particularly, recognize the power and influence of the press and often provide such benefits as free parking or special seating for media personnel. The executive and legislative branches of both the federal and state governments have set up press galleries and special working accommodations for reporters. Although some news organizations, having undergone an ethical revelation in the light of the Watergate scandal in the 1970s, now pay for their space in the press rooms, many still take advantage of this perk.[8] Perhaps they feel that such access is a right rather than a privilege and that they should not have to pay for their proximity to the seat of government.

Checkbook Journalism In February 1994, Jacquee Petchel, head of the investigative unit of WCCO-TV in Minneapolis, was preparing a story on dangerous doctors. When Petchel sought an interview with a woman who had sued a Minnesota doctor for malpractice in connection with her husband's death, the woman told Petchel she would not discuss the lawsuit without getting paid. After the second Rodney King trial, in which several Los Angeles police officers were accused of using excessive force to subdue a speeding motorist, *Los Angeles Times* reporters were effectively excluded from posttrial interviews with certain jurors because they were not willing to pay for them.[9] These two circumstances exemplify a practice that ethical journalists derisively refer to as *checkbook journalism*. It raises serious conflict-of-interest questions because of the traditional journalistic commitment to truth and accuracy. Paying interviewees and sources, it is said, may well taint the quality of the information because of the economic motives involved.

Checkbook journalism came to national prominence in the aftermath of President Richard Nixon's resignation and the subsequent Watergate trials of his top aides. A CBS news producer, Gordon Manning, proposed to the network that it try to line up H. R. Haldeman, in some ways the most powerful and least accessible of Nixon's former staff, for an interview. Haldeman made no secret of the fact that he loathed the press and seldom gave interviews during his White House tenure. But in early 1975, following his conviction for his role in the

Watergate cover-up, he indicated to CBS officials that he was receptive to the idea of an interview. He emphasized, however, that he expected to be paid handsomely for his participation.[10]

After some negotiations, CBS agreed to pay Haldeman $100,000 for the "privilege" of interviewing him on television. When news of this transaction became public, critics accused the network of checkbook journalism. And to add insult to injury, the interviews, which were aired on successive Sundays in the spring of 1975 in the *60 Minutes* time period, were journalistic bombs. Mike Wallace, regarded by many as the most aggressive interviewer in TV news, was unable to budge the unflappable Haldeman, a former advertising man and renowned media expert himself. Haldeman skillfully deflected Wallace's questions and revealed little of real journalistic substance. Thus, the network's folly in shelling out $100,000 for nothing overshadowed the interviews themselves.[11] But ratings and competition are irresistible forces in broadcast journalism, and nine years later CBS paid $500,000 for a ninety-minute videotaped interview with Nixon.

These large payments for interviews with such high-profile public figures attract a lot of attention and a predictable round of criticism, even from within the media establishment itself. Checkbook journalism raises the ethical hackles of some reporters and editors because it encourages the marketing of information that may not be accurate. But this criticism overlooks the fact that much of the checkbook journalism occurs in less publicized ways, involving ordinary citizens. Some news organizations, for example, have been known to pay accident victims for exclusive interviews. The commercial link to newsworthy subjects is sometimes more subtle than direct cash payments. It is not uncommon for news organizations to pay for transportation, lodging, and meals when they fly newsworthy subjects to designated locations for interviews. Such was the case following the hijacking of a TWA flight from Athens to Beirut in 1985, when some families of hostages were flown to Europe by TV news crews anxious for exclusive coverage of the next stage of this dramatic event, the release of the hostages.[12] In addition, reporters operating in foreign countries, in keeping with local customs, sometimes bribe government officials or corporate executives for information. Although most do not condone this practice, some journalists accommodate themselves to cultural norms in order to increase the flow of information to their American audiences.

Although paying sources for news or exclusive interviews is common in other parts of the world, it is still publicly disparaged among most mainstream American news organizations. But the pervasiveness of the practice among TV talk shows and the tabloid media in the 1990s has certainly increased the pressure on all news organizations to conform to the economic realities of the business. For example, during the rape trial of Senator Edward Kennedy's nephew, William Smith, in Palm Beach, *A Current Affair* unashamedly paid Michele Cassone her asking price of $1,000 per interview. Cassone, who was identified as the "other woman" in the alleged rape incident, admitted she knew next to nothing about the case and had only met the alleged victim that night.[13] *A Current Affair* also allegedly paid prosecution witness Anne Mercer $40,000 to appear on the program. When federal authorities laid siege to the compound of a religious cult in Waco, Texas—a siege that ended in a bloody shootout—one of the tabloid TV programs paid the mother of cult leader David Koresh for interviews. In another case, a ratings war turned into a bidding war among several programs that sought to interview several teenage boys who had formed a club that awarded points for sexual conquests of girls at their school.[14] In 1994, figure skater Tonya Harding, following allegations that she conspired to injure Olympic rival Nancy Kerrigan, was paid several hundred thousand dollars for a series of exclusive interviews with *Inside Edition*.[15] *A Current Affair*, which is both credited

and blamed for inventing tabloid TV, announced that it would virtually abandon its long-standing practice of paying for interviews. Checkbook journalism would not disappear altogether, news producers John Tomlin and Bob Young admitted, but they promised to announce on the air when a subject had been paid.[16]

Jerry Nachman, veteran journalist and former vice president of news for NBC-owned stations, in an interview with *Broadcasting & Cable* magazine defended checkbook journalism, at least for nontraditional kinds of information programming: "One of the confusions of the modern era of TV news is expecting nonorthodox magazines and reality shows to play by the same rules as the traditional news divisions do. . . . The key issue is disclosure. If you pay for it, say so, so the viewer can draw whatever inferences are appropriate about the veracity of what he [the paid source] is saying."[17]

Competitive pressures have made the temptation to resort to the herd mentality quite alluring, and checkbook journalism is not that uncommon even among mainstream media, although some are reluctant to acknowledge their participation. For example, such popular magazines as *Sports Illustrated* and *Redbook* have paid for news exclusives. An angry and depressed producer for a popular TV news magazine show recently complained to freelance writer Bruce Selcraig, "We're buying news. We're paying people who are players in the story and calling them consultants. We're buying off local reporters to get their sources. We're acting like the tabloid shows. And what's really distressing is that no one feels bad about it."[18]

In some quarters one can even detect an air of resignation to the ethically controversial practice of paying news sources. For example, in commenting upon the $40,000 that *A Current Affair* allegedly paid Anne Mercer in the William Kennedy Smith rape trial, David Bartlett, president of the Radio-Television News Directors Association, was remarkably restrained: "Is there a substantive difference between paying $150 for a limo drive or $40,000 for an interview? Yes, about $39,850. But does that constitute an ethical difference? I'm not sure I'm prepared to make that call."[19]

Indeed, even the mainstream journalistic community is not of one mind concerning the convention of paying for information and interviews. Some reporters (usually off the record) challenge the orthodoxy that investigative journalism should somehow be immune from economic reality. News is simply a commodity, they argue, not unlike a tangible product that is bought and sold in the marketplace. *Newsweek* Contributing Editor Gregg Easterbrook imbued this argument with an air of respectability when he described the practice as an intellectual property issue: "I don't see why professional reporters should be the only ones to profit from producing news. We in the press seem to think [people] should surrender their privacy and submit to our embarrassing questions so that we can make money off it."[20]

But more traditional reporters deride such reasoning as nothing more than a needless capitulation of journalistic values to commercial interests. If financial incentives for gathering information become a mainstay, they argue, then news organizations will become little more than conduits for those who have an interesting story to tell. In addition, reporters and editors will become economic partners with their sources, thus relinquishing at least some of their editorial independence. In this respect, then, journalists' claims that they are significantly different from PR practitioners will lose its ring of credibility.

Regardless of the particular form of *checkbook journalism*, the practice certainly raises questions concerning the value of the information obtained. Paid interviewees may feel financially obligated to perform or produce something of journalistic interest, which could lead to exaggerations, distortions, or even outright fabrications. Even if these outcomes do not materialize, the question is how much faith an audience should put in an interview that is conducted pursuant to a commercial arrangement between a news organization and a source.

And so how can reporters who do not pay compete with those who do? Some journalists believe that the issue should be made part of the story, thus bringing to public attention the question of payment to news sources.[21] If this becomes a common tactic among investigative reporters, it could at least make for an interesting squabble and might even produce some serious ethical soul searching.

Personal Relationships Of course, conflicts of interest do not always revolve around financial considerations, gifts, or perks. Reporters are human and sometimes develop personal relationships with their sources. They may find it difficult to maintain a sense of detachment when they mingle socially with or develop a genuine fondness for those who are the lifeblood of their existence. For that reason, many reporters prefer to avoid personal relationships with their sources. Of course, this advice is not very helpful if a journalist is married to or otherwise romantically involved with a news source. Such was the case with Donna Hanover Giuliani, a popular anchor at WPIX-TV in New York and the wife of mayoral candidate Rudolph Giuliani. During his 1989 mayoral campaign, Donna Hanover, the journalist, agreed to disclose fully her marriage to the then U.S. attorney, remaining on the air but shunning any news about the campaign.[22] On another occasion, an NBC correspondent became romantically involved with a presidential candidate. NBC learned of the relationship from outside sources and transferred her immediately off the campaign. Although no bias was detected in her reporting, the mere perception of a personal stake in the story was sufficient to merit a reassignment.[23]

Employment of more than one family member by the same organization, particularly if they work in the same department, can be viewed as an ethical problem. A city editor whose wife is a staff reporter, for example, would be under pressure from other newsroom personnel to avoid even the appearance of favored treatment. Because of the potential for conflicts of interest that might develop from these kinds of familial relationships, some institutions have nepotism policies that forbid or limit such employment practices.

The Journalist as Citizen If a man threatens suicide by jumping off a bridge, should a newspaper photographer who witnesses the event attempt to talk the man out of his desperate action, or should he record the event and await the arrival of professional assistance? In other words, should his good samaritan instincts override his journalistic obligations?

Normally, journalists are admonished to maintain a degree of emotional separation from the stories they are covering. And some, who have taken this admonition as a journalistic imperative, have placed "the story" above all other obligations. Other reporters consider this attitude to be morally austere and have become active participants in resolving situations where human lives are at stake.

Consider the following real-life dramas: When a temporary stand seating 125 fans collapsed at the Indianapolis 500, a local newspaper photographer made a series of pictures of the crashing structure and recorded the racing cars as they passed his vantage point. "My first obligation was the assignment the newspaper had given me," Randall supposedly said. "I stayed where I was to cover the race."

On the other hand, when an amateur photographer arrived at the scene of an Atlanta hotel fire that claimed 119 lives, he offered his help to firemen and began taking pictures only after they declined his assistance. In one, which was a Pulitzer Prize winner, he captured a woman in midair plummeting to her death.[24]

Several years ago, Cecil Andrews, an unemployed roofer with a history of mental instability, phoned WHMA-TV in Anniston, Alabama, and said, "If you want to see somebody set himself on fire, be at the square in Jacksonville in ten minutes." The photographer, Ronald Simmons, and the sound technician, Gary Harris, were on duty that night and notified the police. Simmons and Harris were then sent to the scene, but the police were nowhere in sight. The two rolled their camera as Andrews attempted to set himself on fire. Harris eventually intervened, but not before Andrews had been severely burned.[25]

On another occasion, a reporter for WBNS in Columbus, Ohio, was on her way to an assignment with a photographer when they saw some people pulling a fisherman from a river. The man's rescuer asked for some help in administering CPR, and the reporter, trained in CPR, jumped in to help and worked on the man until the rescue squad arrived.[26]

In each of these situations, which involved a conflict between reporters' roles as citizens and their sense of professional detachment, the reporters reacted differently. Media codes usually do not address such contingencies, but we might begin with a threshold standard that appears to be the prevailing view in the industry: Unless a journalist is on a specific assignment to cover an event where people's lives are in danger, he or she should render aid when no one else is present to do so.[27] But even when reporters are on assignment, they do not shed their obligations of citizenship. If someone needs assistance, they should render it (assuming they can do so without peril to their own safety) until emergency personnel have arrived. In this manner, journalists can fulfill their duties as citizens without significantly compromising their journalistic goal of impartiality.

Conflicting Public Participation

The Two Views in Journalism At one end of the ethical spectrum, some news organizations discourage membership or participation in any community organizations. Once reporters become "joiners," according to this view, they become part of the system they are assigned to cover. In addition, this traditional view of journalism holds that news organizations must remain civicly detached, surveying their communities from afar in order to render an "objective" and impartial account of their fates and fortunes. At the other end of the spectrum are those who encourage civic participation and activism as a means to stay attuned to the needs of the community and, not coincidentally, to develop news sources.

Perhaps the best approach to this dilemma is to apply the "rule of common sense." Journalists cannot be social hermits and retreat from all involvement in their communities. In fact, some civic activity sensitizes reporters to the problems they are assigned to cover. In this view, reporters need to be "wired in" to the dynamics of their communities. Thus, in modern society the avoidance of all conflicts of interest may not be feasible, but journalists are still under a moral obligation to disclose such conflicts to the public.

Nevertheless, journalists should be wary of outright political activism, because that is likely to be viewed as a partisan undertaking (which it is!). If reporters might be perceived by the audience as having a vested interest in the story they are covering, they should be reassigned. Some consideration might even be given to alerting the public to the staff's external activities. Can reporters expect public officials whom they cover to disclose their conflicts of interests and not do so themselves?

Some argue, however, that membership in political organizations is not necessarily the cause of reporter bias and that journalists with strong political beliefs would be biased regardless of their official ties with such organizations. Thus, a resignation from such affiliations would be primarily cosmetic and symbolic. The question, of course, is whether the public will be willing to overlook such political memberships, even if the reporter is capable of impartiality under the circumstances.

In recent years reporters have been admonished by their superiors for participating in public demonstrations on controversial issues, even on their own time. The case described at the outset of this chapter, involving reporter participation in an abortion rights demonstration, is just one example. Likewise, gay journalists who are active in gay rights organizations have run into resistance from their editors. A case in point is Sandy Nelson, a reporter for the Tacoma, Washington, *Morning News Tribune*, who sued her employer for allegedly reassigning her to the copy desk because of her activism in a gay rights organization. "Journalists are like serfs," she said. "We have become the company's property twenty-four hours a day." But managing editor Jan Brandt responded that they were just protecting the paper's integrity: "This case is not about lifestyles, freedom of speech or an individual. . . . When a journalist takes a highly visible political role, it undermines the credibility of the paper."[28]

Civic activism by newspaper publishers and station owners presents a related conflict-of-interest dilemma. Media executives are generally well-known, influential members of the community. Most are not journalists and often feel more comfortable in the business world than the newsroom. Nevertheless, their loyalties must lie, first and foremost, with their journalistic enterprises, and civic activities that conflict with those loyalties must be avoided. For example, memberships in such social organizations as the Lions Club or Rotary International would probably pose no problem. But serving on the board of directors of a chemical plant that has been under constant government scrutiny for pollution violations would place the newsroom staff in an awkward position. Of course, the range of civic activities to which media executives might become a party is so great that once again the rule of common sense should be used as a moral guidepost. When conflicts of interests are apparent, they should be avoided. When they are unavoidable or unforeseen, the public should be apprised of the situation, and every effort should be made to insulate newsroom personnel from the pressures for favored treatment.

The Rise of Public Journalism For most of our history, the news media in the United States have adhered to the traditional view that they should serve as society's watchdogs and gadflies and that this role necessitates a respectable psychological distance from the affairs of their communities. But with media credibility continuing to erode (and, with it, newspaper readership), a growing movement is afoot to reconnect journalists and the institutions they represent to their civic roots. Supporters view this ideology as possibly the salvation of American journalism. Opponents see it as a threat to traditional journalistic values. This movement, which has been described as "the hottest secular religion in the news business,"[29] is most commonly referred to as *public journalism*.[30] Alicia Shepard, writing in the *American Journalism Review*, offers this succinct description of the objective of *public journalism*:

> The goal of public journalism—a.k.a. civic journalism, public service journalism or community-assisted reporting—is to "reconnect" citizens with their newspapers, their communities and the political process, with newspapers playing a role not unlike that of a community organizer. According to the gospel of public journalism, professional passivity is passé; activism is hot. Detachment is out; participation is in. Experts are no longer the quote-machines of choice; readers' voices must be heard.[31]

The animating principle of the *public journalism* movement is that news media should serve as agents of change. This practice includes asking readers and viewers to decide what the media should cover and even how they cover it and then becoming active partners with the community in confronting social problems. For example, in 1993 reporters, photographers, artists, and editors at the *Des Moines Register* were assigned to hold open-ended conversations about community concerns with area residents. The paper used the

results to design an opinion poll about major local issues. In still another *public journalism* initiative, the *Wisconsin State Journal* in Madison and a local PBS station convened citizens on mock grand juries and legislatures to deliberate a property tax plan, the national budget, gambling, and health care reform.[32] The Akron, Ohio, *Beacon-Journal* took the lead in its community in confronting racial tensions. Rather than simply "telling the news" of Akron's racial problems and reporting the reactions (the traditional view), Editor Dale Allen placed his newspaper at the vortex of the controversy it was reporting on. The paper not only published a carefully researched series that bashed many racial stereotypes about such subjects as crime, education, and business; it convened interracial focus groups to discuss the implications of the information and possible solutions. It then sought to involve readers who wanted to be a part of the solution by publishing reader coupons with each article to help steer *Beacon-Journal* reporters toward success stories in their neighborhoods.[33]

Although *public journalism* poses a direct challenge to entrenched views about the media's presumed role, it has attracted a rather significant following. In two 1994 University of Kansas surveys of editors and publishers, for example, nearly half of the publishers reported sponsoring town meetings to identify community expectations for newspaper leadership. Ninety-seven percent said they were personally involved with community organizations, and 74 percent said their editors were too. Only 3 percent of the editors responding to the surveys said newspapers should "never" become directly involved in community affairs.[34]

As civic-minded as advocates of *public journalism* appear to be, the notion of abandoning traditional journalistic values of detachment, objectivity, and impartiality is still controversial and raises concerns about conflicts of interests. For example, N. Christian Anderson, editor of the *Orange County* (California) *Register* reflects the attitude among traditional reporters and editors: "I have an obligation not to be involved in a community I write about. It's more important that the people I write about trust that I'm impartial than it is to be involved in that part of the community."[35] One respondent to the University of Kansas survey agreed: "We must stay out of the community power structure if the newspaper is to sustain its credibility," he said.[36] In addition, the critics complain that *public journalism* initiatives too often substitute the judgments of community leaders for those of editors. In responding to referenda, the media are merely feeding citizens what they want to know rather than what they need to know.[37]

Space limitations preclude any exhaustive examination of the implications of the *public journalism* movement. Needless to say, the ethical debate surrounding this phenomenon has just begun. However, if the reformers succeed in subduing the traditionalists in this journalistic tug of war, the aftermath could forever alter the ethical landscape for the practice of journalism within American culture.

Vested Interests and Hidden Agendas

Conflicts between media practitioners' professional duties and their personal interests and agendas pose some intriguing questions. Financial reporters, for example, should obviously not trade in stocks they cover, but does that mean that they should shun the market entirely? The ethical issue usually revolves around the degree to which outside relationships and vested interests are likely to influence one's professional judgment. When such conflicting loyalties remain undisclosed or when hidden agendas motivate the moral agent, then ethical concerns are implicated.

A prime example is one that grew out of the Senate hearings on the confirmation of Supreme Court nominee Clarence Thomas. On October 10, 1991—one day before attorney Anita Hill's Senate testimony concerning her allegations of sexual harassment against Thomas —the *Washington Post* carried a column under the heading "Open Season on Clarence Thomas." In this column, staff writer Juan Williams expressed his outrage over the liberals' "mob action" and smear campaign and asserted that Hill had no credible evidence of Thomas's involvement in any sexual harassment. But what was unknown to the *Post*'s readers was that Williams himself had two weeks earlier become the subject of an internal inquiry into allegations by several female colleagues of sexual harassment. And not until the Senate Judiciary hearings had ended did the *Post* feel compelled to reveal Williams's vested interest in the issue of sexual harassment.[38]

Williams's sin was not in expressing his opinion about an emotional issue that often divides society along gender lines. After all, we do not expect impartiality on the op-ed pages of our newspapers. But we should demand intellectual honesty, and when media practitioners approach their craft with hidden agendas, we expect to be apprised of that fact. In the case of Juan Williams, his personal involvement in sexual harassment allegations while venting his frustrations over the Thomas hearings constituted a conflict of interest. In other words, he did not enter the marketplace of ideas with "clean hands." The newspaper's readers probably expected that Williams, as a columnist, would offer an opinion of the Thomas-Hill confrontation based on an intellectual, reasoned assessment of the evidence or lack thereof. Instead, readers were treated to an emotional diatribe motivated by his own vested interests.

Of course, not all vested interests represent conflicts for media practitioners. For example, you may recall the case described in Chapter 6 in which the PR firm, Hill & Knowlton, failed to acknowledge its connection to the committee holding hearings on alleged Iraqi atrocities in Kuwait. As a PR firm representing Kuwaiti interests, one would not expect Hill & Knowlton to be neutral in this situation. After all, PR practitioners are advocates. The company's ethical transgression was in not disclosing its relationship to members of the Congressional caucus conducting the hearings.

Unfortunately, hidden agendas are not that rare among news organizations. This is particularly true where powerful media industries seek to protect their financial interests in other enterprises. A clash between a media institution's public responsibility and its corporate self-interest is troublesome because of the pervasive influence of media enterprises within our society. In early 1991, for example, the *Columbia Journalism Review* took the Knoxville, Tennessee, *News-Sentinel* to task for "transmitting an editorial message without a proper conflict-of-interest signal." The paper had editorialized against South Central Bell's proposal to develop a fiber optic information and programming network that might directly compete with cable. But the editorial failed to mention that the franchise for Knoxville's cable system was held by Scripps Howard, the paper's parent company.[39] Likewise, the *Chicago Tribune* tried to sway public opinion against congressional proposals to limit so-called "program-length commercials" directed at children, along with their lucrative spinoffs such as toys, lunch boxes, and coloring books. But the paper failed to acknowledge that a Tribune Company subsidiary was affiliated with various producers of nationally syndicated children's programs, including *G.I. Joe.*[40]

All of these situations beg the question: If the parties involved had publicly acknowledged their vested interests, would this have resolved the issue of a conflict of interest? One could maintain that revealing such vested interests, which carry the perception of hidden agendas, is the honest thing to do and fulfills the moral agent's duty to his or her audience. Armed with this information, readers and viewers are perfectly capable, so the argument goes, of determining for themselves how much credibility to place in the communicator's message. On the other hand, audience members, particularly in a fast-paced culture that does not afford many opportunities for quiet reflec-

tion, may have neither the inclination nor the ability to evaluate the moral agent's motivation and sincerity. For example, if Juan Williams had offered a more subdued assessment of the Hill-Thomas controversy rather than one dripping with emotion, is there any reason to assume that readers would have considered his column significantly more credible if they had known of his vested interest in the case? Regardless of whether one prefers the more permissive (full disclosure ethically sufficient) or austere (no reporting or commentary where vested interests are involved) view, most would probably agree that the minimum requirement is for the moral agents to reveal any vested interest or hidden agenda that inspires their public pronouncements.

APPROACHES TO DEALING WITH CONFLICTS OF INTEREST

Obviously, no clear-cut solution can be provided for avoiding every conflict of interest. But the following three-step approach should serve as a guide through this moral thicket and should bring some degree of sanity to the moral reasoning process. First, of course, the goal should be to avoid personal conflicts that are likely to undermine the media practitioner's professional obligations. Duty-based theorists (deontologists) would avoid foreseeable conflicts as a matter of principle. Consequentialists (teleologists) would examine the potential harm to various parties caused by the conflict as a means of resolving the dilemma.

Second, if the conflict cannot be anticipated, every effort to resolve the dilemma, even after the fact, should be made. For example, newspaper publishers may not be able to anticipate that a company in which they hold stock will become the subject of an official investigation. But if their paper is covering the story, they should consider ridding themselves of their financial investment to avoid the appearance of a conflict of interest. We can see this principle in action when public officials who do not choose to divest themselves entirely of their investments nevertheless place them in a blind trust until they have withdrawn from the political arena.

Third, if a conflict of interest cannot be avoided, it should be acknowledged to the public or clients. Those travel writers, for example, who must rely on the good offices and the financial support of the tourist industry to cover their stories should acknowledge their source of sponsorship. A PR practitioner who discovers a conflict of interest in serving two clients with opposing agendas should acknowledge that conflict (as is required by the PRSA code) to both clients. Aristotle's golden mean is sometimes valuable in applying this third principle, because it provides a reasonable accommodation between unrealistic moral purity and the callous disregard of the public's right to know about the existence of the conflict.

CONFLICTS OF INTEREST: HYPOTHETICAL CASE STUDIES

The cases in this chapter provide some insight into the diversity of situations that can pose conflicts of interest for media practitioners. In confronting the dilemmas posed by these scenarios, pay particular attention to the conflicts between the *particularistic*, or role-based, obligations of the moral agents and the universal obligations, as described in Chapter 2. You may also wish to reread Chapter 3, outlining the three primary approaches to ethical decision making: duty-based ethics (deontology), consequence-based ethics (teleology), and Aristotle's golden mean. These will be the keys to stimulating your imagination as you apply the moral reasoning process to the issues raised in these hypothetical cases.

CASE STUDIES

▶ CASE 7-1
A Riverboat Casino Seeks Public Relations Counsel

"Gambling Commission Issues First Casino License." To the local ministerial alliance, this bold headline in the *Athena Herald* signified the commencement of a satanic ritual and the reincarnation of Sodom and Gomorrah along the banks of the Mississippi. Most civic and business leaders were more charitable in viewing the state's first riverboat casino as the salvation of the local tourist industry and a shot of timely adrenalin for an anemic, stagnant economy. Public opinion surveys reflected this moral polarization, with Athena's citizens evenly divided on the evils of legalized gambling. There were few who expressed "no opinion," according to the *Herald's* own polls.

As the state's revenues declined and demands for government services continued unabated, some lawmakers saw legalized gambling as a panacea for their financial woes. But the predictable and unrelenting opposition from a coalition of religious leaders and "quality of life" environmentalists had precipitated a bitter and divisive debate within the legislature. Nevertheless, the gambling lobby had prevailed, and the lawmakers, motivated more by politics than sound fiscal policy, had established an elaborate regulatory infrastructure to oversee the numerous casino and other gambling enterprises that were expected to compete for the commission's blessing.

The *Lady Luck*, under the auspices of Maltese Enterprises, was the first out of the starting gate. Maltese Enterprises was a powerful consortium that had financial interests in casinos in Nevada, Louisiana, Mississippi, and other states that had recently succumbed to the lure of legalized gambling. The *Lady Luck*'s proposal, which included three cruises a day except in inclement weather when the boat could remain moored to the dock, was in compliance with the state's minimum licensing requirements. But Maltese was sensitive to the very vocal and public opposition of some segments of the community and had also promised a major renovation of the dilapidated dockside neighborhood in order to certify its moral worth as a corporate citizen, while securing the *Lady Luck*'s competitive advantage over other applicants.

But opponents of legalized gambling were not placated by what they perceived as a "bribe masquerading as civic virtue" and vowed to continue their campaign to discourage the local citizenry, as well as tourists, from frequenting the slot machines, blackjack tables, and other gaming devices of the *Lady Luck*. To the business community, which had generally supported legalized gambling, this opposition represented a threat to the economic vitality of the community; to the corporate executives of Maltese Enterprises, it represented a challenging public relations problem.

Maltese lost no time in soliciting public relations proposals from three of Athena's most respectable PR firms, one of which would be selected to cultivate the *Lady Luck*'s image as a responsible citizen. Each was asked to respond with a proposal to neutralize the company's opponents and to strengthen the *Lady Luck*'s image among the local citizenry. Deeter & Mather was a large, well-established PR firm that boasted some of the most prominent local and regional companies among its clientele. Smith, Tyler, and Jones, the second contender for Maltese's rather generous PR expenditures, did not include many blue-chip clients among its accounts, but it did have a reputation for developing imaginative and effective campaigns for controversial clients. Mason and Pringle was the newest and smallest among the three firms under consideration by the Maltese management, but it had developed a reputation for aggressive and effective representation of its increasingly impressive client list in the economic marketplace.

As the senior partner of Mason and Pringle, Myra Mason viewed the overtures from Maltese Enterprises with some concern. In the eyes of the local puritans (and this might include other clients), the *Lady Luck* was a public nuisance beyond the pale of redemption. On the other hand, Maltese came to the table with deep pockets, a factor that could hardly be ignored in an increasingly competitive public relations environment.

"The *Lady Luck* has a real problem," said Mason, as she presided over the weekly gathering of her agency's brain trust. "The clergy in this town are fierce in their opposition, and they're obviously having an impact among their parishioners. And the 'quality of life' people are zealots in their own right."

"That may be true," responded Brad Pringle, Mason's spirited junior partner. "But casino gambling is going to be a reality in Athena. It's legal, and the *Lady Luck* has a right to be represented in the marketplace." Pringle was a fervent disciple of the libertarian philosophy that all interests were entitled to representation in the marketplace. He spent little time agonizing over the moral worthiness of prospective clients.

"Perhaps," responded Juanita Lopez, the senior account executive. "But to me gambling is immoral, regardless of whether the state sanctions it. Do we really want to be associated with this kind of client? And I personally would find it difficult to do a quality job for a client whose activities are morally questionable. I'm not the only one. I've talked with Ken, and he agrees with me. He thinks that taking on this kind of client is bad for our agency's reputation." Ken McGraw was Lopez's associate who was out of town on assignment.

Mason was not surprised at Lopez's passionate objection and McGraw's apparent concurrence. She had also heard complaints from a couple of the junior staff, who were sometimes more idealistic than pragmatic, concerning the *Lady Luck*'s interest in seeking PR counsel. This confirmed her belief that institutions, even small firms like Mason and Pringle, are a microcosm of the society they serve.

"I disagree," declared Mike Butler emphatically. Butler was the firm's director of creative services. "I don't care much for legalized gambling either. I think it's poor fiscal policy for the state to stake its economic future on gambling. Nevertheless, we are a PR firm. Attorneys don't usually pick their clients, and neither should we. Everyone is entitled to representation. Besides, the *Lady Luck* is really taking a beating in the media. The antigambling forces really have their attention. The *Lady Luck* is entitled to an opportunity to defend itself. And that's our job."

But Lopez was in no mood for such rhetorical appeals to justice. "I'm not the only member of this firm who opposes gambling," said Lopez. "And quite frankly, I think it's a conflict of interest for a PR firm to take on a client to which many of its employees personally object. The interests of the *Lady Luck* conflict with our personal beliefs. Can we really do a credible job for a client under these circumstances?"

"I think we can," said Pringle. "After all, we've had controversial clients before. And some of their reputations were well deserved. And yet, we did a credible job in repairing their tarnished images, despite the fact that some of us may have harbored personal misgivings about the companies' practices that led to their image problems in the first place."

"But this is different," asserted Lopez. "In those cases it was just a matter of repairing the companies' images. In the case of the *Lady Luck*, several of us object to the company's line of business. I don't know whether there is any way to dignify gambling. I'll admit they're involved in a legal enterprise. And perhaps they are entitled to PR counsel. But I just don't think we should encourage people to gamble. And if we represent the *Lady Luck*, aren't we in a sense doing just that?"

"I wouldn't go that far," said Mason, who had listened intently to the moral jousting of her passionate staff. "The citizens of Athena can decide for themselves whether they want to gamble. Our job is not to promote gambling—just to convince the public that Maltese and its surrogate, the *Lady Luck*, can be responsible citizens. Besides, if we don't accept this account—assuming that we get the bid—then one of our competitors will."

"On the other hand, Juanita may have a point," conceded Mason, as she began to ponder the ethical dimensions of this public relations dilemma. "If our staff is not firmly behind this project—if there is some moral objection to this client—then we may not be able to do a first-rate job. Of course, I could

assign the tasks to those who are willing to work on this project. But that may not be fair to Maltese if they don't have the full support of our agency staff."

As senior partner of the firm, Mason was also concerned about the impact of representing a controversial enterprise on the firm's relationships with its other loyal clients. Would they object to being associated with a PR organization that promoted organized gambling? To some, there was no socially redeeming value in gambling. On the other hand, Maltese was prepared to provide a lucrative contract to any PR firm willing to represent it aggressively in the arena of public opinion. How important was the personal conflict between some employees' moral beliefs and the admittedly lawful activities of Maltese in deciding whether to bid on the Maltese account? If the firm did decide to submit a proposal to represent the *Lady Luck* riverboat casino, did it have an ethical obligation to its prospective client to reveal the objections of some of its staff members?

THE CASE STUDY

As the senior partner in the Mason and Pringle public relations agency, Myra Mason is confronted with competing loyalties. This case represents a potential conflict between the consciences of some staff members and the professional obligations of the firm to its clients and the community at large. This dilemma is captured in this observation from Cornelius B. Pratt, professor of public relations at Michigan State University:

> One, of course, would argue, on the one hand, that a demonstrated loyalty to one's current clients supersedes loyalty to one's potential clients. And that employee reactions to a controversial account need to be considered in evaluating whether such an account should be accepted. On the other hand, such loyalties need to be balanced against the greater loyalty of the organization: loyalty to society.[41]

Should a public relations firm accept a client to which some of its employees have a moral objection? If so, should the client be apprised in advance of this division within the firm? From a management perspective, it would be unthinkable to force employees to ignore their moral beliefs and to work on the *Lady Luck* account. But if the tasks are assigned to other employees—which is particularly problematic in a small agency—then the question arises as to whether the client is receiving the quality service for which it has contracted.

In the final analysis, Mason must decide whether her agency should apply a moral litmus test to this controversial client based on the values of some of its employees. Or should (or can) the institution's values stand apart from those of its individual employees?

For the purpose of resolving this dilemma, assume the role of senior partner Myra Mason. Then, using the SAD Formula for moral reasoning outlined in Chapter 3, render a judgment on whether you will attempt to add the *Lady Luck* riverboat casino to your client list.

▶ **CASE 7-2**
The Gay Journalist as Activist

Oceanside is a community of 475,000 located along California's Pacific coastline. Once a white, middle-class enclave and a politically unassailable Republican stronghold, Oceanside is now a cosmopolitan tribute to racial and cultural diversity. This diversity is also reflected in the city council, which has succeeded in passing a series of ordinances designed to provide legal sanction to the spirit of egalitarianism and cultural tolerance. The most recent and controversial of these is a measure to prohibit discrimination against gays in employment and public accommodations, a concession to the increasingly visible gay population that has been attracted to Oceanside's receptive environment.

This demographic reformation, however, was not an entirely peaceful one, as the entrenched and well-financed conservative political power structure initially resisted what it perceived as a threat to traditional values and their harmonious lifestyle. And now, as the "loyal opposition" on the city council, it has continued its resistance to the new spirit of liberalism, as reflected in its latest attempts at repealing the gay antidiscrimination ordinance.

Nevertheless, despite some public defiance, a small but influential cadre of civic visionaries provided the spiritual and political leadership that paved the way for Oceanside's sociological transformation. Jason Wentworth was one of those visionaries. As the publisher of the *Oceanside Courier*, Wentworth had committed his paper to creating a culture of tolerance and cooperation. He was determined that the *Courier* would be at the vanguard of corporate responsibility in restoring some measure of harmony and sanity to his community's political life. This determination was reflected not only in the paper's liberal editorial policies. At a time when many papers were struggling with the issue of diversity in the newsroom, the *Courier*'s editorial staff was an impressive reflection of the racial, sexual, and cultural demographics of the community it served. As a catalyst for change, the *Courier* had received its share of awards and recognition for its journalistic enterprise in publicizing the problems of racial and cultural minorities.

Wentworth credited Managing Editor Daniel Netterville with much of the paper's success in this respect. Netterville did not believe that only minorities could cover minority issues. Nevertheless, he was convinced that they brought a certain insight and understanding to their beats, a conviction that had paid handsome dividends in terms of access and the cultivation of news sources within the various cultural subgroups. Although Netterville applauded the publisher's commitment to the cause of social justice and the *Courier*'s aggressive editorial stance against discrimination, he was just as strongly opposed to reporter activism on behalf of the causes embraced by the groups they covered, even in their "off-duty" hours. Although the paper's policy manual prohibited staff members from engaging in activities that might compromise their journalistic independence or impugn the paper's credibility, it did not specifically prohibit participation in partisan causes. Nevertheless, Netterville's views on the matter were well known among the *Courier*'s editorial staff.

Katrina Nelson, an avowed lesbian, was the first to challenge the ethical utility of her editor's view. Nelson had joined the newspaper's staff just three years ago and had asked to be assigned to cover the rapidly growing gay community. "They're among our readers and deserve the same consideration as other minorities," she had told Netterville, who did not hesitate in honoring her request.

The editor's decision had paid dividends. Nelson had approached her assignment with compassion and insight, and her in-depth reporting and imaginative writing style had resulted in approbation from both the state's press association and the National Lesbian and Gay Journalists Association. She had also been commended by her peers and many of the paper's readers for her fair and balanced coverage of the gay community.

Nelson had always maintained a psychological distance from any partisanship or activism in gay causes, partly as a result of Netterville's admonitions and partly as a result of her own ambivalence about reporters' involvement in partisan causes. Therefore, Nelson was both flattered and concerned when an invitation arrived from the Gay and Lesbian Alliance.

"I'm aware of your feeling about reporters getting involved in social causes," Nelson began rather cautiously in her meeting with Netterville. Out of loyalty to her editor, who had always been supportive of her journalistic endeavors, she felt an obligation to seek his counsel before confronting this ethical dilemma. "As you know," she continued, "the Gay and Lesbian Alliance is holding a rally downtown on Saturday to protest the proposed repeal of the gay antidiscrimination ordinance. Since I cover the gay community and gay issues, they've asked me to speak. This would be on my own time—and I wouldn't be there as a reporter. You can assign someone else to cover the story."

"You're right—I have a problem with reporters becoming activists," responded Netterville. "Even if they do so on their own time, the paper's credibility could be hurt. The issue is not whether you cover this demonstration or not. You will still be making the news our paper covers. TV cameras will be there. If the public sees you as an advocate, they may question our objectivity."

But Nelson was unpersuaded and aggressively pressed her case. "I disagree. Our readers are sophisticated. I don't think they expect us to be completely divorced from community affairs. We have

as much right as anyone else to express our views on important issues, as long as we don't do it in the pages of the *Courier*. We're citizens too—and citizens should speak out, particularly where social justice is at stake. Just because I'm a reporter, I don't believe that I should have to forsake all involvement in community affairs."

"This paper isn't asking that you become a societal recluse," replied the managing editor. "Many of our reporters are members of organizations. And I certainly don't expect them to shed their political views when they join our staff. But we have to draw the line at political activism, particularly when it relates to issues they cover on a daily basis. If we allow you to speak at this rally, then our other reporters who cover minority affairs will demand the same consideration."

"But we shouldn't be at the paper's beck and call twenty-four hours a day," declared Nelson. "In our off-duty hours, we have a constitutional right to speak out on controversial issues, just like any other private citizen."

"You're right! You do have a constitutional right to express your views on controversial issues," responded Netterville emphatically. "But you don't have a constitutional right to work for the *Courier*."

During this brief exchange, Nelson's ambivalence about reporter activism, at least under some circumstances, had evaporated. However, she had failed to change her editor's view on what she believed to be an outmoded and unreasonable ethical belief as to what constitutes a conflict of interest. Nelson did not believe that her speech before a rally of the Gay and Lesbian Alliance would compromise her independence. After all, she *was* a lesbian covering the gay community, and her sexual orientation had not contaminated the news copy generated during her three year tenure with the *Courier*. Nevertheless, her managing editor's parting shot had left little doubt as to the paper's position on her proposed role, albeit perhaps a brief one, as a political activist in the cause of gay rights.

On the one hand, if she became visibly and publicly active on behalf of the community that she had covered so eloquently for three years, she would either be reassigned to another beat or more likely lose her job. Because of her success in publicizing the concerns of the gay community, including the human tragedy of the AIDS epidemic, perhaps she should subordinate her desire to speak out publicly on the cause of gay rights to the longer-term objective of promoting cultural diversity through her journalistic enterprise.

On the other hand, she worked for an institution that very carefully separated its own political activism on the editorial pages from its so-called objective news coverage. And yet, the paper's management apparently did not believe that reporters could become politically active in their off-duty hours and remain dispassionate and detached in fulfilling their professional responsibilities. And they apparently were even less confident that the readers could make this distinction.

With the demonstration sponsored by the Gay and Lesbian Alliance only three weeks away, Nelson pondered her ethical dilemma. Should she accept, as a matter of principle, the Alliance's invitation to address their rally, or should she acquiesce to the traditional journalistic admonition that reporters should not become involved in partisan causes?

THE CASE STUDY

The debate over whether reporters should become involved in partisan causes is long-standing, and journalists themselves are divided. The disparity of views on this potential conflict of interest is reflected in *Newsweek*'s coverage of the issue in 1993:

> A few reporters and editors refuse to enroll in a party or even to vote because they say it compromises their objectivity. At the other extreme are journalists who contend that objectivity is a fraud because reporters bring their biases to every story. They say as long as they're open about their prejudices, readers can judge for themselves. Most reporters and editors stand somewhere in the middle. They say it's OK to fight for causes as long as you don't cover them and as long as you're not leading the charge.[42]

In the scenario outlined here, the managing editor is concerned that the paper's stock in trade—its credibility—will be compromised if one of its re-

porters becomes a partisan for a cause that she covers as part of her beat. Netterville does not expect the *Courier's* reporters to shed their political views at the newsroom door. But he believes that outright political activism constitutes a conflict of interest. In this view, journalists must sometimes sacrifice their free speech privileges for the overriding responsibilities of their profession.

Reporter Katrina Nelson, on the other hand, rejects the notion that she must relinquish her basic rights of citizenship just because she is a reporter. As an avowed lesbian, Nelson is convinced that she can participate in a public demonstration for gay rights on her own time without jeopardizing her journalistic independence or her paper's credibility. She has also been commended for her fair and balanced reporting of the gay community. Why, she wonders, should converting her private opinions into public proclamations affect her reputation among the paper's readers?

Applying the SAD Formula for moral reasoning outlined in Chapter 3, render a judgment on whether you believe reporter Katrina Nelson should accept the invitation to address the gay rights demonstration or stay aloof from any political activism regarding the issue of gay rights. In so doing, keep in mind that this case has less to do with sexual lifestyle in particular than with the larger issue of reporter involvement in political causes.

▶ CASE 7-3
The NABJ and Divided Loyalties[43]

As the newly elected president of the National Association of Black Journalists (NABJ), Mathias Washington was rightfully pleased with his organization's accomplishments. Washington was a charter member when the NABJ was founded in 1975 to monitor racial discrimination and to help open up employment opportunities for African-American journalists. The initial meetings had been rather sparsely attended, but its founders had infused the organization with a noble mission and a social conscience that increasingly attracted African-American writers, reporters, and editors to its agenda for racial justice. Now, two decades later, the association's annual conventions had become a significant rendezvous point for recruiters and eager job seekers, and its rather modest activities of the early days had given way to lavish concerns where scholarships and awards were handed out.

But it was not scholarships or awards that were on the minds of the NABJ board members as the association prepared for its annual convention in Atlanta. They were preoccupied with the case of Glendell Watts, the charismatic past president of the NABJ who was widely credited with invigorating the organization with its sense of purpose and journalistic camaraderie. But as NABJ members arrived in Atlanta, Glendell Watts was not practicing journalism; he was sitting on death row awaiting the execution of his death warrant.

Watts had been convicted seven years ago in Pittsburgh of shooting a white police officer. From the moment of his arrest and indictment, Watts maintained that he was being beaten by the officer for no legitimate reason and that he acted in self-defense. The prosecutor maintained that Watts had been stopped for speeding and had shot the officer in cold blood without any provocation. Whatever the truth, an all-white jury had taken only two hours to convict Watts, and the former NABJ president was sentenced to death. From the outset, leaders of the African-American community charged that the evidence against Watts was "suspicious" and that he had received an unfair trial because of a lack of minority representation on the jury. They were joined in their protests by Amnesty International and Human Rights Watch. But despite numerous legal appeals, Watts remained on death row.

The Watts case had galvanized some NABJ members and, as the execution date approached, they were pressuring the board to take a public stance in an effort to win a last-minute stay and perhaps eventually a new trial. Mathias Washington had placed the matter on the agenda for the board meeting, which would be held just prior to the convention's opening session. A preview of the debate that was likely to ensue was reflected in the president's "working dinner" meeting with the board's

executive committee: Asa Jackson, Clarence Post, and Tamara Landry.

"I'm not sure we should get mixed up in the Watts affair," said Jackson rather tentatively. "If we do, our stance could turn this organization into an advocacy group. If we're to maintain our credibility as journalists, we need to remain detached."

"I disagree," said Landry. "What's wrong with our getting involved as an organization? After all, other media organizations lobby and take public positions on behalf of their members. That doesn't mean that as individual reporters they can't be objective."

"But when journalistic organizations take positions," responded Post, "such as intervening in litigation involving First Amendment violations, they are usually related to journalistic issues. Watts might be a journalist—in fact, he's a former president of the NABJ—but his case isn't about journalism; it's a criminal case."

But Landry was insistent. "If we remain aloof, some members will view this as an abandonment of our association's commitment to equal justice. They might say we're out of touch with the plight of African Americans who are more likely to face the death penalty than white criminals. And many of our members have covered this issue. That makes it a journalistic issue."

"We may be African Americans, but in our professional duties, we must be journalists first," replied Jackson. "Otherwise we lose our credibility. Remember this: While some of our members work for media targeted specifically to black audiences, many work for white-owned papers and stations that serve diverse audiences. If the NABJ becomes an advocate for a cause, there will always be a suspicion that our own reporting is biased. It will be a case of guilt by association. And we'll be accused of having a conflict of interest."

"That's a point to consider," said Post. "Besides, it may be that Watts didn't receive a fair trial, but I don't think we should risk our reputation and spend the association's capital on this one case. It's definitely a conflict of interest. If we get involved in the Watts case, our professional duties will then become hostage to our personal views on racial justice. Our best approach is to disassociate ourselves from this case. As journalists, we have an ethical obligation to remain detached."

"You act as though the so-called values of detachment and objectivity are moral imperatives for all journalists," responded Landry. "But who set these standards? White reporters and editors. We didn't have any input into the formulation of these standards. Besides, this case isn't just about the guilt or innocence of one man. It's about the disbursement of justice for all African Americans. This high-profile case has received national attention. The black community will watch to see how we handle this. If we don't take a firm stand in support of Watts' right to a new trial, then we might be accused of being disloyal to one of our own. There are times when our consciences must have priority over our professional duties."

Post was concerned about his colleague's apparent belief in race-based journalistic standards. "If we insist on a different set of ethical standards for African-American journalists," he said, "and if we become advocates for a criminal just because he happens to be black, regardless of how unfairly *we* believe he was treated by the justice system, we will be accused of embracing a *double standard* for black journalists—the kind of thing we should be opposed to."

"On the other hand," said Washington, who had listened intently to the impassioned discussion among his three colleagues, "keep in mind that many of our members chose journalism because they wanted to make an impact on society. They certainly didn't go into it for the money. They might feel drawn to the Watts case because it embodies the racist tendencies of the American justice system. Under these circumstances, it's difficult to sit on the sidelines."

But despite this bold assertion, Washington still felt the tug of competing loyalties as the board members continued to travel familiar terrain in their search for moral wisdom. The full executive board would meet later that afternoon to consider the issue. Their decision would then be conveyed to the full membership the following day. The NABJ president knew that Tamara Washington was right about one thing. This case was not just about the guilt or innocence of one man. *The People v.*

Glendell Watts would certainly disrupt the effort at consensus building that had distinguished the association's recent conventions and might even be a defining moment for the NABJ itself.

THE CASE STUDY

Media organizations often take public positions on issues affecting their membership. The Society of Professional Journalists, for example, has been at the forefront on First Amendment issues. But the controversy outlined here does not involve a journalistic issue. It raises the question of whether journalists should abandon their position of neutrality and detachment on matters that do not directly affect their profession. In this scenario, the NABJ executive committee is pondering the dilemma of conflicting loyalties: conscience versus professional duty or journalistic objectivity versus advocacy for social justice.

This case is full of ethical subplots. Of immediate concern to the NABJ board, of course, is whether the association should become an advocate on behalf of Glendell Watts. But beyond the official stance of the NABJ, there is the ethical question of whether individual African-American journalists should become involved. Are they journalists first, or should their allegiance be to one of their own whom they feel has been the victim of racial injustice? Should the answer to this question depend on whether they are working for a news organization targeted to a general audience or a black-owned organization whose constituency is primarily the African-American community? And is there any merit to the argument advanced by Tamara Landry that conventional news values, such as objectivity and detachment, are the product of the white journalistic establishment to which minority journalists do not necessarily owe allegiance?

For the purpose of examining these questions and the issues raised in the scenario, put yourself in the position of an African-American journalist and a member of the NABJ (admittedly, this may be difficult if you are not an African American). And then, applying the SAD Formula for moral reasoning outlined in Chapter 3, explain how you will evaluate and resolve the ethical dilemma posed in this case.

▶ **CASE 7-4**
The Professor and His Book

Professor Byron Wright looked thoughtfully at the sheet just handed him by the departmental secretary. It was time for that annual rite of spring when all faculty members were requested to submit their book lists for the fall semester. For eight years as a member of the journalism faculty, Wright had dutifully selected the texts he felt would best serve his needs and those of the students in his media writing, copy editing, and ethics courses. Normally this was a routine exercise. But not this time.

Wright had retreated to the world of academia after working for fifteen years as a reporter, copy editor, and city editor on three different newspapers. In order to gain respectability within the academic community, he had earned his Ph.D., and he had been eagerly hired by the new chairman of the Department of Mass Communication at Southland College. Southland had a reputation as a solid "nuts-and-bolts" program, and Wright had enjoyed his tenure there. He had entered as an associate professor rather than assistant professor out of deference to his extensive professional experience.

Most of Wright's course load consisted of teaching the basics of journalism, such as writing, reporting, and editing. But he had come to enjoy, above all, the course in media ethics, which was required of all journalism majors. The course was an intellectually stimulating experience for Wright and popular among the students. He used the case approach, in which the instructor provided the students with a hypothetical ethical dilemma and they constructed a written response and presented their conclusions to the class.

Wright had used a variety of ethics texts over the years, but he had not been completely satisfied with any of them. First, most of them were confined strictly to journalism ethics, certainly an important aspect of the course, given his own background. But many of the students in the class were enrolled in the advertising and public relations sequences, and the study of ethical problems in those two fields was no less important. Second, there was a dearth of casebooks in media ethics, and Wright had spent endless hours constructing his own hypothetical cases to pass out to the class. Although most of the books on the market provided plenty of examples of real-life ethical situations, these texts were primarily anecdotal and did not require the students themselves to puzzle and agonize over the dilemmas. Wright believed that a course in media ethics presented an ideal environment for teaching students how to think critically and to reason, skills that had never really been taught as part of the American educational curriculum.

To resolve these difficulties, Wright had decided to write his own ethics casebook. He had done so reluctantly, recognizing how much time it would require. But his colleagues had provided encouragement, and the chairman had even thrown in three hours of release time from his course load to complete the manuscript. Besides, Wright well understood the realities of the academic system of rewards and hoped that a major text in the field would improve his chances of promotion to full professor. The royalties would also be nice, if not lucrative. The writing of college texts, Wright knew, was not the path to a life of luxury.

The text, *Case Studies in Media Ethics*, had been completed in February and was being marketed for the fall semester. And this was what gave Wright pause before completing his book list for the upcoming term. There had been some discussion the previous year in the Faculty Senate about the ethics of professors' writing their own texts and then requiring the students to buy them. The question had been posed in writing to the senators by a young (and undoubtedly naive) faculty member, but he had touched on a sacred cow, and the issue soon died for lack of interest. The young turk, not to be deterred, had then asked the state's attorney general whether requiring students to purchase a text written by the instructor constituted a conflict of interest under the state's ethics in government law. The attorney general had then issued an advisory opinion that such activities were not covered by the law.

However, the fact that his dilemma was not legally unethical did not ease Wright's concerns. He had spent a great deal of time on conflicts of interests in his course, and now the realities of his classroom advice were confronting him like ghosts from the past. On the one hand, he believed his book to be the best on the market. This, of course, was not a profound or even an immodest conclusion, because there were so few casebooks to compete. He had also consulted his faculty colleagues and had been reassured that requiring one's own text was a common practice. If there had been anything wrong with the practice, he was told, it would have been dealt with in the university's policies and procedures. In addition, considering the rather meager financial rewards likely to accrue from his academic authorship, Wright did not feel that he was gaining much at the students' expense.

But he was gaining something! Wright and his students had debated endlessly about how much value had to be involved in an exchange before it constituted a conflict of interest. And sometimes perceptions of a conflict are as important as the conflict of interest itself. How would his students feel about this situation? Should he ask them?

Wright was also concerned about his less mercenary motivations for ordering his own text. Was this book truly the best on the market? How could he be sure? Was he being objective, or was he engaging in rationalization just to salve his conscience? Wright was both judge and jury, and as he stared again at the book order form, he hoped his verdict would be a just (and an ethical) one.

THE CASE STUDY

This case involves a situation confronted by many authors of academic texts, but most do not seem to be concerned about it. One reason, perhaps, is that this practice is common and has yet to be condemned as a conflict of interest. If this were a case of a reporter's accepting a new car from a news source, the ethical dilemma would be clear. Does this case pose any less of a conflict of interest just because it represents a common practice among college instructors? What if Professor Wright's text is really the best on the market? What if it is the only casebook?

Assume the role of Wright, and deliberate the ethics of ordering your own text for this course. You should, first, decide whether there is a conflict of interest. If so, is there a way to resolve the problem while still allowing yourself the luxury of using your own casebook for the upcoming term?

▶ **CASE 7-5**
TV Ads and Conflicting Messages

Ridley Jenkins knew when he had been taken to task. Irma Morris, the president of the local chapter of Mothers Against Drunk Driving (MADD), was angry and had just vented her frustrations to Jenkins, the station manager of one of Phoenix City's three commercially licensed TV stations. Jenkins could only assume that she had similarly confronted his counterparts at the other two stations in the market.

A couple of years before, MADD had begun an aggressive campaign against teenage consumption of alcohol and had sponsored a series of public-service announcements that all three local stations had been dutifully running. It had also cosponsored with one of the local chemical-dependency facilities some antidrug messages aimed at combating the drug epidemic among the city's youths. The local stations, all of which thought of themselves as good citizens and pillars of the community, had also sponsored drug and alcohol awareness campaigns, even sending some of their own celebrities into the high schools to talk to the students. But the results had not been encouraging. The latest figures revealed a 10 percent increase in the number of teenage deaths from alcohol and drugs. Three recent suicides at one of the local high schools had been blamed on the influence of drugs.

Morris believed that more drastic action was warranted. How could MADD's public-service TV campaign against the evils of alcohol and drugs be effective, she asked Jenkins, when the airwaves were inundated with commercials for beer and wine? Morris, never known for her restraint in such matters, demanded that Jenkins take such ads off the air. It was a conflict of interest, Morris argued, for the station to run antidrug and antialcohol ads and to sponsor campaigns of its own while at the same time running commercial messages for beer and wine.

Jenkins could not disagree with the logic of that argument, but he was not prepared to take any precipitous action. The revenues from national spot advertising for beer and wine contributed impressively to his station's income. In addition, there were plenty of commercial tie-ins through local retailers, who often used discount prices on spirits to lure thirsty customers into their establishments. Besides, even if he did remove the ads, there was no guarantee that his competitors would do so. And the network ads would continue to flow, thereby undermining whatever actions were taken locally. The station had always been open to all advertisers, and ads were generally reviewed only for matters of taste or legal considerations. This, Jenkins believed, was a fair (and profitable) way of doing business.

Jenkins was not opposed to drinking, enjoying an occasional cocktail himself. Responsibility was the key, he felt, and removing the ads entirely would not diminish teenagers' determination to experiment. He also wondered about the effectiveness of the ads themselves. Could beer and wine ads influence impressionable juveniles to drink? He had his doubts. And where were the parents in all of this? Still, the conflict-of-interest issue nagged at the broadcaster.

As station manager Jenkins was responsible, first and foremost, for the commercial viability of his station. The removal of alcohol advertising would not be devastating to the profit-and-loss statement, but it would be felt, especially in a soft economy in which revenue projections had remained level for the past year.

But Jenkins also felt a responsibility to the local community. He wondered whether the beer and wine commercials had undermined the credibility of the campaigns against drug and alcohol abuse. A conflict of interest might indeed exist, Jenkins concluded, but how could he resolve it while serving all segments of his viewing audience, including the merchants who depended on the local TV stations to sell their wares?

THE CASE STUDY

This case is really a dispute about consequences. The president of MADD, Morris, is convinced that alcohol ads do influence adolescents. The implication is that by airing beer and wine commercials, the station is canceling out the potential good of its antidrug and antialcohol announcements. Morris sees this matter strictly in terms of a conflict of interest.

But Jenkins is not so sure. He apparently is not convinced of the effectiveness of the ads, and to forego the lucrative revenues for some unproved good might be an unwise decision. But as in many conflict-of-interest dilemmas, perceptions can sometimes be as important as the reality. Will the public, for example, question the credibility of the station's campaign if it continues to air beer and wine commercials?

Jenkins apparently has no personal objection to the ads themselves. The conflict is between opposing messages on the same station. But is this not the nature of the commercial marketplace? Should not all messages and ideas have an opportunity to compete, no matter how objectionable they may be to some? What makes this issue so different? Should juvenile members of the audience be viewed as having the capacity for rational decision making, or are their value systems still too immature to deal effectively with the subtlety of advertising messages?

Applying the facts outlined here and the SAD Formula, assume the role of Jenkins, and render your ethical judgment on this matter. How would you deal with this issue, which has apparently brought commercial considerations into conflict with questions of social responsibility?

▶ **CASE 7-6**
A Controversial PR Client

Alvin Davis was finally returning to the rarefied air of the nation's capital. Davis had been employed for six years as a public information officer for the State Department but had tired of the government bureaucracy and the never-ending rat race of life in Washington. He had departed with exemplary recommendations from his superiors and signed on with a small but growing public relations firm in Atlanta. But after three years, he longed again to be near the center of power and returned to Washington to open his own PR firm, Davis and Associates.

During his tenure at the State Department, Davis had watched the PR landscape with envy, aware that a never-ending parade of special-interest clients was willing to pay handsomely for representation. The rewards were far greater than anything that he could have realized from his civil service position.

In setting up his PR firm, Davis had decided to concentrate on companies seeking access to overseas markets. Although he had not been in a policy-making position at the State Department, his role as a public information officer had brought him into contact with many foreign dignitaries, business executives, and other influential worthies.

Davis's instincts were correct, and Davis and Associates flourished. Although much of his time was spent in dealing with overseas contacts, he was also called on to lobby in Congress whenever a piece of trade legislation was introduced and to promote his clients' causes through the media. To this end, he spent a lot of time with financial reporters from the major newspapers and TV networks.

Davis knew Ahmed Abdul Sharif only by reputation. He had never met the information officer for the Iraqi delegation to the United Nations. But still suffering the consequences of its defeat in the Persian Gulf War in 1991 and the subsequent U.N. sanctions, Iraq was in search of representation in the United States, and Sharif had identified Davis and Associates as a likely prospect. In early 1995, even as Iraqi President Saddam Hussein continued to denounce publicly the United Nations sanctions against his country, he knew that the key to lifting the embargo was through improved relations with the United States. But Iraq still had an image problem as it attempted to overcome its reputation as a renegade nation. And this country's Middle Eastern allies, including Saudi Arabia, had kept the heat on Congress and the White House not to get too chummy with the "enemies of peace in the Middle East."

Sharif wanted Davis to represent the Iraqi cause both with the White House and before Congressional committees concerned with matters of foreign policy and to ensure that the Iraqi story, particularly as it related to the suffering of the Iraqi people as a result of the U.N. embargo, was covered adequately in the media. All he wanted, Sharif assured Davis, was just a fair hearing, an opportunity to compete for the understanding of the American people.

Davis listened attentively as Sharif made his request. He had never represented a foreign client, especially one that aspired to curry favor with policy makers. He wondered whether such a client would present him with an irreconcilable collision of competing loyalties. He had concerns about patriotism that would not go away, although it was not quite clear how helping improve the image of the Iraqi government, including President Saddam Hussein, would be unpatriotic. Perhaps it would be an affront to the American people to represent a client that had only recently been vilified as a brutal aggressor and a threat to American interests in the Middle East.

He had always felt that tensions between the Iraqi government and the United States would not cool until a more cordial dialogue had been established between the two parties. And the United States, Davis believed, was the key to bringing about this dialogue. Not that he necessarily approved of Hussein's political ideas or tactics—he did not. But he felt they had a right to be heard. On the other hand, Davis was politically astute and was certain that some Arab Americans and the more hawkish members of the Jewish community would not look kindly on his taking on the Iraqi government as a client.

He was also concerned about Hussein's sincerity. Had the unpredictable Iraqi president really renounced his aggressive designs, or did he still harbor ambitions of a united Arab world with himself as its leader? Was Hussein really concerned about the suffering of his people under the U.N. sanctions, or did he want the embargo lifted to facilitate the rebuilding of his military machine and deadly arsenal? This situation, like the Middle East itself, was volatile and uncertain.

THE CASE STUDY

This case involves a conflict of loyalties between what Davis perceives as a possibly unpatriotic act, on the one hand, and representing a foreign client whose views and behavior are unpopular, on the other. It presents an interesting dilemma for PR practitioners: should they represent clients with whose ideas they disagree, or should they assume the posture of a defense lawyer, who believes that all clients are entitled to adequate representation?

However, Davis has another very practical problem: is there a way to represent the Iraqi delegation without alienating some of his other clients? A successful campaign on behalf of the organization would probably provide some access to contacts in the Arab world, and this would be appealing to American companies seeking access to those markets. But this gain might not offset the losses that accrued from other clients.

Assume the role of Davis, and, utilizing the moral reasoning formula, come to an ethical judgment in this case. Is a real conflict of interest involved here or just an imagined one? What answer will you give to Sharif?

▶ **CASE 7-7**
The Gray Lobby and Divided Loyalties

Jan Carmack had served as public relations representative for the Senior Citizens' Rights Association (SCRA) for ten years, and she was proud of her accomplishments.[44] The association had been formed in 1975 by several retired business executives in response to what they felt was the need for a senior citizens' lobby in Congress. The "graying" of America and the apparent inattention in the nation's capital to the interests of the elderly, including the fragile health of the Social Security system, had combined to attract thousands of elderly members.

The association, which was open to anyone age fifty-five and over, had begun its operation with rather modest expectations. It had rented a small office in Washington, which was staffed by a director and two salaried employees. Most of their efforts were aimed at pressing members of Congress for legislation that would address the needs of the elderly. A monthly newsletter was also published and distributed to SCRA members.

As the organization gained more visibility and membership recruitment drives began to bear fruit, the SCRA rapidly became a force to be reckoned with. It hired Carmack, who already had several years of impressive experience through her association with one of Washington's most prestigious PR firms, to handle much of its lobbying effort with Congress and to keep the concerns of the elderly before the media and the public. The SCRA, with a potential constituency that included one of every five Americans, also became a marketing enterprise, peddling everything from vacations to discount mail-order items. Despite its tax status as a nonprofit organization, the revenues from the association's business ventures soon outpaced its income from dues. The leadership of the SCRA defended its growing commercialism on the grounds that income generated by these ventures could be plowed back into lobbying efforts at both the federal and state levels.

But Carmack was becoming uneasy. The association's dual roles as lobbyist for the elderly and mass marketer were about to raise some serious ethical questions. For several years, the SCRA had offered low-cost health insurance as a supplement to Medicare. Although the insurance was underwritten by a private company (to protect the association's tax-exempt status), the SCRA collected the premiums and retained part of the income to cover administrative costs. This arrangement provided another lucrative source of revenue for the organization.

Now, after years of wrangling over the costs of a catastrophic health insurance plan, Congress had decided to consider the issue. The plan being considered by the House committee covered 80 percent of the costs of medical expenses, with the remaining 20 percent to be picked up by private supplemental insurance paid for by the consumer, in a manner to similar to the Medicare system. The coverage would be paid for by payroll deductions and underwritten by private insurance companies.

When Carmack joined the association as its PR representative, catastrophic health insurance had been one of her goals. The time had come, and the SCRA's board of directors had thrown its support behind the House bill. Carmack was instructed to lobby vigorously for the catastrophic health insurance plan supported by the association's board and to make sure that the media were aware of the SCRA's concerns. But unlike the fledgling organization she had joined several years before, the SCRA was now a commercial concern with a vested interest in promoting its own insurance ventures. If this bill passed, the association would surely profit from its low-cost health insurance that would be an attractive supplement to the catastrophic coverage.

On the other hand, the SCRA's concerns were legitimate. The "80-20" plan was an expensive proposition for taxpayers but, in the judgment of the SCRA board, had a good chance of passing. Besides, catastrophic health insurance was in the interest of all older people and should be pursued. The 80-20 plan, even if incomplete in some of its coverage, was a reasonable compromise in meeting the needs of senior citizens while holding down the costs to the average taxpayer compared with comprehensive coverage. Even if the SCRA did stand to profit, were these revenues not plowed back into the association's lobbying and other worthwhile endeavors?

Still, Carmack worried about the apparent conflict of interest in lobbying for a bill that would so blatantly be a commercial bonanza for the association. If this issue came up before the committee, the cause of elderly health care could be undermined. The industry, many of whose members stood to lose out to the SCRA on supplemental health coverage, would be sure to point out the potential conflict of interest to the committee. Perhaps she should recommend to the association board that it drop its promotion of supplemental health insurance. This step would be an act of good faith to avoid the appearance of a conflict of interest, but it would deprive the SCRA of a lucrative source of income. However, Carmack considered the possibility of this issue becoming a point of contention among committee members unlikely, because few politicians were willing to attack senior citizens. And, in any event, the real beneficiaries of a catastrophic health plan would be the elderly, many of whom were not even members of the association.

THE CASE STUDY

This case does not involve a personal conflict of interest, but it does concern a conflict for the organization represented by its PR representative. In some respects, this is a conflict of long standing, because the association has for a number of years provided low-cost supplements to Medicare patients. Carmack could recommend that the SCRA drop its insurance promotion, but this plea might fall on deaf ears because of the lucrative nature of the business.

One way of approaching the problem is to evaluate the harm that might result from this apparent conflict of interest. Certainly the public will not be harmed. There is no apparent harm to the elderly, unless one considers the lure of the association's low-cost insurance, thus depriving the elderly of any real opportunity to examine competitive plans. The real losers might be the insurance industry, although it would stand to profit from underwriting the catastrophic health plan.

Assume the role of Carmack, and, using the moral reasoning model, make a decision on this matter. What would you recommend?

▶ ## CASE 7-8
Cable's Friend in Congress

"Sen. McCain Accused of Sexual Harassment." To the readers of the *Washington Post*, this headline was the first public revelation of just another political scandal. For Marcus Conrad, president and chief executive officer of Conrad Communications, Inc., it was the cause of a severe case of indigestion. According to the *Post* article, several of Senator Joseph McCain's female staff members were about to file sexual harassment complaints with the chairman of the Senate Ethics Committee, accusing their powerful boss of everything from groping to French kissing them. Conrad's discomfort was not precipitated by any personal sympathy for the Senator. After all, if he had been an employee of Conrad Communications, he would have been fired if such charges were true. But Senator McCain was no ordinary citizen. He was chairman of the Senate's Commerce Committee, as well as an influential member of the Senate's powerful Finance Committee, which writes tax and trade laws. And he had proven himself to be an important ally of the cable industry as it attempted to unshackle itself from the restraints of government regulation.

Conrad had joined Maxwell Cable Enterprises in 1973, a fledgling cable TV company, as first the assistant manager and then manager of one of its local cable franchises. From his rather modest vantage point, he had become a veteran of the industry's painful economic maturation and often compared this period of his life to trench warfare, as his industry struggled against the opposition of the well-financed, determined over-the-air broadcasters and a Federal Communications Commission that remained hostile to any meaningful deregulation of cable television. Nevertheless, Conrad remained confident that cable TV would someday become an influential participant in what would eventually be referred to as the information superhighway. His enthusiasm, optimism, and creative programming and marketing strategies had caught the attention of Maxwell's corporate executives, and Conrad was swiftly promoted through the ranks to the pivotal position of vice president for marketing.

In 1984 Marcus Conrad, energized by the increasingly favorable climate in Washington toward cable TV, had parted company with Maxwell and, with the backing of several enthusiastic and enterprising investors, established Conrad Communica-

tions. The company had launched two highly successful entertainment cable channels and had significant investments in two others. But Conrad's crowning achievement and the most visible symbol of his daring enterprise was the creation of Cable News Central (CNC), a twenty-four-hour news and information network that competed successfully with Ted Turner's CNN.

Conrad watched with both fascination and concern as the Senate Ethics Committee investigated and then prepared to hold hearings on the alleged misconduct. As expected, the public debate was spirited, with women's groups calling for Senator McCain's resignation and the senator vigorously denying any wrongdoing. With his political life on the line, McCain's friends and supporters quickly established a defense fund to rescue the conservative senator from what they believed were the hysterical manifestations of feminism. The fund resembled a political war chest, as corporate America and their lobbyists bestowed their financial benevolence on the senator for his years of support for favorable tax and trade legislation. Women's groups, underfunded but determined, responded that it was "business as usual in the boardrooms of corporate America" and vowed to appeal uncompromisingly to the court of public opinion.

As the details of Senator McCain's alleged sexual indiscretions continued to provide sensationalistic grist for the journalistic mill, including his own network's news coverage, Conrad sat patiently on the sidelines, but not without some moral ambivalence. As the CEO of Conrad Communications, he had prided himself in his progressivism in employee relations. He was a firm supporter of affirmative action and, from the outset, had taken steps to ensure that his staff reflected, in a meaningful way, the racial, sexual, and cultural diversity of the society they served. In addition, like many corporations, Conrad Communications had stringent rules prohibiting the kinds of behavior of which Senator McCain was accused.

On the other hand, the senator was a powerful ally in the halls of Congress. The cable industry had flourished under the laissez-faire philosophy of the influential committee chairman. Should Conrad Communications, he wondered, come to the aid of the beleaguered senator in the interest of the long-term growth and health of the cable industry?

That was the question on the table as Conrad sought the counsel of his inner circle: Cassandra Clark, vice president for communication and marketing; Michael Jones, vice president for sales and promotion; and Peter Hamilton, president of Cable News Central. Conrad had always been fascinated at how quickly business decisions could develop into ethical dilemmas. This was no exception.

"I'm opposed to contributing to McCain's defense fund," said Clark without hesitation. "It would be hypocritical for a company like ours that has such strong policies on sexual harassment to contribute to a defense fund for a public official accused of conduct for which he could be fired if he worked for Conrad. We could take a public relations bath on this one, especially when women's groups find out. We're probably more vulnerable than most corporations because of our news division."

"But the senator is innocent until proven guilty," responded Jones. "And he's been a real supporter of the cable industry. If the Ethics Committee rules in his favor, he'll remember who came to his defense in his time of need. We need to look at the long-term implications. Let's face it—the list of contributors to this fund already reads like a who's who of corporate America. And that includes other cable interests. If we sit on the sidelines, we'll be conspicuous by our absence."

"I agree that McCain is innocent until proven guilty," said Clark. "But why should we get involved at all? We're different from most corporations; as the parent company of CNC, our mission is different—our responsibility to the public is different."

"We're not just another corporation," agreed Hamilton. "As president of our news division, I am concerned about our independence—or at least the perception among our viewers. Couldn't we be accused of a conflict of interest if we contribute to the defense fund for a senator who is under investigation for sexual harassment and, as such, is the focus of much of our news coverage?"

"But the contribution is from our parent corporation—we're involved in a lot of different enterprises," said Jones. "I don't think the viewers will tie this directly to our news operation. After all, many media organizations lobby for causes that affect their industry and provide support for influential legislators. And we need to consider the future health of the corporation, not just the news division. Our stockholders are interested in the bottom line. And Conrad's future depends on a favorable regulatory environment in Washington."

"In my judgment, whether CNC itself or the parent corporation contributes to this fund is immaterial," responded Hamilton. "In the stockholders' minds, they link Marcus Conrad with CNC in the same way that CNN's viewers link that network with Ted Turner."

As Conrad digested this conflicting advice from his respected staff, he recognized this rather spirited debate as a classic confrontation between the apostles of corporate self-interest and the sanctity of journalistic independence. Of course, what obscured his moral vision somewhat was the fact that Conrad Communications had not hesitated in the past to lobby on Capitol Hill for or against legislation that affected the cable industry. But this situation was different. No legislative agenda was involved; one of their supporters had been accused of moral turpitude. Nevertheless, the political stakes were high. If Senator McCain were forced to resign, Conrad knew, his probable replacement as Commerce Committee chair would be Senator Harold Jamison, whose views on the cable TV industry were less cordial.

THE CASE STUDY

The journalistic enterprise in this country has become big business. Many news organizations are owned by parent companies that are diversified in terms of their corporate interests. Their allegiance is to the bottom line, sometimes at the expense of the public service mandate of their news divisions. Corporate interests are often reflected in lobbying activities and contributions to political candidates in an attempt to influence legislation favorable to their particular industries. As corporate entities, media institutions have often lobbied aggressively for or against legislation that affects their industry.

Trade organizations, such as the National Association of Broadcasters and the National Cable Television Association, are representative of such political involvement. State media organizations, under the banner of the First Amendment, often become partisans in the battle for more liberal sunshine laws allowing greater public access to governmental proceedings.

In this scenario, however, the CEO of a cable enterprise, which also operates a news network, is confronted with the dilemma of whether to come to the rescue of a political ally. Senator McCain has provided a friendly terrain for the cable industry, and Marcus Conrad is confident that Conrad Communications will continue to flourish under his laissez-faire approach to regulation. Corporate America has not hesitated to come to the Senator's defense. Thus, from the standpoint of corporate self-interest, Conrad is tempted to contribute to Senator McCain's defense fund. After all, as Michael Jones, Conrad's VP for sales and promotion, noted, the senator is innocent until proven guilty.

On the other hand, Conrad is afraid that publicly supporting the senator will open his company up to charges of a conflict of interest. He fears the appearance of partisanship by a corporation that also controls a major news organization that is providing coverage of the Senate's investigation of one of their own. But despite the fact that the news division receives much of its revenue from advertising, its economic viability is closely linked with that of the parent corporation, and Conrad is not confident that the cable industry will fare as well under the political auspices of Senator McCain's replacement.

For the purpose of resolving this ethical dilemma, assume the role of cable CEO Marcus Conrad. Then, using the SAD Formula for moral reasoning outlined in Chapter 3, render an ethical judgment on whether you will contribute to the defense fund for Senator Joseph McCain.

▼

Notes

1. "The Bishops under Fire," *Newsweek*, April 23, 1990, p. 24. For a more thorough discussion of this case, see Dennis L. Wilcox, Phillip H. Ault, and Warren K. Agee, *Public Relations: Strategies and Tactics*, 3d ed. (New York: HarperCollins, 1992), pp. 138–142.
2. Stephanie Saul, "Judgment Call," *Columbia Journalism Review*, July/August 1989, p. 50.
3. Jeffrey Olen, *Ethics in Journalism* (Upper Saddle River, NJ: Prentice Hall, 1988), p. 25.
4. Mitchell Stephens, *Broadcast News*, 2d ed. (New York: Holt, Rinehart & Winston, 1986), pp. 309–310.
5. Public Relations Society of America, "Interpretation of Code Paragraph 6."
6. See Dennis L. Wilcox, Phillip H. Ault, and Warren K. Agee, *Public Relations: Strategies and Tactics*, 3d ed. (New York: HarperCollins, 1992), pp. 119–120.
7. H. Eugene Goodwin and Ron F. Smith, *Groping for Ethics in Journalism*, 3d ed. (Ames: Iowa State University Press, 1994), p. 117.
8. *Ibid.*, p. 98.
9. Bruce Selcraig, "Buying News," *Columbia Journalism Review*, July/August 1994, p. 45.
10. Gary Paul Gates, *Air Time* (New York: Harper & Row, 1978), pp. 353–354.
11. *Ibid.*, p. 354.
12. Conrad C. Fink, *Media Ethics: In the Newsroom and Beyond* (New York: McGraw-Hill, 1988), p. 211.
13. "Cheers 'n' Jeers," *TV Guide*, May 18, 1991, p. 37.
14. Goodwin, *Groping for Ethics*, p. 136, citing Ann Hodges, "Cult Interviews Worth Big Bucks to News Shows," *Houston Chronicle*, April 24, 1993, p. 6.
15. Steve McClellan, "Tabloids Pull Out the Checkbook, Proudly," *Broadcasting & Cable*, May 9, 1994, p. 42. The exact amount was not revealed, but most reports put the payment in the $500,000 range.
16. Alan Bash, "A More Wholesome 'Affair' in the Works," *USA Today*, June 14, 1995, p. 3D.
17. Quoted in *ibid.*
18. Quoted in Selcraig, "Buying News," p. 45.
19. "'Checkbook Journalism' Bounces Back," *Broadcasting*, December 9, 1991, p. 5.
20. Quoted in *ibid.*, p. 46.
21. *Ibid.*, pp. 45–46.
22. Sarah Jackson-Han, "Conflicting Interests," *Communicator*, November 1994, pp. 24–25.
23. *Ibid.*, p. 24.
24. Gail Marion and Ralph Izard, "The Journalist in Life-Saving Situations: Detached Observer or Good Samaritan?" *Journal of Mass Media Ethics*, Vol. 1, No. 2, 1986, p. 62, citing J. Faber, *Great News Photos and the Stories Behind Them* (New York: Dover, 1978).
25. William A. Henry III, "When 'News' Is Almost a Crime," *Time*, March 21, 1983, p. 84. For a discussion of this case, see Marion and Izard, "The Journalist in Life-Saving Situations," p. 62.
26. Marion and Izard, "The Journalist in Life-Saving Situations," p. 65.

27. *Ibid.*, p. 66.

28. Quoted in "No Cheering in the Press Box," *Newsweek*, July 19, 1993, p. 59.

29. See Alicia C. Shepard, "The Gospel of Public Journalism," *American Journalism Review*, September 1994, pp. 28–34.

30. For a thorough discussion from one of the foremost disciples of *public journalism*, see Davis "Buzz" Merritt, *Public Journalism and Public Life* (Hillsdale, NJ: Erlbaum, 1995).

31. Shepard, "The Gospel of Public Journalism," p. 29. For an interesting examination of how public journalism was employed to help change the political landscape in one community (Columbus, Georgia), see Jay Rosen, "Community Action: Sin or Salvation?" *Quill*, March 1992, pp. 30–32.

32. *Ibid.*, p. 31.

33. Merritt, *Public Journalism and Public Life*, p. 101.

34. Rebecca Ross Albers, "Going Public," *Presstime*, September 1994, p. 28.

35. Quoted in Liz Viall, "Crossing That Line," *Quill*, November/December 1991, p. 18.

36. Albers, "Going Public," p. 28.

37. Shepard, "The Gospel of Public Journalism," p. 34.

38. "Darts and Laurels," *Columbia Journalism Review*, November/December 1991, p. 37.

39. "Darts and Laurels," *Columbia Journalism Review*, January/February 1991, p. 24.

40. *Ibid.*

41. Cornelius B. Pratt, "Hill & Knowlton's Two Ethical Dilemmas," *Public Relations Review*, 20, Fall 1994, p. 283.

42. "No Cheering in the Press Box," *Newsweek*, July 19, 1993, p. 59.

43. This scenario is based on an actual case reported in 1995 in a national news magazine. However, the facts have been changed for the purposes of this hypothetical case study. See "Should Journalists Also Be Advocates?" *U.S. News & World Report*, July 31, 1995, pp. 278.

44. Some of the ideas for this case were collected from an article on the marketing activities of the American Association of Retired Persons. See "The Big Gray Money Machine," *Newsweek*, August 15, 1988, pp. 38–39.

Economic Pressures and Social Responsibility

ECONOMIC INTERESTS AND MORAL OBLIGATIONS

Ever since the middle class arose from the ashes of the Middle Ages, the profit motive has been the economic mainstay of the Western democracies. The marketplace has become the sacred temple of capitalism, where the bottom line is the measure of corporate success. No doubt, our capitalistic system is responsible for most of our material wealth and commercial prosperity. The predominantly laissez-faire approach to economic regulation has provided the breathing space for aggressive institutional competition and impressive market expansion.

Some have been critical, however, of the excesses of our economic system. "Crass commercialism" and "Let the buyer beware" are expressions often used to describe corporate greed. The critics view the unrestrained pursuit of profits as a parasitical practice that puts self-interest above any sense of social responsibility.[1] According to this view, whenever profit motives and altruistic motives compete for the attention of corporate management, commercial interests always prevail.

There is no doubt that economic considerations are a powerful (and sometimes irresistible) motivator. And herein lies an ethical quandary. In Chapter 1 we noted that one who is motivated primarily by self-interest in situations calling for a moral judgment cannot, by definition, behave ethically. Does that mean, therefore, that moral agents who are driven by economic motives have rejected any allegiance to moral duty and social responsibility?

To answer this question, we should begin with a basic proposition: there is nothing *inherently* immoral in the profit motive or the accumulation of wealth. Many wealthy entrepreneurs and philanthropists have used their considerable economic resources to benefit social causes and charity. Likewise, certain businesses and corporations have revealed a sense of social obligation by plowing some of their profits back into the communities they serve. Self-interest *can* be the servant of the public's interest, because the pursuit of profits can work to the benefit of society at large. Ethical questions do arise, however, when commercial interests are allowed to dominate other social obligations. The issue, in any given situation, is how to *balance* economic pressures against individual or institutional duties to others.

The moral idealist may be tempted to propose that commercial interests should always be subordinated to more noble causes. But suppose, for example, that a major advertiser for a small newspaper threatens to withdraw its support if the editor insists on publishing a story critical of that advertiser. One could argue that, in the spirit of journalistic independence, the editor should proceed with the story, undeterred by the threat of economic reprisal. But if the loss of advertising is likely to pose a severe financial hardship for the paper, it may then be unable to provide a quality service to the public in the rest of its news coverage. The *New York Times* may have the financial security to withstand such pressures, but small hometown newspapers often do not.

In a capitalist society, economic pressures can come from many directions, but they generally originate from three sources: (1) financial supporters, such as investors, advertisers, clients, subscribers, and customers; (2) the competition; and (3) the public at large. The three are interdependent, of course, and economic concerns in one area can have an impact on another area. For example, competitive pressures often force companies to make countermoves in the interest of appeasing institutional financial supporters. Segments of the public sometimes chastise advertisers or even boycott them in order to force them to pressure a network or publisher to withdraw objectionable material.

The media are in a unique position within the American economic system. Unlike most other businesses, they acquire most of their profits not directly from the consumer but indirectly through advertising. The media are also unique because of the constitutional protection accorded them as an institution. Their "product"—news, information, and even entertainment—has been given a legal sanctuary not available to the output of other industries. Thus, from the outset the media have always been viewed as servants of the public interest, a role that transcends purely commercial considerations. Nevertheless, since the turn of the century, the media have joined the ranks of big business, and economic pressures have competed aggressively for influence in management decision making. This uneasy alliance between the media's financial interests and the public's interests has been reflected in three separate but related phenomena: (1) the trend toward concentration of ownership in the media, (2) the rise of the marketing concept, and (3) the influence of advertising on the media.

CONCENTRATION OF MEDIA OWNERSHIP

Since the beginning of the twentieth century, the media have marched relentlessly toward bigness and concentration of ownership.[2] The power of ideas must now compete with the power of the profit-and-loss statement. Nowhere is the evidence of concentration more noticeable than in the newspaper business. Since World War II, most U.S. papers have been gobbled up by groups or chains, a trend that has slowed recently but has nevertheless continued unabated. In 1930, for example, 84 percent of the nation's daily newspapers were independent.[3] By 1994, however, fewer than 30 percent were still independent and family owned. Most daily papers are now the property of such groups as the Gannett Company, Newhouse Newspapers, the Tribune Company, Knight-Ridder Newspapers, and the Times Mirror Company. And fewer than twenty cities now have commercially competitive daily newspapers.[4] Thus, it is clear that the family-owned newspaper is moving steadily in the same direction as the family-owned farm.

However, the threat, if there is one, lies more in the monopoly of information by self-interested institutions than in ownership patterns themselves. As media commentator Ben Bagdikian has noted:

> Concentrated control of the media is not the most urgent danger facing society. It pales before more compelling threats—imminence of economic disorder, deterioration of the planetary environment, growing violence between the world's rich and the poor, and the possibility of nuclear annihilation.

But the ability to cope with larger problems is related to the peculiar industries we call the media, to their ownership and the nature of their operation. They create the popular base of information and political values out of which all critical public policy is made. In a world of multiple problems, where diversity of ideas is essential for decent solutions, controlled information inhibited by uniform self-interest is the first and fatal enemy.[5]

Arguably, media concentration could result in a better product because of the pooling of economic resources. Indeed, chain ownership has allowed many newspapers that might otherwise have died to survive. Corporate ownership often results in an infusion of funds that can lead to an economic rejuvenation and even an improved editorial product. Furthermore, in most cases parent companies do not intrude into the editorial decisions of their news operations.

Another trend that has emerged as a result of economic pressures has been the merging of the noneditorial operations of competitive papers. This practice has been facilitated by the Newspaper Preservation Act, which was passed in 1970 after intense congressional lobbying by the publishing industry. Under this federal law, a "failing" newspaper can enter into a joint operating agreement (JOA) with a competitor, with the approval of the Justice Department. By 1992 there were JOAs in effect in more than twenty communities.[6]

Although such agreements have resulted in the survival of some newspapers, with the continued independence of their news staffs, other publishers who must compete with these joint ventures have charged that they are government-approved monopolies. In 1971, for example, a small publisher went to court to challenge the joint operating agreement between the *San Francisco Examiner* and the *Chronicle*, which had been in effect for five years before the passage of the Newspaper Preservation Act. Bruce Brugman, who published the monthly *Bay Guardian*, told the court that his paper had trouble attracting advertisers because of the lower combined advertising rates set by these two competitors. He

argued that the federal law authorized a media monopoly in San Francisco and violated his freedom of the press. The publisher's arguments were unconvincing, and in 1972 the judge ruled that the Newspaper Preservation Act did not authorize a monopoly.[7]

Perhaps the most serious threat to media institutional independence is the trend toward ownership by outside corporations that have no commitment to the journalistic imperative and spirit. The bottom line often takes precedence over content quality, which is measured by its profitability. This dilemma is noted by Conrad Fink in *Media Ethics: In the Newsroom and Beyond*:

> Search as they will (and must), editors and news directors concerned with ethical, responsible journalism cannot find proof that spending heavily to produce high-quality reporting and writing will assure profitability. No such provable link exists. With business departments and top-management ranks increasingly staffed by accountants, lawyers, and other nonjournalists, the need to cost-justify excellence is no idle exercise, and convincing that type manager to pay for quality becomes crucial to everything else that follows in a newsroom.[8]

While the number of daily newspapers has been inching downward in recent years, broadcast stations and cable systems have been proliferating. In 1994 there were approximately 1,700 daily newspapers, as compared with more than 11,000 broadcast stations and approximately 12,000 cable systems. Until recently, the concentrations of broadcast ownership were not so pronounced, because of the limitation by the Federal Communications Commission on single-market and nationwide station ownerships. Until 1984, for example, no licensee was permitted to own more than seven TV, seven AM, and seven FM stations. But in that year, moved by the spirit of deregulation, the FCC raised the limits to twelve in each category, fueling a merger and station acquisition fever. During the 1990s, there has been a further liberalization of the ownership rules, which could be headed for extinction altogether.

However, the electronic communications industry still offers plenty of diversity. Most markets have more broadcast outlets than they have newspapers, and the rapid growth of the cable industry has enriched program variety.

Perhaps the most ominous concentration of media power is found in the movie industry. The business is dominated by seven major studios that control the distribution of more than 80 percent of the films exhibited in theaters across the country.[9] In addition, the major studios, which were forced in 1949 through a consent decree with the government to sell their chains of theaters, are now quietly reinvesting in movie houses.[10] In some communities, the studios have achieved a major monopoly of ownership.

The verdict is still out on the trend toward media consolidation. In some cases, the quality of content may suffer as corporate executives exhibit a "lowest-common-denominator" mentality in order to increase ratings and circulations and, therefore, the profit margin. On the other hand, some chains, such as Knight-Ridder, generally improve the papers they purchase. Mergers and consolidations do not inevitably result in a diminution of quality, but, in the final analysis, the result depends on whether the corporate managers are committed to the special position traditionally occupied by the media within the American cultural framework.

THE ALLIANCE OF MASS MEDIA AND MARKETING

In order to compete in the economic arena today, a business or corporation must master the principles of marketing. The media are no exception. The fundamental objective of any newspaper, magazine, broadcast station, movie studio, or cable system is profit. Without it, the life span of any media institution will be a short one. In addition, an unprofitable operation is unlikely to attract the investment capital needed for expansion. On the other hand, a profit allows an organization to invest in the talent and hardware necessary for the production of a quality product.

It is little wonder, then, that media managers have adopted the familiar corporate marketing strategies. One book even described marketing as "warfare," in which the competition is the enemy and the consumer is the ground to be won.[11] This analogy may well apply to the media, where the battles for the hearts and minds of the audience are never-ending. Circulations, ratings, shares of audience, and box-office receipts are the barometers of corporate success in the media environment.

As applied to the media, the marketing concept holds that all departments, including news, must contribute to the financial well-being of the organization. Thus, editors and news directors are expected to package their news and information to attract a target audience and to exploit the economic potential of the marketplace.[12] In short, they must search for creative ways to infuse their news and editorial content with entertainment values. In fact, a recent survey of 130 editors and news directors showed that more than 75 percent of the respondents believed that entertaining readers and viewers comes before educating them. They blamed this attitude on economic considerations that compel the media to put entertainment ahead of reporting meaningful information on their hierarchy of values. "As long as Michael Jackson and Tonya Harding get more space on page one than the health care debate or the warfare in Yugoslavia, newspapers are not doing their jobs," lamented one newspaper editor on the comment portion of the survey.[13]

Such surveys have rekindled the age-old question of whether the media should give the public what it wants or what news managers believe it should have.

No recent news event is more illustrative of the impact of marketing values on journalistic decision making than the coverage of the O. J. Simpson trial. In the weeks following the arrest of Simpson for the double murders of his ex-wife Nicole Brown Simpson and her friend Ronald Goldman, the case received more intense coverage than any event since the Persian Gulf War. While critics subjected every aspect of this rather bizarre spectacle to the most exacting scrutiny, many of the concerns revolved around the conflict between the marketing aspects of the trial coverage and the media's role as socially responsible gatekeepers.

The news media devoted hundreds of hours and thousands of inches of copy to exploring every detail—some important, some trivial—of the case.[14] During live coverage of Simpson's preliminary hearing, ratings shot up dramatically, eclipsing even the popular soap operas. However, the public exhibited a degree of schizophrenia in its assessment of the Simpson coverage. At the same time that audiences were devouring every lurid and sensational detail of the case, surveys showed that a large percentage of Americans thought the media's performance was excessive or unfair.[15] Some critics complained about the influence of corporate values (i.e., the "bottom line") and ratings on the journalistic decision-making process. Others complained that such entertainment masquerading as news trivializes real news. "There is a perversion of news values when a presidential visit to Eastern Europe and a presidential visit to a G7 summit cannot get . . . the same amount of time as a pretrial hearing of a former football player," noted Marvin Kalb, a longtime broadcast journalist and director of the Joan Shorenstein Center on the Press, Politics, and Public Policy at Harvard University.[16]

But others defended the media's performance, noting that the sheer drama and compelling public interest in the case were sufficient justifications for the extensive coverage. ABC's Ted Koppel, apparently rejecting the view that the marketing concept and journalism are incompatible, said that the fact that business decisions drive news decisions is a "virtue" because it gives the public a significant voice in shaping the news agenda. In short, the application of marketing principles to journalism has helped to "democratize" the profession.

If so, then nowhere has journalistic democracy thrived more than in the television industry. The marketing approach to electronic journalism is reflected in the discovery in the 1970s of local TV news as a vehicle for enhancing station profitability. Despite some retrenchment in the late 1980s, TV newsroom profitability has continued unabated. In 1994, for example, a survey of TV stations revealed that more stations are programming local news and that 83 percent showed a profit in news.[17] However, critics note that this profitability may be somewhat illusory and may be more the result of cost cutting rather than audience satisfaction, as evidenced by a decline in news viewership levels. Professor S. L. Harrison of the University of Miami, for example, has accused stations of resorting to "Chamber of Commerce boosterism that promotes automobile shows, supermarket openings and boat shows . . . to fill gaps in news time in an effort to pare costs on reporting news."[18] Despite this rather cynical assessment, however, each year electronic journalists win Peabody, AP, and SPJ awards and other honors for their aggressive, hard-nosed news coverage. This is a laudable testament to the fact that some stations have resisted such flights from journalistic sanity and continue to do yeoman's work in the service of their communities.

For the ethical purist, the application of the marketing concept to electronic journalism has been a mixed blessing. As news operations have become profit centers, they have benefited from increased capital investment. In addition, during the 1970s and early 1980s, staffs expanded and salaries rose, although the entry-level pay is still pitifully low for an industry that has such a pervasive influence in the lives of most of us.

On the other hand, local news is at the center of much of the station's marketing strategy, and consultants (sometimes referred to as "news doctors") have descended on newsrooms like the plague, dispensing their wisdom and advice to any client looking for impressive numbers. The result has been nothing short of a revolution in local TV journalism. "Happy talk" news shows, specialized formats, and a move away from hard news to soft news and features have all figured prominently in management schemes to woo the finicky television consumer. Some have followed the lead of the tabloid programs in using graphic violence, human foibles and tragedies, and sensationalism in pursuit of higher ratings in an increasingly competitive marketplace. There is also a disturbing inclination to use news programs as promotional vehicles for the entertainment divisions. A case in point was NBC's hype for the last episode of the highly successful *Cheers* series. In addition to its elaborate promotional effort, NBC also fed additional *Cheers* promo material that masqueraded as news to its affiliates. And the network's Miami affiliate, WPLG, obliged by devoting chunks of its 6 and 11 P.M. newscasts to "interviews" with the series' personalities. On the night of the last *Cheers* episode, the station also devoted virtually the entire newscast to the program.[19]

Interestingly enough, it is the nemesis of mainstream TV news—the tabloids—that have showed some signs of retreating from the sensationalism and exploitation that have energized this program genre. In October 1993, for example, *Broadcasting & Cable* magazine reported that shows such as *A Current Affair*, *Hard Copy*, and *Inside Edition* had softened their approach to news and were trying to shun overly sensational stories and controversial reenactments. This decision, however, was made to appease advertisers and was not the result of moral rectitude on the part of program producers.[20]

Newspapers have not escaped the lure of the mass marketing concept. Confronted with stagnant or declining circulations and profits during the 1980s, many newspapers turned to marketing firms for assistance in helping them reclaim their audience appeal. Marketing surveys have led many newspapers to redefine their news content, much to the dismay of traditional journalists who balked at the notion of abandoning their roles as news gatekeepers. An increasing percentage of the nonadvertising space today is devoted to soft news or features. Articles on health, education, travel, recreation, lifestyles, and community activities are among those that dot the special sections designed to appeal to certain target audiences, as well as to advertisers interested in reaching consumers with such interests.

When it first appeared, *USA Today*, the first American daily to be conceived with the help of marketing experts, was criticized for its use of jazzy graphics to illustrate its short, easily digestible stories. These criticisms subsided as the newspaper began to carry longer, more reflective pieces.[21] Nevertheless, there was a fear that such entertainment-oriented illustrations would become the standard, thus relegating hard-news coverage to second-class citizenship in the journalistic hierarchy. And this fear was not without some justification. When the Knight-Ridder chain, for example, redesigned its paper in Boca Raton, Florida, to feature charts, news-in-brief columns, and graphics, some reporters had to be reassigned to desk jobs to prepare these visuals, thus leaving less time for hard-news coverage and investigative reporting.[22]

Another rather disturbing trend is the blurring of the distinction between editorial and commercial content. Most papers now carry supplements, often referred to as "tabs" (because of their tabloid size), which are special sections built around some theme of interest to the reader. Although these supplements often contain valuable information, the editorial content is really just window dressing for the ads.

A variation on this theme are the so-called *advertorials* published by some newspapers and magazines. These are supplements actually paid for by advertisers but cloaked in the respectability of editorial content. In appearance, they resemble an informative feature article but are in fact a vehicle for delivering an advertiser's message. Although they are identified as commercial matter, this disclaimer is usually printed in small type and may not be discovered by the casual reader. Some drug companies, for example, sponsor special supplements that appeal to health-conscious consumers. These ads are usually labeled as such and often provide valuable information. Nevertheless, the small corporate disclaimers are often overshadowed by the appeal of the editorial-looking content.

Magazine advertorials, of course, have been around since at least the 1930s, when *Life* magazine published one for a clothing manufacturer.[23] Nevertheless, at one time most good magazines were ethical puritans in maintaining the clear distinction between commercial and editorial content. But the money culture and intensely competitive media markets of the 1980s mounted irresistible assaults on the ethical sensibilities of publishers, and in some cases they even altered the very motivation for publishing. Whereas "in the old days" magazines were started because someone had something to say, today publishers are just as likely to start with marketing and build editorial content around that.[24]

The electronic variation of the advertorial concept is the *infomercial*, program-length commercials that have proliferated since the government's deregulation of commercial time limits. Infomercials are today a textbook example of marketing diversity, featuring everything from weight loss regimens, to self-improvement programs, to labor-saving appliances. The financial stakes in the production of infomercials are tremendous. From 1984 to 1994, the industry's annual revenue skyrocketed from $30 to $900 million.[25] And competition for airtime is fierce. In 1993, for example, there were 175 products vying for half-hour time slots.[26]

Whether such program-length commercials should be provided with an unfettered entré to the nation's airwaves and cable systems is a matter of public policy. But when infomercials blur the lines between advertising and entertainment and even editorial content, then serious ethical questions arise. Some journalists and even some advertisers are concerned that a trend in this direction is leading to a kind of "editorial pollution" that compromises the integrity of the media.[27] In fact, the industry's own trade organization, the National Infomercial Marketing Association, has expressed misgivings about infomercials that fail to distinguish between commercial objectives and entertainment.[28] Such was the case when the Federal Trade Commission accused Synchronal Corporation, one of the largest producers of thirty-minute TV infomercials, of false advertising in connection with claims that certain products would dissolve cellulite and cure baldness. The infomercials were also disguised to look like ordinary TV programming, said the FTC, instead of paid advertisements.[29] In another case, a diet product company was cited for using a newscast scenario to promote the "discovery" of the company's weight loss program, thus duping viewers into believing they were watching an actual program.[30]

The packaging of both news and entertainment to achieve some marketing objective is evidenced by the reference to such content as a "product." No longer is the news produced merely as a public service. It must be sold to the consumer and must contribute its share to the success of the marketing plan of the overall operation. Newspapers, for example, must position themselves journalistically to maximize the profit potential of their news product, which means devising a marketing scheme aimed at attracting a well-educated, affluent audience. Marketing directors at many newspapers fear that large numbers of low-income readers would undermine the appeal of the demographics on which high advertising rates are based.[31]

At the outset of this section, we noted the role that the marketing concept plays in the competition of the media marketplace and the apparent inevitability of this trend. And yet, the preceding discussion has a decidedly negative overtone, replete with examples of how the public interest has been subordinated to economic interests. Where then do the ethical problems reside in accommodating the marketing concept to the media's social responsibility mandate?

First, there is a "truth in advertising" problem when news operations dispense promotional content, celebrity profiles, and soft features under the guise of hard news. They are, of course, free to embrace all three within the scope of their newspapers, magazines or broadcast day. But they should not attempt to dignify such material by including it in a "newscast" or packaging it in such a way that the average reader or viewer cannot distinguish it from editorial matter. Second, on a more philosophical level, when marketing strategies result in an unholy alliance between entertainment and journalistic values and undermine the media's imperative to service the democratic system through the discussion of serious and socially relevant issues, then significant ethical considerations are tendered.

Thus, it is within this rising tide of commercial expectations that ethical conflicts arise concerning the media practitioners' obligations to their institutions' own self-interests and their moral duties to the welfare of society. Is the marketing of news, for example, compatible with the journalistic imperatives of reporters, editors, and news directors? There is no law of nature that mandates the sacrifice of quality to the demands of the marketplace. Nevertheless, this is a thorny ethical issue that confronts media managers today, and in the long run its resolution will depend on the moral sensibilities of the policy makers who must ponder the true meaning of social responsibility within an industry that is increasingly infatuated with the marketing concept.

THE ROLE OF ADVERTISING

It is perhaps belaboring the obvious to say that advertising is ubiquitous in the American media system. Advertising is the economic underpinning for both the information and entertainment functions of our mass of communication institutions and thus directly affects the quality of media content. Of course, advertising gives the mass media financial *independence* from government and other political interests, but it also creates a *dependence* on the commercial sector.

The economic pressures exerted by the influence of advertising are apparent in at least three areas. First, the quantity of commercial material determines the amount of space or time remaining for nonadvertising content, that is, news and entertainment. Newspaper editors are obliged to arrange their editorial content in the space remaining after the advertising department lays out its ads on the available pages. In television news, producers have to slot their stories around commercials, so that there is a limit on the amount of time devoted to each "package." And on the entertainment side of TV, programs are constructed to build to a dramatic climax, or peak, going into a commercial break.

Second, there is also a ripple effect when advertisers cut their budgets, as they do in periods of economic recession, or when they switch their buying from one medium to another. In other words, when the advertising industry sneezes, the media catch cold. Even the network giants were not immune to this phenomenon in the 1980s as the impact of cable television steadily eroded the audience levels of ABC, CBS, and NBC. The news divisions suffered severe budgetary cutbacks and layoffs during this economic upheaval, but other network divisions were affected as well. The reduction of advertising revenues directly affects the quality of content, and, in times of economic belt tightening, high-cost functions such as news are likely to come under the budgetary ax.

Another way that commercial interests can affect the nonadvertising content is through direct pressure on media managers. Advertisers are understandably annoyed when they are the subject of unflattering news coverage and sometimes react by withdrawing their ads from the offending publication, station, or network or otherwise pressuring it into refraining from future negative publicity. A representative example is General Motors's decision several years ago to pull a large ad out of *Fortune* after the magazine published a critical cover story about the company. A GM spokesperson defended the move with this pointed reminder: "The purpose of advertising is to try to influence people in a friendly environment."[32]

In another case—one more typical of local markets—automobile dealers in San Jose, California, complained when the *Mercury News* published an article titled "A Car Buyer's Guide to Sanity," in which the reporter counseled consumers, among other things, to rely on factory invoices rather than what the dealer might say. San Jose automobile dealers were not amused and met with the paper's news executives, complaining that the article left the impression they could not be trusted.[33] Angry car dealers pulled at least $1 million in advertising. But in an intriguing reversal of fortunes for the *Mercury News*, the advertiser boycott prompted an antitrust investigation by the Federal Trade Commission, pursuant to which local car dealers agreed to "cease and desist" from their action against the newspaper. This was the first time that the FTC had acted against advertisers for pulling their ads from a news medium. In justifying its actions, the commission noted that the boycott raised antitrust concerns because (1) it deprived consumers of essential price information in the form of newspaper advertising, and (2) the boycott was designed to chill the newspaper from publishing similar stories in the future.[34]

Sometimes the pressure is more subtle than advertising boycotts. For example, a recent study concluded that magazines that rely on cigarette ads—especially women's magazines—publish fewer articles about the hazards of smoking.[35] In some cases advertisers are the objects, rather than the instigators, of such pressures. Such was the case when a beer company withdrew its commercials featuring the rap music singer Ice Cube after Korean-

American merchants in Philadelphia complained about the racist content of one of the artist's songs.[36]

Smaller and competitively inferior organizations sometimes succumb to the demands of advertisers that object to some news story. Consumer complaints, even when they represent a small segment of the audience, can prompt advertisers fearful of offending the buying public to exert economic pressure on media managers. The larger, more stable institutions have the financial resources to withstand an advertiser onslaught, but when commercial self-interests enter the picture, journalistic freedom is sometimes sacrificed on the altar of economic reality.

Nevertheless, even in today's highly competitive market, such repercussions are not a foregone conclusion, and some news executives have valiantly resisted advertiser pressure. Such was the case when San Francisco's KPIX-TV did an investigative series on fast-food chains in which they challenged advertising claims of new low-cholesterol, low-fat hamburgers. The station lost some ad revenues, but the station defended its report on the grounds that it was "in the best interest of the public."[37] In some cases, the media reject entire categories of ads on the grounds that they have "no socially redeeming value." For example, when the *Seattle Times* decided to stop accepting cigarette ads—a decision that cost the paper "a minimum of $120,000 to $150,000" out of an annual total of about $200 million in ad revenue—a tobacco industry spokesman said the ban made him question the *Times*'s commitment to the First Amendment. "Just as we refused advertising for legal products such as handguns, escort services and X-rated movies," responded publisher Frank Blethen, "we have concluded that tobacco advertising has almost no redeeming value."[38]

But despite the influential role that advertising plays in the American media structure, it should be an ethical imperative on the part of media organizations to maintain the industry's traditional separation between church and state. Otherwise, the editorial department's only marketable commodity—its credibility—

will inevitably dissipate. Some news media have been uncompromising in their commitment to this principle. For example, when the advertising department of the *Virginian Pilot* in Norfolk rejected an ad for a winter festival sponsored by a local gay and lesbian group, the paper reported on the decision in an article that not only included the arguments of both sides but also pointed out an inconsistency in the paper's policy: only three weeks earlier, the *Pilot* had published an ad from the Family Research Council denouncing President Clinton's plan to lift the ban on homosexuals in the military.[39] Likewise, the *St. Louis Post-Dispatch* published a story on their advertising department's decision to turn down a three-page abortion ad from Missouri Right to Life. The story, accompanied by the photo of a mutilated doll that contributed to the rejection of the ad, caused some readers to ponder the paper's judgment in publishing a photo it had previously rejected as too tasteless. "That apparent anomaly was the best demonstration of the separateness of a paper's news department and its business offices I've ever seen," observed Larry Fiquette, the paper's ombudsman.[40]

Of course, advertising's influence reaches far beyond the journalistic function of media enterprises. While entertainment executives may complain about the economic influence of advertisers who aspire to exercise more control over program content, they are usually more reluctant than their journalistic colleagues to defy such pressure. Entertainment does not possess the strong tradition of independence as the editorial function. In addition, society is more loath to accord entertainment the same degree of constitutional respect as news and information. It is a courageous (or financially foolish, depending on your point of view) entertainment executive indeed who ignores threats of an advertiser boycott and airs a program on a sustaining basis.

In any event, many advertisers are disinclined to sponsor entertainment programs that they feel are too controversial. For example, six ad spots were pulled from CBS's broadcast of *Moonstruck* because one of the characters was having an extramarital affair. *The Tracy Thurman Story*, an NBC made-for-TV movie about a sexually and physically abused woman, was the network's highest rated movie of the season, but advertisers rejected the movie in droves.[41] And when a major sponsor of NBC's *Sisters* discovered that one episode of the program contained a scene featuring a group of women lolling in a sauna chatting about multiple orgasms, the advertiser threatened to cancel $500,000 worth of ads.[42]

In the final analysis, the ethical pragmatist must search for an accommodation between the role of advertising as an expression of corporate self-interest and the institutional moral imperative of social responsibility. Of course, the two are so intertwined that it is sometimes difficult to examine them separately. Advertising is truly symbiotic with the other mass media functions, news and entertainment. Advertisers, of course, do not entirely share the vision of news managers and entertainment programmers that there should be a complete separation of church and state between the business side and the other mass media functions. Advertisers do *need* the media's vast and instantaneous distribution network to market their products and services. But in the process, they do not consider it unreasonable to exert some influence over the environment in which their valuable economic resources are being expended. And media managers are not entirely unsympathetic to this view. They understand that ad revenue provides the financial sustenance for their entertainment and editorial enterprises. In addition, they believe that advertising contributes to the economic health of society by providing valuable information. Media managers feel that sensitivity to ethical concerns in advertising is an important component of their image-building public relations or marketing effort.[43] On the other hand, they believe that undue advertiser pressure on program content—both news and entertainment—is just as inimical to "freedom of the press" as the power of government. Of course, independence from government control is guaranteed by the First Amendment. But the fragile and often ambiguous wall that insulates news and entertainment from undue commercial pressures is the inescapable collective responsibility of media managers, the ethical chaperons of the public interest.

ECONOMIC PRESSURES: HYPOTHETICAL CASE STUDIES

The diversity of issues surrounding the discussion of economic pressures makes any generalizations risky at best. But the cases in this chapter are representative of the moral dilemmas confronted by media practitioners. In evaluating these cases, apply the SAD Formula for moral reasoning outlined in Chapter 3.

A duty-based theorist applying Kant's categorical imperative, for example, would ask whether the principle applied in a given situation should be universalized to all similar circumstances. In determining whether a newspaper editor should kill a news story because of pressure from a large and influential advertiser, for example, a Kantian would ask what would happen if all editors were to react the same way, thereby making this standard industry practice.

A consequentialist would look at the short and long-term effects of succumbing to economic pressure. At times, of course, discretion is the better part of valor, as when advertisers withdraw their support from a program under threat of a consumer boycott. Advertisers have a right not to sponsor a program, and the decision for the program director is whether there is a compelling reason to air the show in the absence of financial support from advertisers. Caving in to this kind of pressure could result in loss of station credibility, but it might also be appreciated by the audience if the threatened boycott enjoyed broad-based support. From the perspective of a consequentialist, the motivations of the moral agent are not as important as the potential effect of the ethical decision.

Aristotle's golden mean does not always provide a viable alternative in confronting economic pressures. Nevertheless, considering the idea that it is usually impossible or unwise to ignore financial considerations altogether and yet in some situations may be ethically questionable to succumb entirely to these pressures, the goal should be to find strategies that will minimize the conflicts. For some institutions, there is a middle ground between the extremes of commercial self-interest and other competing values. In such cases, profits can be a *means* of accommodating an institution's obligations to society. A case in point is a TV station that avoids the temptation to seek excess profits and plows some of its revenues back into high-quality public-service programming.

CASE STUDIES

CASE 8-1
Consumer News and Advertiser Boycotts

When the *Hartford Journal* published the first installment of "A Consumer's Guide to Buying a New Car," Business Editor Lisa Michaels was proud of her staff's contributions to the paper's public-service mandate. This primer, scheduled to run as part of a Sunday supplement over a four-week period just before the arrival of the new models, was the product of a three-month collaborative effort of reporters Matt Starnes and

Maureen Benedict. Michaels was particularly impressed with their exhaustive research and intelligent analysis of the complexities of shopping for a new car. Although the articles were consumer-oriented features and not hard news, they revealed both a high degree of journalistic enterprise and an imaginative writing style. This series, she believed, would render the process less intimidating for the *Journal*'s readers.

The first article in the series opened with some illuminating tips on comparison shopping for new automobiles. It then moved quickly into how to read a dealer's invoice and a discussion of dealer strategies in countering objections of their prospective customers. It was a virtual "how-to" manual for novice negotiators in challenging aggressive car salespeople on their own turf.

Michaels was confident that the paper's readers would appreciate her staff's journalistic enterprise. She was equally certain that the local automobile dealers, who were always sensitive to any public criticism or attempts to demystify the automobile business, would not welcome the *Journal*'s consumer-oriented initiative. Michaels still remembered the brouhaha caused by a story aired on Hartford's Channel 6 two years ago concerning dealer markups and profit margins on new automobiles. As a result, several car dealers had withdrawn their ads from the local CBS affiliate. The station had survived, and the dealers had eventually reactivated their accounts. But the automobile establishment had demonstrated its willingness to flex its collective muscle in the economic marketplace, a fact that had not gone unnoticed by both journalists and media account executives.

Michaels soon discovered that the past was a prologue to her own paper's ethical dilemma. The first installment in the series was greeted with undisguised hostility by the dealers, many of whom advertised heavily in the *Journal*. And they lost no time in seeking an audience with Managing Editor Jonathan Hamilton, who patiently endured the siege and listened to complaints from three dealers who claimed to represent the local automobile establishment.

"This article is unfair," protested the local Toyota franchisee. "It makes it appear that we can't be trusted—that we're taking advantage of people—

which is not true." Another complained that the series diminished the value of his advertising. "What good are my ads," he said, "if the readers have the impression that they can't get a good deal from us. We advertise in the *Journal* because we expect results; we don't expect to get trashed in the same publication we help to finance." The Oldsmobile dealer was more analytical in his criticism. "The process of buying a new automobile is too complex to be dissected in a consumers' guide," he said. "Our customers are perfectly capable of doing their own research to see if we're competitive or whether they want to do business with us. And your advice on negotiating is misleading because it can't be tailored to specific situations and individual customers."

Hamilton was troubled by the vehemence of his visitors' remarks and promised to take the matter up with his staff. But he recognized the prelude to an advertiser boycott when he saw one. "Cancel the remaining articles in the series," they demanded, "or we'll withdraw our advertising."

With the deadline for the second article in the series rapidly approaching, Hamilton quickly sought the counsel of his business editor and Mona Larson, the industrious and highly successful advertising manager of the *Journal*. Hamilton began the meeting by complimenting Michaels on the enterprise of her two young reporters. As a journalist he was inclined to support his editorial staff against outside influences, but as a manager he was obliged to explore all of the angles to this developing ethical dilemma.

"I realize there's a lot at stake here," said Michaels. "But we simply can't succumb to this kind of intimidation. If we do, we'll be vulnerable to pressures from other advertisers."

"Perhaps," responded Larson. "But most of our advertisers don't have this kind of clout. We currently have thirty dealers on our account list. And their ads bring in over a million dollars to this paper. That's a lot of money."

"I'm aware of the economic implications having these dealers pull their ads," re Michaels. "But if we cave in, we'll lose with our readers. We'll just have to w storm. Besides, advertiser boycotts long. They'll return once this blows o

"I agree with you on the issue of credibility," said Hamilton, carefully assuming his role as devil's advocate. "But we also need to ask ourselves whether these dealers have a point. Are the articles unfair? I personally believe they are well researched and offer some valuable advice to consumers. But perhaps I would feel more noble if we were defending a good piece of investigative journalism against the threats of an advertiser boycott. Is the principle, in this case, worth the financial sacrifice?"

"From the standpoint of whether we should kill this series to appease some of our advertisers, I don't see the distinction between hard news or investigative journalism and this kind of consumer-oriented reporting," replied Michaels. "After all, our readers should come first. If we comply with these advertisers' demands, we'll still lose credibility. And our readers will be the losers."

But Larson was unpersuaded by appeals to credibility. "We might survive this. But in the short run we'll be hurt financially—and don't forget that this will impact the editorial side of this paper as well. If this were an investigative news article about shady practices in the automobile industry, I might be more sympathetic to your position. But as Jonathan has said, these articles are not hard news—and they have made some of our largest advertisers very angry. I think we have more to lose than to gain by not killing this series."

Hamilton listened to this predictable exchange of views between his business editor and advertising manager. As a journalist, his allegiance was to the editorial side of the ledger. But as a manager he also paid homage to the paper's bottom line, which made possible the *Journal*'s successful journalistic venture. In the past, he had resisted attempts by advertisers to pressure his news department to kill unfavorable stories. But in those cases, the amount of revenue involved had been quite modest compared to the collective contracts of the local automobile dealers. With judgment day rapidly approaching, Hamilton pondered the long- and short-range consequences of confronting economic reality and canceling the consumer-oriented series on how to buy a new car.

THE CASE STUDY

With their heavy dependence on advertising revenues for their economic survival, news organizations are finding it increasingly difficult to preserve a healthy separation between their journalistic imperative, with its public service implications, and the commercial values that permeate so much of their corporate decision making. The threat of advertiser boycotts is among the most troublesome ethical concerns confronting media practitioners.

The case outlined here is fairly typical of the kinds of economic pressures that are increasingly plaguing local news media. The ethical landscape is replete with examples of newspapers that have succumbed to pressure from advertisers. Automobile dealers are among the most sensitive because of (1) the intense competition in local markets, (2) the tremendous expenditures on local advertising, and (3) what they feel are unfair portrayals in the media of car sales people.[44]

In an ideal world, Managing Editor Jonathan Hamilton could stand steadfastly behind his paper's ethical imperative to print the truth and serve the public interest. His journalistic instincts propel him in this direction. But Hamilton is also a media manager and is acutely aware that advertising provides the economic sustenance for his journalistic enterprise. Can he succumb to the automobile dealers' demands in this instance and resist future attempts at advertiser intimidation?

Assume the role of Managing Editor Jonathan Hamilton and decide whether you will cancel the remaining articles in the series on how to buy an automobile. In analyzing this case, apply the SAD Formula for moral reasoning outlined in Chapter 3. In so doing, you should incorporate the following questions into your critical thinking about this issue: (1) What are the short- and long-term consequences of responding affirmatively to the advertisers' demands? (2) Although you are satisfied with the journalistic quality of the series, should you even consider the dealers' complaints of unfairness in rendering your decision? (3) Will the fact that the series is not hard news but is instead a "consumer tips" feature influence your decision?

▶ <u>CASE 8-2</u>
The Talk Show as News Lead-In

Dexter Followell was not fond of news consultants. As a twenty-year veteran of television news, he had ruefully witnessed what he considered to be a rather sinister assault on his industry's journalistic integrity. Beginning in the 1970s, Followell had seen local TV news evolve from serious hard news and commentary to soft features and station self-promotion masquerading as news—mostly as a result of consultants' recommendations. Nevertheless, as the news director for Channel 7, a CBS affiliate in the twin cities of Helena–St. Vincents, Followell had reconciled himself to the inevitable intrusion of entertainment values into his professional domain. Local news figured prominently in his station's bottom line, and economic pressures competed with deadline pressures for his managerial attention.

Followell had been hired by General Manager Richard Rosenberg just eighteen months ago with one mandate: restore Channel 7 to number one in the market for the early evening news segment, which consisted of a 5 o'clock news magazine, followed by the *CBS Evening News*, and then the local news from 6 to 6:30. The station had languished in the number two slot for almost two years behind Channel 4, the market's ABC affiliate. According to the latest ratings book, Channel 7 was number one in the 4-to-5 time position occupied by *Myron Casteel*, the latest and currently most popular among the entries in the already crowded talk show marketplace. And like most programs of this genre, its audience feasted on a daily diet of sexual perversion, social misfits, and uninhibited public declarations of abnormal personality traits. But despite *Casteel*'s appeal, Channel 7 was unable to hold its audience, which quickly defected to its competitor's 5 o'clock offering, a loyalty that carried over to *ABC World News Tonight* and the 6 P.M. local newscast.

Rosenberg had promised Followell the full support of the station's resources in overtaking Channel 4's increasingly sizable lead in the 5-to-6:30 time

position. The first "resource," much to the news director's chagrin, was to seek the advice of Mason & Associates, Channel 7's consulting firm that had guided the station's journalistic destiny for eight years. As the station approached the next ratings sweeps, Rosenberg reviewed the consultant's carefully crafted advice with his cautiously optimistic subordinates. Mason had recommended a new set design, reversing anchors for the 5 P.M. news magazine program and the 6 o'clock news, and the incorporation of several new feature segments in the magazine show that had worked in other markets. As the staff reviewed the consultant's recommendations, Followell told his colleagues that, as news director, he had no strong objections to most of the recommendations, which were based on solid research and success stories in other markets. If these changes helped Channel 7 recapture the ratings lead, he reasoned, then he could make the case for greater expenditures to expand what he considered to be more serious news coverage.

However, Mason's last recommendation gave Followell pause. In order to hold the station's audience from the popular *Myron Casteel* for the 5 P.M. magazine show, the consultants advocated regular news tie-ins with the syndicated show. For example, if *Casteel* featured child molesters on a given episode, the follow-up magazine show might include a segment on state laws requiring that convicted child molesters notify their neighbors of their conviction once they are released. Or a *Casteel* segment on teenage prostitutes would be followed by a local feature on that topic.

"I know what the consultants recommended," said Followell. "But I have reservations about using *Casteel* as a tie-in for the 5 o'clock magazine. In effect, this talk show would be dictating our news assignments. Let's face it. Entertainment values already determine a lot of what we do. But *Casteel* should not serve as a cue for our news content."

"I don't see any real ethical issue here," responded Thomas Moreland, Channel 7's general sales manager. "We get ideas for news stories from a lot of sources. Localizing our news coverage based on national events has always been an acceptable—even desirable—journalistic practice. And it certainly makes our news program more attractive and more appealing to our audience. If we can spin off of a popular lead-in talk show, I don't see anything wrong with it as long as we consider the story worthy of our audience's attention. And let's face it—sales for the 5 P.M. show have been soft. This tie-in could be a great angle to help sell the show."

"I agree," said Program Manager Tony Oliver. "The tie-in will probably help our audience flow, especially if we promote it properly. After all, most of the topics discussed on the *Casteel* show, including the offbeat ones, are of interest to our audience. I see no problem with giving them a local spin on the news magazine show. This could help shore up our entire early evening news position. And the increase in ratings will show up on the bottom line. We all benefit, including the news department."

"I don't have a problem with using ideas from entertainment shows, as long as they have news value," replied Followell. "But it's *this* particular show that's the problem. It specializes in the offbeat, sensational, and bizarre. I realize that *Casteel* is popular with our audience. But a direct news tie-in with this show could cost us in terms of journalistic credibility."

"But as long as we don't resort to tabloid treatment of these stories, that should separate us sufficiently from *Casteel*," said Rosenberg. "We can still deal with these issues in a responsible manner, regardless of whether the topic is sex slaves, wife swapping, or child molesters."

"I'm not concerned about our treatment," replied Followell, undeterred by his manager's confidence in his staff's sense of journalistic propriety. "But some topics are simply not matters of legitimate public concern. And I'm afraid that this tie-in will result in our coverage of topics that are nothing more than attention grabbers, with no news value."

"That is a danger," conceded Rosenberg. "But your staff can guard against that kind of temptation by making an independent judgment as to whether a particular story has any real news value. If it does, then what's wrong with taking advantage of a strong lead-in to boost the magazine show? In any event, it's your call, Dexter. I don't care what

you do as long as we see some ratings improvement in our early evening news positions."

THE CASE STUDY

As noted earlier in this chapter, the marketing concept holds that each division of a media organization should contribute to the organization's profitability. In the case of a television station, that includes the news department. And, as the source of most of a station's local programming, news has tremendous profit potential. Thus, the economic pressures to subordinate journalistic values to entertainment values are relentless. But are the two necessarily incompatible?

In the case described here, the station's consultants have recommended that a popular syndicated talk show be used as a journalistic cue for the 5 P.M. news magazine show. The rationale is that if the topic captures the interest of the *Myron Casteel* audience, it will continue to do so for the following time position. And this influence in turn could have a domino effect for the 5:30 network and 6:00 local newscasts. From a programming perspective, this is good strategy.

But the news director's concern focuses on two consequences. First, he fears that the often sensational and salacious content of the *Myron Casteel* show will influence the news judgment for the 5 P.M. magazine segment. Despite his best efforts to ensure that each story is evaluated on its own merits, he is concerned that entertainment values driven by economic pressures will prevail. Second, even if his news staff is convinced of the journalistic merit of specific subjects featured on the syndicated talk show, Followell is still concerned about the public's perception and loss of credibility as a result of the regular tie-ins.

His colleagues, none of whom are journalists, believe that the news department is just as responsible as other departments in contributing to the station's economic viability. They also feel that the news department itself stands to benefit from any move that will boost the ratings of the locally produced news shows. They are convinced that the news department can maintain its credibility, since many of the topics covered on the *Myron Casteel* program interest the public. Why should the news department, they wonder, feel uncomfortable with treating journalistically the rather offbeat subjects featured on a popular talk show?

Station Manager Richard Rosenberg has left the final decision on the controversial consultant's recommendation in the hands of the news director. As the moral agent, Followell must weigh his journalistic concerns against his responsibility to the overall economic welfare of his employer.

For the purpose of confronting this ethical dilemma, assume the role of News Director Dexter Followell, and, using the moral reasoning model outlined in Chapter 3, decide whether you will accept the consultant's recommendation to use the syndicated talk show as a regular tie-in for Channel 7's 5 P.M. news magazine show.

▶ **CASE 8-3**
Billboard Ads in Poor Neighborhoods

Jerry Tanner's entry into the millionaire's club had been nothing short of spectacular. Tanner, twenty-four, had inherited a house, several thousand dollars, and a defunct outdoor advertising agency from his father, by most standards a shaky foundation for financial success. Tanner had an MBA from Harvard, but it was his business acumen and ambition that had prompted him to resurrect his father's advertising agency and turn it into a highly profitable enterprise in Detroit. His father's meager monetary inheritance, coupled with some timely loans, had been sufficient to ensure the temporary solvency of the Tanner Outdoor Advertising Agency, but it was Tanner's own creative energies and promotional strategies that had attracted an impressive array of clients to his doorstep. His position in the outdoor advertising business firmly entrenched, Tanner then expanded his enterprise and opened branch offices in Philadelphia and Boston. Soon he was competitive in those markets as well.

From the beginning, Tanner had assumed a posture much like that of a defense lawyer. He ac-

cepted any client who had money to spend. Tanner believed that any advertiser had a right to promote its wares in the economic marketplace, and he did not accept clients on the basis of whether he personally approved of their products. For example, his two largest clients were a tobacco company and beer distributor, both of whose products had come under criticism from some segments of the public for their allegedly harmful effects on consumers. He did not smoke, but he believed that tobacco companies had a right to deliver their message to those who did. Along with his mercenary tendencies, he also believed that the advertising industry had a responsibility to its audience, and he worked hard to ensure that his ads were tasteful and not deceptive.

Tanner was proud of his role in bringing product information directly to the consumer, but he was chastened by his just concluded meeting with Emma Wise, the chairperson of Citizens for Responsibility in Advertising. The consumer group was concerned about the prevalence and recent proliferation of tobacco and beer advertising in poor neighborhoods, many of them black. Wise was aware that Tanner's ads for these products had appeared on billboards, at bus stops, and in subway stations in the urban ghettos and was appealing for their withdrawal. "These ads are sending the wrong message to our urban youth," Wise declared, "that the way to be happy is to smoke and drink."

Tanner listened patiently but made no promises except to review the situation. He was aware that the targeting of urban poor areas had been a conscious marketing decision on the part of the tobacco and alcohol industries.[45] Consumption in black neighborhoods, for example, was high, whereas consumption within the general population was growing slowly or declining.

In some respects, this decision had been no different from any other in directing an advertising message to a target audience, except that this audience was mostly poor and uneducated and perhaps more susceptible than the average consumer to the subtle lure of seductive persuasion. However, there was no evidence that poor consumers were unable to make informed choices. In fact,

Tanner had never believed that advertising had the power of influencing unwilling consumers, white or black. Do not alcohol and tobacco companies have a right to advertise their products to any audience, regardless of race or ethnic background?

Tanner considered recommending to Wise that she direct her protest at the companies themselves. However, he acknowledged that this was a dead end, because they would probably turn a deaf ear. This left Tanner with his own ethical dilemma. Because the Tanner agency provided the channel for the advertising, what moral responsibility did he have for the alleged effects of these commercial messages? The young advertising executive also had a responsibility to his clients, and he wondered whether he could, in good conscience, recommend that they withdraw their ads from a lucrative market. Of course, his clients would undoubtedly consider this advice unworthy of consideration and might even move their accounts to some other agency.

In Tanner's mind, the battle between his own economic interests and his sense of social responsibility had been joined, and he had to determine his role in an ethical dilemma that extended far beyond the walls of the Tanner Outdoor Advertising Agency.

THE CASE STUDY

National billboard surveys have documented the disparity between the amount of alcohol and tobacco advertising directed at black and white communities. The crux of the debate about targeting minority audiences for alcohol and tobacco advertising is represented by the opposing views of a public health official and a tobacco industry representative, as expressed in a *New York Times* article. Harold P. Freeman, director of surgery at Harlem Hospital and national president of the American Cancer Society, was unforgiving in his criticism of the cigarette industry:

> This marketing strategy is outrageous and immoral. . . . The cigarette industry just wants to make money because they know that poor and uneducated people are their main customers. And black people are disproportionately poor and uneducated.[46]

But Steve Weiss, manager of media relations at the Phillip Morris Company, called this criticism unfair:

> We advertise our cigarettes to anyone who smokes, regardless of their race or background. . . . Adults who smoke in this country are making an informed choice. The argument that minorities are more susceptible to our advertising is at best reprehensible and at worst racist.[47]

It is clear that any advertiser bears ultimate responsibility for the effects of its messages. But what about the advertising agencies themselves? Their economic futures are tied closely to those of the clients they represent. And it is sometimes difficult to reconcile these economic pressures with a clear sense of social responsibility.

One of the problems might be the disagreement over what constitutes social responsibility. Some people, as indicated, believe that it is irresponsible to disseminate tobacco and alcohol ads to poor and uneducated citizens of the inner city. Others would argue, however, that the urban poor have just as much right to product information as other consumers and that the notion that they are more susceptible to persuasion is an insult that carries racist overtones.

Assume the role of Tanner, and, using the moral reasoning model, decide how you will handle this dilemma. Keep in mind your duties to all the parties involved, including your own agency.

▶ **CASE 8-4**

Brand-Name Drugs and Consumer Ads

Concerned about increasingly aggressive marketing techniques and allegations of unfair competition, the pharmaceutical industry had established a self-regulatory trade organization, the National Association of Pharmaceuticals (NAP). One of the first tasks confronting NAP was to devise a professional code of conduct, a general statement of ethical principles.

Lawrence Medica, a renowned pharmacologist, had been appointed to chair the association's Committee on Ethical Standards. The industry's advertising and marketing practices were the committee's first order of business, and in preparation for developing a set of guidelines in this area, Medica decided to examine the controversial trend of direct advertising of prescription drugs to consumers. Drug companies had traditionally promoted their wares directly to physicians through a process known as "detailing."[48] Under this system, a company's representative would make a personal pitch to doctors, provide free samples, and even wine and dine prospective customers. In addition, new prescription drugs were advertised in the medical journals channeled specifically to physicians.

But with the introduction of generic drugs into the marketplace, competitive pressures had increased, and pharmaceutical companies had taken their case directly to consumers. For example, the Upjohn Company, the developer of an antibaldness prescription drug marketed under the generic name Minoxidil, mounted a TV campaign urging men concerned about baldness to "see your doctor." Inasmuch as Minoxidil was the only such drug on the market, the intent of this ad was obvious. In another case, Lexis Pharmaceuticals touted its birth control pill as the cheap alternative to one produced by a competitor. "The same safety and effectiveness—at about half the price," it claimed. "Ask your doctor about switching your prescription."[49]

Medica asked for reactions from consumers, the pharmaceutical industry, the American Medical Association, and individual physicians. He also asked three members of the committee to prepare position papers on the ethical concerns of direct advertising to consumers. An impressive arsenal of documentation was provided by all parties, but stripped of the impressive verbiage, the arguments boiled down to this: Proponents of consumer-directed ads pointed out the educational value of such promotions. Ads kept the public informed about new treatments and apprised consumers of medical alternatives. In addition, with the rising costs of health care, consumers were more interested in participating in decisions affecting their own treatment. And competitive ads could help keep down the costs of prescription medication.

However, the arguments against consumer-directed ads were also persuasive. The critics complained that drug ads could mislead the average consumer. The product characteristics and the effectiveness criteria of prescription drugs were confusing and not likely to be understood by the masses. Television commercials, in particular, were an ineffective vehicle for developing a truly informed consumer market. In addition, consumer-directed ads constituted an unwarranted intrusion into the doctor-patient relationship, because ad-conscious patients sometimes put pressure on their physicians to prescribe or switch medications. It was ironic that patients were often better informed about the prescription drug market than their doctors. Besides, the critics pointed out, the more extensive advertising campaign would be more likely to cause prices to rise, rather than fall, because the increased promotional costs would eventually be passed along to consumers.

Medica was concerned about what recommendations he should propose to the committee. He was acutely aware that all fifty states allowed pharmacists to substitute generic drugs for brand-name prescriptions and that the large pharmaceutical companies were feeling the economic squeeze. In the past several years, generic drug makers had more than doubled their share of the market. Would it be fair, he wondered, to restrict the advertising of name brands directly to consumers when the companies were trying to protect their share of the market?

On the other hand, Medica was sensitive to the views of the critics. A little bit of knowledge can be dangerous, and he was concerned about the disarming effect on physicians if patients began demanding certain drug brands based on a rather cursory knowledge gleaned from some advertisements. What recommendation should he make?

THE CASE STUDY

This case is really a reflection of a trend that has been under way for some time. With consumers taking increasing responsibility for their own physical well-being, they are demanding more information about health products and services. Generic drugs have entered the marketplace at a time when cost-conscious consumers are seeking better health care at affordable prices.

Under the law, a company cannot advertise a prescription drug without including a full and accurate account of potential hazards and side effects.[50] But ethical issues persist concerning this direct marketing of often confusing drug information to consumers.

On the one hand, the brand-name manufacturers have as much right to the advertising marketplace as any other company. But there is some concern that the ads are an ineffective vehicle for conveying important product information and that the result might be confusion rather than illumination. A wrong choice in soaps, toothpaste, or even automobiles is usually a matter of taste and an annoyance from which the consumer will soon recover. The individual characteristics that must be factored in for a choice of prescription medication, however, is another matter. But the question is whether this justification is strong enough to ban brand-name prescriptions from the advertising arena. Perhaps patients and their physicians should be given more responsibility.

Taking into account the arguments set forth in this scenario, assume the role of Medica, and, applying the moral reasoning model, set forth your recommendation to the Committee on Ethical Standards.

▶ **CASE 8-5**
A Controversial Prime-Time Movie

As the network's vice president of programming, Arlen Chase's three-year reign had been disappointing. He had been lured away from a very successful tenure at Fox to add his midas touch to his present employer's rather unimpressive prime-time schedule, but the network still languished behind its commercial competitors. This inauspicious beginning, coupled with the fact that cable viewership continued to erode the audience levels of the four established television networks (CBS, NBC, ABC, and Fox), induced the trade press and media

critics to castigate Chase publicly for his lack of imagination and aggressiveness in the programming marketplace. "When you're number three, there's nothing to lose," wrote one critic in apparent reference to Chase's reluctance to introduce an element of risk into his program decision making.

But despite the network's lackluster performance, Chase was confident that his fall schedule would turn things around. He was impressed with the overall quality of the lineup, and even the critics, who usually approached their tasks with undisguised cynicism, were pleasantly charitable in their evaluation of the network's array of situation comedies, adult dramas, and adventure series. The sales division was impressed too, as advertisers lined up to sample the highly promoted offerings of mass entertainment. Advertisers, according to the latest sales reports, were particularly excited with the lineup of feature films scheduled during the fall ratings sweeps and had quickly gobbled up the inventory of spots available in these dramatic renditions of sex, violence, and intrigue.

The only one that gave them pause was *Presumed Guilty*, a made-for-TV movie about a college student falsely accused of date rape when a jealous girlfriend seeks revenge for his flirtation with a campus rival. Even as the film was still in production, it had been subjected to, along with other proposed series and movies, the traditional advance reviews through the trade press and had received high marks from the critics for its sensitive treatment of a delicate subject. But the Citizens for Rape Awareness (CRA), a national organization devoted to raising the public's awareness of crimes against women, did not share the critics' enthusiasm for what they perceived as a distortion of reality and "an affront to the many victims of sexual abuse." CRA promptly announced its intention of mounting a boycott against any advertiser that bought time in *Presumed Guilty*. "This movie just reinforces old stereotypes that women often falsely accuse men of rape just to get revenge," the CRA said in a letter to one sponsor. "Especially when the female knows her assailant, there's still a strong belief in society that date rape is a myth. *Presumed Guilty* undermines our efforts to change attitudes and to deal with the problem."

Michael Lico, the network's vice president of sales, lost no time in notifying his programming counterpart that advertisers were responding to the organization's threats and refusing to buy time in *Presumed Guilty*. Those that had signed on, fearing the growing controversy surrounding the movie, were defecting from its sponsorship. "If the trend continues," said Lico, "*Presumed Guilty* will have no sponsorship."

"We have to make a decision about whether to keep *Presumed Guilty* in the fall lineup," said Chase during a hastily called meeting with Lico and Lisa Sawyer, the network's vice president of mini-series and feature film development. "As you know, CRA is putting pressure on us; they're getting a lot of coverage, particularly in the trade press. They claim this movie is a distortion of reality—that most men who are accused of rape are guilty. And that this film undermines the organization's ability to deal with the problem."

"But this is a meritorious program," responded Sawyer without hesitation. Sawyer was respected among her peers because of her professional judgment and commitment to quality. She had been instrumental in selecting this program for the fall schedule and strongly believed in its artistic merit. Sawyer harbored little doubt that most men who were accused of rape were guilty. This was no less true, in her judgment, in a date rape situation. She was also painfully aware of the many documented incidences of rape in which the victim herself was put on trial. This reality had been reflected in numerous series and made-for-TV movies. But there was another side, she believed, and her industry had been strangely silent on this issue.

"I realize this movie reflects an unpopular view," she continued. "But the fact is that some men *are* wrongly accused. Count the number of shows that have aired where the rape victim is victimized again by the judicial system, despite the fact that the accused is clearly guilty. And compare that to those where the man is truly innocent, falsely accused by a woman out for revenge. That's an even more distinct possibility in a date rape encounter. I'll admit this is probably rare, but that's what makes this movie so unusual."

"But CRA and our advertisers don't find *Pre-*

sumed Guilty so appealing," responded Lico. "All have pulled out, and we simply can't sell this show. They don't want to be associated with it. And let's face it if you were in their shoes, why risk the adverse publicity from CRA when there are plenty of other *safe* shows to sponsor?"

"Can we sell the show at all?" asked Chase, hoping to detect some ray of optimism in Lico's rather dismal assessment.

"We might be able to attract some bottom dwellers—advertisers who are willing to buy into a high-risk show," responded the sales VP. "But we'll still take a bath financially. They won't be willing to pay the going rate."

"That does concern me," replied Chase. "We need all the revenue we can get. We're losing audience to cable and the Fox network. And the adverse publicity could hurt. On the other hand, sometimes publicity has a way of generating an even larger audience. The show could be popular, especially since it runs counter to the view taken by most of the movies that have dealt with this subject over the past few years."

"But popularity doesn't translate into dollars unless there are advertisers," responded Lico rather bluntly. "And since this movie is at the end of our prime-time schedule, it can't hold the audience for the follow-up program, so there's no revenue benefit on that end. I've seen the movie, and I agree with Lisa. It's a quality show. It has a good script, a talented cast, and a believable story line. But advertisers won't support it. And that's the name of the game."

Sawyer again demurred. "I appreciate your point of view. We obviously can't survive without the support of advertisers. But sometimes we have to bite the bullet and put programs on the air that we strongly believe in—particularly if they are quality shows—even if we can't sell them. This will pay dividends for us later."

"But perhaps CRA has a point," replied Chase, attempting to assume a more noble posture and shift the discussion away from strictly economic concerns. "This movie depicts a situation that doesn't represent the majority of cases. It does tend to reinforce the notion that most so-called date rapes aren't really rapes at all. I realize this is just a work of fiction and that sometimes men are falsely accused. But is *Presumed Guilty* really worth all the fuss just to say we have aired a movie that somehow provides a counterpoint to the abundance of recent movies that show women as being victimized twice—once by the rapist and then by the system?"

Chase was sensitive to the charge that he had succumbed to advertiser pressure in canceling a highly acclaimed program. As an important gatekeeper in the entertainment marketplace, he had a responsibility to serve his audience and present them with quality fare and, in so doing, reflect different points of view on social issues. On the other hand, this programming was paid for by advertising, and he could not ignore his network's duty to those who provided its financial sustenance. As he considered his predicament Chase wondered whether his resolution would be seen as strictly a business decision or whether there were ethical implications as well.

THE CASE STUDY

The kind of economic pressure reflected in this case is not uncommon in the television industry. Advertisers often express their disapproval by refusing to sponsor controversial programs. And while the networks sometimes air sustaining programs (i.e., those without commercial sponsorship), the inclusion of such fare in the prime-time entertainment schedule is unusual. Advertisers come to the networks expecting that they will encounter a friendly environment free of controversy. Network programmers are responsible to their institutions for developing or procuring a quality lineup that will attract the size and kind of audience that is appealing to its sponsors. Usually these goals are compatible, but when controversy engulfs a program and advertisers are threatened with consumer boycotts, they are not reluctant to disassociate themselves from the program's sponsorship.

In this case, programming chief Arlen Chase is not concerned that the failure to obtain sponsorship for a controversial movie will result in financial ruin for the network. While there will be an economic impact, the network can sustain the losses.

Nevertheless, the sales division is unhappy with the prospect of airing a show that will, in effect, reduce the inventory of commercial spots available for the fall ratings period. And Chase is quite sensitive to these concerns. After all, his success is inevitably linked to his employer's financial prosperity. On the other hand, as a programming executive, Chase is an artistic gatekeeper and still feels uncomfortable with his network's refusal to air controversial programming just to appease commercial interests.

Assume the role of network programming chief Arlen Chase, and, using the SAD Formula for moral reasoning outlined in Chapter 3, decide whether you will cancel the controversial movie *Presumed Guilty* or stay the course despite the threat of an advertiser boycott of the film. In rendering your judgment, you should take into account, in particular, your duty to the network's advertisers, your duty to the viewers, and the reputation of the network itself. In working your way through the SAD Formula, you might also keep the following question in mind: Does the scenario outlined here reflect a true ethical dilemma, or is it just a business decision with no real ethical implications?

▶ ### CASE 8-6
Ads with a Journalistic Twist

Modern Lifestyles had been the brainchild of Sandy Radcliffe, the quintessential modern woman with well-focused ambitions and career aspirations. Armed with a degree from Smith College, Radcliffe had gone to work for a small newspaper in New England, but within a couple of years, she had tired of the deadline pressures of daily journalism and had been attracted to a monthly women's magazine published in New Jersey. Radcliffe enjoyed the magazine feature format, in which she could treat single topics with the depth and respect they deserved and in which her creative energies could be accorded literary justice. But in her spare time she also absorbed as much as she could about the business side of magazine publishing.

Radcliffe's endless quest for story ideas frequently took her to New York, where she made it a point to rendezvous with two of her Smith class-mates, who had already taken a respectable bite out of the Big Apple. During one of these luncheon meetings, Radcliffe proposed to her affluent friends that they start a magazine of their own devoted to young, middle-class professionals, both male and female, between the ages of twenty-five and forty-five. She had heard the drumbeat of the yuppies even before the term had become fashionable. With enthusiasm, the three Smith alumnae took out loans, worked out a funding plan for the project, and set their ideas in motion. With her experience in the magazine field, Radcliffe took the position of editor of Modern Lifestyles, a name chosen because of the diversity of contemporary topics to be embraced.

With the revenues from advertisers who saw a receptive target audience in the affluent baby-boom generation and the effective positioning of the magazine in the marketplace, *Modern Lifestyles* had become a financial bonanza within five years. Its colorful and lively writing style and unabashed devotion to materialism and hedonistic values had attracted a loyal, passionate following.

But now, fifteen years after the magazine's inception, Radcliffe was worried. Perhaps *Modern Lifestyles* had become a victim of its own success. In examining the latest edition, for example, the editor noticed, rather regretfully, the advertising inserts that were blended into the editorial content. Advertorials, they were called.[51] One, in particular, caught her eye. In the middle of the magazine was a nine-page insert with its own cover page entitled "Staying Healthy." Its pages were devoted to a variety of pieces on preventive medicine and physical fitness interspersed with ads from pharmaceutical companies and over-the-counter drug manufacturers. Although the cover identified the insert in small type as a "Special Advertising Supplement," this disclaimer would probably be barely noticeable to the average consumer. To Radcliffe, this advertorial appeared to be a magazine within a magazine. Until a few years ago the publication had maintained a strict separation of editorial and advertising content. But *Modern Lifestyles* had succumbed to pressure from advertisers, and now the revenues from these advertorials accounted

for 12 percent of the magazine's advertising income.

In the heady days of continued expansion and healthy profit margins, Radcliffe had not worried too much about the ad formats. She had gladly delegated that concern to the advertising manager. But now the editor worried that *Modern Lifestyles* might lose face with its readers. The magazine had always prided itself on its responsible and well-researched advice on everything from diet and nutrition to buying a condominium. It had no ax to grind except to offer useful information to young professionals attempting to accommodate their own needs to the demands of modern living. But the advertising inserts were submitted by clients that clearly had something to sell, and they had crossed the line into an editorial-looking format in order to gain respectability. Were they likely to cause confusion in the minds of readers?

Radcliffe wondered, however, if she were overly concerned. The magazine's readers were rational and intelligent and should have no problem separating the advertorials from the editorial content. Besides, these inserts were increasingly lucrative for the business side of the publication and were an important subsidy supporting the insightful but sometimes expensive articles. To adopt a policy now of rejecting advertorials would be financially questionable and would be an exercise in ethical elitism that would set *Modern Lifestyles* apart from its contemporaries, including some of the leading news magazines. Besides, if the magazine were to reject such commercial inserts in the future, the advertisers would seek some other platform for their messages. The trend in the industry was unmistakable. Perhaps readers' expectations were now such that they would be forgiving of some blending of journalistic and commercial content.

Still, Radcliffe had nurtured her magazine to a position of credibility with its readers, and she wondered whether it was in the long-term interest of *Modern Lifestyles* to continue to ride along on this commercial bandwagon. Advertorials might be fine for publications in which the editorial and advertising subjects were at least different. But in the case of *Modern Lifestyles,* the content of the ad inserts was similar to the editorial content of the magazine. Radcliffe was aware of the economic pressures to retain the lucrative revenues from these inserts, but she pondered the ethical implications in blurring the lines between the journalistic and commercial content of the magazine.

THE CASE STUDY

The fraternization between advertisers and editors in the mass media is not a new phenomenon. For many years, the Good Housekeeping Seal of Approval has been awarded only to those products that are accepted for advertising in the pages of the magazine. Special-interest sections of newspapers, such as real estate, fashion, and home furnishings, have generally been viewed as something close to adjuncts of the advertising departments.[52] In fact, some newspapers run news stories in conjunction with special advertising supplements. And the early TV programs were often single-advertiser productions, thus planting an unforgettable connection between the advertiser and program content in the collective mind of the audience.

So what has changed? For one thing, some advertisers, in their search for credibility, have turned to the editorial format, which gives the commercial message an aura of seriousness. In addition, some magazines that until fairly recently would have rejected such advertorials have now succumbed to the demands of the marketplace.[53] These supplements are always identified as such, but such disclaimers are often overshadowed by the editorial appearance of the commercial matter.

From an ethical perspective, one could argue that none of the parties involved are harmed by the practice. In a free-market economy, advertisers have a right to persuade, using whatever vehicle is at their disposal, as long as the message itself does not contain falsehoods. The publication maintains a distinction between its editorial and advertising content by labeling the advertorials (albeit not always clearly) as commercial matter. And with proper labeling the public surely is perceptive enough to separate the journalistic content from the ad inserts.

But one could argue just as persuasively that the blurring of the editorial and commercial distinc-

tions is a breach of faith with the audience. The advertorials are sometimes so poorly identified as such that the reader has to search diligently for the disclaimer. In some magazines, the inserts are mixed in with the editorial material in such a way that they are almost an impediment to smooth cover-to-cover perusing of the editorial content.

This marketing concept is well entrenched, and the economic pressures to accept the increasingly lucrative revenues from ad inserts are hard to resist.

For the purpose of confronting the ethical dilemma posed by this scenario, assume the role of Radcliffe, and, using the moral reasoning model, decide whether you will continue to run advertorials in *Modern Lifestyles* or take what may be somewhat of a financial risk in dropping them.

 ## CASE 8-7
The Junket as a Public Relations Tool

The political revolution in Eastern and Central Europe was like a breath of fresh air to Telepac, Inc. As an aggressive and successful player in the competitive telecommunications industry, Telepac's corporate management was increasingly seduced by the commercial opportunities in the emerging democracies of the former Soviet empire as they struggled to master the intricacies and uncertainties of a capitalistic system.

Telepac had been a late entrant in the telecommunications field, but its cadre of ambitious, well-educated young managers, led by president Teri Hance, had quickly developed the company into an attractive Wall Street commodity. Its initial enterprise had been built around cellular phones loaded with novelty features designed to entice both consumers and corporate executives alike. Within a few years, however, Telepac had added other products to its inventory of impressive advanced telecommunications technology. Telepac had indeed become an influential contender in the domestic information marketplace, and Hance began scanning the economic horizons for foreign investment opportunities. She and her management staff were determined to become actors on the global stage, hoping to establish a symbiotic relationship between their own financial self-interest and the proponents of economic reform in emerging democracies.

Hance had traveled to Eastern and Central Europe on both business and pleasure and was impressed by the marketing opportunities that awaited enterprising investors. However, she had also accommodated herself to the reality that any attempt to penetrate these foreign markets would be accompanied by sometimes long and protracted negotiations with government bureaucrats who were capitalistic neophytes. Telepac would have to establish a bond of trust between the company and its foreign suitors. And the public relations division, Hance knew, would play a prominent role in this process.

Earl Kohler, Telepac's vice president for communications and marketing, did not need to be prodded into action. At the first indication of Hance's interest in penetrating the markets of Eastern and Central Europe, Kohler had ordered his small staff to prepare a public relations strategy for maximizing the investment potential in these fledgling capitalistic nations. Sherri McLendon, Telepac's director of public relations, and Dale Knight, a product information specialist, soon developed a rather ambitious plan for providing their company with a PR overture to these foreign markets.

"We're planning to kick off this campaign by bringing some business reporters and editors of the leading newspapers in Poland, Hungary, Slovakia, Bulgaria, and the Czech Republic to this country to tour our plants," said McLendon as she and Knight unveiled the plan to their superior. "We'll set up demonstrations so that they can see what our equipment can do—how it can revolutionize corporate and personal communications in their countries."

"The papers we've selected are among the most prestigious in their respective countries," added Knight. "They're read by government officials and corporate elites. If we get favorable news coverage, this should help pave the way for negotiations with their government representatives."

"It's an interesting idea, but I do have one ethical concern," responded Kohler. "I'm concerned that this will be perceived as nothing more than a junket designed to influence the decision makers in Eastern and Central Europe. Our competitors could have a field day with this. Remember that they're also trying to expand their markets in this part of the world. They could cry foul, and then our plan will backfire."

"But media tours are commonplace in the PR field," replied McLendon. "Our job is to provide information to our publics through the media, and that's all that we would be doing in this case. The journalists will still make their own decisions on what to report."

"That's true," replied Kohler. "But this will be an expensive trip, and we'll be picking up the tab. It may appear as though we're trying to buy influence."

"Let's face it," responded Knight rather candidly. "We spend a great deal of money trying to cultivate our corporate image. I don't see anything wrong with sponsoring a trip for a group of journalists, some of whom probably could not afford to come to this country anyway. Besides, it's mutually beneficial. If we do gain access to markets in these countries, we'll advertise in their papers. And for them, this could be an important event. The attraction of foreign capital and investment is important to their national economic development. This trip will have news value, and that should resolve the ethical dilemma."

"Perhaps. But does news value—or at least what we perceive as news value—really make a difference?" wondered Kohler. "The fact is that we're still setting the agenda for this visit. The reporters and editors will go where we direct them and have access only to certain selective information about our company and our products. In a sense we're paying for access to the news columns of Eastern and Central Europe. How much of what we do here is news, and how much is self-promotion?"

"That's not really our problem," replied McLendon. "The foreign journalists can make that decision. Our job is to provide information and to demonstrate what our products can do. A favorable corporate image will pay dividends later if we should gain access to their markets.

"Besides, self-promotion is part of our job as public relations practitioners. We're responsible for creating a positive corporate image for Telepac in the collective minds of government decision makers in Europe. And I see nothing wrong with inviting foreign journalists to tour our plants, even at our own expense. After all, someday we may be an important source of business news in their countries. This trip will help them familiarize themselves with our operation and get to know us. And I agree with Dale—as a possible future investor in their economy, Telepac should have some news value to their readers."

As Telepac's vice president for communications and marketing, Earl Kohler had carefully nurtured his company's public relations activities, and his efforts had paid dividends in both the general circulation and the trade press. Media events were an important part of Telepac's PR inventory, but the company had never sponsored an all-expenses-paid trip for visiting journalists. In Kohler's mind, his staff's proposal amounted to an ethically troublesome PR initiative. On the other hand, considering the legitimate role of the PR practitioner in the commercial marketplace, it was difficult for him to articulate clearly the exact nature of the ethical dilemma. After all, such activities, sometimes referred to as "junkets" by the media, are commonplace in corporate America. Did the potential news value of such an event, for example, purge it of any moral suspicion? Since the proposed visit by the foreign journalists arguably had some news value, the answer to this difficult question, Kohler knew, would ultimately determine whether he would approve the PR plan proposed by his two energetic and ambitious staff members.

THE CASE STUDY

When Dale Knight, Telepac's product information specialist, states that "[t]his trip will have news value, and that should resolve the ethical dilemma," he may have in mind Article 6 of the ethics code of the Public Relations Society of America. Article 6 admonishes members not to "engage in any practice which has the purpose of corrupting the integrity of channels of communications or the processes of government." However, the code does not prohibit tours when media representatives "are given the opportunity for an on-the-spot viewing of a newsworthy product, process, or event in which the media . . . representatives have a legitimate interest." But what about an all-expenses-paid tour? The authors of one leading text on public relations suggest that PR initiatives that include all-expenses-paid trips are acceptable as long as they have a legitimate news purpose.[54] Such trips for no purpose other than pleasure would be unacceptable. Thus, Knight is apparently concerned that this all-expenses-paid trip should have some journalistic value, thus adding credibility to the lines of communication between his company and the foreign business editors and reporters.

However, Article 6 of the PRSA code has also been interpreted to prohibit "any form of payment or compensation to a member of the media in order to obtain preferential or guaranteed news or editorial coverage in the medium."[55] Does a sponsored trip for foreign reporters and editors constitute a form of payment to obtain guaranteed news coverage?

Media tours and visits sponsored by corporations and government agencies are common tools within the public relations arsenal. Of course, participation in all-expenses-paid "junkets" has increasingly been viewed as a conflict of interest within the journalistic establishment. Should there be any comparable ethical concern from the PR perspective?

There is certainly nothing ethically amiss in cultivating media sources in the hopes of procuring favorable coverage. After all, as autonomous moral agents, reporters are free to render their own decisions on information sources and the kinds of information to include in their news stories.

On the other hand, a moral purist might argue that, while a symbiotic relationship does exist between the media and PR practitioners, a corporate-sponsored junket is an undisguised attempt to influence the news value of an event and therefore undermines the integrity of the communication process. After all, unlike most "pseudo-events" to which the media are invited, reporters are offered a consideration (the cost of the trip) in return for their participation.

Assume the role of Earl Kohler, Telepac's VP for communications and marketing. And then, using the formula for moral reasoning outlined in Chapter 3, decide whether you will approve the proposed all-expenses-paid trip for the business reporters and editors from Eastern and Central Europe. In this case, your decision-making process should be guided by the role of public relations in American society as an embodiment of persuasive communications, as well as what you believe to be a reasonable interpretation of Article 6 of the PRSA code as stated here.

▶ **CASE 8-8**
Crime in the Ghetto Does Not Pay

"A murder in Beacon Hills is news; a murder in Capital Heights is a way of life." The latest addition to the *Petersburg Globe*'s news staff recalled that piece of journalistic wisdom from her city editor, Lance Walls, as she fulfilled her daily ritual of perusing the overnight crime reports. Armed with a journalism degree from the University of North Carolina and two years of experience on the school's newspaper, Paula Campbell had had several job offers on graduation but had opted to join the family-owned *Globe* in her hometown. Campbell was only the second woman hired by the conservative newspaper for its newsroom, and she intended to make the most of it.

Walls first assigned Campbell to the police beat. After only six months on the job, the journalistic neophyte had proven herself more than adequate for the assignment and had lost no time in cultivating the proper contacts in the police department and other law enforcement agencies. Campbell's day always began routinely enough, with a quick perusal of the overnight crime reports gathered by the police department and its detective division. It had not taken her long to discover that the crime rate in Capital Heights, the inner-city black and Hispanic ghetto, was several times that of the rest of Petersburg. This was particularly true of violent crimes, such as murder, armed robbery, and rape, as minority youths seemed determined to wage warfare on one another and anyone else foolish enough to challenge their turf.

Campbell's journalistic instincts, admittedly still in their formative stages, convinced her that these stories deserved greater coverage than merely a police blotter listing buried unobtrusively inside the pages of the Globe. But the city editor quickly disabused her of these intentions.

"There's so much crime down there," he said, "that we don't even consider it news anymore. A murder in Beacon Hills [an affluent suburb] is news; a murder in Capital Heights is a way of life. Our readers are white and middle-class. They're the ones our advertisers are interested in. If there's an unusual or particularly gruesome murder in Capital Heights, sure we'll run a story on it. But our readers are more interested in crime in their own neighborhoods. A simple listing or summary of the crime reports from Capital Heights is all we really need."

For several months, Campbell heeded this advice, realizing that any follow-up investigations to the brief overnight reports provided by the police would probably be a waste of time. The city desk would refuse to run separate stories on crimes committed in Capital Heights. And as a new employee attempting to win her reportorial spurs, she was reluctant to make an issue of the matter.

Nevertheless, Campbell was becoming increasingly frustrated with the city editor's marketing approach to journalistic decision making (which no doubt reflected the philosophy of his superiors). The management at the *Globe* had made it clear that it needed "demographic purity" to justify its high rates for advertisers. And this lucrative advertising revenue had resulted in a salary structure for newsroom personnel that exceeded the national average for a market the size of Petersburg. But Campbell wondered whether such economic concerns had undermined the paper's sense of social responsibility. After all, Capital Heights was a part of the community that the Globe purported to serve. Crime was rampant in the ghetto, but most of the paper's readers were probably unaware of it. More extensive coverage was needed to sensitize the community to the problem and bring more pressure to bear on the city council, which controlled the amount of police protection in Capital Heights.

As Campbell continued to examine the alarming crime statistics reflected in the police reports each day, she contemplated her options. If she saw no prospects of altering the paper's philosophy of covering crime news in the ghetto, she could quit and move to a more enlightened journalistic enterprise. But this was risky, she knew, because there was no guarantee that other papers were any less captive to the marketing approach. She could also stay and resign herself to what was perhaps an inevitable symbiotic relationship between the journalistic and advertising functions of the paper. After all, the *Globe* could not be all things to all people. Journalistic decisions had to be made, and there was always some news that would not get covered. What was wrong with producing an attractive product for the most lucrative segment of the audience? But Campbell still possessed an idealistic streak, and she knew that a third option would be to remain with the paper and try to effect change from within. This approach was a long shot, considering the recent inroads of the marketing philosophy into the journalistic enterprise.

As she contemplated her choices, Campbell wondered whether any of the three was really more virtuous than the others. Was this her own ethical dilemma, or was it exclusively the province of corporate management? How much moral responsibility should she bear for a problem over which she had little direct control in the first place?

owe an obligation to readers, viewers, advertisers, and stockholders to produce an attractive news product. Nevertheless, the marketing concept should not be allowed to taint these institutions' journalistic mandate. Reporters like Campbell believe, and rightfully so, that they must serve a higher master than the bottom line. Nevertheless, the question is what approach they should take in accommodating themselves to this reality while maintaining their own moral purity. Are there strategies that might lead to a mutually satisfactory alliance between the journalistic and marketing concepts? Or are the two hopelessly at odds?

These are complex questions that one cannot hope to resolve within a single case. Nevertheless, they are worthy of discussion within the context of a scenario like this one. Therefore, for the purposes of examining this issue, assume the role of Campbell, and, using the SAD Formula, consider her dilemma.

Needless to say, as an inexperienced reporter, you are unlikely to immediately change the policies of your employer. But you should use this case to examine your own concerns about what some see as an unholy alliance between journalism and the economic pressures of the marketplace. What approaches should practicing journalists take, and why?

THE CASE STUDY

The rise of the marketing concept is a fact of life in today's mass media environment. This reality has been described as follows in the introduction to a contemporary text on media ethics:

> The concept regards newspapers and television news as products to be created in response to marketing research, to be promoted and sold just as other products are. If the concept is permitted to run unrestricted through management ranks, what news products are created—and for whom—is decided by marketing experts whose goal is not fearless coverage of the news on its merits, but, rather, attracting the right affluent readers and viewers who in turn will attract advertisers.[56]

Mass media enterprises are businesses and

Notes

1. Alan H. Goldman, *The Moral Foundations of Professional Ethics* (Totowa, NJ: Rowman & Littlefield, 1980), p. 234.
2. For a thorough examination of this problem see Ben H. Bagdikian, *The Media Monopoly*, 4th ed. (Boston: Beacon, 1992); Robert G. Picard, Maxwell E. McCombs, James P. Wilson, and Stephen Lacy (eds.), *Press Concentration and Monopoly: New Perspectives on Newspaper Ownership and Operation* (Norwood, NJ: Ablex, 1988).
3. See John C. Busterna, "Daily Newspaper Chains and the Antitrust Laws," *Journalism Monographs*, No. 110, March 1989, p. 2.
4. Don R. Pember, *Mass Media Law*, 6th ed. (Dubuque, IA: WCB Brown & Benchmark, 1994), p. 617.
5. Ben H. Bagdikian, *The Media Monopoly*, 4th ed. (Boston: Beacon, 1992), p. 237.
6. *Ibid.*, p. 623.

7. Pember, *Mass Media Law*, p. 619. For the U.S. District Court's full opinion, see *Bay Guardian Publishing Co. v. Chronicle Publishing Company*, 344 F.Supp. 1155 (1972). For three views of joint operating agreements, see *Quill*, January 1989, pp. 27–30, 32.

8. Conrad C. Fink, *Media Ethics: In the Newsroom and Beyond* (New York: McGraw-Hill, 1988), p. 108.

9. Pember, *Mass Media Law*, p. 631.

10. *Ibid.*, p. 630.

11. Al Ries and Jack Trout, *Marketing Warfare* (New York: McGraw-Hill, 1986).

12. See Fink, *Media Ethics*, p. 102.

13. "Entertainment Rules," *Quill*, November/December 1994, p. 10.

14. See Jacqueline Sharkey, "Judgement Calls," *American Journalism Review*, September 1994, pp. 16–26.

15. *Ibid.*, p. 20.

16. *Ibid.*

17. Bob Papper and Andrew Sharma, "Money-Making News," *Communicator*, April 1995, pp. 16–23.

18. S. L. Harrison, "Monday Memo," *Broadcasting & Cable*, July 5, 1993, p. 42.

19. *Ibid.*

20. "TV Violence: What the Market Will Bear," *Broadcasting & Cable*, October 25, 1993, p. 18. See also Alan Bash, "A More Wholesome 'Affair' in the Works," *USA Today*, June 14, 1995, p. 3D.

21. Gene Goodwin and Ron F. Smith, *Groping for Ethics in Journalism*, 3d ed. (Ames: Iowa State University Press, 1994), p. 66.

22. *Ibid.*, pp. 67–68.

23. Paul Farhi, "Time Out from Our Commercial for a Word from Our Sponsor," *Washington Post National Weekly Edition*," March 2–8, 1992, p. 21.

24. Jonathan Alter, "The Era of the Big Blur," *Newsweek*, May 22, 1989, p. 73.

25. Rich Brown, "Operators Take Infomercials into Their Own Hands," *Broadcasting & Cable*, December 12, 1994, pp. 26–27.

26. Christopher Stern, "The Sweet Buy and Buy," *Broadcasting & Cable*, October 25, 1993, p. 20.

27. Farhi, "Time Out from Our Commercial," p. 21.

28. "New Infomercials Test the Growing Industry's Ethics," *TV Guide*, September 4, 1993, p. 38.

29. "Infomercials Maker Agrees to Pay $3.5 Million to Settle FTC Charges," (Baton Rouge) *Advocate*, June 5, 1993, p. 3C.

30. Farhi, "Time Out from Our Commercial," p. 21.

31. *Ibid.*, pp. 114–115.

32. "Will GM Retaliate?" *Newsweek*, February 26, 1990, p. 4.

33. "Those Sensitive Auto Dealers Strike Again, and An-other Newspaper Caves," *American Journalism Review*, September 1994, p. 14.

34. Anthony Ramirez, "The F.C.C. [*sic*] Calls a Halt to Car Dealers' Protest against a Newspaper," *New York Times*, August 2, 1995, p. C3.

35. "Coverage, Cigarette Ads Linked," (Baton Rouge) *Advocate*, January 30, 1992, p. 2C.

36. "Boycott Forces Firm to Pull Rapper's Ads," (Baton Rouge) *Morning Advocate*, November 27, 1991, p. 3A.

37. "The Economics of Ethics: Doing the Right Thing," *Broadcasting*, October 1, 1990, p. 50.

38. "Seattle Times Bans Cigarette Ads," (Baton Rouge) *Advocate*, June 16, 1993, p. 16A.

39. "Darts and Laurels," *Columbia Journalism Review*, May/June 1993, pp. 23–24.

40. *Ibid.*, p. 24.

41. "Program Chiefs Vent Frustrations," *Broadcasting*, February 18, 1991, p. 40.

42. "Sisterhood, Frankly Speaking," *Newsweek*, May 13, 1991, p. 65.

43. Fink, *Media Ethics*, p. 125.

44. For more discussion on auto dealers' boycotts, see Goodwin and Smith, *Groping for Ethics in Journalism*, pp. 75–76; "Those Sensitive Auto Dealers Strike Again, and Another Newspaper Caves, *American Journalism Review*, September 1994, pp. 14–15.

45. See "An Uproar over Billboards in Poor Areas," *New York Times*, May 1, 1989, p. Y32.

46. *Ibid.*

47. *Ibid.*

48. For a discussion of this trend in consumer advertising, see "Pitching to Patients," *Newsweek*, May 9, 1989, pp. 40–41.

49. *Ibid.*, p. 40.

50. See "Advertising in Disguise," *Consumer Reports*, March 1986, p. 180.

51. Before the proliferation of these advertising inserts, the term *advertorial* was often used to refer to advertising space bought by an individual, group, or corporation to express a point of view, usually on a matter of public interest. Now the term includes ads that are designed to resemble editorial content.

52. Jonathan Alter, "The Era of the Big Blur," *Newsweek*, May 22, 1989, p. 73.

53. *Ibid.*

54. See Dennis L. Wilcox, Phillip H. Ault, and Warren K. Agee, *Public Relations: Strategies and Tactics*, 3d ed. (New York: HarperCollins, 1992), pp. 119–120.

55. Public Relations Society of America, "Official Interpretations of the Code," 1988.

56. Fink, *Media Ethics*, p. xxii.

CHAPTER

9

The Media and Antisocial Behavior

THE INFLUENCE OF THE MEDIA ON BEHAVIOR

In 1985, nineteen-year-old James Vance and eighteen-year-old Raymond Belknap listened to six hours of music by Judas Priest and then, following a confrontation with Vance's parents, went to a church playground where Belknap killed himself with a sawed-off shotgun. Vance tried to follow suit but survived the attack. Vance and Belknap's mother sued Judas Priest and CBS Records, claiming that a subliminal message contained in one of the songs had incited them to pull the triggers.[1]

In March 1991, Warner Brothers released the film *New Jack City*, based on the life of Harlem drug lord Nickle Barnes. Death and destruction accompanied the movie's national debut as disturbances erupted in such geographically disparate locations as Chicago, New Jersey, Nevada, and Los Angeles.[2]

Two years later, a baby girl in Moraine, Ohio, perished as the result of a mobile home fire set by her five-year-old brother. The fire chief who investigated the tragedy attributed the boy's sudden burst of pyromania to a popular MTV series. The children's mother said that her son started playing with matches and lighters after watching an episode of *Beavis and Butt-head* in which the two characters amused themselves by setting fires.[3]

In October 1994, a woman and three family members in Pascagoula, Mississippi, were bludgeoned to death by two teenage boys. As the two suspects were taken into custody, the woman's boyfriend identified "gangsta" rap artist Snoop Doggy Dogg as the real culprit. One of the teenagers was apparently fascinated with the song *Murder*, a typical gangsta rap song that features violence.[4]

Events such as these are often used to accuse the media of exerting a powerful influence on the antisocial behavior of readers and viewers. Such incidents provoke publicity and criticism, ranging from mild rebukes to lawsuits and even calls for government regulation. What is lost in these barrages is that the number of injuries, deaths, and other violent acts flowing from any given program, movie, or article is small indeed. Thus, the evidence would appear to suggest a cautionary approach in fashioning a moral framework within which to evaluate the impact of the media on antisocial behavior.

Much of our media content challenges societal norms. Without stories about crime, violence, drugs, and suicides, for example, both news and entertainment would be robbed of their dramatic vitality. It would be unreasonable and unrealistic to delete all controversial content, even when the effects on the audience are unpredictable. The goal should be to devise strategies to promote the responsible treatment of antisocial behavior in the media and to avoid approaches that encourage moral degeneration.

The media occupy a pervasive presence in our lives, and it is at least reasonable to conclude that they affect our behavior in ways yet to be determined. One book, in commenting on the media's impact on criminal conduct, draws this logical conclusion:

> If so many commercial and political interests invest so much money in media advertising, it would seem absurd to believe that the media have no effect on our behavior, including, perhaps, our criminal behavior. Otherwise, billions of dollars are being wasted by advertisers. And if the media changed only the noncriminal aspects of our behavior, that would be only slightly less remarkable.[5]

Concern with the effects of the mass media is not new. When Goethe published *The Sorrows of Young Werther* in the eighteenth century, for example, authorities in several nations worried that readers would commit suicide in imitation of the book's tragic hero.[6] The enduring preoccupation with possible imitation of dangerous behavior is evidenced in this observation of a 1987 *Newsweek* article: "There is no question that news of a youthful suicide often triggers others, and it may be dangerous even to discuss the problem."[7]

Of course, the media should not retreat entirely from controversy just because some viewers are likely to imitate the behavior revealed through its content. From an ethical perspective, the focus should be on the lessons (messages) communicated through the behavior of media practitioners themselves and the values and attitudes reflected in their material.

MEDIA LESSONS AND MORAL RESPONSIBILITY

Because of the media's high visibility and potential influence, they occupy a sensitive moral position in society. Both the conduct of media practitioners and the lessons incorporated into media content in the form of values, attitudes, and symbolic messages can raise ethical questions. The issues surrounding the media and antisocial behavior generally fall into two categories: (1) practitioners' commission of antisocial acts in connection with their professional obligations and (2) the media's influence on antisocial behavior.

Antisocial Acts and Professional Obligations

Media practitioners are watchdogs and gatekeepers, and for that reason they should usually avoid relying on antisocial conduct to fulfill their professional mandate. Like public officials, media practitioners should be expected to seek the ethical high ground in their conduct.

For example, although reporters would like to believe that they would never violate the law in pursuit of a story, many do. Some of the infractions are minor, such as exceeding the speed limit to get to the scene of a story. But what if a journalist illegally records a conversation in order to gather evidence of illegal or unethical conduct? Or suppose that a journalist, in order to demonstrate to the public a lack of military security, decides to gain access illegally to a Defense Department computer system? Does the public's interest in these stories outweigh the reporters' obligations to obey the law?

This was the question in the summer of 1989 when the columnist Jack Anderson breached security and smuggled a gun into the U.S. Capitol for a television show on terrorism. Anderson reported that the United States had been targeted by several terrorist leaders and that political leaders would be in danger. He said he had smuggled the gun (a felony) to demonstrate the lack of security in the building. However, his professional colleagues were not amused, and a committee of journalists reprimanded him.

Regardless of the circumstances, media practitioners are in a weak moral position when they commit serious breaches of the law. Although there are some rare exceptions, such antisocial behavior sends the wrong message to the audience. First, violating the law often places the reporter in the role of participant rather than detached observer, because a story is, in a sense, created out of the reporter's behavior. If journalists are truly representatives of the public, they should not engage in conduct that they would not approve of in their constituents. Second, if the commission of criminal acts in search of a story became commonplace, respect for the rule of law within society would be undermined. And if the public interest became the sole justification for antisocial behavior, many groups within society might have a legitimate claim to exemptions from the standards of moral conduct.

The Media's Influence on Antisocial Behavior

Because of the media's pervasive influence in the affairs of society, they have often been accused of being accomplices to or influencing antisocial behavior. On other occasions, the news media have actually participated in the resolution of some criminal or other antisocial act, which usually brings praise from those who view the journalist as citizen first and criticism from tradition-bound reporters who complain that such participation compromises their independence and objectivity.

Of course, media practitioners are acutely aware of their critics' concerns and over the years have developed moral guidelines and policies. Under the unrelenting stress of deadline pressures and the spirit of competition, however, these guidelines are sometimes ignored, precipitating a fresh round of media criticism. The ethical issues involved in the media's role in influencing antisocial behavior touch on all three functions of the mass media: news, entertainment, and advertising.

News Crime, violence, and human tragedy are an important part of the reporter's stock in trade. It is not surprising, therefore, that the news media should be blamed for perpetuating the cycle of antisocial behavior that appears to have laid siege to U.S. society. Undoubtedly, some immature and impressionable members of the audience may learn lessons in antisocial behavior from news coverage and decide to imitate what they see or read. For example, some evidence suggests that news reports of suicides trigger a temporary increase in the number of people who kill themselves, particularly among the young.[8] Similarly, stories about product tampering often set off a wave of "copycat" incidents or even false rumors of such tamperings. Such was the case when KIRO-TV in Seattle reported that a syringe had been discovered in a can of Diet Pepsi. This set off a chain reaction of phony Pepsi tampering reports nationwide—a phenomenon that federal officials and some media watchdogs blamed on the excessive coverage given to one isolated incident.[9]

As unfortunate as these incidents may be, however, no reasonable person would suggest that the media should retreat entirely from such coverage as a remedy for society's ills. Journalists should use common sense and good taste in balancing the news needs of the audience against the requirements of social responsibility. For example, a journalist might alert the public to the lax security surrounding some of the world's busiest airports but should avoid providing details on how that security might be breached. Likewise, in covering suicides, reporters should avoid assigning celebrity status to a suicide, providing details of the incident, or romanticizing it. In addition, the media should educate the public on how to identify potential suicide victims, discuss solutions to suicide, and provide information on agencies uniquely qualified to treat those who are contemplating suicide.[10]

Perhaps the most dramatic example in recent years of balancing the news needs of the audience with the requirements of social responsibility" (an Aristotle's golden mean, if you will) is the decision by a number of TV stations to reduce or eliminate graphic depictions of murder and brutality on their early evening newscasts. While crime news is still reported, the most graphic and sensational video has been deleted. WCCO-TV in Minneapolis was among the pioneers in this rather daring experiment in January 1994, when it announced a policy of removing violent images from a dinner-hour broadcast easily viewed by children.[11] This was a risky move in a medium that demands visual intensity. Adherents claim they are responding to an audience weary of "hyped" crime coverage and that such relentless exposure to urban mayhem inflames the public's sense of insecurity. Skeptics, including some news consultants, view the move as nothing more than an attention grabber and marketing ploy. Such moves are cosmetic, they complain, because the network newscasts, which usually are juxtaposed next to the local news, and the stations' late news are not affected by such policies.

Nevertheless, an increasing number of journalists and news executives are questioning television's handling of violent news. In Seattle, for example, the American Federation of Television and Radio Artists (AFTRA), the union that represents reporters and anchors, in 1994 began attacking what it called "bodycount journalism." AFTRA organized a public forum on TV news violence and even convinced two of the three local news directors to confront a hostile audience.[12] And in Los Angeles, News Director Bill Lord of NBC-owned KNBC, upset over the broadcast of a surveillance tape showing the murder of a convenience store clerk, ordered staffers not to show violent acts that have been captured on tape. In a staff memo, Lord said such a tape violates "any imaginable standard of good taste or good journalism."[13]

The ethical imperative for journalists is to cover the news responsibly so as not to encourage or incite further crime and violence. Perhaps no genre of story is more journalistically challenging and ethically vexing than the coverage of crisis situations, such as an armed standoff between law enforcement officials

and a defiant group of militants, a hostage taking, or an act of terrorism. Under such stressful circumstances, ethical guidelines (if they exist at all) often fall prey to competitive pressures and the dynamics of newsroom crisis management. A representative case in which the media emerged with mixed reviews was the standoff in Waco, Texas, between the Branch Davidians and government agents. During and following this event, the media received almost as much scrutiny as the confrontation itself. Jay Black and Bob Steele, reviewing the Waco tragedy for the *Journal of Mass Media Ethics*, identified three fundamental journalistic goals that collided during the seven-week siege of the Branch Davidian compound: the gathering and distribution of truthful information, independence of action, and minimalization of harm. The challenge for reporters was to remain at the cutting edge of events without becoming part of the story or being influenced by events. In addition, they had to remain independent and beware of attempts by David Koresh or law enforcement agents to manipulate their coverage. Yet, under such complex circumstances, it was difficult for reporters to act alone, to remain entirely detached from the dramatic and bizarre spectacle that confronted them. But each participatory act—either through competitive instincts or by virtue of some humanitarian instinct to bring the standoff to a peaceful resolution— put journalists at risk of being held accountable for the outcome, including the possibility of a bloody engagement.[14]

The opening act in this journalistic morality play occurred when the *Waco Herald-Tribune* launched its remarkable seven-part series in late February 1993 about a secretive, little-known religious cult that called itself Branch Davidian. Citing their own investigation, officials of the Alcohol, Tobacco, and Firearms (ATF) agency met with the paper's staff and asked that they delay publication of the story. Following this meeting, several staff members discussed the request but decided to move ahead with publication. "We decided we had heard nothing that would mess up what the ATF was planning," said Editor Bob Lott in defending the *Herald-Tribune*'s decision. "I have always believed you should weigh the consequences of publication, but after listening to the final presentation from them, we decided we had heard nothing that would convince us of the harm to society by publication."[15]

From this rather modest request, the ethical and legal turmoil surrounding local media mounted as events quickly unfolded. For example, a Dallas radio station broadcast a request for the Branch Davidians to fly a banner if they were listening. When sect members complied, federal authorities criticized the station for undermining their negotiating strategy, which included isolation. A station executive later said his station's message to cult members might have actually opened up negotiations. On another occasion, at the urging of federal authorities, KRLD-AM, an all-news station in Dallas, broadcast several messages from Koresh, after which the cult leader released pairs of children who had been living in the compound. Koresh then promised to surrender—a promise he later reneged on—if the station would broadcast another of his messages. Station Manager Charlie Seraphin told reporters that his station was not attempting to become part of the story but "was acting at the urging of federal officials."[16] In alluding to the conflict between the station's *particularistic* (objectivity, independence of judgment) and *universal* (humanitarianism, lifesaving duties, cooperation with authorities) obligations, journalism professor Sara Stone of Baylor University defended the station's actions. "I think you deal as a human being first. You have the responsibility as any other citizen has. But I was amazed that they [the ATF] even asked to begin with."[17] Nevertheless, Professor Stone worried that such participatory behavior might establish some kind of worrisome precedent.

Despite such concerns, however, no ethical system, whether deontologically or teleologically based, would condone a principle by which reporters, under the lofty standard of independence, must shun all pretense of humanitarian instincts. For example, at one point during the siege, a TV reporter braved gunfire to make a radio request for ambulances and also used the station's news unit to remove three of the injured federal officers from the compound.[18]

The coverage of terrorist acts and hostage taking has also generated a great deal of controversy concerning the media's role in such events. No one would dispute the fact that such incidents are newsworthy. But a real danger also exists that the media, particularly television, can themselves become hostages to the political agenda of the terrorists. While TV cameras do not *cause* terrorism, there is little doubt that the instantaneous and dramatic coverage afforded by television has an appeal for those who are looking for a forum for some political cause: "Television offers terrorists an initial tactical advantage. They write the script for the opening act. They set the news agenda. Through television, they appeal directly to the people over the heads of the government."[19]

In searching for guidelines for the coverage of crisis situations, particularly where hostages are involved, any advice that might be rendered is more a matter of common sense and journalistic wisdom than divine providence. For example, reporters should avoid reporting, in words or pictures, information that might reveal the positions or tactics of law enforcement officials. They should become involved in hostage negotiations only as a last resort and should avoid the temptation to make contact with a gunman or hostage taker. Journalists should also avoid going live from a crisis scene, *unless there are compelling journalistic reasons for doing so.* And they should notify authorities if a terrorist or hostage taker contacts the newsroom.[20]

Of course, sometimes cooperation with police and other government agents can pose ethical problems. Journalists cannot casually cohabitate with government authorities without jeopardizing their credibility and risking an ethical flogging. When the media "crawl into bed" with law enforcement officials, becoming in effect an arm of the law, they not only compromise their independence. They must also contend with accusations that they have become government pawns. WABC-TV in New York was confronted with such a dilemma when a convict being treated in a hospital escaped and took hostages at gunpoint. He warned that he would kill the hostages unless his demands were broadcast on television. The station chose to assist the police and broadcast the demands. After the incident ended without bloodshed, the *New York Daily News* lamented that the news media can sometimes be "twisted so easily."[21]

Several years ago, the daily newspaper at the University of Missouri set off a fire storm of criticism when it was accused of cooperating with police. In the fall of 1991, student-journalist Beth Darnell earned hundreds of dollars dancing topless or fully nude at parties. She claimed that she had entered a costume shop just a few blocks from the university campus expecting to apply for a clerk's job. When she left an hour later, she was on her way to her first topless dancing engagement. Darnell denied any desire to do nude dancing but acquiesced when the shop's owner, Tom Bradshaw, "made it sound like other girls were doing it." She said she was coerced into doing so by Bradshaw, who allegedly ran a prostitution ring out of the back of his shop. Angry at what she believed was the merchant's manipulation of her, Darnell decided to publish her first-person account of Bradshaw's business in the journalism school's daily newspaper, the *Columbia Missourian*. The story also alleged that other college students had been lured into the sex trade by Bradshaw.

A couple of days before the story went to press, however, the newspaper's faculty managing editor, George Kennedy, agreed to allow a male student reporter to wear a police "wire" (a recorder) both to collaborate Darnell's allegations and assist the police in arresting Brad-

shaw. Kennedy's defense of the *Missourian*'s collaboration with the police was "[T]his was a problem we wanted to help solve—this was not a case where the newspaper would remain neutral. We decided to become an active participant in attempting to enable the police to do an act of public service."[22]

Critics quickly challenged the paper's decision on two grounds. The paper was remiss, according to Don Corrigan, faculty adviser to the student newspaper at Webster University, for publishing a first-person account of highly controversial activities by the person who committed them. "Beth Darnell was not a real investigator sanctioned by the newspaper," noted Corrigan. "She belongs in a news story as a source; we'd have a reporter interview her. But her own report is tainted by her participation in the acts—a reporter has to be seen as above suspicion. Besides, a journalist who's as gullible as she's portrayed herself has some problems with credibility." In addition, the participation of a reporter in the arrest of a suspect compromises the paper's credibility as an independent journalistic organ. While acknowledging that reporters sometimes share information with the police, Ed Lambeth, a professor specializing in media ethics at the University of Missouri, said Kennedy crossed the line when he allowed Darnell's male colleague to step out of his role as journalist to assist in the arrest.[23]

At times an organization's news-gathering activities actually produce evidence—evidence that might be relevant to the solution of a crime. Under such circumstances, unless there are clear-cut reasons for refusing official requests for such materials, the ethical arguments against cooperation become more problematic. Editors and news directors sometimes react defensively, for example, when they are asked to supply photographs or videotape footage that may contain evidence of criminal conduct, such as the actions of looters during a riot or demonstration. Some members of the journalistic establishment view such demands as a violation of their editorial prerogative and believe that cooperation with outside agencies could set a bad precedent.

Although this argument may have some merit, refusal to cooperate under these circumstances should be based on a specific, defensible ethical principle, reflecting a critical analysis of the facts of the case. Reporters and editors should avoid knee-jerk reactions and the invocation of clichés, such as a general claim of "editorial privilege." One can appreciate reporters' fears of being viewed as arms of law enforcement and their desire to keep such outside agencies at a respectable distance. Nevertheless, their societal role does not *automatically* exempt them from the obligations imposed on the rest of us, and such exemptions must still be justified through the normal moral reasoning process. Their decisions must balance the need to maintain journalistic independence and avoid the perception that they are the tools of the police against the universal obligation to comply with subpoenas (or more informal requests) for evidence of specific criminal conduct.

This was the issue in the fall of 1994 when police in Carbondale, Illinois, demanded photographs and videotape of the city's annual Halloween riot involving two thousand people, many of them Southern Illinois University students. Professor Walter Jaehnig, director of the journalism school at SIU, urged university attorneys to resist the subpoenas issued to the school-sponsored *Daily Egyptian* and the university television station, WSIU-TV. Jaehnig said the subpoenas were too broad (they called for 150 to 300 pictures taken by five photographers) and called it a "fishing expedition." University attorneys persuaded the state's attorney general to withdraw the subpoenas and instead provide a list of thirty-nine specific incidents the police were investigating. Jaehnig said that if the *Egyptian* should discover photos relevant to any of the thirty-nine incidents, it would offer to sell prints to the police. While the agreement did not entirely dispel the percep-

tion that the newspaper's photographers might be police agents, said Jaehnig, it at least made it clear that to procure the pictures police must specify they were probing a particular crime. Thus, regardless of the *Egyptian*'s legal standing in this case, the ethical struggle over the police demands for news material was sharply focused. On the one hand, the *Daily Egyptian* wanted to preserve its independence from the police. On the other hand, many of the rioters were SIU students, and the university had tried to stamp out the violence. From that viewpoint, conceded Jaehnig, "We should be willing to cooperate with police."[24]

The decision whether to cooperate with law enforcement authorities must, of course, be made on a case-by-case basis. At times there is no apparent reason for refusing to do so. However, journalists must beware of entering into arrangements with the police and others that compromise their independence and damage their credibility. Such unholy alliances convert reporters into partners in the battle against antisocial behavior rather than mere observers of this unsavory landscape.

Entertainment Does violence on television and in the movies increase the aggressive behavior of children? Do programs about crime contribute to the growing crime rate in society? Is the drug culture glorified in prime-time television drama? Should Hollywood be blamed for the decline in family values?

These are just a few of the ethical questions confronting the entertainment industry. Through their reliance on all kinds of conflicts portrayed through stark characterization, clever dialogue, special effects, and dramatic situations, the entertainment media convey important lessons concerning both beneficial and antisocial behavior. They may, at times, merely reflect reality or, on other occasions, help promote change, but undoubtedly they occupy an important niche in the nation's moral development. Professor Deni Elliott, a frequent commentator on media ethics, has described some of the ethical concerns surrounding the entertainment media as follows:

> Mass media entertainment, in print or broadcast, does more than help people fill time between dinner and bed; entertainment pieces educate and socialize. We learn about moral heroes through feature profiles—people who risk their lives to help strangers. We learn how to deal with child molestation, drug use and other crises through watching prime-time situation comedies. Yet when violence is shown, some of the learning may be not what the writers and producers intended. The basic concern about showing violent acts is that the dramatized event may lead people to commit the same acts. Does a TV movie that depicts gang rape encourage similar acts? Psychological experts disagree. Screenwriters and producers must consider the effect that such scenes could have on some members of the audience.[25]

For more than sixty years, the "effects" of media depictions of various forms of antisocial behavior have been placed under the experimental microscope of social scientists. But even if a definitive link can be established between media content and antisocial behavior, the Constitution would leave little room to maneuver in regulating this content. In the past twenty years, several lawsuits have attempted to hold the media liable for disseminating material that allegedly led to imitative acts of violence.[26] But the courts have consistently held that the First Amendment protects such matters of artistic taste, unless the producer of the content "incites" the audience to unlawful behavior. With the legal protection of violent entertainment thus ensured, the *ethical* concerns surrounding the values being transmitted through the dramatic and sometimes controversial creations of the entertainment industry should assume a renewed sense of urgency.

Few producers of entertainment would intentionally set out to encourage or *incite* antisocial behavior. Such a goal could not be defended under any ethical norm. Nevertheless, regardless of whether the entertainment industry "causes" antisocial behavior, society, particularly vulnerable and impressionable youth, cannot escape the subtle behavioral and psychological cues inhabiting its seductive merchandise. For example, a serious subject like drug abuse, even when dealt with in the sugar-coated format of situation comedy, must be realistic in order to capture the audience's attention. Yet every effort should be made not to glamorize drugs to the point that the antidrug message (if there is one) is lost on the viewers. However, media practitioners are in an ethically delicate position, because they must function at that fragile crossroads between reality and entertainment, attempting to embrace simultaneously both the verities of an uncivil society and socially responsible messages that promote moral values that society itself may no longer be committed to.

Unfortunately, Hollywood is no longer saying no to drugs in its dramatic and entertaining accounts of reality—at least not in any definitive way. For most of the 1980s, drugs either vanished from popular entertainment or were depicted as villainous. But in 1993 *Newsweek* reported that "drug use has gone prime time, and without the cautionary alarm bells or Devil's horns."[27] For example, in one episode of *Roseanne*, one of the top-rated sitcoms in the country, the principal characters discovered a cache of marijuana, lit up, and spent much of the show in stoned bliss. Pot humor was also featured on such satirical offerings as *Saturday Night Live* and *Comedy Central,* while MTV's top-rated Beavis and Butt-head sniffed paint thinner.[28]

The media are accused of promoting every conceivable form of antisocial behavior, from encouraging disrespect for authority to causing an increase in teenage suicide. However, violence continues to be public enemy number one for media critics. And this is not surprising, considering the well-documented epidemic of social violence, particularly among the young. As a cultural value, violence is of classical vintage. Shakespeare's violent scenes in *Julius Caesar*, *Hamlet*, and *Macbeth*, for example, are "classical" examples of the prominence of brutality in our literary heritage. From its inception the movie industry has been under attack for its preoccupation with violence and cavalier attitude toward the deleterious effects of such fare on its audiences. When *The Great Train Robbery* became the first hit movie in 1903, audiences reportedly ran in terror from the screen during a scene in which a "badman" pointed a pistol at the screen. Twenty-eight years later, a reviewer for the *New York Times* denounced the Jimmy Cagney film, Public Enemy, for its "sensationally incoherent murders" ending in "general slaughter."[29]

Of course, by contemporary standards, which embrace graphic portrayals of bloody violence and brutality, these examples stand merely as amusing anecdotes, and today Hollywood remains accused of moral high treason by religious conservatives and presidential candidates alike. In the 1960s, the movie industry, in an effort to blunt some of this criticism, introduced a rating system as an early warning device for their patrons, but media critics consider this step as an insufficient admission of moral responsibility in the value wars between Hollywood and "mainstream" America. Recent trends suggest that the critics may have scored a victory, although not for the reasons they would have preferred. In 1993, for example, the most popular violent fare gave way to the likes of *Huck Finn*, *Dennis the Menace*, and *Teenage Mutant Ninja Turtles 3*.[30] And in 1995 *U.S. News & World Report* felt confident enough to describe Hollywood's new attitude as "family friendly."[31] These developments, however, reflect marketplace dynamics and are not the result of any surge of moral virtue on the part of Hollywood producers. Recent studies reveal that R-rated movies—which constitute a majority of studio films—do not sell as well as PG. As the head of one major film studio acknowl-

edged in 1993: "A movie rated PG is almost three times more likely to reach $100 million [in ticket sales] than a film rated R."[32]

The record industry has also come under moral scrutiny because of its high-volume appeal and sales to teenagers. Such musical genres as gangsta rap and heavy metal, while aesthetically offensive to some musical aficionados, are exceedingly popular among the young. Their lyrics are also often violent and sexually explicit. Time Warner, in particular, has been singled out because of the lyrics produced by some of the rappers under contract to the media conglomerate. The public condemnation of rapper Ice-T's cop-killing song was so great, for example, that Time Warner finally parted company with the artist. However, Time Warner Chairman Gerald Levin did not surrender easily to his critics, embracing the First Amendment as his moral savior. The fact is, however, that much of the gangsta rap music, which glorifies brutality and misogyny, is not the result of spontaneous expression but callous marketing. This reality is reflected in rapper Willie D.'s interview with *USA Today*, in which he expressed reservations about his shocking lyrics now that he has a month-old daughter. The lyrics to which he was referring included the rather startling claim that a woman deserved to get raped and murdered because she left her curtains open. "I have to put food on the table," he said. "For me, it's a business. I say it to get paid."[33]

The music industry has responded to charges of such "cultural pollution" with a voluntary rating system in which some cassettes and compact disks containing violent or sexually explicit material are identified with warning labels. However, in June 1995 the American Medical Association passed a resolution asking the record industry to impose mandatory ratings. "Evidence is mounting of a correlation between aggression and listening to violent lyrics," the resolution said. "Repeated listening may desensitize children to violence without conveying to them the consequences of violent behavior."[34]

Because of television's pervasive intrusion into our home life and its pivotal role in children's lives, this medium has borne the brunt of public censure for its preoccupation with violence and pernicious influence on society. Media watchdogs, government officials, and some industry executives themselves have been unerringly vocal in their denunciation of graphic and often gratuitous televised violence. Headlines such as "Senator Eyes Curb on Violent TV Promos," "FCC Chairman Urges Psychologists to Speak Out against TV Violence," and "TV Networks Agree to Standards on Violence" are among those appearing in recent popular and trade publications.

Despite public protests, Congressional threats, and industry promises,[35] however, violence remains a remarkably durable commodity on television. For example, a recent study found that between 1992 and 1994, TV and cable violence increased by about 41 percent.[36] Nevertheless, media critics should be somewhat heartened, if not entirely pacified, by the industry's adoption of "viewer discretion" advisories for programs with violent, sexually explicit, or otherwise indecent content. And while the effect of such warnings is still unclear, one recent study at Duke University suggests that such warnings may decrease viewership of violent TV programming, at least among children.[37] The cable industry has also assumed a proactive posture in responding to media critics. In March 1994, for example, forty-five cable networks aired programs with antiviolence themes. About the same time, the National Cable Television Association also promised to implement a ratings system of its own.[38] And in 1996 Congress responded to viewers' concerns about televised violence by requiring that TV set manufacturers install "V-chips" that will allow parents to block out objectionable programs.

Research into the effects of violent media content continues and is far from definitive. However, the findings in this area do support one conclusion: TV violence is emotionally arousing, and this arousal can lead to aggressive behavior in children. Under some circumstances, TV-induced aggression can lead to antisocial behavior.[39]

A system of ethics need not demand that violence be eliminated entirely, an absurd prospect at best. But it is not unreasonable to expect producers of mass entertainment to bring to their craft a sense of responsibility toward the medium and audience. A film director, for example, might treat a violent scenario differently for a family TV audience than for a theater audience. Likewise, violence in children's programs should be treated differently from those aimed at adults.

In constructing the guidelines for an "ethics of violent content," we might consider the following questions:

1. Is there an adequate warning by the producer, so that each individual or group in the chain of distribution (advertiser, network, station, movie theater, consumer) can decide whether to reject the content?

2. Is the violence gratuitous, or is it essential to the plot and script?

3. Does the material depict violence as a desirable (or even inevitable) consequence or solution to a problem?

4. Is there just punishment for unwarranted acts of violence, or are such acts rewarded?

5. Are heroes and villains clearly delineated?

6. If there is no just punishment or if the heroes and villains are not clearly identified, is there some higher public purpose to be served by the use of violence in the plot or script?

An ethicist might ask: who should assume moral responsibility for the menu of the entertainment industry? Although the producers of such materials may bear the ultimate responsibility, a reasonable argument could be made that all of the parties in the line of distribution must share in this moral duty: writers, producers, directors, networks, stations, newspapers, magazines, movie theaters, and the audience itself, including the parents of children. Nevertheless, producers of mass entertainment are in a particularly precarious position, because they must entertain and accommodate the needs of the creative community while at the same time being sensitive to the value-laden messages being communicated to a diverse audience. Controversial entertainment materials dealing with social issues are seldom neutral in the lessons they teach. They may be creatively balanced, but social or antisocial values are an inherent component of such dramatic fare.[40] Thus, media practitioners must be sensitive to their industry's role in influencing society's mores and should devise strategies to entertain their audiences while not abandoning them to moral anarchy.

Advertising The relationship between advertising and the problem of antisocial behavior is perhaps not as apparent as that in the news and entertainment functions of the mass media. One reason is that the unabashed purpose of advertising is to persuade, and few media practitioners wish to be accused of promoting illegal or violent conduct. Another reason is that a broad consensus has emerged among the media about the types of ads that are suitable for publishing or broadcasting. Most media institutions have codes that, in addition to rejecting advertising on the grounds of taste, also refuse ads that violate laws or encourage unlawful conduct. Ads that promote illegal lotteries or offer mail-order weapons are two examples.

Among the mainstream media, the primary complaint in recent years has been directed against violence in toy commercials. Cartoon characters, in particular, along with their marketing spinoffs, have been the targets of media critics. However, between 1992 and 1994 toy commercials reduced their violent content by 85 percent, according to a recent study. This led *TV Guide*'s Neil Hickey to observe, "[W]hatever the impetus for change, the recent furor over media violence appears to have drawn a stronger response from advertisers than from the TV industry itself."[41]

Despite advertisers' traditional aversion to controversy, one should never underestimate the economic potency of the marketplace. Even Madison Avenue is not above challenging the limits of ethical convention. In the fall of 1991, for example, *Newsweek* magazine carried this disturbing announcement: "In an attempt to cash in on the multimillion dollar market for urban-inspired goods, experts say, a small but increasingly visible group of marketers is using tough-guy imagery to sell everything from malt liquor to music."[42] The magazine cited as an example a commercial for Snickers featuring a youngster emblazoning an inner-city wall with the candy bar's name—symbolic of a gang practice of "tagging" walls with graffiti. Another spot broadcast on urban contemporary radio stations compared a bottle of the potent St. Ides malt liquor to a Smith & Wesson handgun. The jingle, which *Newsweek* described as having "all the subtlety of a drive-by shooting," was performed by the rapper Ice Cube, former member of the gangsta rap group NWA. And an ad for Coty Wild Musk perfume titled "The Wild Ones" featured a model wearing what resembled a belt full of bullets around his waist.[43]

Ads such as these raise ethical concerns not only because of their questionable content but also because of the audiences to which they are directed. When such gang-related messages are targeted to urban youth, the advertising industry stands accused of introducing still another explosive element into an already hostile, violent environment. Moral agents, of course, are free to seek vindication for their behavior on whatever moral grounds they so choose, but they can never escape moral responsibility for the consequences of their actions.

THE MEDIA AND CIVILITY

If the teaching of ethics means anything, it means we must cultivate respect for others. This "value," which lies at the heart of Immanuel Kant's philosophy and is arguably the energizing force for all ethical behavior, commands us to treat persons as not just a means to an end but as ends unto themselves. In so doing, we should attempt to foster within ourselves the qualities of courtesy, compassion, and respect for the beliefs and opinions of others. In short, we should be civil. A civil society is more likely to be a virtuous society. But unfortunately, in recent years there does appear to be a decline in civility, as evidenced by our growing intolerance and impatience in our relationships, a deterioration in the "quality" of rhetoric with which we express our opposition on public issues, and an overall cynicism toward and disrespect for society's norms.

In searching for answers to this malaise, we should avoid the temptation to blame the media entirely for this disturbing decline in civility. Nevertheless, because of the media's impact, it is certainly fair to inquire what role media practitioners have played in the depreciation of society's cultural life. With the proliferation of computer networks, enabling us to bypass traditional media gatekeepers and communicate at will with other individuals, small target audiences, or large undifferentiated audiences, this is a vital and timely question. Uncivil speech within itself is harmless. But inflammatory and vitriolic rhetoric may also beget antisocial attitudes and behavior. Among the lunatic fringe, it may encourage violence. But even within society's mainstream, such offensive speech can create a culture of incivility in which undisguised hostility is vented in front of millions of zealous onlookers and "trash thy neighbor" becomes a spectator sport. Any attempt to categorize the various kinds of uncivil speech is risky since the lines among them are often blurred. However, for the purpose of a brief discussion, we divide them into two categories: hate speech and dirty tricks.

Hate Speech

In the spring of 1995, right-wing talk show host G. Gordon Liddy said he had used handmade drawings of the President and Hillary Rodham Clinton for target practice and also discussed shooting federal agents if legally justified.[44] He suggested that people, in defending their homes against agents, "shoot twice to the body, center of mass, and if that does not work, then shoot to the groin area."[45] While critics condemned him for his intemperate and shocking remarks, not all agreed. For his "bravado," Liddy was honored with a free-speech award by the National Association of Radio Talk Show Hosts.

Several years ago a conservative radio talk show host, in discussing an Indiana woman who quit her job to go on welfare, leveled this diatribe against his defenseless target: "All these irresponsible whores are the same. They get knocked up by some construction worker, then expect the taxpayers to pay for them to sit around the house all day and watch *Oprah Winfrey*."[46]

The common thread in these two apparently unrelated broadcasts is the genre of *hate speech*—speech "attacking an individual or group on the basis of who they are."[47] Liddy's antigovernment views were manifest in his verbal assaults on federal agents, and the other host cited here made known his disdain for welfare recipients. We cannot just dismiss such mass-mediated rhetoric as the ravings of lunatics wandering in the cultural wilderness. They have struck a responsive chord among some segments of society and command a loyal following. For example, when a Michigan radio station suspended the program of James (Bo) Gritz, a retired lieutenant colonel in the Special Forces who had described the Oklahoma City bombing as a work of art, listener complaints convinced station management to restore the program to the airwaves.[48] And when radio station KCKC near Los Angeles canceled Liddy's syndicated talk show, callers threatened to blow up the station and murder the station manager.[49] One can hardly imagine a more uncivil response to an uncivil program.

The most common variety of hate speech, of course, is verbal or written attacks on various groups because of their racial, ethnic, or national origin. In recent years, for example, right-wing groups have shown an interest in public access cable channels as a platform for disseminating their racist rhetoric. In 1987 a neo-Nazi group calling itself the SS Action Group placed a recruitment message on Warner Cable's access channel in working-class Norwood, a suburb of Cincinnati. The message read, "Join the American Nazis and smash Red, Jew, and Black Power." Shortly thereafter the same message was run on the cable system in Cincinnati under the joint sponsorship of the SS Action Group and the White American Skin Heads. They also aired a one-hour edition of a neo-Nazi program, *Race and Reason*. Local reaction was swift and emotional. The issue dominated the news for several days, as populist leaders denounced hate groups and called for censorship. One member of the cable board even resigned. Eventually reason prevailed in the form of an agreement by a coalition of groups, including the National Association for the Advancement of Colored People (NAACP) and the American Jewish Committee, to produce programs to counter the neo-Nazi message. The Norwood/Cincinnati experience was not unlike conflicts involving neo-Nazis that arose in several other cities as geographically diverse as Atlanta, Georgia, and Sacramento, California.[50]

Two years later the Ku Klux Klan was at the center of a controversy in Kansas City when it sought access to the local cable system. Although the city council attempted to thwart the Klan's initiative, apparently in violation of federal law, the council, faced with a lawsuit it did not think it could win, soon backed down. However, when KKK members showed up in the spring of 1990 to produce a program, they became embroiled in a shouting match with some community members. Police arrested several on concealed weapons charges, and no Klansman returned after the incident.[51]

These cases, of course, concern a legally mandated right of access devoid of management censorship. Thus, media managers—in this case, cable system operators—are left to ponder this question: Should media practitioners simply defend their role in the dissemination of such hate speech on the grounds of legal obligation, or do they have an ethical duty to counter such speech with the presentation of opposing views?

Even college campuses, usually considered repositories of civility, have not been immune from the hate speech virus. Some have expressed their concern and disgust by enacting codes of conduct prohibiting the dissemination of such inflammatory rhetoric. Unfortunately, this prompt codification of moral outrage may have been more a result of a seizure of political correctness than a reasoned balancing of the competing values of free speech against society's interest in combatting racist attitudes and promoting harmony and civility. Thus far, those courts that have undertaken this balancing process have decided in favor of free speech.

Since hate speech is inherently unreasonable and fanatical, it is not surprising that the apostles of hatred would view new technologies, such as those supporting the information superhighway, as a golden opportunity to expand their horizons. Indeed, evidence indicates that cyberspace is already becoming a platform for such uncivil behavior. For example, a week after the terrorist bombing of a federal building in Oklahoma City in April 1995, Rabbi Marvin Hier, dean of the Simon Wiesenthal Center in Los Angeles, discovered this message on the Internet: "I want to make bombs and kill evil Zionist people in the government. Teach me. Give me text files."[52]

In searching for ethical strategies to combat the moral ravages of hate speech, we should remember that free speech is fundamental to a libertarian society. A civil society does not depend on governmental or societal controls on expression, no matter how offensive it may be. The proper antidote to hate speech is not suppression but even more speech. The key to a civil society lies as much with the audiences as the communicators. A talk show host whose stock in trade is shocking epithets and hate-filled messages is sustained through advertising generated by high ratings—in other words, audience appeal. The reality is that if we truly desire and deserve an ethical society, then the apostles of virtue and civility should emerge victorious in the marketplace of ideas in an open encounter with the cynical patrons of hate speech.

Dirty Tricks

In March 1995, the producers of the *Jenny Jones* TV talk show convinced twenty-four-year-old Jonathan Schmitz to appear on an episode dealing with secret crushes. He came on assuming his admirer would be a woman but was instead confronted with a man he barely knew, Scott Amedure. Three days later, after receiving a note from Amedure, Schmitz allegedly drove to Amedure's home and killed him with two shotgun blasts to the chest. Schmitz later told police that the embarrassment from the show (which never aired) had "eaten away" at him.[53]

Such occurrences may be uncommon, but they represent perhaps the fringe of a rather disturbing trend among TV talk shows. Such confrontational programming, which we might refer to as *dirty tricks*, usually consists of "sandbagging" some unsuspecting guest. Consider, for example, a recent episode of the *Jerry Springer* show in which a woman told her husband, John, that she was having an affair with another woman. "You bring me out to Chicago for me to find this out on TV?" John asked in fury.[54]

In the dirty tricks, confrontational mentality of the latest additions to the talk how genre, guests become pawns to be manipulated for the bizarre entertainment of studio and TV audiences and the financial enrichment of producers. Pop therapy becomes a spectator sport. Guests often wind up yelling at each other, and fistfights are not unheard of. "Shows used to do stories that were relevant to people's lives—

whether it was dieting or improving your sex life," said former *Donahue* producer Adrienne Lopez-Dudley nostalgically in an interview for *TV Guide*. "Now they're about the weird lives of a few people who want to get on TV."[55]

Dirty tricks, of course, are not confined to the visually engrossing TV talk shows. Take, for example, the Chicago disc jockey who suggested to listeners that a TV anchorwoman—and recent widow—was pregnant by a Chicago Bulls player. A judge refused to dismiss her defamation suit. In still another case with even more tragic consequences, a St. Louis radio station aired phone messages believed to be a TV weatherman talking about a love affair. Early the next morning, he died in a fiery plane crash believed to be a suicide.[56]

Of course, even when no dirty tricks are involved, the confrontational environment of talk shows sometimes leads to violence. In 1988, for example, Geraldo Rivera's nose was broken by a flying chair when a brawl broke out on the set as he interviewed young white supremacists and a black civil rights leader. Seven years later, his nose suffered the same fate as two men who had been romantically involved with the same woman began arguing about how her children were being cared for. The woman's husband objected, and a fight broke out. Rivera was punched as he tried to shield the woman and two other female guests.

In searching for strategies to confront the cultural ravages of hate speech and mass-mediated dirty tricks, we must reject our natural inclination toward government censorship and instead approach the issue on an ethical plane. Even those who disdain civility have a "right" to search for a hospitable pulpit from which to dispense their messages. But media practitioners, except in cases where the law mandates access, are under no moral duty to accommodate the purveyors of hate speech or dirty tricks. A station executive, for example, is certainly free to reject a talk show that traffics in confrontation and verbal violence. This is a difficult decision, since much of the fare currently on the air is popular with some audiences. Some media managers might argue that the public has a right to all viewpoints, even those that appear to be outrageous to media critics. Fair enough! But the fact remains that such decisions are driven more by market considerations than any altruistic desire to pay homage to the First Amendment or serve the public interest. Besides, the issue here is not toleration of unpopular or even disgusting "views." The view, for example, that the Holocaust never happened—a position that is anathema to many in the Jewish community and elsewhere—can still be presented in a civil, rational fashion, even if it lacks any credible supporting evidence.

Thus, the issue revolves around the use of inflammatory language that is devoid of social value, dehumanizes its target, or *incites* violence or other forms of antisocial behavior. As in all areas of ethical concern, media practitioners are responsible for the content they disseminate, regardless of who actually produces it. And advertisers are ethically liable for providing the financial sustenance to the apostles of incivility. But the stark reality is that as long as audiences continue to patronize or at least indulge the purveyors of hate speech and programs that thrive on violent confrontation, the media will continue to contribute in its own way to the degeneration of cultural civility.

THE MEDIA AND ANTISOCIAL BEHAVIOR: HYPOTHETICAL CASE STUDIES

The cases in this chapter present moral dilemmas concerned with the depiction or encouragement of antisocial behavior by media practitioners. In analyzing these scenarios, keep in mind the three philosophical approaches to ethical decision making described in Chapter 3:

duty-based ethics (deontology), consequence-based ethics (teleology), and Aristotle's golden mean.

A deontologist would examine the motives of the moral agent and would inquire whether the approach under consideration should become a universal rule for resolving such dilemmas. In evaluating gratuitous violence in TV programming, for example, a deontologist would reject this kind of content as being unworthy standard fare for the television entertainment medium, even if there were no demonstrable harmful effects from such programming.

An alternative approach, of course, is to examine the consequences of the ethical decision. The moral agent considers the potential impact on all of the parties affected by the decision and then decides which course of action will produce the best consequences under the circumstances.

In situations involving the depictions of antisocial behavior, Aristotle's golden mean can provide a useful approach to moral decision making. The goal is to find a mean between the two extremes in an ethical dilemma. In applying the golden mean, the strategy should be neither to eliminate controversial material entirely (an extremely paternalistic approach) nor to approve of or encourage antisocial behavior just for the sake of titillating the audience. Rather, programs and published material containing depictions of antisocial behavior should include an appropriate dosage of positive lessons for the audience.

A case in point is a TV series that includes violence but discourages its use as a means of resolving human problems. In cases where the scenes or dialogue are too graphic, warnings could be issued by the producers, thus allowing the audience to render its own judgment on whether to consume the material. Likewise, a TV news crew that covers demonstrations in unmarked cars and with unobtrusive equipment is displaying a sense of responsibility and a healthy respect for Aristotle's golden mean.

◀ C A S E   S T U D I E S ▶

▶ CASE 9-1
Testing High School Security

Despite denials by school officials, to reporter Blake Mathews the evidence was clear: Evanston High had become a blackboard jungle. For more than a year rumors had circulated that Evanston High, one of four secondary schools in this demographically diverse but conservative community of 250,000, had fallen prey to the social maladies normally associated with the urban decay of inner-city schools. Mathews covered the education beat, along with several other government agencies, for the Evanston *Enquirer*, and the rumors of discord within one of Evanston's educational institutions had quickly caught his attention. The education beat was, after all, not usually a fertile field for Pulitzer Prize—winning enterprises, and the young reporter pursued the rumors of moral decay within the local high school with a great deal of enthusiasm.

His initial interview with William Carson, Evanston High's affable but cautious principal, produced little of substance. He acknowledged that a few students had been suspended for possession of drugs but flatly denied that students were bringing guns to school or that violence was a problem in the school's classrooms. But Mathews's interviews with students and teachers, most of whom insisted on anonymity, painted a different picture: an educational institution in which discipline was rapidly disintegrating and violence had replaced decorum as a mode of social interaction.

Within a couple of weeks of Mathews's interview with William Carson, a student was shot and another expelled for bringing a pistol to school. The principal publicly expressed regrets for the incidents but assured the community that they were isolated and that Evanston High was still a secure educational institution. Nevertheless, the school system had invested in a metal detector to screen all students, school personnel, and visitors "just as

a precautionary measure," according to Carson, "to assure parents that their children are safe at Evanston High."

But the reporter's inquiries into the effectiveness of the newly installed security device did little to restore his confidence in the principal's veracity. One teacher compared the system to a leaking dam. "The problem," she said, "is that the school district installed this metal detector, but it doesn't seem to work all the time. It's certainly not foolproof. It's turned up a few weapons, but others have gotten through. I've personally confiscated two pistols from students that went undetected in the screening process. How did they get them through? I don't know."

Mathews's conversations with students confirmed the teacher's story. Nevertheless, he wanted more graphic evidence—a "smoking gun," to use a poorly chosen metaphor—and proposed to City Editor Lenallen Hall that he attempt to penetrate the security system by smuggling a gun through the metal detector. "I can set up an interview with the principal," Mathews told his city editor, "and then if I make it through the detector, I can confront him with the evidence. If I get caught, I can feign embarrassment. After all, I do have a permit to carry a concealed weapon that I acquired after I was mugged last year."

Hall found the reporter's proposed initiative interesting. Managing Editor Cynthia Suyat saw it as an ethical dilemma.

"Is this legal?" asked Suyat. The managing editor was always interested in dispensing with the legal niceties before tackling the more contentious ethical dilemmas.

"As far as we know," responded Hall. "We ran this by our attorney. The school is not in a 'firearm-free zone.' That would be a tacit admission that there's a problem. And there's no law that specifically prohibits carrying a gun into the school. There *is* a school board policy that provides for expulsion for any student who carries a gun to school and sanctions for school personnel discovered with any firearm on school premises. But these are administration penalties; they don't apply to nonschool personnel. Even if Blake gets caught, the most they can do is to confiscate the gun."

"But even if Blake isn't technically violating a criminal law by carrying a concealed weapon into Evanston High, he's still violating the spirit of the regulation. And if he is caught, then that will reflect poorly on us. Our credibility will be hurt. How can we encourage respect for the law on our op-ed page if we are caught flaunting the school's efforts at keeping guns out of the school?"

"This situation is different," replied Mathews, still annoyed by the refusal of school officials to acknowledge the culture of violence within Evanston High. "Carson and his staff have assured the public that the metal detector is just to provide extra security. They're unwilling to admit that there's a serious problem. And our information is that, despite the detector, guns are still showing up in the school. The public has a right to know about this. All that I have now are a few students who claim to have gone through the detector with guns. But I need some confirmation. What better way than to have a firsthand account?"

"But what if we do succeed in proving your point?" asked Suyat. "That might just encourage other students to test the system. At least now the fact that there's a detector in place will probably deter some students from attempting to bring guns into the school."

"But if the system isn't very effective, then most of the students know anyway. The grapevine in a public high school is really amazing," said Hall with a trace of sarcasm.

Suyat conceded that Hall had a point. And since school officials had denied that there was a serious problem at the school and had publicly stated that the security system was entirely effective, perhaps the paper was justified in challenging the regulation for some higher good. But exactly what was the "good"? Even if Mathews did penetrate the school's defenses, he would have succeeded only in debunking the official claims of effective security. The more serious problem of juvenile violence within the academy would remain. In any event, the *Enquirer*'s involvement would probably be applauded by those who were incensed at the principal's public deception and condemned by those who viewed Mathews's behavior as nothing more than misguided journalistic arrogance. As Suyat pondered this ethical dilemma, she wondered whether the ends justified the means.

THE CASE STUDY

Although Mathews's proposal to smuggle a pistol through the school's metal detector might not technically violate a criminal law, it would certainly violate the spirit and intent of school regulations. In addition, Managing Editor Cynthia Suyat is concerned that Mathews's success might encourage others to challenge the security system.

On the one hand, it might be argued that in this case Mathews would be justified in defying school authorities because (1) they have refused to acknowledge publicly the seriousness of the problem, and (2) reporter involvement is the only way to illustrate vividly the inadequacy of the security measure. In this view, reporters, as fiduciaries of the public, should be held to a different standard of moral conduct because of their essential roles within society.

On the other hand, journalists are not above the law and have the same obligations as the rest of us. Violations by such influential members of society breed contempt for law and authority and, in cases such as this one, might even encourage further challenges to the security system.

For the purpose of resolving this ethical quandary, assume the role of the managing editor, and, using the SAD Formula for moral reasoning outlined in Chapter 3, make a decision on whether you will approve Mathews's proposal. In rendering your judgment, keep in mind the interests of students, parents, school officials, your paper, and the community at large.

▶ CASE 9-2
The Uncivil Radio Talk Show Host

Lincoln Hampton had an uncivil tongue. He also had thousands of loyal followers. The *Lincoln*

Hampton Show had made its debut on KAAD in San Francisco in the fall of 1992 while the Democrats were still in control of Congress and George Bush's presidency was under siege. His mean-spirited brand of conservatism and flamboyant, colorful antiestablishment rhetoric had struck a responsive chord among the politically and socially disaffected, as well as those who viewed any public thrashing of the liberal agenda as a spectator sport.

The son of an executive for a large telecommunications company, Hampton had come of age during the early Reagan years, quickly embracing the conservative philosophy that had supplanted the now discredited liberalism of an earlier generation. Hampton held a bachelor's degree in political science and a master's degree in journalism from Stanford, but his liberal arts education apparently had done little to cultivate a tolerance for cultural diversity or respect for others' views. He had originally aspired to a career as a political reporter but came to view journalism (the practitioners of which he also considered as too liberal for his taste) as increasingly irrelevant to social progress. Hampton was also not interested in political office but instead coveted a platform from which to make his own contributions to the conservative cause.

After a couple of years as equipment manager, PA announcer, and publicity director for a minor league baseball franchise in California, Hampton had joined the staff of an AM radio station in a small market in the northern part of the state as the host of an afternoon drive-time program. His maiden voyage on the electronic soapbox began innocently enough, as he entertained his audience and on-air callers with his cheerful banter and interesting commentary on the most mundane of subjects. But as Hampton's ratings improved, his remarks became increasingly assertive and assumed a decidedly antiestablishment political overtone. In addition, his use of intemperate language to punctuate his defiance of conventional mores established common ground with those listeners who felt politically disenfranchised. Talk radio was made for Lincoln Hampton, and after a couple of years he had sent an "air-check" of his present program to Phil Morrow, the general manager of KAAD. Although Morrow had winced at some of Hampton's aggressive commentary, he had also seen an opportunity to "jump-start" his sluggish drive time ratings.

Within a few weeks of its debut, the *Lincoln Hampton Show* had found its niche among what would soon become a sizable following, thus assuring Hampton's present position as the number one drive-time personality in the San Francisco market. This phenomenon quickly attracted the attention of the advertising community, whose generous financial support assured the programming security of KAAD's colorful personality.

While Hampton dominated his electronic platform, his show usually featured a variety of controversial conservative guests, as well as a generous number of callers who usually shared Hampton's contempt for the established order. The occasional dissenter who was unfortunate enough to be selected for airtime was subjected unmercifully to Hampton's linguistic incivility. On one occasion, for example, after one caller, who identified himself as a "gay marine," had taken Hampton to task for his intolerant stance against homosexuals in the military, Hampton retaliated by asserting that "fags like you pose more of a threat to our national security than the communists did at the height of the Cold War." Such mean-spirited broadsides made Morrow increasingly uncomfortable with his talk show host, but Hampton's contribution to the station's bottom line was impressive and could not be ignored.

No topic was beyond Hampton's domain, and he confronted each with a combination of eloquent flourish and tactless diatribes. Beneficiaries of affirmative action programs, welfare recipients, gays and lesbians, feminists, and pornographers were all favorite targets of Hampton's irrepressible disposition.

But it was not gays or feminists that concerned Phil Morrow, as he surveyed the damage from the last week's episodes of the *Lincoln Hampton Show*. Several days before, a terrorist car bomb had destroyed the federal building housing the local office of the FBI, and a little-known organization known as the People's Militia had claimed responsibility. Thirty people had died in the blast and scores had been injured, including several in surrounding buildings. Government officials, various citizens groups, and the media angrily denounced the bombing as (according to one typical newspaper editorial) "the crazed actions of a bunch of lunatics who are willing to sacrifice innocent lives to create a climate of fear and distrust among our citizens."

But one person's lunacy is another's opportunity, and Hampton had seized the moment to share his electronic forum with those who wished to comment on this latest act of domestic terrorism. Some callers condemned the violence outright; others expressed regrets for the loss of innocent lives but sympathized with the antigovernment sentiment that had resulted in the bombing. Hampton also condemned the loss of life, but then tempered his sympathies with the observation that "the government itself was responsible because of its increasing totalitarian tendencies and violation of individual liberties." "I urge all Americans to keep a loaded weapon at home and defy any government agent to cross the threshold uninvited," he said in closing one program. "If we, the people, don't regain control of our government, more innocent lives will be sacrificed, like those here in San Francisco."

"We're under some pressure to pull Hampton off the air," said Morrow to his program director, Darren Baker, as the beleaguered station manager sought counsel on the ethical dimensions of Lincoln Hampton's continuing incivility. Baker was an unwavering proponent of talk shows, both radio and television, which he considered to be the broadcast equivalent of democratic populism. "An electronic town meeting," he often said in referring admiringly to the talk show genre.

"Our calls and mail are running three to one against him," Morrow continued. "Admittedly, some are from those who have always objected to his outspoken views. But others appear to be devoted listeners. And three advertisers have also objected to his recent outburst. They're apparently under a threat of a boycott from some organizations that have consistently complained about Hampton's so-called 'hate speech' in expressing his views. Many of the complaints appear to be well orchestrated. So it's too early to tell how much dissatisfac-

tion there really is out there. Also, it's too early to assess the financial impact."

"I don't think the answer is to pull him off the air," responded Baker. "His most loyal followers aren't likely to leave. And this flap may even add a few just out of curiosity. As long as we produce the numbers, most of our advertisers will stay. Perhaps we could reprimand him, but if we cancel the *Lincoln Hampton Show* because of this one incident, then we'll be caving in to those who have insisted all along that a program such as this doesn't belong on radio. It's a matter of free speech. After all, he has a huge following. Regardless of how offensive his language or even his views, he has a right to express them."

"It isn't his views that worry me, although some find them to be rather extreme," replied Morrow. "Perhaps his detractors have a point. His comments are not only cynical; many consider them to be rude, inconsiderate, and just downright hateful. Does this really contribute anything to the public's intelligent dialogue about issues? Hampton may have a right to free speech, but is it necessary for him to exercise it on our station?"

"You have a point," conceded Baker. "As station manager, you do have the right to fire Hampton. And the station is licensed to operate in the public interest. But you seem to invoke the free-speech argument when it serves the station's purpose. For example, two years ago when the FCC sent us an inquiry as a result of listener complaints about some of our allegedly offensive record lyrics, you raised the free-speech issue then. If we really believe in free speech, we'll defend Hampton even if some of his material is offensive and even hateful."

"But in the long run, if we gain a reputation as a platform for hatemongers who do nothing more than fuel the fires of social discontent—which is often a prelude to violence—then we may lose some of our more reasonable listeners, and some advertisers to boot," replied Morrow. "Is our keeping Lincoln Hampton on the air really in the public interest?"

"But what do you mean by the public interest?" responded an unpersuaded Baker. "Despite this latest episode, Hampton is popular with many of our listeners. He has struck a responsive chord, no matter how offensive it may be to some. So we're giving the audience what it wants. Isn't that what's the public interest is all about?"

"Good question!" Morrow said to himself as he agonized over his difficult personnel decision: to sever the station's relationship with his controversial talk show host or keep him on the air and publicly defend him against the relentless moral onslaughts. He could, of course, admonish Hampton for his outrageous conduct, but the egotistical electronic gadfly would either ignore the warning or perhaps even move his program to another station once his contract expired with KAAD. From a long-term ethical perspective, Morrow saw no middle course. Either he would defend Hampton's intemperate behavior and remarks or dismiss the controversial personality and risk losing a loyal following and the lucrative advertising revenue that, despite the recent flap, would undoubtedly continue to support the *Lincoln Hampton Show*.

THE CASE STUDY

In recent years, the talk show format—particularly that featuring controversial conservative personalities who feed on the public's apparent disaffection with the liberal agenda—has become increasingly popular. A democratic society, of course, should defend the communication of even the most unpopular ideas. Democratic values and tolerance go hand in hand, but when the expression of ideas is devoid of intellectual substance and is conducted instead through a veneer of hate-filled and repulsive rhetoric, one might then question the reasonable limits of tolerance. Such commentary, some believe, just reinforces and perhaps even legitimizes (in the minds of its adherents) the existing climate of incivility that is often the predicate for various forms of antisocial behavior. Opponents might also note that such shows, despite their professed foundation in the expression of ideas on public issues, are really nothing more than entertainment designed to attract an audience through their appeal to the dark side of humanity. Their impertinence, vulgarity, and mean-spiritedness, in this view, overshadow their rather modest contributions to the democratic process.

Not so, say those who believe that free-speech values are precedent to all others. Even if one ac-

cepts the proposition that the primary purpose of controversial talk shows is to entertain, this should not lessen their rightful claim to the marketplace of ideas. Thus, as far as speech is concerned, there should be no limits on tolerance in a free society. Giving the public what it wants, in this view, is a democratic axiom that is as valid in the artistic world as in politics. And the confirmation of this principle lies in the ratings.

In evaluating the dilemma outlined in this case, consider the opposing arguments advanced by General Manager Phil Morrow and Program Director Darren Baker. And then, assume the role of moral agent Phil Morrow, and, utilizing the SAD Formula for moral reasoning outlined in Chapter 3, make a decision on whether you will keep the *Lincoln Hampton Show* as part of your station's programming repertoire.

▶ **CASE 9-3**
Alcohol Ads in the Campus Newspaper

Kendrick Haas was determined to mount an aggressive campaign against substance abuse on his campus, and alcohol was public enemy number one. As president of San Jacinto State University, Haas was accustomed to the casual and morally permissive atmosphere of college life in southern California. But he was chastened by a rather sobering report from his dean of students that alcohol consumption, particularly binge drinking, had shown a dramatic rise among San Jacinto students over the past three years. While the drinking age in California is twenty-one, college upperclassmen were not the only offenders. It was an open secret that many underage students frequented the local pubs using fake IDs.

Under Haas's tutelage, San Jacinto had evolved from a party school, where the class schedule was viewed as a smorgasbord of appetizing "gut" courses, to an institution with rigorous academic standards and a challenging teaching faculty with impressive academic credentials. But he was convinced that his university's commitment to the students' intellectual development should be accompanied by a corresponding devotion to their social and moral welfare. An unabated rise in alcohol abuse, he feared, would corrode the quality of life at San Jacinto and eventually lead to a noticeable decline in academic performance.

The President's Task Force on Substance Abuse, a twelve-person committee composed of both faculty and students, had devised a rather ambitious strategy to deal with the problem, including a three-hour drug awareness seminar during freshman orientation, the distribution to student mailboxes of a wide variety of information pamphlets on the dangers of drug and alcohol abuse, and an intensive training program for dormitory resident assistants on how to detect and manage problems of alcohol overindulgence among their young charges. Even the clergy of the various campus ministries were enlisted to add a spiritual dimension to the university's substance abuse agenda.

The *Daily Sentinel*, the university's student newspaper, editorially applauded the president's decisive action and provided impressive coverage of the task force's deliberations and recommendations. As the forum for student expression at San Jacinto State, the *Daily Sentinel* was a symbol of journalistic excellence. Its reporters and editorial staff had been recognized both regionally and nationally for their enterprise and were perennial finalists in the prestigious Hearst competition. But the *Daily Sentinel* was more than a platform for student expression at San Jacinto State. It was also a profit center, an economic oasis that stood in stark contrast to the university's academic units that existed rather fragilely on austere budgets and increasingly outmoded equipment and facilities.

But Kendrick Haas had not summoned his director of student media, Cassie Lake, to his office to discuss the paper's auspicious status as a campus cash cow. The president, who was not one to waste time on pleasantries, got right to the point. "As you know, we're already four months into our substance abuse campaign," he began. "And I appreciate the editorial support from the *Sentinel*. But I'm concerned about the ads from the off-campus bars that offer all kinds of inducements for students to overindulge. Most of our students read

the *Sentinel*, and they're exposed to these ads. I would like for you to consider dropping them."

"I understand your concern," responded Lake. "But these bars are among our most lucrative and reliable advertisers."

"I understand that," replied the president. "But we're just asking our student paper to be a team player—to help us in our fight against alcohol abuse here at San Jacinto. The university attorney advises me that I might have the administrative authority to ban such ads outright. But I'm not inclined to do so. As you know, I believe in a hands-off approach in dealing with the *Sentinel*. But let me make my position clear: The *Sentinel* is a part of the university community and has a duty to act responsibly. And running ads that glorify alcohol consumption among college students is not ethically responsible."

Lake was grateful that Haas had not played his trump card, the threat of outright censorship of the controversial ads. She was in no mood for a First Amendment confrontation with the president, but he apparently expected her to be his ethical conduit to the paper's business staff. As the director of student media assembled her staff to discuss the president's plea, she was plagued by her divided loyalties both as a university employee and as the head of a student-run journalistic enterprise. Her sounding board consisted of Business Manager Harvey Miller; Lionel Brown, the student advertising manager; and Kenisha Washington, a bright, energetic, and very productive sales representative for the *Sentinel*.

"The president is pushing us to drop all of our alcohol advertising," said Lake. "That includes most of the bars and other student hangouts close to campus. As you know, he has made substance abuse prevention a priority in his program to improve the quality of student life at San Jacinto. And according to information provided to the Office of Student Affairs by the Health Center, alcohol appears to be the drug of choice at this university. Drinking—particularly binge drinking—is on the rise, and President Haas wants us to be a team player in his initiative."

"But I question his logic in this matter," responded Brown. "Ads can't encourage students to drink. They might be effective in helping our student readers decide *where* to go for their entertainment, but those who are already drinkers are going to do so anyway. An ad isn't going to convince a nondrinker to go to a bar."

"Perhaps," replied Lake, who had always been skeptical of claims that advertising was powerless to do more than persuade consumers to switch from one brand to another. "But the ads we run are pretty alluring. Most of these establishments also sell food, but the ads usually focus on what the advertisers believe will appeal most to college students—the alcohol. Many of them feature happy-hour discounts, free snacks with the purchase of certain kinds of beer, tear-off coupons, and other incentives. The student patrons who take advantage of these inducements may already be drinkers, but by running these promotions we're encouraging overindulgence."

"But one of the purposes of advertising is to encourage consumers to behave in a certain way," responded Washington rather defensively. After all, she had negotiated lucrative contracts with several of the clients under scrutiny and was not about to surrender easily to what she perceived as President Haas's moral crusade. "Since it's legal for college students to drink," she continued, "these establishments have a right to advertise. And we're the medium most targeted to the student population. As long as the ads are in good taste, these merchants have a right to compete in the marketplace."

"You have a point, and I understand your concerns," responded Lake. "But I wonder if we aren't a little hypocritical. Our student editors have run columns pointing out the dangers of binge drinking and endorsing the president's program. If we run these ads, isn't the business side of our paper undermining our editorial position?"

"I don't see this as a real problem," countered Brown. "In the professional world, editors insist on a clear separation between the editorial and commercial sides of the paper. Why should a college paper be any different? If we base our decisions on what our editorial staff has done, then we lose our independence."

"But a college paper *is* different," said Lake. "The *Daily Sentinel* is the only paper many of these students will read. We're a forum for student expression. And don't forget that student fees help to support the *Sentinel*. The president has asked for our help in combatting a problem that contributes to antisocial behavior among some of our students. Isn't this a reasonable request? It boils down to a question of what our responsibility is to the students. After all, they're our audience."

"All of our readers are at least eighteen," responded Washington rather emphatically. "They are mature enough to make their own decisions. If we ban these alcohol ads to protect students from themselves, this strikes me as rather paternalistic. And this should not be the role of a student newspaper at a public university."

"I don't have any philosophical problem, as do Lionel and Kenisha, with complying with the president's request," said Miller, who had listened patiently to the debate. "But I am concerned about the financial impact on the paper. We could survive the elimination of the alcohol advertising, but it would seriously erode our profit base. And this would certainly affect our ability to upgrade the *Sentinel*'s physical plant, including investments in new computer technology and software."

"Perhaps we can make the loss of revenue up somewhere else," said Lake, without any clear conviction that she was right. "We'll just have to be more aggressive. Besides, on any issue like this, we don't want to be viewed as irresponsible. I wonder if we shouldn't give in on this and be a team player. After all, alcohol abuse is a serious problem at San Jacinto."

Kenisha Washington, who believed that commercial independence was as sacred as editorial independence, remained unconvinced. "If we thought that these ads really contributed to the problem of alcohol abuse and decided on our own to drop them, then I might feel differently. But if we cave in to administrative pressure, we'll lose credibility. It still comes down to a question of whether we want to be perceived as a student voice independent of administration control."

During this rather impassioned dialogue, Cassie Lake had exhibited a decidedly proadministration posture. But she was unsure of whether she spoke from sincere conviction or more as a devil's advocate in attempting to stimulate the moral imagination of her staff. On the one hand, she was a university staff member who was expected to be a team player and display a certain amount of diligence in implementing administrative policy decisions. On the other hand, she presided over a student-run enterprise that prided itself (both ethically and legally) in serving as an independent voice of student expression. Since President Haas had promised a hands-off approach, at least her ethical capacities would be unfettered by legal concerns. Nevertheless, the mere fact that the president had summoned her to his office constituted a form of pressure that had to be incorporated into the ethical decision-making process. However, if she appeared to accede too easily to Haas's request, she might jeopardize her own credibility with the *Sentinel*'s staff. Thus, like so many moral agents, she approached her ethical dilemma with divided loyalties.

THE CASE STUDY

Much of the ethical debate about alcohol advertising centers around assignment of responsibility. Opponents of such ads claim that youth-oriented messages glamorizing the social prominence of alcohol promote antisocial behavior, which violates advertisers' and the media's moral duty to society. Their defenders usually emphasize the autonomy of the individual to make rational choices from among the many competing voices in the marketplace.

According to the university's president, drinking is a serious health hazard at San Jacinto State University. His proactive stance to deal with the problem has embraced all facets of student life, and he sees no reason that the student newspaper should not contribute to the success of his campaign. Nevertheless, he has pledged an administrative hands-off approach, instead appealing to the ethical sensibilities of the newspaper's staff.

The participants in the *Sentinel*'s staff meeting have staked out various ethical positions. The student staffers, Lionel Brown and Kenisha Washington, emphasize the autonomy of college students to make their own decisions rationally and deliberately. In their view, the *Daily Sentinel* should not make moral judgments about the acceptability of ads, even though some ads may encourage antisocial behavior by some readers.

The paper's business manager, Harvey Miller, is less concerned with social and individual responsibility than with the economic impact on the *Sentinel*. While the loss of this revenue might not be devastating, the *Sentinel*'s future as a state-of-the-art student newspaper could be jeopardized.

Cassie Lake, the director of student media, appreciates the president's dilemma and believes the *Sentinel* has a responsibility to contribute to the quality of student life at San Jacinto State University. Nevertheless, she is sympathetic to the other points of view and does not want to accede uncritically to the president's request.

What is missing from this discussion is any consideration of a middle ground, an Aristotle's golden mean. The two extremes, of course, are a *laissez-faire* approach, in which moral responsibility is focused on the individual readers rather than the paper, and a *paternalistic* approach, by which the paper screens product ads that might encourage some form of antisocial behavior. Is there a reasonable middle ground in this case, or must the *Sentinel* predicate its policy on alcohol advertising on one of the ethical arguments advanced during the staff meeting?

For the purpose of rendering an ethical judgment on whether the *Daily Sentinel* should continue to accept alcohol ads, assume the role of the director of student media, Cassie Lake. Using the SAD Formula for moral reasoning outlined in Chapter 3, make a decision on this matter.

▶ CASE 9-4
The KKK Demands Access to Cable

In the 1960s, as the Federal Communications Commission slowly tightened its regulatory noose around the cable TV industry, the FCC enacted rules to require cable systems to provide access channels for individuals and groups to express their views. But in 1979, the U.S. Supreme Court struck down these requirements on the ground that the commission had exceeded its authority in formulating such rules.[57] Five years later Congress passed the Federal Cable Act, which allows, but does not require, cities to insist that local cable operators provide public-access channels. If a city does require access as part of the cable franchise, however, neither the city nor the system operator may control the content, with the exception of "indecent" content. The constitutionality of this indecency exception was upheld by a federal appellate court in 1995.

Cloverleaf Cable is a small operator in an industry of media giants. Cloverleaf has constructed systems in several small and medium-sized communities and has acquired a reputation as a solid civic-minded citizen that prides itself on its rich diversity of programming at a rather modest cost. There have been few complaints about the maintenance or quality of service.

Cable TV had come to Pittston fifteen years before, and as part of the franchise renewal for the thirty-six-channel system, Cloverleaf was required to provide a public-access channel for anyone seeking a forum. Pittston, a city of 250,000 with three commercially licensed TV stations, is a community of bountiful cultural expression and white middle-class affluence. But this economic prosperity has not been shared by all citizens, especially in the black neighborhoods, and racial tensions surfaced as the city council began to grapple with demands from black leaders for economic and political parity.

Paul Bankston, the manager of Pittston's Cloverleaf Cable franchise, was pleased with the role that his operation had played in confronting the community's social problems. The system's access channel had served as a frequent forum for those with ideas to express and on more than one occasion had been used to stage debates on matters of public importance. Of course, the channel had also been used for announcements and self-serving promotions, but Bankston was convinced that it had been grassroots democracy in action, a video version of the town meeting.

Bankston had always been a little concerned about the "no editorial control" requirements for the access channel. He wondered, for example, how he would react if someone had insisted on making an inflammatory, hate-filled presentation. However, his fears had not been realized, and he had been content to accommodate all requests for access without the added burden of having to make editorial judgments—until now.

Harlan Franks, a Ku Klux Klan leader from nearby East Point, was well known to Bankston and probably everyone else in Pittston. He had been featured prominently on local newscasts whenever there was a racial disturbance or a Klan rally. But Franks apparently believed that the news coverage of KKK activities and views on racial supremacy was either inadequate or biased and had come to Bankston to demand access to the Pittston cable system. The program proposed by Franks would consist of a movie, in which cross burnings were prominently featured, and a panel discussion consisting of remarks from various Klan supporters.

Bankston told Franks that he would consider the request, but the KKK leader knew a stall when he saw one. He told the cable manager that if his demands were not honored, the Klan would go to court and force the cable system to acquiesce.

Hoping to forestall an outcry, Bankston summoned several black leaders to his office and apprised them of the situation. He did not approve of the program, Bankston told his guests, but he felt that he had no choice under the system's franchise. He did not receive the hoped-for sympathy, however, and the black leaders told him that the program would be inflammatory and could lead to violence.

Bankston recognized the legal tenuousness of his position. The cable system's franchise had placed the public-access channel under a no-censorship mandate. But perhaps a sympathetic judge might recognize the volatility of the situation and decide that to allow access by the Klan in a community where racial tensions lay just beneath the surface might pose a clear and present danger of social unrest.

But beyond his legal concerns, Bankston had to contend with the ethical issues and the clash of competing philosophies. Despite his earlier concerns over the prospects of having to accept objectionable material for presentation, the cable manager had embraced the unrestricted philosophy underlying the public-access channel. He believed that all views should have an equitable claim to respectability, no matter how offensive they might be to some, and that no voice should be silenced. Otherwise, the rationale for having an access channel at all would be undermined.

Of course, it was easy for Bankston to wax philosophical as long as the views expressed, even those involving controversial issues, were in the mainstream of political debate. But he wondered whether an exception should not be made for the Klan's demand for access. Its views on racial supremacy were well known, and the program proposed by Franks would be inflammatory and might even lead to violence. Of course, that was a possibility with many contentious issues, including abortion, and Bankston wondered whether a denial of access to the KKK could be justified as a unique situation or whether other demands for censorship would be forthcoming in the wake of this retreat.

As Bankston pondered his dilemma, he wondered whether there were not some benefit to providing access to such groups as the KKK, because the fallacies of their arguments could be exposed in the court of public opinion. But some segments of society did not share this libertarian view, and, after all, Cloverleaf Cable considered itself to be a servant of community interests.

THE CASE STUDY

This scenario is representative of a problem that has emerged in several communities around the country. In such diverse cities as New York, San Francisco, Chicago, Kansas City (Missouri), and Altamonte Springs (Florida), the Ku Klux Klan has sought access on local cable systems, and in some cases it has gone to court to enforce its "right of access."[58] The legal aspects of this issue will be worked out through the courts, but the ethical concerns remain.

Is it possible to fulfill the purpose of public access to cable TV and yet deny entry for some views? Although the ideas on white supremacy promoted by the Klan do not reflect those of mainstream America, the organization does represent a small segment of the community. On the other hand, the airing of a program such as the one proposed in this scenario is likely to cause further racial unrest, and the harm to society would be real.

For the purpose of dealing with the demands for channel access by the KKK, assume the role of the cable manager, Bankston, and, using the model for moral reasoning, make a decision on this matter.

This case requires a great deal of sensitivity. You should not be oblivious to your legal obligations under the cable franchise, but your decision should not rest solely on this foundation. There may be some middle ground for accommodation here, and this avenue should also be explored.

▶ CASE 9-5
The Family-Sensitive Newscast

Channel 5's early evening newscast had occupied the number one position for almost two years, but Alex Kole was unhappy. As news director of the CBS affiliate in South Hampshire, Kole had presided over the station's introduction and cultivation of a highly successful tabloid format into this cosmopolitan market of 750,000. As something of a journalistic purist, he was uncomfortable with such blatant intrusions of entertainment values into TV news. Until two years ago Channel 5's 6 P.M. newscast, which one critic described as "professionally produced but unimaginative in content," was a perennial distant number two to its ABC competitor in a four-station market. But General Manager Michael Hodges, with a cautious eye on the bottom line, had dismissed its news consultants of long standing and had hired a more aggressive firm with impressive successes in comparable markets to invigorate Channel 5's journalistic enterprise. Among their numerous recommendations, the consultants had suggested an early evening news program with "high energy" and "high impact." More specifically, they had recommended a tabloid format to counter the reasonably popular but vulnerable "friendly news" design featured on Channel 5's competitive nemesis.

Kole had dutifully implemented the tabloid newscast, which had immediately captured the imagination of South Hampshire's viewing public and had catapulted Channel 5 into the lead. While the station continued to cover such routine news items as city commission meetings and the controversy over legalized gambling, the ratings sweeps were represented by such seductive features as "Gridiron Studs," "Kids Who Kill," and "Teenage Hookers." But the most prominent visuals, both inside and outside the quarterly ratings periods, were the graphic depictions of violence, mayhem, and grieving relatives. While some segments of the community complained about the explicit video, the numbers spoke for themselves.

Kole was not entirely comfortable with the new format, but even he was awed by his station's sudden resurgence from ratings obscurity. From the outset the print critics, who always seemed to delight in trashing their TV colleagues for the prostitution of journalistic values, were unmerciful in their denunciation of Channel 5's controversial initiative. "If this were a military operation," complained Knox Haygood, the TV critic for the *South Hampshire Sentinel*, "the body count would be impressive."

However, the station had weathered such censure, and the ratings books had confirmed the efficacy of Kole's strategic move. But the news director had never felt at home in the fast-paced and ethically ambiguous world of tabloid journalism. He worried that his station was gradually becoming disconnected from the community it served and that his news department would be perceived as lacking a social conscience. Kole shared his concerns with the general manager. Although Hodges was pleased with the ratings success of the tabloid format and as a nonjournalist appeared to have fewer moral qualms than his news director, he was also proactive when it came to the station's role as corporate citizen. He trusted Kole's instincts and immediately hired a public relations firm to set up a series of meetings with community leaders and to conduct focus groups and a general random sample survey of audience attitudes toward the station's news coverage.

The results were sobering. An overwhelming majority of respondents said they thought the station's coverage of crime and violence was excessive and just helped reinforce the fear also prevalent within the South Hampshire community. They wanted more diversity in the news coverage, with a focus on long-term problems and solutions. To Kole, this public dialogue had produced a clarion call for greater journalistic responsibility; to Hodges, it also represented a significant dent in the bottom line. Community-based investigative reporting, he knew, would require more resources, and there was no way, despite the results of the

surveys, to guarantee that they would hold the ratings lead. Nevertheless, Hodges asked his news director to talk with his staff and make a recommendation concerning the future of tabloid journalism, particularly the high-profile coverage of crime and violence, at Channel 5.

Kole's advisers consisted of Assistant News Director Henrietta Broomfield; Debbie Waldheim, producer of the highly rated 6 o'clock tabloid news program; and Chief Photographer Mike Sayers. Sayers had been invited to join the discussion because of the prominent role that graphic video footage played in the early evening newscast.

"I'm of the old school," Waldheim responded bluntly to Kole's expression of concern about Channel 5's journalistic bearing. "If it ain't broke, don't fix it! We're number one in the market—and have been for two years. That shows we're giving our audience what they want."

"I'm not so sure," said Kole. "It's true our ratings have soared since we adopted the tabloid format. But our focus groups and other meetings with a cross-section of our community indicate that viewers are tired of so much violence on TV, including the 6 o'clock news. There's a lot of fear out there, and there's a perception that we may be part of the problem."

"But that's a typical reaction when journalists are just doing their jobs," asserted Sayers rather defensively. "The public always wants to kill the messenger. We're just reflecting what's going on in our community. TV is a visual medium. Our pictures, as graphic as they are, are part of the story. Our job is to report. If we filter out all the offensive or violent video, then we could be compromising factual accuracy. Pictures—even the most offensive ones—often provide context. And isn't that the role of the journalist?"

Henrietta Broomfield, who had expressed reservations about the tabloid format at the time of its highly publicized introduction, was finally beginning to feel vindicated by her own station's audience surveys. "I share Alex's concern," she responded in her typically understated manner. "We are number one, and it's risky to set a new course when you're on top. In fact, most news directors would probably say we're crazy. But we have to examine the truth behind our numbers. If you look at our performance over the past year, there are a lot of peaks and valleys. When we feature a hot and sensational topic, our ratings soar. But for newscasts that don't have a heavily promoted sexy topic, there has actually been a decline in the ratings. To continue the momentum, each time we have become even more outrageous."

But Waldheim, who presided over the top-rated newscast in the South Hampshire market, was undeterred. "We decided two years ago to adopt the tabloid format because of its popularity. The track record is sound. Even our network's prime-time magazine shows resemble the tabloids. If we abandon our present format, the critics will applaud our sense of social responsibility, but many of our viewers will leave."

"I'm not so sure," responded Kole. "I'm not proposing that we abandon all crime coverage and provide nothing more than 'happy news.' We'll continue to cover the important stories—violent crime included—but we'll tone down the graphic depictions of actual violent acts, blood, and bodies. If we do a good job of promotion, our viewers will appreciate the fact that Channel 5 has a social conscience—that we're actually involved in trying to dispel the public's fear about the world they live in."

"I don't think we'll lose viewers if we do a good job journalistically," agreed Broomfield. "Our marketing surveys, focus groups, and various meetings within the community have convinced me that the public is ready for a change."

"But people often say one thing in surveys and behave differently in their viewing habits," responded Sayers, still confident that the ratings data were the more accurate barometer of the public mood. "Besides, if viewer sensitivity is more important than just covering the news as it happens—warts and all—then we should consider sanitizing our 10 o'clock news. And what about the network lead-in to the 6 o'clock newscast? It sometimes contains graphic violence, but we have no control over it. I just don't think our role should be to try to calm the public's fear. This smacks too much of paternalism."

"You have a point," conceded Kole. "We can't control what the network does. But I selected the 6 P.M. newscast because that's when there are a lot of children in the audience. It's the family dinner hour. At least it's a start in the right direction."

"But aren't you being a little disingenuous?" replied Waldheim. "On the one hand, you say this is the socially responsible thing to do. But you're basing your arguments on our own surveys that supposedly indicate our viewers are tired of the nightly televised violence and mayhem. So you're suggesting that we *give the people what they want*. But how does that differ from the point I made earlier to justify the tabloid format?"

As Kole ended the meeting in preparation for his meeting with the general manager, he had to concede Waldheim's last point. Besides, the tabloid format was popular and it was making money. A change in direction defied conventional wisdom. It was certainly financially risky. But as he pondered his dilemma, he also worried that a daily diet of sex, violence, and mayhem trivialized the more serious intelligence of the day and in the long run would erode Channel 5's reputation as a credible news organization. Once again, commercial values appeared to be on a collision course with journalistic values unless, of course, Kole could convince the general manager that responsible journalism, in the long run, is also good business.

THE CASE STUDY

The values and ethical issues reflected in this scenario have been debated in several newsrooms across the country. Some stations have made deliberate moves to remove graphic depictions of violence from their newscasts. Of course, for a highly rated news program, this can be a risky move.

Producer Debbie Waldheim and Chief Photographer Mike Sayers appear to define journalistic values in terms of giving the people what they want—as documented in the ratings, of course. And this might be a defensible position, ethically speaking, if we define TV news as a "product" to be marketed in such a way as to produce maximum audience appeal. And if Waldheim and Sayers appeal to industry "standards," then it would be hard to argue with the tabloid format as a viable news vehicle.

On the other hand, Kole is uncomfortable with tabloid journalism, particularly the graphic and offensive video. He believes that responsibility lies in truly reflecting and reporting on community problems (of which crime and violence are only a small part), even if such coverage lacks pizazz and "high energy." But is Waldheim correct? Is Kole appealing to the "give the public what it wants" rationale (the same one used in defense of the tabloid format) as reflected in the station's own research to justify a change in format? Or, to put it another way, would Kole feel as strongly about dispensing with the sensational coverage of tabloid news if the surveys had revealed the public's approval of such a journalistic genre?

For the purpose of resolving this dilemma and making a recommendation to General Manager Mike Hodges, assume the role of News Director Alex Kole, and, using the SAD Formula for moral reasoning outlined in Chapter 3, render a judgment on this matter. Keep in mind that if you should recommend a change of format, you should include a rationale as to why you believe such a change will be to the station's long-term benefit. In constructing your response, you might keep a couple of questions in mind: Does this case really just involve a business decision, or are there truly serious ethical implications? Can the two really be separated?

▶ ### CASE 9-6
Heavy-Metal Music and Suicide

George DeSilva always looked forward to the annual convention of the National Association of Broadcasters. It was an opportunity for him to escape from the relentless pressures of managing a top-rated progressive rock radio station in a medium-sized market and share ideas with his broadcast peers. The NAB spared no expense in producing its annual extravaganza, and the sessions generally featured experts in such fields as management, programming, station brokerage, engineering, news, and communications law. DeSilva enjoyed these presentations and usually left the convention with some fresh ideas and a renewal of managerial spirit.

This year was no exception. DeSilva was impressed, once again, by the overall quality of the panel presentations during his week-long stay in Las Vegas. He enjoyed the sessions on "New Radio Computer Software and Digital Technology" and "Trends in Broadcast Regulation." But it was the panel on "Broadcast Music and Licensee Responsibility" that really caught his attention and also left him somewhat chastened.

Although there was some discussion of drug lyrics, most of the time was devoted to the effects of heavy-metal music on teenagers, particularly songs that deal with the occult, suicide, and Satanism in their lyrics. Two cases were cited as causes of concern. In 1988 a fourteen-year-old New Jersey youth murdered his mother and then shot himself, allegedly after he had spent several weeks studying the occult and listening to heavy-metal music. In another case, the families of two teenagers filed a lawsuit against Judas Priest, CBS Records, and others, contending that listening to the band's suggestive lyrics and hypnotic rhythms and beat had caused two teenagers to enter into a suicide pact. One of the youths actually committed suicide, and his friend made an attempt.

The panel consisted of four members: a child psychologist, a representative from a major record company, a program director from a progressive radio station in Chicago, and the general counsel of the Federal Communications Commission. The discussion was lively. The psychologist contend that it was doubtful whether a particular style of music could control anyone's behavior, even an impressionable youth's. But as a reflection of a youth culture in crisis, the music might trigger those already contemplating suicide. The representative from the record manufacturer agreed but argued that troubled juveniles derived their ideas from many sources and that the music industry should not bear the brunt of the blame. If we ban Judas Priest or any other group from the airwaves, she asked, where will this censorship end? It would be a sterile culture indeed if all offensive or questionable content were deleted just because of the possibility that some member of the audience might engage in some form of antisocial behavior. The program director, however, noted that heavy-metal music was unique because of its association with pentagrams and other satanic symbols. Adolescents feel a kinship with music because it is a reflection of their concerns and insecurities, he said. It creates a bond with others of their own age, he added, and the impact of negative symbols and lyrics in music can be magnified through group reinforcement. The fourth member of the panel, the FCC's general counsel, was concerned about the alleged connection of heavy-metal lyrics and satanic symbolism to the two suicide cases discussed. However, he maintained that the commission's general policies on licensee responsibility for program supervision were adequate and that no further regulatory action was contemplated. Broadcasters should be aware of the content of the albums on their playlist and should withdraw any selections they feel are detrimental to the public interest.

DeSilva's own station's playlist included some heavy-metal albums, some of which included the kinds of lyrics referred to during the NAB panel discussion. DeSilva now wondered about his own moral responsibility in continuing to air such musical selections. The number of suicides with any reported connection to the heavy-metal culture was small. No suicides in the Greenville area, which boasted a large and enthusiastic teenage radio audience, had been connected to heavy metal. There is always a danger, DeSilva knew, in overreacting to a problem that receives more publicity and press than it deserves.

But it was also difficult to find anything really positive about the suggestive lyrics, unless one viewed them merely as an outlet for normal adolescent frustrations. Could these heavy-metal words and rhythms perhaps have a cathartic effect that had been overlooked by concerned adults?

DeSilva wondered whether, as station manager, he should take any action in this situation. He had always prided himself on being a responsible entertainer for his youthful audience, one who was capable of capturing their musical soul without corrupting it. Some of the heavy-metal groups were among their favorites. Would the removal of the selections with questionable lyrics be an act of moral courage or one of needless paternalism?

THE CASE STUDY

Teenage suicides have received much media attention in recent years. Both news organizations

and movie directors have explored the tragic causes of teen suicide. Some researchers believe that there is a link between media coverage of suicide and an increase in the number of juveniles who take their own lives;[59] others disavow any statistical link.[60]

In any case, producers of material directed at juvenile audiences are treading a rocky ethical path because of the fragile nature and anxieties of the adolescent experience. Much of the news coverage and many of the fictional portrayals of teenage suicide also include information on how to seek help or at least how to cope until help arrives. But the suggestive lyrics of some heavy-metal songs, according to critics, are a glorification of the occult and suicidal rituals.

Because most of this music is directed at a juvenile audience, is there a moral responsibility on the part of media gatekeepers, such as station managers and program directors, to ban such music? Or do teenagers, as part of a consuming public capable of making rational choices, have a right to purchase and listen to the entertainment of their choice? And what responsibility do parents have in this ethical dilemma?

For the purpose of confronting the concerns of DeSilva, assume his role and, using the model for moral reasoning, make a decision on how you will deal with the problem of suggestive heavy-metal lyrics on your station.

▶ CASE 9-7
Drug Scenes on Prime-Time Television

Mackie Walters did not like the label "censor," but as the head of his network's much-maligned divisions of standards and practices, he was responsible for scanning the program schedule for affronts to taste and decency. Walters was the ultimate gatekeeper for the network's entertainment division, a position that required him to walk a thin moral line. He was often vilified both by Hollywood producers, who accused him of prudery, and the religious right, which was convinced that his network was in league with the devil to capture the soul of the nation's TV viewers. The network had long-standing guidelines on programming and commercial acceptability, but at times even Walters worried that the decisions made by his division were somewhat arbitrary. For example, just a couple of years before he had insisted that a producer delete the word *condom* from a prime-time situation comedy while the weekday afternoon soap operas rolled right along with their passionate love scenes and graphic portrayals of bedroom encounters.[61]

Television emerged from its adolescent innocence in the 1960s and for the next decade entered a period of liberation during which society's moral revolution had entered TV entertainment with a vengeance. But now the pressure was again on the networks to ensure that their programming conveyed the right message. This was easier said than done, Walters believed, because of the symbolism and nuances inherent in any dramatic presentation. The goal when dealing with controversial issues was to make scenes believable without glamorizing antisocial behavior. And this was the dilemma that confronted Walters as he previewed an upcoming episode of *Family Strife*.

Family Strife had premiered during the network's fall season and within four months had become a ratings leader in its 9-to-10 P.M. time slot. The program revolved around two professionals, one a lawyer and the other a doctor, who were in their second marriage, each having contributed two children to the new relationship. *Family Strife* was a serious-comic adventure into the agonies of raising four children in today's complex urban environment.

In the episode under review, the two eldest children, seventeen-year-old Michael and sixteen-year-old Richie, were invited to a party at a classmate's house, at which drugs were used. The party was held in a middle-class neighborhood, and most of the guests were rather attractive teenagers who nonchalantly retired to the bedrooms to smoke pot or crack cocaine. Richie, who was depicted in the series as the paragon of juvenile responsibility, soon left the party, clearly distraught by the turn of events, but Michael stayed behind. As the show unfolded, Michael eventually resisted the peer pressure to consume drugs, although he did

not condemn his classmates. He later confided to his parents that he had been humiliated by the experience.

Walters appreciated the antidrug message in this episode. Sugar-coating controversial content with an entertainment format was sometimes more effective than preaching at teenagers through information programs and public-service announcements. And in this show, both Michael and Richie made the socially correct choice in declining the opportunity to consume drugs. The setting was realistic, one with which most teenagers could identify, and the subject matter was certainly relevant for both parents and their children.

But Walters was also concerned that the antidrug message had been lost in the glamorous setting of the party. The party was staged in an affluent middle-class neighborhood, and the participants were all teenagers from respectable families. When Michael finally left, the party was still in full swing, and the stoned teenagers appeared to be having fun. This was hardly the image that he felt should be portrayed to young people, but Walters had to admit that the scenes were realistic.

The humiliation over not going along with their peers that Michael and Richie experienced was an emotion with which most teenagers could identify, but this scene might, in Walters's opinion, serve to reinforce the security of conformity rather than the necessity for saying no. At no time during the party scene did either of the major characters give a lecture to his contemporaries about the dangers of drugs. Under the circumstances, that might have been unrealistic, but at least the message would have been loud and clear. On the other hand, teenagers usually reject heavy-handed preaching, and antidrug messages wrapped in the veneer of entertainment have to be handled with care and subtlety. But Walters was also aware that children imitate the behavior of others and wondered whether the graphic drug scenes should be edited out.

As the primary programming gatekeeper for the network, Walters was aware of his moral responsibility to the network's audience, particularly children. He believed that programs such as this episode of *Family Strife* could be a powerful tool in promoting positive values. But how should it be done? If he felt that the antidrug message might be overshadowed by the more glamorous aspects of the program, he could just delete the episode from the network's schedule. At the other end of the spectrum, he could insist on an unmistakable antidrug message, but this demand would collide with the producer's insistence on creative control, a complaint that in this instance might be justified. Walters wondered, however, whether there were a way to maintain the credibility of the dramatic plot while toning down the more graphic scenes of the drug party. Perhaps not, because above all it was imperative to relate to the teenage audience while subtlety inculcating it with society's view of life.

THE CASE STUDY

In the early days of television, a network censor's time was devoted primarily to guarding against sexual innuendo and certain pejorative references that by today's standards would be tame. But now few topics are beyond the pale of network entertainment. Such diverse and controversial issues as abortions, AIDS, homosexuality, drugs, incest, and child abuse have been explored in prime-time programming.

Network censors occupy a rather uncomfortable moral position, because they must try to be all things to all people. With approximately two hundred affiliates to serve, they must be sensitive to a wide range of tastes and social mores. Thus, by their very nature these programming gatekeepers are fairly conservative and sensitive to charges that the media, and TV in particular, have played a significant role in undermining the moral values of today's youth.

But television audiences demand reality (or at least believability), which sometimes necessitates graphic portrayals of antisocial behavior. Some believe that this shock therapy approach is an effective tool in sending a positive message. Others feel that such graphic scenes are unnecessary and might overshadow the message. It is better to sacrifice some realism, they believe, for the sake of presenting heroic characters who always know right from wrong and state their case in clear terms. But adolescents are finicky TV viewers, and there is some question whether they will respond to characters who come across as unrealistic models of

moral virtue. Dealing with the drug issue is particularly difficult because it requires the Hollywood producer to balance the realities of the youthful drug culture with the demands of good entertainment.

How would you, as a network programming executive, approach this dilemma? Put yourself in the shoes of Walters, and, using the model for moral reasoning, make a decision on this episode of *Family Strife*. Your options appear to be three: (1) reject the program on its face as too controversial, (2) accept this episode uncut, or (3) require that some changes be made by the producer before inserting it into the network's schedule.

▶ ### CASE 9-8
Television and Sports Violence

It had been a tense day for Byron Harris, producer for that Sunday's nationally televised National Football Conference matchup. The game, between the Chicago Bears and the Detroit Lions, had lasted three hours and forty-five minutes instead of the usual airtime allotment of three hours. There had never been any love lost between these two teams, but this game had been particularly brutal. On one occasion, a defensive player for the Bears had taken what the Lions believed to be a "cheap shot," which had resulted in a bench-clearing brawl. Not content with the action on the field, a couple of fans had aimed some bottles at the Bears' coach and players as the team left the field at halftime. And all of the actors, players and fans alike, had been immortalized on national TV.

Harris had ten years of experience in producing and directing sports events, six of it in local markets before joining the network four years before, and he had become concerned with the increasing level of violence in professional sports. He was accustomed to the extracurricular activity in hockey, but fights and brawls had also become commonplace in football, basketball, and even the civilized sport of baseball. Harris realized that such events might just be a reflection of the increased violence in society. But he was concerned about the role that television played in such dramatic affronts to the rule of law on the playing field.

As he reviewed the day's coverage with his production staff, Harris realized that his options were limited in covering the on-field confrontations. They were a part of the game and could not be ignored. Using alternate shots would just leave the TV audience bewildered. Fan violence was another matter. The bottle-throwing incident had occurred as the cameras were following the Bears to the locker room, and there had been no way of anticipating this act of fan aggression. But there had been occasions in other games, such as fans streaking across the field to gain attention, when the cameras could have shied away from such behavior.

Harris realized that football was a contact sport that could sometimes become violent. But he was concerned that the technology of his industry had magnified the role of violence within the sport. The never-ending replays often focused on the most dramatic and furious contact, and even brawls on the field were repeated. The slow-motion replay was, when used correctly, a marvelous addition to the sports director's repertoire, but Harris feared that it often drew the viewer's attention to the more violent aspects of televised professional sports. And the color commentators, usually former players themselves, did not help matters when they dismissed intentional acts of aggression in football as just part of a contact sport or a bean ball in baseball as a warning to the hitter. Such comments served to legitimize sports violence.

As a television producer, Harris was unsure how to confront this dilemma. His job was to record the action of the game and, above all, to entertain the fans. In a highly competitive and costly environment, the network expected him to produce an interesting, dramatic contest that would attract a large audience. Violence, superstars, and slow-motion replays were now an inevitable part of the professional sports landscape, and it was his job to convert this volatile mixture into high video drama for the sports faithful. Why should he feel guilty about merely documenting a social phenomenon over which he had little control?

On the other hand, Harris was concerned that TV did have a hand in the level of sports violence because of fan expectations. The emphasis on winning encouraged an intimidating style of play, and these paid gladiators were only too willing to accommodate the millions of admiring fans watching the combat on television. The selection of replays for their dramatic effect, including those showing fights and particularly violent action, perhaps focused needless attention on the more troublesome aspects of the contest. He also wondered whether the on-field activities were responsible for a heightened level of violence in the stands, because the unruly fans might have been seeking media attention for themselves.

During the postgame review of the Bears-Lions coverage, Harris vented his anxieties to his production staff, which had a cathartic effect. But he wondered whether his concerns were justified and, if so, whether he could make any changes in coverage that would play down the more violent aspects of televised sports coverage while maintaining a high level of entertainment and drama for the fans.

THE CASE STUDY

The increase in sports violence, even among fans, is apparent, but what is not so clear is the role that TV plays in this phenomenon. There are undoubtedly a number of reasons for this increase in violence, but as Arthur Miller, a Harvard law professor and occasional TV commentator, has observed, television should assume part of the blame:

> An influence often cited is the intense media coverage, particularly by television, which tends to focus on the more violent aspects of the game, either because these elements are more photogenic or because they will appeal to the largest audience. Often it's the crushing tackle or the bone-rattling fore check that gets emphasized by the television commentators and the replay technology, rather than the perfectly run pass pattern or the superb display of skating. By giving so much attention to what is only one part of the game, the media impose a subtle pressure on players, coaches, and owners to live up to the violent image of their sport.[62]

Thus, from the standpoint of moral responsibility, the following questions might be posed: Is television really an objective bystander, or is the medium so intrusive and omnipresent that the athletes feel they must live up to a certain level of expected intimidation? Does the attention paid to the more aggressive aspects of sports through both live coverage and instant replays, particularly in contact sports like football, help legitimize violence at the expense of the finer points of the game? What lessons are being communicated to youthful sports fans, many of whom view professional athletes as role models? And what responsibility do the media, particularly TV, have in this process?

The answers to questions such as these are sometimes elusive because of the role that televised sports play within our society. In many respects they are a hybrid of reality and fantasy, spectacular events staged to entertain a mass audience. If sports violence is merely a reflection of society's violent nature, one could argue that television is no more than a chronicler of this phenomenon. On the other hand, all sports have rules, and to the extent that the coverage focuses on violent conduct that exceeds the bounds of propriety, TV legitimizes this kind of behavior for the audience.

For the purpose of confronting the issues posed by this scenario, assume the role of Harris, and, using the SAD Formula, formulate a recommendation on how to deal with the problem of televised sports violence. You should begin by deciding, first, whether TV really does have some moral responsibility in this matter and whether anything can realistically be done. If so, what changes would you recommend that would accomplish your objectives without robbing the events of their entertainment value?

▼

Notes

1. See Juliet Dee, "Subliminal Lyrics in Heavy Metal Music: More Litigation, Anyone?" *Communications and the Law*, 16, September 1994, p. 5.

2. "Violence in Theaters Has Filmmaker on Defensive," (Baton Rouge) *Morning Advocate*, March 12, 1991, p. 3A.

3. "Cartoon Culprits," *Newsweek*, October 18, 1993, p. 10.

4. "Slaying of Four in Family Blamed on 'Gangsta' Rap," (Baton Rouge) *Advocate*, October 27, 1994, p. 5B.

5. James Q. Wilson and Richard J. Herrnstein, *Crime and Human Nature* (New York: Simon & Schuster, 1985), p. 337.

6. *Ibid.*, citing D. P. Phillips, "The Influence of Suggestion on Suicide: Substantive and Theoretical Implications of the Werther Effect," *American Sociological Review*, 39, 1974, pp. 340–354.

7. "The Copycat Suicides," *Newsweek*, March 23, 1987, p.

28. Social scientists generally agree that television can contribute to "modeling," or imitative behavior. What is missing in this research, however, is an adequate explanation of the conditions under which viewers will accept a TV role model's behavior as a guide to their own actions. See Shearon A. Lowery and Melvin L. De Fleur, *Milestones in Mass Communication Research*, 2d ed. (White Plains, NY: Longman, 1988), pp. 304–305.

8. See Phillips, "Influence of Suggestion on Suicide"; D. P. Phillips, "Motor Vehicle Fatalities Increase Just after Publicized Suicide Stories," *Science*, 196, 1977, pp. 1464–1465; "TV Coverage Linked to Teen Suicides," *Science News*, September 20, 1986, pp. 182–183; Elizabeth B. Ziesenis, "Suicide Coverage in Newspapers: An Ethical Consideration," *Journal of Mass Media Ethics*, 6, No. 4, 1991, pp. 234–244.

9. "Media Blamed in Spread of Pepsi Scare," (Baton Rouge) *Advocate*, June 19, 1993, p. 7C.

10. Ziesenis, "Suicide Coverage in Newspapers," pp. 241–242.

11. For a discussion of how the station changed the focus of its newscast, see John Lansing, "The News Is the News, Right? Wrong! 'Family Sensitive' Shows Another Way," *Poynter Report*, Fall 1994, pp. 6–7.

12. Bob Simmons, "Violence in the Air," *Columbia Journalism Review*, July/August 1994, p. 12.

13. Richard Cunningham, "No More," *Quill*, July/August 1995, p. 13.

14. Jay Black and Bob Steele, "Beyond Waco: Reflections and Guidelines," *Journal of Mass Media Ethics*, Vol. 8, No. 4, 1993, pp. 239–245.

15. Quoted in Joe Holley, "The Waco Watch," *Columbia Journalism Review*, May/June 1993, p. 53.

16. *Ibid.*, p. 52.

17. Quoted in *ibid.*

18. *Ibid.*

19. *Ibid.*, p. 38.

20. For a more complete list and discussion of such guidelines, see Black and Steele, "Beyond Waco," pp. 244–245.

21. See Conrad C. Fink, *Media Ethics: In the Newsroom and Beyond* (New York: McGraw-Hill, 1988), p. 212.

22. Ed Bishop, "J-School Paper Criticized for Breach of Ethics, Cooperating with Police," *St. Louis Journalism Review*, December 1991–January 1992, pp. 1, 9.

23. *Ibid.*

24. Richard P. Cunningham, "Police Go Fishing, but Student Press Not Biting," *Quill*, January/February 1995, p. 12. See also Richard P. Cunningham, "Southern Illinois Dismisses Jaehnig, Citing Differences," *Quill*, March 1995, p. 12.

25. Deni Elliott, "Mass Media Ethics," in Alan Wells (ed.), *Mass Media and Society* (Boston: Heath, 1987), pp. 66–67.

26. E.g., see *Olivia N. v. NBC; Zamora v. Columbia Broad-*

casting System et al., 480 F. Supp. 199 (S.D. Fla., 1979); *DeFilippo v. National Broadcasting Co. et al.*, 446 A.2d 1036 (Rhode Island, 1982); *Herceg v. Hustler*, 13 Med.L.Rptr. 2345 (1987). The one notable exception in which a media defendant was held negligent is *Weirum v. RKO General, Inc.*, 539 P.2d 36 (1975). In this case a radio station was held liable for having broadcast a promotional contest that led to a motorist's death.

27. John Leland, "Just Say Maybe," *Newsweek*, November 1, 1993, p. 52.

28. *Ibid.*

29. Michael Medved, *Hollywood vs. America: Popular Culture and the War on Traditional Values* (New York: HarperCollins, 1992), p. 184.

30. "When Money Talks, Violence Walks," *Newsweek*, March 29, 1993, p. 8.

31. "Hollywood: Right Face," *U.S. News & World Report*, May 15, 1995, pp. 66–72.

32. "When Money Talks, Violence Walks."

33. Quoted in John Leo, "Stonewalling Is Not an Option," *U.S. News & World Report*, June 19, 1995, p. 19.

34. "Song Lyric Ratings Are Backed by A.M.A.," *New York Times*, June 23, 1995, p. A10. See also "Shame Isn't Fleeting," *U.S. News & World Report*, June 19, 1995, p. 57.

35. E.g., see "Networks under the Gun," *Newsweek*, July 12, 1993, pp. 64–66.

36. Neil Hickey, "New Violence Survey Released," *TV Guide*, August 13, 1994, p. 37.

37. "Washington Watch," *Broadcasting & Cable*, March 20, 1995, p. 55.

38. "Cable Programming Tackles TV Violence," *Broadcasting & Cable*, December 19, 1994, p. 50.

39. See U.S. Department of Health and Human Services, *Television and Human Behavior: Ten Years of Scientific Progress and Implications for the Future* (Washington, D.C.: U.S. Government Printing Office, 1982); J. L. Singer and D. G. Singer, *Television, Imagination and Aggression: A Study of Preschoolers' Play* (Hillsdale, NJ: Erlbaum, 1980); L. D. Eron and L. R. Huesmann, "Adolescent Aggression and Television," *Annals of the New York Academy of Sciences*, 1980, pp. 319–331. However, some studies involving other media have not found such increases in aggression resulting from violent content. See Alexis S. Tan and Kermit Joseph Scruggs, "Does Exposure to Comic Book Violence Lead to Aggression in Children?" *Journalism Quarterly*, 57, Winter 1980, pp. 579–583.

40. One study found an increase in the number of homicides after stories about prizefights, in which violence is rewarded, and a decrease in homicides after stories about murder trials and executions, in which violence is punished. See David P. Phillips and John E. Hensley, "When Violence Is Rewarded or Punished: The Im-

pact of Mass Media Stories on Homicide," *Journal of Communication*, Summer 1984, 34, pp. 101–116.

41. Hickey, "New Violence Survey Released," p. 39.

42. "Do Gang Ads Deserve a Rap?" *Newsweek*, October 21, 1991, p. 55.

43. *Ibid.*

44. See Donna Petrozzello, "Talk Show Hosts Dispute Clinton's Criticism," *Broadcasting & Cable*, May 1, 1995, pp. 6–7.

45. David Stout, "Broadcast Suspensions Raise Free-Speech Issues," *New York Times*, April 30, 1995, p. 18.

46. See Brian Simmons, "Hate Radio: The Outer Limits of Tasteful Broadcasting," in Philip Patterson and Lee Wilkins (eds.), *Media Ethics: Issues and Answers*, 2d ed. (Dubuque, IA: WCB Brown & Benchmark, 1994), pp. 239–241.

47. For a more exhaustive definition and discussion of hate speech, see Richard Alan Nelson, *A Chronology and Glossary of Propaganda in the United States* (Westport, CT: Greenwood, 1995).

48. Stout, "Broadcast Suspensions Raise Free-Speech Issues."

49. Richard Reeves, "We're Talking Ourselves to Death," (Baton Rouge) *Advocate*, May 2, 1995, p. 6B.

50. Mark D. Harmon, "Hate Groups and Cable Public Access," *Journal of Mass Media Ethics*, Vol. 6, No. 3, pp. 149–150. For a brief discussion of the use of cable by extremist groups, see "Extremist Groups Spread Message via Cable Access," *Broadcasting & Cable*, May 1, 1995, p. 8.

51. *Ibid.*, pp. 148–149.

52. "Hate, Murder and Mayhem on the Net," *U.S. News & World Report*," May 22, 1995, p. 62.

53. Janice Kaplan, "Are Talk Shows Out of Control?," *TV Guide*, April 1, 1996, p. 10.

54. *Ibid.*, p. 12.

55. *Ibid.*

56. Sharon Cohen, "Radio Stunts, Reports Push Medium to Edge," (Baton Rouge) *Advocate*, April 16, 1994, p. 13A.

57. *FCC v. Midwest Video Corp.*, 440 U.S. 689 (1979).

58. "Klan Sues to Get Public Channel Access," *News Media and the Law*, 13, no. 1, Winter 1989, pp. 21–22.

59. See "TV Coverage Linked to Teen Suicides," *Science News*, September 20, 1986, pp. 182–183; "The Copycat Suicides," *Newsweek*, March 23, 1987, pp. 28–29.

60. *Ibid.*

61. For a discussion of the difficulties confronting prime-time shows in achieving the delicate balance between entertainment and sending the right message, see Joanmarie Kalter, "Drugs on TV," *TV Guide*, April 1–7, 1989, pp. 14–16.

62. Arthur R. Miller, *Miller's Court* (Boston: Houghton Mifflin, 1982), pp. 109–110.

Morally Offensive Content: Freedom and Responsibility

SOCIETY'S SURVEILLANCE OF OFFENSIVE MATERIAL

When ten-year-old Anders Urmacher, a student at the Dalton School in New York City, received a mysterious E-mail file from a stranger on his computer, he downloaded it and then called his mother. When Linda Mann-Urmacher opened the mysterious file, the screen filled with ten small pictures depicting couples engaged in various acts of sodomy, heterosexual intercourse, and lesbian sex. A shocked Mann-Urmacher said, "I was not aware that this stuff was on-line. Children should not be subjected to these images."[1]

In 1986, papers across the country engaged in what can best be described as linguistic gymnastics to avoid quoting verbatim a Washington state high school student who had been suspended for three days for including sexual double entendre in a speech at a school assembly. This reluctance to include the exact language was puzzling, considering that the real news in that year was the U.S. Supreme Court's 7-to-2 decision upholding the right of the high school to discipline the student.[2]

Several years later, many readers praised the Minneapolis *Star Tribune* for its story on mammography. But sixty readers objected to the ac-

companying photo that depicted a woman giving herself a breast examination. One woman complained that her husband had died of testicular cancer and doubted that the paper would illustrate an article on that subject with a picture of testicles.[3]

In February 1995, NBC aired a timely fact-based movie focusing on the Pentagon's policy regarding gays in the military. The film, *Serving in Silence: The Margarethe Cammermeyer Story*, starred Glenn Close as a nurse who was drummed out of the army because she was a lesbian and included a dramatic scene of two female lovers kissing. Weeks before the airdate, controversy engulfed the movie as conservatives, outraged that such a scene would be televised, squared off with liberals, who were outraged that anyone would be upset.[4]

When Universal Studios released *The Last Temptation of Christ* in 1988, many theaters across the southern Bible Belt decided not to show the film in response to protesters. The film was a skillfully produced depiction of the more human qualities of Jesus. Religious critics were unwilling to tolerate this "revisionist" view of Scripture and accused the studio of blasphemy.

Pornography in cyberspace, indecency in the local newspaper, lesbian relationships in prime time, blasphemy at the box office—just a few examples of controversial subjects that reflect people's sensitivity to what might be described as morally offensive content. Any material that offends the moral standards of certain segments of society could conceivably fall into this category, and thus the issues are often intertwined with those relating to the antisocial behavior dealt with in Chapter 9. Nevertheless, the continuing debate over the mass distribution of morally offensive material justifies a separate chapter devoted to an exploration of these concerns.

Society's watchdogs are never far from center stage when it comes to their moral surveillance of the nation's mass media. In some respects, the issue of offensive content is one of the most troublesome ethical dilemmas for media practitioners. The ethical dimensions of this problem are made more apparent by the fact that virtually all morally offensive content, except for the most blatant forms of obscenity, are protected by the First Amendment. Although most ethical transgressions prompt complaints only from media critics and perhaps those most affected, condemnations of morally offensive material can sometimes lead to mass protests and demonstrations. For example, some might object to pornography on the grounds that it offends the community's standards of decency. Others object to shocking photographs published in the local paper. Religious conservatives protest the local showing of a movie they consider to be blasphemous. Some even object on moral grounds to ads for abortion clinics or beer and wine commercials. Morally offensive content is a broad and perhaps ill-defined subject.

Attempting to placate the moral sensibilities of all segments of society is, of course, impossible and even undesirable. Any such strategy would deprive our culture of its artistic vitality and render it aesthetically sterile. Nevertheless, media practitioners must be sensitive to these concerns and should blend their legal rights

under the First Amendment with a healthy dose of social responsibility.

Pornography, Indecency, and Moral Responsibility

In 1967 Congress, apparently believing that the proliferation of obscene and pornographic materials was a matter of grave national concern, established the Commission on Obscenity and Pornography. Its mandate was to initiate a thorough study of such materials and make recommendations for their regulation. Three years later, however, the advisory panel issued a recommendation that Congress did not want to hear: because of the lack of evidence to support a causal relationship between explicit sexual materials and social or individual harm, all legislation prohibiting the sale, exhibition, or distribution of sexual materials to consenting adults should be repealed.[5] Since the commission's findings were issued in 1970, other governmental bodies have investigated the problems of obscenity and pornography, the most recent being the so-called "Meese Commission."

The Supreme Court has ruled that obscenity is not constitutionally protected speech, but it has frequently struggled to define it. The justices may come to the Court with impressive legal credentials, but they are not literary critics. After all, one person's pornography may be another's art. A former justice, Potter Stewart, in a candid concession to pragmatism, once observed that he could not define obscenity but knew it when he saw it.[6] For more than a decade following its 1957 *Roth* decision, in which the Court first decided definitely that obscenity was not protected by the First Amendment,[7] the justices seemed unable to agree on a common meaning for obscenity. But, in 1974, a majority of the Court, including Chief Justice Warren Burger, settled on a definition in *Miller v. California*.[8] It held that material is obscene if (1) an average person, applying contemporary community standards, finds that the work, taken as a whole, appeals to prurient interest; (2) the work depicts in a patently offensive way sexual conduct specifically defined by applicable state law; and (3) the work in question lacks serious literary, artistic, political, or scientific value.[9]

Of course, these standards are still full of ambiguities, and subsequent court decisions have attempted to supply meaning to this elusive three-part test.[10] One theme that underlies *Miller* and subsequent decisions, however, is that the Court is concerned with the idea that obscenity is harmful to society and may adversely affect a community's quality of life. In this respect, the Court's latest pronouncements on obscenity are more than just constitutional dogma. They also reflect a profound concern with a community's *ethical* standards.[11]

Nevertheless, sex sells, and the proliferation of home video recorders and computers has resulted in a lucrative market for X-rated movies. Pornography is a billion-dollar industry that continues to appeal to some segments of society. Despite the fact that obscenity is not protected by the First Amendment, the standards are such that criminal prosecutions in many states are unusual. In addition, even when an overzealous prosecutor does file obscenity charges against a purveyor of pornography, juries find it difficult to make sense out of the law of obscenity and are reluctant to convict.

As the debate over obscenity continues, new emotional and political lineups have emerged. In the 1980s, for example, some feminists aligned themselves with the forces for moral restraint by condemning pornography as an expression of the notion of male supremacy.[12] In some communities they won passage of ordinances that defined pornography as the depiction of the sexual subordination or inequality of women through physical abuse. A federal judge in 1984 declared one such ordinance in Indianapolis unconstitutional on the grounds it was vague and did not meet the *Miller* standard for obscenity.[13] A three-judge panel of the Seventh U.S. Circuit Court of Appeals, in up-holding the ruling, observed that the antipornography ordinance did not refer to prurient interest, offensiveness, or community standards, as required by *Miller*. Furthermore, it made no provision for judging the literary, artistic, political, or scientific value of the work.[14]

Shortly thereafter, Attorney General Edwin Meese kept the debate over obscenity in the public consciousness by releasing the final report of the U.S. Attorney General's Commission on Pornography, commonly referred to as the "Meese Report." Meese was the Reagan administration's point man in the "war on crime," and before the report was even released, charges were made that the commission had already made up its mind about the detrimental effects of obscenity.[15] Although the panel was accused, even by some of its own members, of questionable interpretations of social-scientific evidence and was unable to establish a definitive link between some kinds of pornography and sexual violence, some groups used the study to pressure stores to remove sexually explicit material.

The Constitution has been an enduring instrument for protection of *legal* rights, but it has not always proved to be a worthy moral compass, as evidenced by the continuing debates over abortion and the death penalty. Some states, for example, have enacted laws regulating the dissemination of recorded music containing indecent or obscene lyrics. There have been prosecutions of music store owners for allegedly violating these laws. But despite the ultimate disposition of these cases, the moral debate will rage on in those communities that feel strongly that such music is offensive to societal mores.

The practice of journalism resides at the core of First Amendment values, but reporters are often confronted with an ethical quandary when it comes to including material that might offend the moral sensibilities of the audience. Should a videotape of nudity, for example, be included in a TV news report if such visuals contribute to the public's understanding of the story? Should public figures be subjected to a different standard from ordinary citizens when deciding whether to include quotes containing "colorful" and indecent language? Should offensive language be deleted from a quote or cleaned up to avoid embarrassment to the interviewee and offense to the readers or viewers?

Of course, altering a quote raises an ethical question within itself from the standpoint of truth and accuracy. Some publications employ what they believe to be a reasonable compromise by printing the first letter of the questionable word followed by a series of dashes. TV stations often "bleep" offensive language uttered by newsworthy subjects, which again raises questions of journalistic accuracy. Many local newspapers, because of their role as a community-based family medium, are still fairly conservative on the matter of offensive and indecent language. The size and nature of the market often determine how liberal media practitioners can be toward reproducing scatological language, but most are still reluctant to challenge the public's tolerance for such material.

When public figures (including professional athletes) are concerned, the question of whether to report profane language becomes a matter of ethical gamesmanship. Some editors take the position that if the questionable comments are essential to the story, they should be left in. Others are more comfortable with the use of euphemisms and indirect quotes in which the offensive remarks are sanitized. This is often a close call and may depend on the news figure's status and the context in which the remarks are made. It may also depend on the specific expressions used.

Sports figures are particularly troublesome, because their interviews are often peppered with colorful expletives. Sports editors usually sanitize these remarks before publication, although some use the "bleep" technique as a substitute for offensive language. Such editing can be justified, according to the rule stated earlier, because the rough language found in most interviews with sports figures is seldom essential to an understanding of the story. Nevertheless, sometimes an athlete's reaction to a situation is so revealing that an exact quote is justified.

This decision may depend, of course, on the readership of the publication. *Sports Illustrated*, which appeals to fans, might feel more comfortable with including offensive quotes from athletes than would magazines with a more diverse audience. In 1989, for example, the magazine published an article featuring the newly hired coach of the Chicago Blackhawks hockey team, Mike Keenan. In response to a question concerning his reputation as a tough-minded coach, Keenan said, "I've matured as a coach. My public persona is still the hard ass, the son of a bitch, but that's not accurate."[16] It is unlikely that many of the readers of the magazine would have been offended by this remark. One might also argue that this language was no more offensive than that offered up in prime time by the commercial networks. Cultural norms do change, and language that was unacceptable just ten years ago is now common in the mass media.

The English language contains many words that are offensive to society's linguistic norms, but some are considered more indecent than others. Certain references to specific sexual acts and other bodily functions are usually taboo in the mainstream media, whereas some words that were once forbidden, such as *bastard*, are now commonplace. In fact, until recently even the word *condom* was shunned by the networks' program decision makers.

Indeed, despite the moral squeamishness of some news media in reporting offensive language, some taboos appear to be fading. The list of words considered to be offensive has narrowed considerably. In fact, the only common bond between Anita Hill and Lorena Bobbitt may be that they both have been instrumental in journalistically legitimizing some heretofore forbidden expressions. During the Clarence Thomas hearings before the Senate Judiciary

Committee, Hill's graphic live testimony captivated a national TV audience with her repeated references to "large breasts," "penis," and the porn star "Long Dong Silver."[17] Perhaps because of the seemingly clinical descriptions of Hill's allegations of sexual harassment, the words that were once considered too raunchy for radio and TV barely caused a murmur. And in 1993 when the world was treated, through extensive media coverage, to the lurid details of how Lorena Bobbitt had taken a knife to her husband's penis, no significant demonstrations of moral outrage were apparent. And how did news executives decide that the Bobbitt case should make the headlines? "It was a story of public interest," said Richard Wald, ABC's senior vice president for editorial quality. "There is no such thing as a totally inappropriate news story. The problem is to figure out how you should tell it."[18]

These shifting journalistic sands at the national level may have resulted in some liberalization of standards at the local level. For example, in April 1994, the president of Arkansas State University was accused by his two secretaries of masturbating in his office. During the public hearing on the matter, the school official denied the charges and said it was impossible for him to have an erection because he was impotent. Radio station KBTM in Jonesboro, Arkansas, included both *masturbation* and *erection* in its news accounts without one critical phone call. "Does this mean," news director Wayne Hoffman wondered, "that 'masturbation' and 'erection' are okay to say on the air?"[19]

Nevertheless, despite the increasing acceptability of such clinical language, the use of scatological counterparts for such body parts and functions and other "curse" words still gives news gatekeepers pause. For example, in the O. J. Simpson case, when the 911 tapes made by Nicole Simpson a few years before her murder were released, ABC chose to air the obscenity-filled tapes unedited in its *Nightline* program. Prior to the program, which airs after the late news in most markets, the network warned viewers of what they were about to hear. ABC justified its decision on the grounds that the tapes "were the real thing and they indicated his anger and her fear."[20]

Of course, the use of indecent language in electronic media raises another host of moral problems because of the intrusion of radio and TV into the privacy of the home and the presence of children in the audience. Ever since the Federal Communications Commission first fined a Pennsylvania radio station for broadcasting an interview with the rock musician Jerry Garcia, of the Grateful Dead, that contained several indecent phrases, the commission has been concerned about the use of offensive language on the nation's airwaves. This concern was graphically reflected in the famous "seven dirty words" case, in which the FCC upheld a complaint against a New York radio station owned by the Pacifica Foundation. The complaint involved the broadcast of a satirical recording by the humorist George Carlin in which he repeated several words that one would never hear on the public's airwaves. In its order, the FCC described the language as "patently offensive as measured by contemporary standards for the broadcast medium."[21] The fact that children are in the audience at certain times of the day was also cited as justification for channeling indecent content into certain time periods. The commission's decision was upheld by the Supreme Court in 1978, thus putting licensees on notice that they were forbidden to broadcast indecent language for shock value.[22]

At first, few broadcasters saw this decision as a problem, but things have changed dramatically in the broadcast industry since 1978. Cable television and videocassettes have siphoned off the audience for over-the-air television. And because cable is not governed by the same rules as broadcast stations, there is a choice of explicit material not found in conventional broadcasting.[23] Competition in radio has also heated up, and some stations have resorted to talk shows that, to say the least, challenge the limits of moral propriety.[24]

The FCC has responded by attempting to channel indecent programming into times when children are unlikely to be in the audience. The time periods for this so-called "safe harbor" have varied, because of both some administrative indecision and legal challenges to the FCC's policy. Nevertheless, explicit broadcast chatter has continued unabated, and the FCC has been busy policing the nation's airwaves. In 1987, for example, it moved against three stations for airing indecent programming. A Philadelphia station was cited for comments made by a drive-time "shock jock," and a student-run station was cited for playing a song containing indecent lyrics. A Pacifica station in Los Angeles was even sanctioned for broadcasting excerpts of a serious drama concerning AIDS in the gay community.[25] The play consisted of telephone conversations between two homosexuals dying of AIDS in which they share their sexual fantasies. The FCC said such references were patently offensive.[26] These actions were followed by sanctions against stations as geographically disparate as Chicago, San Jose (California), and Indianapolis. All of the material aired by these shock jocks was intended to be humorous, and most of it was heavy on double entendre.[27]

The most renowned and controversial apostle of shock radio is Howard Stern, whose program is syndicated nationwide. Characterized by humor full of sexual innuendo, pejorative language, and ridicule, critics consider Stern's programs to be offensive and tasteless.[28] Stern's brand of "entertainment" is also very popular, consistently garnering high ratings and the lucrative advertising revenues that naturally accompany such success. He has also defied the government's attempts at regulation, having accumulated at one time more than $1 million in fines while he challenged the FCC's sanctions in court.

However, the issue of government regulation of indecency over the public's airwaves is far from settled. The battle has been joined between those who believe that government has a role in preventing the dissemination of morally offensive material and those who feel that such choices should be left to the marketplace. Critics like Bob Larson, a nationally syndicated minister who hosts a weekly debate program, note that electronic media are not a Las Vegas nightclub where the young and innocent are excluded. Civil libertarians respond that the FCC should not be a national nanny and that the monitoring of programs should be a parental responsibility.[29] But regardless of the legal resolution of the use of indecent language in the electronic media, the ethical concerns will remain at the vortex of the social debate on this matter.

The latest and what could prove to be the bloodiest battle over pornography and indecency is in "cyberspace." As the largest and most accessible on-line service, the Internet represents a virtually infinite marketplace of ideas, the purest form of democracy. It is also an endless menu of some of the most perverse sexually explicit material. While much of this material can be found in adult bookstores, pornography is different on computer networks, as *Time* magazine noted in a recent cover article on "cyberporn":

> You can obtain it in the privacy of your home—without having to walk into a seedy bookstore or movie house. You can download only those things that turn you on, rather than buy an entire magazine or video. You can explore different aspects of your sexuality without exposing yourself to communicable diseases or public ridicule.[30]

Much of the early debate has reverberated around the easy access to cyberporn of children, many of whom are more computer literate than their parents but may not be emotionally prepared for what they see. It is under this banner that some concerned parents are supporting government regulation, a view that many legislators are only too willing to indulge. Thus far, the American public is divided on the issue, as evidenced in a 1995 Time/CNN poll in which 42 percent of the respondents favored government control of computer networks, and 48 percent were against it.[31]

If the past is truly a prologue, however, then the Constitution will once again prove an unworthy taskmaster in the service of moral virtue, and society's combatants will again be forced (as in the case of abortion) to wage their ethical skirmishes in the marketplace of ideas. The Internet and other computer networks will, of course, increase the accessibility of pornography for children as well as for adults. But from an ethical perspective, the solution (if there is one) does not differ appreciably from that recommended to combat the pernicious influences of sex and violence on television and cable: parental control and supervision.

A Matter of Taste: Shocking and Disturbing Visuals

Offensive content does not always involve indecent or obscene material. Some photographs and TV news footage are so graphic as to shock the sensibilities of the average reader or viewer. Suppose, for example, that a state official who has just been convicted of a felony calls a news conference to announce his resignation. But instead of the expected resignation announcement, he pulls a gun and, with cameras rolling, places the barrel in his mouth and pulls the trigger. Would you air this graphic footage? That was the question confronting TV news directors in Pennsylvania in January 1987, when R. Budd Dwyer, the state treasurer, convened a news conference in his office the day before his scheduled sentencing on counts of mail fraud, racketeering, and perjury. Following a brief, rambling statement critical of the justice sys-

tem, the press, and the outgoing governor, he shot himself. As he slumped to the floor with blood gushing from his nose and mouth, the cameras followed him.[32]

This tape was quickly fed by satellite to stations across the state. Most news directors chose not to show this public suicide, but a few made the contrary decision. The most common reason cited by those who decided not to show the moment of death was the graphic nature of the footage. They felt it would be in bad taste and would shock the audience. Closely related to these concerns was the observation that showing the suicide itself was not necessary to the reporting of the story.[33] The three stations that chose to run the footage during the noon hour defended their decision on the values of newsworthiness and immediacy. They also argued that the footage they had shown was not particularly graphic.[34]

Most of the newspapers in and around the state capital of Harrisburg also refused to publish graphic photos of the suicide. Many editors gave the same reason: readers do not want to see such sensational photos. Only two papers in the region published some of the photos. James Dible, publisher of the *Lewistown Sentinel*, said he had no second thoughts about using the "gun in the mouth" shot and that reaction from the readers had been minimal. "A curious thing," he said, "is that much of the adverse reaction was linked to what people saw on television. The moving pictures were more startling."[35]

However, viewers in central Louisiana apparently were not offended by similar graphic coverage provided by a TV station in Alexandria. Although some objected, 80 percent of those who called the station supported the decision to air the drama.[36]

A sheriff's deputy, who was distraught over his pending divorce, killed his wife in the courthouse garage and then fled across the street where he threatened suicide. An eyewitness said that during the 2½-hour episode, the man pointed a gun to his head. As a priest and friends tried to talk him out of it, KALB-TV cameras carried the event live, including the moment when he placed the barrel of the pistol to his jaw and fired. Blood splattered and his body slumped.[37]

"We did not televise a suicide," News Director Jack Frost said. "The incident we televised was a situation that put the downtown area in danger, and our public needed to be aware of that." Frost also said he was unable to cut away because he did not have a tape delay mechanism. Roy Peter Clark, senior scholar at the Poynter Institute for Media Studies, refused to second-guess Frost and said there is value in seeing events as they unfold: "That's the ultimate sense of immediacy and, in a way, you get to vicariously experience a public event that may have some danger." However, Clark acknowledged that, when stations go live, they relinquish some measure of editorial control, thus running the risk that harmful consequences will occur.[38]

But Pat Monk, mental health therapist at an agency near the suicide scene, criticized the station for not turning the camera away at the crucial moment. "They must question whether unstable people will fulfill their threats," she said. "You can't base your coverage on the possibility they will not."[39]

Such forays beyond what some believe to be the limits of aesthetic and dramatic propriety usually subject journalists to charges ranging all the way from poor taste to voyeurism. In deciding whether to use potentially offensive and shocking pictures, media practitioners must weigh newsworthiness against other values. Unfortunately, many editors appear to be oblivious to the impact of photos. They view them as supplements to news stories, ignoring the fact that the impact of a story is often determined by the accompanying photograph.[40]

Television news directors may be more sensitive to visual effects because of the fact that pictures are an inherent part of any TV report.

News video does not always explain the meaning of a story, but it can create powerful images.[41] For example, the nightly visual coverage of the gruesome battlefield casualties in Vietnam has been credited with influencing the public opinion about the continued U.S. commitment to that conflict. Likewise, powerful news pictures also hastened the demise of the Ferdinand Marcos government in the Philippines.[42]

Given the inevitable psychological impact of visual images, it is little wonder that graphic photos of human tragedies evoke such strong reactions from the audience and even the professional community. In the Dwyer case, for example, the popular press was uniformly critical of the airing of his suicide. At one station, some advertisers even withdrew their support in protest of the coverage.[43] Following the terrorist bombing of a federal building in Oklahoma City, some readers of the *Sunday Advocate* in Baton Rouge, Louisiana, took the newspaper to task for running a photo that showed a fireman cradling a child in his arms, tenderly looking down at the small limp form. "There was no shortage of photographs we could have used," the *Advocate* commented editorially. "None of them, however, captured the essence of the bombing like that one photograph. It showed, as no other photo did, and as no written or spoken words could hope to convey, the horror that had taken place in Oklahoma City."[44] On another occasion, the *Advocate* published photos of a man in South Africa being dragged from a bus and stabbed in the top of his head. One reader was unmerciful in his denunciation of what he referred to as "shock" journalism. "Obviously we are not intelligent enough, as Baton Rouge citizens, to read about the tribal violence of South Africa and gain sufficient understanding," he complained. "We have to be shown what it's like when someone jabs a knife in another man's skull."[45]

Photographs of the casualties of war are always disturbing and often gruesome. Who can forget the televised scenes of the mass victims of the Iraq-Iran war? And then there was the photographic coverage of the summary execution of a Viet Cong soldier, who was shot with a pistol at close range by a South Vietnamese officer. The graphic visual evidence of the genocide in Bosnia-Herzegovina was a shocking testament to the darker side of the human experience. Of course, the ethical consequences of such agonizing decisions often extend beyond expressions of moral indignation. Americans were horrified, for example, when TV news programs aired footage of jeering Somalis dragging the body of a dead U.S. soldier through the streets of Mogadishu. Newspapers ran similar photos. Following this coverage, thousands of Americans called Capitol Hill to demand that U.S. troops be withdrawn from this ill-fated operation. Members of Congress referred to the pictures in demanding that President Clinton withdraw the troops immediately. The pictures and the public reaction precipitated a national debate about the political and ethical implications of the pictures and the media's influence on foreign policy.[46]

Of course, examples such as the Dwyer case and the casualties of combat are subjected to more public and professional scrutiny than most photographic coverage. Despite the alleged newsworthiness of such visuals, media practitioners have a moral obligation at least to consider the sensibilities of family, friends, and relatives of the victims. Nevertheless, pictures of tragedies are a staple of photojournalism, and some editors feel that because they are so compelling and memorable, such graphic representations must be used, even at the risk of distressing readers and family members. Many scenes of auto accidents, shootings, drownings, and suicides are prizewinners in annual news photography competitions.[47]

Media gatekeepers are confronted with another decision involving taste when news coverage includes nudity. Pictures of the human body often offend the moral sensibilities of the audience, prompting charges of sensationalism. Once again, editors and news directors must balance the news value of such pictures against other considerations. Assume, for example, that a TV news crew accompanies police officers on a raid of a topless bar. Should the evening news, presented during the dinner hour, graphically depict the arrest of naked dancers? Because television is a visual medium, these shots are arguably at the heart of the news story. Nevertheless, many audiences are offended by such journalistic candor, so some stations sanitize this kind of material by electronically blocking out the bare breasts.

Many editors refuse to run nude photographs of even those involved in newsworthy events or matters of public interest. Despite the prevalence of sexually explicit material in our society, they apparently do not believe that the public will accept nudity in their hometown newspapers. When one considers that the audience is an important ingredient in the moral reasoning process, it is difficult to fault such caution.

News managers are essentially *teleological* in their approach to publishing or airing offensive language or visuals. For an ethical journalist, the reactions of their audiences and the consequences for the family and friends of those featured in the coverage should be a dominant concern in their decision making. In deciding whether to include morally offensive material in news coverage, we should keep one guideline clearly in mind: such visuals should not be used just for shock value or to increase circulation or ratings. These pictures should be justified according to the same rules of good journalism as any other editorial matter. They should, first of all, be *newsworthy*. Once the news value of such photos has been ascertained, a determination should be made whether they are *essential* to the story. Do the graphic visuals, for example, provide significant information or understanding that would otherwise be lacking in the story? These factors should then be weighed against other competing values, such as good taste and a respect for human decency.

The Lingering Legacy of Blasphemy

In 1811, a Mr. Ruggles was convicted in New York of having made blasphemous remarks about Jesus and Mary. A few years later, the courts of Boston convicted Abner Kneeland for circulating irreligious remarks in a newspaper. In 1928, a warrant was issued but never served for the arrest of a well-known editor for suggesting that Socrates and Jesus had been anarchists. In the same year, an atheist was convicted in Arkansas of the "crime" of ridiculing the Christian religion.[48] And as late as 1937, a Connecticut man was convicted of violating that state's blasphemy statute.[49]

Although a few states still have blasphemy statutes, today the *crime* of blasphemy is primarily a historical artifact. But despite the fading of blasphemy from the legal arena, the ethical dimensions of the debate remain problematic. In 1979, for example, six theater managers in Louisiana were pressured into canceling the Monty Python film *Life of Brian*, described by some as delightful and hilariously funny but condemned by conservative religious groups as blasphemous and even obscene. In Valdosta, Georgia, *Brian* was closed by court order until a judge could view it.[50] As noted earlier, the controversy surrounding *The Last Temptation of Christ* a few years ago demonstrates the continued vigilance of religious conservatives over what they consider to be blasphemy and irreverence in the mass media.

However, it was not American Christianity but Islamic fundamentalism that stimulated the most fervent and emotional indictment for blasphemy in recent years. When Indian-born British author Salman Rushdie published his novel *Satanic Verses*, the Iranian spiritual leader, the Ayatollah Khomeini, accused him of blasphemy against Islam and imposed a death edict against the writer. Rushdie then went into exile in Great Britain. To an American, this rather harsh sanction might have remained just one more manifestation of the zealotry of Middle East fundamentalism had it not been for the fact that some bookstores in the United States pulled *Satanic Verses* from their shelves for fear of reprisals.

These examples notwithstanding, charges of blasphemy against media practitioners are relatively rare today. Nevertheless, blasphemy is considered by some to be among the most offensive forms of content, because it challenges the fundamental principles of religious doctrine.

The controversy over morally offensive content, perhaps more than any other media ethics issue, touches on the kind of society we want to be. Our libertarian heritage propels us in the direction of freedom. But even in an open society there are limits, and much of the ethical debate has focused on them. The ferocity of this moral dialogue would challenge even the wisdom of Socrates in forging an accommodation of competing values in the intellectual marketplace.

On the one hand, a system of ethics based on moral prudishness would lead to such austere media content that it would probably be rejected by a majority of the audience. On the other hand, absolute freedom leads to moral chaos and destruction of cultural continuity. Practically speaking, neither extreme is workable. Thus, in a diverse society the strategy should be to reach some middle ground, an accommodation between the excesses of moral prudishness and moral chaos.

THE CASE FOR MORAL LIMITS

A search for an ethical meeting of the minds on the issue of morally offensive content must begin with an understanding of the arguments for and against societal controls. One way of approaching the matter of moral limits is to note the grounds that might be advanced to justify those limits. Four liberty-limiting principles are relevant to this inquiry: (1) the *harm* principle, (2) the principle of *paternalism*, (3) the principle of *moralism*, and (4) the *offense* principle. Although these grounds have most often been cited to justify the legal regulation of obscenity, they are equally applicable to the control of other forms of morally offensive content.[51]

The Harm Principle

Under the first concept, based in part on the ideas of John Stuart Mill in *On Liberty*, individual liberty may be reasonably restricted to prevent *harm to others*. For example, some allege that exposure to pornography is directly related to sex crimes such as rape. Even in a libertarian society, few would disagree with the harm principle as a general notion. But there is little evidence that morally offensive content causes physical or psychological harm to others. Thus, the supporters of this principle have turned their attention to the detrimental impact on cultural values and the exploitation of certain segments of society. This view is reflected in an observation from Professor Franklyn S. Haiman in *Speech and Law in a Free Society*:

> If communication is so vital to the functioning of a free society as to warrant the extraordinary protection afforded to it by the First Amendment, it must have the power—we are often reminded—for harm as well as good. If speech can enlighten, it can also exploit. If literature can enrich our values, it can also debase them. If pictures can enhance our sensitivities, they can also dull them.[52]

The harm principle does attract an interesting cast of supporters, on both the right and left of the political spectrum. In 1986, for example, a feminist, Andrea Dworkin, testified before the Meese Commission in favor of the regulation of pornography. Invoking images of women being brutalized and even killed for the profit of pornographers, Dworkin explained, "The issue is simple, not complex. Either you're on the side of women or on the side of pornographers."[53] Such a view shows that the cause of censorship is not the exclusive preserve of conservatives or liberals.

The Principle of Paternalism

Under the second principle, morally offensive content should be controlled to prevent *harm to self*. In other words, exposure to obscene and other sexually explicit matter is harmful because it dehumanizes individuals and even corrupts their value system. In common parlance, we need to be protected from ourselves. If nutritionists believe that we are what we eat, then proponents of paternalism believe that we are what we read (or view).

Some accuse the media of emphasizing freedom at the expense of responsibility. A recent study, for example, found that there had been an increase in the depiction of sexual behavior on television but little portrayal of the possible consequences, such as pregnancy and venereal diseases.[54]

The paternalistic view is captured in an unequivocal comment attributed to Larry Parish, who once prosecuted the porno star Harry Reems in Memphis, Tennessee.[55] Parish, who apparently viewed the elimination of obscenity as a divine mission, told a reporter, "I'd rather see dope on the streets than these movies," because drugs could be cleansed from the body, but pornography's damage was permanent.[56]

The Principle of Moralism

According to the third view, morally offensive content should be controlled by society in order to prevent *immoral behavior* or *the violation of societal norms*. This principle raises the question of the kinds and degrees of regulation that should be tolerated in a pluralistic society. Some believe that ready access to pornographic material, for example, encourages promiscuous sexual behavior. But even if there is no demonstrable harm from exposure to content such as pornography and blasphemy, some support societal controls merely because this material offends community standards. This is an extreme position, because it could lead to social ostracism of even those who choose to consume controversial content within the privacy of their homes.

The Offense Principle

Some argue that society is justified in restricting individual liberty to prevent *offense to others*. In this context, offensive behavior is understood as behavior that "causes shame, embarrassment, discomfort, etc., to be experienced by onlookers" in public.[57] This principle is usually employed to justify the protection of nonconsenting adults from public displays of offensive material. Likewise, objections to the publication of gruesome or disturbing photographs are usually made on the basis of taste and the desire to avoid offending the moral sensibilities of the audience. When newspapers agree to accept only listings for adult theaters but no promotional ads, or when bookstores conceal adult magazines behind the counter for sales by request only, these decisions are grounded primarily on the offense principle.

THE CASE AGAINST MORAL LIMITS

The arguments against societal censorship are based primarily on the notion of individual autonomy and a rejection of the liberty-limiting principles just described.[58] Proponents of this view have little trouble, for example, dispensing with the harm principle as a viable foundation for regulation. No evidence shows, they say, that morally offensive material harms others (e.g., by causing an increase in sex-related crimes) and that the so-called societal harm is so speculative as to pose no immediate threat to the cultural order.

Likewise, libertarians find paternalists are wrong when they argue that pornographic and blasphemous material harms the individual. But even if such harm did occur, according to those who oppose restrictions, paternalism is an unacceptable liberty-limiting principle.

The principle of moralism is also rejected, because the alleged consensus on what constitutes community standards does not exist. But even if it did, moralism would be unacceptable, because standards vary tremendously from community to community. Undoubtedly, the liberal cultural environment of New York City would be anathema in the Bible Belt. In addition, reliance on such fluid and often elusive criteria imposes the majority's will without respecting individual autonomy and minority interests.

Civil libertarians also argue that "offensiveness" is an ambiguous and virtually unproductive standard both legally and ethically. Some group might be offended by any controversial content, they argue; in a democratic society, offensive content actually serves as an invigorating influence in the diversity of the marketplace. Besides, it is a rare occasion when autonomous individuals become captive audiences for such fare, and critics of offensive content often base their views on an abstraction rather than any personal experience or knowledge or insights into the nature of the material. How many respondents of the Time/CNN poll described earlier, for example, have actually seen any of the sexually explicit material supposedly polluting the cyberspace?

The anticensorship position is rather persuasive from a legal standpoint, especially in view of the Constitution's expansive protection of speech and press rights. But it remains for the ethicist—and each of us should participate in this process—to search for that balance between individual autonomy and the need for moral standards.

THE SEARCH FOR STANDARDS

The notion of morally offensive content poses a problem for deontologists. These duty-based theorists would not desire that such material become common within society. The production and distribution of offensive material just for the sake of commercial exploitation cannot be justified, because (1) the purpose of artists in producing such content does not flow from any universal moral obligation, and (2) exploitation does not show the proper respect for persons as ends unto themselves.

On the other hand, deontologists also acknowledge the right to free expression.[59] Under the duty-based approach to ethical decision making, the value of actions lies in motives rather than in consequences. Artistic freedom by itself does not justify such material, but works of art that in some way contribute to cultural enrichment should be protected. Thus, the deontologist would examine the purpose and motive of the author in producing the allegedly morally offensive work, regardless of the ultimate consequences of the material. The problem with this approach is that it requires an exploration of the vast recesses of the author's mind, a perilous and uncertain journey. Sometimes the author's motives are evident, but at other times they are concealed.

Consequentialists (teleologists), as always, would look to the probable effects of the content. So far there does not appear to be any demonstrable physical or psychological harm resulting from the consumption of some forms of morally offensive material, such as obscenity. Nevertheless, a teleologist must still consider the more fundamental effects on societal values and attitudes. For example, does the viewing of sexually violent pornography result in the degradation and subordination of women in society's collective consciousness?

If there is no demonstrable harm to others or to society, perhaps censorship is unwarranted. Of course, teleologists rest more comfortably on this position than deontologists, because they are not really concerned with the author's motives but only the consequences. And some believe that even hard-core pornography, regardless of whether it is produced for the purposes of commercial exploitation, can have beneficial effects. For example, G. L. Simons, an Englishman who has written extensively on various aspects of human sexuality, believes that exposure to pornography can aid normal sexual development and that it can invigorate sexual relationships.[60] But even if one were to reject Simons's observations, a teleologist might conclude that the consequences of censorship are fraught with dangers in that some material possessing social value might be swept aside with that containing no demonstrable literary or cultural utility.

Aristotle's golden mean, on the other hand, seeks the middle ground between the excesses of moral prudishness and moral chaos. An ethicist applying the golden mean would examine the content, the medium of distribution, and the audience to which it is directed. The real centerpiece of the golden mean is "information and reasonable control." Distributors of potentially offensive content have a moral obligation to provide consumers with adequate information and warnings so that they can make rational choices about their reading or viewing. The film ratings system and the disclaimers included at the beginning of controversial network programs are two well-known examples.

The principle of reasonable control ensures the availability of material for consenting adults while protecting the sensibilities of nonconsenting adults and children. Zoning laws, bans on public promotions for offensive material, and the placement of adult magazines behind the counters at retail outlets would appear to be a reasonable middle ground between the excesses of prudishness and affronts to pubic morality.

The various media deserve different levels of control, depending on audience accessibility. Radio and TV, for example, are still predominantly family media and are almost ubiquitous. Newspapers, magazines, movies, and books, on the other hand, require consumers to make more active and conscious decisions.

Where children and nonconsenting adults are concerned, greater controls would also be justified. This is the principle on which the FCC has built its programming standards regarding indecent content, as evidenced in the Pacifica case described earlier. But the technology that has made possible the information superhighway has also challenged traditional ethical approaches and precipitated a public debate about its role as an instrument of cultural enrichment. Thus, the old strategies may no longer be feasible as distinctions among media rapidly disappear and all communication becomes increasingly electronic. The Internet is a classic example, as proponents of regulation argue that cyberspace should be governed according to the "broadcast" model, whereas free-speech advocates favor a "print" model with little or no regulation.

MORALLY OFFENSIVE CONTENT: HYPOTHETICAL CASE STUDIES

The following cases afford the opportunity to apply the ethical guidelines described here to the media distribution of what some consider to be morally offensive content. The issues surrounding the production and dissemination of pornography and other varieties of material that offend some people's moral sensibilities are among the most emotional and contentious confronting media practitioners. It is a classic confrontation between the libertarians and the proponents of governmental paternalism. You may have personal feelings toward such material, but in resolving the ethical dilemmas posed here, try to keep an open mind, and apply the principles of sound moral reasoning outlined in Chapter 3 to the facts of these cases.

CASE STUDIES

▶ **CASE 10-1**
"Skin" on the Evening News

By no stretch of the imagination could the Sommerville Road section of Manderville be considered a cultural oasis. Manderville is a growing midwestern community of 200,000 and, like many expansion-minded cities of its size, has already begun to experience the ravages of urban blight. The city fathers viewed with concern the gradual decay of the Sommerville Road section, once an attractive habitat for the working class. But crime and drugs took control, and Sommerville Road became populated primarily by nightclubs, pawn shops, adult bookstores, and a variety of greasy-spoon restaurants.

Although an occasional drug raid or arrest for prostitution was made on Sommerville Road, the former district attorney and the police had shown no interest in attacking the problem of pornography or indecent exposure in the topless clubs. The chances of a conviction were so small and the penalties so light, according to Police Chief Nathan Camp, that he could not even justify turning his attention to such matters.

But the newly elected district attorney, Oscar Jones, had won his post in part on his pledge to clean up Sommerville Road. One of his first targets was the Pink Lady Club, one of the most notorious nude dancing bars on the strip. With the promise from the new DA that he would prosecute pornography and indecency to the "limits of the law," Camp now viewed the problem in a new light, as Howard Stein soon discovered. Stein was the news director of WWW-TV (Channel 4), one of three network affiliates in the Manderville market. The irrepressible Camp, never one to forgo favorable publicity for himself and his department, had phoned Stein and informed him that he was about to "bust" the Pink Lady Club. The officers expected to arrest those in charge and any women who were performing nude for the patrons. Would a news crew from Channel 4 like to accompany the officers on their raid of this unsavory establishment, Camp wanted to know?

Stein consulted with his assignment editor, Marlin Shaw, on the matter, but both knew an exclusive when they saw one. Shaw dispatched a reporter, Jerry Mars, and a crew to cover the raid on the Pink Lady Club, and the news team followed the officers into the establishment. Although the raid was carried out in the middle of the afternoon, the club was full of patrons, most of whom ducked for the exits. The manager was surprised by the raid and made a half-hearted objection to the presence of the news crew, but not before the camera had accomplished its mission.

An hour before airtime, Stein and Mars were viewing the footage in the editing room. Even Stein was impressed with the graphic coverage of the raid. The camera had captured the police officers as they entered the club, the patrons fleeing from view, and the arrests of the owner, manager, and assistant manager. The cameras had also focused on two women dancing on a runway stage in front of the bar as well as their subsequent arrests. The scenes showed full frontal nudity as the startled performers stood dumbfounded before they regained their composure and sought the security of their robes.

Even before the unedited footage had completed its run, Mars was arguing that the nude scenes should be broadcast. They were essential to the reporting of the story, he said. After all, the nude dancers were the reason for the DA's interest

in the Pink Lady Club to begin with. Without the nude scenes, even if they were offensive to some, the story would lose its visual impact. Even Mars acknowledged the need for discretion in the station's entertainment fare, but he believed that news should be held to a different standard.

But Stein was hesitant. The troubled news director did not want to dilute the visual impact of this exclusive story, but he had always been mindful of the need for good taste, especially in this essentially conservative community. The graphic footage would undoubtedly offend some viewers, although audiences were in some respects less puritanical today. Could the scenes be justified on the grounds that they were essential to the reporting of the story? Stein did not want his station to be accused of tabloid journalism. Of course, such material was not standard for Channel 4, and perhaps the majority of viewers would forgive this temporary detour into journalistic voyeurism.

Nevertheless, Stein wondered whether a less graphic means of portraying the video aspects of this story were possible. There were a couple of shots of shoulders and legs as the performers fled from the stage. Perhaps these seminude scenes could be used to convey the idea of the story without offending the audience.

But Mars insisted that the nude scenes alone could convey the importance of the story. If such raids were going to become commonplace under the new DA's regime, this was an opportunity for the audience to see their tax dollars at work.

As airtime for the evening newscast approached, Stein considered his options. He had little doubt that such graphic scenes, even within a newscast, would be viewed as tasteless and morally offensive by some segments of the audience, and he wondered whether the interest of journalism would be served by challenging their aesthetic prudishness.

THE CASE STUDY

How far (and under what conditions) should television news go in showing nudity that the audience may consider to be in poor taste? Most journalists would agree on one point: the facts of this story can be conveyed without the nude scenes. But beyond that is the question of whether a TV news story loses its impact when interesting video is omitted. TV is a visual medium that sometimes must rely on graphic scenes to convey the essence of a story.

But what if the scenes involve questions of taste? There is plenty of precedent in TV news for deleting graphic scenes of brutality and violence on the grounds that it is likely to be offensive to some segments of the audience. In cases when such scenes are deemed essential to the story, a warning is often issued to the viewers. Would that be an ethically acceptable compromise in cases involving nudity?

Paradoxically, TV audiences are more readily receptive to the portrayal of violence in news than to graphic nudity. Thus, many stations are reluctant to include nudity in their stories, even when such scenes go to the heart of the coverage of a particular event. Does such journalistic squeamishness distort the reality of the event, or is this self-censorship justified out of a consideration for the sensibilities of the audience?

In approaching this dilemma, assume the role of the news director, Stein, and, using the SAD Formula, make a decision on whether you will include the nude footage as part of your report on the Pink Lady Club.

▶ **CASE 10-2**
The Little Boy in Sarajevo[61]

It was a human tragedy of unimaginable proportions. In the first three years of the bloody civil war in Bosnia-Herzegovina, tens of thousands of innocent civilians had died and thousands more had been left homeless, as the Serbs carried out their relentless campaign of genocide, referred to as "ethnic cleansing." And many of these had been children—Serbs, Muslims, Croats—too young to have any political allegiances or embrace the unmistakable hatred of their adult predecessors.

Masonville was a New England town thousands of miles from the "killing fields" of Bosnia-Herzegovina. But the citizens of this urbane, ethnically diverse community were visibly troubled

by events in the former Yugoslavia, as they lamented the impotence of the United Nations in stopping the carnage and debated the moral obligation of the United States to get directly involved in this bloody civil war.

The *Masonville Globe* was firmly attuned to the journalistic interests of its readers. While the paper provided a comprehensive and intelligent account of the local political, economic, and cultural landscape, it also prided itself on its international coverage, a concession both to the sophistication and the immigrant heritage of many of its readers. Almost from its inception, the civil war in the former Yugoslavia had been front-page copy, as the *Globe* documented both narratively and visually the tragic consequences of that bloody conflict. The paper's editorial staff had examined hundreds of photos since the outbreak of hostilities, as foreign correspondents risked their own lives to document the savagery and futility of the war. Many of the photos had been gruesome, but most had been serious candidates for inclusion in the *Globe*'s regular front-page coverage of international events.

But the *color* photo of a little boy in Sarajevo who had been shot to death was different! The seven-year-old youth lay face down on the street in a pool of blood. Managing Editor Jim Rainwater, Assistant Managing Editor Laura Hatfield, and Photo Editor Mannie Fernandez were emotionally in harmony in their reactions to the dramatic picture. Where they differed was in their ethical perspectives on publishing the color photo on the front page of their newspaper.

"This is pretty grim stuff," said Rainwater, who would be the ultimate moral agent in deciding whether to publish the gripping visual. "This is the photo that accompanies this sidebar story to today's account of the fighting in Bosnia. The boy was apparently killed yesterday by a sniper as he and his mother were running across the street."

"I vote against publishing this picture on the front page," said Hatfield with a grimace. "This would be too big of a jolt for our readers. I have a twelve-year-old daughter and wouldn't want her to see this photo as the first thing when she picks up the paper in the morning."

"You have a point," responded Rainwater. "I feel uneasy just by looking at it. And some readers will undoubtedly find it offensive and tasteless. But we are a news organization. Sometimes we have to publish pictures and copy that may offend our audience. After all, this photo is an accurate account of the horror in Bosnia. Children are as much the victim of this civil war as adults."

"I agree," replied Fernandez. "I'll admit this is strong stuff. But we pride ourselves on providing visual, as well as narrative, accounts of the news. And sometimes the truth is hard to take. But as conduits for the people's right to know, our business is telling the truth."

"If we omit this picture, I don't see where the truth will really be compromised," responded Hatfield as she became increasingly uneasy with this gruesome documentation of the reality of war. "Publishing this photo would just be gratuitous. Our readers will learn from the story that the boy was killed. They don't need to see blood oozing from his head."

"That's a good point," conceded Rainwater, as he became increasingly uncomfortable with his original position. "Besides, no one has even mentioned respect for this dead boy and whatever family he has remaining. It's true that this is just one casualty in a war thousands of miles away. Surely none of our readers know him or his family. But it does give me pause to publish this bloody picture on the front page."

"But we publish graphic photos all the time of people who are victims of accidents or even casualties of war," said Fernandez. "And some of them are pretty bloody. And just look at some of the visuals on the nightly news!"

"This is different," replied Hatfield, as she sought to expose the weakness in the photo editor's argument. "Pictures of children are more emotionally wrenching than those of adults. Readers react differently to them. When innocent children are killed, it just magnifies the tragic proportions of this conflict. Do we really have to show such bloody photos on the front page?"

"It's not a pleasant thought," admitted Fernandez. "But as tragic as it is, this is a high-profile news event. War is hell! And what better way to show this. After all, some good may come from publishing such photos. If enough pictures of dead children are published, maybe the world community will be outraged enough to do something about this bloody war. And there is already sufficient precedent for this view. If the American people had not seen the bloody photos and film of the Vietnam War, thousands more U.S. soldiers might have been killed while the government remained committed to that useless conflict. Perhaps even in death this child can serve a higher purpose."

Rainwater fell silent for a couple of minutes while he stared at the photo, a grisly emblem of both a tragic private moment and a legitimate matter of public interest. As the deadline for publication approached, the managing editor acknowledged that he was not entirely comfortable with either option but told his assistant and the photo editor that he would consider their advice carefully. While in college, he had once taken a course in moral philosophy, but at times like these the advice of Aristotle and Immanuel Kant eluded him. He wondered whether they would speak to him forcefully in the two hours remaining before deadline.

THE CASE STUDY

This case is not unlike the real-life dilemmas confronted by editors across the country each day. Visuals are an important ingredient in the journalistic mix, and they often convey information that cannot be graphically communicated in a narrative account. But when they depict the stark reality of human tragedy in a horrific, often bloody way, then ethical concerns arise in attempting to balance journalistic responsibilities against the audience's sensibilities, as well as respect for the victim and the victim's family and friends.

In this scenario, one could argue, as Mannie Fernandez did, that "war is hell" and that the paper's responsibility is to report the truth. Perhaps the relentless publication of such photos will convince the world community to put an end to such carnage.

On the other hand, graphic photos of dead children are more prone to offend the audience's moral sensibilities than the typical pictures of war casualties. Under such circumstance, perhaps some of the truth must be sacrificed for other humanitarian concerns.

For the purpose of confronting this ethical

dilemma, assume the role of Managing Editor Jim Rainwater, and then, using the formula for moral reasoning described in Chapter 3, decide whether your newspaper will publish this photo. In working your way through this ethical thicket, you may wish to keep the following two questions in mind: (1) Would the publication of this picture, as Laura Hatfield suggested, really be gratuitous, or is there an overriding journalistic purpose in publishing this picture? (2) Since the photo is designed to accompany a sidebar story on the dead youth, is it essential to support the vivid narrative description of the tragedy?

In addition, the discussion among the three editors concerned the ethics of publishing this picture as a color photo on the front page of the *Globe*. Is there a middle ground between this option and not publishing at all? If so, will this ethical middle ground resolve all of the concerns raised in the scenario, or will there still be some lingering doubts?

▶ **CASE 10-3**
Live! From Death Row!

Wilbert Lacey had languished on death row for ten years, but now his rendezvous with justice was apparently at hand. His last appeal having been exhausted, Lacey awaited the inevitable enforcement of the warden's third and final death warrant. After a six-month reign of terror in the usually tranquil community of Manderville, Lacey had been convicted for the brutal slayings of three families, all of whom had been ritually dismembered and some of their body parts stored in Lacey's refrigerator. Lacey's attorney had invoked the insanity defense, but the jury was in no mood for such legal ploys and lost no time in convicting him on all counts. He was subsequently sentenced to die in the electric chair.

A decade after his incarceration, feelings were still running high in Manderville, whose citizens had grown impatient with the judiciary's indulgence of the convicted murderer's interminable appeals. Nevertheless, a small cadre of death penalty foes

had assembled at Hapeville State Prison, just thirty miles from Manderville, to protest this "state-sponsored brutality" and "cruel and unusual punishment" prohibited by the Constitution.

But it was Robert Eaton's unexpected invitation, not the small gathering of vocal demonstrators, that attracted the attention of the state's journalistic establishment. Eaton was the warden at the Hapeville state penitentiary and was an avowed supporter of the death penalty. The warden had never cultivated a close relationship with the media, but in an abrupt change in both custom and policy he announced that the execution would "be available to live TV coverage to show that swift and certain punishment awaits convicted murderers." The only conditions, according to the warden's surprise announcement, would be that only one pool camera could be installed for the event and the faces of all witnesses would be electronically blurred. Thus, as Lacey, through his attorney, pronounced himself "at peace with the Lord" and prepared to suffer the consequences of his foul deeds, the state's television news departments found themselves pondering the ethical dimensions of an issue that was not entirely of their own making: Should they take advantage of Warden Eaton's offer of live coverage of Wilbert Lacey's execution?

Channel 10, one of two network affiliates in Manderville, was among the first to render its own collective moral judgment and publicly proclaimed that it would disassociate itself from the televising of such a gruesome spectacle. Rondell Hayes was pleased that his counterpart at Channel 10 was apparently not plagued by moral ambiguities in this matter. As news director of Channel 7 in Manderville, Hayes shared his competitor's discomfort at the prospect of carrying the state's first live telecast of an execution. However, the station's assignment editor, Martha Klein, and Sydney Fielding, the producer of the late-night news who would also handle the execution telecast if it were approved by station management, disagreed in their ethical assessment of Eaton's offer.

"I don't think much of this idea," said Klein unequivocally in the hastily arranged meeting with Hayes and the spirited young news producer. "The televising of an execution is just too grotesque. Our audience may be overwhelmingly in favor of the death penalty, but I don't think they're ready for this."

"The execution isn't scheduled for prime time," replied Hayes. "It'll happen around midnight. And of course, we'll issue the usual warnings."

"A lot of people will stay up and watch out of curiosity," said Klein. "I realize that's their choice. But should we cater to the public's fascination with the macabre? And besides, if we televise this event live at midnight we'll probably wind up airing tapes of the execution on the next day's newscasts. These things have a life of their own. Our competitor has already declined to televise this execution, and they have already generated a lot of publicity about their decision. Whatever the public feels about the death penalty, they certainly won't fault Channel 10 for declining the warden's invitation."

"I don't think we should take our cues from our competitor," responded Fielding who, as a news producer, had applauded the TV media's success in introducing televised coverage into the state's court system. "As journalists, I think we have an obligation to televise this execution. The print media have for many years witnessed such executions. All we're seeking is parity, and the warden is apparently willing to give it to us, even if we didn't file a petition requesting this unprecedented access to an execution. After all, the camera provides a more accurate portrayal of the event than the vivid account presented narratively by our print brethren. The people of this state convicted Lacey; they now have a right to see the results. Considering the sentiment in this state for the death penalty, our viewers might even applaud our initiative."

But Klein was unmoved, partially because of her own opposition to the death penalty and partially because she did not believe that such ghoulish renditions of the state's handiwork belonged on public display. "There's also a matter of privacy here," she said. "Lacey has been convicted, and he's about to pay his price. We'll cover the execution, just like we would any other news story. But why is it essential, from a journalistic perspective, to televise Lacey's last gasp?"

"Lacey lost his right to privacy when he murdered his victims," said Fielding in a rejoinder to what he felt was a specious argument. "And this

kind of televised execution might even serve as a deterrent to others."

"But that's an ideological argument, not a journalistic one," responded Hayes. "If we make our decision on that basis, then we're making a rather subtle editorial statement. The same would be true if we decided to televise Lacey's execution on the grounds that the horrific nature of such an event might convince the public that the death penalty is immoral or at least unconstitutional. Such reasons are good from an ideological perspective, but they don't serve the cause of journalism well."

"You have a point," conceded Fielding, who was sensitive to any insinuation that his reasoning was not journalistically sound. "But we have a history of public executions in this country. This wouldn't really be that new. We have a tradition in this country that government proceedings should be open to the media and the public. And until now the TV media have been closed out."

"It's true that many executions in the nineteenth century were public events," said Klein. "But TV is different. Bringing an execution live into the privacy of the home is going too far. I'm a journalist too, and I'm sensitive to the public's right to know and our role in fulfilling that responsibility. But there are times when other values have to be considered. Televising an execution is gruesome without any clear-cut journalistic rationale."

"I think you're overreacting," responded Fielding. "Executions are not exactly unheard of on television. Take, for example, the execution of Romanian President Ceaucescu, the beheadings in Saudi Arabia, and executions in Iraq, Iran, and Vietnam. All of these were shown on the nightly news."

Klein was willing to acknowledge this appeal to precedent but not its moral standing." I've seen some of the footage of these executions," she said. "Most of these were fairly rapid events and even edited for broadcast. In addition, these were public events; they took place in front of news cameras. At least in recent years in this country, with the exception of a few witnesses, executions have been conducted outside of public view. And while death comes relatively quickly when the switch is pulled, the televising of this execution will last several minutes. It will just enhance the morbid nature of the event. Besides, the fact that there have been visual news accounts of other executions does not automatically justify providing live coverage of the Lacey execution."

As Hayes listened to both the ideological and ethical arguments advanced by his producer and assignment editor, he felt emotionally fatigued. Because of the controversial nature of this matter, any proposal to go live with Lacey's execution would have to be approved by the station's manager. But he would rely heavily on Hayes' recommendation.

On a personal level, Hayes felt emotionally repulsed by the idea of televising an execution. But he also had to concede the validity of the journalistic, if not ideological arguments, advanced by Sydney Fielding. In some respects, perhaps this was just another governmental proceeding to which the media deserved to have access. On the other hand, in his mind the very nature of an execution —actually killing a human being (albeit a very wretched one) in front of a live TV camera—relegated this kind of event to a special category. Were there sound journalistic reasons, he wondered, for televising Wilbert Lacey's last moments, or was this act tantamount to electronic brutality?

Channel 10 had already provided its response to this question. That his competitor had declined the opportunity to beam Lacey's demise into his community's living rooms weighed heavily on Hayes's mind. "What an interesting twist," he thought as he began to ponder his ethical dilemma. "Normally I have to worry about taking a certain course of action because of what our competitor might *do*. In this case, I'm concerned about our own conduct because of what the other station is *not* planning to do."

THE CASE STUDY

"Should a TV station broadcast an execution?" That was the question explored in a 1991 *Newsweek* article following a request by a public TV station in San Francisco to televise the execution of Robert Alton Harris, convicted of the murders of two San Diego teenagers.[62] A federal judge eventually upheld California's ban on cameras at executions, and the station's petition was denied. However, this was not the first interest displayed by the TV industry in providing visual coverage of executions. In

1977, for example, a federal appellate court upheld Texas regulations prohibiting camera coverage of executions.[63] And more recently, Phil Donahue, in another cutting-edge initiative, sought permission to televise an execution in North Carolina. His request was denied, but the determined Donahue turned his attention to a scheduled execution in Ohio when a county judge actually urged the media to televise the execution of a convicted double murderer.[64]

The televising of executions is not among the most hotly debated issues in newsrooms. Nevertheless, as long as the death penalty itself remains controversial and with the relentless competitive pressures that have driven the industry increasingly toward the sensational, it is probably just a matter of time before the debate begins for real. One could argue that the televising of an execution cannot be justified because it demeans respect for life and is nothing more than an electronic catharsis for those who seek vengeance.

On the other hand, at a more detached and unemotional level, a journalist might argue, as did Sydney Fielding, that the issue here is one of access to governmental proceedings and that the public has a right to witness the ultimate consequence of its system of justice. This argument tracks closely that usually offered in support of TV camera access to criminal trials. In addition, proponents of access could claim that televised executions could help to shape public attitudes (either pro or con) in the ongoing public debate about the morality of the death penalty.

For the purpose of discussing the ethical issues raised in this case, assume the position of News Director Rondell Hayes. Using the SAD Formula for moral reasoning outlined in Chapter 3, decide whether you will accept the warden's offer and televise Wilbert Lacey's execution.

▶ **CASE 10-4**
The Aborted Fetus as Political Speech

Harvey Dastuge was truly a one-issue candidate. He had thrown his hat into the political ring for his district's soon-to-be-vacant house seat for the sole purpose of restoring some measure of moral virtue to his state through the enactment of a strict antiabortion law. As a religious fundamentalist, Dastuge was determined to challenge what he considered the ill-conceived 1973 Supreme Court decision in *Roe v. Wade* legalizing abortion. And since that decision more than twenty years ago, the Court had turned decidedly more conservative. Dastuge believed that a majority of the justices were poised to overturn *Roe*, and he wanted to be at the vanguard of that effort.

Dastuge was a minister by training but had abandoned his pulpit ten years ago to "do God's work" among the underprivileged. He had established a nonprofit, charitable organization to provide food, money, and clothing to the needy. But having attended to the material needs of the economically disenfranchised, he reasoned, it was now time to administer to the souls of his state's inhabitants. Conventional wisdom (fueled by political pollsters) predicted a more conservative legislature would emerge from the fall elections, and Dastuge was confident that the like-minded freshmen lawmakers would support the codification of his moral vision.

Despite his lack of a comprehensive political agenda, Dastuge embarked on a grassroots campaign both to take advantage of the strong antiabortion sentiment in the state's rural communities and to cultivate the 15 percent of the electorate that were "undecided" on the legal if not moral issue of abortion. While some of his political activities were dutifully covered by the media's political reporters, as the campaign progressed most of the state's news organizations directed their scarce resources at Dastuge's more "mainstream" opponents since they viewed him as a fringe candidate with little chance of political success. Dastuge attributed this journalistic snub to "just another example of the biased liberal press" and was determined to take his case directly to the people through the unfiltered lens of TV advertising. Since his opponents had already invested heavily in the state's television commercial inventory, Dastuge knew that federal law—Section 315 of the Communications Act, to be exact—required that stations accept his commercials and run them

unedited. Apparently the authors of Section 315 never envisioned a political candidate who would actually produce a commercial featuring an aborted fetus.

And neither could Clayton Talbert, general manager of Channel 3, the ABC affiliate in Greenville. During Talbert's twelve-year tenure as GM, Channel 3 had aired a true diversity of political spots during campaigns, ranging from "attack" ads to soft-sell emotional appeals, but none had truly tempted him to defy the no-censorship provision of Section 315. While some ads occasionally provoked his outrage, none had offended his sense of moral propriety. Until now!

Talbert was cautiously optimistic that, with a rather limited campaign chest compared to his opponents, Dastuge would overlook Channel 3 in planning his campaign strategy. But his optimism quickly faded when a member of Dastuge's campaign team delivered a videocassette of the controversial spot to the station's traffic department. Talbert's quick review of the tape confirmed what his managerial colleagues around the state had already told him: the one-minute commercial contained graphic depictions of an aborted fetus.

At times like this, Talbert was usually eager to seek the advice of the station's attorney, but he had recently been updated on his legal obligations under Section 315. Although stations were still prohibited from censoring the content of commercials submitted under Section 315, the Federal Communications Commission had recently issued a policy by which broadcasters, who determined that an ad was indecent, could "time-shift" it to the late night or early morning hours when children were unlikely to be in the audience. In FCC parlance, this time period was known as a "safe harbor." Indecent content, according to the commission, was material that depicted or described, in a patently offensive manner, sexual or excretory activities. Although this ad did not exactly fit the government's concept of "indecency," it clearly offended Talbert's sense of moral propriety, especially when viewed from the perspective of TV as a family medium.

"So that's what we're up against," said Talbert as he aggressively hit the off switch on his office VCR. Before making a decision on the placement of the Dastuge commercial, he had summoned

General Sales Manager Sally McCoy and Terri Breaux, Channel 3's director of community relations, for a private screening of the candidate's rather coarse contribution to the marketplace of ideas. "Most candidates show pictures of their families or themselves kissing babies," he continued. "Dastuge has to show an aborted fetus. As you are aware, we can't just refuse to air this commercial, no matter how offensive it may be. Section 315 requires that we show the spot. Dastuge is requesting prime time for this commercial, but we can time shift it to late at night or early in the morning. We've notified Dastuge that we're considering this, and through his attorney he has registered a strong objection."

"I admit that this is strong stuff," responded McCoy. "I don't personally approve of abortion, but this ad offends me. Nevertheless, this is Dastuge's way of getting his message across. It's not unusual to see aborted fetuses displayed at antiabortion rallies, and we cover these in the news. Doesn't he have a right to compete on a level playing field? Let the viewers decide if he has gone too far. Maybe he'll self-destruct."

"But this goes beyond his views on abortion," replied Breaux unsympathetically. "Certainly he has a right to express his opinions on any subject free of censorship. But this goes too far. This ad is indecent. And if we run it in prime time, we're sure to have a lot of complaints from our viewers."

"But let me play devil's advocate," said McCoy. "Dastuge's position is that abortion is murder. He apparently believes the only way to communicate the horrors of the abortion process is to show it graphically to the electorate. Sure it's offensive to some. But that's going to be true even if we just time shift the commercial to a later hour."

"But children are less likely to be in the audience late at night," said Talbert. "We'll probably have fewer complaints if we run the spots at midnight or 1 A.M."

"You have a point," conceded McCoy, who visibly felt uncomfortable defending Dastuge's intellectually barren and indecent contribution to the marketplace of ideas. "However, there's no guarantee that, particularly in today's permissive society, children won't be in the audience even at that hour. But even assuming the validity of your assertion, time-shifting the spot doesn't really confront the issue of airing this offensive commercial, even to a smaller number of adult viewers late at night. What about our responsibilities to them?"

"We have a responsibility to all our viewers," replied Breaux. "And we may still get some complaints. However, we have no choice but to air this spot. We're just trying to schedule it where it will do the least damage. We won't make as much money off these spots in this time position, but I think it's the responsible thing to do."

"I'm not concerned about the revenue," the sales manager shot back, apparently offended at the subtle reference to her perceived preoccupation with commercial values. "In terms of our station's bottom line, as a percentage of income we don't derive that much from these spots anyway. But I still think we should run them in prime time with an advisory to our viewers. We shouldn't be in a position of making content judgments on political commercials, even to the extent of time shifting them. After all, that's why the 'no censorship' provision was written into Section 315—to allow candidates to express their views without interference from broadcast licensees. If we shift this spot because we happen to believe it's offensive, then what will be next?"

Indeed, Clayton Talbert had no intention of serving as gatekeeper for the diversity of political spots that consumed much of his commercial inventory during various campaigns. His station had lived in harmony with Section 315 for too long and had accommodated itself to this electronic packaging of candidates that usually made a rather questionable contribution to the quality of political discourse. However, Dastuge's antiabortion spot went beyond the bounds of moral propriety. Surely any reasonable viewer would be offended by such graphic representations of the abortion process. Should his station's management abandon all responsibility in the matter on the grounds that "offensiveness" is too subjective a standard? On the other hand, this one-issue candidate did have a following, although not in sufficient numbers (according to the polls) to provide him with a seat in the legislature.

Sally McCoy had framed this dilemma in terms of a free-speech issue. But at times like this, Talbert found it difficult to invoke First Amendment values. He worried that even the time shifting of Dastuge's commercial, despite the recent FCC ruling, would be met with a legal challenge. But his more immediate concern was with the ethical dimensions of airing an offensive political message that would clearly be offensive to a significant segment of his audience.

THE CASE STUDY

This case is not strictly about the competing philosophies of unbridled libertarianism versus paternalism or the conflicting values of censorship and free speech. After all, federal law still requires that these offensive ads be aired but does allow broadcasters to shift them to times when children are unlikely to be in the audience. Of course, many mature adults will not be in the audience either, and some of these may be supporters of this antiabortion candidate.

The station's general manager, Clayton Talbert, has initially responded as most reasonable people would—with an acute sense of revulsion. On what moral grounds, one might wonder, can such a revolting ad without any apparent socially redeeming value be justified? And since the station cannot refuse the ad altogether, what is wrong with minimizing the harm by relegating it to a period when audience levels are low? Indeed, it might be hard to imagine any TV station airing this spot in prime time. On the other hand, one could argue that, while the "no censorship" language of Section 315 is *legally* unambiguous (despite the FCC's interpretation), its intent is also to remove licensees from the business of making moral judgments about political messages, no matter how offensive they might be.

Channel 3's community relations director agrees with Talbert; but the sales manager, Sally McCoy, while not approving of the ad's offensive content, believes the Dastuge campaign has the same moral claim to the station's prime time audience as other candidates. She apparently believes that "offensiveness" is a poor test for determining the suitability of political content. Or, to put it another way, McCoy is willing to allow the strict interpretation of the law (no censorship) to serve as the

station's ethical standard as well. Her solution is to include a viewer advisory. Is this sufficient from an ethical perspective?

For the purpose of evaluating the ethical dilemma posed in this scenario, assume the position of General Manager Clayton Talbert, and, using the SAD Formula for moral reasoning outlined in Chapter 3, decide whether you will afford Harvey Dastuge access to your prime-time commercial lineup or relegate his offensive political spot to more remote time periods of your broadcast schedule.

 CASE 10-5
The Holocaust Myth and Free Speech[65]

Hermann and Marta Weiss were among the more than six million Jews who died in Nazi concentration camps in World War II, victims of Adolph Hitler's campaign of annihilation. This policy of genocide came to be known as the Holocaust, an unimaginable event that soon became a prominent feature of the Weiss family's oral history. And now, more than half a century later after her grandparents' persecution at the hands of the Nazis and their subsequent execution at Auschwitz, Myra Weiss was confronted with her legacy in a rather brutal fashion.

Myra Weiss was a senior majoring in journalism at Cornwallis University, a prestigious private college in Connecticut. As editor of the university's student newspaper, the *Intelligentsia*, Weiss was no stranger to controversy. Her uncompromising and often linguistically harsh editorials on such contentious topics as abortion, the proposed "hate speech" amendment to the Code of Student Conduct, and the university's irresolute sexual harassment policies distinguished the young student journalist as a person of conviction. Despite the fact that Cornwallis was a private university and thus not subject to the same First Amendment constraints as public institutions of higher learning, the administration had committed itself to a hands-off posture. And Weiss took full advantage of that noble concession. In the editorial staff meetings,

Weiss had often expressed the view that the *Intelligentsia* was a forum for free expression and that no ideas should be denied admittance to its pages just because they offended some of the paper's readers. But the ad that arrived one morning in the mail gave her pause.

Michael Kaplan, the *Intelligentsia*'s advertising manager, had first brought the ad to the editor's attention. The ad, with its four-column narrative layout, resembled a magazine feature rather than an advertisement and had been delivered as camera-ready copy, along with a $500 check, to the paper's advertising and circulation department. It was written under the byline of someone named Bradley R. Smith and was titled "The Holocaust Controversy: The Case for Open Debate." The ad was clearly an exercise in historical revisionism, a denial of the reality of the Holocaust. As Weiss read the ad, she became increasingly offended at Smith's unmistakable message. While Smith did not dispute the fact that many Jews had suffered during the Nazi era and many had been killed, he challenged the documented fact that the deaths had resulted from any systematic policy of extermination. The deaths in many of the camps were due to natural causes, he claimed, rather than execution. Smith challenged the eyewitness testimony, on which much of the historical evidence of the Holocaust is based, as being notoriously unreliable. He blamed this historical cover-up on Zionists who were perpetuating the "myth" simply to justify the continuing existence of the state of Israel. Smith also accused college administrators and faculty of "political correctness" in denying revisionists access to their campuses to discuss their views and to debunk the Holocaust myth.

Weiss was offended by this potentially explosive ad at a university with a significant Jewish population. But her journalistic instincts and curiosity could not be disquieted, even by the prospect of publishing what in her opinion were such distasteful falsehoods. She quickly retreated from the hectic pace of the newsroom to the more tranquil surroundings of the library to acquaint herself better with the Holocaust denial movement. She also interviewed Professor Dale Martin, an eminent scholar in the history department who also taught a course on Nazi Germany.

Weiss had approached her self-imposed assignment in the hopes that Smith would turn out to be merely an anti-Semitic kook, a lone voice in the wilderness. That alone might justify refusing to publish his ad, since under those circumstances his radical claims would lack credibility. But Weiss was disappointed. Smith, it turned out, was the head of the Committee for Open Debate on the Holocaust and spent much of his time producing ads and videotapes and distributing them to college papers. Some student editors found his ideas repugnant and refused to accept them, but many other reputable college papers published them in either advertisement or opinion form. Although Smith's thesis had been rejected by most reputable scholars as nothing more than a reflection of his anti-Semitic views, revisionism was given its impetus with the publication in 1977 of the book *The Hoax of the Twentieth Century* by Arthur R. Butz, a professor of electrical engineering and computer sciences at Northwestern University. In addition, Smith's brand of historical revisionism was supported by international contingents in such diverse locations as Europe, South America, the Middle East, and Japan. It was clear, as Weiss met with her paper's editorial board, that Bradley Smith was no lone voice in the wilderness. The Holocaust denial movement, in Weiss's view, might be composed of historical charlatans, but they had already achieved some credibility for their preposterous beliefs.

The *Intelligentsia*'s editorial board consisted of Weiss, Managing Editor Joseph Bell, Advertising Manager Michael Kaplan, and Faculty Adviser Sally Stevens. Weiss began the meeting by briefing her colleagues on her investigation. "I've done some research in the library on the revisionist movement," said Weiss, "and I've also talked with Professor Martin in the history department. He teaches a course on Nazi Germany. Bradley Smith is no kook. If you read this ad, his arguments are well presented. If you aren't tied to that period in history, you might well be persuaded by this ad."

"Smith may be articulate and he may deny that he's anti-Semitic, but the claims in this ad are simply untrue," noted Bell. "No event in history has been better documented than the Holocaust. If we're part of a university whose purpose it is to search for truth, I don't think we should be a party to disseminating these kinds of blatant falsehoods."

"Let me play devil's advocate for a moment," responded Stevens, who always delighted in socratically challenging her journalistic neophytes. "We're not a public university, so First Amendment concerns are off the table. We aren't *required* to publish this ad. Nevertheless, this revisionist movement does have support across the country. It's true that most respectable scholars have debunked Smith and his cohorts. But the best way to expose false ideas is to debate them openly. From an ethical perspective, we should believe in First Amendment values even if we aren't legally required to do so."

"But 30 percent of our student body is Jewish," replied Kaplan emphatically. "If we publish this ad, it will be morally offensive to many of our readers. Even today, this is a very sensitive issue among the descendants of those who died in the Nazi death camps. The *Intelligentsia* will be savaged if we publish Smith's outrageous piece of historical revisionism."

Despite her revulsion at Smith's blatant denial of the Holocaust, Weiss prided herself on her unwavering support of First Amendment values. In board meetings such as this, she had often stated that no ideas should be denied access to the student paper just because of their moral offensiveness. She remained resolute in her commitment to principle. "Many of our readers will be offended," said Weiss, without a trace of doubt. "I'm Jewish and I'm in sympathy with this position. But if we refuse to publish content—editorial or otherwise— just because the *ideas* are offensive, then we could be accused of moral hypocrisy. We cling to a strong belief in the First Amendment when it comes to our own views; yet, we appear to have reservations when it comes to someone else's ideas that are offensive. If the First Amendment means anything, it should offer sanctuary for the most offensive of views. I'm in favor of holding our collective noses and publishing this ad."

Because Myra Weiss was Jewish, Bell was surprised at her tolerant stance in the face of one of the most historically offensive desecrations to the memories of the Holocaust victims. Nevertheless, he was undeterred in his opposition to publication of Smith's ad. "We're not talking about just offensive ideas," he said. "This ad is loaded with falsehoods. We know it's false; the evidence supporting the Holocaust is undeniable. If we run this ad, we'll become a party to this historical revisionism. In a sense, just by publishing it, these falsehoods achieve a certain amount of legitimacy."

"But don't you think your classmates are savvy enough to see through these falsehoods?" asked Stevens. "The content may be offensive to some of our students, but I doubt that any of these ideas will be viewed as credible among the student body. And keep in mind, there's no overt racist language in this ad. Smith may or may not be anti-Semitic, but he has advanced some intellectual arguments in support of his ideas. They may be wrong and not stand up to historical scrutiny, but if anything is offensive about this ad, it's the ideas, not the language. And doesn't the First Amendment protect offensive ideas?"

"I'm not so sure," replied Bell. "This ad contains some historical falsehoods. I thought the First Amendment was designed to promote the search for truth. It's morally offensive without having any redeeming value. This ad is nothing more than anti-Semiticism concealed by a clever facade of intellectual rhetoric. Unfortunately, it looks and sounds credible, and there could very well be some converts among our non-Jewish population. This ad could cause some further division among students and faculty."

"Professor Martin has an interesting perspective on the matter," conceded Weiss, acknowledging a reality that could undermine her own position. "He says that we must keep in mind that today's students are three generations removed from the Holocaust and World War II. They have no ties to that era. They're also more cynical, according to Professor Martin, and view history and the media with a great deal of skepticism. Of course, skepticism can be healthy, and it's often essential to good scholarship. But unfortunately, today's students are also more ignorant. A recent poll of high school students found that almost 40 percent weren't familiar with the Holocaust. Students are more likely to believe in conspiracy theories and historical hoaxes."

"But according to that logic," responded

Stevens, "perhaps we should avoid any discussion of the conspiracy theories surrounding the assassination of President Kennedy. We can't control what people believe. If this university really believes in freedom of inquiry and First Amendment values—and the *Intelligentsia* is a part of the university community—then we should publish this ad, even if we believe it to be false."

"But we wouldn't publish a news story that we know is false," replied Kaplan. "Why publish this ad? What does it contribute of value to the story of the Holocaust?"

"That's not a very persuasive argument," responded Weiss. "We do check our stories for accuracy, and we try to avoid publishing knowingly defamatory information to avoid a lawsuit. But news stories are a result of our own enterprise. They reflect on us. Although this ad does resemble editorial copy, it's clearly identified as an ad under the byline of Bradley Smith. We've accepted other editorial ads on other topics. How can we in good conscience turn this one down just because of the offensive nature of its ideas?"

"This subject is different," insisted Kaplan. "The other 'advertorials' dealt with such subjects as abortion, capital punishment, and the environment. All of these are emotional issues, and sometimes the viewpoints in these ads have been expressed in fairly strident language. Public sentiment is divided on these issues. But no one endorses genocide, and the insinuation that the Holocaust was a hoax is highly offensive to the Jewish community. I don't see where there is another side to this issue. If we run this ad, this paper will be accused of a lack of sensitivity and respect for a large segment of our readers, many of whom have ancestors who died at the hands of the Nazis."

"I appreciate this 'lack of respect' argument," replied Stevens. "And I'm certainly not insensitive to the feelings of our Jewish readers. But they are mature college students. Surely they can handle this controversy, even if it does offend their sense of moral propriety. Their ancestors have admonished the world to *never forget* the Holocaust. Revisionists like Bradley Smith will ensure that this never happens. And I don't agree that publishing this ad will afford legitimacy to his cause. It may even serve as a catalyst to educate other students on campus as to the horrific nature of arguably the worst case of genocide in history."

Under the university policy establishing the *Intelligentsia*, the editor was the ultimate gatekeeper in determining the content of the voice of student expression at Cornwallis University. Nevertheless, Myra Weiss valued the input of the other board members, as well as the views of her editorial and advertising staffs. As she confronted the conflicts between her belief in free expression and Bradley Smith's affront to her heritage that she knew would also be morally offensive to many of her classmates, Weiss decided to take a straw poll of her staff to bring as much wisdom as possible to bear on her troublesome dilemma.

THE CASE STUDY

Should some opinions be denied access to the marketplace of ideas because of their morally offensive and inflammatory nature? Is the fact that the claims underlying the opinions are demonstrably false (at least according to the most credible scholarship and evidence) relevant to this inquiry?

While this scenario is essentially hypothetical, it is based on a controversy that has erupted on college campuses nationwide, as well as in mainstream society. Putting aside the legal questions underlying the First Amendment protection of such expression, one view is that the moral imperative of the First Amendment commands absolute protection for all speech regardless of its falsehood and offensive nature. In the marketplace of ideas, according to this view, historical revisionists without credible evidence on their side will be readily debunked and their views discredited. And since any controversial subject might be offensive to some, this is an insufficient test for regulating speech.

On the other hand, some people argue that some speech by its very nature is so offensive that it has no socially redeeming value. Racially motivated hate speech, for example, falls into this category. Thus, for a student newspaper to give legitimacy to a thesis supported by false claims by publishing it to a population that is vulnerable to its message is immoral. And since the university is intellectually committed to the search for truth, knowing dissemination of false information is unacceptable. The paper, in effect, becomes an accomplice in spreading such malicious falsehoods.

Before making her decision, Editor Myra Weiss has decided to take a straw poll of the newspaper's staff. Assume the role of a staff member of the *Intelligentsia,* and, using the moral reasoning model outlined in Chapter 3, reveal how you would vote on the publication of Bradley Smith's ad.

▶ ### CASE 10-6
Cyberporn and Free Speech

"Obscenity in Outer Space: The Marketing of Cyberporn." This snappy headline in the Southwestern University *Chronicle,* the university's student newspaper, highlighted a two-page article on the marketing of sexually explicit material through the Internet. It also presaged a public relations nightmare for university president William Calders.

The article, published under the byline of student reporter Scott Winters, had been the culmination of several weeks of painstaking research "surfing the net" for any trace of on-line pornography, which he found in surprising abundance. Winters had availed himself of the university's connection to the World Wide Web that was available to students both in the library and a special computer-equipped room in the student union. The *Chronicle*'s editorial offices were also hardwired for ready access to cyberspace. Winters had not targeted commercial bulletin boards that housed adult pictures and narrative since those were available only upon payment of a fee. He was interested primarily in the availability of such adult-oriented fare on-line, including explicit "sample" materials (both pictures and narrative) that served as promotional and marketing tools for the commercial adult bulletin boards.

Not only was Winters surprised at the accessibility of such morally offensive content; he was also able to identify the computers from which requests for pornographic materials originated, since the Netscape "browser" tool provided by the university

to facilitate student access to the Internet also made a copy of each transaction. And much to the dismay of the university's administration, the young journalist had dutifully noted his classmates' keen interest in the material under investigation. Southwestern University students, it seemed, viewed the Internet as more than just an engaging medium for intellectual pursuits.

"I'm really catching some heat about this *Chronicle* article—or more precisely, what the article represents," said President Calders as he convened a strategy session on what he called the "cyberporn flap." With him were Nathan Moses, vice president for academic affairs; Morris Feldman, director of university public relations; Joanne Michaels, the dean of students; and Jacob Samuelson, student government president. Calders usually consulted the president of student government on matters affecting student life at the university, because he liked to think of himself as "student oriented" and considered Samuelson as a good source of intelligence about student opinion.

"I've had calls from several parents wondering why we're allowing students to have access to this kind of material," continued Calders. "And the chairman of the board of regents isn't thrilled about it, either. On the other side, the president of the local chapter of the American Civil Liberties Union heard we were considering blocking student access to this material and called to urge us to reconsider. I told him no decision had been made on the matter."

"It's been only a week since publication of this article, but my office has already handled numerous inquiries from the media, including the *Chronicle of Higher Education,*" volunteered Feldman.

"There's a lot of interest at every level," admitted the university president. "This is a complex issue—for us, it involves free speech, academic freedom, our responsibility to the students and their parents. And since whatever we decide will also affect the image and credibility of the university, it's also a troublesome PR problem. And that's your domain, Morris!"

"I think I speak for the faculty in opposing any limitation on access to any part of the World Wide Web," said Moses. "We invested heavily in this system to facilitate both faculty and student research. I'm aware that some of this usage may not be for legitimate research purposes. But I don't think we should spend our time policing how the students and faculty use this facility. This is a public university, and I don't think there should be censorship of any kind."

"I don't see this as censorship," responded Michaels. "Since we're facilitating the students' access to this material, why can't we control the conditions under which they have this access? I realize our students are adults. But our mission is to encourage earnest intellectual pursuits. Surfing the Net to gawk at pornography is not my idea of serious research. Besides, some of this material is probably illegal under current obscenity laws. Do we want to be in a position of providing access to material that may not even be legal to begin with?"

"But how can we recommend values to our students that promote freedom of inquiry and freedom of expression and then tell them that they are too immature to view this material?" asked Moses. "It's too paternalistic to try to distinguish between legitimate research interests and prurient interests."

"There are other values that are just as important as freedom of inquiry and expression," stated Michaels unequivocally. The dean of students was not bothered by the accusation of paternalism, since she viewed the moral behavior of many college students to be subject to the whims of unbridled youth. Their psychological maturity, she reasoned from her own experience, was not matched by their ethical development.

"Just three years ago," she continued, "this university decided that the teaching of ethical values was important enough that now all students are required to take a course in moral philosophy. And two years ago the Faculty Senate approved an amendment to the Code of Student Conduct punishing hate speech directed at racial and ethnic minorities. Although a federal judge has just declared this provision to be unconstitutional, the point is that the faculty decided that the promotion of campus civility and tolerance was just as important as free speech. If we limit access to this so-called cyberporn, this will send a message that this kind of material has no socially redeeming value and

doesn't contribute anything of significance to intellectual discourse. I don't see this as a free-speech issue since it's not the students' speech that's at stake."

"Part of the free-speech equation," responded Moses, "is the right to receive information. I realize that much of this material is trash. But I don't see how we can control access without interfering with legitimate research. Besides, even if we could, these students are mature enough to make their own decisions."

"But our situation isn't exactly comparable to making a rational choice to see a movie or purchase an adult magazine," said Calders. "It's true that students don't have to log on to this material. But it's certainly tempting. Should we be using public money to facilitate access to cyberporn?"

"How do the students feel about this?" Calders directed this question to Jacob Samuelson.

"There's some difference of opinion," responded Samuelson, who had patiently awaited his turn to join this engaging exchange. "But most seem to oppose any censorship by the administration. They feel they are mature enough to make their own decisions, especially since the university has set up this system partially for their benefit. However, there are a few who find pornography repugnant and would have no problem if the university blocked access to this material."

Calders then turned to the university's PR director. "How do you assess the public fallout from all of this?"

"From a PR perspective, there are two concerns: image and intellectual credibility," replied Feldman. "On the issue of credibility, quite frankly I don't think the public understands our intellectual debates about academic freedom. We'll catch some heat from our own faculty and probably from scholars across the country. And, of course, the civil libertarians will be heard from on the issue of free speech. But the public—and that includes the parents of our students—is fairly conservative. They aren't likely to understand why this university is providing access to pornography for our student body. We may suffer some short-term damage in terms of image. But it'll blow over. Most parents aren't likely to refuse to send their students here because of this flap, unless some other problem arises. What it boils down to is what this university feels is more important: students' right as autonomous individuals to choose their own materials, regardless of how morally offensive they might be to some, or the university's responsibility to set standards and to promote virtuous behavior and attitudes. Of course, the two might not be mutually exclusive."

"This has been a productive dialogue," said Calders sincerely as he adjourned the meeting. "This is a serious matter. I want each of you to give this issue some thought and have your individual recommendations on my desk within a week. And then before a final decision is made, we'll reconvene to consider whether cyberporn will continue to be a prominent feature of Southwestern University's information superhighway."

THE CASE STUDY

Even as the ethics of the distribution of and access to sexually explicit and other morally offensive content through conventional media remain controversial, new technologies now pose more daunting challenges to society in confronting the ethical dimensions of their cultural influence. The traditional regulatory mechanisms constructed to control the flow of pornography seem inadequate in the face of unrestricted access to the World Wide Web by adults, adolescents and children alike.

In this case, a public university is a facilitator in this process. University administrators, in order to remain technologically competitive, have provided their students and faculty with a system that is interactive with the Internet and other computer systems. While the purpose of this access is research, there is little supervision of how the system is used. And now that the public is finally realizing the potential of this information technology, they are demanding accountability. And even the administration is divided. On the one hand, the dean of students rejects the notion that the university, having set up this system for students and faculty, must now abandon any control over the kinds of material that are examined or downloaded by its users. She sees this as another opportunity to

teach values and virtuous behavior, to which the university has supposedly committed itself. She is also concerned about whether the university should provide unsupervised access to content that may not even be legal under current obscenity statutes.

On the other hand, the vice president for academic affairs sees this as a matter of academic freedom and free speech. Both positions, of course, raise the question of what role the university should play in facilitating access to content along the information superhighway that some consider to be at least morally offensive or perhaps even legally obscene under current law.

President Calders has requested each of those present at the meeting to submit a recommendation on whether to regulate access to the Internet. Much of the analysis, of course, will focus on the ethical dimensions of the issue. For the purpose of responding to the university president's request, assume the role of university PR Director Morris Feldman. Then, using the SAD Formula for moral reasoning outlined in Chapter 3, formulate a recommendation to the president, defending your position.

▼

Notes

1. Philip Elmer-Dewitt, "On a Screen Near You: Cyberporn," *Time*, July 3, 1995, p. 40.
2. For a discussion of how the press reported this case, see Linda Lotridge Levin, "Dirty Words and Blushing Editors," *Quill*, September 1986, pp. 22–25.
3. "Mama Mia! Breast Pic Offends Readers," *Quill*, April 1992, p. 5.
4. Dennis McDougal, "The Static over 'Silence,'" *TV Guide*, February 4, 1995, pp. 30–31.
5. *The Report of the Commission on Obscenity and Pornography* (Washington, D.C.: U.S. Government Printing Office, 1970). However, the commission recommended retention of some laws dealing with displaying and distributing pornographic materials to nonconsenting adults.
6. Stewart made this comment in his concurring opinion in *Jacobellis v. State of Ohio*, 378 U.S. 184, 197 (1964).
7. *Roth v. United States*, 354 U.S. 476 (1957).
8. 413 U.S. 15 (1973).
9. In 1987, the Court clarified the third prong of the

Miller standard by ruling that deciding whether a work is obscene does not require the application of contemporary community standards to determine whether the material lacks serious literary, artistic, political, or scientific value. Instead, the Court said, the aim should be to assess whether a "reasonable person" would find such value in the material taken as a whole. *Pope v. Illinois*, 14 Med.L.Rptr. 1001 (1987).

10. See *Pinkus v. U.S.*, 98 S.Ct. 1808 (1978); *Hamling v. U.S.*, 418 U.S. 87 (1974); *Jenkins v. Georgia*, 418 U.S. 153 (1974).

11. One author who takes this position is Harry M. Clor in *Obscenity and Public Morality: Censorship in a Liberal Society* (Chicago: University of Chicago Press, 1969).

12. For a discussion of the relationship between women's rights, pornography, and the First Amendment see Dwight L. Teeter, Jr., and Don R. Le Duc, *Law of Mass Communications*, 7th ed. (Westbury, NY: Foundation Press, 1992), pp. 360–361.

13. *American Booksellers Association, Inc. v. Hudnut*, 598 F.Supp. 1316 (S.D. Ind., 1984).

14. 771 F.2d 323 (7th Cir., 1985).

15. For a summary of this controversy, see Don R. Pember, *Mass Media Law*, 6th ed. (Dubuque, IA: WCB Brown & Benchmark, 1993), pp. 444–445.

16. Austin Murphy, "Toothsome Sacrifice," *Sports Illustrated*, May 8, 1989, p. 26.

17. See "Toppling the Last Taboos," *Newsweek*, October 28, 1991, p. 32.

18. Quoted in Wayne Hoffman, "No Longer Taboo," *Communicator*, October 1994, p. 85.

19. Hoffman, "No Longer Taboo," p. 85.

20. *Ibid.*

21. See *FCC v. Pacifica Foundation*, 3 Med.L.Rptr. 2553, 2554 (1978).

22. *Ibid.*

23. For a discussion of this issue, see Howard M. Kleiman, "Indecent Programming on Cable Television: Legal and Social Dimensions," *Journal of Broadcasting and Electronic Media*, 30, Summer 1986, pp. 275–294.

24. See Pember, *Mass Media Law*, pp. 573–574.

25. *Ibid.*

26. For a discussion of this case, see T. Barton Carter, Marc A. Franklin, and Jay B. Wright, *The First Amendment and the Fourth Estate*, 6th ed. (Westbury, NY: Foundation Press, 1994), p. 823.

27. See "FCC Turns Up the Heat on Indecency," *Broadcasting*, August 28, 1989, p. 27.

28. For some examples of Stern's comments, see Franklin, *The First Amendment and the Fourth Estate*, p. 823.

29. Alan Sayre, "FCC Crackdown Sparks Debate," (Baton Rouge) *Morning Advocate*, September 15, 1989, p. 14C.

30. Elmer-Dewitt, "On a Screen Near You," p. 40.

31. *Ibid.*, p. 42.

32. See Patrick R. Parsons and William E. Smith, "R. Budd Dwyer: A Case Study in Newsroom Decision Making," *Journal of Mass Media Ethics*, 3, no. 1, 1988, pp. 84–85.

33. *Ibid.*

34. *Ibid.*, pp. 89–90.

35. "News Photo of Public Suicide Placed Many Editors in Quandary," *ASNE Bulletin*, February 1987, p. 5.

36. Chevel Johnson, "Viewers Back Decision to Air Suicide Drama," (Baton Rouge) *Advocate*, September 17, 1994, p. 4B.

37. *Ibid.*

38. *Ibid.*

39. *Ibid.*

40. William L. Rivers and Cleve Mathews, *Ethics for the Media* (Upper Saddle River, NJ: Prentice Hall, 1988), pp. 137–138.

41. See Conrad Smith and Tom Hubbard, "Professionalism and Awards in News Photography," *Journalism Quarterly*, 64, Summer–Autumn 1987, p. 352.

42. See Thomas Griffith, "The Visuals Did Marcos In," *Time*, March 17, 1986, p. 72.

43. Parsons and Smith, "Budd Dwyer," p. 92.

44. "A Photograph That Said What Words Could Not," (Baton Rouge) *Sunday Advocate*, April 23, 1995, p. 14B.

45. "No Excuse for Gory Photos," (Baton Rouge) *Morning Advocate*, September 25, 1990, p. 6B.

46. Jacqueline Sharkey, "When Pictures Drive Foreign Policy," *American Journalism Review*, December 1993, pp. 14–19.

47. See John L. Hulteng, *The Messenger's Motives: Ethical Problems of the News Media*, 2d ed. (Upper Saddle River, NJ: Prentice Hall, 1985), pp. 148–149.

48. See Thomas L. Tedford, *Freedom of Speech in the United States* (New York: Random House, 1985), p. 152.

49. Harold L. Nelson, Dwight L. Teeter, Jr., and Don R. Le Duc, *Law of Mass Communications*, 6th ed. (Westbury, NY: Foundation Press, 1989), p. 380, citing the *New York Times*, October 14, 1937, p. 29.

50. Thomas L. Tedford, *Freedom of Speech in the United States* (New York: Random House, 1985), p. 147.

51. These categories are based on those described by Joel Feinberg in *Social Philosophy* (Upper Saddle River, NJ: Prentice Hall, 1973), Chaps. 2–3. However, they are also dealt with in some detail in Thomas A. Mappes and Jane S. Zembaty, *Social Ethics: Morality and Social Policy*, 3d ed. (New York: McGraw-Hill, 1987), pp. 284–287; and Tom L. Beauchamp, *Philosophical Ethics: An Introduction to Moral Philosophy* (New York: McGraw-Hill, 1982), pp. 270–297.

52. Franklyn S. Haiman, *Speech and Law in a Free Society* (Chicago: University of Chicago Press, 1977), p. 164.

53. Described in Alan M. Dershowitz, *Taking Liberties: A Decade of Hard Cases, Bad Laws*, and Bum Raps (Chicago: Contemporary Books, 1988), pp. 179–180. The commission issued its report and conclusions in 1986. See U.S. Attorney General's Committee on Pornography, *Final Report*, 2 vols. (Washington, D.C.: U.S. Government Printing Office, 1986).

54. Dennis T. Lowry and David E. Towles, "Prime Time TV Portrayals of Sex, Contraception and Venereal Diseases," *Journalism Quarterly*, 66, Summer 1989, pp. 347–352.

55. Reems's real name was Herbert Streicker.

56. Quoted in Alan M. Dershowitz, *The Best Defense* (New York: Random House, 1982), p. 158.

57. Mappes and Zembaty, *Social Ethics*, p. 285.

58. For a discussion of the pros and cons of these liberty-limiting principles, see Mappes and Zembaty, *Social Ethics*, pp. 285–287.

59. For a discussion of the public's right to pornography, see Ronald Dworkin, *A Matter of Principle* (Cambridge, MA: Harvard University Press, 1985), pp. 335–372.

60. G. L. Simons, "Is Pornography Beneficial?" in Mappes and Zembaty, *Social Ethics*, pp. 301–306; Walter Berns, "Beyond the (Garbage) Pale or Democracy, Censorship and the Arts," in Harry M. Clor (ed.), *Censorship and Freedom of Expression: Essays on Obscenity and the Law* (Chicago: Rand McNally, 1971), p. 63.

61. This case is based on an ethical dilemma confronted by editors at the Baton Rouge, Louisiana, *Advocate* in November 1994. See Edward Pratt, "Horrible Photo Had to Be Seen," (Baton Rouge) *Advocate*, November 26, 1994, p. 7B.

62. "'Live, from San Quentin . . . ,'" *Newsweek*, April 1, 1991, p. 61.

63. *Garrett v. Estelle*, 556 F.2d 1974 (5th Cir., 1977), *cert. denied*, 438 U.S. 914 (1978).

64. "Judge Wants Execution Televised," *Broadcasting & Cable*, December 5, 1994, p. 89.

65. Some of the information and ideas for this case study were derived from a recently published article describing the controversy over Bradley Smith's ads. See Gayle Forman, "Denying History," *Flux 1995*, pp. 17–20.

11

Media Practitioners and Social Justice

THE PRINCIPLE OF FORMAL JUSTICE

There are many ways of viewing the idea of justice, but common to all of them is this fundamental principle: *like cases should be treated alike*; there should be no double standards.[1] This notion, which has traditionally been attributed to Aristotle, is sometimes referred to as the *principle of formal justice*, because it is a minimal requirement for any system of justice but advances no criteria for deciding the question of when two parties should be considered equal.[2] The formal principle of justice provides a point of departure for debates about social justice but must be supplemented with other principles to serve as a blueprint for meaningful moral reasoning about the matter.

For example, many people believe that race, gender, or sexual preference should not be used as bases for hiring, but nothing in Aristotle's view precludes using them. In fact, race has been used as a legitimate employment criterion in order to compensate for past injustices. Thus, theories other than Aristotle's formal principle must be brought to bear to justify the consideration of race as a just hiring practice. It remains for the individual or institution dispensing justice to establish the criteria for equitable consideration. But once the standards are in place, the formal principle of justice requires that all parties be treated alike in the application of those standards. This idea is reflected in the salary scales of journalists, who deserve the same pay as their colleagues with similar experiences and job profiles.

MEDIA PRACTITIONERS AND SOCIAL JUSTICE: TWO VIEWS

Most of us would not quibble with a system of justice that seeks equality of treatment for all members of society. It is certainly a noble goal. But how this goal is to be achieved has posed some interesting political, legal, and philosophical questions and has precipitated some sharp cultural divisions. At one extreme are those who believe that justice can best be achieved by relying on individual freedom and marketplace forces to provide for equal opportunity. This view is represented by the traditional libertarian theory that media practitioners should be independent and autonomous, without any moral obligation to society. At the other extreme are those who doubt that justice can ever be achieved through a blind faith in the self-interests of individuals and that some form of social responsibility, enforced through public pressure or governmental action, is often necessary to ensure equal opportunity. Proponents of this view believe that the media have a moral duty to promote equality and justice. These opposing philosophies have influenced the media's institutional role in achieving social justice and are reflected in such practices as employment, responsiveness to the cultural needs of minorities, and the coverage of controversial issues.

The Libertarian Concept of Justice

The libertarian conception of justice is closely aligned with the traditional view of the media's role in U.S. society.[3] Having grown from the writings of such notables as John Milton, John Locke, and John Stuart Mill, the libertarian philosophy is characterized by the marketplace of ideas as the primary determinant of social and political truths.[4] Under this theory, justice consists of the maximizing of individual freedom from both government coercion and demands for special attention by segments of society. Freedom of the press is codified in the First Amendment, and media practitioners have historically favored an independent press, responsible to no one except their own consciences. This philosophy is reflected in a comment attributed to William Peter Hamilton of the *Wall Street Journal*: "A newspaper is a private enterprise owing nothing whatever to the public, which grants it no franchise. It is therefore affected with no public interest. It is emphatically the property of the owner, who is selling a manufactured product at his own risk."[5]

Media practitioners may report on social injustices but do not necessarily feel any responsibility to crusade on their behalf. Libertarians reject mandated rights of access for political and social groups and prefer to leave it to the competitive forces of the marketplace to determine the extent of media exposure for various causes. Thus, libertarians advocate the right to espouse a cause in the belief that competing views will provide a "self-righting" effect if all have the same opportunity to speak. Critics of this philosophy point out that not all members of society have the same opportunity. Political, social, and economic considerations often serve as barriers to the marketplace of ideas.

Libertarianism is clearly concerned with self-interest. But proponents of this theory, such as the economist Milton Friedman, argue that individuals' and institutions' pursuit of their own interests will ultimately benefit society. Involvement in righting social wrongs, according to this view, compromises the media's role as an objective observer and threatens journalistic and artistic freedom.

Even when media coverage itself threatens the cause of justice, libertarians prefer to seek alternatives to governmental coercion. A case in point is the extensive and sometimes sensational publicity surrounding the trial of a defendant accused of committing a particularly heinous crime. Such news coverage, especially when it involves the release of incriminating evidence before a jury can be selected, threatens the defendant's right to the fair administration of justice. Libertarians stress the alternatives to "gagging" the press, such as a change of venue, postponing the trial, and uncovering bias through the jury selection process. The objective is to protect both the right to a free press and the right of the defendant to a fair trial, which can sometimes precipitate an awkward balancing act.

One could argue that this issue of free press versus fair trial is more a legal matter than a question of social justice. But because the issue raises questions of media responsibility, the ethical concerns underlying the dangers of "trial by media" are worthy of consideration. The media are the representatives of the public in maintaining vigilance over the criminal justice system. Thus, to the extent that their coverage is prejudicial and irresponsible, they have violated their public trust and perhaps undermined society's commitment to the principle that a person is innocent until proven guilty. It is not overstating the matter to point out that the media's interest in a defendant's right to a fair trial is as great as that of the society they serve.

The Egalitarian Concept and Social Responsibility

Whereas libertarianism emphasizes individual self-sufficiency, egalitarianism focuses on ensuring equality for all members of society. Egalitarians are more willing to sacrifice individual liberty in the name of justice than are libertarians. Thus, these philosophers would argue that media practitioners should relinquish some editorial discretion to ensure that various segments of society have access to the nation's organs of mass communication.

In its most extreme form, egalitarianism appears to be implausible as a foundation for a system of justice, because it demands equality regardless of what people deserve. But most egalitarian theories are highly qualified. Some take the form of *distributive justice*, in which such things as property, rights, and opportunities are allocated to members of society in equal shares according to merit. A system of equal pay for equal work is such an example. Others emphasize a theory of *compensatory justice*, which holds that whenever an injustice occurs that results in harm, some form of moral compensation is required. Affirmative action programs, for example, are designed to afford this kind of equal opportunity in employment and to remedy past injustices. Likewise, the increasing visibility of minorities in prime-time programming might be viewed as an attempt to compensate for the historical absence of minorities from television except in the most stereotypical of roles.

Those who oppose affirmative action programs reject the very notion of compensatory justice on the grounds that it is unfair to attempt to remedy past wrongs by holding the present generation accountable. Individuals, they argue, should be rewarded strictly on the basis of merit. But even a meritocracy poses some rather intriguing questions. Assume, for example, that a managing editor hires an African-American reporter over a more "journalistically" qualified white reporter to cover inner-city racial problems. Clearly race was instrumental in this hiring decision. But it is also true that the editor considered race to be a "merit" in providing qualitative coverage of the African-American community.

The egalitarian approach to justice clearly offers an alternative to libertarianism's endorsement of unfettered individual choice. Although there are many variations of this theory, one of the most influential contemporary versions is that proposed by John Rawls in *A Theory of Justice*.[6] As noted in Chapter 3, Rawls introduces the concept of the "veil of ignorance" behind which all participants in a moral situation would serve as "ideal observers." These moral agents would behave as rational thinkers, free from the knowledge of special talents, socioeconomic status, political influence, or other prejudicial factors concerning the other parties to the arrangement.[7] Media practitioners, therefore, would make their ethical decisions without regard for whether the other participants in the situation were women, members of racial minorities, corporate vice presidents, bag ladies, or politicians. The goal is to protect the weakest or most vulnerable parties in the relationship from injustice.

One application of Rawls's theory is in the coverage of news events. Journalists should report on the activities of an individual based on the person's inherent newsworthiness rather than merely on his or her social status. Thus, behind the veil of ignorance reporters and their subjects would establish a working relationship in which not all politicians would be depicted as dishonest, cultural labels and stereotypes would be discarded in news and advertising, the media would base their coverage on a group's legitimate claim to representation rather than merely marketing considerations, and journalists would approach their assignments with a respect for people rather than undisguised cynicism. Under this approach, a more harmonious relationship would develop between reporters and society.

The Mainstream: A Philosophical Blend

The ethical concerns of the contemporary media are too complex to fit neatly into a two-theory configuration of social justice. Most media institutions do not conform nicely to either the libertarian or the egalitarian view but fall somewhere between these two extremes. Thus, it is more accurate to speak of an organization's tendencies to be more or less concerned about its commitment to social justice.

A newspaper, for example, might make a concerted effort to attract African-American employees while at the same time exhibiting little interest in improving its coverage of black urban problems. On the other hand, another paper might view the hiring of African-American reporters as an opportunity to appeal to minority audiences through better news coverage. Some news organizations might distribute their content to minority audiences only if it were profitable to do so. Others might view this profitability as an obligation to use their resources to produce material targeted to the culturally deprived. Under this hybrid philosophy, the media's role in the cause of social justice usually revolves around four concerns: access to information, media coverage and representations of minorities and the disadvantaged, diversity in the workplace, and the media's impact on criminal justice.

Information Access Is access to information a fundamental "need" like food, shelter, and medical care? Skeptics might argue that this is just another absurd rights-based claim of those who cannot afford to travel the information superhighway. Neither media practitioners nor the government has a moral obligation, they argue, to ensure that the disenfranchised are full beneficiaries of today's information-rich culture. Or, to put it another way: On what moral basis is society obligated to ensure that all citizens have access to an abundance of information regardless of economic status or geographic location? This view, of course, represents the orthodoxy that information is just another economic resource and that the marketplace should be the ultimate determinant of access to this resource. Social reform-minded egalitarians counter that society, and the media as wealthy and powerful members of that society, should subsidize those who cannot afford access (such as offering reduced-rate cable TV to the inner-city poor). As a model for such humanitarianism, proponents of this view might cite public utility companies that often subsidize the poor (sometimes through contributions from their customers).

This issue embraces pivotal political, economic, and social policy questions. Perhaps the point of departure should be to pose the question of whether information is indeed a fundamental need. From a purely physical survival perspective, one can hardly envision information as economic soul mates of food and shelter. After all, most of us survive the exigencies of life in various stages of ignorance, and while knowledge (part of which is based on "information") may be essential to rational decision making and effective political and economic participation in the democratic process, access to information is more akin to a luxury than a "need." Information is just another commodity to be merchandised (as evidenced by the resurgence of checkbook journalism), just another manifestation of an affluent society. In pursuing this argument, one might also point out that even the disadvantaged have access to a minimum level of information through our system of compulsory education. In addition, radio and television are prominent fixtures even among the urban poor; thus, there is no ethical imperative for society to subsidize their access to the vast array of services that are available on a 500-channel capacity cable TV system or the information-rich Internet.

In a society founded on the principles of individual achievement and initiative as the measures of "deservedness," these arguments are undoubtedly appealing from an ethical perspective. On the other hand, one could contend that in an information-rich society, there is a moral obligation to share the benefits of that wealth, based not so much on what one deserves (after all, who are *we* to judge?) but on the common good of society. If "knowledge is power," then access to a diversity of information empowers the disenfranchised and makes them full partners in the democratic experiment. Rather than being marginalized, they become key players. Even if the media or society must subsidize their access to the full range of information services, this is a small price to pay to improve the psychological (if not always the economic) state of the poor. According to this view, a "need" should not be defined as something that is essential to survival but any commodity that contributes to one's humanity and makes him or her a productive member of society. This philosophy is captured in this ethical appeal from media ethicists Clifford Christians, Mark Fackler, and Kim Rotzoll:

> People as persons share generic endowments that define them as human. Thus, we are entitled—without regard for individual success—to those things in life that permit our existence to continue in a humane fashion. Whenever a society allocates the necessities of life, the distribution ought to be impartial. Free competition among goods and services has been the historically influential rationale for media practice, but in the case of a total national structure performing a vital function, the need-based criterion appears to be the more fitting ethical standard.[8]

Media Coverage and Representations In the fall of 1982 when *Washington Post* reporter Howard Kurtz asked his editors whether he could cover the Department of Housing and Urban Development (HUD), he had one advantage. No one else wanted the job. Poverty was no longer politically relevant. Under the watchful eye of the Reagan Administration, HUD's costly social programs took a direct hit. Journalistically speaking, HUD quickly became a "sleepy backwater," unable to compete with places like the Pentagon where untold billions were being poured into modern high-tech military hardware.[9] Kurtz describes this phenomenon in his recently published critique of the newspaper industry:

> The problems of big cities seemed intractable, and if federal housing programs appeared mainly to benefit blacks and Hispanics, well, their concerns had nearly vanished from the political radar screen.... Newspapers were running upbeat profiles of canny corporate leaders and takeover artists. It was OK to be rich in America; there was no need to feel guilty about the poor. And the press, increasingly disconnected from its downscale readers, went along for the ride.[10]

Kurtz's stark assessment is perhaps a microcosm of one of the most serious indictments of the media: that they have virtually ignored those elements of society that do not reflect substantially in their readership or ratings profiles or are not perceived to have the kinds of purchasing power that will attract advertisers. As noted in Part One of this text, in its review of the media landscape in the 1940s, the Hutchins Commission chided the press for its inattention to the demands of minorities and challenged it to present a "representative picture of the constituent groups of society."[11] Critics contend that the commission's challenge still has not been met and that the problems of minorities and the disadvantaged are still underrepresented in the media except to the extent that sporadic news events (such as an urban riot) dictate otherwise. Of course, this kind of spot news coverage lacks a social conscience since it tends to be event oriented, reactive rather than proactive, and often ignores the contextual truth underlying the events.

Despite this rather dismal assessment, some significant achievements have been made. Television, for example, was instrumental in converting the civil rights marches of the 1960s into a national mandate for social justice. In recent years media practitioners have been more active in combating racial and sexual stereotypes. And Howard Kurtz's experience notwithstanding, more attention has been paid in the past few years to social ills such as poverty and homelessness.

Nevertheless, in the 1990s the matter of diversity has reinvigorated media critics who accuse the media of a continuing moral indifference to the needs of society's constituent groups. For example, *Entertainment Tonight* correspondent Garrett Glaser has called for more fair and accurate news coverage of homosexual issues. While urging news directors not to ignore issues that are unflattering to the gay community, Glaser is also critical of terms like "innocent victims of AIDS" because "that implies that gay men who are AIDS patients are innocent, and I don't agree with that."[12] Elaine Kim, professor of Asian-American Studies at the University of California—Berkeley, complains that there is a tendency to portray Asian Americans as "foreign invaders."[13] African Americans contend that the media magnify their guilt when blacks are accused of crimes but minimize their pain when they are the victims of crimes. This complaint is exemplified in the comparative coverage of two cases in New York, one in which a white woman was attacked and raped in Central Park by a gang of black youths and the Howard Beach and Bensonhurst incidents where black men were killed by gangs of whites for "being in the wrong neighborhood at the wrong time."[14] The media's coverage, which many African-American viewers felt was racist and unfair, was described in a 1990 article in the *Communicator*, the trade publication of the Radio-Television News Directors Association:

> [A]fter the attack in Central Park, the media often described the teens who were arrested as acting like animals and beasts. Donald Trump took a newspaper ad calling for the restoration of the death penalty. But in the Bensonhurst and Howard Beach cases few ever referred to the white youths in terms that were less than human. No millionaires took out ads calling for the death penalty, even though two people had actually died. The white communities of Bensonhurst and Howard Beach were not portrayed as brutal and uncivilized though they can clearly be pretty brutal if you're black.[15]

Such anecdotal evidence aside, some empirical data support such claims. According to a recent article in the *Journal of Broadcasting & Electronic Media*, for example, a content analysis of reality-based shows (e.g., *Cops*) revealed that white characters were more likely to be portrayed as police officers than criminal suspects, whereas black and Hispanic characters were more likely to be portrayed as criminal suspects than police officers.[16]

The entertainment industry has also been taken to the public woodshed for the lack of a fair representation of minority groups. "Not only are we underrepresented on television, but when they do show us, it's frequently in a negative, stereotypic fashion," complains Gary Kimble, head of the Association on American Indian Affairs.[17] A recent study commissioned by the Screen Actors Guild and the American Federation of Radio Television Artists found that women and minorities are vastly underrepresented in prime-time roles in comparison to their representation in the population as a whole, and only a little more than 1 percent of major TV characters are poor, compared to 13 percent of the population as a whole.[18]

The demands for change are becoming more vociferous, particularly from those groups with increasing economic clout. In early 1995, for example, the leaders of a coalition of forty-five national Latino organizations, complaining that the TV industry is rampant with institutional racism toward Latinos, said they would use their $190 billion in purchasing power to punish the major networks with actions ranging from viewer boycotts to angry demonstrations outside TV stations. They also accused ABC of reneging on promises it made to Latino leaders to schedule a Latino-themed show for the 1994–95 season and to air more programs featuring Latinos.[19]

However, there have been some recent incremental efforts to respond to some of these concerns. For example, the number of minority characters in commercials has increased dramatically as Madison Avenue discovers the buying power of middle-class minorities. In 1992 the Chicago-based Tribune Entertainment Company announced that it was creating a new "target marketing" division to market black and Hispanic programming to the advertising community.[20] Similarly, in an effort to beef up its programming for the Latino population in the United States and production of programming for Latin American markets, Fox television announced in 1994 that it would fund a production company to be headed by a Hispanic programmer.[21] And in 1994 and 1995, Hollywood producers began work on a number of projects featuring Hispanic and Latino characters.[22]

But this sudden flurry of artistic enterprise featuring minority characters and directed at minority audiences should not obscure the marketing reality. Economic considerations and ownership patterns have traditionally deterred the media from becoming full partners in the cause of social justice. Ratings and circulation are the driving forces of media institutions, and content, including advertising messages, has traditionally been directed at white middle-class audiences.[23] But there is cause for optimism. For several years program producers and advertising executives have been responding to an increase in consumer spending among minorities, particularly African Americans. In fact, it was only after the TV industry discovered the black middle class that African-American characters (with a few notable exceptions) made significant inroads into television's lucrative prime-time schedule. Likewise, the recent sensitivity to the Hispanic and Latino audiences is a reflection of the fact that the annual buying power of these groups has nearly tripled to $200 billion since 1973, a not inconsiderable sum that has caught the attention of programmers.[24] In addition, some companies have moved to rid their ads of obvious stereotypes, and others have incorporated elements of authentic black pop culture in their ads. Some large publishing companies, recognizing the African-American audience as a potent consumer force, have invested in general-interest magazines targeted for upscale blacks.[25]

The social responsibility theory of the press is really an offshoot of the egalitarian approach to justice, because it promotes access for various segments of society. Although such a theory puts the individual liberty of media practitioners at some risk and makes them accountable to society, it provides a niche for public opinion in advocating social justice through the media.

Diversity in the Workplace   It is unlikely that media coverage and representations of minorities will improve without a corresponding improvement in the employment picture for minorities within the media establishment. The latest statistics in this respect are somewhat encouraging, although not all minorities are fairly represented. In TV news, for example, the employment of racial minorities, which stood at about 13 percent in 1986,[26] had risen to 20 percent in 1994.[27]

In those stations with rather dismal minority staff profiles, news directors often say they cannot find qualified minority candidates for jobs in their newsrooms, especially in small or medium-sized markets. Some admit they are likely to give minorities more of a break in order to attract minority candidates, a practice that again sparks debates about the dimensions of social justice.

The number of minority journalists in the newspaper business is even less than for its electronic counterpart, standing at just 10 percent in 1993.[28] The American Society of Newspaper Editors has set a target of 17 percent for minority employment by the year 2000, but it is questionable whether it will achieve this goal.[29] There are a number of reasons that nonwhites have traditionally shunned careers in the newspaper field, some of which may be difficult for media managers to overcome: a lack of role models, relatively low pay, feelings of isolation, inadequate language skills, and poor advising in high school, to name a few. But in addition, large metropolitan newspapers usually have policies of hiring mostly experienced reporters who have cut their journalistic teeth on smaller papers. And to compound this problem, nonwhite reporters are reluctant to seek out beginning newspaper jobs on smaller papers in rural areas.[30] Thus, the traditional hiring practices within the newspaper business become self-defeating where minorities are concerned.

With the number of minority media practitioners still pitifully low, almost 6,000 African-American, Asian, Hispanic, and American Indian journalists convened in Atlanta in 1994 to map strategies for improving their visibility within the nation's news establishment, to improve employment opportunities, and to eliminate stereotypes in news coverage. Members of the National Lesbian and Gay Journalists Association also attended in an observer capacity.[31]

The advertising and public relations industries have also displayed an increasing interest in gays and lesbians, directing some of their communications strategies at this increasingly vocal, visible, and economically influential group. This trend led the prestigious public relations firm, Hill & Knowlton, in 1995 to form a unit for marketing communications efforts that address gay men and lesbians.[32]

Meanwhile, the public relations industry has had a public relations problem of its own. Some agencies refuse to hire minority practitioners because clients will not work with them.

"Perceptions are that minorities may not be as well educated as whites and that minorities don't know how to write," lamented one PR executive in an article in the *Public Relations Journal*.[33] There is clearly a "culture gap" between employers and prospective minority employees. Cultural differences are often not appreciated by PR employers, and the unwritten standards or rules for success are often unknown among minorities. In other cases, minorities are reluctant to choose careers in public relations because of their own cultural heritage. Asian Americans, for example, rarely aspire to be PR practitioners because drawing attention to oneself contravenes their cultural values. "Asians are discouraged by their parents from entering this profession—it's considered tantamount to show business," observed the head of one prestigious advertising and PR firm in Los Angeles.[34]

The available data indicate that women have fared better than racial minorities in some segments of the media industry. For example, a recent study revealed that women now comprise nearly 35 percent of the workforce in TV news and 31 percent in radio. In addition, more than 15 percent of the TV news director positions were held by women. One in four of the news director slots in radio were occupied by women.[35] These figures are still far below the percentage of women in the population at large, but they do reflect some progress in promoting women into decision-making roles within the broadcast industry. On the print side, there are more women in top journalism jobs in markets of all sizes, and with the number currently in the pipeline, the industry should see a continuing increase in women occupying management-level positions.[36]

The most recent claimant for social justice in the nation's newsrooms is the National Lesbian and Gay Journalists Association that had its genesis in 1990. Just three years after its formation, the group held its first job fair in New York—an event that was underwritten by a $40,000 grant from the *New York Times* and attended by such prestigious media institutions as the *Washington Post*, the Associated Press, and ABC News.[37]

Despite the noble intentions of those who embrace the egalitarian philosophy, including programs that advocate compensatory justice for those who have been denied employment opportunities, for some white males "diversity" has become a code word for reverse discrimination. The perception is fueled by both rumor and the aggressive manner in which media organizations are recruiting minorities: hiring consulting firms, conducting sensitivity seminars, participating in minority job fairs, and announcing special hiring policies.[38]

In searching for strategies to confront the ethical dimensions of this issue, some troubling and complex questions must be raised. In so doing, perhaps we should begin with the common ground: In the cause of social justice, it is wrong to deny a person employment simply on the basis of color, gender, sexual preference, or any other artificial characteristic. But beyond the issue of employment per se, we must ask ourselves exactly how diversity can best serve society's interests. There is an unstated assumption that diversity in the workplace will improve the qualitative diversity of the content. But does diversity, for example, automatically improve the *quality* of the news product? Or, more specifically, are middle-class black reporters more attuned to the problems of the inner city than their white counterparts, or are urban problems as much a matter of economic class as race? Are gay and lesbian journalists more understanding of and compassionate in their treatment of the gay community than heterosexual reporters? Can only a reporter with disabilities empathize with the physically challenged in their daily struggles for respectability? Must journalists be over fifty-five to write about the problems of the aged? And the list goes on.

Of course, a certain impertinence arises in such questions, and they should not deter media managers from attempting to develop an employment profile that more closely mirrors the society of which they are a part. But they must also be careful that whatever policies they implement do not lead to an unhealthy balkanization in the workplace environment that is in the long run inimical to the cause of social justice.

The Media and Criminal Justice   Six murders were committed near Evansville, Indiana, in 1954 and 1955, and a man named Irvin was eventually indicted for one of the murders. The crimes, extensively covered by the news media, caused great excitement and indignation in this rural community. The media, both print and broadcast, were merciless in their coverage of the defendant, reporting that "Mad Dog Irvin" was "the confessed slayer of six" and that he was "remorseless and without conscience." The media also included references to his prior convictions as a juvenile and his military court-martial for going AWOL. When time came to seat the jury, all twelve told the judge they would be fair and impartial. And yet, eight of the twelve also said they thought Irvin was guilty. Irvin was convicted, and for the first time in its history, the Supreme Court overturned a conviction specifically on the grounds of prejudicial media publicity.[39]

Two years later, the Court reversed the conviction of a defendant in Lake Charles, Louisiana, charged with kidnapping, bank robbery, and murder after a local TV station televised a filmed jailhouse confession. At least three of the jurors were among the thousands of viewers who had seen the confession.[40] In 1966, the Court overturned the conviction of Dr. Sam Sheppard who was accused of bludgeoning his wife to death in the couple's home in Bay Village, Ohio. The media, in what can best be described as a textbook example of yellow journalism, were relentless and highly prejudicial in their coverage of the case. There was no pretense of fairness, as the press eagerly reported every rumor and damning piece of evidence, much of which was never presented at trial. Journalistic deportment during the trial was, to say the least, uncivilized. In his opinion, Justice Clark criticized the "carnival atmosphere" surrounding the trial in which reporters "took over practically the entire courtroom, hounding most of the participants in the trial, especially Sheppard."[41]

Concerned about the role that an irresponsible press plays in such sensational cases, trial judges during the 1970s began resorting increasingly to injunctions and restraining orders (referred to by the media as "gag" orders) to protect defendants and insulate defendants from the effects of prejudicial publicity. However, in 1976 the Supreme Court declared such orders to be unconstitutional except where there is an immediate danger to the rights of the defendant and where the trial judge has exhausted all alternative means of protecting those rights.[42]

The Sixth Amendment to the U.S Constitution guarantees a criminal defendant the right to a fair trial—the right to a public trial before an impartial jury of his or her peers. The First Amendment guarantees the media freedom from government censorship or sanction. That these two bold declarations of individual and institutional liberties should sometimes clash is perhaps ironic since they are both predicated on a healthy distrust of government. The criminal justice system revolves around juries that are unprejudiced before trial as to guilt or innocence. While they may indeed hear prejudicial information during the trial, there are also safeguards that regulate the introduction and evaluation of evidence and witness testimony. No such precautions prevent the media from disseminating such information to the public before or during the trial.

Thus, those who consider the right to a fair trial the most fundamental among our constitutional guarantees criticize the media, particularly in high-profile cases, for their irresponsible dissemination of inflammatory and incriminating evidence and even "extrajudicial" statements (e.g., comments by opposing attorneys outside the courtroom), resulting in a trial before the court of public opinion rather than a court of law. Free-press advocates, on the other hand, respond that only through media access to the judicial process and the right to serve as surrogates for their constituents can the citizenry be confident that justice is indeed being dispensed.

The American judicial system, despite its shortcomings and occasional failures, is considered to be a paradigm of justice, a reflection of our culture's fundamental commitment to fairness and equality of treatment. Strictly speaking, the Supreme Court's vigilance in balancing the rights of a criminal defendant against the media's right to cover judicial proceedings, particularly when couched in constitutional terms, is a matter of law. But in reality, the criminal justice system reflects our more general concern for social justice, with its emphasis on fairness, procedural safeguards, and dispensing rewards and punishments based on what people deserve. And when the media act irresponsibly and a defendant is denied the right to a fair trial because of pervasive and sensational publicity, then serious ethical questions are implicated.

At times, of course, the media have performed admirably in fulfilling their ethical imperative in pointing out the imperfections in the judicial system, such as the disparate sentencing patterns of whites and African Americans convicted of similar crimes. At other times, however, the herd mentality consumes the media, and trial coverage takes on a circuslike atmosphere. Such cases usually reflect the conflict between news as a commodity to be marketed and the notion that the news media, because of their First Amendment protections, also have a social responsibility. And the presence of cameras in the courtroom, providing live coverage, has introduced a high degree of irresistible drama into this conflict.

The best example of recent vintage is the O. J. Simpson trial. From the outset, there was a great deal of skepticism that Simpson could get a fair trial because of the exhaustive and sometimes sensational coverage. Although the concerns underlying "trial by media" are at the heart of all high-profile cases, the Simpson case was unique in at least three respects: the amount of coverage, dismissal of a *grand jury* because of potentially prejudicial publicity, and the unprecedented access of media to information.[43] And much of the press coverage was centered in the exact location where an impartial jury was supposed to be impaneled, Los Angeles County. But it was the quality of information, not the amount of coverage, that threatened the justice system.

First, many of the items reported were either false or unsubstantiated. Second, even some of the matters that were reported accurately were so compromised by the level of media coverage that they similarly compromised the search for truth in the criminal process. For example, one witness reported seeing the defendant near the crime scene. Unfortunately, after it was learned that reporters had paid the witness for her "exclusive story," the prosecutor decided not to use the witness's testimony before a grand jury or during a preliminary hearing because she had been hopelessly compromised as a credible witness.[44]

In any high-profile trial, it might be expected that the contending parties—both prosecution and defense—would appeal to the conscience of public opinion. And there is nothing unethical in doing so. Public opinion, after all, has an invigorating influence on the democratic process. Thomas Jefferson understood this vital principle more than 200 years ago when he courted public opinion in search of support for the Declaration of Independence. Although the judiciary is supposed to remain aloof from the political influences of public opinion, at least since the Aaron Burr treason trial in 1807 the media have often served as public advocates or conduits for those who have sought a hearing before the court of public opinion.[45] Attorneys, of course, have never hesitated to serve as their own publicists

in the interests of their clients.[46] For example, several weeks after Timothy McVeigh was charged with bombing a federal building in Oklahoma City, McVeigh's court-appointed attorney released a videotape, which received national TV coverage, showing a decidedly more relaxed and "friendly" McVeigh than had been portrayed in media coverage.

But the recent proliferation of high-profile trials and particularly the ubiquitous coverage of television have led some attorneys to solicit professional assistance in creating favorable images for their clients. This alliance between the PR and legal professions has become increasingly collaborative, as evidenced by the frequent reference in the literature to "litigation public relations." The list reads like a virtual "Who's Who" of criminal defendants: John De Lorean, Ivan Boesky, Michael Miliken, William Kennedy Smith. The perceived "need" for litigation PR is captured in this observation from Professors Susanne Roschwalb and Richard Stack writing in *Communications and the Law*:

> A big error many lawyers make, according to public relations executives, is in failing to recognize that while silence should be accorded a presumption of innocence in the court, it is likely to be taken as a sign of guilt in the pressroom. The innocent, when accused, are expected by the public to proclaim their innocence promptly and emphatically. Absent such proclamation, any courtroom claim of innocence may be more skeptically perceived.[47]

The introduction of the public relations function into the criminal justice system does raise some serious ethical concerns for everyone involved: attorneys, PR professionals and the media themselves. The reasons for using communications strategies vary among attorneys and even from case to case, but proponents of "litigation PR" cite at least two reasons in its defense. First, although prosecutors portray themselves as "above PR," they have an effective media network. Prosecutors have an early advantage in the court of public opinion because the government initiates and controls the criminal investigation, evaluates the evidence first, and often conducts news conferences to announce indictments. Under such a scenario, the first message the public receives about the accused is a negative one. Defense attorneys are then pressured to remind the public that their clients are innocent until proven guilty.[48] Second, advocates often target the public in order to sway potential jurors. A well-orchestrated PR campaign on behalf of a client is sometimes effective in at least softening the harsh image generated by the prosecution. And such publicity does not threaten the criminal justice system since jurors are carefully screened and then admonished to render a verdict based solely on the evidence and testimony introduced during the trial.

Critics counter that it is absurd to believe that jurors can completely separate the publicity generated in the (sometimes circuslike) court of public opinion from the carefully scrutinized evidence and testimony adduced in a court of law. Despite the best intentions of the attorneys and the judge, it is impossible to ferret out all bias. In addition, opponents argue that, depending on the communications strategy devised, the use of PR professionals can leave the impression that the defense team is attempting to massage the facts. Under such circumstances, PR practitioners can quickly become co-conspirators in frustrating the search for truth. Consider, for example, the role that the PR firm of Robinson, Lake, Lerer and Montgomery played in the case of "junk bond king" Michael Miliken, who pleaded guilty to securities fraud. The goal of the PR campaign was to turn public opinion from outrage to admiration. The strategy was to build a positive image of Miliken through human interest stories involving his relationship to his children and reports of his charitable gifts. According to reporters who covered the Wall Street financial scandals of the 1980s, the Robinson agency encouraged journalists to publish stories that would discredit witnesses cooperating in Mili-

ken's prosecution. A former Robinson employee also accused the firm of generating favorable "op-ed" pieces that appeared under the bylines of corporate leaders.[49] Miliken spent millions on a misguided campaign that seemed to have no moral compass—a campaign that, according to Washington defense lawyer Reid Weingarten, had a negative effect and stands as an example of "PR gone wrong."[50]

Even more subtle efforts at changing the public perception of criminal suspects can raise ethical questions concerning the search for truth and justice. A case in point is the police investigation of the brutal murder of five college students in Gainesville, Florida, in 1990. Police and media attention quickly focused on eighteen-year-old Edward Humphrey, who had been arrested (and later convicted) for assaulting his grandmother. Though he was never charged with the multiple murders, the court of public opinion lost no time in its rush to judgment. The initial public image of Humphrey, disseminated through news stories and photographs taken during his battery trial, was that of a deranged killer, a wild-eyed, disheveled boy with scars on his face from an automobile accident who beat his grandmother.

A year after the murders, Humphrey's attorney hired Marty Mackenzie as a PR consultant to change his client's image. As part of the communications strategy, Mackenzie produced a seven-minute video portraying Humphrey as a man wronged by police and the media, wrongly convicted in the court of public opinion and a manic depressive who was now receiving medical treatment for his unpredictable mood swings. The objective, which apparently succeeded, was to change the perception of Humphrey from that of a maniacal serial killer into that of a mild-mannered, kind young man.[51] This image transformation and the corresponding change in public opinion led one commentator to make this cautious assessment: "What is clear in the Humphrey case is that the individual had the right to defend himself in the court of public opinion as well as in the courtroom. The question is whether he is defrauding or misleading the public while defending himself."[52]

The demands of the justice system are subjected to their most compelling challenges in cases like the Sam Sheppard and O. J. Simpson trials. Judges, of course, are the ultimate repositories of judicial fairness, and they have at their disposal an arsenal of legal devices to protect a defendant's right to a fair trial, including a careful screening of the jurors. In a democratic system, the media are charged with both a mandate and a responsibility. Reporters should understand that their ethical imperative to provide meaningful and comprehensive intelligence on the performance of the judicial system is not incompatible with a simultaneous commitment to the cause of justice. Each time that a criminal defendant is accorded a fair trial, uninfluenced by prejudicial publicity, society itself is the beneficiary. On the other hand, the media should be mindful that unfair or slanted coverage (which may include publicity generated by either prosecutors or defense attorneys or their PR consultants) has the potential for compromising the integrity of the process of criminal justice. Thus, the potential consequences both to the cause of justice and the credibility of the media are too serious to ignore.

SOCIAL JUSTICE AND ETHICAL DECISION MAKING

Justice is a central moral principle of society.[53] At the most formal and abstract level, as noted, it relates to giving individuals what they deserve. But what is each due? And how are competing interests to be balanced when justice for one might result in injustice for another?

These are complex questions, particularly for institutions that serve such a pivotal and pervasive role as the mass media. Libertarians tend to focus on individual media practitioners and the liberty to make decisions free from outside coercion. Egalitarians emphasize social responsibility and the duty to ensure justice for all segments of society, even at the expense of infringing on the liberty of media practitioners. Although these two concepts appear to be at the opposite ends of the philosophical spectrum, each has something to offer in constructing an ethical framework for social justice. The self-interest orientation of the libertarian concept must be rejected as contrary to sound moral reasoning. But the emphasis on individual autonomy places the focus where it should be: on the individual moral agent. As noted in Chapter 2, media practitioners are singularly accountable for the institutional decisions of their corporations. When a newspaper, for example, decides not to publish special inserts directed at minorities because of a perceived lack of advertiser interest, this decision is made by individuals acting on behalf of the institution. These executives are morally responsible for this decision.

Nevertheless, we often speak of "institutional responsibility" when referring to the various cultural roles of the mass media. Thus, from the egalitarian camp we can draw the notion of social responsibility in constructing an approach to ethical decision making for social justice. Because the media draw their sustenance from the communities of which they are a part, society has a right to expect media institutions to at least be sensitive to the cause of social justice. The question, of course, is how far this responsibility should extend and how this commitment to justice should be balanced against other obligations. The media, for example, have obligations to their subscribers, advertisers, and audiences (and perhaps stockholders), and these must be weighed carefully before honoring the demands of special segments of society.

In considering a dilemma involving issues of social justice, a duty-based theorist (deontologist) would examine the motives of the moral agent. Under this approach, media practitioners act out of a sense of duty regardless of the consequences.

Duty-based theorists view justice as fairness, without consideration of whether the results of the ethical decision will benefit the greatest number of people. For example, a television executive who programs to minority audiences out of a sense of duty rather than because the decision is commercially viable is following this approach to moral reasoning.

On the other hand, those who consider *consequences* to be important (teleologists) examine the potential effects of a decision on the cause of social justice. The positive consequences are weighed against the possible harm to the various parties in arriving at a just solution for the problem. In those cases where the goal is to achieve positive ends for particular groups within society, some believe that individual liberties, such as freedom of expression, may be restricted in the name of social justice. This principle has been invoked by some feminists who support censorship of pornography on the grounds that it exploits and dehumanizes women.

Aristotle's golden mean can also be a welcome companion in confronting complicated situations in which the ethical extremes are unacceptable. Suppose, for example, that a TV news crew is sent to cover a prison riot. Such civil disturbances always pose a danger that news organizations will become a part of the story and be used as pawns by those who seek publicity. The vices at either extreme involve providing no coverage, on the one hand, and covering every detail and angle regardless of the consequences, on the other. The challenge is to provide responsible reporting of the disturbance without offering a platform for the rioters to solicit public support.

Of course, not all moral dilemmas involving social justice can be accommodated through the golden mean. Sometimes fairness resides at one extreme or the other, and then the moral agent must approach the situation from the perspective of either the consequentialist or the duty-based theorist.

To Aristotle, justice was a virtue consisting, among other things, of equality of treatment based on merit. The problem, of course, is to determine whether the criteria for merit are just, which can challenge even the most rational media practitioner. For example, in deciding which spokespersons are to be accorded publicity during the news coverage of minority issues, should editors rely on those who appear to represent the largest constituency, the most articulate community leaders, or those who are the most vocal in pressing their cause? This is a practical journalistic problem because spokespersons, even within the same segments of society, do not always have the same agenda and may not even represent a significant following. As Paul Sagan, news director of WCBS-TV in New York, has observed, "But in doing a story about the minority community, I think a lot of us don't know who speaks for them. We tend to listen to whoever talks the loudest, or who holds news conferences."[54]

The golden mean also allows for compensatory justice in order to rectify past injustices.[55] Thus, affirmative action programs and demands by minority groups for fair treatment from media producers are viewed as compensation for past injustices and an attempt to equalize social relationships.

In the final analysis, the approach that one takes to social justice depends on how one perceives the functions of the media in a complex society. Should the media be true participants in the social arena, or should they be viewed merely as transmitters of information? Should media practitioners see themselves as merely reflectors of the social landscape, or should they consider themselves as catalysts for change? The role of the media as instruments of social justice will depend on how we, both as individuals and collectively as a society, answer these questions.

THE MEDIA AND SOCIAL JUSTICE: HYPOTHETICAL CASE STUDIES

You will confront a variety of issues in this section. Some involve traditional questions of social justice, such as racial discrimination in the media and coverage of the poor. Others are more recent issues of social justice, such as "liti-gation public relations." Still others concern conflicting values that extend beyond what most of us think of as social justice. The diversity of these cases demonstrates that the concept of justice exists at every level of our cultural experience. In reasoning through these cases, you should consider which ethical guideline described in Chapter 3 and the previous section best serves the cause of justice.

CASE STUDIES

▶ **CASE 11-1**
Litigation PR as a Tool of Justice

The prosecutor called Heidi Van Cunningham "a cold-blooded, calculating teen without conscience or remorse." Her attorney depicted her as "a victim of an undisciplined childhood who sought on the streets the love she never received at home." On one thing they both agreed: Heidi Van Cunningham would be tried twice—once in a court of law and again in the court of public opinion.

Van Cunningham had been born into a family of privilege on Manhattan's Upper East Side, the daughter of Michael Van Cunningham, a prominent Wall Street broker, and his socialite wife, Martha. Despite Heidi's natural beauty, charm, and genuine affection for others, her parents' social agenda deprived their young daughter of their companionship and supervision during her formative years and left her to the erratic discipline of various nannies. Despite her luxurious surroundings, Heidi's childhood was an unhappy one. Her teachers remembered her as "an unruly child, lacking in direction and longing for affection." By the time she was fourteen, according to acquaintances, Heidi had become sexually promiscuous and hooked on drugs, two clear signs of youthful rebellion that apparently went unacknowledged by her parents.

It was during her sophomore year in high school that she met Joseph Picone, a thirty-five-year-old dress designer who serviced her mother's lavish and expensive wardrobe. But Picone, according to police reports, was more than a dress designer. He was also a child pornographer, who marketed his wares through cleverly disguised promotions in a variety of publications and on the Internet. Attracted as much by Picone's attentiveness as his offer of financial rewards, Heidi readily succumbed to her suitor's seductive advances and eagerly joined his growing list of adolescent models. As the bond of trust between Picone and his incorrigible victim grew, he promoted her from model to procurer, and she responded enthusiastically by surveying the youthful landscape for fresh recruits to her benefactor's illicit occupation.

But their relationship soon soured as the teenager, who was both streetwise and financially savvy, began to demand a larger commission for her procurement activities. Heidi's attorney later described this situation as a simple business disagreement. The prosecutor called it a motive for murder.

According to police reports and evidence produced by the district attorney's office, Picone's body was discovered in his rather lavishly apportioned apartment by a business associate. He was lying in bed and had been shot once in the head by a small-caliber pistol. Heidi became an immediate suspect because her parents told police that their daughter had gone to Picone's apartment to pick up some dresses for her mother. The teenager confessed to the killing but, in keeping with her parents' version of their daughter's whereabouts, said she had gone to Picone's apartment to procure some dresses for her mother. Picone had tried to rape her, she claimed, but she had managed to retrieve a pistol from her purse to defend herself against his unwelcome advances. The police did not believe Heidi's plea of self-defense, and after an investigation, Heidi was indicted for murder.

Because of her family's social prominence and the shocking consequences surrounding the murder, the Big Apple was riveted by the case of *The People v. Heidi Van Cunningham*. "Manhattan Lolita Indicted for Murder," heralded one tabloid headline. "Judgment Day for Kiddie Porn Queen," proclaimed another, in an obvious exaggeration of Heidi's role in her former employer's nefarious enterprise. Even the mainstream media became preoccupied with this tragic story of squandered youthful innocence, although their headlines were less sensationalistic than their tabloid counterparts. No friend, acquaintance, or family member escaped the probing inquiries of the news media, and opinion polls reflected the public's increasing impatience with the "criminal as victim" mentality that had invigorated the liberals' sense of justice for so long. The court of public opinion had begun its deliberations.

The renowned defense attorney Lewis Spencer was hired by Heidi's parents to handle her case. Spencer was joined in his trial preparations by his associate, Mark Mayfield. Spencer was confident that he could raise a reasonable doubt as to his client's guilt in the collective minds of an impartial jury. He was less confident of actually *finding* an impartial jury. He needed someone to help offset the negative images portrayed through the media's relentless coverage—someone like Alford Cane.

Alford Cane had met Lewis Spencer at a social function six months ago, but he knew the prominent attorney primarily by reputation. Cane was the senior partner of Cane, Perez, and Bascomb, a small PR firm that had a reputation for developing creative strategies for their limited but impressive registry of corporate clients.

In his first meeting with Cane, Spencer exchanged pleasantries and then got right to the point. "My associate and I can handle the courtroom strategies," said Spencer. "But we're taking a beating in the media. Finding an impartial jury might be difficult. We need your assistance in changing—or at least neutralizing—the public's negative perception of Heidi. In the two weeks that I've represented her, I've gotten to know and like her. Heidi Van Cunningham is not a monster. She's a teenager who went astray. All I'm asking for is fairness. And we're not getting it from the media."

Cane was impressed by Spencer's concern for his client's badly tarnished public image and promised to consider the attorney's invitation. As senior partner, Cane would render the final judgment on whether to defend the controversial teenager in the court of public opinion, but he soon found himself listening to a spirited debate between the firm's two junior partners, Belinda Perez and Alan Bascomb.

"One question is whether we should represent someone like this unless we believe in her innocence," said Perez. "I don't know whether she's guilty or innocent. But the evidence seems to be mounting against her."

"The only thing that's mounting against her," responded Bascomb, "is public opinion. And she's innocent until *proven* guilty in a court of law. And that's what we really should be worried about. Heidi Van Cunningham is entitled not only to fairness in a court of law; she deserves the right to let the public know the 'real' Heidi. After all, the prosecutor has a lot of contacts in the media. He can trash her at will, and she has no defense. Her lawyer can deflect some of the criticism, but he's not an expert in molding public opinion. That's where we come in."

"But does a public relations firm, this one included, have an obligation to accept any client who walks through the door?" asked Perez. "Spencer is asking us to change her public image, to present her in a different light to the public. In short, our job is to make her appear to be a victim and a believable witness in her own defense in the public's mind. We could wind up creating a false impression that has little to do with the search for the truth."

"We create images for clients all the time," responded Bascomb, annoyed by what he perceived as Perez's rather puritanical view of a PR practitioner's role. "We emphasize the good and ignore the bad. And there are certainly *some* likable things about Heidi Van Cunningham. She may not be the model teenager. But since she's been savaged in the media, she has a right to respond. That's no different from our corporate clients, who feel they should have as much control as possible over the flow of information to the media concerning their activities. There's no doubt that so far the cards have been stacked against Van Cunningham from a publicity standpoint. Perhaps even she is entitled to some compensatory justice in the court of public opinion."

"I'll admit that she could use some image repair," said Cane, who had been uncharacteristically silent during this exchange between his two junior partners. "The first pictures I saw of her on TV during her arrest were those of a disheveled, wild-eyed young woman who, quite frankly, was dressed more like a hooker than a seventeen-year-old high school student. And this image has been reproduced daily on the nightly news and the tabloids. But Heidi isn't a corporate client. She's on trial for murder, and I'm always concerned about the impact of publicity on our justice system. Just look at the William Kennedy Smith and O. J. Simpson cases. She may be guilty. But what if we succeed in generating enough favorable publicity and changing her image to such an extent that she is acquitted or gets a hung jury? Will justice have been served?"

"That isn't our concern," responded Bascomb unhesitatingly. "Keep in mind that our system is weighted in favor of the defendant—and justifiably so. The defendant is entitled to fairness, not the state. It's the accused who is guaranteed the right to a fair trial by the Constitution. So when pretrial publicity is prejudicial to the defendant, as it is in this case, then the defendant has a right to respond. But in a high-profile case like this one, that may not be possible without professional help."

"You're correct that the Constitution guarantees only the defendant a fair trial," conceded Perez. "But that's only true from a criminal justice perspective. From the much broader vantage point of *social* justice, the people of New York are also entitled to fairness. Should we be involved in changing a defendant's image that could alter the outcome of a case? If we play the publicity game in a criminal case, are we any better than the tabloid media that generated the negative publicity to begin with?"

"Let's be realistic," responded Bascomb. "We can't alter the outcome of this case. The judge and the attorneys will select the jurors, and it'll be up to them to reach a verdict based on the evidence. All that we can do is to try to humanize Heidi—to try to counteract those grotesque images of her when she was arrested."

"I realize that she probably isn't the monster that the media have portrayed her to be," replied Perez, unimpressed by Bascomb's eagerness to assist Spencer in rescuing his client from her public crucifixion. "Few people are one-dimensional. But Heidi could be manipulative enough that we wind up creating a false image. I don't mind being fair, but in balancing the negative publicity, we should at least portray an image that's accurate."

"But it's all a matter of perception," said Bascomb. "When we represent corporate clients, our job is to get their story out—and in the process to create a favorable image with the public and their customers. This image, of course, is never the whole story. And, for that matter, it never constitutes the whole truth. In this case, our job is simply to help level the playing field and to ensure that Heidi Van Cunningham gets a fair hearing—that justice prevails in the court of public opinion, as well as in the court of law."

Alford Cane listened to the impassioned arguments of his two junior partners. If his firm accepted Van Cunningham's attorney as its client, they would join an impressive array of other PR professionals and firms that had represented high-profile, controversial clients in the court of public opinion. But he wondered whether "image cultivation" for criminal defendants—or litigation PR, as it is called—was a suitable role for the public relations industry. Would it be perceived by an already skeptical public as analogous to the "packaging" of political candidates, a marketing technique that often obscured the search for truth?

On the other hand, regardless of the accused's guilt or innocence, she must still be *presumed* innocent, a presumption that became increasingly fragile with each sensational news account. The competing values weighed heavily on the mind of Alford Cane as he contemplated whether to join Lewis Spencer's defense team.

THE CASE STUDY

For many years the impact of prejudicial publicity on a defendant's right to a fair trial has been the concern of courts and media critics alike. Of course, defendants are legally entitled to competent counsel to challenge prejudicial influences within a court of law. This case raises the question of whether defendants are also at least *ethically* entitled to a defense in the court of public opinion. If so, that entitlement then implicates the role of communication strategies in the criminal justice system.

There are two philosophies regarding the role of PR practitioners within society: (1) as skilled representatives of something they personally believe in or (2) as hired technicians representing a point of view they may or may not believe in.[56] Under the first view, there is little evidence in the scenario here that any of the partners believe personally in the defendant's innocence or necessarily her moral worth, except for the admission by Alan Bascomb that "there are certainly some good things about Heidi Van Cunningham" and Belinda Perez's comment that "she probably isn't the monster that the media have portrayed her to be." However, there is some discussion concerning an accused's *entitlement* to a defense in the court of public opinion. Thus, there is some belief in the cause of justice if not in the defendant herself. Is this sufficient to meet the requirements of the first philosophy described earlier?

Under the second philosophy, the decision to represent the defendant does not revolve around the practitioner's belief in either Heidi Van Cunningham or, for that matter, whether she may or

may not receive a fair trial as a result of prejudicial publicity. But a certain entitlement to representation prevails in the court of public opinion, and PR professionals, in this view, would not spend a great deal of time agonizing whether their role in "image-building" obscures some underlying truth about Heidi's character. Public reactions to a high-profile individual are based on perceptions anyway, under which "truth" about the person becomes relative to any given point in time anyway. This notion is reflected in this comment in a recent issue of the *Journal of Mass Media Ethics*:

> [E]ach of us operates within his or her perceptual shield and the perceptions that it generates are the truth to us. Understanding that the truth is a relative concept, and that judgmentalism is a destructive behavior (including that constantly foisted upon us by the media), practitioners strive to build positive consensus among stakeholders, whatever the situation. This is a uniting act.[57]

For the purpose of deciding whether your firm should become a part of Lewis Spencer's defense strategy, assume the role of senior partner Alford Cane. Using the moral reasoning model outlined in Chapter 3, make a decision on whether you will defend Heidi Van Cunningham in the court of public opinion.

 ## CASE 11-2
The African-American Publisher and Divided Loyalties

Washington Roundtree's credentials as a longtime crusader for civil rights were unimpeachable. As a young college student in the early 1960s, he had marched with Dr. Martin Luther King in Alabama and participated in the black voter registration drives in Mississippi. He had challenged the segregated lunch counters in Montgomery and had been arrested in Birmingham for taking part in a peaceful demonstration to protest segregation in the city's public transportation system. For this act of civil disobedience, Roundtree had spent three nights in jail. He had emerged from these experiences convinced that black Americans were on the precipice of a new era of social justice in which these descendants of slaves would finally share in the economic opportunities and social parity that had symbolized the white middle class. On a philosophical level, his emotional spark had been stoked by the doctrine of nonviolence embraced by Dr. King. From a political and legal perspective, his optimism was sustained by the passage of landmark civil rights legislation during the Johnson administration and the continuing vigilance of the federal courts in their determination to eradicate constitutionally the vestiges of segregation.

Upon his graduation from Morehouse University, a historically black college in Atlanta, Roundtree had found employment in a black-owned print shop in Jackson Falls, a racially diverse city of 500,000 in the heart of the Deep South. But despite the demands of earning a livelihood and attending to the needs of his family, Roundtree continued his commitment to the ongoing struggle for racial equality through his participation in the NAACP and support for black legislative candidates. The redundancy of his print shop responsibilities were not intellectually challenging, and the young civil rights activist applied for and was hired as a reporter for the *Jackson Falls Gazette*, whose progressive-minded publisher was eager to have minority representation in his newsroom. At a time when most newspapers in the South were neglecting their black audiences partly because of their lack of commercial appeal to advertisers, the *Gazette*'s publisher was determined that the problems of the black community would have a forum in the pages of his newspaper. And Washington Roundtree would be his representative in the economically impoverished and socially volatile black enclaves of Jackson Falls.

For ten years Roundtree chronicled the struggles and triumphs of the black residents of Jackson Falls, but despite his publisher's alleged commitment to racial equality, the activist-turned-journalist was disappointed in the rather modest amount of space accorded his stories by the *Gazette*'s editorial staff. "You're doing a great job, and we feel the black community is fairly represented in our paper. But we also have to sell papers, and our advertisers aren't interested in targeting audiences with no purchasing power"

became an increasingly frequent rejoinder when Roundtree challenged his editors' decision to cut or eliminate one of his stories.

With this journalistic seasoning and a low-interest loan, Roundtree had founded the *Freedom Fighter*, a paper that would service exclusively Jackson Falls' African-American citizens, while it continued his campaign for social justice and cultivated the growing black middle class. From his perch as publisher and editor of the *Freedom Fighter*, Roundtree was an unapologetic advocate for compensatory justice. He editorially promoted affirmative action initiatives, government antipoverty programs, and busing as a means of achieving school desegregation. And as the corridors of political power became increasingly accessible to African Americans, Roundtree had enthusiastically endorsed black candidates for local office, the statehouse, and Congress. He was particularly pleased when, in 1986, the legislature, under pressure from members of the influential black caucus, had redrawn his 10th Congressional district to ensure a majority black voter representation. Black legislators referred to this as social justice; their opponents called it racial gerrymandering. Nevertheless, the move had guaranteed the election of an African-American representative, as conservative white politicians abandoned the 10th District race as a lost cause, politically speaking.

But in 1994, an increasingly conservative Supreme Court had ruled that the 10th District had been unconstitutionally redrawn specifically for the purpose of ensuring black congressional representation. Within a few months, the legislature complied with the Court's edict as it revisited the 10th District's geographic configuration. Thus, Washington Roundtree's residence once again became an attractive plum for the white political establishment.

Elections normally did not pose a moral dilemma for the *Freedom Fighter*'s publisher/editor. In the past he had simply endorsed and actively supported African-American candidates in their races against white opponents, reasoning that a commitment to racial justice could easily compensate for political inexperience. In the past two contests in the 10th District, in which no white candidates had run, he had supported the incumbents because of their proven track record. But the upcoming congressional race—the first since the legislature's most recent redesign—challenged Roundtree's racial loyalty.

Thomas Whatley, the white candidate in the race, had survived the Democratic primary by virtue of a formidable coalition of white progressive, pro-choice female, and black middle-class voters. Whatley depicted himself as a political moderate, but his liberal record on civil rights, government assistance for the disadvantaged, and a woman's right to choose an abortion were undeniable. The Democratic entry was also politically experienced, having served two terms as a city councilman and two terms as a state senator.

Whatley's black Republican opponent, on the other hand, was a political neophyte, but it was not his political inexperience that concerned Washington Roundtree. Brewster Fields was the product of a black middle-class environment, undoubtedly a significant factor in what Washington perceived to be an opportunistic endorsement of Republican conservatism. Fields had not publicly repudiated affirmative action—a move that would be political suicide in a district in which African-American voters were still influential—but in interviews with the media, he consistently preached the gospel of individual initiative and self-help, not "paternalistic indulgences," as the keys to economic prosperity. Fields professed his support for civil rights but did not apparently share Roundtree's commitment to compensatory justice in a society that appeared to be less racially tolerant today than at any time since the struggles for racial equality in the 1960s.

As the election neared, Roundtree was confronted with the nagging uneasiness of his competing loyalties as he considered his editorial posture on the congressional race. If he broke with tradition and supported the white candidate, his constituency might accuse him of abandoning them in their continuing efforts to maintain black political representation. Fields might be conservative, but he *was* an African American and could probably be educated as to the viability of affirmative action. Fields was also politically inexperienced, but Roundtree had never considered that to be a litmus test for public office, especially when blacks

were trying to gain access to the corridors of political power. In addition, Fields's election would ensure that the 10th District seat would remain in the hands of an African American. This would at least preserve the visible trappings of social justice if not guarantee its ideological progression.

On the other hand, Whatley's liberal credentials appealed to Roundtree's sense of social justice. His civil rights record was undeniable, which made him, in Roundtree's judgment, the better qualified of the two candidates. If he publicly supported the Democratic candidate, he could explain his reasons in his editorial endorsement, and his black readers might forgive his political transgression. He could, of course, refuse to endorse either candidate as being unworthy of his blessing, but this position carried the same risk as not supporting Brewster Fields.

As a respected publisher and editor of a newspaper devoted to the cause of racial justice, Roundtree wondered, where should his allegiances lie in this election: race or affirmative action? During his more activist days in the service of Dr. King, the now middle-aged journalist never dreamed that his dual commitments to his race and the greater cause of social justice might be politically incompatible. Which candidate, he wondered, would better serve the cause of racial justice, and what role should the *Freedom Fighter* play in bringing about that candidate's election?

THE CASE STUDY

During his professional career as a publisher and editor, Washington Roundtree has, without exception, supported African-American candidates for public office on the grounds that racial progress can best be achieved through those who truly understand the black experience. Thus, in Roundtree's view the notion of race and his own vision of social justice for African Americans are inevitably linked. But Brewster Fields, a conservative Republican black candidate, does not share Roundtree's vision. In fact, Fields's white opponent appears to be more firmly committed to Roundtree's views on civil rights than Fields himself. And this has posed a dilemma for the publisher/editor of the *Freedom Fighter*. He must choose between his loyalty to race or loyalty to a particular vision of racial justice (i.e., compensatory justice) that is more closely aligned with that of a white candidate.

For the purpose of analyzing this ethical dilemma, apply the SAD Formula for moral reasoning outlined in Chapter 3 and render a decision on which course of action available to Washington Roundtree would better serve his view of social justice.

▶ **CASE 11-3**
Campus PC, Racial Justice, and the Student Press

The campus at Houston State University had become decidedly less civil in the past five years. The university's students were increasingly more conservative than their predecessors and less appreciative of the administration's commitment to a system of compensatory justice designed to increase the minority presence among the faculty and student body. They were particularly incensed at the campus orthodoxy known as "political correctness."

For more than two decades, the administration of Houston State had prided itself on its commitment to racial equality as reflected in its affirmative action programs for faculty and students. The university's aggressive recruitment of minority students had resulted in a student population that was now 23 percent non-Caucasian, including 19 percent African-American. However, the academy's efforts in this regard were not without controversy. When Houston State had abandoned its open admissions policy ten years earlier and replaced it with minimum grade point average and SAT performance requirements, the administration also initiated a "minority access program" in which students who did not meet these standards would be considered for admission. The university also established a minority scholarship program, funded by private and corporate donors but administered by Houston State's Office of Financial Aid.

Although there appeared to be some self-segregation of the black students, the campus, until recently, had been a reasonably tranquil and decorous academic environment. Although from time to time some isolated incidents of racial harassment occurred, the first real signs of the deep-seated prejudices that festered among the white students occurred following a request by a contingent of African-American students for a black student union. Since that time, the number of racially motivated incidents on campus had increased significantly. On one occasion, racial epithets had been painted on the dormitory room doors of several black students. In another incident, African-American students had hurled rocks at a white fraternity in protest as the members paraded in front of their fraternity house in black face. Letters to the student newspaper, the *Beacon*, denounced the administration's acquiescence to the request for a separate student union and accused the African-American students of attempting to set up a black enclave on the Houston State campus.

The dean of students, alarmed by the visible manifestations of racial prejudice and the climate of intolerance, proposed that the university adopt a student speech code in order to promote domestic tranquility on the Houston State campus. As approved by the Faculty Senate, the university could discipline any student for addressing an epithet to another individual member of the campus community that was intended "to demean the race, sex, religion, color, creed, disability, sexual orientation, national origin, ancestry, or age of the person addressed" and was intended "to create a hostile educational environment for that individual." While this action was applauded by the more liberal members of the faculty, it was condemned by the Student Government Association as a "misguided attempt at political correctness and an unprecedented violation of free expression on the Houston State campus."

As the voice of student expression, the *Beacon* had faithfully covered the growing campus controversy over political correctness and the university's affirmative action policies, with both sides appealing to "justice" to vindicate the morality of their respective positions. Until now, the *Beacon* had assumed an even-handed editorial posture on the race relations issue with its denunciation of both the highly publicized incidents of racial harassment and the university's speech code as an unconstitutional overreaction to a few isolated episodes.

Alvin Green, a journalism major and a weekly columnist for the student newspaper, was in his senior year at Houston State. His intellectual urbanity, sophisticated wit, and rhetorical flair were a welcome departure from the insignificant subject matter, shallow analysis, and occasional immature whining that had characterized his predecessors' writing. Green was an uncompromising supporter of student rights, and his views often clashed with those of the university's leadership. Nevertheless, the paper's irrepressible columnist, who was energized by virtually any campus controversy, had restored a measure of respect to the op-ed page with his thoughtful commentaries motivated by his youthful skepticism.

Green's latest masterpiece, scheduled for publication in Friday's edition of the *Beacon*, lived up to the columnist's usual standards of engagement, but it was not its intellectual rigor that concerned faculty newspaper adviser Margaret Hightower. The column was a direct assault on the university's affirmative action program and what Green described as "the administration's alliance with the totalitarian orthodoxy known as political correctness." Green was particularly critical of his institution's two-tiered admission standards, citing statistics to prove that the mean grade point average and SAT scores of minority students admitted to Houston State were significantly below those of entering white freshmen. "Compensatory justice," wrote Green, "in the form of double admission standards increases resentment among those who were admitted on merit, thus perpetuating a *de facto* system of racial apartheid on the Houston State campus. And the administration's failure to confront the moral impoverishment of this system constitutes nothing more than an appeasement to the forces of political correctness."

"This column will be inflammatory," said Hightower, as she began her hastily arranged meeting with Alvin Green and Cameron Pugh, the editor of the *Beacon*. As an employee of the university, Hightower exercised no power of censorship over the student newspaper, but she did attempt to render sage advice to her enthusiastic neophyte journalists. To encourage more critical decision making, she often played devil's advocate, thus skillfully concealing her own views on the issue at hand.

"The administration is already concerned about the increase in racism on campus," she continued, "and this column will just add fuel to the fire."

"But the facts in my column are true," responded Green, "including the statistics on minority admissions. And I have a right to express my opinions about the facts. It's a matter of free speech. I just don't believe it's fair to give minorities special advantages. Equal opportunity, yes—but not preferential treatment."

"We're not here to debate the merits of affirmative action," replied Pugh. "As a student newspaper, we do have the *right* to publish our views on such things as double admission standards, race-based scholarships, and the campus hate speech code. The question is what our role should be in promoting racial justice on campus."

"But what about justice for the rest of the student body?" responded Green indignantly. "Racial preferences are inherently unfair. We have a responsibility to speak out against them. This political correctness movement on campus is a threat to free speech, and it's more likely to increase racial tensions than to reduce them."

"You have a point," conceded Hightower who, as the faculty adviser, was emotionally divided between her commitments to the students and the administration. "But keep in mind that we serve the interests of all students, not just the white majority. Almost a fourth of our student body are minorities, and they also deserve to be represented. As faculty adviser to this paper, no one values free speech more than I do. But we're not really talking about your *right* to express your views. The administration hasn't threatened us with censorship. But there is a question of our *wisdom* in publishing this column at this time. After all, there are other values that may be just as important. If this campus becomes a hostile place because of racial prejudice, then the quality of dialogue on the issue of justice will greatly diminish. Perhaps our role should be to promote racial tolerance rather than open old wounds by denouncing the administration's affirmative action initiatives."

"But Alvin objects to these policies on the grounds of reverse discrimination," said Pugh. "And he sees the speech code as a threat to free expression, which of course could affect this newspaper as well. If we remain silent, then the advocates of political correctness will prevail. If we hold strong views on an issue and fail to take a stand, then we will be engaging in self-censorship. Personally, I believe that a frank exchange of views serves the cause of social justice more than policies designed to remedy past wrongs. There are plenty of African-American students who could gain admittance here without preferential treatment. The administration's policies, including its efforts to enforce PC through the speech code, are the cause of much of the resentment on campus. We have a responsibility to speak out against such policies because in the long run they undermine rather than promote racial tolerance."

Hightower silently conceded that Pugh might have a point. But at times like this, perhaps discretion was the better part of valor. "You may be right," she said. "But the right to speak does not always carry with it an obligation to do so. If we run this column, then we may become part of the racial problem on campus. We've already been taken to task because of our lack of minority representation on staff. But the *Beacon* is a part of the campus community. I think we can help promote campus harmony without falling victim to the PC movement. The administration has made a good-faith effort to attract minority students to this campus. No one can argue with that goal. Perhaps some aren't qualified to be here, but it's difficult to judge because many of them are from school districts where the educational quality is substandard. They haven't had the advantages of most of our white students. Normally, I would have no problem with criticizing particular administration policies, but Houston State is at a crossroads. Incidents of verbal harassment and even violence are increasing. A column like this will just add fuel to the fire."

"That isn't our problem," replied Green. "If my column were filled with racial slurs, then it might be a different matter. I'll admit that it does include some very strong statements, but the arguments are well reasoned. Quite frankly, I think this paper is on the side of the angels in this debate about PC. Racial preferences, race-based scholarships, and the student speech code are all unfair to a majority of our students. Social justice doesn't consist of treating groups differently because of their race. And it's our duty to point that out. And for those who disagree, there is always the letters to the editor column."

"It's true that some minority students are admitted who might not otherwise be eligible," replied Armstrong. "But who is really being harmed? Houston State has no quota on admissions—all qualified white students are admitted. And as far as the minority scholarship program is concerned, the money comes from private and corporate donors. It's their money and they can do with it as they please. And there's still plenty of money for scholarships for other students."

"That's an interesting perspective on the matter," acknowledged Pugh. "This is quite a dilemma. As a forum for student expression, we need to take a position on this matter. If we come out against the administration's policies, we'll be seen as undermining the university's efforts to provide educational opportunities for minorities in an academic setting free of racial harassment. Also, our minority readers will accuse us of racism. On the other hand, if the *Beacon* supports these policies—and by implication the PC movement—then we'll lose credibility with a majority of our readers who see political correctness as a threat to individual liberties. Not everyone will applaud our decision to run Alvin's column, if that's what we decide to do, but it's important that we maintain credibility with our readers—minorities included."

"I realize that, as editor, the final decision on whether to run Alvin's column is mine," continued Pugh in acknowledging his inescapable role as moral agent. "Although this is a column and not, strictly speaking, an editorial stance of our paper, it will still be perceived as such. We're responsible for everything we publish. What it boils down to is what we believe is in the best interest of the campus community and in the long-term interest of *all* our readers."

THE CASE STUDY

What should the college newspaper's role be in promoting racial justice on campus? In this case there are many stakeholders: the administration, the minority students, the aggrieved white student majority, and the newspaper itself as the forum for student opinion.

Campus papers do not stand in the same relative position to their readers as their professional counterparts. Like the *Beacon*, many are funded in part by mandatory student fees. Thus, they owe at least some allegiance to the demographic diversity that exists within the university setting. In addition, the campus community is a geographically confined environment in which students mingle and live in close proximity to one another. Their associations, in both their housing facilities and classrooms, are often involuntary. Thus, the potential for uncivil behavior is exacerbated, particularly in a racially mixed environment.

In this scenario, the university's administration has committed itself to an aggressive affirmative action program to attract minorities. With the increase in campus racial unrest, they have also instituted a student speech code to discourage racially motivated harassment that could lead to violence. Proponents of such initiatives argue that values such as justice, equality, and human dignity are as important as free speech. Opponents see such moves as the imposition of officially sanctioned orthodoxy known as "political correctness."

However, this is not a case about the merits of affirmative action or political correctness. The issue is whether the student paper should publish a column that will be perceived as anti-affirmative action and an attack on the university's efforts at achieving some measure of social justice within the academy. Editor Cameron Pugh could run the column, thus ingratiating himself to most of Houston State's white student body majority. Of course, the paper's African-American readers would accuse the *Beacon* of racism. On the other hand, if Pugh "kills" the column, he might be accused of acquiescing to the forces of political correctness. Is there a middle ground here that fulfills the *Beacon*'s duty (assuming there is one) to speak out while preserving the paper's obligation to *all* of its readers? Is the letters to the editor column, as suggested by Alvin Green, a sufficient solution to the concern for maintaining the paper's credibility with its diverse readership, minorities included?

For the purpose of confronting this troubling decision, assume the position of student editor Cameron Pugh; then, using the SAD Formula for moral reasoning outlined in Chapter 3, decide whether you will publish Alvin Green's column.

▶ **CASE 11-4**
The Media as Social Do-Gooders

"Jane Roe," a single woman whose real identity was never revealed, had sought refuge in one of Graniteville's homeless shelters, and soon thereafter she went into labor. She was transported by ambulance to a nearby public hospital, where she gave birth prematurely to a baby boy. From the outset, it was clear to the medical staff that the infant was suffering from cardiac distress, and "Baby Doe" was placed in the high-risk nursery. A heart specialist, after a thorough examination, decided that nothing short of a heart transplant would save the child's life and that the operation would have to be performed in a matter of days. An infant donor was needed.

It was this crisis that brought Karen Caldwell and Jane Roe together. Caldwell was the director of community relations for Channel 10 in Graniteville and for two years had been featured twice a week on the station's 5 P.M. news magazine show. Caldwell's "Community Helpline" spot was designed to assist viewers in dealing with government bureaucracies, recovering from personal tragedies, and confronting a variety of other social injustices. On more than one occasion she had rallied community support for those who needed help in securing such human necessities as housing or clothing or in paying their staggering medical bills. "Community Helpline" was a popular feature and had won several public service awards. And it did a lot for Channel 10's image, a fact that did not go unnoticed by the station's management.

A couple of days following the birth of Baby Doe, a social worker who had taken an interest in the case contacted Caldwell and asked her assistance in seeking an infant donor for the heart transplant. The social worker said Jane Roe was willing to be interviewed for the "Community Helpline" segment. Caldwell was enthusiastic. The plight of Baby Doe had been a topic of considerable local interest since the infant's birth, but this would be the mother's first interview.

Jane Roe, as it turned out, was an attractive nineteen-year-old who had been unemployed for more than a year. She had lived with the baby's father for several months, but he had abandoned her when she told him she was pregnant. The short interview went smoothly, with Jane Roe tearfully asking for the public's help in finding a donor for her baby. Following the program, the station's switchboards lit up with offers of financial support for the mother and the infant's operation. Jane Roe had become a TV celebrity.

The next day an attorney representing a family whose infant daughter had just died contacted Caldwell and offered to donate the baby's heart to Baby Doe. Caldwell relayed the offer to hospital officials, who lost no time in preparing for the lifesaving operation.

Once again, "Community Helpline" was applauded for its role in bringing about this "miracle." Letters to the editor published in the *Graniteville Gazette* reflected the depth of the public's vicarious participation in this event through Jane Roe's emotional television appearance. The Chamber of Commerce even commended the station for its outstanding service to the cause of humanity, a commendation that was followed several months later by an award.

However, not everyone was impressed by Jane Roe's television appearance. A local media critic, writing in the *Gazette*, questioned the fairness of giving priority for organ transplants to those who are fortunate enough to be the beneficiary of media publicity. He was pleased at the unselfish benevolence of the parents who had donated their daughter's heart but questioned the fundamental fairness to others who were also in line for transplants. A team of local physicians, expressing a similar ethical concern, also signed a letter to the editor complimenting Channel 10's humanitarian gesture but also raising the specter of the media's influence in deciding the priority for organ transplants.

Two other babies in nearby communities had been awaiting donors at the same time as Baby Doe, the letter noted, but their cases had attracted no public attention.

The criticisms did not go unnoticed by Caldwell. Although she was proud of the station's accomplishments, she had always been sensitive to the media's role in bestowing celebrity status on ordinary people. Normally, no harm was done, but when benefits accrued to some simply because they had been exposed to the glare of publicity, ethical questions arose. In the case of Baby Doe, the concerns involved both media ethics and medical ethics. Caldwell wondered whether in her haste to assist Jane Roe and her infant son she had been unjust to those who had no access to the media to plead their case.

But Caldwell also wondered whether her station was being unduly chastised for its role in saving Baby Doe's life. The "Community Helpline" segment had made a humanitarian gesture, and the results had been gratifying. Caldwell felt comfortable with Channel 10's altruistic motives in seeking the organ donor for the baby, but she reflected on her own eagerness to do the interview without considering the possible consequences. Had she seen this as yet another opportunity to promote the station's image? Caldwell could not be sure, but there was little doubt that station management had viewed her twice-a-week spot as a vehicle for demonstrating Channel 10's commitment to public service.

Caldwell considered the concerns of her critics, as well as the social good that had come about as a result of her efforts. Now that she had time to reflect, she wondered how the station should respond if another Baby Doe (or anyone else in need of an organ transplant) were to seek the assistance of "Community Helpline."

THE CASE STUDY

Ethical issues concerning matters of social justice arise when media intervention benefits some but harms others. A case similar to this one arose in 1986 when the parents of "Baby Jesse," having been rejected for a heart transplant by officials at the Loma Linda University Medical Center in California because they were unmarried, took their case to the media. While they were being interviewed live on the *Donahue* show, a couple whose son had died at birth offered to donate their baby's heart to Jesse. Following this episode, *Time* magazine made this observation: "Another ethical issue was brought to light by the Baby Jesse case: the growing role of the media in determining who gets organs."[58]

But what TV had failed to reveal was that another infant, in Louisville, Kentucky, had been waiting even longer for a transplant. The child's parents had eschewed media publicity, choosing instead to work quietly through the organ procurement program. Upset that they had been passed over in favor of Baby Jesse, they asked Congress for an improved system of donor identification. To them it seemed as if "publicity is the only method that's working."[59]

The media can create inequitable social relationships because of their intrusive coverage, but in the process they also have the capacity to benefit the cause of humanitarianism. Because the media, and television in particular, rely on human drama for much of their appeal, it is perhaps inevitable that they will become pawns for those who do not feel that they can receive justice through society's established institutions. The goal should be to harness the media's power for good while remaining alert for abuses that compromise social justice.

For the purpose of analyzing the problem posed by this scenario, assume the role of Caldwell, and decide whether you feel the station was wrong in broadcasting the plea of Jane Roe on behalf of her infant son. In doing so, employ the SAD Formula for moral reasoning.

▶ **CASE 11-5**
Media Employment and Compensatory Justice

The managing editor of the Sparta *Sentinel*, Tyler Moore, had narrowed the job search to two candidates. The newspaper had been without a full-time

city editor for six weeks, but Moore had taken his time in evaluating the applicants. This position was too important for any rush to judgment, and he wanted to be comfortable with his selection.

Sparta is a vibrant, culturally diverse New England community of 350,000, but its racial tensions and pockets of poverty belie the city's appearance of progressivism. The previous census had revealed Sparta's population to be 35 percent black and 10 percent Hispanic, and the failure of these groups to make what they believed to be sufficient inroads into the city's political power structure was a continuing source of agitation. The leaders of the black community, in particular, had accused the *Sentinel* of ignoring the problems of the minorities and responding only when a crisis arose. The fact that the paper employed only a few blacks and Hispanics, and none in management or reportorial positions, had also subjected the *Sentinel* to criticism.

Moore was not insensitive to the complaints of the black leaders, but he believed that they were unfair. He had felt the need to improve coverage of minority problems and to that end had mounted a campaign to employ more African-American and Hispanic reporters. He had contacted several journalism programs seeking minority applicants but discovered that the potential applicant pool was small. Those whom he had interviewed had either elected to take jobs with larger papers where the pay was better or had been reluctant to work for a paper where minorities were virtually invisible, especially in the newsroom. They did not, in other words, want to think of themselves as a "token hire."

But Moore had not abandoned his goal of improving the paper's sensitivity to the problems of the African-American and Hispanic communities, and he had kept this aim in mind as he read the stack of applications for the city editor's position. Only two black candidates had been in the pool, and one had been rejected on the basis of limited experience and an unimpressive letter of application.

Jeremy Blanchard, however, had caught Moore's attention. Blanchard's résumé revealed that he had a bachelor of arts in journalism, with a minor in political science, and had worked for six years as a reporter for the *Marionville Gazette*, a paper comparable in size to the *Sentinel*. He had been both a general assignment and political affairs reporter and had compiled an impressive list of by-lined articles. He had also worked briefly on the copy desk, although his experience there was limited. Moore had contacted Blanchard's references, and all had given him high marks. "Bright," "aggressive," and "sharp" were frequently used adjectives to describe the young reporter. Moore's interview with him had confirmed these observations.

But despite Blanchard's credentials as a reporter, Moore knew that the other finalist for the position was perhaps even more qualified for the job. Jim Hardy had also worked for the *Marionville Gazette* for six years before joining the *Sentinel* as a governmental reporter. Hardy had performed impressively in that position until moving to the copy desk and eventually to assistant city editor six months before. Since his arrival in Sparta, he had immersed himself in the affairs of the community and knew the city intimately. As a reporter he had cultivated contacts among the political and social elite and had a good news sense.

Under normal circumstances, this decision would not have been so challenging for Moore. The managing editor preferred to hire from within the organization, a practice that was definitely a morale booster. In addition, both copy editor and assistant city editor were natural stepping stones to city editor. Copy editors usually understood more about the internal operation of the paper than did reporters. It would be an unusual move, Moore knew, to hire a reporter from another paper, with limited experience on the copy desk, to be city editor. Moore had also been impressed with Hardy's cool demeanor, organizational skills, and ability to work well with others. Blanchard might possess all of these qualities, but they were yet to be demonstrated.

Moore considered his decision. The hiring of Blanchard might well have a devastating effect on newsroom morale, especially since Hardy appeared to be better qualified. Blanchard was also unfamiliar with the Sparta community and would have to depend on subordinates until he learned the ropes. Although Moore had more than a passing interest in hiring minorities, he also had to keep in mind that the city editor had to be sensitive to all community interests.

On the other hand, Blanchard had demonstrated his journalistic prowess and had some experience, albeit limited, on the copy desk. He had apparently impressed his references, and Moore's interview with his young black applicant had left the impression that Blanchard would be a quick study for the role of city editor. Of course, placing a black into a managerial position would not immediately solve the *Sentinel*'s deficiencies in minority news coverage, but Blanchard's presence might stimulate minority recruitment and help blunt some of the criticisms from the leaders of the black and Hispanic communities.

The safe decision, Moore realized, would be to hire Hardy. He could, after all, reject Blanchard in good conscience, because the *Sentinel*'s assistant city editor appeared to be more qualified, at least according to traditional criteria for the position of city editor. The hiring of the black reporter from the *Marionville Gazette* to be city editor, moreover, would be contentious. Moore would be accused of "reverse" discrimination, a controversial form of preferential treatment to remedy the effects of past discrimination. The managing editor wondered what his responsibilities were to advance the cause of social justice and how far they should extend.

THE CASE STUDY

Affirmative action, which some refer to as "reverse" discrimination, is one of the most hotly debated issues of our time. It is also a classic illustration of the ethical conflicts inherent in the principle of social justice. In recent years, demands have been placed on businesses to correct past employment discrimination against women and racial minorities. As commercial institutions, the media have been at the vortex of this controversy because of their visibility and perceived influence on public opinion and societal values.

The two most often cited justifications for preferential treatment are the principle of compensatory justice and the principle of utility. Compensatory justice holds that whenever there has been a prior injustice resulting in harm, compensation is morally required. This is the principle usually cited to justify preferential hiring practices.[60] But are such practices fair to those who are better qualified and yet are passed over for promotions or other employment opportunities?

When discrimination is viewed as compensation for a lost opportunity to compete on equal terms, a case could be made for its fairness.[61] The relatively few members of minority groups in management-level positions in the media attests to the effect of past discrimination. Without affirmative action, would those doors remain closed to the victims of past discrimination?

The second principle, utility, denies that the primary purpose of preferential employment practices is the rectification of past injustices. Rather, the central concern is the morally good consequences to be produced for minorities and the society as a whole by eliminating the continuing effects of past discrimination.[62]

But those who are affected by reverse discrimination are not usually responsible for the past discrimination against minorities. Thus, should social justice for minorities be extracted at the expense of those who deserve promotions and other rewards of the workplace?

Moore seems as concerned with appeasing the leaders of Sparta's minority communities as with improving the paper's commitment to affirmative action. However, if he employs what he considers to be the standard criteria for hiring a city editor, the white assistant city editor should be chosen. No evidence suggests that the criteria themselves are discriminatory, but the following question might be posed: Considering the black reporter's credentials, is there any reason to believe that he would be clearly unqualified for the city editor's position? Another way to put it is to ask whether injustices suffered by minorities have made race a relevant criteria in employment considerations.[63]

When the problem is stated in this manner, the focus in comparing the two applicants shifts away from the amount of their professional experience to one of institutional goals—in this case, an increase in minority recruitment. But if Moore hires Blanchard, he is still left with the question of fair-

ness to Hardy and the effects on newsroom morale.

For the purpose of making a decision on these applicants, assume Moore's role, and, using the moral reasoning model, render a judgment in this matter. In analyzing this case, you might consider the following questions: (1) Is it morally wrong for those media practitioners in charge of hiring to use race as a criterion in a hiring decision? (2) If a minority candidate who is less qualified than a white is hired, has the white employee been treated unfairly? (3) Should media employers alter their traditional hiring criteria in order to promote minorities into management-level positions? (4) In general, is the cause of social justice for minorities, which may necessitate some preferential treatment in some cases, more important than the occasional harm done to other employees in the hiring and promotion process?

► CASE 11-6
A PR Practitioner Considers Pro Bono Work

Father Gerald Michaelson was a man with a mission and a champion of the downtrodden. The young priest had been assigned to a Catholic church in a poor neighborhood of Augustine, and from the beginning he had committed himself to the cause of social justice for the poor and homeless. When he was not dispensing food and shelter to the outcasts among his parishioners, he was pleading their cause to the city leaders. He also spent much of his time seeking assistance from doctors and lawyers who were disposed to offer their services in the spirit of charity.

Augustine is a city of contrasts. Located in the New England corridor, it is a thriving community of 475,000 with a healthy diversification of light industry, small business, and white-collar occupations. But not all of the citizens of Augustine have shared in this prosperity. The unemployment rate among the community's ethnic minorities has been triple that of the white population, and within the previous three years the homelessness among poor whites also showed a dramatic increase. The government's refusal to fund more low-cost housing had made a bad situation worse, and the city's recent destruction of a public housing project to make way for a high-rise condominium revealed, in Michaelson's opinion, an alarming insensitivity to the problems of the urban poor.

Michaelson understood the necessity for mobilizing public support for his cause. On more than one occasion he had appeared before the city council to plead for more assistance, events that had merited all of thirty seconds on the local TV news. The crusading priest had even led a band of homeless people to the Government Center to protest their economic plight. Once again, there was some media coverage of the demonstration but not sufficient interest in the story to sustain its coverage.

Not easily discouraged, Michaelson decided to seek professional help in arguing his case in the court of public opinion. The poor and homeless, he knew, had no access to the media, and thus their agenda was shoved aside by those who could command the attention of the nation's powerful organs of mass communication. Michaelson first sought the assistance of a large public relations firm in a nearby city, noting that he had no funding for this project and appealing to its sense of charity. His request was summarily rejected. Another firm responded that it occasionally took on projects at no charge for charitable institutions but that it had filled its quota. These rejections brought Michaelson to the doorstep of Jason Blackwell.

Blackwell had set up his small PR firm in Augustine eight years before and had worked hard to attract a steady clientele of local and regional institutions. The firm had not made Blackwell a wealthy man, but it had provided a comfortable income. Michaelson was a very passionate, persuasive man. He began by describing the plight of the poor and homeless in Augustine. "No one seems to care," he said. "The city council says it can't afford to do more without federal assistance—and that's unlikely. And the media coverage has been so sparse that I don't believe the citizens of Augustine are really aware of the problem or understand

what it's doing to an important segment of this community." Blackwell had to admit that he had not been fully aware of how bad things were.

Michaelson then asked for Blackwell's assistance in waging his campaign for poor people through the media and keeping their cause in the public spotlight. "They need an advocate," he said, "someone who can ensure access to the local media." The priest then told Blackwell that he had no funding for the campaign but asked the PR executive whether he would consider taking on the project pro bono—without charge and for the good of society.

During Michaelson's impassioned presentation, Blackwell had taken copious notes. He was impressed by the young priest and told him he would consider his request. The idea of pro bono work, a social obligation often associated with the legal profession, was something new to him. His firm still had a relatively small client list. Blackwell and Associates had represented a couple of charitable organizations but never free of charge. If he took on this responsibility, where would it stop? Would every unfunded cause seeking publicity come to his door? How could he decide which were worthy of consideration? Why not leave the pro bono work to the other agencies with greater resources? Blackwell sympathized with Michaelson's predicament but wondered whether justice required that all segments of society seeking access to the media be granted an audience.

On the other hand, Blackwell questioned the wisdom of a system of social justice that determined media access strictly by economic and political considerations. The economically disenfranchised were virtually without representation in the court of public opinion. Despite some government support, things would not improve until the public was mobilized in favor of helping the downtrodden improve their lot. Of course, the media had not been completely inattentive to the plight of the poor. Blackwell had seen an occasional newspaper article and even some features and documentaries on TV. But they had been spotty and certainly not consistent.

As a PR professional, Blackwell pondered his moral duty to devote some of his time and energy (and profits) to clients who could not afford the cost of his services. Most lawyers do some pro bono work; many physicians administer to the sick regardless of their ability to afford quality health care. What responsibilities, Blackwell wondered, do PR practitioners have to the cause of social injustice?

THE CASE STUDY

The mass media are at the vortex of the public opinion process, but not all segments of society have access to the media to state their case. The public must depend on the news judgments of editors and reporters to provide a surveillance of the environment. But persistent social problems such as poverty do not hold the media's attention for long. Despite some excellent stories produced by the commercial TV networks and some of the nation's leading newspapers, the coverage has not been consistent.

Part of the problem is a lack of access and the inability of some groups to generate publicity. Economic considerations, of course, enter into the equation because publicity is expensive unless an event is staged to draw media attention, and this kind of coverage is short-lived. Do the media have a moral obligation to ensure access for all groups, and, if so, how is this objective to be accomplished?

PR practitioners are central to this issue, because they are uniquely qualified to develop programs to maximize the opportunities for media access. The question is, What moral obligations should be imposed on the profession of public relations to contribute to the cause of social justice through pro bono work? Nothing in the "Code of Professional Standards for the Practice of Public Relations" commits PR practitioners to this effort. Thus, moral agents must decide where their ethical obligations reside in the practice of public relations and whether, like other professionals such as lawyers and doctors, they have a comparable role in contributing to the cause of social justice.

For the purpose of considering this problem as reflected in this scenario, assume the role of Blackwell. Then, using the SAD Formula, decide whether

you will honor Michaelson's request and represent the plight of the poor pro bono.

Notes

1. See Tom L. Beauchamp, *Philosophical Ethics: An Introduction to Moral Philosophy* (New York: McGraw-Hill, 1982), p. 223.
2. Aristotle considers the subject in Book V of the *Nichomachean Ethics.*
3. For a discussion of the relationship of libertarianism to institutional press freedom, see John C. Merrill, *The Dialectic in Journalism: Toward a Responsible Use of Press Freedom* (Baton Rouge: Louisiana State University Press, 1989), pp. 113–114.
4. Fred S. Siebert, Theodore Peterson, and Wilbur Schramm, *Four Theories of the Press* (Urbana: University of Illinois Press, 1956), pp. 39–71.
5. *Ibid.*, p. 73.
6. John A. Rawls, *A Theory of Justice* (Cambridge, MA: Harvard University Press, 1971).
7. For a discussion of the relationship of Rawls's theory, as well as those of other influential philosophers, to the notion of "responsibility," see Merrill, *Dialectic in Journalism*, pp. 37–54.
8. Clifford G. Christians, Mark Fackler, and Kim B. Rotzoll, *Media Ethics: Cases & Moral Reasoning*, 4th ed. (White Plains, NY: Longman, 1995), p. 97.
9. Howard Kurtz, *Media Circus: The Trouble with America's Newspapers* (New York: Random House, 1993), pp. 31–32.
10. *Ibid.*, p. 31.
11. Commission on the Freedom of the Press, *A Free and Responsible Press* (Chicago: University of Chicago Press, 1947), pp. 26–27.
12. Quoted in Regina Burns, "Covering Minority Communities," *Communicator*, November 1992, p. 32.
13. *Ibid.*
14. Paul Ruffins, "What's Fair in Black and White?" *Communicator*, October 1990, p. 75.
15. *Ibid.*
16. Mary Beth Oliver, "Portrayals of Crime, Race, and Aggression in 'Reality-Based' Police Shows: A Content Analysis," *Journal of Broadcasting & Electronic Media*, 38, Spring 1994, pp. 179–192.
17. Neil Hickey, "Many Groups Underrepresented on TV, Study Declares," *TV Guide*, July 3, 1993, p. 33.
18. *Ibid.*
19. Greg Braxton and Jan Breslauer (*Los Angeles Times*), "Latinos Protest Invisibility, Even Negative Image on TV," (Baton Rouge) *Advocate*, March 20, 1995, p. 8A.
20. Mike Freeman, "Tribune Targets Minority Audience," *Broadcasting*, March 9, 1992, p. 26.

21. "Fox Creates Hispanic programmer," *Broadcasting & Cable*, October 3, 1994, p. 28.

22. See "Listening to Their Latin Beat," *Newsweek*, March 28, 1994, pp. 42–43; David Tobenkin, "Latinos Unhappy with TV Portrayal, Representation," *Broadcasting & Cable*, January 9, 1995, p. 51.

23. For an insightful commentary on news coverage of groups outside the mainstream, see Clifford Christians, "Reporting and the Oppressed," in Deni Elliott (ed.), *Responsible Journalism* (Beverly Hills, CA: Sage, 1986), pp. 109–130.

24. "Listening to Their Latin Beat," p. 42.

25. "A Long Way from 'Aunt Jemima,'" *Newsweek*, August 14, 1989, pp. 34–35.

26. Vernon A. Stone, "Trends in the Status of Minorities and Women in Broadcast News," *Journalism Quarterly*, 65, Summer 1988, p. 289.

27. Vernon A. Stone, "Status Quo," *Communicator*, August 1994, p. 17.

28. Ellis Cose, "A City Room of Many Colors," *Newsweek*, October 4, 1993, p. 82.

29. Donald L. Guimary, "Non-Whites in Newsrooms of California Dailies," *Journalism Quarterly*, 65, Winter 1988, p. 1009. For an examination of the organization's plans to improve minority recruitment and hiring, see "Minorities in the Newsroom," *ASNE Bulletin*, February 1985, pp. 3–35, and May–June 1987, pp. 16–23.

30. *Ibid.*

31. Michael Giarruso, "Minority Journalists Gather to Break Down Bias in News," (Baton Rouge) *Advocate*, July 25, 1994, p. 9A.

32. Stuart Elliott, "Hill & Knowlton Forms a Unit to Direct Public Relations Efforts toward Gay Men and Lesbians," *New York Times*, June 23, 1995, p. C5.

33. See Marilyn Kern-Foxworth, "Minorities 2000," *Public Relations Journal*, August 1989, pp. 14–22.

34. *Ibid.*, p. 16.

35. Stone, "Status Quo," p. 17.

36. Christi Harlan, "Role Models in Transition," *Quill*, July/August 1995, pp. 39–40.

37. "Newsrooms Recruit Gay Journalists," *Quill*, November/December 1993, p. 8; Cal Thomas, "Group Urges Media to Hire Homosexuals," (Baton Rouge) *Advocate*, September 22, 1993, p. 4B.

38. See Alicia C. Shepard, "High Anxiety," *American Journalism Review*, November 1993, pp. 19–24.

39. *Irvin v. Dowd*, 366 U.S. 717 (1961).

40. *Rideau v. Louisiana*, 373 U.S. 723 (1963).

41. See *Sheppard v. Maxwell*, 384 U.S. 333 (1966).

42. *Nebraska Press Association v. Stuart*, 427 U.S. 539 (1976).

43. Kathy R. Fitzpatrick, "Life after Simpson: Regulating Media Freedom in Judicial Matters," *Media Law Notes* (Newsletter of the Association for Education in Journalism and Mass Communication Law Division), 22, Spring 1995, p. 4.

44. "O. J. Simpson Coverage: Reflecting on the Media in Society," *Poynter Report*, Fall 1994, p. 3.

45. Susanne A. Roschwalb and Richard A. Stack, "Litigation Public Relations," *Communications and the Law*, 14, December 1992, p. 6.

46. E.g., for a good discussion of how O. J. Simpson's lead attorney manipulated the media, see Robert L. Shapiro, "Secrets of a Celebrity Lawyer," *Columbia Journalism Review*, September/October 1994, pp. 25–29.

47. *Ibid.*, p. 3.

48. *Ibid.*, p. 13.

49. *Ibid.*, pp. 18–19, citing James B. Stewart, *Den of Thieves* (New York: Touchstone Books, 1991), particularly pp. 356, 378.

50. *Ibid.*, p. 19.

51. For a thorough analysis of the ethics of the role of PR in this case, see Barbara K. Petersen, Doug Newsome, Patrick Jackson, Betsy Plank, and Cornelius B. Pratt, "Public Relations for the Defense," *Journal of Mass Media Ethics*, Vol. 8, 1993, pp. 247–256.

52. Doug Newsome, "Commentary #1," in *ibid.*, p. 249.

53. For a discussion of the relationship of justice to various disciplines, see Ronald L. Cohen (ed.), *Justice: Views from the Social Sciences* (New York: Plenum, 1986).

54. Joann Lee, "New York City NDs Reflect on Their Coverage of the Tawana Brawley Story," *Communicator*, August 1989, p. 29.

55. Aristotle's conception of compensatory justice is sometimes described as "rectifying justice." See Norman E. Bowie, *Making Ethical Decisions* (New York: McGraw-Hill, 1985), p. 268.

56. Doug Newsome, "Public Relations for the Defense: A Right to Defend Himself (Commentary #1)," *Journal of Mass Media Ethics*, 8, No. 4, 1993, p. 248.

57. Patrick Jackson, "The Real Question: Can Journalists Be Fair (Commentary #2)," in *ibid.*, pp. 250–251.

58. "Of Television and Transplants," *Time*, June 23, 1986, p. 68.

59. *Ibid.*

60. Joan C. Callahan, "Social Responsibility and Justice," in Joan C. Callahan (ed.), *Ethical Issues in Professional Life* (New York: Oxford University Press, 1988), p. 346.

61. George Sher, "Justifying Reverse Discrimination in Employment," in Callahan, *Ethical Issues*, p. 356.

62. Thomas A. Mappes and Jane S. Zembaty, *Social Ethics: Morality and Social Policy*, 3d ed. (New York: McGraw-Hill, 1987), p. 187.

63. *Ibid.*, p. 189.

Stereotypes in Media Communications

THE CONCEPT OF STEREOTYPES

A stereotype is a "fixed mental image of a group that is frequently applied to all its members."[1] In a world full of complexities and ambiguities, we are constantly seeking ways of confronting and simplifying the confusion of everyday reality. Most of our knowledge of the universe is experienced vicariously, and we tend to compartmentalize this secondhand information and fit it into our preconceived notions about other groups of people. When this happens, we are participating in the process of stereotyping. The concepts discussed in this chapter are related closely to some of those in Chapter 11. Stereotyping can lead to social injustices for those who are its unfortunate victims, and when this happens, serious ethical questions arise. Stereotypes sometimes extend beyond the matter of social justice, however, and thus they deserve to be examined in a separate chapter.

There is a tendency to associate stereotypes with such visible issues as sexism and racial and ethnic prejudice. These are undoubtedly the most controversial of our stereotypes, but unfair labeling extends to all areas of social interaction. Overweight people, for example, are often pictured as slovenly and lazy. Young people are often described rather disparagingly as "Generation X" and depicted just as unflatter-ingly as unmotivated, economically pampered whiners. The homeless are all lumped together as bums and social misfits who have chosen their unconventional lifestyle and economic circumstances. Certain nationalities are depicted as romantic and fun-loving, and others are pictured as cold and authoritarian. The media's unflattering portrayal of such groups as the Russians and Arabs has done little to advance the cause of international understanding.

Stereotyping is a human trait of ancient vintage. Aristotle, the patron saint of "virtue ethics," was guilty of stereotyping. In his defense of slavery in the fourth century B.C., he justified treating slaves differently from free men because, he insisted, nature had intended to make the bodies of slaves suitable for "servile labors."[2] He constructed this stereotype to justify the distinction, which was not otherwise apparent to the casual observer, between Athenian slaves and the free citizens of this classic city.

The modern concept of stereotyping was introduced into our social consciousness by the distinguished author and columnist Walter Lippmann. Writing in his often quoted *Public Opinion* in 1922, Lippmann made the following observation about the necessity (or perhaps inevitability) of relying on stereotypes to manage our environment and social relationships:

For the attempt to see all things freshly and in detail, rather than as types and generalities, is exhausting, and among busy affairs practically out of the question. . . . Modern life is hurried and multifarious, above all physical distance separates men who are often in vital contact with each other, such as employer and employee, official and voter. There is neither time nor opportunity for intimate acquaintance. Instead, we notice a trait which marks a well known type, and fill in the rest of the picture by means of the stereotypes we carry about in our heads.[3]

In other words, stereotypes are an economical way of viewing the world. Because individuals cannot personally experience most of the events in which they have an interest, they rely on the testimony of others to enrich their impoverished knowledge. The mass media, of course, are an important window for this vicarious experience and function as our eyes and ears for that part of the universe we cannot directly observe.[4] Thus, media practitioners have a moral responsibility to understand the differences between stereotypes and reality.

Lippmann notes, quite correctly, that a "pattern of stereotypes is not neutral." Because stereotyping involves our personal perceptions of reality, it is "highly charged with the feelings that are attached to them." Thus, as he instructs us, stereotypes are a vital defense mechanism behind which "we can continue to feel ourselves safe in the position we occupy."[5] This view suggests that stereotyping, as a natural process, has a role to play in maintaining sanity and that to arbitrarily reject it as unsavory or unworthy of our respect would be a mistake:

We need categories to group things that are similar in order to study them and to communicate about them. We have stereotypes about many categories, including mothers, fathers, teenagers, communists, Republicans, school teachers, farmers, construction workers, miners, politicians, Mormons, and Italians. These stereotypes may contain some useful and accurate information about a member in any category. Yet, each member of any category will have many charac-

teristics that are not suggested by the stereotypes and may even have some characteristics that run counter to some of the stereotypes.[6]

Nevertheless, in our egalitarian society, stereotypes are unfair. Their use leaves little room for perceiving individual differences within a group.[7] Thus, to the extent that we judge others according to some misguided stereotype, we have undermined their right to self-determination, a basic value within our society.[8]

The use of stereotypes can also violate the fundamental human values of honesty and sincerity. Professor Peter Orlik, commenting on the use of stereotypes in the broadcast media, makes this thoughtful observation in his book *Electronic Media Criticism*:

When ages, occupations, genders, religions, or racial groups are represented in stereotypical ways, the treatment becomes potentially more dishonest the longer it is allowed to remain on microphone or on camera. All Texans, all Native Americans, all Baptists, or police officers are not the same; and to depict each member of such groups as exactly the same is to be functionally dishonest and insincere . . . to the concept of individual *human dignity*.[9]

However, it would be a mistake to equate stereotypes with falsehoods, because some stereotypes do have a foundation in reality. It is when we make inaccurate judgments about others on the basis of these mental images that ethical questions arise to confront our prejudices.

For example, the media have traditionally depicted male homosexuals as flamboyant and effeminate, traits that do represent a segment of the gay population but are not necessarily representative of the group as a whole. Because such images often erect psychological barriers between the gay community and society at large, the question is whether they should be avoided entirely, even if they are an accurate portrayal of a segment of the offended group.

The media have been the focal point for much of the criticism of the perpetuation of stereotypes. In recent years, they have become increasingly sensitive to these accusations, and some offensive stereotypes have been eliminated. Ironically, some critics have occasionally chastised media practitioners who presented nonstereotypical portrayals. A case in point is the criticism of the controversial Spike Lee film *Do the Right Thing*. Some movie reviewers observed that the film's ghetto neighborhood is not populated by addicts and drug pushers and thus is not a true depiction. This criticism ignores the fact that millions of black Americans live in neighborhoods that are not populated by drug dealers and street gangs.[10]

Nevertheless, media professionals must still struggle with the moral dilemma of responding to the concerns of those who object to unflattering or unrealistic portrayals while protecting the legitimate and acceptable roles that some stereotypes play in the presentation of media content. In other words, some stereotyping in the production of media content may be inevitable, but strategies should be deployed to confront those that are particularly offensive and unfair to certain segments of society.

THE ROLE OF STEREOTYPES IN MEDIA CONTENT

If stereotypes are indispensable for the individual's comprehension of the environment, as Lippmann suggested in 1922, stereotyping is probably important to the media's repertoire. In the production of entertainment programming for television, for example, the technology of the medium and the insatiable demand for material make the use of standardized images inevitable. In addition, the necessity for formulaic genres in TV drama produces stereotypical characters to whom the audience can relate week to week.

T. W. Adorno noted this phenomenon in the early 1950s, when TV was still in its infancy, but his comments are just as applicable today:

The very standardization indicated by set frames of reference automatically produces a number of stereotypes. Also, the technology of television production makes stereotypy almost inevitable. The short time available for the preparation of scripts and the vast material continuously to be produced call for certain formulas.... It appears inevitable that the kind of person the audience faces each time should be indicated drastically through red and green lights.... Since stereotypes are an indispensable element of the organization and anticipation of experience, preventing us from falling into mental disorganization and chaos, no art can entirely dispense with them.[11]

Nevertheless, Adorno warns us, there is a danger zone surrounding the use of stereotypes, because "people may not only lose true insight into reality, but ultimately their capacity for life experience may be dulled by the constant wearing of blue and pink spectacles."[12] In other words, ethical issues arise when the employment of media stereotypes becomes so pronounced as to dull the audience's critical faculties in making value judgments concerning individual members of society. In a pluralistic culture such as ours, media practitioners have an obligation to consider the fundamental fairness of a system that has traditionally projected stereotypical images of certain segments of society.

Racial Minorities

In particular, stereotypes of minorities, women, and the elderly in the media have been among the most visible and most criticized. Generations of Americans, for example, were treated to conventional images of blacks as depicted by the movie actor Stepin Fetchit, a slow-moving and dim-witted caricature, and the children's book and cartoon character Little Black Sambo. Early programs such as *Amos 'n' Andy* perpetuated black stereotypes on radio and television.

By the late 1970s, however, it was clear that some changes were being made, and in the 1980s black family comedies held a position of prominence among the networks' program offerings. *The Cosby Show*, for example, had its debut in the 1984–85 season and featured a black obstetrician living with his wife and children in a New York Brownstone. The following year *227* joined the network lineup, starring Marla Gibbs as a tenant living in an urban neighborhood.

By the early 1990s, prime-time TV had more programs than ever dominated by black characters, and surveys showed that black households were watching TV in record numbers,[13] a discovery that did not go unnoticed on Madison Avenue. But some critics and even industry executives have greeted this trend with some cynicism. For example, at his induction into the Academy of Television Arts & Sciences Hall of Fame, Bill Cosby castigated the networks for churning out "drive-by images" that he said reinforce shallow stereotypes. A case in point is *Here and Now,* a black sitcom produced by Bill Cosby, that featured a Stepin Fetchit character that was depicted in such degrading situations as hustling Knicks tickets in exchange for stolen snow tires.[14]

The reasons for this state of affairs lie both in the artistic and commercial realities of the marketplace. Whites still control most shows about blacks, and producers and writers often miss the nuances of the ethnic landscape they are writing about. Such a cultural gap is difficult to bridge without an adequate representation of minorities on the writing teams for such programs. In addition, while black-dominated sitcoms are fairly prominent features in prime time, network executives are still reluctant to invest heavily in black dramatic series. In 1988, for example, CBS canceled after just one season the highly acclaimed but low-rated drama *Frank's Place,* starring Tim Reid as a New Orleans restaurateur.[15]

Another group that has long suffered from media stereotypes are American Indians (sometimes referred to as Native Americans).[16] Portrayals of the "savage Indian" did not begin in the movie studios of Hollywood. In the nineteenth century, long before the emergence of film, news reporting about American Indians was distorted in such a way that it encouraged or at least condoned brutal treatment of them. Mass-produced books reinforced the popular image of American Indians as subhuman renegades. With the rise of the giant film studios, Hollywood succeeded in erasing the cultural and ethnic distinctions among the over 400 distinct American Indian tribes and nations by developing one-dimensional figures who mercilessly slaughtered innocent women and children.

However, such stereotypes die hard and are not merely a historical relic of Hollywood's fantasy. Hollywood is increasingly under siege by American Indian activists to eradicate stereotypes. For example, in an unprecedented news conference in 1994, a council of Indian actors, actresses, and advocates called for the film and TV industries to stop "the inaccurate or demeaning stereotypical portrayals of American Indians." They also protested the use of non-Indians to portray Indians, referring specifically to such TV series as *Dr. Quinn Medicine Woman* and the animated film *Peter Pan.*[17]

The news media, which we depend on for an accurate representation of our national fabric, are not blameless in the perpetuation of stereotypes. For example, blacks are often depicted as welfare recipients and drug pushers, as poverty-stricken and uneducated. This image undoubtedly fits a segment of the black community, but the news media have usually ignored the sizable black middle class. How many black attorneys, for example, are interviewed on television concerning their opinions of Supreme Court decisions (unless, of course, the ruling involves civil rights)?

Such insensitivity may lie in the fact that the minority representation in media management positions is still relatively low. But part of the problem is inherent in the nature of the news business. Social problems are newsworthy, and coverage of these problems inevitably focuses on those who are most likely to represent perceived stereotypes, such as inner-city blacks who are school dropouts and gang members, and Hispanics who are illegal aliens.[18]

But while the news media, in the interest of fairness, should not unnecessarily perpetuate stereotypes, there are limits to their responsibility. Should a newspaper, in the interest of being perceived as "politically correct," simply delete stereotypically offensive proper names from its coverage? Consider the Portland *Oregonian*'s decision in the spring of 1992 to ban from its sports pages the names Indians, Braves, Redmen, and Redskins. The change was met with mixed reviews in the journalistic community. A reporter for the *Seattle Times*, for example, applauded the decision because "[t]oo often what is traditional is considered normal, when in effect it is often abnormal and derogatory and biased." But one of the *Oregonian*'s own executives probably reflected the views of most reporters and editors when he said, "I'm not sure it's appropriate for a newspaper to act as a censor in policing the language and labels used by others. The *Oregonian*'s action seems almost like changing a quote because the newspaper disagreed with what the person said."[19]

The advertising industry must also plead guilty to stereotyping racial and ethnic minorities. Because advertisers are in the business of creating images and selling a product within a brief message, stereotyping is inevitable. And before the 1960s and 1970s, the economic reality that campaigns were produced primarily for a white audience led advertisers to appeal to the perceived attitudes and prejudices of the majority. Ads featuring stereotypical racial and ethnic characters, such as Chiquita Banana and Aunt Jemima, were commonplace until groups representing the various minority groups began protesting vigorously, thus forcing a retreat by agencies and companies.[20]

Of course, a danger always persists that old stereotypes might be replaced by newer ones. For example, as these domestic racial and ethnic stereotypes began to disappear, the advertising industry began to capitalize on the resurgence of patriotism of the 1980s under Ronald Reagan's administration. Russians, in particular, were fair game, as evidenced in a Wendy's commercial featuring a fashion show in which an overweight, unattractive, and drab Slavic woman was portrayed.[21] In another

commercial, a Russian spy was banished to the frigid outdoors for his failure to procure for his party superiors a Bud Light.

Women

The depiction of women has traditionally been one of the media's most pervasive stereotypes. In the 1950s most women were homemakers, and ads often portrayed them as being preoccupied with better ways to do the laundry and discovering new ways to please their husbands. Television programs featured the perfect wife, who maintained a spotless home for the family patriarch and the children and displayed none of the signs of stress that one associates with contemporary living. Such early TV fare as *Father Knows Best*, *Leave It to Beaver*, and *The Adventures of Ozzie and Harriet*, some of which are still in syndication, were fantasy insights into the model American family.

Other programs, such as *I Love Lucy*, featured silly and trouble-prone wives, a stereotype that continues to attract and amuse the mass audience. Nevertheless, neither image of women in the 1950s was an accurate portrayal of reality, although one might struggle to find real fault with these programs in light of the hours of clean entertainment they have provided television viewers. In the 1970s and 1980s, the TV roles of women began to change as such popular shows as *M*A*S*H*, *The Mary Tyler Moore Show*, *One Day at a Time*, *Murphy Brown*, and *The Golden Girls* began to feature female characters who were assertive and self-sufficient. And more recently we find such popular TV personalities as Roseanne Arnold as an independent wife and also a working-class hero.

However, regardless of its ethical appeal, confronting stereotypes is culturally risky, and in the 1990s there has been a backlash against the feminist messages of the last two decades. "Too much freedom causes women unhappiness" is the theme of the new generation of female-focused entertainment. We see this trend reflected, for example, in such films as *The Hand That Rocks the Cradle*, in which a "psycho nanny" wreaks havoc on a trusting family, thus reinforcing the message that women who work and leave child rearing to others are flirting with disaster. We see similar antifeminist overtones in *Fatal Attraction*, in which Glenn Close plays the part of a crazed career woman, and the TV series *Thirtysomething*, featuring Mel Harris as the submissive housewife.[22]

The advertising industry has also thrived on female stereotypes. The submissive housewife has virtually disappeared from television commercials, but she was supplanted in the 1980s by the "supermom," who calmly and skillfully balances the demands of family and career. Both images are unrealistic, of course, and they exemplify the difficulties of constructing media content that is devoid of stereotyping. Images of women as preoccupied with beauty, sex appeal, and youth still abound in commercial messages directed at the mass audience. For example, a recent study of MTV commercials found that female characters had more beautiful bodies, were more physically attractive, wore more sexy and skimpy clothing, and were often the objects of another's gaze than their male counterparts.[23] In the 1990s, traditional gender roles returned with a vengeance. Consider, for example, the Brut ad featuring a gorgeous young woman in a lacy black dress, her car stuck by the side of the road. A sexy young man arrives, slowly removes his T-shirt, uses it to remove her overheated radiator cap, and then ignores her "come hither" look as he saunters away. An appreciative female voice, her words appearing on the screen as they are spoken, says, "Brut. Men are back."[24] And then there was the Diet Coke commercial in which a group of women look longingly from an office window as a construction worker "hunk" strips to his waist and enjoys a "Diet Coke Break."

Although these diverse images of women, like many other stereotypes, are probably an accurate reflection of some segments of the female population, they reinforce the notion of a culture anchored in superficial values. Of course, if this cultural portrayal is realistic, a related ethical question arises: what is the media's

moral responsibility in promoting such transparent values? This discussion brings us back to the perennial question of whether the media should merely reflect societal norms or whether they have an affirmative obligation to promote positive images.

The Elderly

In our youth-oriented culture, the elderly have been among the most psychologically abused segments of society. Negative stereotypes about older people appear to be ingrained in U.S. society.[25] And because the media generally reflect our value system, it is little wonder that the elderly have been the victims of stereotyped characterizations. They are often depicted as infirm, forgetful, childlike, and stubborn.

In Wendy's 1984 campaign, for example, a crusty grandmother is shown recklessly speeding from one drive-in to the next demanding, "Where's the beef?" This promotion raised Wendy's sales, but it also insulted the aged by portraying them as crotchety, ridiculous, and bad drivers.[26] Several years later, an ad featured a grandmother sneaking away from her rocking chair to take a spin in Dad's new Subaru. An ad for Denny's featured two elderly sisters, one of whom was too hard of hearing to get the name of the restaurant right.[27] Although these images might be applicable to some segments of the elderly population, they are clearly unfair to many others. Many elderly people concur. In a survey by the Ogilvy and Mather advertising agency, 40 percent of the respondents over age sixty-five agreed that Madison Avenue usually presented older people as unattractive and incompetent.[28]

Like many other stereotypes, distorted images of the elderly in the media are now undergoing some slow renovation. Pressure groups, such as the Gray Panthers, have raised the collective consciousness of society to the plight of the elderly. More positive images are beginning to emerge in the media, as evidenced by the increasing depiction of the elderly in TV commercials as alert, energetic, and perfectly capable of sustaining romantic feelings. One of the commercials in a recent Bud Light campaign, for example, showed an elderly couple in a romantic exchange in a living room. An American Airlines print ad promoted its Senior Savers Club by featuring an attractive couple in a powerboat.

Nevertheless, the stereotypes persist. In one recent television commercial, the delivery of a Pizza Hut pizza to a group of card-playing senior citizens caused them to chase one another around over who gets one rather than two slices of pizza. *TV Guide* took the spot to task for reinforcing old-age stereotypes. "[W]hat's meant to be funny is the very idea of anyone over sixty-five being in tune with the times and enjoying an active life," the magazine said.[29] In a Frito-Lay ad campaign in 1993, an elderly woman walks in front of a runaway steamroller at a construction site as she munches a bag of Doritos Tortillo Thins. Comedian Chevy Chase, seeing the impending disaster, jumps on a swinging wrecking ball to rescue the bag of chips. The woman is plowed into wet cement. However, in a follow-up Doritos ad several months later, the woman was allowed to get the better of Chase. Some seniors saw that as a tacit admission by the company that the previous ad was offensive to elderly viewers.[30]

People with Disabilities

People with mental and physical disabilities have been among the most misunderstood and forgotten groups. To the extent that they have been allowed at all into the public's media consciousness, they have usually been portrayed as helpless and incapable of fending for themselves and meeting the challenges of our complex society. But there are signs of change. NBC's highly acclaimed *LA Law* featured a mentally handicapped office worker in the law firm. In the fall of 1989, ABC premiered *Life Goes On*, a family program starring Chris Burke, an actor with Down's syndrome who plays a teenager with the same condition. And

more recently, the physically impaired have assumed a more prominent role in commercials. Some TV ads, for example, featuring the hearing impaired are now done in total silence with the main characters "signing," while the narrative is superimposed on the screen.

These positive examples notwithstanding, however, critics still complain that the coverage of disability issues continues to rely on images of people with disabilities as either objects of pity or courageous individuals struggling against adversity in order to "inspire" others. These persistent stereotypes have spawned an alternative disabled press, with such descriptive titles as *Mainstream* and *New Mobility*. Although their coverage is diverse, the goal of such publications is to counter the negative images of pity and hero worship with one of people leading independent, active lives.[31]

As these examples illustrate, stereotyping of all kinds has traditionally been pervasive in media content. In some respects, it is a tool for communicating with the mass audience. But used in the improper context, stereotypes can also lead to human degradation and prejudice. Thus, the moral responsibility for media professionals is to search for strategies that will discourage such pejorative stereotypes while not abandoning the commitment to artistic freedom and cultural diversity.

STRATEGIES FOR CONFRONTING MEDIA STEREOTYPING

The production of media content that is intended to perpetuate patterns of discrimination and prejudice cannot be justified under any of the ethical theories examined in Chapter 3. Duty-based theorists (deontologists), such as those applying Kant's categorical imperative, would argue that racism and prejudice should never become universally recognized standards of conduct. Stereotypes promoting such practices undermine the fundamental idea of respect for persons, which plays such a crucial role in ethical decision making.

Deontologists would examine the motives of the moral agent without regard to the specific consequences of the decision. For example, the television producer Norman Lear had high hopes for his classic series *All in the Family* when it premiered in the early 1970s. The lead character, Archie Bunker, was clearly and blatantly a bigot, a composite of all the dominant prejudices of U.S. culture. Lear used stereotypes as a means of confronting society's racist attitudes, a video version of "reality therapy" that was designed to satirize bigotry and prejudice. Unfortunately, there was some disagreement about whether all viewers recognized the program as a satire or whether this family comedy served to reinforce and to sanitize prejudice.[32]

Teleologists (consequentialists), of course, are interested in the potential consequences of their decisions. The teleologist is not necessarily concerned with the motives of the media practitioner, which may not flow from moral purity. Because degrading stereotypes are unfair and offensive to certain segments of society, they must be rejected as harmful to the self-image of those groups. But beyond the specific harm to the targeted group, such stereotypes breed prejudice and discrimination within society at large. Nevertheless, sometimes potentially damaging stereotypes may serve a useful purpose by forcing society to confront the reality of its prejudices. Under such circumstances, the teleologist must weigh the positive and negative consequences before abandoning the use of controversial images altogether. For example, a documentary's use of stereotypes in exploring the issue of genetic racial differences would undoubtedly be controversial. But such a program might be justified as beneficial for society on the ground that it is better to confront the issue and examine the evidence publicly than to allow such stereotypical myths to fester beneath the surface of societal discourse.

The golden mean is particularly useful when stereotyped characters are representative of some individuals within a group (such as the flamboyant gay or the traditional housewife) but are seen as prejudicial to the group as a whole. Under such circumstances, media practitioners should treat these characters with sensitivity while not holding them up as typical of the entire group. In addition, the golden mean calls for diversity in media presentations. Media practitioners, in other words, should strive for overall balance in attempting to portray the range of lifestyles within a particular group, not just those that are the most prejudicial to the group.

Regardless of the moral theory employed in a specific circumstance, those who create media images have an obligation to the mass audience. Elimination of all stereotypes would infringe on artistic freedom and sterilize our vicarious experiences through the media. Nevertheless, efforts should be made to change those that are particularly degrading and prejudicial. Increases in minority employment and minority media ownership should help make media institutions more sensitive to this moral dilemma.

But we should also recognize that a society cannot retreat entirely from its cultural heritage and that many classic works of art and literature contain stereotyped characters. Huckleberry Finn, for example, has been attacked in some quarters as racist, and there have even been calls to ban it. Such drastic actions would be an affront to a democratic society. Under such circumstances, the contemporary artistic marketplace should be the proper mechanism for remedying whatever prejudicial lessons might be reflected in American cultural history.

STEREOTYPES AND THE MASS MEDIA: HYPOTHETICAL CASE STUDIES

The cases in this chapter cover a wide range of ethical concerns involving stereotypes, though they are by no means exhaustive. As you evaluate these cases, keep in mind that perpetuation of offensive stereotypes can result in a diminution of social justice. Thus, some of these cases have a close kinship with those of the preceding chapter.

Several kinds of moral agents are represented in these hypothetical scenarios: journalists, advertisers, those who make decisions regarding TV entertainment, and even those who market professional sports franchises through the media. In working your way through the ethical thicket of stereotypes, review again the principles of sound moral reasoning and the philosophical guidelines discussed in Chapter 3.

CASE STUDIES

CASE 12-1
Television News and Stereotypical Symbols

The state had just executed its third convicted murderer in eighteen months, and on each occasion the event had been marked by candlelight vigils by civil libertarians and cries for vengeance from supporters of the death penalty. Capital punishment had been the state's ultimate form of retribution for fifteen years, but each execution brought howls of protest from the liberal members of the legislature. The conservatives, who represented the majority view on the issue, according to the latest polls, always countered with protests of their own, lamenting what they saw as the slow pace of justice and the endless appeals of those on death row.

The state's large black population was represented in the court of public opinion by the NAACP and the American Civil Liberties Union, which accused prosecutors and judges of racism in disproportionately seeking and imposing the death penalty for blacks. Thus, the public and legislative debates concerning the morality of the death penalty had taken on racial overtones, obscuring the more fundamental question of whether capital punishment really was a deterrent to crime.

Channel 10 in Greencastle had never been far from the controversy, dutifully showing up outside the state prison to record both the emotional condemnations and the rejoicing at each inmate's appointment with the electric chair. But on the fifteenth anniversary of the capital punishment law,

the station's news director, John Smith, believed it was time to do more than cover these executions as routine news events. The state was number two in the nation in the number of executions and first in the number of inmates on death row, and Smith wondered why the media had not done a better job of examining some of the assumptions underlying the death penalty. The most recent crime statistics, including those for homicide, were not encouraging, prompting renewed condemnations of the death penalty as an ineffective deterrent to crime.

Smith assigned his most experienced reporter, Sandy Stiles, to produce a five-part series on capital punishment for the station's evening news. The series would examine the disparity in sentencing between black and white defendants, but it would also explore the opposing views on the morality of capital punishment as well as the more practical question of its deterrent effect. Stiles and her news crew accepted the assignment enthusiastically, and the project went smoothly until the week before the airdate set for the start of the highly promoted series. Smith had been summoned to the editing room, where he found Stiles and a tape editor, Victor Maze, engaged in an animated discussion. Maze was black, the only minority-group member on the production staff.

Maze asked Smith to review the raw footage for the story, because he felt that the story might be perceived by the black community as racially biased. "If you look at this stuff," Maze said, "you'll see that it just reinforces stereotypes about blacks." The footage contained the usual exterior shots of the state's county jails and prison as well as scenes inside the penal facilities. There were also interviews with several inmates on death row, prison officials, and families of the victims. Stiles wanted the comments from the inmates juxtaposed with those of the victims' families for dramatic effect. There was also a cassette of file footage of death row inmates that could be used to provide historical perspective to the series.

When the last frame disappeared from the monitor, one thing was abundantly clear to the news director: all of the interviewees from death row, as well as those on the file footage, were black; the victims were all white. Maze argued that this contrast would send a symbolic message to the viewers that blacks committed most of the murders and that their victims were usually white. He knew that most victims of black crime were also black, a fact often overlooked by the news media. He pointed out to Smith that there were whites on death row, although a majority of the inmates were black. But this situation was a result of racial discrimination in sentencing patterns, he said, and the footage would just make it appear that most cold-blooded murders were committed by blacks. "But how many whites accused of a capital crime have received life sentences instead of the death penalty, which might have been the case if they were black?" he asked. "This should be included in the story."

Stiles, who had remained silent during most of the dialogue between Smith and Maze, objected to the editor's arguments. She acknowledged that there was probably racial discrimination in the state's sentencing patterns and that this bias should be part of the story. But Stiles rejected Maze's complaints about the taped footage. Some white inmates were on death row, she admitted, but most were black. "When Troy Jones [a producer] and I set up these interviews," she said, "we didn't intentionally select all black subjects. The warden arranged for the interviews. They just happened to be black."

Their next mission, Stiles explained, was to seek out the victims of these convicted criminals, all of whom were white. "These are facts," she declared testily. "Our job is to report, not try to balance a story that can't be balanced."

But Maze responded that journalists had an obligation to be fair and that televised symbols could have a tremendous impact on the audience. Information was conveyed through the visuals as well as the narrative, and reporters had to be careful about the impressions they communicated, not just the so-called facts. Without the inclusion of some white inmates in this story, he said, the old stereotypes of blacks as more violent and crime-prone would be reinforced.

The news director appreciated Maze's observations. As a white journalist, Smith had to admit that he would probably not have been sensitized to this problem had it not been for his editor's acute awareness of racial prejudice and stereotypes. He had never approached a story from the standpoint of balancing racial symbols, and even now he wondered whether that should become a part of a reporter's value system. Journalists should strive to be fair, but death row was, in fact, populated more by blacks than whites. This would serve to make the point, in Smith's view, that more blacks than whites were sentenced to die in the electric chair. In addition, many of their victims had been whites, a fact that could not be ignored.

Nevertheless, Smith wondered whether his news team should have attempted to interview at least one white inmate. Prison officials had arranged for the interviews, but considering the allegations that the judicial system was prejudiced against blacks, the news director was suspicious of the warden's motives in selecting four black inmates to meet with Stiles and her news crew. On the other hand, the selection process might have just been pure coincidence. As a reporter Stiles should have perhaps insisted on racial balance in her interviews.

Smith had now become sensitized to the problem, but his immediate dilemma was how to approach his five-part series on capital punishment under the threat of a rapidly approaching deadline. The story had already received the usual hype from the station's aggressive promotions department, and conventional wisdom suggested that it be aired according to schedule. Perhaps if a point were made in the narrative and accompanying video of the disparate sentencing policies for blacks and whites, the station could avoid charges of racial stereotyping. On the other hand, the station could try again to interview some white inmates and perhaps even some black victims. This would be difficult to do before the deadline, but Stiles could make a good-faith effort.

The news director was not sure that this problem justified postponing the series just to accommodate the need for balance. He also wondered whether TV journalists should, in the future, strive for visual racial balance in all of their stories in order to combat what minorities perceived as a subtle form of stereotyping. Above all, he wondered what his position would be if he were to step into the shoes of a black journalist confronted with the same dilemma.

THE CASE STUDY

Television is a symbolic medium, and the visual portrayals that appear on the screen can communicate subtle, as well as obvious, messages. These messages can influence our view of the world (including reinforcing stereotypes) in ways that are not always immediately clear. But under the stress of gathering television news, journalists cannot always be aware of audience perceptions of their stories. They strive for accuracy and fairness without any intent of offending minority audiences. But the visual symbols sometimes communicate ideas that go beyond the pure facts of the story.

Thus, this question might be posed: should TV news strive to ensure racial balance in visuals of controversial stories, such as crime, welfare, drugs, and juvenile delinquency, in order to avoid the appearance of stereotyping? We see such intentional balance, for example, in commercials featuring children, where at least one of the actors belongs to a minority. Should TV journalism strive for the same balance, or are there reasons to avoid such symbolic affirmative action in news reporting?

A journalism teacher, Trace Regan, in cautioning reporters to be more sensitive in the use of file video and stories that might perpetuate stereotypes and inadvertently offend the black community, makes the following observation:

> I don't think that journalists should duck newsworthy issues or in any way alter the substance of the stories they report or "tone down" relevant information,

no matter whom it embarrasses. What I have suggested embraces the ideals of journalism and . . . simply allows a reporter to make changes in the non-substantive elements of a story to minimize any effect that might sustain racism.[33]

Are the visual portrayals reflected in this scenario part of the nonsubstantive elements of the story? Should they be racially balanced? If so, would that alter the focus of the story?

For the purpose of confronting this problem, assume the role of Smith, and, using the SAD Formula for moral reasoning, evaluate this problem from an ethical standpoint. Keep in mind that the reasons underlying your decision should be applicable under similar circumstances in the future.

▶ CASE 12-2
Gender Wars and Sexual Stereotyping

Lydia Caldwell was a veteran of the gender wars. She had matriculated at Briarfield College, a prestigious women's school in Connecticut, and had embraced the controversial ideology of the feminist movement with undisguised zeal. Upon graduating with honors, Caldwell accepted a position as copywriter for a large ad agency in New York, where her youthful idealism was quickly challenged by the commercial socialization process of her newly adopted corporate culture. She had struggled for recognition and advancement in a male-dominated world—a world that she was convinced, at least initially, was responsible for the perpetuation of commercial sexual stereotypes. However, as she moved from agency to agency in search of new challenges and career advancement, Caldwell's perspective had gradually evolved from one of idealism to marketplace reality. As a market-sensitive commodity, advertising, she believed, reflected rather accurately the state of gender relations in society at large. And from her present vantage point as creative director for the Patterson and Rheinhold agency in Chicago, things had changed for the better. Caldwell had applauded her industry's growing cultural sensitivity in the 1980s as career professionals, capable of skillfully balancing both career and family, replaced the harried housewife as the typical commercial caricature, a market-driven monument to the incredible success of the women's movement. She was concerned, however, that such "supermom" commercials might place even more pressure on women to fulfill society's heightened expectations.

Even in her most activist days, Caldwell had never equated feminism with being "anti-male" and believed strongly that her industry could play a crucial role in bringing the gender wars to an end. Advertising, she believed, could be an important catalyst in the cause of social equality. Therefore, she was particularly interested in her creative team's campaign concept for the agency's newest client, Lancelot Malt Liquor.

The proposed commercial featured an athletic-looking male (or a "hunk," to use the vernacular) holding a can of Lancelot Malt Liquor in a lounge, while two very attractive and "leering" women looked on from across the room. As the camera focuses on various aspects of the male's physique, his two female admirers engage in a subtle dialogue concerning his athletic prowess. The spot ends with the man looking toward the women and holding up the Lancelot Malt Liquor can in a toast, as a female narrator's voice says rather enticingly, "Lancelot Malt Liquor . . . the choice of champions . . . and their fans."

"These are the storyboards and the script for the Lancelot account," said Caldwell as she displayed her unit's handiwork to Nancy Tibbs and Todd Austin. Tibbs was the agency's media director, and Austin was senior account manager. Caldwell often solicited input from Tibbs and Austin because of their units' roles in commercial placement and marketing among various media outlets.

"There's a quality of egalitarianism about this spot," continued Caldwell, as she pointed to the storyboards displayed in front of her two colleagues. "At last women have the right to express their sexual desires in commercials, just as men always have had the right to admire beautiful women."

"I'm not so sure," responded Tibbs. "Aren't we replacing one stereotype with another? It's not just a question of male dominance or female independence. In the past, too many female characters

were depicted as sex objects. And men were portrayed as being interested in only one thing—sex appeal. Now we have a role reversal. Doesn't this ad promote false values?"

"I don't think so," insisted Austin. "The message in this spot is that now women can be just as candid in their sexual attraction to men. The fact is that this commercial will be successful. *It sells!* And the reason it sells is that it appeals to traditional sex roles. Women *do* place physical attractiveness of men high on their list of values, and in this sense I don't see sex appeal as a false or superficial value."

"I disagree," responded Tibbs. "In this spot the male is a sex object. His sex appeal is all that matters. The message is that, if you're a hunk, the world is at your feet, sexually speaking. This is nothing more than stereotyping. Whereas women use to be leered at in commercials, now men are accorded the same treatment."

"I'm a feminist, but that doesn't mean that we have to ignore traditional gender roles in our commercials," said Caldwell. "The fact is that women are just as interested in men's sexuality as men are in female sex appeal. However, I must concede, Nancy, that perhaps a spot such as this is one-dimensional. Perhaps it does promote superficial values, even as it reflects reality to a certain degree."

"I don't see equality as the issue," responded Tibbs with an air of moral superiority. "Crudeness is crudeness, regardless of who is doing the leering. We use to criticize men for being interested in only one thing. This commercial just reverses the roles. And you consider that liberating?"

"I don't see anything distasteful about this spot," responded Austin. "It just reflects the reality of gender relationships in today's society. It's OK for women to be as aggressive as men—to admire openly the male's sexuality. Advertising is market driven. And the market reflects contemporary cultural norms. All we're doing is exhibiting in commercial form the current state of gender relationships."

Lydia Caldwell had approached this discussion with her two management-level colleagues confident that the proposed Lancelot Malt Liquor commercial would serve their client well. And she still believed that it reflected the contemporary reality of gender relationships. But as she pondered the arguments advanced by Nancy Tibbs and Todd Austin, she also wondered whether the agency's media director had a point. Did the Lancelot Malt Liquor spot replace one stereotype with another and in the process depict women as one-dimensional? Perhaps it was inevitable that in a thirty-second commercial the dimensions of complex human relationships had to be accommodated to the production requirements of the television medium, as well as the realities of the marketplace.

THE CASE STUDY

Critics accuse the advertising industry of stereotyping large segments of society—that is, ascribing certain characteristics to the undifferentiated group (e.g., women) without sufficient sensitivity to individuality. In a sense, this issue comes back to an age-old question of whether advertising helps shape society's values or just reflects them. Proponents of the "value-shaping" view argue that advertisers should be particularly sensitive of how they portray different groups and that they should strive to eliminate or at least minimize stereotyping.

On the other hand, those who ascribe to the "reflective" view argue that since ads mirror society sponsors have a responsibility to ensure that their ads accurately depict the constituent groups within society. Commercials are perhaps the most market driven of television content, they note, even more so than entertainment programming. As such, they reflect our cultural values and our worldview. And stereotypes are undeniably one paradigm that helps shape our worldview. There are times, of course, when stereotypes are clearly unfair to individual members of a group and help perpetuate harmful prejudices.

In this case, the debate appears to center around whether advertisers and advertising agencies have a responsibility to erase sexual stereotypes entirely as a means of pacifying the so-called war between the genders. On the one hand, such stereotypes based on little more than sex appeal are viewed as the promotion of superficial values for both males and females. In this view, the advertising industry should attempt to eliminate stereotypes to the extent that men and women are

depicted as dependent on one another from the perspective of sex appeal.

On the other hand, traditionalists argue that some stereotypes are permissible because they reflect reality. And the *reality* in the scenario here appears to be that the modern woman now feels comfortable with expressing openly her admiration for a male's sexuality. In this view, such portrayals are not inaccurate or unfair. In the past, of course, men were often depicted as interested in only a woman's sexuality, and women were often depicted in this fashion in commercials. Does a role reversal replace one stereotype with another, and if so, is this unfair, or could it reinforce some harmful prejudice? Or, to put it another way, does the proposed commercial for Lancelot Malt Liquor raise important ethical questions concerning sexual stereotypes?

For the purpose of discussing these issues, assume the role of Lydia Caldwell, and, using the SAD Formula for moral reasoning outlined in Chapter 3, render a judgment on this matter.

▶ CASE 12-3
Television Comedy and the Flamboyant Gay Lifestyle

Max Crawford was clearly a hot property. His string of prime-time hits for three commercial TV networks had elevated him, according to the trade press, to a position as one of the most successful television producers of the previous decade. His incredible sense of timing and ability to be on the cutting edge of audience tastes and aesthetic norms had provided him with an open invitation to produce network pilots for a new series.

Crawford had begun his television career twenty-five years before as a production assistant but had moved steadily through a succession of jobs, including stints as a writer and director for two of Hollywood's leading TV production studios. Through it all, he had maintained a constant vigil on the changes in the television industry and had gradually become a student of the unpredictable mass audience and its finicky tastes in entertainment. He had apparently learned his lessons well, and in 1980 he formed his own production company, Crawford Television Enterprises, and lost little time in gaining an entry into the networks' prime-time schedules. Crawford's first three hits had been situation comedies, two of which had stayed on the air for more than five years, but his most recent triumphs had revolved around the hour-long continuing dramatic series.

As the ratings from the November sweeps began to signal another successful series for Crawford Television Enterprises, the producer propped his feet up on his mahogany desk in his Hollywood office and began reading Richard Denton's latest proposal for a television series. Denton was no stranger to Crawford. He had been the creator of one of Crawford's most successful sitcoms and had submitted his latest idea and format proposal for the producer's perusal.

Denton sat patiently while Crawford digested the material with a critical eye. The half-hour comedy series was tentatively entitled *Wilderness Inn* and revolved around a resort inn in rural New Hampshire run by two brothers, Bruce and Frank Pitts, and Frank's young wife, Sarah. Each episode of the weekly series, according to Denton's proposal, would bring a bizarre and colorful array of vacationers to the resort and would produce a host of absurd and unexpected challenges for the three proprietors of the Wilderness Inn. Several supporting regulars also provided continuity.

According to Denton's proposal, the younger brother, Bruce, was a flamboyant gay with exaggerated behavioral traits, whose unusual lifestyle and mannerisms, as contrasted with those of most of the conservative guests at the inn, were designed throughout the series to provide the catalyst for comedic ridicule. Bruce was described in the format outline as a sensitive individual who did not mind flaunting his gay lifestyle. Frank was supportive of his brother's sexual orientation, but Sarah's ill-concealed contempt and embarrassment were a point of contention from week to week.

In response to Denton's expectant demeanor, Crawford began with words of praise for the program series idea. Staffed with a clever and creative team of writers, he believed it could be a hit. However, he was concerned about the depiction of the gay character in the series. Crawford's experience with the network programming gatekeepers had taught him that they were still sensitive about the treatment of homosexuality in prime-time television. *Wilderness Inn* posed no problem in terms of taste, but the television industry had received complaints about the stereotypical depiction of gays as "sissies with limp wrists and effeminate characteristics." One gay rights organization had even taken out full-page ads in several leading newspapers to object to the image of homosexuals as projected through the media. Crawford wondered whether they should soften the outrageous nature of the gay lead in the series. This character, while clearly a humorous and sensitive figure, might be viewed by some as nothing more than a caricature who did not typify the majority of homosexuals. In addition, the continuing ridicule of Bruce's lifestyle might not be a laughing matter to some segments of the gay community.

But Denton objected vehemently to Crawford's suggestion. Television is a symbolic medium, he observed, and the audience had to be made constantly aware of this character's sexual orientation in a humorous manner. The only way to do this was through Bruce's flamboyant behavior and exaggerated mannerisms. Denton also pointed out—and Crawford had to concede the merits of this argument—that some gays are flamboyant. Although all homosexuals do not fit this image, some certainly do.

Crawford agreed with Denton's views on dramatic license for stereotyping when essential to the script and the plot. The audience can relate to stereotypes, and in the short time spans on television, characterizations must be developed quickly. The complexities and subtleties of human traits must be simplified for the electronic audience.

Crawford saw potential in Denton's proposal as a prime-time series but hesitated to recommend its approval. He still worried that such a blatantly exaggerated image would be offensive to some segments of the community. Still, heterosexual relationships, some of which perpetuated male-female role stereotypes, were the subject of prime-time comedy. Crawford wondered whether humorous treatments of homosexuality had become forbidden territory for the television entertainment industry.

THE CASE STUDY

This scenario implies that some stereotyping may be inevitable in mass entertainment on television. Characters have to be clearly delineated, and the subtleties and complexities of the real world sometimes have to be compromised for the requirements of the medium and the audience's understanding. Sometimes characteristics have to be exaggerated to communicate their symbolic meaning to the viewer. Is this a sensationalized version of the truth or an acceptable concession to the technical demands of the medium?

As noted earlier in this chapter, stereotypes are not necessarily false representations. They sometimes reflect a slice of reality, albeit perhaps an overly simplified version. The flamboyance depicted in this case is clearly present among some segments of the homosexual population. But is the use of a stereotype that accurately reflects the lifestyle and behavior of only some members of a group unfair to the group as a whole?

In pondering this question, assume the role of Crawford, and, utilizing the moral reasoning model, make a decision on whether you will agree to take this TV series idea to one of the networks for their consideration. In so doing, keep in mind that your instincts have told you that this program, if staffed with a good team of writers, will probably be a hit with the mass audience. However, it may also elicit protests from the gay community. Is this a sufficient reason for you to have second thoughts about producing such a program?

▶ **CASE 12-4**
The American Indians' Battle with the Major Leagues

Peter Backus was determined to return baseball to its rightful position as America's pastime. As the newly installed commissioner of major league baseball, Backus had assumed command of a professional sport under siege. He was confronted, first of all, with rescuing the major leagues from the ravages of a devastating players' strike the preceding season that left in its wake disaffected fans

from coast to coast and what might be charitably described as an uncivil relationship between the players and team management. The dramatic decline in attendance and television revenues even threatened the financial security of the franchises in the smaller markets, but Backus, with his business and Wall Street background, was confident that he could at least secure the economic stability of his athletic domain.

He was also determined that the American League's most recently approved expansion teams in Jacksonville and Oklahoma City enter the competitive arena in an environment of relative tranquility, as well as demonstrable fan support. The owners of the Jacksonville franchise had selected "Sharks" as their nickname, while Oklahoma City had tentatively settled on "Warriors," reflecting the state's rich Native American heritage. The owner of the Oklahoma City franchise had also selected the team's logo—a fierce-looking, scowling image of an American Indian warrior with a decidedly red cast.

As Backus settled into his position as baseball commissioner, he was also troubled by the recurring complaints of racism against some team owners. His egalitarian and nonjudgmental instincts were offended by such charges, but he was also astonished that such prejudice existed in light of the fact that both African-American and Latino players had been featured so prominently in the sport for many years. Not one to let such problems fester, Backus had dispatched the director of team relations as his ambassador to consult with team owners on the matter.

But racism comes in many guises, as the commissioner soon discovered in a meeting with a delegation from the American Indian Movement (AIM) only three months after taking office. AIM's visit was unexpected since the power centers of major league baseball were the leagues and team owners. And in the past, AIM had lodged its complaints about the use of Indian names, logos, and mascots directly with team owners. Apparently, the organization, which admittedly did not reflect the views of all American Indians, had decided that an assault on the commissioner's office would generate greater national publicity.

In just the past three weeks, as the major league teams prepared for the season's opener,

AIM had held two well-attended press conferences in which it denounced professional sports franchises for their "institutionalized racism in the form of stereotypical use of American Indian names and logos." AIM had also called on the commissioner to use his influence to eliminate such stereotypes from the game. Backus had also noticed, much to his chagrin, that AIM had taken out full-page ads in several newspapers complaining about the use of Indian names and logos in professional sports.

Backus said little but listened attentively as John Hawks, the leader of the AIM delegation, made his appeal to major league baseball's social conscience: "We're here to protest the use of American Indian names, mascots, and logos in some major league franchises. We're conveying similar concerns to the National Football League. Such symbols are degrading; they perpetuate offensive stereotypes. They are nothing more than caricatures. You have a reputation as a person of fairness, committed to social justice. AIM is asking that you develop a plan to eliminate such vestiges of racism from major league baseball. We know it isn't practical to change all the team names immediately—like the Cleveland Indians and Atlanta Braves—but we just want a pledge that you'll work toward it.

"But there is something you can do about the proposed name for the new Oklahoma City franchise. Their name and logo—the Warriors, depicting a scowling savage-looking brave—is offensive to us, and we're demanding that this name be rejected. They don't start play until a year from now, so there's still time to change the name. As you know, we have already set up pickets at the construction site of the new stadium in Oklahoma City. And on opening day, we plan to picket all stadiums with teams that have Indian names. This is how strongly we feel about this issue."

The thought of approaching Ted Turner with the suggestion that he should consider changing the name of his Atlanta Braves was not one that brought a smile to the commissioner's face. The Oklahoma City franchise was perhaps more within reach but still problematic. Nevertheless, Backus, responding both diplomatically and truthfully, told the Indian delegation that he appreciated its concerns but that they should, as in the past, be directed at team owners and perhaps the Executive Committee of Major League Baseball.

Since AIM had already moved aggressively in appealing to the court of public opinion through its public protests, press conferences, and newspaper ads, the organization's next strategic move on the eve of a new season was to again confront the owners concerning their use of offensive stereotypes. Its first target was the league's newly enfranchised but still inoperative team in Oklahoma City. AIM's leadership did not plan to relinquish its pressure on the teams in Atlanta and Cleveland, but it was not naive about its chances of exerting any immediate influence on the ownership and management of those well-established, traditional franchises. Oklahoma City, however, was a different matter. There was still time, AIM reasoned, to block the proposed name and logo for a team with no tradition and no established fan loyalty.

Margaret Roundtree, the daughter of a recently deceased wealthy Oklahoma businessman, was the owner of the Oklahoma City team. She listened patiently as the same AIM delegation that had pleaded its case to Commissioner Backus again stated its objections to the unfair appropriation of Indian names by professional sports franchises. "If our voices go unheard," John Hawks promised, "we will continue our public campaign against major league baseball, including picketing of offending teams and encouragement of fan boycotts."

As a community-minded owner who was culturally sensitive to the Sooner State's most visible minority, Roundtree was not entirely unsympathetic to AIM's concerns. Nevertheless, she promised only to discuss the issue with her staff. AIM obviously viewed its plea as a humanitarian issue; Roundtree saw it as both a public relations and marketing problem.

Roundtree lost little time in convening her "brain trust" to discuss AIM's vociferous complaints about her team's name and logo. She was joined by team President and General Manager Michael Davenport; Director of Publicity Jonathan Salters; and Frank Antoine, the Warriors' marketing director. Roundtree had asked Antoine to participate in the discussion because of the financial and marketing aspects of team names and logos.

"The commissioner and some team owners are concerned about this protest from the American Indian Movement," noted Roundtree as she opened the meeting with her enthusiastic young staff. "They're threatening to throw up pickets at every stadium that hosts one of our teams with an Indian name or mascot: Cleveland, Atlanta, and Oklahoma City, if we go through with our plans to call ourselves the Warriors. In fact, they're already picketing the construction site for our stadium."

"What exactly is their complaint?" asked Antoine. "Even if we should concede to them, the fans will be unhappy. The polls we conducted before settling on this name reflect public support for the Warriors. And we've already tied up capital in marketing and the initial negotiations on licensing agreements. If we back down now, it'll cost us, both financially and in terms of public credibility."

"They say the use of Indian mascots and the commercialization of Indian names result in demeaning stereotypes," responded Roundtree. "They say this is nothing more than institutional racism."

"I can see their point," replied Salters, who was under no illusions about the unpopularity of his view, especially within the multimillion-dollar entertainment enterprise known as baseball. However, the team's owner had hired Salters precisely because he was known as somewhat of a gadfly who was both enterprising and unafraid of risky initiatives. He carried a reputation as a person with a social conscience and humanitarian instincts. "The symbols associated with these mascots and team logos," he continued, "such as the fierce, scowling face of an Indian warrior, as proposed for Oklahoma City, for example, do tend to perpetuate negative images. And this in turn affects society's attitudes toward the American Indian. I think AIM realizes that Indian names for established franchises aren't likely to disappear overnight. But they apparently are convinced they have a realistic chance of blocking expansion teams from following the same path as their predecessors."

"But I would think they would be proud of having their names associated with so many public institutions," said Davenport. "I view team names and mascots as a celebration of the American Indian."

"This is not a peripheral issue for them," replied Salters. "They're serious about eliminating the use of stereotypes in team names. And they've had some success. I know of one newspaper—the Portland *Oregonian*, I believe—that has actually banned from its sports pages such names as Indians, Braves, and Redskins."[34]

"That's carrying political correctness too far," responded Davenport. "It shouldn't be the media's job to censor such names, even if they are offensive to some. But we're the *source* of such names and thus have the power to do something about them—assuming, of course, that there really is a problem here. I wonder if AIM isn't being sensationalistic about this issue."

"In their meeting with the commissioner, I think AIM was quite clear on this point," said Salters, as he became increasingly comfortable with playing devil's advocate. "They don't consider this as a peripheral concern. AIM's position is that the use of these symbols, particularly in connection with professional sports, perpetuates the stereotype of Indians as savage warriors. They argue that they should be able to set their own agenda, to define themselves on their own terms."

"I sympathize with them," said Antoine, "but many of these team names have been around for years. There's a tradition built up around these franchises, like the Cleveland Indians and the Atlanta Braves, not to mention a lot of money invested in their logos. I suppose that we could reconsider the proposed nickname for the Oklahoma City team, but then every group with an objection to a team name would surface. The fact is the fans are on our side; most consider this issue as sensational. If we even consider removing the Indian logos and nicknames, we'll have more to worry about than AIM."

"There's another consideration," said Davenport. "AIM has generated a lot of publicity, but they don't speak for all Native Americans. For some, the use of Indian names by professional sports franchises may not be that important. In fact, some have even profited off this phenomenon. You may recall several years ago when the tomahawk chop became popular in Atlanta, and AIM protested. And then it was discovered that the Cherokees were actually making some of the tomahawks and marketing them to the Braves."

"The issue is *not* whether all tribes agree with AIM's objectives," responded Salters. "The fact is that Native Americans have complained for a number of years of unfair stereotyping. The only question is whether these names and logos are fair representations. AIM's position, if I understand it correctly, is that Indians—not non-Indians—should determine how they're depicted. Other minority groups—African-Americans and Hispanics, for example—have made inroads into removing offensive stereotypical symbols from products. Aunt Jemima and Chiquita Banana are two examples that come to mind. But they have more clout. Shouldn't Native Americans be accorded the same consideration?"

"Let's face it, Jonathan," replied Antoine, who was becoming increasingly irritated at what he perceived to be the irrational idealism of the team's publicity director. "Caricatures such as Aunt Jemima had no constituency. Who would really complain if it disappeared altogether? Team names are a part of American culture; they're as much a part of some cities' history as politics. There's a lot of fan support out there, and they're the ones we have to appeal to, through both our marketing and the stories in the media. I think AIM is being sensational; team names, in my judgment, don't denigrate American Indians. If we cave in to them, even in the case of Oklahoma City, the fans will really be unhappy—*and most of them aren't Indians*."

"Thanks for your sensitivity," responded Salters with undisguised sarcasm. "You appear to be more interested in the impact on marketing and the fans' reactions rather than the justice involved. I'll admit that the fans must be taken into account. But if we develop a plan to change team names over the long term—after all, we're not talking about a large number of franchises—that'll give us breathing space to help educate the fans. I agree it's unrealistic to consider changing all of our team logos immediately, but it's not too late here in Oklahoma City. Perhaps AIM will accept this as a good-faith effort to work toward the elimination of stereotypes. Some other name will work just as well for this franchise. All I'm suggesting is that we should at least be sensitive to AIM's complaint."

Roundtree had learned from experience that there would never be a meeting of the minds between the idealistic Jonathan Salters and the market-driven Frank Antoine. But as the team owner, the decision would ultimately reside with her. Roundtree was aware that she was the proprietor of a potentially hot media property whose marketing capabilities could be lucrative for both the team's corporate structure and the community that it served. Her decision would be closely scrutinized by the media, the fans, the general public, the baseball industry, and Native Americans themselves, some of whom lived in the shadows of the American League's newest franchise. In such an environment, the question of social injustice as perpetuated by unfair stereotyping was inevitably challenged by marketplace realities and public apathy toward the cause of Native Americans.

Roundtree knew that sports writers were almost uniformly unsympathetic to AIM's concerns. And its complaints about unfair stereotyping were just as unconvincing to baseball fans and team owners alike. With so little support, Roundtree reasoned, perhaps she should dismiss its pleas as nothing more than an attempt by a handful of activists to use the high-profile institution of major league baseball as a vehicle for furthering its own political agenda. On the other hand, Roundtree's sense of fairness and sensitivity to the plight of Native Americans compelled her to consider AIM's complaints with the same degree of respect as those of other minorities who had persevered in the face of so much initial public apathy to their charges of racism.

THE CASE STUDY

This case is not so much about the unfair portrayal of American Indians by the media per se as it is about the use of stereotypical symbols (i.e., team names and logos) in promotion and marketing that in turn are conveyed through various media channels and other avenues of dissemination. In recent years, some members of the Native American community have expressed their displeasure at what they perceive as "institutional racism" in the use of such symbols.

In this case, the path of least resistance would be to recommend that AIM's protest be rejected as unworthy of consideration—a position that might appear to be insensitive but would certainly draw no protest from the fans. There is a danger that AIM might become more aggressive in the arena of public opinion, but it is unlikely that it would garner much support from non-Indians, especially since Native Americans do not appear to speak with one voice in this matter. On the other hand, major league baseball is an American institution, and perhaps some team owner should take the lead in eradicating offensive stereotypes from the sport. Clearly, the matter of changing established team names is a long-term proposition, but the Oklahoma City franchise has not yet received final approval for its name. Nevertheless, developing public relations strategies to convince fanatical fans of the social worth of this cause could prove to be a daunting task.

In this case, Margaret Roundtree, who is the moral agent, is not a media practitioner in the strict sense of the word, but she holds a franchise for a potentially hot media property, through both national licensing arrangements and the sales of local TV rights. And much of her staff's efforts are devoted to public relations, publicity, and marketing. The team's name and logo will be featured prominently in both the journalistic and the more entertainment-oriented aspects of this multimillion-dollar enterprise.

For the purpose of analyzing this case, assume the position of team owner Margaret Roundtree. Using the moral reasoning model outlined in Chapter 3, evaluate the concerns of the leadership of the American Indian Movement and decide how you will respond.

▶ **CASE 12-5**
Black Athletes and the Perpetuation of Stereotypes

The TV network's documentary unit had been revived after several years of dormancy. The unit had been disbanded in the early 1980s, much to the chagrin of the news division, as a concession to the budgetary crises confronting all three major networks. But with the recent corporate merger and signs that the news operation was emerging from its ratings doldrums, additional funding had arrived just in time to lift the sagging spirits of reporters, producers, and staff members.

The news division's president, Macy Atwater, had personally approved the appointment of Ron Howser to be executive producer of the reactivated documentary unit, and Howser had promised that the unit's first documentary would be a controversial blockbuster. His promise was not an idle one. Intrigued by the earlier firing by CBS of Jimmy "The Greek" Snyder because of his intemperate remarks concerning the superiority of black athletes due to their "breeding" during slave times, Howser decided to explore the problem further.[35] The controversy swirling around Snyder's remarks had generated a lot of heat but little light, and Howser believed it was time to confront the problem head-on. The executive producer assigned a producer, Sandy Frank, and a reporter, Peter Hunt, two of the news division's most experienced journalists, to undertake this assignment.

The documentary unit worked for months on the project, and by the end of August the program was nearing completion. The hour-long special, tentatively entitled *The Black Athlete—Myth and Reality*, pulled no punches and explored in some detail the issue of the dominance of black athletes. Although it would undoubtedly offend some segments of the black community, Howser believed the documentary was balanced. For example, the program cited studies by Professors Carl Marxton and Daniel Herschel suggesting that genetic differences in blacks provided them with physical superiority over whites in most sports. However, these findings were rebutted by other researchers, who questioned the scientific conclusions of the Marxton and Herschel studies.

Some of the sociologists and anthropologists interviewed for the program attributed the black dominance in some sports to cultural and environmental factors. One interviewee, for example, noted that sports was the only avenue of escape from poverty for many blacks and that they were "programmed from youth" to develop their athletic abilities. To balance this cultural-environmental perspective, some of the coaches interviewed for the documentary attributed blacks' dominance to their work ethic but also said that many had a natural talent for sports. However, one black track coach interviewed for the broadcast compared the genetic theories to those of Hitler, who promoted the idea of the superiority of the "Aryan race."

The documentary had not yet been slotted into the network's fall program schedule, but it was already causing trouble for Atwater. Word of the project had leaked out, and several college athletic directors and black coaches sent letters of protest to Atwater, criticizing the network's project as nothing more than a subtle form of racism and asking that the documentary not be aired. Several civil rights groups weighed in with opinions of their own, faulting the network for perpetuating the stereotype of blacks as physically dominant, thus implying mental inferiority. One group even threatened to boycott any advertiser foolish enough to sponsor such a program.

To worsen an already unpleasant situation, the network was taking a public relations bath in the media, as various black leaders offered their assessments (both solicited and unsolicited) of the proposed airing of *The Black Athlete—Myth and Reality*. It was time, Atwater believed, to review the situation with his executive producer, Ron Howser. During the meeting, Atwater played devil's advocate.

"Perhaps the blacks have a point," he told the executive producer. "This idea of black dominance is really just another stereotype. Regardless of the Marxton and Herschel studies, the jury is still out on this matter. Even if we present other points of view to counter the idea of black superiority in athletics, the fact that we have even raised the issue is going to reignite this controversy." Atwater went on to note that several black leaders had called the perpetuation of the stereotype of black dominance a form of racial labeling, from which future generations of black youths might find it difficult to extricate themselves.

Howser acknowledged these concerns but told the news president that the issue was a timely one.

The hour-long special was sure to be controversial. "But what's the purpose of a documentary except to confront controversy?" Howser wanted to know. "Besides, this documentary is balanced. It provides a variety of views and allows viewers to draw their own conclusions." On a more practical note, and one that he felt Atwater would understand, Howser said that the news division had a lot of money invested in this project. "To cancel it now because of outside pressure," he said, "would undermine the morale of the entire news division."

As an admirer of President Harry Truman, Atwater had placed a sign on his desk with the message "The Buck Stops Here." At times like these, Atwater regretted his haste in adopting this motto. Nevertheless, he had been thrust into the position of moral agent, and the decision would ultimately be his. He could yield to the complaints of the black community and cancel the documentary. But Howser was right: that move would adversely affect staff morale. Besides, on a more noble level, Atwater had always believed that no issue, regardless of the nature of the controversy, was beyond the reach of TV journalism. Should he now subordinate his ideals to more practical considerations?

On the other hand, despite the journalistic balance that he perceived in this documentary, black viewers might not be so charitable. There was no doubt that some of the interviewees in this program, including Marxton and Herschel, had again raised the racial stereotype of black superiority in athletics. This was a sore point for whites and blacks alike, and a reasonable person might question the whole point of the documentary, inasmuch as the scientific evidence on this matter was still inconclusive.

As a former journalist himself, Atwater sympathized with his news staff. Nevertheless, as an executive he had to be mindful of his responsibilities to the parent company and the charges of racism that would inevitably be leveled against the network. As he pondered his options, he realized that even if he canceled the broadcast of this documentary, the controversy over black dominance of college and professional athletics would not soon disappear.

THE CASE STUDY

Although all stereotypes are tinged with various degrees of unfairness, the notion of black physical superiority as an explanation for African Americans' athletic dominance is highly offensive to the black community. Why? Because it suggests that talent rather than work is responsible for blacks' success in some sports. It also implies that their physical prowess overshadows their mental capabilities, which is a stereotype of long standing.

This issue has been just below the surface of public discourse for some time, but the dismissal of Snyder by CBS in 1988 rekindled the debate. An NBC documentary the following year added fuel to the controversy. The question posed by the scenario here is whether the news media should avoid such racially inflammatory controversies, which some charge do nothing more than perpetuate stereotypes. Or should they make a concerted effort to dispel stereotypes by confronting them head-on? Stereotypes, of course, are a part of our cultural heritage and are often used as a vehicle to search for answers. Some would even argue that documentaries such as the one described here, although clearly offensive to some, might even stimulate more research and soul searching on the issue of black genetic physical superiority.

Beyond the specific facts of this scenario, this case also raises the question of whether some stereotypical depictions are so offensive that the media's rights of free expression and inquiry should, out of fairness, be subordinated to the sensitivities of those being stereotyped. This is a dilemma that calls for a very patient approach to the moral reasoning process.

For the purpose of considering this issue, assume the position of Atwater, and, using the SAD Formula, make a decision on the future of *The Black Athlete—Myth and Reality*.

Notes

1. Charles Zastrow and Karen Kirst-Ashman, *Understanding Human Behavior and the Social Environment* (Chicago: Nelson-Hall, 1987), p. 556.
2. *Politics*, Book 1, Chapt. 5.
3. Walter Lippmann, *Public Opinion* (New York: Macmillan, 1922), pp. 88–89.
4. See Bruce E. Johansen, "Race, Ethnicity, and the Media," in Alan Wells (ed.), *Mass Media and Society* (Lexington, MA: Heath, 1987), p. 441.
5. *Ibid.*, 96.
6. Zastrow and Kirst-Ashman, *Understanding Human Behavior*, p. 487.
7. Peter B. Orlik, *Electronic Media Criticism: Applied Perspectives* (Boston: Focal Press, 1994), p. 23.
8. *Ibid.*, p. 516.
9. Orlik, *Electronic Media Criticism*, p. 23.
10. Patricia Raybon, "A Case of 'Severe Bias,'" *Newsweek*, October 2, 1989, p. 11.
11. T. W. Adorno, "Stereotyping on Television," in Alan Casty (ed.), *Mass Media and Mass Man* (New York: Holt, Rinehart & Winston, 1968), p. 64.
12. *Ibid.*
13. Joshua Hammer, "Must Blacks Be Buffoons?" *Newsweek*, October 26, 1992, p. 70.
14. *Ibid.*, p. 71.
15. *Ibid.*
16. For a discussion of contemporary stereotyping of Native Americans, see Richard Hill, "The Non-Vanishing American Indian," *Quill*, May 1992, pp. 35–37; Cynthia-Lou Coleman, "Native Americans Must Set Their Own Media Agenda," *Quill*, October 1992, p. 8.
17. "American Indian Group Asks Hollywood to Stop Stereotyping," (Baton Rouge) *Advocate*, October 12, 1994, p. 5C.
18. For a viewpoint on the continuing biased and stereotypical portrayal of blacks in news coverage, see Raybon, "A Case of 'Severe Bias,'" p. 11.
19. Richard P. Cunningham, "Racy Nicknames," *Quill*, May 1992, p. 10.
20. Johansen, "Race, Ethnicity, and the Media," p. 444.
21. *Ibid.*
22. Nancy Gibbs, "The War against Feminism," *Time*, March 9, 1992, pp. 50–55.
23. Nancy Signorielli, Douglas McLeod, and Elaine Healy, "Gender Stereotypes in MTV Commercials: The Beat Goes On," *Journal of Broadcasting & Electronic Media*, Vol. 38, Winter 1994, pp. 91–101.
24. "Old-Fashioned Gender Roles Are Back—in a Commercial," *TV Guide*, November 6, 1993.
25. Zastrow and Kirst-Ashman, *Understanding Human Behavior*, p. 431.
26. "Madison Avenue's Blind Spot," *U.S. News & World Report*, October 3, 1988, p. 49.
27. *Ibid.*
28. *Ibid.*
29. "Cheers 'n' Jeers," *TV Guide*, June 6, 1992, p. 6.
30. "Senior Citizen Gets Last Laugh in New TV Ad, (Baton Rouge) *Advocate*, February 5, 1994, p. 3A.

31. Douglas Lathrop, "Challenging Perceptions," *Quill*, July/August 1995, pp. 36–38.

32. See Christopher Lasch, "Critical View: Archie Bunker and the Liberal Mind," *Channels of Communication*, 1, October–November 1981, pp. 34–35, 63.

33. Trace Regan, "Color the News Accurately," in Wells, *Mass Media*, p. 461.

34. This issue is discussed in Robert Jensen, "Banning 'Redskins' from the Sports Page: The Ethics and Politics of Native American Nicknames," *Journal of Mass Media Ethics*, 9, No. 1, 1994, pp. 16–25.

35. The ideas for this scenario are based on a controversy surrounding an NBC documentary aired in 1989 entitled *Black Athletes—Fact and Fiction.*

Media Content and Juveniles:
Special Ethical Concerns

JUVENILES AND CULTURAL PATERNALISM

Juveniles occupy a special niche in U.S. society. And because the juvenile audience is unique, media messages directed at that audience warrant our undivided attention in a separate chapter of this text. Americans have committed themselves to the protection of youthful innocence and to the rehabilitation of those who have lost or been deprived of that innocence. Cultural paternalism is greatest when applied to children and adolescents, and this moral obligation has even been codified in the legal system. The juvenile justice system, prohibitions against child pornography, child labor laws, and laws establishing the legal age for buying alcoholic beverages and exchanging marriage vows without parental consent reflect this interest in protecting society's youth.

This web of legal paternalism would appear to defy the principles of freedom and autonomy that have been alluded to several times in this book as necessary for making rational decisions about ethics. But children are not autonomous, depending on others for their moral guidance and sustenance. Conventional wisdom holds that the value systems of juveniles are still immature and, therefore, need protection and nurturing. In recent years, the U.S.

Supreme Court has acknowledged this lack of intellectual and emotional maturity by restricting free-speech rights in secondary school.[1]

This immaturity rationale for insulating youth from undesirable influences was addressed directly by the thinkers of the European Enlightenment, the architects of the libertarian tradition. Although these philosophers advocated individual freedom—a prerequisite for autonomous moral reasoning—they did not believe that such rights should be extended to those below the age of majority. John Locke, for example, notes children's limited capacity to rationally exercise the privileges of freedom and argues for special protection:

> To turn him [the child] loose to an unrestrained liberty, before he has reason to guide him, is not allowing him the privilege of his nature to be free, but to thrust him out amongst brutes, and abandon him to a state as wretched and as much beneath that of a man as theirs.[2]

John Stuart Mill also addresses the subject in his classic work, *On Liberty*. In promoting the notion of individual liberties, Mill observes that "this doctrine is meant to apply only to those human beings in the maturity of their faculties. We are not speaking of children, or of young persons below the age which the law may fix as that of manhood or womanhood."[3]

Such observations provide credible support for the need to treat juveniles as special. It must be acknowledged, however, that this vision of children as innocent and weak has changed dramatically as the "psychological space" between childhood and adulthood has shrunk in our complex, fast-paced society. The disintegration of traditional family structures and the diminishing tranquility of the nurturing environment have accelerated the maturation process.

This altered view of the juvenile segment of society is reflected in cracks in the legal protections for children and adolescents. For example, states have traditionally shielded youthful offenders from the glare of publicity by closing juvenile courts and records to the public, asserting a "compelling state interest" in the rehabilitation of juvenile delinquents. The embarrassment caused by the publication of the names of youthful offenders, it was felt, would hamper the states' efforts to restore some sense of moral direction in their younger citizens.

In recent years, however, the U.S. Supreme Court has struck down state laws that prohibit the publication of juvenile offenders' names lawfully obtained.[4] And an increasing number of states have opened their juvenile courts and records for public inspection.[5] The trend toward trying the more violent youths as adults, even to the extent of imposing the death penalty in some cases, is further evidence of the erosion of special legal sanctuary for juveniles.

Of course, this changing reality is of more than passing sociological interest. As the lines between childhood, adolescence, and adulthood become less distinct, ethical questions remain. Because the mass media are important agents of socialization,[6] some consideration must be given to what role the media should play in the lives of a youthful audience that is admittedly more knowledgeable and less innocent than its predecessors.[7] Should media content aimed at children merely reflect reality, or should it attempt to inculcate the young audi-ence with positive values? What responsibility do media practitioners have when they develop programs targeted to adults but accessible to children? How graphic should mass media material be in confronting the juvenile audience with discussions of sensitive and controversial subjects? What moral obligations do media practitioners have in dealing with children and adolescents as consumers?

These are difficult questions, and the challenge, given the current permissive environment, is to construct strategies that will avoid the intellectual and emotional prudishness of a bygone era while maintaining a sense of moral obligation toward children and adolescents as impressionable audiences in the media marketplace. It should be remembered that the juvenile audience is not monolithic. Media content prepared for young children should be considered differently from that prepared for adolescents. Thus, age and maturity are important considerations in evaluating media content aimed at the younger generation.

INFLUENCES ON THE JUVENILE AUDIENCE

The concern with the protection of the youthful audience from the harmful effects of artistic subversion is of ancient vintage. Plato in his *Dialogues*, for example, advocates the censorship of "bad fiction" to insulate children from its undesirable influences:

> And shall we just carelessly allow children to hear any casual tales which may be devised by casual persons, and receive into their minds ideas for the most part the very opposite of those which we should wish them to have when they are grown up?
>
> We cannot.
>
> Then the first thing will be to establish a censorship of the writers of fiction, and let the censors receive any tale of fiction which is good, and reject the bad.[8]

Plato's counsel would be welcomed by those who continue to be concerned about the artistic and literary tastes of American youths.

Books

Book banning has been a familiar part of the educational landscape in the twentieth century, and even such literary masterpieces as Mark Twain's *Huckleberry Finn* and Shakespeare's *The Merchant of Venice* have not escaped the censor's wrath for their allegedly racist views.

Since the beginning of this century, public schools have felt increased pressures within their communities to maintain a cautious vigil over the materials used in teaching children. For one thing, more literature is available for children and young people than ever before.[9] In addition, over the past thirty years literature designed for the juvenile reader has changed dramatically. This literary revolution has reflected society's own loss of innocence.

> Realistic literature, based on the changes in society, began to be published. Former literature patterns, designed to be uplifting and to free the imagination of the child (the books read by parents), were changing with the times. Young readers, whose life styles differed from those of their parents, had different interests. Authors began writing books about the new life styles that interested youth. Personal and social problems often became the theme of the new books.[10]

This "new realism" in literature for children and adolescents has explored topics formerly reserved for adult audiences. Such themes as one-parent households, divorce, estranged parents, living on welfare, death and dying, homosexuality, drugs, and changing sexual roles are representative of the candor displayed in contemporary literature. Of course, within this plethora of controversial subjects are both good and bad books. Some deal with these themes with sensitivity and a respect for human dignity; others use mature themes and language for shock value in order to sell a product.[11]

These changes in literature targeted to the youthful audience illustrate the moral dilemma confronting the producers of mass media content, even those who do so with purity of purpose. On the one hand, the new themes are often appealing to the young audience, and from the perspective of publishers and authors, such literature can be a valuable introduction to the real world of social change for children and adolescents. On the other hand, media practitioners must be sensitive to community standards and charges by pressure groups that exposure to controversial material at such an early age undermines the moral stability of the youthful audience. Under such circumstances, publishers and authors are warned that traditional books must also be available in the marketplace. "The pendulum must not swing too far."[12]

Movies

Of course, this concern with the special nature of the juvenile audience extends far beyond what young people read. The film and sound-recording industries are essentially youth-oriented enterprises. Teenagers are a significant part of the movie audience, and Hollywood has not been oblivious to this fact of economic life. Although producers have been far from puritanical in their approaches to films designed for teenagers, the movie ratings have at least served as a warning to parents and adolescents.

The ratings system grew out of the ashes of the movie code, which by the late 1960s was considered by Hollywood to be a virtual failure. The code had incorporated strict standards for depictions of, among other things, violence, sexually explicit material, crime, and racism. But film producers ignored these lofty standards, thus rendering the code a moral failure.

In 1968 the Motion Picture Association of America (MPAA) formalized the current ratings system. Films were originally accorded a G, PG, R, or X rating.[13] In 1984 the MPAA added the PG-13 rating to warn parents that some material might not be suitable for children under thirteen, and in 1990, because of the appropriation of the X designation by the adult film industry, the MPAA replaced it with NC-17. Although no one is required to submit a film for a rating, most producers do so. The ratings may be evidence of Hollywood's sensitivity to its moral obligations to all audiences, but the effectiveness of the system depends, in the final analysis, on the good-faith efforts of both theater managements in enforcing the code and parents in maintaining an interest in their children's cinematic tastes. And the proliferation of movies on videocassettes, at rental rates often below the price of a theater ticket, makes this task more formidable.

Recordings

Teenagers and even preteenagers are the largest segment of the record-consuming audience. Although some parents whose musical tastes are more reserved might find rock music aesthetically offensive, the lyrics often reflect the frustrations and uncertainties of adolescence and strike a responsive chord in impressionable teenagers. Music is a powerful communication medium for adolescents, who often associate the music with such emotions as excitement, happiness, and love.[14] But when the musical lyrics and album covers contain obscenities, indecencies, and glorifications of certain forms of immoral conduct, such as drug abuse, ethical considerations arise in connection with the distribution of such material to a youthful audience. In some communities, concerned citizens have complained about the sexually explicit lyrics and record covers often associated with "raunchy rock" and rap albums.[15] The Federal Communications Commission has launched a crackdown on stations that air "shock jock" programs, featuring bawdy commentary, as well as stations that consistently play records containing indecent language.[16] The commission's policy on indecency is aimed particularly at the airing of offensive program material at

times of the day when children are likely to be in the audience.[17]

This paternalistic attitude reflects a sensitivity to the special interests of the juvenile audience. From an ethical perspective, indecency and obscenity are not essential to the communication of socially relevant messages to adolescents, even within rock lyrics. But the challenge for media practitioners, in an era of liberated youth, is to develop artistic models that avoid the extremes of moral puritanism and moral anarchy.

Television

Television has also been at the forefront of the debate over freedom versus responsibility in programming content to which children and adolescents are likely to be exposed. And perhaps for good reason. In a print culture, before the advent of television, adult characters in children's books were traditionally depicted as positive and even stereotypical role models. In this idealized world, parents really did know best, politicians were usually honest, and teachers were respected and omnipotent. In addition, parents were worthy gatekeepers who channeled their children's reading habits and maintained a constant vigil over their literary consumption. But television is omnipresent, and both newscasts and TV dramas now confront the juvenile audience with political corruption, dysfunctional families, and ambiguous role models that challenge the moral affiliation between parents and their children. Such portrayals have a leveling effect and tend to narrow the gulf between childhood and adulthood.

There was a time when childhood consisted of a parade of fictional heroes, youthful icons whose virtuous qualities and messages were unambiguous. Such heroes were influential in reinforcing positive values and helping build self-esteem. The comic books that children read and the TV shows that were derived from those comics, such as *The Adventures of Superman*, reflected that belief in heroes.

The social upheavals and the counterculture movement of the 1960s and 1970s severely undermined our faith in heroes.[18] Children's programs reflected this new sad reality as a new generation of action-packed adventure cartoons, in which the "good guys" were virtually indistinguishable from the "bad guys," confronted the nation's youngest viewers in a cultural environment already adrift in a sea of ethical relativism. The moral poverty of such content is summed up in this assessment from clinical psychologist Dr. Arietta Slade, in a recent *TV Guide* article:

> A clear-cut hero is a very important component in children's art, and the lack of clear-cut heroes on action shows is a big problem. Most of these shows don't have one hero you really get to know, and the stories are very confusing and incoherent. The good guys often seem violent or ominous.[19]

However, the industry has not been entirely unresponsive to such concerns. In 1993, for example, DIC Entertainment, producers of a number of popular children's shows, announced a twelve-point plan to guide writers and directors who work for the company. The standards included development of story lines to enhance self-esteem and foster cooperative behavior and an admonition against portraying antisocial behavior as glamorous or acceptable.[20]

The TV program decision makers have also been criticized for the rather subtle and not so subtle messages that their prime-time offerings send to the adolescent audience, particularly those who lack parental guidance and whose moral anchors are adrift. In Chapter 9, we discussed the potential impact of excessive televised violence on its young audience. But the concerns go beyond graphic depictions of such antisocial behavior. For example, TV critic Faye Zuckerman recently took NBC to task for airing "A Family Torn Apart," a fact-based film in which a teenager, apparently chafing under his parents' strict disciplinary code, decides to kill them. "Here the weak script so narrowly defines its characters," complained Zuckerman, "it irresponsibly delivers the message that it's acceptable for a teenager to kill both of his parents because they refuse to let him date."[21]

Does this mean that Hollywood producers and TV programmers should maintain a healthy distance from any reality-based story lines? In a diverse society, where artistic expression is a virtue, that would be unrealistic and undesirable. But Zuckerman's complaint is not so much that such a program was aired but that it portrayed the attacker as the victim and thus preyed on parents' "worst fears about their kids."[22]

The influence of television in the lives of children and adolescents poses an ethical dilemma for producers of entertainment programming. They must have the artistic freedom to develop quality shows that reflect the realities of contemporary society for a mass audience, a segment of which is children and adolescents. But there is now little doubt that juveniles learn values, social roles, and behaviors from watching television. For example, TV portrayals of minorities, sex roles, and family relationships can have a profound effect on children's attitudes about society.[23]

Thus, in light of this electronic influence on the socialization process, producers and programmers should at least pause to consider the nature and extent of their moral responsibility to develop positive role models for children and adolescents. They must be sensitive to the moral needs of young viewers who might be less innocent than their predecessors but are nevertheless still vulnerable and impressionable. This obligation is particularly important in an era of declining parental supervision and influence.

Of course, this responsibility does not absolve adults of their parental mandate to guide children's viewing habits.[24] Nevertheless, many parents are imperfect gatekeepers, either because they are not present to witness their children's program selections or have not learned how to "just say no." Under such distressing circumstances, the pressure inevitably would be on the producers and distributors of television programming to step into the moral vacuum left by this parental abdication.

Advertising

Media critics are also concerned about the influence of advertising on children. Much of their attention has focused on the commercialization of TV programs produced for children.[25] Moreover, broadcasters themselves have not been unmindful of their special responsibilities in this area. For more than half a century, the National Association of Broadcasters worked with the TV networks to limit the amount of commercialization in programs designed for children. But in 1982 the Justice Department filed an antitrust suit against the NAB, charging that its commercial codes were a restraint of trade. Shortly thereafter, the NAB agreed to abandon all efforts to negotiate further limitations on broadcast advertising.[26]

Since the early 1970s, Action for Children's Television (ACT), a citizens' group, has pressured the Federal Communications Commission and Congress to regulate the commercialization of children's programming. And until recently the FCC did provide guidelines, limiting the number of commercial minutes per hour of programs designed for children. But in 1986 it eliminated those guidelines,[27] and the industry's reaction was swift: many stations increased the number of commercial minutes in children's programming, and the networks began airing what were really program-length commercials, cartoon shows built around popular toys like G.I. Joe and Smurfs.[28] The ACT mounted a legal challenge to this deregulation and won a technical victory when a federal court ruled that the FCC had failed to justify adequately its policy change.[29] But in 1991 Congress passed legislation reinstituting commercial limits on children's programming— 10.5 minutes per hour on weekends and 12 minutes on weekdays—and also ordering

broadcasters to serve children's special educational needs.

These efforts at legal regulation aside, the ethical questions remain for the television and advertising industries. Those who view juveniles as a special audience argue that children and adolescents are vulnerable and should not be exploited by TV advertising.[30] Their concerns may well be justified, because research findings suggest that children do not always understand that the primary purpose of advertising is to sell and that very young children have difficulty distinguishing between advertising and program content.[31]

This situation poses a dilemma for those who aspire to insulate juveniles completely from the allegedly harmful influences of advertising. After all, young people are in the audiences when the ads aimed at adults are aired. Advertising of alcoholic beverages, for example, is not directed at teenagers, but one study concluded that young people who said they had seen more TV and magazine ads for beer, wine, and liquor generally drank more or expected that they would begin drinking.[32]

Of course, the influence of advertising extends beyond the electronic media. Consider, for example, the recent campaign for Camel cigarettes, featuring a cartoon character known as Old Joe Camel. From the moment of his American debut in 1988 (he was an immigrant from European ads), he maintained a pervasive presence on billboards, phone booths, and magazine pages.[33] Suspecting that the campaign was really aimed at children (a charge that R. J. Reynolds, the manufacturer of Camels, denied), three teams of researchers attempted to find out. While there was no evidence that Joe Camel affected the overall teenage smoking rate, the findings suggested a phenomenal increase in Camel's share of the youth market. In addition, Old Joe also had an impact on much younger children. For example, fully 91 percent of the six-year-olds surveyed could match Old Joe with a Camel cigarette—nearly the same proportion that could pair Mickey Mouse with the Disney Channel.[34]

Younger segments of the public are more impressionable than adults and more likely to be deceived by production values that increase the attractiveness of products in the minds of the viewers.[35] Thus, commercials aimed at children, especially younger children, take advantage of those who are the least powerful among consumer groups and the least capable of making rational and independent decisions in the marketplace.[36]

In addition, children are actually secondary consumers, because they have no real buying power of their own. Nevertheless, the available research suggests that heavy TV viewers do, in fact, approach their parents with requests for toys, games, and other products that they have seen featured in commercials.[37] Some critics believe that "this places an unfair burden on parents, who are required to spend significant portions of their parental energies vetoing purchases of new toys, breakfast cereals, candy products and soft drinks."[38]

However, this mass marketing to the child audience is not confined to the TV industry. The highly acclaimed film *Jurassic Park*, for example, featured a scene in which the child characters pass through a Jurassic Park gift shop where the shelves are lined with "JP" shirts, caps, toys and other souvenirs—an inside-the-movie ad for the many Jurassic Park products that were being marketed around the country. This tactic evoked this complaint from Alan Entin, past president of the family psychology division of the American Psychological Association: "They're doing an awful lot to sell that movie and all its spin-offs. And it's misleading. I think it's taking advantage of kids and a market and parents who feel they are coerced into buying these things for kids and taking them to the movie."[39]

Some people, however, do not approach the role of commercialization in the lives of children with such a caustic eye. Children are consumers, too, they argue, and nothing is inherently evil or immoral in attempting to influence their product choices. This view is reflected in a statement by an FCC commissioner, Glen O. Robinson, in a policy statement on children's television:

> Like adults, children are consumers. Like adults, their tastes are not genetically determined. Among the influences upon the tastes of consumers—be they adults, or children—is advertising. Irrespective of its target, its purpose is to motivate behavior that would not otherwise, but for the advertising, have occurred. For better or for worse, commercial messages, even those involving significant amounts of non-information mental massaging, have long been tolerated in our society. Some people even regard them as economically and socially useful. . . . I suggest that we candidly acknowledge that within proper limits it is not a sin, and certainly not a crime, to try to influence the consumption desires of children.[40]

In a society where advertising is ubiquitous and mass marketers attempt to cultivate consumer behavior at an early age, developing strategies to reconcile the views outlined here could be a formidable task. But as a point of departure we might consider the following guidelines for TV ads targeted to the child audience:

1. Commercials directed at children should avoid high-pressure tactics to compel the young consumer to purchase the product.

2. Children's commercials should not make exaggerated claims or mislead their audiences about the characteristics or benefits of the product advertised.

3. In commercials directed at children, premiums or other promotional inducements should be depicted as clearly secondary to the original product being advertised.

4. Children's commercials should never use violence, verbal abuse, or other forms of antisocial behavior as a selling technique, nor should such behavior be depicted as socially beneficial or acceptable.

5. Children's commercials should avoid the use of "weasel" words, such as *only* and *as low as* to promote price or exclusivity claims.

6. In programs targeted to children, program content should be clearly separated from commercial content, and the major characters in the programs should not also be used to promote products to the juvenile audience.[41]

In conclusion, the media do play a significant role in the lives of children and can be influential in the formation and adoption of attitudes and values. Some media content is a reflection of the youthful subculture, but it also has something to say about the moral tone of that subculture. Thus, society has an ethical imperative to examine the media messages aimed at its youthful members.

THE JUVENILE AUDIENCE: HYPOTHETICAL CASE STUDIES

The cases in this chapter reflect a diversity of situations in which media content is directed at youthful audiences, both children and adolescents. In reading and evaluating these scenarios and providing your own solutions to the ethical dilemmas, keep in mind the special nature of the audience involved. You may wish to review the three philosophical guidelines for ethical decision making described in Chapter 3. Then, as you have done in the preceding chapters, examine each situation from the perspective of the duty-based moral agent (deontologist), the consequentialist (teleologist), and Aristotle's golden mean. Base your judgment on one of these philosophical foundations, and defend your decision.

◆ C A S E   S T U D I E S ▶

▶ CASE 13-1
The High School Newspaper: A Lesson in Responsibility

Bill Trammell had viewed the evolution of the scholastic press with both respect and concern. He had graduated from high school in 1962, before the Vietnam War and the racial unrest of the 1960s robbed the nation's youth of its innocence. Now, as the principal of Harding High in Columbus, twenty-eight years later, he often reflected nostalgically on his own high school newspaper, in which the election of class officers and the selection of the prom queen were usually front-page copy. An occasional satirical commentary on some school policy would bring a mild rebuke from the principal, but in those days student reporters maintained a respectable distance from controversy.

But the youthful rebels of the late 1960s, who

had challenged traditional values and demanded constitutional parity with society at large, had discovered a forum in the scholastic press. And during the 1970s, some federal courts seemed eager to recognize a more expansive constitutional role for student journalists, thus unshackling high school newspapers from the paternalism of school officials.

As a math instructor at Walding High, his first teaching assignment, Trammell had watched as the student journalists tested the limits of their newfound freedom and antagonized the school's principal over the coverage of various controversial issues. He had envied their sense of youthful independence but had nevertheless been shocked by some of the topics they had chosen to explore.

In 1986, after a brief stint as an assistant principal at Walding, Trammell was appointed principal at Harding High, a crosstown rival of Walding. Trammell had welcomed his new assignment but had not looked forward to the inevitable confrontation with Michael Ford, the journalism teacher and faculty adviser to the *Falcon*, Harding High's school newspaper. Ford had served as adviser to the paper for twelve years, acquiring a reputation as an uncompromising defender of student press freedom. He had infected his students with his enthusiastic defense of the First Amendment, and Trammell's predecessor had spent his tenure at Harding in a state of perpetual confrontation with the unrepentant journalism instructor. No issue was off limits to his eager young charges, in Ford's view, and the *Falcon* was clearly a force to be reckoned with.

As Trammel assumed command of Harding High in 1986, he was aware of the limitations on his authority to rein in the student newspaper and restore what in his judgment was some modicum of responsibility. Twelve years earlier a federal court in Columbus had ruled that the principal could screen material and prevent its publication only when it "would be likely to lead to substantial disorder and disruption." Some federal courts had not gone so far, and the authority of school officials to restrain the school newspaper was at best uncertain. The *Falcon* was often controversial, but in Trammell's view it never really posed a threat to Harding High's educational mission. Nevertheless, he questioned the suitability of some of the articles on sex, abortion, and birth control for the younger members of the student body.

In his second year as principal, Trammell read with interest the news accounts of the *Hazelwood* decision. In early 1988, in what he regarded as a welcome note of reason, the U.S. Supreme Court issued its first ruling on high school press freedom. School officials may, the Court said in its majority opinion, exercise editorial control over the style and content of student speech in school-sponsored expressive activities as long as their actions are reasonably related to legitimate "pedagogical" (teaching) concerns.[42]

Although Trammell was pleased with the restoration of his authority over the *Falcon*, he was determined not to be precipitous in his actions. He promised Ford and the student reporters and editors that he would review each article objectively and exercise his powers of censorship with restraint.

Trammell's tolerance was soon tested by the newspaper's adviser and student editors. As he was reviewing the copy for the paper's last edition of the school year, the principal noticed two articles that gave him pause. One was entitled "The Facts about Sex Education and Birth Control," under the byline of Jeremy Bowers. The article was a critique of the effectiveness of the school's six-year-old sex education course, which was available to all students with parental consent. It was based on interviews with students who had completed the course and those who had not. In his comparison of the two groups (admittedly, not a scientific survey), Bowers had concluded that although knowledge about birth control seemed to be greater among those who had enrolled in the course, the actual use of contraceptives did not vary appreciably between the groups. In essence, the article, which also contained some rather graphic descriptions of sexual attitudes and references to birth control devices, was hardly a ringing endorsement of the effectiveness of the school's sex education program.

The other article was a report on five members of Harding's highly touted football squad who had received failing grades in several courses and had been suspended indefinitely from the team for cheating. Although the players were not mentioned by name, the paper's sports editor had apparently acquired the information from other team members and had solicited their reactions concerning how the suspensions might affect the team's performance in the next season. One member of the offensive line observed caustically that cheating was widespread at Harding and that he did not think his teammates should be singled out. This comment was followed by another containing an interesting combination of indecent utterances. It was clearly an expression of adolescent frustration. Although the editor had used only the first letter of the obscenities followed by a series of dashes, there was no doubt what words were intended.

Trammell was troubled by these two articles and summoned Ford to his office for a chat. The principal began by taking issue with Bowers's story about sex education at Harding. "This is poor journalism," the principal told Ford. "This student reporter has conducted an unscientific survey and has concluded that our sex education class is ineffective. We don't really know how effective the course is. Our pregnancy rate has dropped since it was implemented, but this isn't even mentioned in the article. The reporter never asked my opinion on the matter. At this point, we're unsure of whether we're getting through to the kids. In any event, an article like this undermines the credibility of our sex education efforts." Trammell also contended that some of the graphic descriptions in the article were unsuitable for younger students.

Ford defended the story, noting that even the professional media often ran unscientific surveys reflecting the opinions of those who agreed to be interviewed. "All we're trying to do," he said, "is to find out how much students at Harding High really know about birth control and whether those who have taken the class have really learned anything from their instruction. And as far as whether some of this material is suited for the younger students, let's face it. Most teenagers today know more than we give them credit for. There aren't many shrinking violets left."

After some further verbal sparring, Trammell turned to the article on the football players. His first concern was whether the cheating incident should be reported at all, because such matters were usually kept confidential. The omission of the names was beside the point, he believed, because it would take little ingenuity to figure out who the players were from the editor's description of the situation. "This should not be published in the *Falcon*," he said emphatically. "In addition, this quote with the poorly concealed obscenities is in poor taste and should be deleted."

Once again, the paper's adviser came to the defense of his student staff. "This cheating 'incident,' as you call it, is newsworthy. It could affect the performance of the team next season. The editor obtained this information legally from other members of the team. Our students have a right to know about what's going on at their school. Besides, with or without this story, everyone will know about the suspensions through the rumor mill.

"As far as that quote is concerned," Ford continued, unmoved by Trammell's criticism, "I think it was done responsibly. Within the context of the story, it was an important statement. Many professional newspapers print such quotes when they are essential to the story. How can we teach 'real-world' journalism if we put unrealistic restraints on these kids?"

The principal's confrontation with the adviser of the Falcon ended in a stalemate. Trammell promised, however, to take Ford's comments into account and render what he considered to be a fair decision, a decision that had to be made expeditiously because of the rapidly approaching deadline to submit the newspaper copy to the printer.

Now that the *Hazelwood* decision had bestowed the role of publisher on school officials themselves, Trammell was uncertain how to wield his authority. On the one hand, he believed that high schools should prepare students for their participation in a democratic society. This meant, of course, encouraging student expression and dialogue on controversial issues. Trammell wondered whether he could square his decision to censor Harding's newspaper with the academic instruction on the Bill of Rights that Norman Kenney set forth so eloquently in his course on American government. Would the principal's heavy hand of censorship negate the civics lesson on the diversity of ideas that underlies First Amendment freedoms?

And perhaps Ford was right. The practices represented by the two articles in question were not uncommon in the professional media. The story about the effectiveness of the sex education class was certainly a matter of interest, even if it fell short journalistically. And there was little doubt that the article about the suspensions for cheating would be of profound interest to Harding High students.

Nevertheless, Trammell had always considered the scholastic press to be a learning experience, a laboratory in which students were taught ethics and responsibility. Student journalists, despite their unbridled enthusiasm, had to learn that there were limits, even in the real world. He doubted whether some of the young reporters were mature or experienced enough to deal responsibly with some of the issues that confronted them.

Trammell also fretted about his moral duty to the student audience that would read the articles in the *Falcon*. He was particularly concerned about the material in the sex education article and the offensive references in the sports story. He also questioned whether the student paper should publish the story on the suspensions, even though the accused were members of the football team. And how would the parents respond to the newspaper's enterprising reporting?

Nevertheless, Trammell recognized that the school paper had a responsibility to provide information of interest to its student readers. Teenagers today were interested in more than the selection of the prom queen, although such stories were still common in the *Falcon*. The paper provided a sense of community for the students, a vehicle for sharing information about one another. Trammell wanted to maintain the *Falcon* as a forum for student expression without completely abandoning the paper to the unpredictable whims of adolescence. As the deadline approached, he wondered how he should balance his responsibilities to the newspaper's young journalists, their student audience, and the parents who depended on school officials to provide moral leadership for their children.

THE CASE STUDY

This case involves student journalists addressing an adolescent audience. Although the *Hazelwood* decision has settled, at least for now, the constitutional authority of school officials to control the style and content of the high school press, some questions still remain open for debate: What should be the role of scholastic journalism? How much freedom should high school reporters and editors be granted? What is the best way to instill a sense of responsibility in adolescent journalists? What is the moral duty of school officials to the student journalists, the audience they serve, and the parents of the students?

In this scenario, Trammell has several concerns: (1) the lack of maturity of both the student journalists and some members of their audience, (2) the suitability of some of the content for the younger students at Harding, (3) the questionable journalis-

tic quality and taste of some of the material, and (4) the parents' reaction to the articles in question. Are these legitimate concerns, or should the *Falcon* be viewed as a forum for the free flow of information to the students at Harding High?

Despite these objections, Trammell acknowledges the potential hypocrisy of teaching the students in class about the constitutional guarantees of free speech and then exercising the heavy hand of censorship in the school newspaper. He probably wonders how these students, who are rapidly approaching adulthood, can be inculcated with democratic values while being told that they must wait awhile before participating fully in this process. Even if the articles in question are unfair or perhaps unbalanced, the self-righting philosophy of the marketplace of ideas suggests that competing voices will help correct any misinformation disseminated to the audience. In the high school, however, there are no competing media voices, and thus the marketplace of ideas is not an effective model in this environment.

Should student journalists enjoy as much freedom as they might in the outside world, or are there reasons inherent in the school environment that would justify moral restraints on their activities?

For the purpose of resolving this issue, assume the role of Trammell, and, using the SAD Formula, offer a judgment on the two articles in question.

▶ CASE 13-2
Advertising in the Public Schools

Braxton Hutto surveyed the fallout from Saturday's school bond election with a profound sense of pessimism. As the superintendent of the Parkersville School District, Hutto had led a television and newspaper advertising campaign to convince taxpayers to rescue the financially destitute system from economic ruin. But the voters had once again rejected the educational establishment's plea, apparently unconvinced that increased funding would appreciably improve the academic quality of their community's schools. The vote had been close—51 percent to 49 percent—but "close counts only in horseshoes," Hutto remarked rather dejectedly to one of his assistants.

Hutto grappled with his melancholy for a few days, and then decided to take matters into his own hands. The Parkersville School District had once been among the state's most exemplary, and there was no reason, in his judgment, why it could not once again aspire to academic excellence. If he could find outside sources of funding for books, supplies, lab equipment and state-of-the-art computers, the superintendent reasoned, then perhaps he could encumber some money in the budget to provide small pay increases for both faculty and staff.

Hutto's natural instincts inclined him toward the rather lucrative benevolence of the corporate world, which had provided an abundance of educational materials to his district during his tenure. Of course, there was a trade-off in that each company's corporate logo was featured prominently on each packet, and there was always a suspicion concerning the educational balance of materials provided by institutions with a vested interest. Nevertheless, teachers had found them to be a welcome addition to their other pedagogical tools.

The superintendent wondered whether the time had come to become more fully engaged with corporate sponsorship of the educational enterprise. His proposal, which would have to be approved by the school board, would not be revolutionary since other school districts around the country had already given corporate sponsors an entré into their schools, including Channel One television, which also included commercials and was beamed directly into the nation's classrooms. Specifically, Hutto's plan called for the selling of advertising space along school hallways, a virtual arcade of target marketing. The money raised by such a commercial venture, Hutto reasoned, could pay for a lot of computers, software, and supplies.

Hutto viewed his plan as an economic necessity. He also recognized it as a potential public relations problem, a perception confirmed by Robert Lane, the school district's affable publicity director. Lane suggested that they move cautiously by introducing the concept on a one-year trial basis at Parkersville High and that they solicit as many views as possible on the proposal.

"We should begin," Lane said, "by meeting with the head of the teachers' union, the president of the PTA, the Parkersville High principal, Leslie Holiday, and perhaps even a teacher and the president of the school's student council. In this way, all of the constituencies will be represented." Lane also suggested that they meet together since group dynamics, in his judgment, often produced more reasonable results.

Hutto convened the meeting in his office after school hours. He was joined by Leslie Holiday, Parkersville High principal; Sandra Land-Johnson, president of the district's PTA; Marsha Braxton, union president and a social studies teacher at the high school; and Lisa Stanley, student council president. Robert Lane was also in attendance to assess the public relations implications of the proposal and to consider the advice that he would recommend to his superior concerning whether the plan should be implemented.

"I assume you have all read my proposal," Hutto said as he began his pitch in support of corporate sponsorship of his educational enterprise. "Simply put, we would like to sell ads to companies like McDonald's, Pepsi, and others that appeal to the youth market. We don't plan to saturate our school buildings, of course. The ads would be strategically placed along the hallway and in our cafeteria. The revenue from this venture can help support a lot of our needs that taxpayers apparently are unwilling to pay for."

"I support the proposal," responded Braxton. "The teachers haven't had a raise in several years, and we have little money for supplies. And in this information age, our students need computers. If the taxpayers are unwilling to approve a bond issue to help pay for these necessities, then we have to take matters into our own hands."

"I'm the principal of Parkersville High," said Holiday, "and I'm certainly sympathetic with our financial plight. But this seems rather drastic to me. We could open ourselves to charges of selling out to corporate interests. In addition, if we can so easily raise money through this means, that will take the state legislature and the local taxpayers off the hook. Politically, a better approach might be to let things get so bad that our citizens have no choice but to support the schools."

"I'm not concerned with the politics of this matter," responded Land-Johnson indignantly. "We should put the kids first. The fact is that if we allow advertising in our schools, these sponsors will have a captive audience. We'll be assisting them in taking advantage of these students. The purpose of school should be to teach, not to promote products."

"But isn't that rather elitist?" replied Hutto, unable to resist the temptation to defend his proposal at this point. "After all, these kids have grown up on advertising. It's ubiquitous in their world—on television, in shopping malls, and even on the scoreboard in the municipal stadium where we play our games. What's the difference here? These students are mature enough to make their own buying decisions."

"The difference," stated Land-Johnson, "is that in this case we would become in a sense partners in commercializing our public schools. Advertisers would have a captive audience. And we would be helping them to take advantage of these students. Having these ads—many of which are cleverly done and very entertaining—in our hallways and cafeteria would distract from the seriousness of our schools' educational mission."

"I agree with Sandra," said Holiday. "Schools are supposed to be institutions that students trust. If these ads go up in the public schools, they will assume a certain amount of credibility. Our community role and responsibility to these students distinguish us from advertising in other contexts. And we don't have the personnel or the time to sift out the good ads from the bad."

"I realize it's a trade-off," responded Braxton. "I'm not crazy about the idea of having ads in our hallways and lunchroom. But the bottom line is we need the money. The materials provided by corporate sponsors so far have been helpful. In a market-driven world, I just don't agree that we're somehow taking advantage of impressionable youths. They're more worldly and materialistic than many of their parents."

The superintendent then turned to Lisa Stanley, who had been uncharacteristically quiet, for the student perspective. "I'm not concerned about the ads," she replied, without hesitation. "After the newness wears off, most of the kids at Parkersville High will probably pay little attention to them. Besides, we're mature enough to make our own judg-

ments about products. Our whole world is saturated with ads. If these advertisements produce money for the district, the students certainly won't complain."

"I am concerned about the public's perception," said Lane. "Our critics might accuse us of selling out to commercial interests, thus diluting the quality of the educational environment. And if our relationship with corporate sponsors continues for an extended period, we might even be publicly indicted for propagandizing rather than educating our students. On the other hand, in our advertising and media-saturated world, even the public may not care. This just may not be a big issue for them. In any event, from a PR perspective, we might use this plan to convince taxpayers how desperate our financial condition is. Perhaps, then, they'll come to our rescue."

As Superintendent Hutto brought the meeting to a close, Lane began to ponder the ethical dimensions of the proposal. Although Hutto was certainly favorably disposed toward some kind of marketing alliance with corporate America, he would lean heavily on his publicity director's recommendation, especially since the proposal had to have school board approval and eventually public endorsement. On the one hand, Lane agreed with the superintendent that the support from advertising revenues could be the economic salvation of the district's educational support system. And besides, in a commercially saturated youth culture, what harm could result from placing a few ads in the school's passageways?

On the other hand, it did seem rather unseemly to introduce commercial values into an institution that was committed to academic concerns, particularly to a captive audience for which the school assumed responsibility for its educational maturation. He had visions of an ad adorning the Parkersville High cafeteria that read, "This lunch break is brought to you today by . . . ."

THE CASE STUDY

Because of economic concerns, many school districts across the country have provided access to corporate sponsors to promote their products directly to students within their educational environment. However, such a practice is not without controversy, as noted in this observation from a recent article in *U.S. News & World Report*:

> Once relatively free from reminders of the outside commercial world, schools today are fast becoming billboards for corporate messages. . . . Whatever their port of entry into the schools, advertisements and product endorsements are creating a stir across the country. While supporters argue they are harmless, critics blast school-based commercial plugs as not only distasteful but manipulative.[43]

In this case, the superintendent feels his options are limited considering the district's bleak financial picture. Teacher union president Sandra Land-Johnson agrees and sees the corporate sponsorship as a means of at least improving the district's educational support system. And student council president Lisa Stanley does not anticipate any objection from the students because of the commercial environment in which they have matured.

On the other hand, the school's principal is reluctant to have his institution become a marketing vehicle despite the financial benefits that might accrue. But he also cites political motives; that is, accepting outside funding sources might send the wrong signal to the legislature and taxpayers. The PTA president, who supposedly speaks for the parents' concerns, is unconditionally opposed to the proposal because of its potential impact on the students.

Thus, all of these concerns might be addressed in response to this question: Does the placement of ads in the public schools in order to enhance the quality of the educational enterprise raise ethical concerns, or is it really more of an amoral business decision based on economic reality?

You are the school's publicity director, Robert Lane, and must now make a recommendation to the district superintendent on whether to go forward with his proposal to the school board. Using the SAD Formula for moral reasoning outlined in Chapter 3, render a judgment and defend it. In so doing, you should keep in mind the public relations aspect of this dilemma. If you should recommend approval, what strategies might you use to sell the idea to the public (assuming, of course, that you anticipate some resistance)?

▶ **CASE 13-3**
A TV Movie's Lesson for Troubled Teens[44]

Like most network television executives, Peter Angelo had developed a siege mentality. For forty years the TV industry had been a favorite whipping boy of the politicians in Washington, but now the conservative majority was relentless in its determination that the commercial networks become a repository of family values. Sex and violence were their mantras, but clearly their agenda included nothing less than an indictment of the entertainment industry for its role in the moral demise of the nation's youth. While children's programming was a favorite target of the moral philosophers in the nation's capital, they had also targeted all prime-time programming that contained what they believed to be morally destructive messages. As a network vice president whose responsibility included the commissioning, licensing, and scheduling of feature films and miniseries, Angelo was caught between the political realities of "give the people what they need" mentality in Washington and the market-driven "give the people what they want" capitalistic ideology. However, even the market had recently retreated from its toleration of artistic liberalism as opinion polls began to indicate an increasing conservatism among viewers, a reflection perhaps of the prevailing political climate.

Angelo was not entirely insensitive to the concerns of his industry's critics. As a parent of two children, he believed that television—still the entertainment of choice for many children and adolescents—should be a positive force in their lives. On the other hand, the TV audience was heterogeneous, and the networks had an obligation to serve the interests of both the cosmopolitan viewers in New York and the more conservative viewers in Des Moines. This was an unenviable challenge, in Angelo's view, but one that could be managed through artistic diversity and symmetry.

Although Angelo accepted his industry's social responsibility mandate, he also believed that television should be the showcase for Hollywood's most creative energies, and, considering TV's voracious appetite for new material, he was constantly amazed at the overall quality of the output. He also believed that it was unreasonable to expect television to retreat to its sanitized, entirely unrealistic world view of the 1950s and that continuing audience support depended on the realism of its dramatic renditions. In short, television's continued salience depended on its ability to entertain the mass audience on its own turf, reflecting a world with which they could relate. And that was particularly true of teens, who were notorious for rejecting material that was alien to their culture.

Nevertheless, Angelo believed that there were limits and that his industry had a role to play in the moral development of the juvenile audience. Particularly within the entertainment genre, realism could be balanced with messages that at least were morally unambiguous.

These conflicting ideals were uppermost in the TV executive's mind as he reviewed the latest proposal and script for a feature film from David Zellner, an independent Hollywood producer who had already compiled an impressive résumé of successful network programs. It was Angelo's responsibility to accept or reject the proposal, or perhaps to accept it subject to changes. The process was fairly routine, as he examined such submissions for marketplace potential and artistic quality. But the overall dramatic slant of *Family Secrets*, the working title of the proposed film, concerned Angelo.

Family Secrets was a made-for-TV movie based on a real case history of a family named Beckworth, in which the father, Alan Beckworth, is portrayed as a strict disciplinarian, a virtual tyrant, and the teenaged son and daughter are depicted as victims of an unreasonably austere moral code. For example, the children are not allowed to date and subjected to an extremely early curfew (which is unreasonable, in the children's view) even when they are visiting their friends. They are also subjected to a never-ending barrage of criticism with little corresponding praise, a classic case of the destruction of self-esteem. According to the script, the mother, Janet Beckworth, comes across as a rather

pathetic character, subservient to her husband's authority while secretly emotionally engaged with her children's plight. Nevertheless, to her children she is a willing partner in their father's authoritarian demeanor and thus shares in the resentment that gradually manifests itself as the plot unfolds.

The story itself, as reflected in the script, is one of relentless psychological abuse, in which the children's perception of their own self-worth is gradually eroded. The uncompromising discipline and paternal criticism eventually lead the two children to rebel as they plot to murder their parents upon their return from a social engagement. The act is consummated, when the teenage assailants lie in wait in their garage and kill their parents with their father's shotgun. The children are tried as adults and convicted, although the trial scene, through a series of flashbacks, is decidedly sympathetic to the plight of the young defendants.

Angelo did not doubt the overall quality of the project from an aesthetic perspective. But the moral ambiguity of the film troubled him, and the network vice president sought counsel from Marvin Kingsley, his assistant for special projects, and Celeste Brown-Walters, a trusted aide who was in charge of prime-time scheduling.

"This film has a lot to commend it," said Kingsley, after reviewing the script while sipping a cup of Colombian coffee in Angelo's spacious, well-appointed office. "The writing is sharp, the characters are well defined, and there's a lot of conflict. This is an emotional film, and I think the audience will connect with it. The writers did take some license with the facts, but this isn't a docudrama. It's based on a true story, but the real version isn't quite as dramatic as this film. I think it'll be a winner in the marketplace."

"Perhaps," replied Brown-Walters. "But *Family Secrets* sends the wrong message to troubled teens: that if you don't agree with your parents' strict discipline, it's OK to blow them away."

"But that's what happened in this case," responded Kingsley. "Perhaps these two teenagers weren't physically or sexually abused, but they clearly were psychologically abused by their parents. I agree that murder isn't the solution, but in today's permissive society—especially in a household where teenaged children aren't permitted to have a normal teenage existence—it's inevitable that they might respond in this way. Again, I don't approve of their solution, but most teens in the audience can probably identify with their frustrations. This program, in my judgment, will connect with today's teenagers."

"But the writers have taken a lot of liberties with the script," countered Brown-Walters. "In the original case, according to news accounts and court transcripts, the father was a stern, strong disciplinarian, but he was not the tyrant portrayed in this film. In fact, some witnesses testified that he was a loving father, although he didn't often express his affection. Also, in the actual case, the mother was a dominant figure and reinforced her husband's strict disciplinarian code. In the film, however, she comes across as being a compliant character who supports her husband out of fear rather than conviction. At times, when the father isn't around, she even appears to sympathize with the children. What bothers me is that this is another film where the attackers are depicted as victims. *Family Secrets* is at best morally ambiguous. The producer needs to send a strong and unmistakable message that regardless of how bad things are at home, murder is not the solution. There are other ways of dealing with this difficulty."

"I have no problem with the writers taking a certain amount of poetic license in their character development," responded Kingsley, undeterred by what he believed to be his colleague's austere moral stance. "Television is about conflict. In order to depict the children's frustrations, the writers had to contrast them to a father that was pretty unreasonable. In *Family Secrets* there has to be a dramatic justification for the children's actions. A father who was stern but loving would have been insufficient. And, again, since this film is not being promoted as an actual case history, I see no problem with the fictionalized account of events."

"That's not the point," said Brown-Walters. "This is a film that, if we accept it, will air in prime time—probably during the ratings sweep. Teens will be in the audience, as well as their parents. What is at issue is not so much whether the facts are accurate as how the writers choose to slant the dramatic interpretation of the facts. I just simply don't believe the film should portray the children as victims. This

tends to justify their actions. And while I don't expect all teens who resent parental discipline to take their moral cues from this film, the fact is that it might reinforce tendencies that are already prevalent among troubled teens."

As Angelo listened to this exchange between his two colleagues, he felt increasingly uncomfortable in his role as moral agent. *Family Secrets* would be a quality program from an artistic perspective, and Angelo was convinced of its potential for success in the highly competitive marketplace during the quarterly ratings sweeps. But most of his experience in confronting the critics' assaults on the amoral posture of his industry had involved content that was too sexually explicit or too violent. But in this case, he was sitting in judgment of a Hollywood producer's fictionalized account of a real event that went to the very essence of dramatic license. "One person's victim is another's culprit," he said to himself as he pondered the opposing perspectives of Marvin Kingsley and Celeste Brown-Walters. Nevertheless, the "attacker as victim" syndrome represented an increasingly unpopular view, and Angelo was not insensitive to Brown-Walters's concerns about the film sending the wrong message to troubled teens.

In rendering a decision on Zellner's proposal and script, Angelo had three options. He could accept the proposal, reject the proposal, or tentatively accept it pending revisions, which would probably include a film that more closely tracked the real-life experiences of the Beckwith family. This would, of course, intrude directly into Zellner's artistic domain, but it would at least accommodate his concerns (and undoubtedly those of media critics if the current version were aired) about the "victimization" theme that pervaded this movie.

THE CASE STUDY

The proposed TV movie, *Family Secrets*, is not targeted to children or adolescents. Nevertheless, a TV executive is concerned that it sends a negative message to troubled teens who might be in the audience: that it is socially acceptable to rebel violently (including murder) against your parents if their disciplinary code is not to your liking.

Peter Angelo, the network vice president in charge of feature films and miniseries, is not concerned about the overall theme of the movie. After all, it is based on a true story and appears to be a quality product that is likely to garner ratings for the network. But he is troubled by the degree to which the writers and producer appear to be taking poetic license in developing sharply contrasting characters: an uncompromising tyrant of a father, a subservient mother who shares the blame in the eyes of her children, and two teenagers who are "victimized" by their parents' strict discipline and, no longer able to withstand this "psychological abuse," decide to take revenge. In the real-life version, of course, the relationships were not so neat, and the children received little sympathy from their community.

Hollywood and the TV industry have come under fire, not only for their preoccupation with sexual and violent content but for their overall contributions to the decline in morality. The commercial networks, syndicators, and the cable industry are the primary vendors for Hollywood producers. Should their decisions be confined to the aesthetic quality (which includes artistic freedom) and marketplace potential of dramatic productions, or should program executives also serve as moral censors to ensure that the "lessons" integrated into such offerings promote positive values? Is that even possible or desirable, considering the diversity of the TV audience?

The program proposal under review, *Family Secrets*, has definitely taken an "assailant as victim" point of view, one that has increasingly come under attack. But in a marketplace system, where both commercial values and artistic freedom are considered virtues, one could argue that a program reflecting such a perspective should be accommodated, with the expectation that other offerings will eventually balance what some consider to be an antisocial message for troubled teens. In addition, the majority of teens in the audience will certainly not identify with the ideas advanced in *Family Secrets*. On the other hand, TV can exert a powerful influence on children who are the products of dysfunctional families. Is there any social value in airing a program that, in effect, justifies the violent actions of teens against their parents? Does the de-

cision to televise a program such as *Family Secrets* depend on its social worth, or should commercial and entertainment values be the only criteria for selection?

Network executive Peter Angelo is both troubled and ambivalent about such questions. For the purpose of resolving the dilemma concerning the proposed TV movie *Family Secrets*, assume his position and, using the moral reasoning model outlined in Chapter 3, fashion a response to Hollywood producer David Zellner.

▶ CASE 13-4
Music Videos and the Teenage Audience

Ben Campbell was a product of the cable television generation. Unable to land a job as a TV news reporter with his newly earned journalism degree in 1968, Campbell had signed on as a sales representative for a fledgling cable company in the small midwestern community of Clarkston. The pay had been low, and the position had really demanded little in the way of salesmanship abilities, but the young sales rep had bided his time until the moment when some news director would recognize his considerable talents as a broadcast journalist.

During what he believed would be a short tenure in cable TV, Campbell had read with interest the various futuristic predictions about the industry and the unlimited diversity that cable television would someday provide for the viewing audience. He had been skeptical about many of these predictions but had been nevertheless impressed by his company's ability to offer twelve channels to a community that only two years before had been limited to two local network affiliates. Most of the channels, of course, were retransmissions of both local and distant over-the-air signals, but he had been intrigued by the industry's potential for growth.

Campbell's initial complacency had been replaced by a sense of commitment to Clarkston Cable's success, and his interest in the glamour of TV news had slowly waned. Within three years, he was named assistant manager and, two years later, manager of the local system. The 1970s witnessed a steady growth in the number of cable subscribers, and the introduction of satellite-delivered services in the latter half of the decade revolutionized the industry, resulting in an impressive increase in revenues with only modest capital investments.

By 1980 Clarkston Cable, which had entered the marketplace on a financial shoestring in the mid-1960s, had acquired a twenty-channel capacity, many of which were satellite-delivered services. Campbell had been pleased to be on the cutting edge of his company's role in the cable revolution, but he had grown restless and in 1986 accepted his present position as manager of a thirty-six-channel system in Donaldsonville, a thriving service industry and white-collar community along the banks of the Mississippi River.

Campbell had embarked on his new assignment with enthusiasm. Donaldsonville Cable was steadily growing, and the revenue projections for the following five years were impressive. On assuming the helm at his new company, Campbell surveyed the virtual smorgasbord of program offerings and marveled at the creative and artistic diversity available to the Donaldsonville community. Cable television had certainly come a long way since his rather modest introduction to the medium in the 1960s.

As a manager of a cable system in a medium-sized market, Campbell had never considered himself an arbiter of the public's tastes. The program selections ran the gamut from the family-oriented Disney Channel to one recently added adult service, but the soft-core porn that was the standard fare had been slotted into a pay channel. Although some of the programming offered on Donaldsonville Cable's "basic tier" did not appeal to the manager's personal tastes, the audience appeared reasonably happy with the diversity and the quality of content. Most of the complaints centered on the steadily rising costs of cable service and the occasional distribution outages that still plagued the system.

But the Coalition against Violence and Pornography had not come to Campbell's office to complain about cable bills. The coalition was a group of citizens concerned about the proliferation of sex, violence, and drug-related musical lyrics on televi-

sion. Melba Sills, the spokesperson for the group, was blunt. She told Campbell that the members considered the channels that featured rock videos, such as the Music Television (MTV) channel, to be unsuitable for a teen audience. "Many of these videos glorify casual sex and violence and feature themes of social protest and alienation," she complained. "This is hardly the stuff we should be feeding our teenagers."

Sills told Campbell that the group had written letters of protest to the MTV network, but to no avail. It had no choice, she said, except to ask the local system to remove this kind of programming from its lineup. "You have a responsibility to this community," she declared.

Campbell listened attentively to the coalition's grievances and was somewhat chastened by Sills's visit. On the one hand, he shared her feelings toward the music video phenomenon. Much of the material, particularly the bizarre blend of music with striking imagery, quick cuts, and suggestive choreography, tested the outer limits of artistic decorum and was probably unsuitable for a generation of adolescents already morally adrift. Even if the music video producers were insensitive to the abuses reflected in some of their creations, Campbell reasoned, he was in a position to respond to the concerns of groups like the Coalition against Violence and Pornography. But should he?

The coalition represented a segment of the community, but it was unclear how many citizens of Donaldsonville really shared its critical views. Market research revealed that the MTV channel had a loyal following among local youths. The teenagers of today, after all, were products of both the rock and the TV generations. The artistic marriage of lyrics and video was, therefore, a natural cultural progression for the youthful audience.

Besides, Donaldsonville Cable offered sufficient diversity to accommodate a wide range of tastes. Teenagers, after all, were an important segment of the audience and certainly entitled to some respect in the consumer marketplace. The rather questionable content, Campbell rationalized, was just a reflection of adolescent frustration and uncertainty.

Nevertheless, during the previous several years, music videos had become bolder in their graphic portrayals of sexual situations, and Campbell wondered whether they had exceeded the bounds of propriety. Above all, he pondered the extent of his own moral responsibility, as manager of Donaldsonville Cable, for programming such material for a teenage audience.

THE CASE STUDY

Although music video is not an entirely new concept, it became a highly visible force with the launching of the MTV cable channel in 1981. Within just three years, an estimated 22.6 million viewers were receiving the twenty-four-hour rock video signal through cable.[45] Music video's continue to be a prominent feature on cable's diverse programming menu. MTV's rapid maturity as a cultural phenomenon is evidenced by the fact that it now boasts of its own nationally televised video music awards.

Although music videos appeal to some segments of the young adult audience, a significant percentage of the viewers are teenagers.[46] The themes are really no different from those that have always driven rock and roll: rebellion and sex. MTV has written guidelines on program content, but there is much flexibility in these vaguely worded standards.[47] One early study of sixty-two MTV music videos found that sex, crime, and violence were common themes. Much of the sexual and violent content was characterized by innuendo and suggestiveness, perhaps reflecting MTV's adolescent audience.[48]

Little scientific evidence documents the harmful effects of music videos on teenagers.[49] And it is unlikely that the impact of viewing violence or sexual innuendo on MTV is likely to be any more profound than the impact of watching similar content on commercial television. The visual dramatizations just add meaning to rock lyrics that are already available and purchased by the teen audience.[50] However, critics worry that music videos are just one more challenge in a world where too many external stimuli already compete with parental guidance for moral control of impressionable adolescents.

But cable is a medium devoted to diversity, where the artistic tastes of all segments of society can be represented. Does this role undermine the moral claim of those who object to certain kinds of content on the ground of taste? The idea of diversity, of course, does not confront directly the question of whether the distributors of content directed at teenagers have a special responsibility to that audience. Should cable operators, for example, serve as gatekeepers and arbiters of tastes for adolescents (or for any other segment of the audience, for that matter)? On the other hand, should cable operators be any less responsive to public concerns about taste than over-the-air broadcasters?

For the purpose of confronting these questions, assume the role of Campbell, and, using the SAD Formula, respond to the concerns of the Coalition against Violence and Pornography.

▶ **CASE 13-5**
The Adolescent Audience and Moral Choices

As a producer of children's programs, Alvin Weintraub was unrivaled in Hollywood. His cartoon characters had occupied a prominent position for ten years on the networks' Saturday morning schedules. Weintraub's creative genius had managed to attract a loyal audience of youthful viewers without resort to violent fantasies or the program-length commercials to which many television critics objected. Although consumer groups occasionally complained about commercials on children's programs (a fact of life over which he had no control), his "wholesome" cartoons had kept the wolves away from the door, and the networks were appreciative.

Weintraub had also caught the attention of programming executives with his production of three successful specials aimed at adolescents that had been aired as the lead-in program to the Sunday night prime-time schedule. He had even dabbled occasionally in the rarefied atmosphere of public broadcasting, with the production of two docudramas on drugs and teenage pregnancy.

Thus, Weintraub's talents were well known to network executives when the call came from Andrea Beach. Beach had been in her present position for only six months, but she was already looking to expand her turf. She was the network's executive responsible, among other things, for developing ideas for programming directed at children and adolescents. She had scored what to her was a coup in convincing the network to give her an hour of time once a month late in the afternoon for a dramatic special aimed at the teenage audience. This program would necessitate an occasional preemption of the regularly scheduled and popular soap opera, but the network brass had apparently been willing to make this minor concession.

Beach had asked for proposals from several producers, but Weintraub's had been the most impressive. His submission had outlined a series of dramatic specials, entitled *Choices*, that would feature various teenage characters confronted with the agonizing dilemmas and decisions of adolescence. Some would involve moral issues, such as the drug culture; others would feature the more mundane adolescent concerns, such as learning how to drive and personal grooming. However, all programs would have a common theme: convincing teenage viewers that despite peer pressure to conform, they did have choices and demonstrating through the use of dramatic dialogue and plot development how to make those choices.

Despite Beach's enthusiasm for the concept and Weintraub's reputation, she had asked the producer for a pilot program before giving final approval to the project. Weintraub eagerly obliged, and several months later the pilot of *Choices* and a completed script for another episode had been entrusted to the care of the young network executive. This was followed a couple of weeks later by a pilgrimage to New York to review the results of his latest creation.

Beach began the meeting by complimenting Weintraub on the quality of the scripts, casting, and production work. The pilot dealt with the issue of teenage sexuality, hardly a novel idea for television but certainly one that was always timely and of continuing interest to the youthful audience. The program's primary focus was on birth control and safe sex, an appropriate subject in light of the AIDS epidemic. There were several scenes inside a class on sex education, where birth control and sexual practices were discussed candidly. The characters were then confronted with how to apply these lessons in the outside world.

But Beach was concerned with what she referred to as "moral closure" in the program. Although the pilot was effective in revealing to its audience the choices in teenage sexual development, it did not espouse a moral point of view. Sexual abstinence was an option, but the program made no value judgment about the morally correct course of action. Beach perceived the same flaw in the completed script that Weintraub had submitted. This episode dealt with classroom cheating, an issue that was sure to hold the attention of a juvenile audience. But in Beach's view, the drama had lost its moral flavor by concentrating on the grade and peer pressures that prompted cheating rather than the unethical nature of the act itself. The real message had been obscured, Beach believed, by the program's reluctance to assign clear moral responsibility to those who cheat. She believed that *Choices should* go the extra mile and express a point of view on ethical issues.

Weintraub objected vociferously to Beach's evaluation of his *Choices* pilot and the script. "The concept of the program," he stated emphatically, "is to teach adolescents how to make decisions—to show them they do have choices in life. It's a mistake to moralize to these kids. Although most of the viewers might be teenagers, we're still dealing with a diverse audience. Some are happy and well adjusted; others are from broken homes. Some are middle-class; others are from the inner city. They come from different cultural backgrounds." Weintraub also noted that teenagers were caught in the crossfire of competing values. "The one thing they don't need," he said, "is to be preached to by the mass media. Moral education is the responsibility of parents and schools."

Beach listened attentively to the producer's defense of his proposed program. Taking the most charitable view of his rebuttal, she had to admit that some of Weintraub's comments made sense. Perhaps her hopes for *Choices* were too ambitious. The program did an effective job of outlining the options available to adolescents when they were confronted with a dilemma. That was, after all, a worthwhile goal for any TV program. If every episode tried to present a point of view, the audience might reject the candid messages as too "preachy."

Beach had always felt that the broadcast industry should be socially responsible, but now she wondered how far that obligation extended. Should networks distribute programs that reflected a particular moral point of view? With the continuing decline of moral direction among the nation's youth, she was convinced that television had a positive role to play. But what kind of role?

Beach closed the meeting with Weintraub by telling the producer that she would consider his views and let him know shortly whether she would insist on revising the program concept for *Choices*.

THE CASE STUDY

Should television promote particular moral views to the adolescent audience? This idea is certainly not new; television programming has traditionally suggested answers to various dilemmas. But one could argue that TV programs targeted at adolescents should be wary of espousing particular ethical values. Moral training should be left to the parents, in this view, and TV's responsibility is to entertain and deal with society's problems realistically without rendering value judgments.

Of course, few programs that confront social issues are entirely devoid of value judgments. Nevertheless, some believe that TV should become an active partner in the fight against moral relativism and help restore traditional values. Thus, programs aimed at teenagers should express an unambiguous point of view on moral issues.

But in this scenario, the network might be accused of ethical schizophrenia. Beach's motives seem pure enough, but she is operating in a cultural environment in which much of the programming, both the daytime soap operas and some of the prime-time content, is countering the lessons to be taught by programs such as *Choices*. For example, can one take the moral high ground on the issue of teenage sexuality in some programming while featuring casual sex so prominently throughout the schedule?

And then there is the issue of artistic freedom and diversity. The commercial television networks

appeal to a mass audience and should not be expected to direct all of their energies into a single-minded programming philosophy. They appeal to mature adults as well as impressionable teenagers. Thus, the ethical issue represented by this scenario should be confined to the question of what responsibilities ought to be borne by the producers and distributors of program content directed specifically at adolescent audiences.

For the purpose of confronting the concerns of Beach, assume her role. Using the formula for moral reasoning, make a decision on whether you will acquiesce to Weintraub or insist that the *Choices* concept be altered.

▶ ## CASE 13-6
Kids as PR Strategy

Alan Noles had never heard of the chemical raminozide, but its more common name, Molnar, was front-page news. As the senior partner of Noles and Barkham, a small public relations firm in Washington, D.C., specializing in consumer-oriented and environmental issues, Noles was about to become part of the controversy that surrounded the alleged harmful effects of Molnar.

Molnar was a synthetic hormone that had been approved by the Federal Drug Administration to spur greater milk production in cows and increase the nation's supply of milk. But within a few years after the agency's approval, the evidence had begun to mount that Molnar caused tumors in laboratory animals. The Consumer Protection Coalition (CPC), an uncompromising activist organization that served as a self-appointed watchdog over the nation's food supply, had petitioned the FDA to ban the production and use of the synthetic hormone. However, under pressure from the dairy industry and its lobbyists in Washington, the agency became increasingly deliberate in its rush to judgment over the alleged harmful effects of Molnar. And despite the negative publicity surrounding Molnar, there appeared to be no groundswell in opposition to the chemical agent. Patience was not a virtue, however, for the CPC. Not content to wait for further government study and deliberation, the CPC had decided to take its case to the court of public opinion in an aggressive campaign of mass persuasion.

With its track record on environmental and consumer-related issues and geographic location in the nation's locus of news activity, Noles and Barkham was a natural candidate to represent the CPC in its public campaign against the manufacturers of Molnar and the milk producers who continued to flaunt the scientific evidence, in the opinion of CPC's leadership, of the health risks of the agricultural chemical. Alan Noles and his junior partner, Toni Barkham, did not hesitate when Linda Carroll, CPC's publicity chair, approached the firm about developing a PR campaign to focus the public's attention on this alleged threat to the nation's milk supply. "If we can convince consumers to stop buying milk," she said in her first encounter with the two partners, "Molnar will be history."

Noles and Barkham considered the CPC's concerns to be a perfect match for their firm's increasingly activist posture, but they were not naive about the formidable opposition that would be arrayed against them. The dairy industry's pockets were deep, and their PR representation exceptional and powerful. Nevertheless, Noles and Barkham were undeterred and looked forward to the competition of the marketplace.

The partners assigned the CPC account to Tasha Herrington, a young but seasoned account manager. Within a couple of weeks, Herrington had outlined her strategy for their newest environmental client, which included press conferences in a dozen cities and appearances by CPC leaders on several national radio and TV talk shows. Overall, the two partners were suitably impressed with the proposal produced by their young colleague—a plan that would guarantee that the dangers of Molnar would figure prominently on the nation's political agenda.

The well-financed CPC enterprise also included national print and TV advertising, and it was the theme of this campaign that enlivened the evaluation process. Herrington's objective was to concentrate on consumers' most vulnerable spot: their kids. One TV spot, for example, would be filled with cherubic-looking children who were being slowly poisoned by the harmful chemical

agent Molnar through their rather innocent consumption of milk. While the spot was skillfully conceived to avoid being outright offensive, the message was unmistakable.

"I don't have any problem with the overall strategy," said Barkham, as she thumbed through Herrington's proposal in search of her notes in the margin. "However, I am concerned about one theme," she continued, "that seems to pervade part of this plan: the impact of Molnar on children. It seems pretty alarmist, and it could backfire. It appears that we're using children as pawns." Noles shared her concern, but considering the heavy artillery that was arrayed against his firm, he was willing to concede that extreme measures might be justified.

"I don't see it that way," responded Herrington. "Adults might be concerned about the use of growth hormones to stimulate milk production, but there have been so many alarms in recent years that many have stopped paying attention. But when their children are involved, that's a different matter. We need to focus this campaign where it will be most effective—on the effects of Molnar on children."

"We need to be careful about how we use the available research," replied Noles, who had used his share of marketing data to his own advantage and was painfully aware of the rather elusive meaning of so many of the studies that had been done in support of various causes. "Most of what I've read has related to research done on laboratory animals. The effects of Molnar on humans haven't been tested. And the fact is that in many of these studies lab animals are fed tremendous doses to get the results. I wouldn't be so concerned if we were just issuing an early warning for adults. But our client is interested in an immediate victory against the manufacturers of Molnar. I'm afraid that we might be perceived as being hysterical, particularly with the campaign we've devised centering on children."

"But children are more vulnerable than adults," declared Herrington emphatically. "Their systems are not as well developed as adults, and they're more at risk. In addition, our statistics show that they consume much more milk than adults, both at home and in school cafeterias. I see nothing wrong with pointing out the obvious: that there is evidence that Molnar is a health hazard, particularly to children. Then their parents can decide whether to stop feeding their kids milk, and school officials can decide whether to stop serving it in their lunch rooms until they're convinced the milk supply is safe."

"But not all dairies use growth hormones to spur milk production," countered Noles. "We don't really know how many children are drinking milk from cows that have been injected with Molnar. And even better labeling may not be sufficient for the average consumer."

"That's the point," replied Herrington. "We don't know. It's like Russian roulette with our children's health. And the most effective way to get this across is to use children in our advertisements and get their parents emotionally engaged. We're certainly not being deceptive. Our goal is just to alert parents to potential dangers and let them make the choice."

"Let's assume we're successful," replied Barkham, "and let's assume that some parents stop buying milk and schools pull their milk inventories until they are assured the supply is safe—thousands of children will be deprived of a beneficial food. And in the long run, that could be more harmful than the effects of Molnar itself."

"But if we *are* successful," responded Herrington, "the lowered demand for milk will only be temporary. Our goal is to eliminate the use of Molnar as a stimulant to milk production. It's a potential carcinogen and could pose a risk to children. Why take a chance? That's the message we're trying to get across."

"In general, I don't have a problem with focusing on children as a PR strategy," replied Barkham. "After all, they are a concern of our client, and if there is a risk to kids, then the public should know. But the emotional impact of these spots is pretty awesome. Who wouldn't respond to a commercial with beautiful children who are being harmed by a chemical in the nation's milk supply? The manufacturers of Molnar will be savaged. Again, in the interest of our client, I have no problem with going after this chemical agent. There apparently is at least some risk involved. Perhaps that should be our approach—appeal directly to adults based on the evi-

dence we do have—rather than use kids in these commercials."

But Herrington was unmoved. "Our job is to do the best we can for our client. And children have an emotional impact," she said. "Is there anyone here who disagrees with the notion that focusing on children as the primary consumers of milk will probably be the most effective public relations strategy?"

Noles and Barkham did not challenge their young colleague's assessment. Her campaign strategy was sound. But as senior partner and the moral agent who would be the final gatekeeper in the approval of Herrington's proposal, Alan Noles was still troubled by the ethically slippery slope of using children to convince the public of a potential danger to the nation's milk supply.

THE CASE STUDY

A public relations practitioner's first obligation is to serve the client. However, such loyalty is not unlimited, and no ethical system (including the PRSA Code) would sanction the use of a clearly unethical strategy to accomplish some goal that does nothing more than serve the client's self-interest.

In this scenario, a citizens' group is sincerely concerned about the effects of a chemical agent on the nation's milk supply and has hired the Noles and Barkham PR firm to represent it in promoting its cause in the marketplace. The strategy devised by account manager Tasha Herrington is designed for maximum effectiveness—to convince parents that their children may face risks from drinking milk, particularly that produced from cows injected with Molnar, a growth hormone. One way of doing this, of course, is to introduce persuasive messages (in this case, ads) to convince parents to boycott milk until the government assures them that this product is safe. As the largest consumers of milk, children have been chosen as the focus of this campaign. There is no reason to believe the ads themselves are in poor taste. Thus, under the circumstances, is this an ethically defensible strategy, or will the PR firm be perceived as using children as pawns to create a hysteria about the potential harmful effects of milk?

The research on which this "scare" is based, like much research, is still inconclusive in terms of the effects of this hormone on humans. Of course, the purpose of the campaign is just to serve as an early warning to parents, but the use of children in the ads will have a greater emotional appeal than the more hard-sell messages using adults. Is such an approach warranted under the circumstances? Is there any ethical problem with this strategy, or are the concerns of Alan Noles and Toni Barkham unjustified?

For the purpose of responding to these questions, assume the position of senior partner Alan Noles, and, using the formula for moral reasoning outlined in Chapter 3, make a decision on Tasha Herrington's proposal to use children as the focus of her PR/advertising campaign.

▼

Notes

1. See *Hazelwood School District v. Kuhlmeier*, 14 Med.L.Rptr. 2081 (1988); *Bethel School District No. 403 v. Frazer*, 106 S.Ct. 3159 (1986).
2. John Locke, "Second Treatise on Civil Government," in J. Charles King and James A. McGilvray (eds.), *Political and Social Philosophy* (New York: McGraw-Hill, 1973), p. 117.
3. John Stuart Mill, "On Liberty," in King and McGilvray, *Political and Social Philosophy*, p. 186.
4. See *Smith v. Daily Mail Publishing Co.*, 99 S.Ct. 2667 (1979).
5. For a discussion of this issue, see Louis A. Day, "Media Access to Juvenile Courts," *Journalism Quarterly*, Winter 1984, pp. 751–756, 770.
6. *Ibid.*, pp. 471–480; Charles R. Wright, *Mass Communication: A Sociological Perspective*, 3d ed. (New York: Random House, 1986), pp. 185–201; Karl Erick Rosengren and Sven Windahl, *Media Matter: TV Use in Childhood and Adolescence* (Norwood, NJ: Ablex, 1989), pp. 159–241.
7. For an examination of some of the early research on the effects of mass media on children, see Ellen Wartella and Byron Reeves, "Historical Trends in Research on Children and the Media: 1900–1960," *Journal of Communication*, 35, Spring 1985, pp. 118–133.
8. Plato, *The Republic, The Dialogues of Plato*, 2 vols., ed. and trans. B. Jowett (New York: Oxford University Press, 1892), Vol. 2, p. 323; quoted in Joseph E. Bryson and Elizabeth W. Detty, *The Legal Aspects of Censorship of Public School Library and Instructional Materials* (Charlottesville, VA: Michie, 1982), pp. 14–15.
9. Bryson and Detty, *Legal Aspects*, p. 41.
10. *Ibid.*, p. 51.
11. *Ibid.*, pp. 52–53.
12. *Ibid.*, p. 54.
13. Most producers of pornographic films do not submit their works to the ratings board but instead just self-supply an X rating and go to market.
14. Alan Wells and Ernest A. Hakanen, "The Emotional Use of Popular Music by Adolescents," *Journalism Quarterly*, Vol. 68, Fall 1991, pp. 445–454.
15. See "A Rap Album in the Dock," *Newsweek*, October 16, 1989, p. 72.
16. "FCC Crackdown Sparks Debate," (Baton Rouge) *Morning Advocate*, September 15, 1989, p. 14C.
17. 56 F.C.C. 2d 94, 98 (1975).
18. James Kaplan, "Superheroes or Zeros?," *TV Guide*, October 29, 1994, p. 33.
19. *Ibid.*, p. 34.
20. "Cartoons with a Conscience Are in the Works," (Baton Rouge) *Advocate*, December 15, 1993, p. 8A.
21. Faye Zuckerman, "NBC Movie Sends Wrong Message to Troubled Teens," (Baton Rouge) *Advocate*, November 20, 1993, p. 11C.
22. *Ibid.*
23. See F. Earle Barcus, *Images of Life on Children's Television* (New York: Praeger, 1983).
24. For an examination of this problem, see Aimee Dorr, Peter Kovaric, and Catherine Doubleday, "Parent-Child Coviewing of Television," *Journal of Broadcasting and Electronic Media*, 33, Winter 1989, pp. 35–51.
25. For a recent study of the role of children's advertising in electronic media, see Dale Kunkel and Walter Gantz, "Children's Television Advertising in the Multichannel Environment," *Journal of Communication*, 42, Summer 1992, pp. 134–152.
26. See *United States v. National Association of Broadcasters*, 536 F.Supp. 149 (D.D.C., 1982).
27. "Programming Commercialization Policies," 60 RR 2d 526 (1986).
28. See Don R. Pember, *Mass Media Law*, 6th ed. (Dubuque, IA: WCB Brown & Benchmark, 1993), p. 569.
29. *Action for Children's Television v. FCC*, 821 F.2d 741 (D.C.Cir., 1987).
30. An examination of the prevalence of commercials aimed at children is provided by John Condry, Patricia Bence, and Cynthia Scheibe in "Nonprogram Content of Children's Television," *Journal of Broadcasting and Electronic Media*, 32, Summer 1988, pp. 255–270.
31. See Laurene Krasny Meringoff and Gerald S. Lesser, "Children's Ability to Distinguish Television Commercials from Program Material," in Richard P. Adler et al. (eds.), *The Effects of Television Advertising on Children* (Lexington, MA: Heath, 1980), pp. 32–35.
32. Charles Atkin, John Hocking, and Martin Block,

"Teenage Drinking: Does Advertising Make a Difference?" *Journal of Communication*, 34, Spring 1984, pp. 157–167.

33. "I'd Toddle a Mile for a Camel," *Newsweek*, December 23, 1991, p. 70.

34. *Ibid.* The cigarette industry has recently responded to criticism that they are targeting the young. In 1995, for example, Philip Morris announced a comprehensive program to discourage juvenile smoking. See Glenn Collins, "Philip Morris Seeks to Curb Cigarette Sales to the Young," *New York Times*, June 28, 1995, p. A11.

35. There is also evidence that younger viewers do not distinguish between the real and unreal on television. See Peter Nikken and Allerd L. Peeters, "Children's Perceptions of Television Reality," *Journal of Broadcasting and Electronic Media*, 32, Fall 1988, pp. 441–452.

36. For example, one study that examined children's understanding of network commercial techniques found that they did not understand the concept of a "balanced breakfast." See Edward L. Palmer and Cynthia N. McDowell, "Children's Understanding of Nutritional Information Presented in Breakfast Cereal Commercials," *Journal of Broadcasting*, 25, Summer 1981, pp. 295–301.

37. *Ibid.*

38. *Children's Television Report and Policy Statement*, 31 R.R.2d 1228 (separate statement of Commissioner Glen O. Robinson, at 1255), *affirmed*, 564 F.2d 458 (D.C.Cir., 1977).

39. "'Jurassic Park' Hype Masks Disturbing Question," (Baton Rouge) *Advocate*, June 21, 1993, p. 3E.

40. *Ibid.*

41. For a summary of the Fox television network's policies on children's TV commercials, see Helen Boehm, "Monday Memo," *Broadcasting*, October 1, 1990, p. 17.

42. See *Hazelwood School District v. Kuhlmeier*.

43. Betsy Wagner, "Our Class Is Brought to You Today by . . . ," *U.S. News & World Report*, April 24, 1995, p. 63.

44. The idea for this case was derived from a column by TV critic Faye Zuckerman distributed nationally in November 1993. E.g., see "NBC Movie Sends Wrong Message to Troubled Teens."

45. Jane D. Brown and Kenneth Campbell, "Race and Gender in Music Videos: The Same Beat but a Different Drummer," *Journal of Communication*, 36, Winter 1986, p. 94; citing *MTV Networks, Inc.*, "MTV Fact Sheet," Press Release, New York, 1984.

46. See "MTV Faces a Mid-Life Crisis," *Time*, June 29, 1987, p. 67.

47. "MTV's Message," *Newsweek*, December 30, 1985, p. 55.

48. Richard L. Baxter, Cynthia De Riemer, Ann Landini, Larry Leslie, and Michael W. Singletary, "A Content Analysis of Music Videos," *Journal of Broadcasting and Electronic Media*, 29, Summer 1985, pp. 333–340.

49. "MTV's Message," pp. 54–55.

50. Se-Wen Sun and James Lull, "The Adolescent Audience for Music Videos and Why They Watch," *Journal of Communication*, 36, Winter 1986, pp. 115–125.

14

The Global Community and Shared Ethical Values

American media practitioners are not just citizens of their native land; they are also citizens of the world community. With the diversity of cultural norms, mores, and customs that inhabit our planet, it might seem paradoxical and somewhat pretentious to describe ourselves as a "community." But at a very basic level we share certain human qualities and moral inclinations, regardless of whether we reside in Russia, India, Argentina, or the United States. Rushworth Kidder, a former correspondent and the president of the Institute for Global Ethics, refers to these common ethical traits as "shared values."[1] Regardless of the specific code to which we pledge allegiance, we are all moral agents who must make certain ethical judgments that will either enhance or diminish the virtuous quality of our own culture.

So far in this text, we have examined a variety of ethical issues from an American perspective, and the philosophical foundations outlined in Chapter 3 are based on the great ideas of Western civilization. This approach is certainly reasonable since most readers of this text are Americans and are a product of the moral environment that currently exists within this country. But some of you may become players in the global arena, perhaps as foreign correspondents or practitioners of international public relations. And many of you will experience culture shock in your first encounter with the unfamiliar foreign customs and behavioral norms. When such traditions involve ethical concerns, your own moral imaginations will be challenged. Sometimes, of course, you can justify adhering to local custom without significantly compromising your own ethical standards. At other times, however, you may have to decide whether to invoke your own profession's ideal of moral virtue or simply to "go with the flow," ethically speaking, and capitulate to the demands of your host country.

The good news is that, with the proliferation of all forms of media practice around the world, including advertising and public relations, there is a discernible interest in the "professionalization" of the various media activities. For example, the number of cultural exchanges among media practitioners and media educators has increased dramatically in the past twenty years. Nations where university training for media professionals was virtually nonexistent until recently have turned to the West in setting up degree-granting programs in media studies. And many of these programs and cultural exchanges have included ethics as a discrete field of study.

These cooperative ventures among nations with diverse cultures and political systems suggest that there is keen interest in at least exchanging views on the professional standards that should be applicable to practitioners in such diverse fields as journalism, advertising, public relations, and even mass entertainment. A moral optimist might even suggest that such shared information could eventually result in some agreement on shared values for media practitioners across cultures. The fact is that the information society of the twenty-first century is a vastly different place from its historical predecessors. The psychological and geographic distances that have divided the world's cultures since the beginning of time are becoming obsolete under the relentless pressures of economic and political interdependence and the communications technological revolution. Whether this fortuitous trend portends an increasingly virtuous global environment will depend on how we respond to this question: Are there universal moral values that the world community might agree on as standards of international behavior, or are cultural diversities too great to reach any kind of common ground in this area?

On the one side are the proponents of cultural relativism, who contend that ethical judgments are culturally determined and that the notion of any kind of universal standards or moral code is a myth. On the other hand, there are those who believe passionately that our very survival depends on discovering at least some shared values and that ample evidence suggests that such universal ethical norms currently exist. This debate has serious implications for media practitioners in all nations since the mass communication process both captures the essence of a culture's moral value system and influences its maturation. Thus, they must take the lead in either searching for ethical common ground with other societies or rejecting their overtures and resisting the moral progress that often results from a cross-cultural exchange of ideas.

THE MEDIA AND CULTURAL RELATIVISM

The Nature of Cultural Moral Relativism

The defining principle of moral relativism, as it relates to the practices of different cultures, is that there can be no agreed-on standards of right or wrong. The notion of moral relativism based on the distinct characteristics of various cultures is of ancient vintage. In commenting on the diversity of moral codes among various cultures, for example, the Greek historian Herodotus writes:

> For if anyone, no matter who, were given the opportunity of choosing from amongst all the nations of the world the set of beliefs which he thought best, he would inevitably, after careful consideration of their relative merits, choose that of his own country. Everyone without exception believes his own native customs, and the religion he was brought up in, to be the best.[2]

Reflected in this observation is a certain amount of moral conceit, perhaps even arrogance, of the superiority of one's own cultural norms. American media practitioners undoubtedly believe that their system, for all of its flaws, is superior to all others. Their foreign counterparts might even find common ground with the Americans in acknowledging the virtual absence of governmental restraint on the media in the United States, but they would be unlikely to concede its moral and ethical superiority. Media practitioners in the Middle East and some Asian societies might point to the proliferation of indecent, sensational, and seemingly trivial material as an inescapable sign of moral decadence. On the other hand, the European media, which sometimes include overt nudity in their advertising, might accuse American advertisers of moral prudery for their aversion to the use of such content. Similarly, journalists in Western Europe, where news stories often include a healthy dose of analysis and opinion, might admonish the more fact-oriented American reporters for their failure to provide meaningful context for their readers.

The world is a virtual smorgasbord of cultural norms, a reality that appears to provide ample validation for the moral relativist position. Proponents of cultural relativism begin with the principle that different cultures have different moral codes. The notion of universal truth in ethics, the relativists declare confidently, is a myth. Ethical standards are neither correct nor incorrect because there is no independent (i.e., universally recognized) standard for evaluating the ethical "quality" of a society's standards of behavior. Our own culture's standards are not superior to others, and it is arrogant for us to try to judge the conduct of other peoples. Therefore, we should adopt an attitude of tolerance toward the practices of other cultures.[3] Thus, according to this view, American journalists should not criticize Russian reporters for their eagerness to pay for information, although so-called "checkbook journalism" is still considered unethical among the mainstream American media. Likewise, American PR practitioners representing their companies abroad should not condemn foreign officials for demanding financial incentives (bribes) as a cost of doing business, although such practices are illegal under American law.

In all fairness, cultural relativism has served as a buffer against the forces of moral dogmatism in which some societies, particularly those based on religious fundamentalism, have attempted to impose their moral views on others. In other words, one consequence is tolerance of cultural diversity, a seemingly worthwhile objective. And even opponents of moral relativism would not favor an imperialistic approach to cross-cultural ethical communication. Thus, we must pose this question: Can the world have cultural diversity and also a system of shared values? If so, then we must begin a search for strategies that can best accommodate the demands of both. In so doing, we must first acknowledge the deficiencies of moral relativism and then ask ourselves whether there are any universal ethical tendencies that are candidates for a system of shared values.

The Negative Consequences of Moral Relativism

Because of its emphasis on tolerance, moral relativism on an international scale does have some appeal. It would appear to move us away from our ethnocentricity and enhance our respect for the values and norms of other societies. Of course, carried to the extreme American media practitioners could just leave their own moral baggage at home and simply accommodate themselves to the ethical standards of their host country. This "When in Rome, do as the Romans do" philosophy might be a worthy traveling companion in the realm of habits and customs, but as a moral beacon it leaves something to be desired. While ethical standards do vary significantly among cultures, several troublesome consequences are possible of blindly accepting culturally based moral relativism and summarily repudiating the notion of universal moral standards.[4]

First, *relativism rejects the notion of moral superiority based on objective criteria*. Thus, a culture should be judged only according to its own definition of good and evil. However, if carried to its logical conclusion, then genocide might be justified if it does not offend the moral standards of the nation engaged in the practice. Likewise, under moral relativism American media practitioners should refrain from criticizing the practices of foreign cultures since their own ideas of moral virtue have no standing outside the United States. American journalists, for example, should not condemn the Chilean media for their timidity in discussing controversial issues, such as abortion, or in assuming an aggressive posture in covering governmental affairs.

But while American media practitioners must often, for political reasons, remain silent when confronted with such abuses, they should not abandon their efforts to set an example for their counterparts in their host country. For example, the refusal of American journalists to pay interviewees in Russia sends a clear signal to government officials and Russian journalists alike that such practices are inimical to journalistic virtue, at least from an American perspective. While such a stance may not immediately be applauded or even understood by their foreign hosts, it at least exposes them to the standards adhered to by ethical journalists in the United States. This within itself might be educational with the increasing number of cultural exchanges between these two nations.

Second, *cultural relativism not only precludes us from criticizing the practices of other societies; it also inhibits criticism of our own*.[5] In other words, if notions of right and wrong are relative among cultures, this must be true of our own culture. If moral values such as truth, fairness, justice, and respect for persons mean anything, then they must be considered fundamental and applied universally. Otherwise, relativism can easily become the dominant philosophy in which various subgroups within a culture make a claim for special exemption from the ethical norms of the society at large.

Third, *cultural relativism is antithetical to the idea of moral progress*.[6] Cultural relativism presupposes an absence of external criticism, and without criticism there can be no reevaluation of values. Societies are most progressive when they exchange ideas and learn from each other. A case in point is the keen interest among Russian and former Eastern Bloc journalists, as they struggle to implement a free-press system, in the ethical standards adhered to by American journalists. They are well aware that an American-style system cannot be simply transplanted in their own cultures, but as privately owned media proliferate in this region, the study of ethics has assumed a prominent role among their concerns.

THE CASE FOR UNIVERSAL VALUES

The question of whether there are indeed universal values eludes empirical confirmation. It is not possible to survey the world's population or even most of its opinion leaders to ascertain their views on or commitment to a set of shared values. In making the case for a system of universal values, two questions must be addressed: (1) Is there a *need* for a set of universal ethical precepts, and (2) are there such common values that diverse cultures might agree on?

The Need for Universal Values

As residents in the global community, all cultures have a stake in the moral worth of the world's habitat. The transmigration of peoples and the inescapable interdependence of diverse populations result in a form of ethical spillover as cross-cultural interaction and assimilation continue unabated. Communicators, regardless of whether they are professional mass communicators or individuals who disseminate their messages via the Internet, are an indispensable ingredient in this process. They are at the vortex of the information flow within and across cultures and are in a position to influence the ethical quality of this intelligence, both the significant and the trivial.

Kidder has identified three trends that will distinguish our future significantly from our past. These trends are particularly relevant to the issue of whether there is a need for shared values in an increasingly shrinking global environment. They also have important implications for media practitioners, who should be key players in the identification and ratification of any system of universal values. Kidder identifies these trends as worldshrink, technobulge, and consensus building.[7]

Worldshrink is another formulation for global interdependence. The convergence of pressures associated with population, economics, and communication are rapidly transforming the world into one community in which the problems of one society have increasingly become the concern of others. The global media quickly disseminate stories and pictures (often live) of natural disasters, wars and political upheavals to audiences thousands of miles away. Thus, a Russian invasion of one of its former provinces in which innocent civilians are massacred rapidly becomes a concern of the international community. Drought and starvation in Ethiopia, the visual images of which are fed almost daily into millions of culturally diverse homes, stimulate the humanitarian tendencies in all of us.

If the natural consequence of *worldshrink* is indeed a greater feeling of community, then such a community cannot exist without a shared ethic. As Kidder has observed, if this world community is to survive then the search for a set of universal values is a cultural imperative:

> Without a common set of values, communities are no more than unstable collections of individuals coexisting uneasily within common boundaries. It may not be too much to say, then, that our very survival as a global community will depend on our shared ethic. It will depend, in other words, on our willingness to identify and come together around a core of common values that allows us to interact successfully. Without that common ground, we risk being a community only in name, experiencing an ever-increasing intensity of interaction, but lacking the agreement on central values that makes coexistence possible.[8]

Media practitioners, because they are in a unique position to take the pulse of their own cultures and to share their experiences with their professional colleagues abroad, should be conspicuous among the moral gatekeepers in identifying such shared values. And the proliferation of international conferences and cultural exchanges among global journalists, public relations professionals, and media educators is evidence that this process is well under way.

Technobulge—the rapid expansion of technology—has altered the ethical dimensions of human interaction, in both quantity and quality. Ethical concerns no longer conform to natural boundaries as the information superhighway penetrates into every corner of our global sphere. The fear of cultural imperialism, which has always been problematic, has been exacerbated by the ability for both mass communicators and individuals to communicate directly with foreign audiences. Content, such as nudity and violence, that some societies consider morally offensive is now readily available both on the Internet and through direct satellite broadcast. The threat of such culture wars, however, should be viewed as a mandate to find common ground on some shared values before technology becomes the master rather than the servant of international ethical discourse.

The third trend, according to Kidder, that justifies the search for global moral common ground is the need for *consensus building.* The world, as never before, is confronted with difficulties that need problem solving on an international scale. Environmental problems, overpopulation, and continuing human rights abuses are representative of the moral challenges that confront the inhabitants of the global community. And global problem solving requires a shared set of values.[9] Again, the media have a pivotal role in building constituencies both domestically and internationally because they serve as an important transmission belt for our cultural heritage. They can contribute immeasurably to the sense of community because of the shared experiences of their audiences. However, consensus building is more complicated in free societies than authoritarian ones, and both journalists and those who provide information, such as PR practitioners, must have an ethical commitment to truth and accuracy in order to forge a bond of trust with their audiences.

In Search of Universal Values

Are there universal values to which media practitioners in all countries might aspire? This is a tricky topic, since the diversity of cultural practices would appear to make the identification of shared norms implausible. Nevertheless, as noted in this insightful observation in the *Journal of Mass Media Ethics*, the study of ethics itself can provide common ground for the discovery of universal values:

> The question of whether ethics is an inherent aspect of human communication seems by now almost obsolete. How could we deny that values and, thus, questions of ethics, are essential to the phenomena of human communication, which is a fundamental element in social relations? Ethics should indeed be understood as a *pervasive* [italics added] aspect of communication.[10]

This is not to suggest that the goal should be to construct a *written* international code of ethics, since the experience with such codes in our own country is not promising. But even among the variety of customs practiced in the global community, there do appear to be, based on the literature of international communications ethics, some universal ethical concerns shared by media practitioners. While the interpretations of these values might vary, an element of commonality about them exists that could provide the foundation for a system of universal standards.

First, a worldwide interest prevails in the "quest for *truth*," which includes such familiar journalistic values as *objectivity* and *accuracy*.[11] While governments may vary in terms of their regulation of the media and the amount of disinformation disseminated to the citizenry, audiences share a common bond in their desire for truthful, accurate information. Given a choice between truth and falsehood, they will choose the former. In other words, media audiences "value" truth, even while they are skeptical of the quality of information provided by their own media. Similarly, journalists and editors, regardless of their cultural heritage, expect truthful information from their public relations sources. In fact, it is hard to conceive of a journalist who would value falsehood over truth.

Second, there appears to be an international concern for *responsibility* among public communicators. While the emphases may vary by region, the notion of responsibility generally manifests itself in such constructs as professionalism, accountability, justice, equality, and loyalty to certain constituencies such as government, the public, and peers. A concern is also expressed for motivational issues, such as conflicts of interest and self-promotion, and adherence to social mores, with secrecy, privacy, and protection of sources being the most prominent.[12]

At this juncture in our search for universal ethical values, we must be cautious. Some of these concerns are more prevalent in some societies than others, and their appeal as moral norms are certainly culturally based. In some countries, for example, it is not uncommon for journalists also to hold public office. In others, including the United States, this dual role would be considered a conflict of interest. Such disparate views, of course, often reflect a disagreement about the roles of media practitioners as much as the ethical standards that should govern their behavior.

The third area of concern is what might be referred to as the "call for *free expression*."[13] Obviously, the world's media systems vary significantly in terms of their freedom and independence from government control. Thus, it might appear strange indeed to sanctify *free expression* as a candidate for universal moral esteem. Nevertheless, a lot of debate has been heard in various international forums on such issues as the free flow of information, censorship, media independence, and government regulation of the media. And with the emergence of the Internet and other computer-generated forms of transnational communication, the interest in the free flow of information has assumed new dimensions.

It is true that "freedom" has many different meanings and is often culturally based. However, despite these surface differences, which often are reflected in media codes or national constitutions, media scholar Thomas Cooper argues that the call for free expression is inherently a human trait, although there is still disagreement over who should control the channels of communication:

> "[T]he call for free expression" may in fact be indigenous to human beings, and thus focuses upon the concern that organisms (whether individuals, institutions, governments, classes, or minorities, and the media they use) should not be muzzled. However, there is not widespread agreement about whose voices should be heard, to what extent, and through which media.[14]

In addition to discussions within the literature on international communications and spirited debates at various conferences attended by government officials, scholars, and media practitioners, further evidence indicates that the values of *truth*, *responsibility*, and *free expression* have some universal salience. The flow of information, for example, has been a concern of the United Nations from its inception.[15] Article 19 of the Universal Declaration of Human Rights states, "Everybody has the right to freedom of opinion and expression; this right includes freedom to hold opinions without interference, and to seek, receive and impart information and ideas through any media and regardless of frontiers." Since the adoption of this noble document in 1948, the United Nations Educational, Scientific, and Cultural Organization (UNESCO) has sponsored numerous conferences dealing with the issue of

information flow and at its biennial meetings has adopted many resolutions with the objective of raising the levels of information flow in all parts of the world.[16]

However, the debate within UNESCO has revealed a serious breach between Third World countries and the Western nations. The developing nations are critical of the Western news media for reporting only negative events in the Third World, such as terrorism, famine, and political upheavals. They attribute this negative news flow to its marketability based on audience appeal. In response, the Third World nations have proposed a New World Information and Communication Order (NWICO) that would grant all nations the right to regulate access to information and license foreign journalists covering events in these regions. The NWICO would also give each country the right to reply to false news reports. The goal, in the view of the developing nations, is to create a more balanced two-way flow of information. Not surprisingly, the Western nations have objected to this proposal on the grounds that it would impede access to information by foreign journalists and the right to report on it without government interference.[17] No substantive progress was made on this issue, although some new news agencies and national media enterprises were initiated to try to balance the one-way flow of information into the developing nations.

When viewed from an international political perspective, this would appear to be a serious intellectual breach (and it is!) and one that would not bode well for consensus on freedom of information. But one could argue, too, that this dispute is also about the "mechanism" for achieving *fairness*, *balance*, and *quality of information flow* (values embraced also by Western journalists) rather than about the values themselves.

The work of various international and regional organizations of working journalists, often under UNESCO's sponsorship, has also resulted in the codification of certain ethical principles. These codes and domestic media codes around the world, despite varying expressions and interpretations, reflect an unusual amount of agreement on such concepts as truth, responsibility, and freedom.[18] For example, the International Principles of Professional Ethics in Journalism, issued in 1983 after meetings in Prague and Paris of working journalists, states that "[p]eople and individuals have the right to acquire an objective picture of reality by means of accurate and comprehensive information as well as to express themselves freely through the various media of culture and communication." The code also declares that the "journalist's social responsibility requires that he or she will act under all circumstances in conformity with a personal ethical consciousness."

Such concerns are also reflected in the constitutions of many nations, although when examining codes and constitutions, one must be cautious to consider the cultural contexts of the articulated values. Indeed, while there may be agreement on such values as truth, responsibility, and free expression, these concepts are interpreted differently when mediated through cultural biases. In some societies, for example, the media are considered responsible when they serve as watchdogs and adversaries on government. In others, responsibility is a positive force tied to nation building and supporting government and nongovernmental institutions. Nevertheless, even agreement at a very general level on universal values can provide common ground for developing a more virtuous environment for the practice of media ethics across cultures.

Admittedly, cultural diversity is still a barrier to recognition of these values as truly universal, except in a general, abstract fashion. However, one recent trend has emerged that, as far as media practitioners are concerned, might lead us inevitably toward more common ground on shared values. This trend is known as *the democratic impulse*.

The Democratic Impulse and Shared Media Values

In August 1989 in Poland, for the first time in more than forty years, a communist party agreed, without civil war or foreign invasion, to accept a minority role in a government headed by non-Communists.[19] This momentous event was symbolic of a movement that had been under way for much of the decade in such diverse parts of the world as Latin America, Asia, and the Philippines—a movement that virtually overnight transformed the political landscape of Eastern Europe and the former Soviet Union. French philosopher Jean-Francois Revel refers to this political reformation as *the democratic impulse*.

It would be premature to predict democracy's victory as the political system of choice for all of the inhabitants of the global community, as reflected in this stark reminder from media scholar John Hamilton and George Krimsky, former director of the Center For Foreign Journalists:

> The fall of communism justifies hope for democracy, but by itself the fall of the Iron Curtain does not mean the rise of a more independent press system. The more important question is, What kind of social, economic and cultural system exists in the wake of its departure? All of these factors are crucial in determining how a new press system will develop in these countries.[20]

And the reality is that, despite the proliferation of advertiser-supported newspapers in the former communist nations, excessively high taxes, the cost of newsprint, and reliance on government-controlled printing facilities still threaten their independence and even their existence.

Nevertheless, while in many countries democracy is still struggling for survival against the resistant forces of authoritarianism, the influence of democratic values on an international scale has never been greater. Of course, democracy itself is a diverse political ideology, and its practice varies significantly from culture to culture. Thus, while democracy will not erase all vestiges of cultural differences (indeed, this would probably be undesirable), it provides the best hope of finding at least some common ground among media practitioners on a global basis. Why? Because all democracies share certain values, such as freely elected political representatives and open debate with tolerance for unpopular opinions. In addition, a system of mass communication is indispensable to the cultivation of the democratic impulse as a means of providing the vital information that is essential to intelligent decision making. And the free flow of information, public discourse, and tolerance for unpopular ideas are most likely to occur in a media system free from government restraint.

This is not to suggest that there is complete accord even among established democracies on a common set of values to guide media practitioners. For example, reporters and editors in Western Europe are often chastised by their peers in the United States for their lack of objectivity in practicing "opinion-oriented" journalism as opposed to the "fact-based" journalism that is so prevalent in this country. Nevertheless, there is still substantial agreement on such fundamental values as press independence, media credibility, and the free flow of information.

While an independent press is vital to the full flowering of democracy, there is significant disagreement, even within the United States, over what role the media should play in the democratic process. For example, in this country some people believe that the press should stand in an adversarial role to government. Some view the press as the watchdog of government, a fiduciary of the public in holding government officials accountable for their deeds. Still others believe the media should play a constructive role in democratic nation building, with an emphasis on social responsibility rather than unbridled freedom. However, regardless of what role(s) the media are assigned within the

democratic framework, one characteristic is shared by all of them: the need for the free flow of accurate and truthful information.

Since democracy itself is predicated on certain fundamental values, media practitioners in newly emerging democracies over time appear to share some of the same concerns as their counterparts in well-entrenched democratic systems, such as the United States. The demise of communism in Eastern Europe and the former Soviet Union, for example, has precipitated a keen interest by journalists in those nations in the intricacies of how a free press functions, not only in a structural sense (newsroom management, advertising, circulation, etc.) but also from an ethical perspective. This region of the world has witnessed an unprecedented invasion by American journalists and journalism educators in an effort to share ideas with reporters and editors and even to assist them in setting up media education programs in their own countries. Of course, an American-style press system cannot be imposed on cultures with no recent history of individual liberties or experience with the capitalistic enterprise. Any such attempts at cultural imperialism are doomed to failure. After all, the democratic experiment is still under way in this country. It would be naive to assume that former communist nations will accomplish overnight what it has taken the United States more than two hundred years to nurture. But the fact that they are fascinated by the democratic impulse and its symbiotic relationship with a marketplace economy suggests that there is the potential for the development of shared values, including ethical values.

For example, those American journalists and educators who have traveled to Eastern Europe and Russia on training missions have discovered a keen interest in media ethics that was unheard of under communism, where the parameters of journalistic behavior were essentially a product of the legal controls of the totalitarian system. Surprisingly, in these emerging democracies the ethical concerns are not unlike those confronted daily in the United States: protection of news sources, conflicts of interest, checkbook journalism, independence from government control, and the influence of advertisers on the editorial product. We see similar patterns in other newly minted democratic systems, such as those in Latin America.

Of course, such ethically questionable practices (from an American perspective) as bribery, payment of news sources, subservience to special interests, and publishers and editors who also hold political office are still endemic in many of these emerging democracies, but the fact that they are turning increasingly to the West for moral guidance is a cause for optimism in the cultivation of shared ethical values. Although the specific concerns might vary from culture to culture, a common thread that emerges from dialogues with journalists in these cultures relates to media credibility. As a fundamental value, *credibility* can serve as a stimulus for discovering other shared values that unify media practitioners across cultures.

The democratic enterprise is more than just a political ideology fueled by an independent press and the free flow of information. Economic development and the accumulation of wealth under a capitalistic system are most likely under democratic liberalism. One salutary effect of a capitalistic system, in addition to economic development, is the diffusion of power among governmental and commercial institutions, which must all compete to develop constituencies in the competition of the marketplace. To accommodate these needs, we see the emergence of public relations practitioners representing a variety of commercial and noncommercial institutions in many of these emerging democracies. Of course, as compared to the United States, where public relations is most highly developed, the practice in many of these societies is fairly primitive. It would be premature to predict to what extent the standards adhered to by ethical PR practitioners in America will be attractive to

their foreign counterparts. But the demands of a democratic system for truthful and accurate information from credible sources justifies a certain degree of optimism that the practice of public relations can also achieve a set of shared values on an international scale.

A free marketplace also makes possible an independent press supported by advertising revenues rather than government subsidies. Advertising, in turn, creates consumer demand for products, the consumption of which helps sustain the vitality of the marketplace. Thus, clearly a symbiotic relationship exists among the requirements of political democracy, a marketplace economy, and an independent media system.

In summary, the democratic revival in the former communist nations and elsewhere could provide the occasion for media practitioners to reach some common ground on certain fundamental moral values, although there will always be cultural differences on specific issues. However, this situation should not be regarded as an opportunity just to export American ethical standards. There is a temptation in this direction considering the ubiquitous presence of American media practitioners abroad. But a frank exchange of views—an international Socratic dialogue, if you will—is more likely, in the long run, to produce a system of shared values that will serve as guideposts for all ethical media practitioners in the global community.

AMERICAN MEDIA PRACTITIONERS ABROAD

American media practitioners working abroad are ambassadors. They have a pervasive influence in the global community, and in that respect, they are unofficial instruments of foreign policy. The conduct of our media representatives, as well as the content produced by them, conveys a strong message to their foreign hosts concerning their moral values and beliefs and those of their native land. The ethical dilemmas confronting American practitioners doing business in foreign lands represent the four kinds of media-related activities discussed throughout this text: journalism, public relations, advertising, and entertainment.

Journalism

American journalists are stationed in virtually every corner of the globe and not only provide daily intelligence of world events to their native audiences but also communicate American values and ideas to foreign audiences and governments. But in their news-gathering activities, they encounter a myriad of local customs and traditions, some of which may involve simply matters of decorum and taste but others of which might pose a challenge to their moral imagination.

American reporters will also confront different attitudes toward the practice of journalism itself among foreign journalists, many of whom may be important sources of information. For example, American journalists enter their profession through a variety of avenues, none of which involve licensing or any formal requirement for a degree from an accredited university. Italian journalists, on the other hand, are licensed after they negotiate a national examination that attests to their journalistic skills. German journalists are not licensed, but they are undoubtedly among the best educated in the world. It is not uncommon, for example, for those writing for the most respected publications to hold Ph.D.'s in the disciplines about which they write. And many German journalists are required to sign a pledge to their employer of honesty in reporting. In Japan, journalists are well educated, too, but obtaining a position in the media is very competitive. Japanese reporters, unlike their counterparts in the United States and Western Europe, have no duty to keep the public informed. In fact, the

collaboration among industry, government, and the news media would startle most American reporters who operate within an adversarial environment.[21]

These differences among cultures can strain the professional kinship that should exist, but clearly domestic norms determine the roles that journalists play within their societies. However, these roles also influence the expectations of foreign news sources and institutions, both governmental and nongovernmental, thereby placing greater pressure on American journalists to conform to local tradition. So, what are ethical American journalists to do when confronted with situations that challenge their own ethical values?

A good point of departure is to reject any notion of casually abandoning one's own ethical standards just because of local custom. To do so raises questions as to the commitment of the moral agent to sound ethical conduct in the first place. However, according to one morally defensible position, even in our society journalists are sometimes justified for deviating from accepted practice for some higher purpose. When projected into the international arena, Professor John Merrill has constructed the argument as follows:

> I am convinced that ethical communicators must be flexible; therefore they must consider situations and contexts. But they should, I think, have some basic rules or principles of ethics which they are dedicated to and from which they deviate only after much deliberation. Maybe they could be dedicated to some such principle as this: Have some overriding universal principles to which you are dedicated, but be willing to deviate from these when you think you can, by such deviation, reach a higher good.
>
> Many persons will say that such a journalist would be compromising basic ethical principles by rationally deviating from them. There is no doubt but that he does compromise his principles, but in the name of, and for the sake of, *a higher ethics.* In other words, his motives

—his will—is good, and even Kant would approve of that. Why? Because it shows a good will or indicates ethical motivation. It is a sound ethical stance for the international journalist who treasures loyalty or commitment and at the same time desires a flexibility of action based on reason.[22]

Thus, we see reflected in Merrill's observation a refrain that has guided much of the discussion in the preceding chapters. Journalists should recognize a set of fundamental principles (such as to avoid deceptive news-gathering practices or never to break a promise to a news source) and should deviate from them only to serve some higher principle or purpose (i.e., there must be a morally defensible reason for doing so). This sage advice can serve American journalists not only in their native land but in the international sphere as well.

Public Relations and Advertising

Journalists, of course, are not the only media practitioners who serve as American ambassadors. With the increase in tourism and international communication since World War II and the lowering of trade barriers in the 1980s, the practice of public relations has also assumed a position of prominence within the global community. The heightened demand for communicators who can represent their clients successfully in cities distant from New York, Chicago, and Los Angeles has enriched PR firms, both large and small. In fact, the fifteen largest public relations organizations now generate more than 40 percent of their fees outside the United States.[23]

Although advertising is still not permitted in some countries, particularly through the electronic media, the trend internationally is toward media systems supported, at least in part, through advertising. International acquisitions and mergers of giant PR and advertising firms have precipitated a new age of global marketing,

fueled by an impressive array of communications technologies.[24] In the 1990s, almost one-third of U.S. corporate profits are generated through international business.[25] American enterprises such as Coca-Cola, Kodak, Nabisco, IBM, and McDonald's are among those who are prominent players in the global marketing arena.

International public relations may be defined as "the planned and organized effort of a company, institution, or government to establish mutually beneficial relations with the publics of other nations."[26] Although its origins are generally regarded as a product of the American economic system, public relations practitioners are now a common feature on the cultural landscape of many nations. In fact, American PR principles and strategies have been adopted on an international scale, although the specifics of such techniques must still conform to domestic norms.

American PR practitioners operating abroad, of course, encounter a multitude of local customs, laws, and mores. Practitioners who expect to transplant their own standards to a foreign culture are likely to be disappointed. However, just because local ethical standards are different does not necessarily mean that they are right or wrong. American practitioners abroad must quickly develop an acute sense of cultural sensitivity to understand the context within which ethical issues arise before pronouncing judgment on them. Nevertheless, sometimes PR professionals representing U.S. interests must draw an ethical line in the sand and stand on principle.

For example, gift giving, junkets, and even outright bribery are traditional among some foreign governments and their PR and lobbying representatives. Such practices, however, are antiethical to sound PR practice from an American perspective. Unfortunately, the American corporate enterprises can hardly claim the moral high road in their own dealings with foreign governments. In the competition of the international marketplace, some have willingly and greedily become ethical relativists in their determination to gain concessions in foreign markets. In fact, gift giving reached such troublesome proportions in the 1970s that Congress in 1977 enacted the Foreign Corrupt Practices Act that forbids corporations from offering major gifts or bribes to foreign business contacts or government officials.

Thus, the point of departure for PR practitioners overseas is to make sure they are in compliance with American law. This is a necessary but insufficient condition for the ethical practice of public relations in foreign cultures. After all, corruption comes in many guises, some of which may not be strictly illegal but which may reflect unfavorably on those who engage in it. For example, in some countries it is not unusual for PR practitioners to pay journalists to have favorable stories for clients placed in publications. But participation in such activities does have its price, as noted by Barbara Burns, a PR consultant and a member of the board of directors of the International Public Relations Association: "But everyone knows which publications these are—so placement is not so valuable to the client. And if you start paying off, it undermines your credibility, and finally your business."[27]

In addition, if American PR practitioners simply acquiesce to such practices as official corruption and the payment of foreign journalists to publish their stories, then governments and other institutions have no incentive to clean up their act. On the other hand, if they refuse to condone such behavior, then their own moral scruples might, in time, have a subtle influence in altering the ethical climate for the practice of public relations in foreign cultures. And with the current attractiveness of American PR techniques on a global scale, this is not an unrealistic expectation.

As a strategy for improving the ethical environment of the global market, PR Professor Dean Kruckeberg has also recommended an international code of ethics for PR professionals. Again, while the practicality or even the wisdom of international codes of ethics for media

practitioners might be questioned, the underlying principles of honesty, integrity, and respect have already been incorporated into a code adopted in 1965 by the International Public Relations Association and followed by PR professionals in more than seventy countries.[28] Of course, as Kruckeberg has acknowledged, a code of ethics by itself is insufficient, but it would provide another mechanism for influencing the policies and actions of transnational corporations.[29]

Advertising, of course, is the energizing force of free-market economies, and as capitalism, in its variety of manifestations, takes roots in heretofore tightly controlled economies, opportunities have abounded for mass marketers and advertising practitioners. International ad agencies, many of them American based, have set up shop in foreign cultures to service both American corporations that sell their products abroad, as well as local industries that compete aggressively in the commercial marketplace. McCann-Erickson, Ogilvy and Mather, and Young & Rubicam are typical of those agencies that have exported their creative energies into foreign markets.

The opportunities that have arisen in Russia and Eastern and Central Europe since the demise of communism have not been lost on American corporations and the ad agencies that construct their messages targeted to domestic audiences. Patience is a virtue as each nation in this region struggles to replace its state-controlled enterprises with those privately owned and operated. Advertising is playing an increasingly important role as privately owned newspapers and magazines proliferate.

Of course, each nation has been confronted with its own problems. In Russia and Hungary, for example, advertising has been instrumental in ensuring some measure of media financial independence, but at the same time advertising in Poland virtually stopped as the nation was confronted with a staggering unemployment rate because of their rapid transition into a market economy. During this period in the early 1990s, the few ad agencies that existed either went bankrupt or made draconian cutbacks in their staffs and services.[30]

Even in those nations where capitalism is still not the dominant form of economic philosophy, advertising is assuming an increasing (though cautious) position of prominence. The People's Republic of China is a classic example. The Chinese have recently enacted a law to regulate domestic ads, a testament perhaps to the government's recognition of the potential cultural influence of such content.

Needless to say, American advertisers operating abroad should not suddenly abandon their ethical standards just because they are directing their messages to foreign audiences. However, advertising is perhaps the most market-driven form of content, and acceptable practices vary among cultures. The ethical debates surrounding advertising in the United States tend to cluster around such concerns as falsehood and deception, puffery, promotion of superficial and even undesirable cultural values, offensive content, stereotyping, and targeting vulnerable audiences, such as children. When filtered through a myriad of languages, customs, cultural taboos, and even governmental concerns, these problems are exacerbated. Many developing countries, for example, resent Western-style advertising because it creates demands that cannot be met by the local economy, promotes materialistic values, and even offends local customs. In traditional cultures, such as Saudi Arabia and China, nudity is a taboo, whereas in Western Europe it is a common feature of commercial content. In some countries children cannot be targeted by advertisers. In the United States, on the other hand, advertising directed at children is still acceptable, although the practice is becoming increasingly controversial.

Before the advent of satellite communications, governments served as the primary gatekeepers for the introduction of foreign content into their cultures. Satellite communication, particularly such technological developments as direct broadcast satellites and the Internet,

has made governments increasingly irrelevant in the process. From a market perspective and with a world community increasingly committed to the free flow of information across national boundaries, there is nothing inherently unethical in appealing directly to foreign audiences. Regardless of culture, from an ethical perspective consumers are rational decision makers and are likely to reject messages that are not culturally sensitive. However, that point does not absolve advertisers of the responsibility to respect the dignity of foreign consumers as autonomous individuals. After all, American corporations and the ad agencies that represent them are "guests" in their host countries.

Since advertising is market driven and advertising appeals are culturally based, it might be tempting to retreat to a relativist position on the question of advertising to foreign audiences. Indeed, some practices that are acceptable in the United States would send moral shock waves if implemented in some foreign markets (and vice versa). But even here most would probably agree that "respect" for the audience and cultural norms is a universal standard that should guide American advertising agencies as they prepare their clients' campaigns for introduction into foreign markets. And certain kinds of content, such as false advertising and exaggerated product claims, should be universally condemned since it is unlikely that such practices would be applauded by consumers and autonomous moral agents in any culture.

Entertainment and Media Imperialism

In the entertainment field, no ethical problem has been debated more vociferously in the international community than that of *media imperialism*. Media imperialism occurs when one country's mass media dominate another country's national culture.[31] And no nation's entertainment output, particularly in TV programming and films, has been as dominant as that of the United States. In the late 1950s, Hollywood began using its existing film distribution system to syndicate TV programs to foreign markets, a move that coincided with the development of television systems around the world that were in the market for cheap products to fill the airtime. Since that time, the American TV syndication business has turned into a multibillion-dollar industry overseas, with some of the most popular American TV series and films attracting audiences worldwide. Such cultural exports are market driven, revealing an unusual degree of shared tastes in entertainment.

Many TV series are more profitable overseas than in the United States, and some producers shape their programs to maximize their profits in foreign markets.[32] In response to this invasion of American mass entertainment, many countries have imposed quotas, thereby ensuring that their own domestically produced programs and films remain the dominant feature on their population's artistic menu. For example, in 1989 the European Economic Community decided to require member nations to carry at least 50 percent of TV programming produced within Europe. Because of the adverse impact on American TV programming sold to Europe, Hollywood and U.S. government officials protested, but to no avail.[33]

American and British popular music is experiencing the same degree of popularity, and many of the same artists can be found on the radio and in music stores around the globe. In Russia, for example, where Western music was deemed morally decadent, American rock and pop music has enjoyed a renaissance in night clubs and among street musicians.

This exportation of American values, through its popular mass entertainment, is not universally applauded. Some complaints involve competition with domestic entertainment industries. However, from an ethical perspective, the globalization of American entertainment has focused more on the messages that are deemed offensive to foreign audiences, some of which remain controversial in this country: violence, sex, drugs, gender roles, and racial images and stereotypes that clash with local mores. In many cases, the concerns are similar to those expressed in the United States—that such content will adversely affect the nation's youth and eventually erode the culture's moral anchors.

In searching for strategies to combat the so-called problem of media imperialism, we should probably avoid the temptation to retreat to an admittedly unrealistic position of moral prudery in our dealings with foreign cultures by exporting only our least controversial entertainment offerings. First, this would contradict our commitment to the principles of free trade, free enterprise, and the free flow of information (which might include entertainment as well) and would be counterproductive for a nation committed to democratic liberalism. Besides, competition is already reducing the perils of media imperialism. More nations at all levels of economic development are producing more of their own entertainment fare and distributing much of this into the international marketplace.

Second, such a sanitized output of artistic material would provide a distorted view of American society, and while this might be desirable from a foreign policy perspective, it would be dishonest. In the field of mass entertainment, our cultural self-portrait is reflected through this nation's TV programming, films, and music and captures, albeit in a somewhat refracted and dramatic form, the character of our aesthetic and moral worth. To the extent that we should be troubled about the ethical cues and antisocial messages (and we clearly should be) inherent in some of our overseas entertainment exports, in a market-driven global economy these concerns should really be no different than they are for domestic audiences. Those foreign institutions that purchase the programs can decide which ones are unsuitable for their audiences. However, where direct satellite transmissions to foreign nations are concerned, then American distributors should assume a moral obligation to consider the cultural sensitivities of those audiences for whom the programs are destined. However, some studies have even suggested that the very notion of media imperialism has been overblown, as audiences interpret foreign entertainment exports in line with their own interests and cultural biases.[34]

IN CONCLUSION

The foregoing discussion does suggest that there is reason to be optimistic about developing a system of shared ethical values without entirely compromising the attractive features of cultural diversity. The democratic impulse, assuming its continuing vitality, can provide the impetus for a frank exchange of views and information, which in turn can lead to a meaningful dialogue and the ultimate discovery of at least some universal values. Indeed, ample evidence shows that the process is well under way. At the same time, some culturally determined values will remain that will distinguish one society from another. This is not a cause for concern as long as there is accord on some basic universal ethical constructs.

For their part, American media practitioners working in other cultures should continue to reflect the ethical ideals of their profession. They should not attempt to impose their values on others, since this will ultimately be counterproductive. But if they believe in the moral worth of those standards, they should not hesitate to convey this message to their foreign hosts. In so doing, they may facilitate the search for shared values that could eventually lead to the international professionalization of the communication process.

THE GLOBAL COMMUNITY AND SHARED ETHICAL VALUES: HYPOTHETICAL CASE STUDIES

Three of the following four cases concern ethical issues confronted by American media practitioners in foreign cultures. Although specific countries were selected for these hypotheticals, the locales are less important than the issues. Ethical dilemmas such as these could occur in many countries, including some in our own hemisphere. The fourth case involves a PR firm that is asked to represent in the United States a foreign government that has a reputation for human rights abuses.

C A S E   S T U D I E S

▶ **CASE 14-1**
A PR Dilemma: Blowing the Whistle in Bulgaria

The revolution in Eastern and Central Europe had been like a shot of adrenalin for Union Lacewell Enterprises. With its domestic market at the saturation point and increasing production costs in Western Europe, Union Lacewell, a manufacturer of home appliances and household goods, had looked with economic lust on the investment pos-

sibilities in the newly emerging democracies of the former Soviet empire. Thus it had quickly joined other corporate giants like McDonald's, Pepsi, and General Electric in making overtures to the more promising of the fledgling capitalistic systems. The company had abandoned its production facilities in Austria and Germany in lieu of a manufacturing base in Hungary, where labor costs were a fraction of those in Western Europe and environmental regulations were not nearly as austere. From the outset, Hungary had been among the most hospitable of the Eastern and Central European economic cultures. From this vantage point, Union Lacewell could join the corporate trend known as "outworking"—the manufacture of goods in the low-production-cost markets of Eastern and Central Europe for sale in the more advanced countries of Western Europe.

With its footprint firmly established in Hungary, Union Lacewell had then entered into discussions with the newly installed government in Bulgaria, a more politically unstable and economically risky nation. Nevertheless, Bulgaria's leadership had demonstrated an unmistakable interest in foreign investment, and the company's corporate management had decided to assume the risk of being among the vanguard of American corporate presence in that former member of the Soviet Bloc. Union Lacewell's initial negotiations with the Bulgarian government, represented by Todor Petrov, an official in the Ministry of Finance and Economic Development, had not gone well, as endless bureaucratic delays and red tape consistently thwarted the company's efforts to begin operations in Bulgaria. Nevertheless, corporate management waited patiently as their negotiating counterparts, none of whom were experienced in the intricacies of a free-market economy, deliberated among themselves about Union Lacewell's bid to avail themselves of Bulgaria's economic potential.

At one point in the negotiations, Petrov informed company officials that his government had offered cash bonuses to those ministry representatives who procured lucrative foreign investment contracts but that those bonuses were to be paid by the foreign corporations as a cost of doing business in Bulgaria. Petrov referred to these as "incentive commissions." Union Lacewell management recognized them as bribes and notified Petrov that American law prohibited the corporation from providing such inducements to do business in a foreign country.

Confronted with this reality and the pressing need for industrial investment, government officials had relented and licensed Union Lacewell to open a plant in a leased facility in Sofia, the nation's capital, with an option to build a more modern plant within five years on land that would be privatized for economic development. The company's maiden voyage in what once had been among the

most hard-line of communist regimes was a mixed blessing. While the American corporation's foreign subsidiary contributed to its parent company's bottom line, as well as to the economic prosperity of Sofia and its environs, each negotiation with the Bulgarian government for additional concessions (e.g., licenses for exports to foreign markets) was accompanied by further bureaucratic delays and sometimes demands for cash incentives to expedite the approval process.

Despite these frustrations, Union Lacewell had concentrated its public relations arsenal on developing a rapport with the newly independent Bulgarian press and cultivating amicable relations with the citizens of Sofia who welcomed the American corporate giant and its economic benevolence. Jefferson Niemus, the company's vice president for corporate communications and marketing, was the ultimate PR gatekeeper, but Jeanne Burnett, the director of international public relations, and Earl Truman, the on-site director of external relations in Bulgaria, masterminded the daily PR regimen for Union Lacewell's foreign subsidiary. Within corporate headquarters, Truman was generally credited with rapidly establishing a professional bond with the Bulgarian media, particularly those in Sofia and surrounding communities, a tribute perhaps to his journalism background and his emotional engagement with "the people's right to know."

In its second year of operation in Sofia, Union Lacewell decided to exercise its option to build a more modern and permanent facility and entered into negotiations with the Ministry of Finance and Economic Development for a site located near Blagoevgrad, just sixty miles from the nation's capital. Again, government officials made overtures to corporate management concerning some kind of financial inducements to facilitate approval of Union Lacewell's new manufacturing enterprise. In a now all too familiar reprise, the company refused and filed a formal complaint with President Milko Petev. News of the negotiations, which in their initial stages were kept secret, had been leaked to the Bulgarian media in both Sofia and Blagoevgrad, and local business reporters began to press Truman for some kind of timetable for completion of Union Lacewell's new plant. "What is the delay?" they wanted to know, although Bulgarian journalists were not naive about the intractable government bureaucracy.

In countries accustomed to official secrecy, Niemus had admonished his team to be cautious in developing corporate PR strategies for use in Eastern and Central Europe. "What works here may not work there," he reminded them in stating the obvious. And it was this admonition that energized his discussion with Burnett and Truman as he met with them during a three-day visit to Sofia to gain some personal perspective on the stalled negotiations for the company's new manufacturing facility in Blagoevgrad.

"Petrov is still asking for a bribe for approval to build a plant near Blagoevgrad," said Niemus. "As always, we've filed an official complaint with his superior, Minister Ekaterina Naidenov, but I don't know how much good that will do."

"As you know, such tactics are fairly common in some of these former communist countries," remarked Truman. "Even though they've been told corporate bribery is a violation of American law, they still persist. Perhaps we need to take more drastic measures since official protests don't seem to work. We have good contacts with the *Balkan Financial Reporter* [English translation—a leading business newspaper in Bulgaria]. It's an independent paper and even carries some of our ads. It's also reform minded and often takes the government to task for the slow pace of economic development. In fact, in just the past couple of years I've noticed an increased aggressiveness among some of the papers. A story in the *Reporter* might work to our advantage in the long run and make Bulgarian officials more sensitive to our own ethical standards."

"I'm not so sure," responded Burnett. "As the director of international public relations, I'm as interested in honesty as anyone else. I've always tried to play straight with the media, particularly in our own country. But we have to look at the big picture. The bureaucrats here—some of whom are truly reformists but others of whom are former communists—don't understand such moral squeamishness over paying for economic concessions. If we go public with this, we may have even more problems down the road. Perhaps it's better to remain quiet and just work within the system."

"But we have taken great pains to cultivate domestic constituencies—not only the media but also the local communities," replied Truman. "We have always made it a point to play it straight with the media in the United States. That's good public relations. I think we should use the same approach here. We have established good relations with many of the Bulgarian media—both government supporters and those in opposition. And we've had some inquiries concerning the delays in building our plant in Blagoevgrad. If we don't play straight with them, we'll lose credibility."

"But we may have more to lose than credibility," said Niemus. "If the government breaks off negotiations, we may lose this plant, but the citizens of Blagoevgrad will be the ultimate losers. And the government could actually blame us. And then we'll *really* have a PR problem."

"I'll admit that's a calculated risk," conceded Truman, whose own philosophy of public relations leaned toward revelation rather than secrecy. Nevertheless, she was also a firm believer in spin control. "But Bulgaria needs this new plant. Even the minister understands this. Perhaps under some of these communist regimes corruption was a way of life. And the people may accept it. But in the long run we'll benefit by showing that we're above this. What's wrong with bringing our ethical standards with us, along with our capital investment?"

"That may be a little pompous," said Burnett. "Our ethical standards in this case are determined by American law. Perhaps we would follow the same course without the law. I would like to think so. But the fact is that bribery is not uncommon in Eastern and Central Europe. I'm not sure that exposing it will do much good. And some of our competitors from other Western nations have paid them. I'm not suggesting that we should follow suit. But if we publicize the demands of some government officials for payoffs to gain concessions, we may find investment opportunities suddenly hard to come by."

"But from a public relations perspective, our responsibilities are to the media and their audiences," replied Truman. "The newspapers here are newly independent. They're just learning what it means to operate in a capitalistic system, as primitive as it is, and how a market-driven economy operates. And as economic development increases, corporate PR will become more important. If we aren't credible, then we'll lose an important ally in our effort to establish good community relations. The citizens of Blagoevgrad have a right to know why we haven't started building in their city and providing much needed employment for the local economy."

Truman paused to let his comments register with his two colleagues and then continued. "And keep in mind that the government here is democratically elected. They have to be more responsive to the public than under communism—at least in theory."

"I'm still not convinced that government officials are as sensitive to public exposure as those in our own country," observed Burnett with an air of finality. "And if the government is unhappy with our strategy of openness, they could stall forever. And no one will benefit economically—Union Lacewell *or* the residents of Blagoevgrad."

On that note, Niemus concluded his meeting with his two subordinates. It would be his decision whether to publicize the ethically nefarious activities of the Bulgarian government. As the vice president for corporate communications and marketing, Niemus was the ultimate gatekeeper for Union Lacewell's public relations activities.

On the one hand, he believed that exposing what he viewed as government corruption might serve some higher good and might pave the way for a more just system of foreign investment in Bulgaria. On the other hand, such behavior was not uncommon in some countries in the former Soviet bloc and might be greeted with less concern than similar behavior in the United States. In addition, there was a danger that such a strategy, while establishing a certain degree of corporate credibility with the Bulgarian press, might further erode the company's opportunities for economic expansion within this emerging democracy.

THE CASE STUDY

Since 1977, it has been illegal for American companies to offer major gifts or bribes to foreign business contacts or government officials. Thus, in a sense the law has established the threshold ethical standard for American companies doing business abroad.

But this case does not revolve around the question of whether American corporations should follow local custom and pay bribes to government officials. Union Lacewell Enterprises, in following the spirit and letter of the law, has refused to pay the financial incentives demanded by Bulgarian officials to facilitate the construction of the company's proposed new modern manufacturing center. Corporate management has filed a protest with the government, but they are under no illusions that such procedures will prompt any significant change in government behavior.

Thus, their dilemma is whether to expose publicly through the Bulgarian media, some of which are manifestly antigovernment, what they perceive to be unethical behavior on behalf of government officials. Clearly, Union Lacewell has adhered to American ethical standards (or at least those imposed by Congress) by refusing to pay the bribes. But should they now attempt to change the system itself by exposing this corruption, or should they remain silent and continue to work within the system? As with most such dilemmas, there are potential winners and losers in this ethical equation.

For the purpose of confronting this troublesome question, assume the role of Jefferson Niemus. Then, using the SAD Formula for moral reasoning outlined in Chapter 3, make a decision on this issue.

▶ **CASE 14-2**
Checkbook Journalism, Russian-Style

Nikolai Kurzenko was a symbol of the worst of the new Russian social order. As the acknowledged head of the rapidly growing and increasingly feared Russian Mafia, he was considered perhaps the most powerful and influential figure outside the government itself. The breakup of the Soviet empire had been accompanied by an expected period of political and economic instability as the

Russian leadership attempted to implement re-forms and master the intricacies of the democratic process. But the Russian people, who had suf-fered under communist domination for seventy years, greeted their newly won freedoms with mixed emotions, as fear of the KGB was replaced by fear of crime in a society where law and order was rapidly dissipating.

The new economic order provided a fertile field for organized crime's nefarious activities as various Mafia families from Moscow to Vladivostok waged their turf battles in defiance of established authority. While such threats to the nation's tran-quility concerned both local officials and their West-ern benefactors who had invested heavily in the new Russian economic order, they were hopeful that such rivalries would serve to diffuse the influ-ence of organized crime until an effective law en-forcement system could be established.

Their confidence had been shattered, how-ever, as the far-flung Mafia families, apparently out of self-preservation and self-interests, had entered into an unholy alliance accompanied by an alarming consolidation of power. Nikolai Kurzenko, the head of the largest syndicated crime family in Moscow, had emerged as the first among equals, quickly assuming the mantle of the "Russian godfather."

In many respects, Kurzenko's empire was stereotypical of organized crime elsewhere, with its domestic control of the drug traffic, trade unions, and prostitution and its audacious contributions to political corruption. As Russian officials searched for strategies to combat this threat to internal security, they relied increasingly on American expertise in the form of FBI consultants to rescue them from Kurzenko's ubiquitous criminal domain.

John Chambers was an American freelance journalist who had covered stories for several of his country's leading newspapers and had on several occasions reported for ABC from trouble spots in which that news organization had no correspon-dents on location. During his journalistic career as a foreign correspondent, Chambers had established an impressive network of sources throughout the world, particularly in Western and Eastern Europe. The intelligence provided by these sources allowed

him to survey the global community with uncom-mon insight and to convey his impressions through the media to America's opinion leaders, govern-ment officials, and political pundits.

As a journalist, Chambers was both fascinated and concerned about the Russian Mafia's threat to that nation's social and political tranquility and had kept a watchful eye on Kurzenko's consolidation of power. He had written several stories concerning the growing influence of organized crime in the "new" Russia but had failed to penetrate the rather shadowy and secretive apparatus of the organiza-tion itself. Like most organized crime families, the code of silence appeared to be impenetrable—that is, until Kurzenko made a strategic mistake.

In an effort to expand his organization's in-fluence as a player on the international stage, Kurzenko authorized his operatives to offer what-ever financial inducements were required to pur-chase plutonium from Russia's impressive and expansive nuclear network for sale on the interna-tional black market. Kurzenko knew that some cus-tomers, particularly those renegade nations that engaged in state-sponsored terrorism, would pay handsomely for such potentially deadly resources.

Within a few months after Kurzenko's consoli-dation of power, several foreign businessmen had been arrested in Munich and Paris for attempting to smuggle small amounts of plutonium through customs. Western intelligence experts immediately suspected that most of the material had originated from Russian nuclear stockpiles and were destined for countries such as Libya, Iran, and Iraq. However, the real source of this black-market plutonium was unknown, as Russian authorities denied that their nuclear inventories had been compromised.

But as German authorities, with the assistance of American and Israeli intelligence, continued their investigation, Kurzenko's decision became increas-ingly controversial within the Russian Mafia hierar-chy. Nevertheless, the code of silence remained intact. That is, until Maxine Kukushkin made over-tures to John Chambers.

Kukushkin was a member of the inner circle of the most influential crime family in Vladivostok, who had apparently become disaffected with Kurzenko's leadership, particularly his decision to lead the organization along the perilous path of trafficking in stolen nuclear materials on the international black market. Kukushkin's disillusionment appeared to be motivated more by his concern that such activities, because of the international attention directed at any unauthorized movement of plutonium, put at risk the economic prosperity of his organization's infrastructure rather than any concern for global security.

Chambers was first apprised of Kukushkin's disaffection while in Vladivostok for two weeks covering a story concerning Russia's Pacific fleet. A source, on whom Chambers had relied on several occasions to ferret out hard to acquire information, represented the disaffected crime figure in his negotiations with the reporter.

Kukushkin, according to Chambers's source, was prepared to document the Mafia's involvement in the sale of plutonium from Russia's vast nuclear stockpiles and to provide details of how this transfer of such deadly materials from under the noses of Russian security agents was carried out. He was also prepared to identify the customers who had arranged for such purchases through their contacts in Munich, Germany. Chambers recognized Kukushkin's story for what it was: a bombshell that posed a threat to world security. In return for his story, according to Chambers's source, Kukushkin made two demands: a promise of confidentiality and 5 million rubles, or about $2,000 according to the current exchange rate. The $2,000 was twice the asking price for most interviews, according to accounts from some of Chambers's professional colleagues who had also encountered the Russian version of checkbook journalism. The pledge of confidentiality was no problem for the experienced international reporter, since he often relied on anonymous sources to harvest the fruits of his journalistic enterprise. Besides, Kukushkin's life would be in danger if the origin of the plutonium story became known to his partners in crime. Kukushkin's demand for payment, however, was more problematic.

As a professional journalist, Chambers had always disparaged checkbook journalism, a practice that had been routinely repudiated by the newspapers for which he had once worked before embarking on his freelance career. Although some news organizations, particularly the tabloids, had occasionally paid high-profile interviewees, the practice was still not condoned among mainstream American media. Nevertheless, in an information society the pressures to offer financial inducements for exclusive interviews in a marketplace economy were unremitting. And in many parts of the world, including the former Soviet Union and its satellites, demands for compensation in exchange for information were commonplace.

As an American journalist, Chambers was confronted with the quintessential dilemma of gathering information in a culture where the tradition of journalistic independence was not well established. Although so-called independent newspapers were now a prominent feature of the Russian media terrain, many Russian journalists did not display the same ethical reservations as their American counterparts in purchasing information from their news sources. The Kukushkin story was of international import, and the young Mafia defector was clearly for sale. If Chambers refused his demand for compensation, he would simply peddle his frightening intelligence elsewhere. The veteran reporter wondered whether he should leave his American values at the Russian border and rationalize his flirtation with checkbook journalism as an exceptional case necessitated by local custom. Besides, this was an exceptional story with international implications. His interview with a member of the Russian Mafia's inner circle could provide the "smoking gun" for the Western nations' confirmation of the source of the black-market uranium discovered in Munich and Paris. And because of Kurzenko's increasingly precarious position within the organization, such publicity might even lead to his demise and could prompt Russian authorities to tighten security around their nuclear stockpiles.

On the other hand, such journalistic compromises, in Chambers's view, often became precedential in the eyes of potentially greedy news sources, and he wondered whether other controversial interviewees would demand the same consideration. In addition, Kukushkin clearly had an ax to grind within the Mafia empire, and Chambers's readers might be forgiven if they read his accounts with some skepticism, particularly if they were apprised of the arrangements under which the information was procured. In fact, some news organizations might reject his account because of the payment to Kukushkin. But Chambers had no doubt that he would find an outlet for his story, although any reputable news organization would at least insist that the financial arrangements between the reporter and his interviewee be revealed to their readers.

Following his conversation with Kukushkin's envoy, Chambers returned to his room in Vladivostok's Gavan Hotel and reviewed his notes from the previous day's interview with the commander of the Russian Pacific fleet. But his moral beacon was focused more on Maxine Kukushkin's commercially valuable and journalistically explosive insights into the Mafia's latest terrifying enterprise than on the Russian navy's strategic importance to the international community's military balance of power.

THE CASE STUDY

In this case, a journalist is confronted with a dilemma that often confronts American media practitioners operating abroad. In this country, while the incidents of checkbook journalism appear to have increased in recent years, perhaps because of the influence of the tabloids, the practice is still discouraged by most mainstream media. But in some parts of the world, payments for information and interviews with important figures are commonplace.

On the one hand, John Chambers is inclined to invoke his traditional American journalistic values and refuse to pay Maxine Kukushkin for his unique, terrifying information. Such financial inducements could compromise his credibility with readers, and such a practice does raise questions about the motivations of the interviewee.

On the other hand, in some cultures information is just another commodity, for sale to anyone who is willing to pay. Since journalists' stock in trade is information, perhaps there are times when they must accommodate themselves to local custom, particularly when the story is as compelling and of such international significance as Kukush-

kin's firsthand account of the Russian Mafia's involvement in the black market sale of plutonium, an essential ingredient for the manufacture of nuclear weapons. In this case, do the significance of this story and the fact that Kukushkin has uncommon and never before revealed insights into the Russian Mafia's activities justify the reporter's compensation to this disaffected crime figure?

For the purposes of confronting this dilemma, assume the role of American freelance journalist John Chambers and, using the SAD Formula for moral reasoning outlined in Chapter 3, decide whether you will pay Maxine Kukushkin for this interview.

▶ CASE 14-3
Advertising American Computers in Hungary

It had been five years since the Templeton and Mason (T&M) Advertising Agency had established an economic beachhead in Hungary, an undeniable validation of its global strategic perspective. T&M had been the brainchild of Roy Templeton, Sr., and Todd Mason thirty years ago, when the Cold War was the cornerstone of American foreign policy and capitalism and communism were uncompromising ideological adversaries. As they struggled to maintain the viability of their fledgling agency in the late 1960s, they could not have imagined the rapid demise of communism following the breakup of the Soviet Union that would, three decades later, pave the way for their successors in the international marketplace.

Templeton and Mason had launched their enterprise in Chicago to service regional clients, with only modest success in an increasingly competitive environment. Templeton, in one of his few pessimistic assessments, had once described the agency's account list as "the backwaters of American commercialism." Nevertheless, the partners had persevered, and T&M had eventually established itself as one of the most creative and successful agencies in the Midwest. Templeton and Mason, in an effort to capitalize on their prosperity, then moved aggressively to open branch offices in

New York, Los Angeles, and Dallas and within a few years had authenticated their agency's influence and prominence on a national level.

Roy Templeton, Jr., had inherited his father's unrelenting ambition, and with the downfall of communism in the former Soviet bloc and economic reforms in Eastern and Central Europe, the T&M Advertising Agency had moved swiftly to cultivate the struggling market economies in the most progressive of these nations. Templeton's efforts were directed initially at establishing some representation in Hungary, where in 1988 the Trade Ministry had issued guidelines that had essentially opened the door for the advertising of all products. Within two years, all of Hungary's thirty daily newspapers and major magazines were accepting ads, as well as radio stations and the two state TV channels.[35]

Although advertising had existed under the communist regime, it was strictly utilitarian in nature, devoid of any of the creative genius, puffery, and the blend of both aggressive and subtle salesmanship to which Americans are so accustomed. Thus, for the T&M agency Hungary was virgin territory, and its account list soon included both American companies who had invested in the Hungarian economy, as well as Hungarian-run enterprises. While Hungary was an active trading partner with the industrialized nations of the West and thus imported many of its consumer goods, the government was committed to protecting its domestic manufacturers, particularly those that were struggling to convert from the centralized and inefficient planning system of the communist regime to the competitive environment of a free-market economy. Thus, the Hungarians had misgivings about manufacturers that remained culturally disengaged by refusing to invest in the local economy, while exporting products from their home countries to compete directly with Hungarian-produced goods that were often of inferior quality. For the Hungarian government, this was an economic problem. For American advertising executive Roy Templeton, Jr., it was an ethical dilemma.

"Compumax has asked us to represent them in the Hungarian market," Templeton said in laying the foundation for the subsequent discussion in the agency's rather cramped quarters in downtown Budapest. The senior partner had arrived in the Hungarian capital the day before to consult with Angela Kast, the agency's local account manager, and Gustav Dajka, an agency account executive. Dajka was a local national fluent in English and indispensable, in Templeton's judgment, in infusing his American-dominated firm with a healthy dose of cultural sensitivity.

"As you know, Compumax is now a big player in the PC industry in the States," Templeton said. "They also are making significant inroads into industrial computer designs. But unlike some other American companies, Compumax has not invested directly in the local economy. They have no plants here. They still build most of their computers in the States and import them into Hungary. Compumax wants to mount an aggressive ad campaign in the local media to capture a share of the Hungarian market."

"This should be fairly simple," responded Kast. "The Hungarians are strong in computer software, but quite frankly their hardware is of poor quality. It can't compete with the Western computer industry. Many of their plants are still suffering from the poor management and production quality of the communist system. Once the Hungarians—and that includes individuals, as well as commercial enterprises—become aware of the Compumax name through advertising, it will become synonymous with quality."

"I realize that this agency's role is to represent clients in the marketplace and Compumax could become a big account," observed Dajka. "And Compumax has been given access to the Hungarian market, at least on a limited basis. But the government is very sensitive about companies that import but don't invest in the local economy. T&M represents other American clients, but all of them have plants here. Although they do in some instances compete with Hungarian manufacturers, at least they are contributing to the economic health of the country, including employment. But the computer hardware industry is vulnerable to companies like Compumax. Local manufacturers may not be able to compete, and the Hungarian government is interested in encouraging domestic production and protecting Hungarian-owned and -operated plants."

"That is a concern," replied Templeton in a sincere display of cultural understanding. "If we believe in the effectiveness of advertising to create demand—and we obviously do—then Compumax could drive some of these local plants out of business."

"But I don't see that as our problem," said Kast, who believed strongly that a nation that embraced capitalism must also accept the competitive risks of the marketplace. "Compumax has been given permission to import its computers, although there are quotas to provide some protection for the domestic industry. Thus, they have a right to create demand through a domestic ad campaign. Although Western-style advertising is relatively new in Hungary, creative strategies, tailored for a domestic audience, work well here."

"But you're looking at this issue through the economic prism of your own country," insisted Dajka. "In the States most similar product lines are competitive. Thus, ads concentrate on superficial or advertiser-created distinctions. There is little real difference among products in terms of quality. But there is a big difference between the Hungarian-produced computer hardware and that produced in America. And a national ad campaign will just accentuate those differences. In the United States an effective campaign might simply readjust the market shares among competitors. Here, the Hungarian computer industry is vulnerable to foreign competition."

"But this could serve as an incentive for the Hungarians to become more competitive in the computer marketplace," responded Kast, who showed no signs of retreat from her marketplace ideology. "Besides, they have a right to advertise their products to stimulate demand."

"They do advertise," noted Dajka. "But many of their managers still have the communist mentality. They don't understand creative ad strategies as practiced in the West. They view advertising as a means of promoting the utility of their products, rather than the more emotional and stimulating appeals found in American ads. And they just can't compete from a quality standpoint. They have little to advertise, at least not from a Western perspective."

"But we represent other American clients who compete against Hungarian manufacturers and service industries," objected Kast. "That's why we're here. The Hungarian market is increasingly competitive. And all companies that do business here have a right to advertise their wares."

"That's true," admitted Dajka. "But many Hungarian products are now competitive with those produced in the West. The quality may still be somewhat less, but at least they are competitive. And as I said before, our government welcomes those industries that invest in the Hungarian economy and manufacture their goods here. However, the computer hardware industry is not competitive; the home-grown computers are inferior. The government would like to change that, and they may resent American companies that simply import their products into the Hungarian market. I'm not sure that we should represent a client that raises such a politically sensitive issue."

"That *is* a concern," agreed Templeton. "All of our clients who advertise in Hungary are either American corporations or Hungarian industries. A couple are even joint American-Hungarian ventures. But all manufacture their products here. They contribute to the economy directly, including providing jobs for Hungarian workers. And our campaigns have been successful in helping them compete in the marketplace. But Compumax doesn't fit this profile. We have a good working relationship with the media and our Hungarian clients. That could change if we take on Compumax as a client. We need to think of the future as well."

"But we're an American agency, and an American company has asked us to represent them in the Hungarian marketplace," Kast said. "Whether they manufacture their computers here or in the States should not concern us. They are a reputable company and have a right to compete here. And that includes advertising their products. I don't know why we should concern ourselves with the economic health of the domestic computer industry. If they can't compete, they're not going to survive anyway."

As an unapologetic proponent of capitalism, Templeton could not deny the unassailable truth of Kast's assessment. And yet, having traveled to Russia and the Eastern Bloc countries both before and after the fall of communism, he understood the challenges of moving from a communist-run economic system to a free-market economy. Eventually, there would be unrestrained competition, but some industries in these emerging democracies needed time to master the intricacies of the capitalistic ideology. As senior partner, Templeton would decide whether his agency should represent Compumax in the Hungarian marketplace. And the more Templeton reflected on his discussion with Angela Kast and Gustav Dajka, it became increasingly difficult to assess the ethical dimensions of this dilemma.

THE CASE STUDY

Does Templeton's dilemma simply involve a calculated business decision, or does it raise serious ethical questions as well? Viewed strictly from a free-market perspective, it appears to be more of a business decision. However, T&M is an American agency that has become an active participant in the development of the Hungarian economy. It is a "guest" of the Hungarians, but their relationship is symbiotic. The agency has expanded its own horizons into what could become a lucrative market, while contributing to the development of the Hungarian economy through the advertising of consumer goods. The advertisers represented on Templeton's client list have a good relationship with the Hungarian people because they either invest in the economy (in the case of American firms) or are Hungarian-run enterprises.

But Compumax could be viewed as an interloper since its products are merely imported into the Hungarian economy in direct competition with a struggling domestic industry. If the agency represents this American manufacturer and succeeds in increasing demand for Compumax computers, T&M could be viewed as part of the problem. Indeed, Templeton is concerned about the impact of his decision on the agency itself, and its future relationship with other domestic clients, which could include the Hungarian computer industry as it struggles to become competitive.

On the other hand, one could argue that in the spirit of free trade the company has been given access to the Hungarian market and has a right to

agency representation. T&M's first loyalty, therefore, should be to this American client rather than the struggling Hungarian computer industry. Thus, when viewed from the perspective of the behavior of American advertising agencies in foreign cultures and the problem of divided loyalties that sometimes emerge as a result of such relationships, ethical concerns are implicated.

For the purpose of making a decision on whether your agency will represent Compumax in placing its ads in Hungarian media, assume the role of advertising executive Roy Templeton, Jr. Then, using the SAD Formula for moral reasoning described in Chapter 3, render a judgment on this matter and defend it with sound ethical reasoning.

 CASE 14-4
Public Relations and Morality in Foreign Policy

"U.S.-China Relations Hit New Low," reported the headline in the *New York Times*. "China's Most Favored Nation Status in Jeopardy," according to a *Washington Post* account of Congressional reaction to Beijing's latest diplomatic dispute with the White House. "A Cold Wind in Beijing," declared *Newsweek*'s cover story in another journalistic validation of the most recent rift in the administration's relations with one of this country's most enigmatic trading partners.

Since the Nixon administration's overtures more than twenty years ago to the leaders of the People's Republic of China that eventually led to a normalization of relations between our two countries, the U.S.-Sino alliance had remained politically fragile. American foreign policy had adopted a controversial strategy of pressuring the Chinese to end its human rights abuses, while at the same time pursuing the more pragmatic path of cultivating an economically viable trade policy with Beijing. On the one hand, the White House continuously expressed its moral indignation at China's use of forced labor to produce goods for export, an inhumane practice that had been documented by a naturalized American citizen and scholar who had returned to the People's Republic and secretly videotaped the abuses inside that country's exploitative prison system. On the other hand, administration pragmatists, as well as their supporters in Congress, argued that it was in our national interest to negotiate with the Chinese to open their markets to American goods and that Congressional confirmation of most favored nation status, which the Chinese currently enjoyed but was now in jeopardy, was essential to that foreign policy objective.

However, even as the Chinese appeared to covet most favored nation treatment that would also ensure greater access to American markets, they stubbornly refused to acknowledge American charges of human rights violations and expressed their resentment, both publicly and privately, at such insulting indictments. The most recent fracture in the already fragile Sino-U.S. relationship came when the State Department issued a visa to a prominent visiting professor from Taiwan, Dr. Wang Wai, who had been invited to give a series of lectures at Harvard University. Wang, a frequent critic of the communist regime on mainland China, was not reticent during his three-day visit to Cambridge in once again condemning the Beijing government for its dismal human rights record. This action prompted a swift protest from the Chinese ambassador in Washington, followed by a suspension of the most recent negotiations between the United States trade representatives and their Chinese counterparts.

But despite these highly publicized diplomatic repercussions, the Chinese government persisted in its efforts to procure congressional reaffirmation of its most favored nation status. However, recent evidence that China was selling medium-range missiles to Pakistan, as well as the continuing allegations of human rights abuses, had put the issue in doubt, particularly in a politically conservative Congress where any Communist regime was viewed with suspicion. And the enduring balance of trade deficit with the People's Republic did little to soothe Congress' bipartisan pique at what they perceived to be the moral callousness of the Chinese leadership.

To Dong Teng-hui, the Chinese trade representative assigned to the embassy in Washington, the message both from his diplomatic contacts and in America's news media was unmistakable: his country's most favored nation status was in jeopardy. And it was within this environment of political uncertainty that Dong sought counsel from Knopp & Bryce, a Washington, D.C., public relations firm with branches in five countries. The firm's client list included both domestic and multinational corporations, but Knopp & Bryce had also been a successful advocate within the halls of Congress for foreign governments and commercial enterprises.

Anne Barker-Lane was Knopp and Bryce's director of international relations and served as the gatekeeper in selecting those clients who were worthy of her firm's attention. But despite the autonomy that she enjoyed within her company's hierarchy, Barker-Lane often sought the advice of her coworkers. Thus, Dong's overtures and the issue of whether human rights violations should be used as a benchmark in representing the Chinese government soon became a point of contention among Barker-Lane; Bryan Hardy, the firm's congressional liaison; and Jacob Wiley, the international account manager.

"The Chinese have approached us about representing them before Congress on the most favorable nation issue," began Anne Barker-Lane, as she briefed her two colleagues on Dong's visit. "Despite their offense at the visit of Dr. Wang and his comments at Harvard, trade is still economically vital to them. American markets are important, if not absolutely essential, to the leaders in Beijing."

"This will be tough," remarked Hardy. "The mood on Capitol Hill isn't very good. In the Senate, some of the older and more conservative members still resent our recognition of the People's Republic. Taiwan still has friends in Congress. Some are just looking for an excuse to withdraw most favored nation status from the Chinese."

"It may be a tough sell," responded Wiley. "But that's our job: to represent our clients as faithfully and skillfully as we can, even when the odds aren't good. And as you know we have represented many clients on Capitol Hill, including foreign governments. But this one is different. The Chinese government is still seen by many as a repressive regime. The pictures of the Tiannamen Square massacre are still vivid in America's consciousness. In fact, recent polls indicate a majority of Americans are in favor of holding the Chinese accountable for their alleged human rights violations."

"It's true that they would be an unpopular client in some quarters," countered Hardy. "But should we select our international clients based on our own country's sense of morality? If the Chinese were clearly an outlaw regime, committing such atrocities as genocide, then I would have no problem with rejecting such a client out of hand. But even our own government continues to deal with the People's Republic. And as long as we still have diplomatic relations with this nation, don't they have a right to be heard in America's court of public opinion, as well as have representation in the halls of Congress?"

"I'm not so sure," replied Wiley, who had on several occasions expressed the opinion that any economic affiliation with a nation where human rights abuses could be documented amounted to an abdication of moral virtue in foreign policy. "We are an American PR firm. As such, our values should count for something. As long as these human rights abuses continue, we should refuse to represent the Chinese. What do we stand to gain by taking on the regime in Beijing as a client? This could be an unpopular decision that might reflect unfavorably on this agency."

"It's true that we could take some heat if we sign the People's Republic as a client," conceded Hardy. "But I don't see this as an issue of moral virtue. The administration and its supporters in Congress apparently feel that the most effective means of combatting the human rights abuses is to reach out to the Chinese and provide them with most favorable nation status. Over the long run, this relationship may provide us with more influence over China's domestic behavior. The integration of the People's Republic into the international community has to be gradual. And our own efforts on behalf of the Chinese could be significant."

"But this is speculation," responded Wiley. "In my judgment, the Chinese should earn the right to be represented in America's court of public opinion. Unless there's some movement on the human rights issue, I don't think we should represent them."

"The standard has already been set by the administration and several before it," said Hardy.

"Despite the Beijing regime's sensitivity and resentment, the White House continues to press them on the human rights issue, but the president and his Congressional supporters feel it's in our national interest to cultivate a meaningful trading relationship with the Chinese. This may not be the most desirable approach, but politically it may be the most sensible."

"I appreciate the political delicacy of this matter from a foreign policy perspective," replied Wiley. "But our position is different. I don't think we can do a good job for a client that we don't really believe in, particularly when they have such a dismal record on human rights. When Knopp & Bryce does business overseas or represents foreign clients in this country, we shouldn't abandon our own moral beliefs and standards. American corporations and the PR firms that represent them are unofficial ambassadors. It may be true that, if we refuse to represent the Chinese, they'll go to some other firm. But that's not our problem. We have to make a decision that we'll be comfortable with."

As Barker-Lane began to ponder the solicitation from the Chinese trade representative, she appreciated the competing philosophies just advanced by her two colleagues. Jacob Wiley favored moral virtue over political reality, even on the international stage, and believed that American values, as imperfect as they might be, should dominate our relations with foreign governments. And that was particularly true, in Wiley's view, of American firms in their international activities. On the other hand, Bryan Hardy was a pragmatist who believed that all clients, even those who might be morally suspect, deserved some representation in the corridors of American political power. Anne Barker-Lane was painfully aware that her decision could have political consequences, not only for her firm but for American foreign policy as well.

THE CASE STUDY

At one level, this case involves a familiar question in the practice of public relations: Should a PR firm be a "hired gun" for all who seek representation, or should it assume representation only for those whose causes it can, in good faith, support? But from a much broader perspective, this case also raises the issue of whether, in dealing with foreign enterprises (either private or governmental), American PR firms should apply their own culture's moral values or whether they should provide representation for any foreign patron regardless of that client's moral worth.

According to one recent survey, more than 150 American PR firms work in this country for nations as diverse as Egypt, Japan, Hungary, and El Salvador. These client countries pursue both political objectives and commercial interests.[36] One could argue that, in a democratic system that prides itself on an unfettered marketplace of ideas, all speakers (including unpopular governments) have a right to be represented in the court of public opinion. In this view, PR practitioners should assume a politically pragmatic posture in which the primary consideration is the "fit" between the client and the capabilities of the firm. Thus, the application of American moral standards, particularly as they apply to other nations, becomes secondary to the decision-making process.

A counterpoint to this view is that, while foreign governments have the right to attempt to influence American foreign policy, PR firms also have a right to select their clients based on their own self-interests (or the interests of others) and that moral behavior of the client can and should be an important consideration.

For the purpose of rendering a judgment on whether Knopp & Bryce should assist the Chinese government in salvaging its most favored nation status, assume the role of Anne Barker-Lane. Using the formula for moral reasoning outlined in Chapter 3, make a decision on this matter.

▼

Notes

1. See Rushworth M. Kidder, *Shared Values for a Troubled World* (San Francisco: Jossey-Bass, 1994).
2. Quoted in James Rachels, *The Elements of Moral Philosophy* (New York: Random House, 1986), p. 24.
3. *Ibid.*, pp. 14–15.
4. These are discussed in greater detail in *ibid.*, pp. 17–19.
5. *Ibid.*, p. 18.
6. *Ibid.*, pp. 18–19.
7. Kidder, pp. 5–11.
8. *Ibid.*, p. 7.
9. *Ibid.*, p. 11.
10. Tom Cooper, "Comparative International Media Ethics," *Journal of Mass Media Ethics*, 5, No. 1 (1990), p. 13, quoting K. Nordenstreng and A. Alanen, "Journalism Ethics and International Relations," *Communication*, 6 (1981), p. 225.
11. Thomas W. Cooper, "Global Universals: In Search of Common Ground," in Thomas W. Cooper, Clifford G. Christians, Frances Forde Plude, and Robert A. White (eds.), *Communications Ethics and Global Change* (White Plains, NY: Longman, 1989), p. 21. These are also examined in Cooper, "Comparative International Media Ethics," pp. 3–14.
12. *Ibid.*, pp. 20–21.
13. *Ibid.*, p. 21.
14. *Ibid.*, pp. 35–36.
15. E.g., see J. Herbert Altschull, *Agents of Power*, 2d ed. (New York: Longman, 1995), pp. 316–324.
16. *Ibid.*, p. 208.
17. For fear that UNESCO's policies would give too much power to governments, at the end of 1984 the United States even decided to withdraw from the organization in protest. For a discussion of this issue, see Michael W. Gamble and Teri Kwal Gamble, *Introducing Mass Communication*, 2d ed. (New York: McGraw-Hill, 1989), p. 441–442.
18. Cooper, "Global Universals," pp. 31–37.
19. Jean-Francois Revel, *Democracy against Itself: The Future of the Democratic Impulse* (New York: Free Press, 1993), p. 5.
20. John Maxwell Hamilton and George A. Krimsky, "Exporting American Media," in *Media Studies Journal: Media and Democracy*, The Freedom Forum Media Studies Center, Summer 1995, p. 95.
21. See Stephen Anderson, "Successfully Working with International Journalists," *IABC Communication World*, September 1994, pp. 30–32.
22. John C. Merrill, "Global Commonalities for Journalistic Ethics: Idle Dream or Realistic Goal?," in Cooper et al., *Communications Ethics and Global Change*, pp. 287–288.
23. Keith Elliot Greenberg, "Going Global," *Public Relations Tactics*, September 1995, p. 1, citing the 1995 edition of *O'Dwyer's Directory of Public Relations Firms*.
24. For a good discussion of international public relations, see Dennis L. Wilcox, Phillip H. Ault, and Warren K. Agee, *Public Relations: Strategies and Tactics*, 4th ed. (New York: HarperCollins, 1995), pp. 413–446.
25. *Ibid.*, p. 414.
26. *Ibid.*
27. Philip Seib and Kathy Fitzpatrick, *Public Relations Ethics* (Fort Worth, TX: Harcourt Brace, 1995), p. 52, quoting Andrew W. Singer, "Ethics: Are Standards

Lower Overseas?" *Across the Board*, September 1991, p. 34.

28. This code, known as the Code of Athens, has been recognized for its universal principles. For an outline of the code's principles, see Seib and Fitzpatrick, *Public Relations Ethics*, pp. 53–54.

29. *Ibid.*, pp. 52–53.

30. William Wells, John Burnett, and Sandra Moriarity, *Advertising: Principles and Practices*, 3d ed. (Upper Saddle River, NJ: Prentice Hall, 1995), p. 744.

31. Gamble and Gamble, *Introducing Mass Communication*, p. 442.

32. Joseph Straubhaar and Robert LaRose, *Communications Media in the Information Society* (Belmont, CA: Wadsworth, 1996), p. 127.

33. *Ibid.*, p. 127.

34. E.g., see *ibid.*, p. 126.

35. The Freedom Forum, *Looking to the Future: A Survey of Journalism Education in Central and Eastern Europe and the former Soviet Union* (Arlington, VA: Freedom Forum, August 1994), p. 35.

36. Wilcox, Ault, and Agee, *Public Relations: Strategies and Tactics*, pp. 424–425.

◀ E P I L O G U E ▶

A COUPLE OF LESSONS FROM THIS TEXT

This book has forged a rather broad path through the moral landscape. There is certainly no dearth of ethical dilemmas confronting the media, but the text material and hypothetical cases have explored what, in my judgment, are the most important of these. However, as noted at the outset, the purpose of this book is not to furnish an encyclopedia of media issues but, rather, to provide training in moral reasoning in the context of some of the most important ethical problems confronting media practitioners.

Critical thinking, of course, can be applied to virtually any decision-making situation, which should be sufficient justification for its role in the educational process. But the teaching of ethics and moral reasoning should also assume a position of respectability in view of the ethical malaise that has engulfed U.S. society. Surveys continue to show a youthful culture afloat in a sea of relativism without any clear-cut moral guideposts. Cheating and plagiarism, for example, in high schools and on college campuses are stark reminders of this youthful moral infirmity. But an individual's moral blueprint should be well developed before he or she enters the working environment. How can reporters, for example, be expected to challenge deception as a tool of investigative journalism when they enter the newsroom with little respect for truth telling as a fundamental societal value?

The ethical standards of media practitioners do not stand apart from the rest of society. Those in the media must resolve their ethical quandaries through the same process of moral reasoning as the rest of us. That, at least, is one lesson of this book. And since they occupy such a pivotal and prominent position in society's communication channels, journalists, advertising and public relations professionals, and producers of mass entertainment should be among the leading moral critical thinkers of our diverse society.

Another lesson of this book is that, at least insofar as universal moral principles are concerned, the conduct of media practitioners should be judged by the same standards as those applied to the rest of us. As John Silber, the president of Boston University, observes in *Straight Shooting: What's Wrong with America and How to Fix It*:

> Correctly understood, there is one ethics, one set of principles for the guidance of human conduct. And it is wholly consistent with the objectivity and universality of ethical principles that they are applied differently in a variety of fields. The moral obligations of doctors, soldiers, scientists, and other professionals may differ from the moral obligations of farmers, bankers,

bureaucrats, bus drivers, chimney sweeps, and homemakers, but the ethical principles by which their conduct is guided and judged in these various contexts are the same.[1]

Of course, as noted throughout this book, several approaches can be brought to bear on any ethical dilemma. But the fundamental values underlying such decisions do not vary with the occupation of the moral agent.

Hypothetical textbook cases obscure the pressures, tensions, and moral uncertainty of the real world. Nevertheless, they can serve as at least a starting point for the teaching of moral reasoning, a skill that is no less important for media practitioners than reporting and writing.

THE STATE OF MEDIA ETHICS: MIXED SIGNALS

As the United States enters the twenty-first century, the moral direction of its media institutions and the practitioners who work in them is unclear. Because of the gradual erosion of public confidence in the media, as evidenced by polls, there appears to be a heightened sensitivity within the industry to ethical issues. This concern is reflected in the fact that the media have begun to turn the spotlight on themselves and debate the moral dilemmas that confront the creators of mass-produced content. For example, a recent survey by the Associated Press managing editors found a surprising level of concern among editors over new ethical issues and eroding standards. More than 30 percent of the respondents acknowledged that they spend more of their time today dealing with ethical issues.[2]

In addition, media practitioners are participating in ethics seminars and workshops in ever-increasing numbers. And media organizations are paying more than lip service to moral issues at their professional conferences. For example, ethics programs and workshops are now a prominent feature at the annual conventions of the Society of Professional Journalists and the Radio-Television News Directors Association.

There also appears to be an increasing awareness of the growing disenchantment within society and the profession itself with some of the questionable news-gathering techniques that have characterized investigative reporting for twenty years. For example, more criticism within the industry has been leveled toward such practices as simulations and re-creations and even undercover reporting. Although some news organizations may still use deception to get a news story, some within the industry question whether such tactics are desirable or even necessary. Promises of confidentiality to news sources are less common today than in the past, and when such promises are essential, many organizations now require management approval.

It is still too soon to tell what impact this internal reexamination of moral values will have. But trends such as these signify a growing recognition that some of the techniques of investigative journalism raise ethical issues and that reporters cannot operate on a moral plane separate from society at large.

The development of written statements of principles has also been a step forward in at least codifying the moral precepts of the various media enterprises. As noted in this text, all areas of media communications—journalism, advertising, public relations, and the entertainment industry—are represented by codes. Many media organizations now have their own codes, and "company policy" is often cited in support of why a particular course of action was followed. Although these codes may not offer solutions in ticklish ethical situations, they do reflect a philosophy about the moral values to which homage should be paid.

The development of codified ethical standards can imbue the cause of self-regulation with a certain amount of credibility and dignity, but these are still rather modest steps. In the final analysis, the moral environment of media institutions will depend on the determination of individual practitioners to aspire to lofty standards of ethical conduct.

On this score, there is still much to be done. The ethical boundaries of contemporary journalism are rather broad and not always well defined. Such practices as "pack journalism," by which reporters descend in a competitive fervor upon a "hot" news story; unwarranted invasions of the privacy of ordinary citizens; news gathering with hidden cameras; and the use of sensational and dramatic language to "hype" a story are representative of the perennial ethical concerns of the journalistic profession. Of course, media practitioners still disagree about the ethical acceptability of some news-gathering techniques. But the issue is not whether the occasional deviation from ethical norms can be justified according to some more important principle but whether particular forms of behavior, such as the use of deception or invasions of privacy, should become the industry standard. Unfortunately, too many decisions are still made on an ad hoc basis—a form of situation ethics, if you will—rather than from any set of well-constructed ethical principles.

Even in the midst of a spirited debate involving the more traditional ethical issues, we are confronted with new concerns engendered by the explosion of the information age and the new technologies that service the information superhighway. The proliferation of computer data banks, the digitalization of information storage and retrieval, and the staggering potential, for both good and evil, of cyberspace have already challenged the moral imaginations of ethicists and media practitioners alike. And colleges around the country have responded in kind, as courses in computer and cyberspace ethics have been added to the curricula.

What should be remembered, however, is that the fundamental values that have served us well in moral reasoning about the more conventional ethical issues—truth, respect for persons, fairness, and so forth—are timeless and should serve us well in confronting the challenges of the information age. For example, while the use of the Internet to transmit pornography might facilitate the dissemination of sexually explicit content, the ethical concerns underlying the proper balance between moral anarchy and moral prudery remain the same. Likewise, the alteration of news photos and visuals raises basic questions of honesty, regardless of whether it is accomplished through the use of digital technology or more conventional methods. Thus, the lesson is clear: regardless of how they occur, such ethical lapses will do little to restore the public's confidence in the media as moral leaders of society.

There also does not appear to be any abatement to the intrusion of the marketing concept into the editorial side of journalistic institutions. Competition is inherent in the media system, of course, but marketing principles elevate commercialism to such a position of influence and prominence as to undermine the independence of the news process. Many of the ethical views of media managers can be attributed to economic concerns that lead them into decisions that are not always socially responsible. As you may recall, this consideration cropped up time and time again in the hypothetical cases in this text.

Although some recent ethical consciousness raising has occurred within the community of media practitioners, consistent and systematic self-criticism is still rare. A relatively small number of the more than 1,600 daily newspapers have ombudsmen to evaluate the complaints of readers. In fact, the number of ombudsmen has actually decreased in recent years, as some newspapers have chosen to eliminate such internal watchdogs. The demise of the National News Council several years ago also left a void of organized media soul searching at the national level.

Despite some public grumbling over the ethical conduct of the media, there is surprisingly little consistent external criticism. A number of citizen media watchdog groups exist, but they are usually narrowly focused toward an agenda of self-interest, as is the ideologically conservative Accuracy in Media (AIM), or some special concern, as is Action for Children's Television (ACT). However, such organizations do serve a useful purpose in expanding the diversity of media criticism in the intellectual marketplace.

Some journals, including the *Columbia Journalism Review* and the *American Journalism Review*, offer incisive and illuminating media criticism. And the debut several years ago of the *Journal of Mass Media Ethics* reflects the concern of the scholarly community with the academic exploration and critical analysis of ethical standards within the media professions. Nevertheless, as worthy as these contributions are, they are still modest and unlikely to result in any systematic and broad-based program of external media criticism.

Even as we agonize over the direction of media ethics in this country, the debate continues at the international level on the question of whether there are universal values that might provide the foundation for a shared system of ethics by the global community. And while cultural diversity and the forces of nationalism are formidable obstacles to such a prospect, some hopeful signs suggest that the democratic movements around the world may provide the common ground upon which such a system might be cultivated.

TOWARD GREATER ETHICAL AWARENESS: WHAT CAN BE DONE?

Beyond study in the classroom, several things can be done to improve the ethical environment of media institutions. First, media managers should take the lead in identifying the moral standards of their organizations and codifying those principles. These codes should then be published and explained to employees. Unfortunately, the national codes are too abstract and general to serve as a foundation for a pragmatic ethical blueprint. But the detailed standards of some newspapers and the commercial television networks, for example, can be valuable in at least serving as guideposts for journalists and other media practitioners as they confront moral dilemmas.

Some organizations have declined to commit to writing what they believe to be appropriate ethical behavior. They apparently believe that in our litigious society, such codified principles will be used against them in lawsuits accusing them of negligent conduct. But the existence of such codes can also be cited as evidence of a socially responsible institution that is unwilling to condone unethical practices.

It is insufficient, however, to confine publicity about these ethical codes to the institutions and employees themselves. The public should be informed of the existence of organizational codes of conduct and the standards of behavior expected of media professionals. For example, newspapers could periodically publish the codes for their readers, an acknowledgment of public accountability.

Another means of improving the moral climate of media institutions is for media managers to conduct regular sessions on ethical standards and conduct. Other problems are discussed at staff meetings at all levels; ethical issues should be included, especially at the moment when they arise. Media managers should not be afraid to invite critics and moral philosophers to offer their own analyses and counsel on ethical dilemmas that confront staff members. Consultants have been helpful in improving the commercial posture of media organizations. In a similar fashion, ethicists have something to contribute to the moral tone of such institutions. And why not occasionally invite representatives of the reading or viewing audience to participate in these internal ethics discussions? This avenue of external criticism not only would provide a different perspective on the issues under discussion but would also increase public awareness of the media's sensitivity to ethical concerns. Above all, every employee should be involved in this process. Employee involvement usually results in a more congenial work environment. "Come let us reason together" should be the hallmark of corporate ethical decision making.

In addition, media practitioners could benefit from attendance at workshops on ethics and moral behavior. Professional organizations, such as the Society of Professional Journalists and the Public Relations Society of America, often sponsor such seminars. Some colleges and universities and media-supported institutes, such as the Poynter Institute for Media Studies in St. Petersburg, Florida, have also been instrumental in providing continuing education in ethics and moral reasoning.

Finally, media practitioners should continue the periodic public examination of ethical issues that is now evident. As noted in the preface, various news organizations have discovered the ethical malaise to be a social ill worthy of their attention. One can only hope that this is not a transitory infatuation that receives intense scrutiny while the topic is hot, only to fade from the media's consciousness. Of course, as part of their coverage of the ethics issue, the media should engage in their own rigorous self-examination. This process would both sensitize media professionals to the moral dilemmas confronting their own enterprises and enhance their credibility with the public.

However, such a self-examination will take serious reflection on the part of journalists. In fact, one wonders how long journalists can continue to report on and expose the moral foibles of others without getting their own house in order. Should publishers and reporters, for example, accept honoraria for speeches when they discourage this practice in elected officials? Can print journalists continue to cover the health hazards of cigarette smoking while their own institutions accept millions of dollars in advertising from the tobacco industry? Can news organizations in good conscience offer pervasive coverage of the drug addictions of college and professional athletes if similar problems exist in the newsroom? The lesson is simple: media practitioners should pay at least as much attention to their own ethical conduct as to the moral behavior of others.

One means of approaching this matter of self-criticism is for media organizations to reverse the trend against the use of ombudsmen and hire such internal critics to review public

and internal complaints of ethical misconduct. For the larger institutions the ombudsman might be a full-time staff member. Others might choose to employ ethics "experts," such as university professors, in a consulting capacity to handle such complaints. The results of these internal reviews should then be published as a means of reassuring the public that the media are serious about their own policies of self-regulation.

One could argue that media institutions merely reflect the moral relativity of their culture and that any significant change in the ethical standards of the media must await a similar metamorphosis in society at large. But one could argue just as convincingly that media practitioners should be leaders in this moral revival, willingly serving as role models for their audiences.

There is no reason to believe that the more traditional ethical issues that have confronted the media for many years will be any less troublesome in the future. What we can hope for, however, is a move away from situation ethics and toward a system based on more reasoned judgments and a positive set of moral principles.

These recommendations are fairly modest, but they can serve as a starting point for confronting the crisis in public confidence that has beset some of our media institutions. With the subject of media ethics now at center stage, media practitioners should become more aware in the future of the fallacies of situation ethics and should be more prone to engage in a dialectic regarding their industry's moral standards. The optimistic view is that they will do so willingly. The more pessimistic view is that they will have no choice, because the public will demand greater accountability.

The media are important transmitters of our moral heritage. In this information age they also sit at the vortex of the democratic process and our pluralistic social structure. Thus, media practitioners have a special responsibility to the culture of which they are a part and should consider it a professional mandate to improve the ethical climates of their own institutions. Because this book will be read primarily by future media practitioners, perhaps the lessons learned here in the pursuit of sound moral reasoning will someday pay dividends in the fulfillment of this professional mandate.

Notes

1. John Silber, *Straight Shooting: What's Wrong with America and How to Fix It* (New York: Harper & Row, 1989), p. 244.
2. David Hawpe, "Questions of Ethics," *APME News*, May–June 1993, pp. 3–6.

1

Society of Professional Journalists: Code of Ethics*

The Society of Professional Journalists believes the duty of journalists is to serve the truth.

We believe the agencies of mass communication are carriers of public discussion and information, acting on their Constitutional mandate and freedom to learn and report the facts.

We believe in public enlightenment as the forerunner of justice, and in our Constitutional role to seek the truth as part of the public's right to know the truth.

We believe those responsibilities carry obligations that require journalists to perform with intelligence, objectivity, accuracy, and fairness.

To these ends, we declare acceptance of the standards of practice here set forth:

I. RESPONSIBILITY

The public's right to know of events of public importance and interest is the overriding mission of the mass media. The purpose of distributing news and enlightened opinion is to serve the general welfare. Journalists who use their professional sta-

tus as representatives of the public for selfish or other unworthy motives violate a high trust.

II. FREEDOM OF THE PRESS

Freedom of the press is to be guarded as an inalienable right of people in a free society. It carries with it the freedom and the responsibility to discuss, question, and challenge actions and utterances of our government and of our public and private institutions. Journalists uphold the right to speak unpopular opinions and the privilege to agree with the majority.

III. ETHICS

Journalists must be free of obligation to any interest other than the public's right to know the truth.

1. Gifts, favors, free travel, special treatment or privileges can compromise the integrity of journalists and their employers. Nothing of value should be accepted.

2. Secondary employment, political involvement, holding public office, and service in community organizations should be avoided if it compromises the integrity of journalists and their employers. Journalists and their employers

---

* This code was adopted in 1926 and revised in 1973, 1984, and 1987.

should conduct their personal lives in a manner that protects them from conflict of interest, real or apparent. Their responsibilities to the public are paramount. That is the nature of their profession.

3. So-called news communications from private sources should not be published or broadcast without substantiation of their claims to news value.

4. Journalists will seek news that serves the public interest, despite the obstacles. They will make constant efforts to assure that the public's business is conducted in public and that public records are open to public inspection.

5. Journalists acknowledge the newsman's ethic of protecting confidential sources of information.

6. Plagiarism is dishonest and unacceptable.

IV. ACCURACY AND OBJECTIVITY

Good faith with the public is the foundation of all worthy journalism.

1. Truth is our ultimate goal.

2. Objectivity in reporting the news is another goal that serves as the mark of an experienced professional. It is a standard of performance toward which we strive. We honor those who achieve it.

3. There is no excuse for inaccuracies or lack of thoroughness.

4. Newspaper headlines should be fully warranted by the contents of the articles they accompany. Photographs and telecasts should give an accurate picture of an event and not highlight an event out of context.

5. Sound practice makes clear distinction between news reports and expressions of opinion. News reports should be free of opinion or bias and represent all sides of an issue.

6. Partisanship in editorial comment that knowingly departs from the truth violates the spirit of American journalism.

7. Journalists recognize their responsibility for offering informed analysis, comment, and editorial opinion on public events and issues. They accept the obligation to present such material by individuals whose competence, experience and judgment qualify them for it.

8. Special articles or presentations devoted to advocacy or the writer's own conclusions and interpretations should be labeled as such.

V. FAIR PLAY

Journalists at all times will show respect for the dignity, privacy, rights, and well-being of people encountered in the course of gathering and presenting news.

1. The news media should not communicate unofficial charges affecting reputation or moral character without giving the accused a chance to reply.

2. The news media must guard against invading a person's right to privacy.

3. The media should not pander to morbid curiosity about details of vice and crime.

4. It is the duty of news media to make prompt and complete correction of their errors.

5. Journalists should be accountable to the public for their reports and the public should be encouraged to voice its grievances against the media. Open dialogue with our readers, viewers, and listeners should be fostered.

VI. PLEDGE

Adherence to this code is intended to preserve and strengthen the bond of mutual trust and respect between American journalists and the American people.

The Society shall—by programs of education and other means—encourage individual journalists to adhere to these tenets, and shall encourage journalistic publications and broadcasters to recognize their responsibility to frame codes of ethics in concert with their employees to serve as guidelines in furthering these goals.

2

American Society of Newspaper Editors: Statement of Principles*

PREAMBLE

The First Amendment, protecting freedom of expression from abridgment by any law, guarantees to the people through their press a constitutional right, and thereby places on newspaper people a particular responsibility.

Thus journalism demands of its practitioners not only industry and knowledge but also the pursuit of a standard of integrity proportionate to the journalist's singular obligation.

To this end the American Society of Newspaper Editors sets forth this Statement of Principles as a standard encouraging the highest ethical and professional performance.

ARTICLE I—RESPONSIBILITY

The primary purpose of gathering and distributing news and opinion is to serve the general welfare by informing the people and enabling them to make judgments on the issues of the time. Newspapermen and women who abuse the power of their professional role for selfish motives or unworthy purposes are faithless to that public trust.

---

* This statement was adopted with permission of the ASNE board of directors in October 1975.

The American press was made free not just to inform or just to serve as a forum for debate but also to bring an independent scrutiny to bear on the forces of power in the society, including the conduct of official power at all levels of government.

ARTICLE II—FREEDOM OF THE PRESS

Freedom of the press belongs to the people. It must be defended against encroachment or assault from any quarter, public or private.

Journalists must be constantly alert to see that the public's business is conducted in public. They must be vigilant against all who would exploit the press for selfish purposes.

ARTICLE III—INDEPENDENCE

Journalists must avoid impropriety and the appearance of impropriety as well as any conflict of interest or the appearance of conflict. They should neither accept anything nor pursue any activity that might compromise or seem to compromise their integrity.

ARTICLE IV—TRUTH AND ACCURACY

Good faith with the reader is the foundation of good journalism. Every effort must be made to assure that the news content is accurate, free from bias and in context, and that all sides are presented fairly. Editorials, analytical articles and commentary should be held to the same standards of accuracy with respect to facts as news reports.

Significant errors of fact, as well as errors of omission, should be corrected promptly and prominently.

ARTICLE V—IMPARTIALITY

To be impartial does not require the press to be unquestioning or to refrain from editorial expression. Sound practice, however, demands a clear distinction for the reader between news reports and opinion. Articles that contain opinion or personal interpretation should be clearly identified.

ARTICLE VI—FAIR PLAY

Journalists should respect the rights of people involved in the news, observe the common standards of decency and stand accountable to the public for the fairness and accuracy of their news reports.

Persons publicly accused should be given the earliest opportunity to respond.

Pledges of confidentiality to news sources must be honored at all costs, and therefore should not be given lightly. Unless there is clear and pressing need to maintain confidences, sources of information should be identified.

These principles are intended to preserve, protect and strengthen the bond of trust and respect between American journalists and the American people, a bond that is essential to sustain the grant of freedom entrusted to both by the nation's founders.

Radio-Television News Directors Association: Code of Broadcast News Ethics

The responsibility of radio and television journalists is to gather and report information of importance and interest to the public accurately, honestly and impartially.

The members of the Radio-Television News Directors Association accept these standards and will:

1. Strive to present the source or nature of broadcast news material in a way that is balanced, accurate and fair.

    A. They will evaluate information solely on its merits as news, rejecting sensationalism or misleading emphasis in any form.

    B. They will guard against using audio or video material in a way that deceives the audience.

    C. They will not mislead the public by presenting as spontaneous news any material which is staged or rehearsed.

    D. They will identify people by race, creed, nationality or prior status only when it is relevant.

    E. They will clearly label opinion and commentary.

    F. They will promptly acknowledge and correct errors.

2. Strive to conduct themselves in a manner that protects them from conflicts of interest, real or perceived. They will decline gifts or favors which would influence or appear to influence their judgments.

3. Respect the dignity, privacy and well-being of people with whom they deal.

4. Recognize the need to protect confidential sources. They will promise confidentiality only with the intention of keeping that promise.

5. Respect everyone's right to a fair trial.

6. Broadcast the private transmissions of other broadcasters only with permission.

7. Actively encourage observance of this Code by all journalists, whether members of the Radio-Television News Directors Association or not.

4

American Advertising Federation: Advertising Principles of American Business

1. Truth—Advertising shall reveal the truth, and shall reveal significant facts, the omission of which would mislead the public.

2. Substantiation—Advertising claims shall be substantiated by evidence in possession of the advertiser and the advertising agency prior to making such claims.

3. Comparisons—Advertising shall refrain from making false, misleading, or unsubstantiated statements or claims about a competitor or its products or services.

4. Bait Advertising—Advertising shall not offer products or services for sale unless such offer constitutes a bona fide effort to sell the advertised products or services and is not a device to switch consumers to other goods or services, usually higher priced.

5. Guarantees and Warranties—Advertising of guarantees and warranties shall be explicit, with sufficient information to apprise consumers of their principal terms and limitations or, when space or time restrictions preclude such disclosures, the advertisement shall clearly reveal where the full text of the guarantee or warranty can be examined before purchase.

6. Price Claims—Advertising shall avoid price claims which are false or misleading, or savings claims which do not offer provable savings.

7. Testimonials—Advertising containing testimonials shall be limited to those of competent witnesses who are reflecting a real and honest opinion or experience.

8. Taste and Decency—Advertising shall be free of statements, illustrations, or implications which are offensive to good taste or public decency.

5

Public Relations Society of America: Code of Professional Standards for the Practice of Public Relations*

DECLARATION OF PRINCIPLES

Members of the Public Relations Society of America base their professional principles on the fundamental value and dignity of the individual, holding that the free exercise of human rights, especially freedom of speech, freedom of assembly, and freedom of the press, is essential to the practice of public relations.

In serving the interests of clients and employers, we dedicate ourselves to the goals of better communication, understanding, and cooperation among the diverse individuals, groups, and institutions of society, and of equal opportunity of employment in the public relations profession.

We pledge:

To conduct ourselves professionally, with truth, accuracy, fairness, and responsibility to the public;

To improve our individual competence and advance the knowledge and proficiency of the profession through continuing research and education;

And to adhere to the articles of the Code of Professional Standards for the Practice of Public Relations as adopted by the governing Assembly of the Society.

CODE OF PROFESSIONAL STANDARDS FOR THE PRACTICE OF PUBLIC RELATIONS

These articles have been adopted by the Public Relations Society of America to promote and maintain high standards of public service and ethical conduct among its members.

1. A member shall conduct his or her professional life in accord with the *public interest.*

2. A member shall exemplify high standards of *honesty and integrity* while carrying out dual obligations to a client or employer and to the democratic process.

3. A member shall *deal fairly* with the public, with past or present clients or employers, and with fellow practitioners, giving due respect

---

* This code was revised in 1988.

to the ideal of free inquiry and to the opinions of others.

4. A member shall adhere to the highest standards of *accuracy and truth,* avoiding extravagant claims or unfair comparisons and giving credit for ideas and words borrowed from others.

5. A member shall not knowingly' disseminate *false or misleading information* and shall act promptly to correct erroneous communications for which he or she is responsible.

6. A member shall not engage in any practice which has the purpose of *corrupting* the integrity of channels of communications or the processes of government.

7. A member shall be prepared to *identify publicly* the name of the client or employer on whose behalf any public communication is made.

8. A member shall not use any individual or organization professing to serve or represent an announced cause, or professing to be independent or unbiased, but actually serving another or *undisclosed interest.*

9. A member shall not *guarantee the achievement* of specified results beyond the member's direct control.

10. A member shall *not represent conflicting* or competing interests without the express consent of those concerned, given after a full disclosure of the facts.

11. A member shall not place himself or herself in a position where the member's *personal interest is or may be in conflict* with an obligation to an employer or client, or others, without full disclosure of such interests to all involved.

12. A member shall *not accept fees, commissions, gifts or any other consideration* from anyone except clients or employers for whom services are performed without their express consent, given after full disclosure of the facts.

13. A member shall scrupulously safeguard the *confidences and privacy rights* of present, former, and prospective clients or employers.

14. A member shall not intentionally *damage the professional reputation* or practice of another practitioner.

15. If a member has evidence that another member has been guilty of unethical, illegal, or unfair practices, including those in violation of this Code, the member is obligated to present the information promptly to the proper authorities of the Society for action in accordance with the procedure set forth in Article XII of the Bylaws.

16. A member called as a witness in a proceeding for enforcement of this Code is obligated to appear, unless excused for sufficient reason by the judicial panel.

17. A member shall, as soon as possible, sever relations with any organization or individual if such relationship requires conduct contrary to the articles of this Code.

SELECTED BIBLIOGRAPHY

The following books and articles, some which are cited in this text, are recommended for further reading.

Adams, Julian. *Freedom and Ethics in the Press.* New York: Rosen, 1983.

Adler, Richard P., Gerald S. Lesser, Laurene S. Robertson, John R. Rossiter, Scott Ward, Bernard Z. Friedlander, Leslie Isler, Ronald J. Faber, and David B. Pillemer (eds.). *The Effects of Television Advertising on Children.* Lexington, MA: Heath, 1980.

Algraawi, Mbark A., and Hugh M. Culbertson. "Relation between Specificity and Accessibility to News Sources," *Journalism Quarterly*, 64, pp. 799–804.

Bagdikian, Ben H. *The Media Monopoly*, 4th ed. Boston: Beacon, 1992.

Bailey, Charles W. *Conflicts of Interest: A Matter of Journalistic Ethics.* New York: National News Council, 1984.

Baker, Lee W. *The Credibility Factor: Putting Ethics to Work in Public Relations.* Homewood, IL: Business One Irwin, 1993.

Barcus, F. Earle. *Images of Life on Children's Television.* New York: Praeger, 1983.

Bayles, Michael. *Professional Ethics*, 2d ed. Belmont, CA: Wadsworth, 1989.

Beauchamp, Tom L. *Philosophical Ethics: An Introduction to Moral Philosophy.* New York: McGraw-Hill, 1982.

Blake, George. "Rebuilding Credibility: Banning Anonymous Sources Is a Start," *The Quill*, April 1988, pp. 21–23.

Bok, Sissela, *Lying: Moral Choice in Public and Private Life.* New York: Vintage Books, 1978.

Bok, Sissela. *Secrets: On the Ethics of Concealment and Revelation.* New York: Pantheon Books, 1982.

Bowie, Norman E. *Making Ethical Decisions.* New York: McGraw-Hill, 1985.

Brody, Baruch. *Ethics and Its Methods of Analysis.* New York: Harcourt Brace Jovanovich, 1983.

Brogan, Patrick. *Spiked: The Short Life and Death of the National News Council.* New York: Priority, 1985.

Brown, Jane D., and Kenneth Campbell. "Race and Gender in Music Videos: The Same Beat but a Different Drummer," *Journal of Communication*, 36, Winter 1986, pp. 94–106.

Busterna, John C. "Daily Newspaper Chains and the Antitrust Law," *Journalism Monographs*, No. 110, March 1989, p. 2.

Callahan, Joan C. (ed.) *Ethical Issues in Professional Life.* New York: Oxford University Press, 1988.

Chazan, Barry L., and Jonas Soltis (eds.). *Moral Education.* New York: Teachers College Press, 1973.

Christians, Clifford G., John P. Ferré, and P. Mark Fackler. *Good News: Social Ethics & the Press.* New York: Oxford University Press, 1993.

Christians, Clifford G., Kim B. Rotzoll, and Mark Fowler. *Media Ethics: Cases and Moral Reasoning*, 4th ed. White Plains, NY: Longman, 1995.

Clor, Harry M. (ed.). *Censorship and Freedom of Expression: Essays on Obscenity and the Law.* Chicago: Rand McNally, 1971.

Clor, Harry M. *Obscenity and Public Morality: Censorship in a Liberal Society.* Chicago: University of Chicago Press, 1969.

Cohen, Ronald L. (ed.). *Justice: Views from the Social Sciences.* New York: Plenum, 1986.

Commission on the Freedom of the Press, A Free and Responsible Press. Chicago: University of Chicago Press, 1947.

Cooper, Thomas W., Clifford G. Christians, Frances Forde Plude, and Robert A. White (eds.). *Communication Ethics and Global Change.* White Plains, NY: Longman, 1989.

Courtney, Alice E., and Thomas Whipple. *Sex Stereotyping in Advertising.* Lexington, MA: Heath, 1983.

Deats, Paul (ed.). *Toward a Discipline of Social Ethics.* Boston: Boston University Press, 1972.

Elliott, Deni (ed.). *Responsible Journalism.* Beverly Hills, CA: Sage, 1986.

Endres, Fred F. "Influences on the Ethical Socialization of U.S. Newspaper Journalists," *Newspaper Research Journal,* 6, No. 1, Spring 1985, pp. 47–56.

Feinberg, Joel. *Social Philosophy.* Upper Saddle River, NJ: Prentice Hall, 1973.

Fink, Conrad C. *Media Ethics: In the Newsroom and Beyond.* New York: McGraw-Hill, 1988.

Frankena, William K. *Ethics,* 2d ed. Upper Saddle River, NJ: Prentice Hall, 1973.

Gert, Bernard, *Morality: A New Justification of the Moral Rules.* New York: Oxford University Press, 1988.

Goldman, Alan H. *The Moral Foundations of Professional Ethics.* Totawa, NJ: Rowman & Littlefield, 1980.

Goodwin, Eugene H., and Ron F. Smith, *Groping for Ethics in Journalism,* 3d ed. Ames: Iowa State University Press, 1994.

Gross, Larry, John Stuart Katz, and Jay Ruby (eds.). *Image Ethics: The Moral Rights of Subjects in Photographs, Film and Television.* New York: Oxford University Press, 1988.

Hare, R. M. *Moral Thinking: Its Levels, Method and Point.* New York: Oxford University Press, 1981.

Hastings Center. *The Teaching of Ethics in Higher Education.* Hastings-on-Hudson, NY: Hastings Center, 1980.

Howie, John (ed.). *Ethical Principles and Practice.* Carbondale: Southern Illinois University Press, 1987.

Hulteng, John L. *The Messenger's Motives: Ethical Problems of the News Media,* 2d ed. Upper Saddle River, NJ: Prentice Hall, 1985.

Hunt, Todd. "Raising the Issue of Ethics through Use of Scenarios," *Journalism Educator,* 37, No. 1, Spring 1982, pp. 55–58.

Jaska, James A., and Michael S. Pritchard. *Communication Ethics: Methods of Analysis,* 2d ed. Belmont, CA: Wadsworth, 1994.

Johannesen, Richard L. *Ethics in Human Communication,* 3d ed. Prospect Heights, IL: Waveland, 1990.

Johnson, David. "The Anonymous-Source Syndrome," *Columbia Journalism Review,* November–December 1987, p. 54.

Jones, W. T. *The Classical Mind.* New York: Harcourt, Brace & World, 1969.

Journal of Mass Media Ethics (all issues).

Kant, Immanuel. *Foundations of the Metaphysics of Morals,* trans. Lewis White Beck. Indianapolis: Bobbs-Merrill, 1959.

Kidder, Rushworth M. *How Good People Make Tough Choices.* New York: Morrow, 1995.

Kidder, Rushworth M. *Shared Values for a Troubled World.* San Francisco: Jossey-Bass, 1994.

Klaidman, Stephen, and Tom L. Beauchamp. *The Virtuous Journalist.* New York: Oxford University Press, 1987.

Kohlberg, Lawrence. *The Philosophy of Moral Development.* San Francisco: Harper & Row, 1981.

Lambeth, Edmund B. *Committed Journalism: An Ethic for the Profession.* Bloomington: Indiana University Press, 1986.

Langley, Monica, and Lee Levine. "Broken Promises," *Columbia Journalism Review,* July–August 1988, pp. 21–24.

Lazere, Donald (ed.). *American Media and Mass Culture.* Berkeley: University of California Press, 1987.

Lippmann, Walter. *Public Opinion.* New York:

Macmillan, 1932. (Reprinted from the original of 1922.)

Ludwig, Arnold M. *The Importance of Lying.* Springfield, IL: Charles C. Thomas, 1965.

Mappes, Thomas A., and Jane S. Zembaty. *Social Ethics: Morality and Social Policy,* 3d ed. New York: McGraw-Hill, 1987.

Mauro, Tony. "The Name of the Source: Editors Want to Know," *Washington Journalism Review,* September 1987, pp. 36–38.

Merrill, John C. *The Dialectic in Journalism: Toward a Responsible Use of Press Freedom.* Baton Rouge: Louisiana State University Press, 1989.

Merrill, John C., and Ralph D. Barney (eds.). *Ethics and the Press: Readings in Mass Media Morality.* New York: Hastings House, 1975.

Merrill, John C., and Jack S. Odell. *Philosophy and Journalism.* White Plains, NY: Longman, 1983.

Meyer, Philip. *Ethical Journalism: A Guide for Students, Practitioners, and Consumers.* White Plains, NY: Longman, 1987.

Meyers, Chet. *Teaching Students to Think Critically.* San Francisco: Jossey-Bass, 1986.

Miller, Arthur. *Miller's Court.* Boston: Houghton Mifflin, 1982.

Moore, Timothy E., and Reet Mae. "Who Dies and Who Cries: Death and Bereavement in Children's Literature," *Journal of Communication,* 37, Autumn 1987, pp. 52–64.

Moyers, Bill. *A World of Ideas.* New York: Doubleday, 1989.

Newsome, Doug, Alan Scott, and Judy VanSlyke Turk. *This Is PR: The Realities of Public Relations,* 4th ed. Belmont, CA: Wadsworth, 1989.

Nikken, Peter, and Allerd L. Peeters. "Children's Perceptions of Television Reality," *Journal of Broadcasting and Electronic Media,* 32, Fall 1988, pp. 441–452.

Olen, Jeffrey. *Ethics in Journalism.* Upper Saddle River, NJ: Prentice Hall, 1988.

Orlik, Peter B. *Electronic Media Criticism.* Newton, MA: Butterworth-Heinemann, 1994.

Pember, Don R. *Privacy and the Press.* Seattle: University of Washington Press, 1972.

Picard, Robert G., Maxwell E. McCombs, James P. Winter, and Stephen Lacy (eds.). *Press Concentration and Monopoly: New Perspectives on Newspaper Ownership and Operation.* Norwood, NJ: Ablex, 1988.

Piper, Thomas R., Mary C. Gentile, and Sharon Daloz Parks. *Can Ethics Be Taught?* Boston: Harvard Business School, 1993.

Rawls, John. *A Theory of Justice.* Cambridge, MA: Harvard University Press, 1971.

Reep, Dina C., and Faye H. Dambrot. "Effects of Frequent Television Viewing on Stereotypes: 'Drip, Drip' or 'Drench'?" *Journalism Quarterly,* 66, Autumn 1989, pp. 542–550, 556.

Report of the Commission on Obscenity and Pornography. Washington, D.C.: U.S. Government Printing Office, 1970.

Ries, Al, and Jack Trout. *Marketing Warfare.* New York: McGraw-Hill, 1986.

Rivers, William L., and Cleve Mathews. *Ethics for the Media.* Upper Saddle River, NJ: Prentice Hall, 1988.

Robinson, Deanna Campbell, Elizabeth B. Buck, Marlene Cuthbert, and the International Communication and Youth Consortium. *Music at the Margins: Popular Music and Global Cultural Diversity.* Newbury Park, CA: Sage, 1991.

Rosengren, Karl Erick, and Sven Windahl. *Media Matter: TV Use in Childhood and Adolescence* (especially pp. 159–241). Norwood, NJ: Ablex, 1989.

Rosenthal, David M., and Fadlou Shehaili (eds.). *Applied Ethics and Ethical Theory.* Salt Lake City: University of Utah Press, 1988.

Rubin, Bernard (ed.). *Questioning Media Ethics.* New York: Praeger, 1978.

Russell, Nick. *Morals and the Media: Ethics in Canadian Journalism.* Vancouver: UBC, 1994.

Ryan, Michael, and David L. Martinson. "Ethical Values, the Flow of Journalistic Information and Public Relations Persons," *Journalism Quarterly,* 61, Spring 1984, pp. 27–34.

Seiter, Ellen. "Stereotypes and the Media: A Reevaluation," *Journal of Communication,* 36, Spring 1986, pp. 14–42.

Shibles, Warren. *Lying: A Critical Analysis.* Whitewater, WI: Language Press, 1985.

Siebert, Fred S. Theodore Peterson, and Wilbur Schramm. *Four Theories of the Press.* Urbana: University of Illinois Press, 1956.

Smith, Ted J. III. "Journalism and the Socrates Syndrome," *The Quill*, April 1988, pp. 14–20.

Stiles, Lindley J., and Bruce D. Johnson (eds.). *Morality Examined: Guidelines for Teachers.* Princeton, NJ: Princeton Book, 1977.

Sun, Se-Wen, and James Lull. "The Adolescent Audience for Music Videos and Why They Watch," *Journal of Communication*, 36, Winter 1986, pp. 115–125.

Swain, Bruce M. *Reporters' Ethics.* Ames: Iowa State University Press, 1978.

Tan, Alexis S. "Television Use and Social Stereotypes," *Journalism Quarterly*, 59, Spring 1982, pp. 119–122.

Thayer, Lee (ed.). *Ethics, Morality and the Media.* New York: Hastings House, 1980.

Tivnan, Edward. *The Moral Imagination: Confronting The Ethical Issues of Our Day.* New York: Simon & Schuster, 1995.

Van Gerpen, Maurice. *Privileged Communications and the Press.* Westport, CT: Greenwood, 1979.

Wedberg, Anders. *A History of Philosophy. Vol. 1. Antiquity and the Middle Ages.* Oxford: Clarendon, 1982.

Whaley, Bennett A., William I. Gordon, and Edmund P. Kaminski. "Docudrama from Different Temporal Perspectives: Reactions to NBC's 'Kent State,'" *Journal of Broadcasting*, 27, No. 3, Summer 1983, pp. 285–289.

Williams, Bernard. *Ethics and the Limits of Philosophy.* Cambridge, MA: Harvard University Press, 1985.

Williams, Bernard. *Morality: An Introduction to Ethics.* New York: Harper & Row, 1972.

Wood, Donald M., and Arvo A. Leps. *Mass Media and the Individual.* St. Paul, MN: West, 1983.

Young, Robert E. (ed.). *New Directions for Teaching and Learning: Fostering Critical Thinking.* San Francisco: Jossey-Bass, 1980.